The 'Jewish Question'
in German Literature
1749–1939

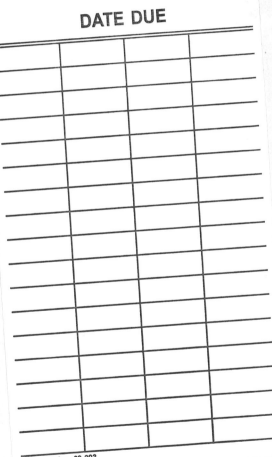

DATE DUE

Demco, Inc. 38-293

The 'Jewish Question' in German Literature
1749–1939

Emancipation and its Discontents

RITCHIE ROBERTSON

OXFORD
UNIVERSITY PRESS

#47824746

3-30-04

OXFORD
UNIVERSITY PRESS

Great Clarendon Street, Oxford OX2 6DP

Oxford University Press is a department of the University of Oxford.
It furthers the University's objective of excellence in research, scholarship,
and education by publishing worldwide in
Oxford New York

Athens Auckland Bangkok Bogotá Buenos Aires
Cape Town Chennai Dar es Salaam Delhi Florence Hong Kong Istanbul
Karachi Kolkata Kuala Lumpur Madrid Melbourne Mexico City Mumbai
Nairobi Paris São Paulo Shanghai Singapore Taipei Tokyo Toronto Warsaw
and associated companies in Berlin Ibadan

Published in the United States
by Oxford University Press Inc., New York

First published 1999
First published in paperback 2001

British Library Cataloguing in Publication Data
Data available

Library of Congress Cataloging in Publication Data
Data available
ISBN–0–19–818631–2 (hbk)
ISBN–0–19–924888–5 (pbk)

1 3 5 7 9 10 8 6 4 2

Typeset by J&L Composition Ltd, Filey, North Yorkshire
Printed in Great Britain
on acid-free paper by
Biddles Ltd
Guildford and King's Lynn

To Edward Timms

Contents

viii   *Contents*

Abbreviations

Editions

A   Arthur Schnitzler, *Aphorismen und Betrachtungen*, ed. Robert O. Weiss (Frankfurt, 1967)

BH   Richard Beer-Hofmann, *Gesammelte Werke* (Frankfurt, 1963)

Br i   Arthur Schnitzler, *Briefe 1875–1912*, ed. Therese Nickl and Heinrich Schnitzler (Frankfurt, 1981)

Br ii   Arthur Schnitzler, *Briefe 1913–1931*, Peter Michael Braunwarth *et al.* (Frankfurt, 1984)

BT   Theodor Herzl, *Briefe und Tagebücher*, ed. Alex Bein *et al.*, 7 vols. (Berlin, Frankfurt, Vienna, 1983–96)

D   Arthur Schnitzler, *Die Dramatischen Werke*, 2 vols. (Frankfurt, 1962)

DD   *Your Diamond Dreams Cut Open My Arteries: Poems by Else Lasker-Schüler*, tr. Robert P. Newton (Chapel Hill, NC, 1982)

DKA   Johann Wolfgang Goethe, *Sämtliche Werke: Briefe, Tagebücher und Gespräche*, Deutsche Klassiker-Ausgabe, 40 vols. (Frankfurt, 1986–)

E   Arthur Schnitzler, *Die Erzählenden Schriften*, 2 vols. (Frankfurt, 1961)

FS   Karl Kraus, *Frühe Schriften 1892–1900*, ed. J. J. Braakenburg, 2 vols. (Munich, 1979)

G   Else Lasker-Schüler, *Gedichte*, ed. Karl Jürgen Skrodzki, 2 vols. (Frankfurt, 1996)

H   Heinrich Heine, *Sämtliche Schriften*, ed. Klaus Briegleb, 6 vols. (Munich, 1968–76)

HA   Johann Wolfgang Goethe, *Werke*, Hamburger Ausgabe, ed. Erich Trunz, 14 vols. (Hamburg, 1949–60)

J   Arthur Schnitzler, *Jugend in Wien*, ed. Therese Nickl and Heinrich Schnitzler (Vienna, 1968)

K   Karl Kraus, *Schriften*, ed. Christian Wagenknecht, 20 vols. (Frankfurt, 1989–94)

L   Gotthold Ephraim Lessing, *Werke*, ed. Herbert G. Göpfert *et al.*, 8 vols. (Munich, 1970–9)

M   Thomas Mann, *Gesammelte Werke*, 13 vols. (Frankfurt, 1974)

PS   Else Lasker-Schüler, *Prosa und Schauspiele*, ed. Friedhelm Kemp (Munich, 1962)

R   Wilhelm Raabe, *Sämtliche Werke*, ed. Karl Hoppe *et al.*, 20 vols. (Göttingen, 1960–)

SE   *The Standard Edition of the Complete Psychological Works of Sigmund Freud*, ed. James Strachey, 24 vols. (London, 1953–74)

T   Arthur Schnitzler, *Tagebuch* (Vienna, 1981–)

ZW   Theodor Herzl, *Gesammelte zionistische Werke*, 5 vols. (Tel Aviv, 1934–5)

Periodicals

DVjs   *Deutsche Vierteljahrsschrift für Literatur und Geistesgeschichte*
F   *Die Fackel*
GLL   *German Life and Letters*
LBY   *Leo Baeck Institute Yearbook*
MAL   *Modern Austrian Literature*
MLR   *Modern Language Review*
TLS   *Times Literary Supplement*
ZfdP   *Zeitschrift für deutsche Philologie*

Introduction

> Oh, the literature on the 'Jewish question'! I don't know all
> the books, but I'm afraid I know many of them; to read them
> all is beyond the strength of an ordinary mortal—the entire
> literature for and against the Jews has been read, perhaps,
> only by Hercules.[1]

The 'Jewish question', the problem concerning the position of
Jews in Germany and Austria, was widely discussed from the
1770s onwards. Early landmarks include G. E. Lessing's philosemitic dramas, *Die Juden* (*The Jews*; written in 1749, and taken
as the chronological starting-point for this study) and *Nathan der
Weise* (*Nathan the Wise*, 1779); C. W. von Dohm's plea for Jewish
emancipation (inspired by the Berlin Jewish philosopher Moses
Mendelssohn), *Über die bürgerliche Verbesserung der Juden* (*On
the Civil Improvement of the Jews*, 1781); and, in the same year,
the beginning of emancipatory legislation with the Patent of
Toleration issued by Joseph II in Austria. Emancipation culminated in 1871 with the bestowal of equal rights on all Jewish
citizens of the newly formed German Empire (four years after
similar legislation in Austria). And, along with progress towards
emancipation, the Jewish presence in German and Austrian
culture became increasingly conspicuous, reaching a peak of
brilliance and diversity in the Weimar Republic, before being
annihilated or sent into exile by the National Socialist regime.
The focus of this book is on the Jewish presence in German
literature.

It was also in the 1870s, however, that public discussion of the
'Jewish question' became sharply more hostile, as Jews were made
the scapegoats for the drawbacks of modernity. The eminent
Prussian historian Heinrich von Treitschke wrote in a much-
noticed article in 1879: 'Even in the most highly educated circles,
among men who would reject with loathing any idea of religious

[1] Constantin Brunner, *Der Judenhaß und die Juden* (Berlin, 1918), p. 4.

intolerance or national arrogance, the cry resounds as though from a single mouth: "The Jews are our misfortune!"[2] The construction of a 'Jewish question', and the respectability given to antisemitism by Treitschke and his more extreme contemporaries, created an atmosphere of unease, tarnished the Jews' attainment of emancipation, and provided at least a precondition for the still unimaginable horrors of the mid-twentieth century.

My aim in this book is to render the 'Jewish question' more intelligible by looking at its literary expressions. There is now a large body of first-rate historical work on German–Jewish relations, and research is still proliferating, but studies of German-Jewish literary history are less numerous. While my main focus is on the period 1880–1930, I have also gone back to the eighteenth century to show how the project of Jewish emancipation was closely tied to an Enlightenment philosemitism which was problematic from the outset. I have not attempted a continuous history, still less an encyclopaedic survey, of relevant literature, but selected a number of texts in order to illustrate the problems of emancipation.[3] These are texts both by Jewish and non-Jewish writers which thematize aspects of Jewish identity.

In doing so, I have followed the example of recent historians in trying to distance myself from two older and well-established historiographical patterns.[4] One of these models treated the history of emancipation as a success story that was cut short by brutal intervention from outside, ignoring the unease and tensions that were part of the process of emancipation. It often used the metaphor of 'symbiosis'. Thus, in March 1939, shortly before leaving Germany, Martin Buber wrote: 'The symbiosis of the German and Jewish characters (*Wesen*), as I experienced it in the four decades I spent in Germany, was the first and only one, since the Spanish Middle Ages, to have received the highest confirmation that history can confer: confirmation by *fruitful-*

---

[2] Treitschke, 'Unsere Aussichten', *Preußische Jahrbücher*, 44 (1879), 559–76 (p. 575).

[3] For surveys, see Alfred D. Low, *Jews in the Eyes of the Germans: From the Enlightenment to Imperial Germany* (Philadelphia, 1979); and Sander L. Gilman and Jack Zipes (eds.), *The Yale Companion to Jewish Writing and Thought in German Culture, 1066–1996* (New Haven and London, 1997).

[4] See Shulamit Volkov, *Jüdisches Leben und Antisemitismus im 19. und 20. Jahrhundert* (Munich, 1990), p. 166.

ness.'[5] Zionist historiography violently rejected such a conception, arguing instead that assimilation was a mistaken ideal which achieved only a delusory success. According to Gershom Scholem, no real cultural contact, no dialogue between Jews and Germans, ever took place: instead, the Jews only spoke to themselves, or uttered an unanswered 'cry into the void'.[6] Scholem's bitterness betrays his resentment at feeling unwanted and hence the intensity of his own attachment to Germany.

Inevitably, our view of the past has been affected, and in some respects distorted, by the catastrophe of the Holocaust. Understandably, early historians (Eva G. Reichmann, Paul Massing) could only see German-Jewish history in the shadow cast by the crematoria. They thought that the all-too-frequent hostility of Germans towards their Jewish neighbours formed a continuous history of antisemitism which culminated in the Holocaust. More recently, some historians (Lucy Dawidowicz, Paul Lawrence Rose, Daniel J. Goldhagen) have depicted German history as a mounting frenzy of exterminationist antisemitism. These accounts do not carry conviction. Despite the virulent public discussion of antisemitism that began in the late 1870s, the German Empire did not enact any repressive measures against Jews—in striking contrast to its persecution of Roman Catholics in the mid-1870s and its banning of Socialism from 1878 to 1890. Looking eastwards to the Russian pogroms, German Jews could be forgiven for thinking that their situation was so different, and the rule of law so firmly established, that nothing remotely similar could happen to them. Even in the 1920s most observers thought that Hitler, if he came to power, would be no worse than Mussolini. Far less could they foresee the enormity of the 'final solution' that Hitler would put into practice. The 'functionalist' approach to the Holocaust suggests that the full extent of the 'solution' was not envisaged even by its perpetrators before 1940.

If one retrospectively deplores the blindness of German and Austrian Jews, one will be tempted to interpret their history as

---

[5] 'Das Ende der deutsch-jüdischen Symbiose', *Jüdische Weltrundschau* (10 Mar. 1939), repr. in Buber, *Der Jude und sein Judentum* (Cologne, 1963), pp. 644–7 (p. 645).
[6] Scholem, 'Against the Myth of the German–Jewish Dialogue', in his *On Jews and Judaism in Crisis* (New York, 1976), pp. 61–4 (p. 62).

tragedy.[7] A phrase like 'the German-Jewish tragedy', invoking a prestigious literary genre, seems to acknowledge both the magnitude of the events and the dignity of the victims. But does it? Glib talk of tragedy assimilates the real experiences of real people to a literary form, making them into an aesthetic structure which can be contemplated with a mixture of feelings including pleasure. Moreover, tragedy centres on recognition. Oedipus realizes too late that the strangers he respectively killed and married were his father and his mother; Othello learns too late that the wife he has murdered was devoted to him. To call the Holocaust tragic is to blame its victims for failing to read the signs: for hastening to accept German culture without foreseeing that their adoptive nation would turn and rend them. That is in turn to abuse the hindsight that is ours only because we happen to live later. As Michael André Bernstein rightly says, in his invaluable polemic against apocalyptic history, such hindsight 'drains all meaningful reality (that is, a reality made up of specific choices and decisions) from the lives of the people being described'.[8]

I have accordingly tried to go back to the period when the Holocaust was still unimaginable and understand the age of assimilation as contemporaries did. I have chosen 1939 (the date when Freud published *Moses and Monotheism*, the last German-Jewish text considered here in detail) as my terminal date, both to avoid the many difficulties of writing about the Holocaust, and because the character of literature by Jews in Germany since 1945, whether elegiac or bitter, is strikingly different from literature before the catastrophe.[9]

In the age of assimilation, however, it is not always clear who may rightly be described as a Jew. There are (at least) five possible criteria for this description. First, according to the traditional legal criterion, a Jew is the child of two Jews, or of a non-Jewish father and a Jewish mother, or else a convert to Judaism. However,

---

[7] See Saul Friedlander (ed.), *Probing the Limits of Representation: Nazism and the 'Final Solution'* (Cambridge, Mass., 1992).

[8] Bernstein, *Foregone Conclusions: Against Apocalyptic History* (Berkeley and Los Angeles, 1994), p. 17.

[9] See Sander L. Gilman and Karen Remmler (eds.), *Reemerging Jewish Culture in Germany: Life and Literature since 1989* (New York and London, 1994); Jack Zipes, 'The Negative German–Jewish Symbiosis', in Dagmar C. G. Lorenz and Gabriele Weinberger (eds.), *Insiders and Outsiders: Jewish and Gentile Culture in Germany and Austria* (Detroit, 1994), pp. 144–54.

this definition only pushes the problem further back. What made one's mother Jewish? The answer must be the second, religious criterion: a Jew is a member of the people that has a special relationship with God. God has singled out Israel and given her the Torah; Israel has freely accepted this choice, and is voluntarily separate from the other nations of the world.[10] Since, however, one remains a Jew even if one renounces Judaism, either for a secular existence or for another religion, a third criterion is implied, which is biological or racial. In the late nineteenth century, as I describe in Chapter 3 below, enormous efforts were made to discover physical features that distinguished Jews from other people. No answer was ever found. The physique of the Jew seemed infinitely malleable. And so one turns to the fourth or cultural criterion. According to this criterion, being a Jew is not a fixed, stable identity; it is not guaranteed by one's relation to God or one's physical being; it is a matter of meanings which change continually throughout history. On this criterion, Jews, like members of all other cultures, ceaselessly reinvent themselves, through their interaction with changing historical contexts.

Here we encounter the central problem of present-day identity politics. I want an identity: I want to be able to identify myself with a larger group outside myself; I want to associate my fleeting, unstable self with something at least relatively fixed. But culture is not fixed; it is continually reinvented, as we know from the plethora of books with 'Invention' or 'Inventing' in their titles.[11] When the fashion for such titles began, they had a polemical, debunking ring, as though their authors wished triumphantly to undermine other people's false certainties. Now the invention of tradition is accepted as normal: 'the invention or construction of tradition is a key activity in a healthy culture,' affirms Robert Crawford.[12] But the whole point of tradition is that I did not invent it. It exists independent of me. If I am so self-aware that I know tradition or identity to be a fiction, it can no longer sustain

---

[10] See David Novak, *The Election of Israel: The Idea of the Chosen People* (Cambridge, 1995), esp. p. 10.

[11] e.g. Eric Hobsbawm and Terence Ranger (eds.), *The Invention of Tradition* (Cambridge, 1983); Adam Kuper, *The Invention of Primitive Society* (London, 1988); Larry Wolff, *Inventing Eastern Europe: The Map of Civilization on the Mind of the Enlightenment* (Stanford, Calif., 1994); Keith W. Whitelam, *The Invention of Ancient Israel: The Silencing of Palestinian History* (London, 1996).

[12] Crawford, *Devolving English Literature* (Oxford, 1992), p. 14.

me. Ironic self-awareness may give me self-satisfaction as I reflect
in my study, but it cannot help in the trials of life. If the fictions of
culture, identity, or nationhood are to be effective, I have to forget,
or never realize, that they are fictions. Hence, as Ernest Gellner
has said: 'Generally speaking, nationalist ideology suffers from
pervasive false consciousness.'[13] A Jewish cultural identity, like
any other cultural identity, is unstable and unreliable. The invention and reinvention of culture means a constant race against
oneself to outstrip the awareness that it is merely a fiction.

There is another problem with the invention of culture. Who
invents it? Do I invent my own culture, or accept what someone
else has invented for me? This problem becomes acute when we
consider the fifth criterion of Jewishness: the reactive criterion.
On this criterion, Jews remain Jews because antisemites insist on
regarding them as Jews and provide them with unwelcome and
hostile definitions of Jewishness which are hard or impossible to
escape from. The acceptance and internalization of such hostile
definitions leads to the phenomenon known, controversially, as
'Jewish self-hatred'. The argument that Jews are made Jews by
antisemites has a long history. Spinoza, rejecting the concept of
divine election, argues forcefully that the Jews 'have been
preserved in great measure by Gentile hatred'.[14] Three hundred
years later, Sartre maintains: 'The Jew is one whom other men
consider a Jew.'[15] The reactive definition of Jewishness underpins
the recurrent argument that when Jews are allowed to assimilate,
they will vanish into the surrounding population. The demo-
grapher Felix Theilhaber argued in 1911 that the increasing
number of mixed marriages would lead to the racial extinction
of the western European Jews, and recently the historian Bernard
Wasserstein has maintained that the dissolution of European
Jewry is far advanced.[16] Against such arguments one can point
to the Jews' fertility in reinventing a cultural identity. But it should
be clear that a reactive conception of Jewish identity puts one at

[13] Gellner, *Nations and Nationalism* (Oxford, 1983), p. 124.
[14] Benedict de Spinoza, *A Theologico-Political Treatise; A Political Treatise*, tr.
R. H. M. Elwes (New York, 1951), p. 55.
[15] Jean-Paul Sartre, *Anti-Semite and Jew*, tr. George J. Becker (New York, 1948),
p. 69.
[16] Felix A. Theilhaber, *Der Untergang der deutschen Juden* (Munich, 1911);
Bernard Wasserstein, *Vanishing Diaspora: The Jews in Europe since 1945* (London,
1996), p. 283.

the mercy of antisemites and implies that one finds no intrinsic value in Jewishness.

Since the terms 'Jew' and 'German' do not simply label independently existing entities but themselves help to construct and reshape those entities, it is here that the literary historian can make a contribution. For the texts I examine in this book do not simply register an independently existing historical reality. They help to form that reality by redefining the terms 'Jew' and 'Jewishness'. They construct Jewish identities out of materials which come both from Jewish tradition and also—often more—from the German culture in which their writers grew up. Joseph Roth said in 1933: 'We come from emancipation, from humanity (*Humanität*), from humanism, rather than from Egypt. Our ancestors are Goethe, Lessing, Herder, no less than Abraham, Isaac and Jacob.'[17] The definitions articulated in fictional texts are themselves—inevitably—unstable: while recognizing the author's intentions, one can also read the texts against the grain to reveal the presence of counter-meanings whose implications might be developed in later texts and realized in history.

The structure of this book is primarily thematic, only secondarily chronological.[18] The first chapter examines the link between Jewish emancipation and the Enlightenment, exploring the difficulties of adapting Judaism to the secular world without sacrificing its distinctive character. The second chapter pursues this narrative, focusing on varieties of nineteenth-century liberalism with which Jews were identified, and examining how three Viennese writers, Schnitzler, Stefan Zweig, and Freud, exposed the limitations of the enlightened liberalism to which they were vitally attached. Turning to antisemitism as an external obstacle to Jewish integration, the third chapter investigates the diversity of antisemitism, and looks at the representation of Jews in selected texts by Gentile writers. Chapter 4 considers Jewish responses to the evident failure of their hopes for integration, including the 'self-hatred' with which some internalized antisemitic stereotypes and the defiant 'hyperacculturation' in which others sought to be

---

[17] Letter to Stefan Zweig, 22 Mar. 1933, in Roth, *Briefe*, ed. Hermann Kesten (Cologne, 1970), p. 257.
[18] In organizing this material I have found a particularly useful model in Steven Beller's book *Vienna and the Jews, 1867–1938: A Cultural History* (Cambridge, 1989).

more German than the Germans. The final chapter turns to what historians have recently called 'dissimilation', the affirmation of Jewishness in response to an unwelcoming society. It inquires into new ways of being Jewish and reinventing Jewish identity: the rediscovery and revaluation of the traditional Jewish communities of eastern Europe; the notion that the Jew was really an Oriental and hence endowed quite differently from the Europeans among whom he was stranded; and finally the Zionist movement, typified by Theodor Herzl, which sought to solve the Jewish question by transporting the Jews to a new, or old, home in the East.

In writing this book I have incurred many debts. Mark Anderson, David Rechter, and Edward Timms read large parts of it and supplied detailed comments. The Humboldt Foundation enabled me to start the project in 1992 during a six months' stay in Germany, where I received much kind help from Barbara Klose and Gerhard Kurz. The Wiener Library in London was an invaluable resource. David Groiser, Desmond King, Karen Leeder, and Helen Watanabe provided encouragement in various forms. I also owe much to the doctoral theses on German-Jewish topics by Anita Bunyan, Hannah Burdekin, Dafna Clifford, and Ena Pedersen which I had the good fortune to examine or supervise.

Since this book is intended to explain an aspect of German cultural history to readers who may not know German, all quotations are given in English, with the original provided when it is of particular poetic or linguistic interest, and reference is made whenever convenient to English translations. The select bibliography lists those works referred to more than once in the footnotes.

I
Enlightenment

Before emancipation, the Jewish population in many German towns was normally restricted to a ghetto.[1] This *Judengasse* consisted of narrow streets crowded with tall, dingy buildings, often in an unpleasant part of town. Thus the Jews of Hamburg lived close to the city refuse dump, the Dreckwall. Some ghettos, like those of Worms and Hanau, had a gate which was shut at night; the Frankfurt ghetto, explored by the young Goethe, was locked every night until 1796.[2] They were overcrowded: in the Frankfurt ghetto in the late seventeenth century, 3,000 people lived in 200 dwellings. Its appearance over a century later was described thus by the journalist Ludwig Börne, who (as Löb Baruch) was born there in 1786:

Ahead of us a long alley with no end in sight, beside us just enough space to reassure us that we could turn back whenever we felt like it. Above us is no more sky than the sun needs to spread out its disc; there is no sky to be seen, nothing but sun. Everywhere a foul smell rises, and the cloth that keeps us from infection serves also to catch a compassionate tear or to hide a malicious smile from the gaze of the lurking Jews. As we wade laboriously through the mud, our slow pace provides us with leisure needed for contemplation. We step timidly and cautiously so as not to trample on any children. The latter are swimming about in the gutter, crawling around in the mud, innumerable as a swarm of insects which the sun's power has bred from dung.[3]

---

[1] This account of pre-emancipation German Jewry relies especially on Herman Pollack, *Jewish Folkways in Germanic Lands (1648–1806): Studies in Aspects of Daily Life* (Cambridge, Mass., 1971).

[2] See Johann Wolfgang Goethe, *Sämtliche Werke: Briefe, Tagebücher und Gespräche*, Deutsche Klassiker-Ausgabe, 40 vols. (Frankfurt, 1986–), I. xiv. 165–6. Henceforth cited as DKA.

[3] Börne, 'Über die Stättigkeit' (1808), in *Sämtliche Schriften*, ed. Peter and Inge Rippmann, 5 vols. (Dreieich, 1977), i. 47.

Börne's disgust with this slum shows his aversion to the setting from which he had escaped. Non-Jews could be more tolerant, for, as Goethe's example shows, the ghetto did not prevent contact between Jews and non-Jews: non-Jews might be employed as servants in Jewish homes, especially to run errands on the Sabbath; Jews and non-Jews would meet in inns to transact business; visitors, like Goethe, would stroll through the ghetto on Sundays. Despite lingering antipathy, there is considerable evidence for mutual toleration in the seventeenth and eighteenth centuries.

However, we must not imagine the pre-emancipation Jewish community as homogeneous. It was divided into a patrician class, a middle class, and a lower class.[4] The patrician class consisted of old-established families with special charters of protection, like the Oppenheimers of Frankfurt, the Wertheimers of Worms, or the Gumpertz family of Cleves; very wealthy Jews who were Court suppliers, bankers, and manufacturers; and scholars, rabbis, and doctors. They were widely separated from the middle and lower classes, consisting of merchants, traders, craftsmen, and community officials, who looked on the relatively privileged patricians with envy. While the diversity of criteria for membership of the patrician class—education alongside wealth—probably prevented the community from becoming rigidly stratified, educational opportunity of course usually depended on whether one's family could support one. In other ways, too, wealth defined one's social position: as a conspicuous example, it was the better-off members who had the distinction of being called to read from the Torah at Sabbath services.

Most Jewish communities were small and rural.[5] At the beginning of the nineteenth century, some 90 per cent of Jews living in German-speaking countries lived in villages and small towns. Many of them were traders, dealing in cattle, horses, hides, farm produce, and second-hand goods. Above them was a thin crust of contractors and financiers. Below these commercial strata was a growing mass of transients: the homeless, refugees from

    [4] Selma Stern, *The Court Jew* (Philadelphia, 1950), pp. 188–90.
    [5] See especially Werner Cahnman, 'Village and Small-Town Jews in Germany', in his *German Jewry: Its History and Sociology. Selected Essays*, ed. Joseph B. Maier, Judith Marcus, and Zoltán Tar (New Brunswick, NJ, 1989), pp. 43–68 (originally in *LBY* 19 (1974), 107–30).

pogroms, professional beggars (*Schnorrer*), and wandering singers. Poor Jews suffered from restrictions and special taxes (the *Leibzoll*, a transit tax otherwise levied only on cattle) and could not gain the right of residence. Although Jews were required to receive mendicants kindly, they often did so reluctantly, expecting to suffer petty theft; the Jewish-German word *Gascht*, we are told, designates not a welcome guest but one who is a nuisance.[6] It would be mistaken to exaggerate the solidarity of the pre-emancipation Jewish community.

One can also exaggerate its distance from its Gentile surroundings. Traders dealt with non-Jews; moneylenders lent them money. Gentiles often consulted Jewish doctors, and occasionally a Jewish doctor might be allowed to stay overnight in a Gentile's house if it were far from the ghetto.[7] Despite the social contacts promoted by commerce, Jewish traders were readily suspected of being sharp, dishonest, and excessively rich. When the bandit Johannes Bückler, known as Schinderhannes, systematically robbed Jews in the Hunsrück district south of Trier in the years 1798–1802, he could usually count on passive and even active support from the non-Jewish population.[8]

The stratified Jewish community was held together by the hostile, or at best unreliable, society surrounding it. The ghetto imposed physical proximity, but since Jews might often be expelled from a town (as from Vienna in 1670, from Prague in 1745) and return years or even generations later, they were united less by their physical setting than by the religious and legal traditions and folk customs that held their lives together. The key points of the life-cycle—birth, marriage, and death—were occasions for communal ceremonies. In addition, the community was held together by its members' physical appearance—the men's beards, the married women's covered hair; by allegiance to the rabbinic dietary laws; and of course by their language, a form of German with a large admixture of Hebrew words. Unlike the

---

[6] Cahnman, 'Village and Small-Town Jews', p. 46.

[7] See Robert Jütte, 'Contacts at the Bedside: Jewish Physicians and their Christian Patients', in R. Po-Chia Hsia and Hartmut Lehmann (eds.), *In and Out of the Ghetto: Jewish–German Relations in Late Medieval and Early Modern Germany* (Cambridge, 1995), pp. 137–50.

[8] See Cilli Kasper-Holtkotte, '"Jud, gib dein Geld her oder du bist des Todes". Die Banditengruppe des Schinderhannes und die Juden', *Aschkenas*, 3 (1993), 113–88.

Yiddish spoken in eastern Europe, however, this 'Jewish-German' (*Jüdisch-Deutsch*) was not so distinct as to hinder communication with non-Jews.[9] Sabbath religious practices reinforced a sense of physical restriction because the distance one could walk on the Sabbath was defined as 2,000 ells (Exod. 16: 29), an ell being two feet. One way of overcoming this restriction was the *eruv*, the legal fiction whereby one established another residence: this could by done by depositing a plate of food in a place that would symbolize the location of one's home; eating this food represented a change of dwelling. Some communities were surrounded by a wire marking the limit of Sabbath travel.[10]

The Jewish community was also held together by its self-government. The local *kehilla* comprised all Jews who were permanent local residents. *Halakha*, the Jewish religious law, was supplemented by many local by-laws. Communal leadership was in the hands of four to ten *parnassim* (wardens), assisted by lower officials. From the late Middle Ages onwards, these wardens tended to be drawn from the wealthiest members of the community, thus reinforcing its oligarchic character.[11] A large *kehilla* would have a high official, the chief elder or *shtadlan*, who acted as intermediary with the non-Jewish world. The rabbinate was independent of the *kehilla* organization. The basic religious observance required was public prayer twice daily in the synagogue, which thus reinforced the community's awareness of itself. Before daybreak every day, the *shammash* (sexton) would go from house to house calling people to the synagogue. There are, however, many complaints of inadequate synagogue attendance. The synagogue also served as a social centre, since business negotiations

---

[9] See Matthias Mieses, *Die Entstehungsursache der jüdischen Dialekte* (Vienna, 1915), repr. with introd. by Peter Freimark (Hamburg, 1979), pp. 85–6; Werner Weinberg, 'Die Bezeichnung Jüdischdeutsch: Eine Neubewertung', *ZfdP* 100 (1981), Sonderheft, 253–90. Weinberg shows that until after the First World War Jewish linguists emphasized the German character of their forebears' language, but subsequent linguists have stressed the autonomy of Yiddish and sought to extend this autonomy also to the Jewish-German dialect.

[10] See Pollack, *Jewish Folkways*, p. 166; Peter Freimark, 'Eruw/"Judentore". Zur Geschichte einer rituellen Institution im Hamburger Raum (und anderswo)', in Freimark et al., *Judentore, Kuggel, Steuerkonten: Untersuchungen zur Geschichte der deutschen Juden, vornehmlich im Hamburger Raum* (Hamburg, 1983), pp. 10–69.

[11] See Lionel Kochan, *Jews, Idols and Messiahs: The Challenge from History* (Oxford, 1990), pp. 32–5.

and gossip were permitted there. Festivals and holy days served even more to bring the community together.

Great importance was ascribed to education. The child was supposed to start school (*heder*) at 5 and stay at least until the age of 13. This includes at least some girls, according to community records. Glückel of Hameln tells us in her autobiography (which is written in Jewish-German and shows considerable knowledge of the Torah and contemporary moral literature) that she attended *heder* as a child.[12] The *melamed* (teacher) was supposed to instruct eight to ten children at one time; children of pre-school age might be sent just to sit and listen; as for length of study, the communal legislation of Hamburg–Altona in 1726 required the *melamed* to teach eight hours a day in winter and ten hours a day in summer.[13] The *heder* was a crèche as well as a school. Many reports stress the incompetence and brutality of the teachers, who had often failed at other professions, but the philosopher Lazarus Bendavid, no friend to traditional education, tells us that children were normally treated with kindness: his teacher went for walks with the pupils and took part in their games.[14] Children were started on Hebrew by reading the Pentateuch and moved as soon as possible to the Talmud. The main purpose of teaching was to enable pupils to follow prayers and readings in the synagogue; this took precedence over any systematic instruction. Gifted scholars graduated to a *yeshiva* when they were 12 or 13, normally in a different town.

However, these arrangements did not go unquestioned. Critics complained that the *heder* should have aimed to inculcate a thorough knowledge of the Bible and the Mishnah, instead of regarding these as mere preliminaries for the production of Talmud scholars. Moreover, the knowledge of Judaism inculcated in the seventeenth and eighteenth centuries had a particular character. David Sorkin has called it 'baroque Judaism', by analogy with the ceremonial elaboration of Counter-Reformation

---

[12] *The Life of Glückel of Hameln, written by herself*, tr. and ed. Beth-Zion Abrahams (London, 1962), p. 14. On her reading, see Natalie Zemon Davis, *Women on the Margins: Three Seventeenth-Century Lives* (Cambridge, Mass., 1995), pp. 22–8.

[13] Pollack, *Jewish Folkways*, p. 65.

[14] Bendavid, 'Selbstbiographie', in *Bildnisse jetzt lebender Berliner Gelehrten mit ihren Selbstbiographien* (Berlin, 1806), pp. 14–15; cf. the lecture 'Über den Unterricht der Juden' in his *Aufsätze verschiedenen Inhalts* (Berlin, 1800).

Catholicism, and described it as follows: 'Its strength was its single-minded concentration on the study of Talmud and law, which it often supported with mystical i.e. kabbalistic ideas. Its weaknesses were the method of Talmud study—a casuistry often at odds with literal meaning—its neglect of Hebrew, the Bible and the Jewish philosophical tradition and its cultural insularity manifest in a disdain of foreign languages and science.'[15] This casuistry, called *pilpul* or dialectics, valued ingenuity for its own sake, and was equally indifferent to philological scholarship and to the day-to-day practical questions on which rabbis were required to pronounce. It was opposed by the *musar* ('ethical') tradition that emerged in the seventeenth century; *musar* teachers wanted to guide the behaviour of ordinary Jews, and preferred simple discussion related to practical matters.[16] The meticulous observance of the Law required many precise definitions. For example, at the Passover *seder* meal one must eat unleavened bread. How much must one eat? The traditional answer is: a quantity at least as large as an olive. But how big is an olive? The *Shulḥan Arukh* (the sixteenth-century legal code by Joseph Karo) defines it as slightly less than half an egg. But, asked the eighteenth-century rabbi Ezekiel Landau of Prague, how do we know that olives and eggs are the same size now as in ancient times? The controversy continues to the present day.[17] *Pilpul* flourished above all among Polish Jewry: Salomon Maimon, who was brought up in Lithuania and found his way to Enlightenment Berlin, tells us that it favoured such conundrums as these: 'How many white hairs can a red heifer have and still remain a red heifer? Did the High Priest put on his shirt before his trousers, or the other way round? If the *yabam* (a man whose brother has died childless and who is obliged by law to marry his widow) falls off the roof and sticks in the mud, is he relieved from his duties or not?'[18] These are less absurd than they may seem: the first

[15] Sorkin, 'Jews, the Enlightenment and Religious Toleration—Some Reflections', *LBY* 37 (1992), 3–16 (p. 10).

[16] See Pollack, *Jewish Folkways*, pp. 77–8; David Sorkin, *The Transformation of German Jewry, 1780–1840* (New York and Oxford, 1987), pp. 45–8.

[17] This example is taken from Menachem Friedman, 'Life Tradition and Book Tradition in the Development of Ultraorthodox Judaism', in Harvey E. Goldberg (ed.), *Judaism Viewed from Within and from Without: Anthropological Studies* (Albany, NY, 1987), pp. 235–55 (p. 237).

[18] Maimon, *Lebensgeschichte*, ed. Jakob Fromer (Munich, 1911), p. 93.

concerns the definition of the 'red heifer without spot' required for sacrifice in Numbers 19, and incidentally illustrates the sorites paradox; but clearly such inquiries could easily promote pedantic over-ingenuity.

The seventeenth and eighteenth centuries saw various new currents within Judaism. The mysticism of the Kabbalah had some impact: it made Judaism more inward-looking by commending the performance of good actions (*mitsvoth*) less for their moral value than as means to assist the rekindling and reunion of the divine sparks that had been scattered by a primal catastrophe.[19] In 1666 the whole of European Jewry was convulsed by the appearance of the false Messiah Sabbatai Zvi, which seemed to confirm the doctrine of the Kabbalist Isaac Luria that the world was approaching the messianic era. Glückel of Hameln recalls how letters concerning Sabbatai Zvi were read to great enthusiasm in the Hamburg synagogue, and how many people sold up all their possessions, expecting the imminent restoration of the messianic kingdom.[20] After Sabbatai Zvi had disappointed his followers by adopting Islam, his influence lingered on in the antinomian movement led by Jacob Frank, which, as we shall see, penetrated the consciousness even of classical German writers.

In eastern Europe, disillusionment with Sabbatai and dissatisfaction with a narrowly intellectual tradition which seemed the only alternative gave rise to the Hasidic movement.[21] This originated in the eighteenth-century Ukraine with Israel ben Eliezer (c. 1700–60), known as the Baᶜal Shem Tov ('Master of the Holy Name'). Working within a well-established tradition of mysticism and shamanism, the Baᶜal Shem won followers by advocating a joyous communion with God which did not require ascetic feats or talmudic erudition. Hasidic leaders (*tsaddikim*)

---

[19] See Gershom Scholem, *Major Trends in Jewish Mysticism* (New York, 1946).

[20] *The Life of Glückel of Hameln*, p. 46.

[21] See S. A. Horodezky, *Religiöse Strömungen im Judentum, mit besonderer Berücksichtigung des Chassidismus* (Berne, 1920); Simon Dubnow, *Geschichte des Chassidismus*, tr. A. Steinberg, 2 vols. (Berlin, 1931); Stephen Sharot, *Messianism, Mysticism, and Magic: A Sociological Analysis of Jewish Religious Movements* (Chapel Hill, NC, 1982), chs. 9–11; Moshe Idel, *Hasidism: Between Ecstasy and Magic* (Albany, NY, 1995); Moshe Rosman, *Founder of Hasidism: A Quest for the Historical Baᶜal Shem Tov* (Berkeley and Los Angeles, 1996).

came to be credited with miraculous powers, including that of intercession with God. Their office became hereditary; some of them acquired wealth and maintained splendid courts which were thronged with their adherents and petitioners.

Although Hasidism underwent what Max Weber called the 'routinization of charisma', it was a genuine spiritual renewal, comparable to contemporaneous Protestant movements like Pietism or Methodism. If it had penetrated western Jewry, traditional Judaism might have put up far stronger resistance to the secularizing pressure of the Enlightenment. As it was, western Judaism could easily appear obsessed with superstition and scholasticism. In the 1750s this impression was reinforced by the much-publicized dispute between Jonathan Eybeschütz and Jacob Emden, two eminent rabbis living in Altona. Emden accused Eybeschütz of supplying pregnant women with protective amulets containing covert references to Sabbatai's magic powers. This controversy, which drew in the Senate of Hamburg and the King of Denmark, encouraged both Jews and Gentiles to regard mainstream Judaism as superstitious, disputatious, and hopelessly out of touch with real moral and intellectual issues. Traditional Judaism was ill equipped to face the new challenges that came to it from the society of the Enlightenment.

The first such challenge was political. Self-governing Jewish communities had an anomalous and precarious position within the absolutist states of early modern Europe. Princes were intent on creating unified states by removing the sovereign rights of aristocratic corporations and transferring power to the princely bureaucrats. These officials believed in the Roman legal theory of the unrestricted power of the state; in the theory of natural law, according to which any corporate body interposed between the sovereign ruler and his subjects threatened the unity of the state; and in theories of mercantilism which maintained that a state should as far as possible be economically self-sufficient. Arguing that a state's wealth depends on the happiness and prosperity of its subjects, mercantilism concluded that their lives should be regulated in considerable detail by a benevolent 'police state' (*Polizeistaat*), meaning 'a state in which the good of the ruler is indistinguishable from the good of the populace; the administrative apparatus is devoted to the increase of the ruler's wealth through the optimization of the happiness of his subjects'.[22]

These principles drew German Jews further into the surrounding society. From the early eighteenth century onwards, Jewish communities were brought under governmental control, so that the elders of the communities were obliged to present their financial and administrative reports to royal commissions, and to keep records in German instead of Hebrew. Thus, after the Jews were allowed to resettle in Prussia, their affairs were supervised by state officials, and their self-government was further limited by the *Judenreglement* of 1750, which restricted rabbinical jurisdiction to the religious sphere (ceremonies, marriages, wills, etc.) but forbade it to deal with civil and economic actions. Often the chief elder became a kind of royal official, serving as an intermediary between the community and the government.

But while Jews lost communal autonomy, they gained a kind of power through the rise of the Court Jews. Mercantilism assumed that Jewish merchants and financiers could benefit the state, and they were usually placed under the personal protection of the monarch. Belonging to an international financial network with its centre in Amsterdam, the Court Jews were able to supply food, weapons, clothing, and horses for the armies deployed in the period's continual wars, to provide princes with large sums on credit, and also to assist in secret diplomatic negotiations. In return, they were freed from many restrictions, being permitted to buy land, ride in carriages, and acquire titles of nobility. They might even mix socially with princes: Glückel of Hameln, who was married to the wealthy jeweller Chaim Segal, tells us how her daughter's wedding with Kossman Gumpertz was attended by Prince Frederick of Cleves and Prince Maurice of Nassau.[23] Despite wealth and comfort, however, German Court Jews maintained a conservative life-style: even Samson Wertheimer, the *Judenkaiser* in Vienna who raised vast sums for the Emperor, retained his beard, dressed 'like a Pole', and acquired few possessions except for books and manuscripts.[24] In the eighteenth

---

[22] Keith Tribe, *Governing Economy: The Reformation of German Economic Discourse 1750–1840* (Cambridge, 1988), p. 34.
[23] *The Life of Glückel of Hameln*, pp. 78–9.
[24] See Jonathan I. Israel, *European Jewry in the Age of Mercantilism, 1550–1750* (Oxford, 1985), pp. 132–3, 143.

century this changed: the famous Joseph Süss Oppenheimer, known as 'Jud Süss', who in 1734 was placed by the Duke of Württemberg in charge of the state's finances, dressed like a nobleman, professed deism, and immersed himself in secular culture. His arrest and execution after the Duke's death showed dramatically how vulnerable the Court Jews were: they depended wholly on the favour of potentates, and their necessary identification with their international financial network made them national as well as religious aliens. Many Court Jews died in poverty, cheated by the Gentile rulers to whom they had advanced money: Selma Stern remarks that their fates resemble the downfall of protagonists in seventeenth-century martyr dramas.[25]

Mercantilism in the eighteenth-century German states stimulated home manufactures and discouraged imports, thus reducing the Jews' economic role in trade between states. Some Jews prospered in industry, like Moses Mendelssohn in Berlin: originally a clerk in Isaak Bernhard's silk-weaving factory, he was made manager and, after Bernhard's death in 1768, ran the factory jointly with the widow, eventually employing over a hundred weavers, who, because of government regulations, must mainly have been non-Jews. The Jews' economic activities were carefully supervised: large sums were demanded as dues (*Schutzgeld*); the Jews of Berlin were compelled to establish factories (in order to prevent them from engaging in petty trading), and on obtaining an economic concession, or on marrying, they were also obliged (from 1769 on) to buy a large quantity of china and sell it (at a loss) outside Prussia, to assist Prussian manufactures.[26] One could not even choose one's china: thus Mendelssohn was obliged to buy twenty life-size china monkeys, some of which were still family possessions over a hundred years later.[27] Meanwhile, a growing proportion of German Jews sank into poverty. Of the sixty or seventy thousand Jews who are thought to have lived in 1750 in the territories that later became Imperial Germany, over half lived

---

[25] Stern, *The Court Jew*, p. 248, with many examples. On Jud Süss, see ibid., ch. 4; also Stern, *Jud Süß: Ein Beitrag zur deutschen und zur jüdischen Geschichte* (Munich, 1929); Barbara Gerber, *Jud Süß: Aufstieg und Fall im frühen 18. Jahrhundert* (Hamburg, 1990).

[26] Ludwig Geiger, *Geschichte der Juden in Berlin*, 2 vols. (Berlin, 1871), i. 65–6.

[27] Sebastian Hensel, *Die Familie Mendelssohn 1729–1847*, ed. Konrad Feilchenfeldt (Frankfurt, 1995), p. 12.

a marginal existence of petty trade, begging, and thievery. Mercantilist policy dictated that these 'Trödel-und Betteljuden' should be expelled, as they were from Prussia in 1750.

As relations between Jewish communities and absolutist bureaucracies grew closer, the question arose whether education should acknowledge the secular world. The prominent rabbi Jacob Emden maintained that the study of philosophers would offer nothing that was not already stated in the Bible and rabbinic literature; he felt a need for instruction in languages, politics, and other religions, but also opined that 'whoever brings into his house books other than the Bible introduces confusion' and found that secular studies caused him 'considerable pain, anguish, and intense suffering'.[28] The efforts of such conservatives, however, did not prevent the growing secularization of urban Jewish communities. Thus Lazarus Bendavid describes his upbringing in Berlin in the 1760s, making it clear that he belonged to the second generation that had absorbed outside influences:

My parents had both enjoyed a liberal education. They both wrote very correctly in Hebrew and German letters, both spoke good French, and in particular my father wrote very fine commercial documents and was well read in the classical French authors. Their religious ideas were formed on a system of their own, and deviated, much for the better, from those of most Jews at that time. Thousands upon thousands of petty ceremonial laws, the transgression of which was considered by other Jews the utmost sin, were scarcely known in our house even by name. [. . .] I was simply taught to lead an orderly and upright life, with my parents as exceptionally conscientious models, and, as my only religious practice, to recite the morning and evening prayers.[29]

Parallels can be drawn, for example, with the parents of Heinrich Heine. His mother, Peira van Geldern (known as Betty), born in 1771, daughter of a prominent doctor and descended from a family of Court Jews, still wrote German in Hebrew characters but was well versed in French literature and an adherent of Rousseau's progressive ideas on child-rearing; his father, Samson Heine, born in 1764, evidently had a relaxed attitude to ritual

---

[28] Quoted in Pollack, *Jewish Folkways*, p. 80.
[29] Bendavid, 'Selbstbiographie', pp. 6–7. For comment and other examples, see Steven M. Lowenstein, *The Berlin Jewish Community: Enlightenment, Family, and Crisis, 1770–1830* (New York, 1994), pp. 51–2.

observance, for he was a Freemason, socialized with his Christian fellow-citizens in Düsseldorf, and gave his son only a rudimentary Jewish education; there is no evidence that Heine had a bar mitzvah.[30]

Many educated Jews believed that contact with secular thought, far from harming Judaism, could provide much-needed renewal. From the 1760s onwards we find an increasing number of Jews, known as *maskilim*, who are schooled in the Torah but also acquainted with foreign languages and secular culture. Eventually they formed a coherent movement, the Haskala or Jewish Enlightenment.[31] Their great prototype was Moses Mendelssohn, whose ambiguous position between preserving the traditions of Judaism and contributing to its dissolution will be discussed later, and who had pointed the way with a short-lived journal, the *Kohelet Musar* ('Preacher of Morals', 1758), which combined the *musar* tradition with the educational mission of the German moral weeklies. Accepting the arguments put forward by Locke in *A Letter on Toleration* (1689) and by Mendelssohn in *Jerusalem* (1783) for the separation of church and state, the *maskilim* criticized rabbinical jurisdiction, especially the use of the ban (*herem*) as a penal sanction. They wanted to enlarge the scope of Jewish education by promoting the study of Hebrew and a wider interest in science, philosophy, and mathematics. Naphtali Herz Wessely's Hebrew pamphlet *Words of Peace and Truth* (1782), regarded as the manifesto of the Haskala, argues that a partially secular education would pose no danger to Judaism, for while the 'teaching of God' can be known only through revelation, the 'teaching of man' (history, science, languages) is necessary for social existence. In 1783 they founded a Hebrew journal, *Ha-Me'asef* ('The Collector'), to promote the study of the plain meaning of the Bible, unencumbered by talmudic ingenuity, and to encourage the use of the Hebrew language in contrast to Jewish-German.

The *maskilim* seem to have been right in thinking that the Jewish corporate community was in rapid decline. Besides external pressure, there was also pressure from within the Jewish community to integrate with external society: this came especially

---

[30] See Jeffrey L. Sammons, *Heinrich Heine: A Modern Biography* (Princeton, 1979).
[31] On the Haskala, see Sorkin, *The Transformation of German Jewry*, chs. 2 and 3.

from businessmen, bankers, and Court agents, but also from the Jewish educated middle class. The Jews of Enlightenment Berlin were the pacemakers of acculturation. By the late eighteenth century Jewish men dressed indistinguishably from non-Jews, with wigs or three-cornered hats instead of the traditional flat hat (*Barett*); many were beardless, as was normal for Gentiles, and even Mendelssohn retained only a small narrow beard. Berlin Jews were conspicuous at the theatre, on promenades, and in coffee-houses, where interaction with Gentiles rapidly increased. From the 1780s religious observance declined sharply. In a letter of 1783 the artist Chodowiecki declared that the Berlin Jews, apart from the lower classes, were far from orthodox: 'They buy and sell on Saturdays, eat all forbidden foods, keep no fast days, etc.'[32] Such changes of lifestyle further divided the community and weakened rabbinical authority. So did the requests made by priv-ileged Jews, such as financiers, for release from rabbinical jurisdic-tion, and their preference for taking legal disputes to the civil courts. The wider society was no longer seen simply as a source of economic advantage, but also as a source of social and intellectual pleasure. In comparison, the previous closed community had little to offer. 'All that keeps us together', wrote the historian Isaak Markus Jost in 1822, 'are impressions received in our youth, nothing more. Our children are living in a different world; they have no reason to sacrifice their whole existence in order to be called Jews, which they aren't.'[33]

On the one hand, therefore, the intellectual leaders of German Jewry were seeking to renew Judaism and reconcile it with the Enlightenment. On the other, the social vanguard of German Jewry felt less and less compunction about discarding those customs and practices that had hitherto kept Jews distinct. Was it really possible to renew Judaism while accepting the values of the Enlightenment? When no longer protected by the closed community, was Judaism not bound to dissolve? In any case, while the new generation of educated Jews was anxious to enter the society of the Enlightenment, that society was decidedly lukewarm about welcoming them.

---

[32] Quoted in Lowenstein, *The Berlin Jewish Community*, p. 53.
[33] Letter to S. M. Ehrenberg, 16 Aug. 1822, in *Leopold and Adelheid Zunz: An Account in Letters 1815–1885*, ed. Nahum N. Glatzer (London, 1958), pp. 34–5.

HOW THE ENLIGHTENMENT SAW THE JEWS

Many Enlightenment thinkers held deeply negative opinions of Jews and Judaism.[34] These followed from their scepticism towards revelation and their view of God as the Supreme Being and first cause who had created the world as a well-functioning machine that required no subsequent intervention. Nature and reason were thought sufficient to convince one of the existence of a supreme being and of universal principles of morality. This deism, which attacked not only the revelation of Christ but also the revelation made to Moses on Sinai, denied the Jews any significant part in history. For if the essential truths of Christianity were as old as the creation, then Judaism could lay no special claim to moral excellence, and it could be seen as consisting largely of ceremonies suitable for the primitive state of the ancient Hebrews but irrelevant to subsequent history. The ceremonial laws ordained in the Pentateuch, argued Spinoza, 'formed no part of the Divine law, and had nothing to do with blessedness and virtue, but had reference only to the election of the Hebrews, [and] therefore they were only valid while that kingdom lasted'.[35]

Many writers drew an unflattering picture of Old Testament Jews, charging them with gloom, intolerance, immorality, and xenophobia.[36] The English deist Matthew Tindal dwells on how Jacob cheated his brother, how the Israelites exterminated the unoffending Canaanites, how Rahab betrayed her country, how David cursed his enemies, and how the prophets called down arbitrary punishments on their antagonists; he calls the spirit of the Old Testament 'a Spirit of Cruelty'.[37] Voltaire's article 'Juifs' in the *Dictionnaire philosophique* denounces the Old Testament

[34] See Isaac Eisenstein Barzilay, 'The Jew in the Literature of the Enlightenment', *Jewish Social Studies*, 18 (1956), 243–61; Arthur Hertzberg, *The French Enlightenment and the Jews* (New York and London, 1968); Klara Carmely, 'Wie "aufgeklärt" waren die Aufklärer in Bezug auf die Juden?', in Ehrhard Bahr, Edward P. Harris, and Laurence G. Lyon (eds.), *Humanität und Dialog: Lessing und Mendelssohn in neuer Sicht* (Detroit and Munich, 1982), pp. 177–88.

[35] Spinoza, *A Theologico-Political Treatise*, p. 69.

[36] See e.g. Anthony Ashley Cooper, Earl of Shaftesbury, *Characteristics of Men, Manners, Opinions, Times, etc.*, ed. John M. Robertson, 2 vols. (London, 1900), i. 22; Christian Wilhelm von Dohm, *Über die bürgerliche Verbesserung der Juden* (Berlin and Stettin, 1781), pp. 20–1.

[37] Tindal, *Christianity as Old as the Creation* (London, 1730; repr. New York and London, 1978), p. 268.

Jews for massacring their enemies, denies them any philosophy, art, or learning, complains of their material conception of the soul, and charges them with cannibalism, bestiality, and human sacrifice.[38] In his *Essai sur les mœurs* he says of the Jewish nation: 'It dares to spread irreconcilable hatred against all the nations; it revolts against its masters. Always superstitious, always greedy for others' property, always barbarous, servile in misfortune, and insolent in prosperity.'[39] Voltaire of course is using the Jews as a stick with which to beat the Christianity that acknowledges its descent from them. As an alternative to the Christian scheme of sacred history, he puts forward a non-Eurocentric historical narrative which seeks everywhere for anticipations of the deism of the Enlightenment and professes to find it among the Chinese and the Indians. Yet his ostensible cosmopolitanism is actually self-centred, for he is not trying to appreciate the otherness of other cultures, but searching for equivalents to his own beliefs.[40]

The figure of Moses was particularly controversial for the Enlighteners.[41] They inherited from the Renaissance an inclination to value the supposed wisdom of the Egyptians, and to adopt the scurrilous ancient tradition, recorded by Josephus and repeated by Tacitus, that the Jews were originally leprous Egyptians banished from their country.[42] Thus for Giordano Bruno 'the Jews are without doubt the excrements of Egypt' while Egypt is 'the grand monarchy of letters and nobility'.[43] Radical Enlightenment thinkers, like John Toland, imagined that the Egyptians had anticipated their own deism or pantheism.[44] Hermann Samuel Reimarus, whose biblical criticism was published only after his death by his friend Lessing, depicted Moses as an unscrupulous political manipulator, while the notorious *Traité des trois imposteurs* portrayed him, along with Jesus and Muhammad, as

[38] See Voltaire, *Œuvres complètes*, ed. Condorcet (Paris, 1879), esp. xix. 513–23.
[39] Voltaire, *Essai sur les mœurs*, ed. René Pomeau, 2 vols. (Paris, 1963), i. 151.
[40] See J. H. Brumfitt, *Voltaire Historian* (Oxford, 1958), p. 77.
[41] See Wolf-Daniel Hartwich, *Die Sendung Moses: Von der Aufklärung bis Thomas Mann* (Munich, 1997).
[42] See J. N. Sevenster, *The Roots of Pagan Anti-Semitism in the Ancient World* (Leiden, 1975), pp. 142–3.
[43] Frances A. Yates, *Giordano Bruno and the Hermetic Tradition* (London, 1964), p. 223.
[44] See Jan Assmann, *Moses the Egyptian: The Memory of Egypt in Western Monotheism* (Cambridge, Mass., and London, 1997), pp. 91–6.

a deliberate fraud.[45] One pamphleteer compared his appeal to the Jews with the propaganda about 'la grande nation' employed by Napoleon.[46] But the fullest debunking of Moses comes from Friedrich Schiller. His 1790 lecture 'Die Sendung Moses' ('The Mission of Moses'), which he delivered as professor of history at Jena, follows the work of a Jena colleague who had argued that the Egyptian priests were the world's first Freemasons. Drawing on Tacitus, Schiller describes the Jews in Egyptian exile as a contemptible, degenerate, and probably leprous people, similar to the pariahs of Hinduism. Moses, however, had been brought up among the Egyptians and learnt all the wisdom of their priests, including the idea of monotheism. Resolving to liberate his people, he first had to imbue them with heroism, and this he did by proclaiming the true God with the aid of fables and miracles suited to his public's limited understanding. Thus Moses, a well-intentioned charlatan, enabled the Jews to preserve the pure doctrine of monotheism: 'We must esteem them as a mean and unclean vessel in which something precious was preserved; we must honour in this nation the channel which, however unclean it might be, was chosen by Providence to bring us the noblest of all goods, the truth, but which Providence broke as soon as it had done what it should.'[47]

Schiller's essay has disturbing implications for the situation of Jews in eighteenth-century Germany. For it was widely accepted that the authority of rabbis and the practice of Talmud exegesis had reduced Diaspora Jews to a state of degeneracy such as Schiller ascribes to the followers of Moses. Lessing in *The Education of the Human Race* complains that 'the very way in which the Rabbis handled *their* sacred books' was, by over-interpretation and gratuitous allegorization, to impart 'a petty, crooked, hairsplitting understanding' and make their pupils 'full of mysteries, superstitious, full of contempt for all that is comprehensible and

[45] See 'Viertes Fragment eines Ungenannten', in Gotthold Ephraim Lessing, *Werke*, ed. Herbert G. Göpfert *et al.*, 8 vols. (Munich, 1970–9), vii. 398–403 (henceforth cited as L); *Traité des trois Imposteurs*, ed. P. Rétat (Grenoble, 1973), pp. 46–7; H. B. Nisbet, '*De Tribus Impostoribus*: on the genesis of Lessing's *Nathan der Weise*', *Euphorion*, 73 (1979), 365–87.
[46] Johann Wilhelm Kosmann, *Für die Juden: Ein Wort zur Beherzigung an die Freunde der Menschheit und die wahren Verehrer Jesu* (Berlin, 1803), pp. 8–9.
[47] 'Die Sendung Moses', in Schiller, *Sämtliche Werke*, ed. Gerhard Fricke and Herbert G. Göpfert, 5 vols. (Munich, 1958), iv. 784.

easy'.[48] The modern rabbinate attracted the enmity which the Enlightenment reserved for priestly power, especially because they were able to excommunicate dissidents by the *herem* or ban. Its best-known victim was Spinoza, who was expelled by the Amsterdam community in 1656. It was widely thought that Moses Mendelssohn had similarly been excommunicated for publishing a German translation of the Pentateuch.[49] This exaggeration shows how ready the Enlighteners were to demonize their chosen antagonists.[50]

Rabbinic Judaism was considered not only authoritarian and obscurantist, but fossilized. Kant thinks it merely external, a church without religion. Towards the end of *Religion within the Bounds of Reason Alone* Kant dismisses as fetishistic religious practices regarded as means of grace, like ritual fasting, washing, praying, and pilgrimages in Islam; without doubt the Jewish ceremonial law would fall under the same condemnation. He thinks Judaism must expect a peaceful annihilation by being transformed into a pure morality: 'The euthanasia of Judaism is purely moral religion, abandoning all ancient doctrines.'[51]

Kant shared common prejudices against Jews. A footnote to the discussion of honesty and deceit in his *Anthropology from a Pragmatic Viewpoint* describes the Jews as a nation of merchants and hence of deceivers: 'Since their exile the Palestinians living among us have, as far as the great majority is concerned, acquired a not unfounded reputation for deceit', a national character which Kant attributes to the location of Palestine at the intersection of many trade routes.[52] In private conversation, he disapproved of Lessing's *Nathan* because he disliked Jewish heroes; he described Jews as social vampires; and he complained that Salomon Maimon's comments on his philosophy had a characteristically Jewish self-importance.[53] Yet

---

[48] *Lessing's Theological Writings*, ed. Henry Chadwick (London, 1956), p. 91.

[49] See Alexander Altmann, *Moses Mendelssohn: A Biographical Study* (London, 1973), p. 387.

[50] See Andreas Gotzmann, 'Rabbiner und Bann. Zur Problematik der Analyse und Bewertung zweier Topoi des aufklärerischen Diskurses', *Aschkenas*, 4 (1994), i. 99–125.

[51] *Der Streit der Fakultäten*, in Kant, *Werke*, ed. Wilhelm Weischedel, 6 vols. (Frankfurt, 1964), vi. 320–1.   [52] Kant, *Werke*, vi. 517–18.

[53] See Gunnar Och, *Imago judaica: Juden und Judentum im Spiegel der deutschen Literatur 1750–1812* (Würzburg, 1995), pp. 23–4; Carmely, 'Wie "aufgeklärt" waren die Aufklärer in Bezug auf die Juden?', p. 185.

he also praised Maimon's understanding of his work, corresponded with Moses Mendelssohn, and was friendly with the
Jewish doctor Marcus Herz.

Similar condemnations are found in the work of the Romantic
generation of philosophers. They apply the Enlightenment critique
of rabbinical Judaism to Jewish history as a whole. The young
Hegel draws an over-sharp distinction between the legalism of
Moses and Jesus' gospel of love, evidently unaware of such figures
as the saintly pre-Christian teacher Hillel. For Hegel, Judaism is
legalistic, external, alienated from nature and the world of the
senses. He evidently did not know about such renewals of Judaism
as Kabbalistic mysticism and Hasidic spirituality. According to
Hegel, Abraham established his people in loveless isolation from
the rest of the world; Moses freed the slavish Jews from Egypt,
only to establish his own tyranny; their ideals were merely
animal—a land flowing with milk and honey; their relation to
God was similarly servile, and enforced by the Law in which 'the
holiest of things, namely the service of God and virtue, was
ordered and compressed in dead formulas'.[54] Although some
Jews, like the Essenes and John the Baptist, had loftier conceptions of virtue, the multitude were unable to recognize the divinity
of Jesus: 'The lion has no room in a nutshell, the infinite spirit
none in the prison of a Jewish soul, the whole of life none in a
withering leaf.'[55] In Hegel's mature philosophy of history, Jewish
history is played down and described, despite its 'grand features of
character', as exclusive, xenophobic, superstitious, and lacking in
culture.[56] Feuerbach takes Hegel's critique of Judaism to the point
of caricature, not only defaming it as a narrowly practical,
utilitarian and egoistic religion but maintaining that it is
essentially gastronomic: 'The Israelites opened to Nature only
the gastric sense; their taste for Nature lay only in the palate;
their consciousness of God in eating manna.'[57] Nor do these

---

[54] G. W. F. Hegel, *Early Theological Writings*, tr. T. M. Knox and Richard Kroner
(Chicago, 1948), p. 68. See Reinhard Sonnenschmidt, 'Zum philosophischen Antisemitismus bei G. W. F. Hegel', *Zeitschrift für Religion und Geistesgeschichte*, 44
(1992), 289–301.

[55] Hegel, *Early Theological Writings*, p. 265. Translation amended: Hegel wrote 'in
einer Nuß', which Knox mistranslates as 'in a nest'.

[56] Hegel, *The Philosophy of History*, tr. J. Sibree (New York, 1956), p. 197.

[57] Ludwig Feuerbach, *The Essence of Christianity*, tr. George Eliot (New York,
1957), p. 114.

philosophers expect any renewal of Judaism: 'Judaism has long been a dead religion,' writes Schleiermacher in 1799, 'and those who at present still bear its colours are actually sitting and mourning beside the undecaying mummy and weeping over its demise and its sad legacy.'[58]

But while the philosophers dismiss Judaism and urge conversion, Schiller reveals a deeper unease about Jewish emancipation in his first play, *Die Räuber* (*The Robbers*, 1781). Besides the two brothers Karl and Franz, who revolt in contrasted but explosive ways against patriarchal authority and indeed against the moral order of the universe, we have Karl's fellow-student Moritz Spiegelberg, implicitly identified as a Jew, who joins his robber band, secretly hoping to lead it. Spiegelberg's ambitious fantasies begin with the reconquest of Jerusalem from the Turks and move on from there:

> Great thoughts are taking shape in my soul! Mighty plans are fermenting in my ingenious mind. Curse me for sleeping! [*striking his forehead*] for letting my energies lie fettered, my prospects barred and thwarted; I am awake, I feel what I am—what I must and shall be!
> MOOR: You are a fool. The wine has gone to your head.
> SPIEGELBERG [*in greater excitement*]: Spiegelberg, they will say, are you a magician, Spiegelberg? What a pity you did not become a general, Spiegelberg, the King will say, you would have beaten the Austrians into a cocked hat. Yes, I can hear the doctors complaining, it is wicked that he didn't take up medicine, he would have discovered a new powder for the goitre. Ah! and that he didn't study economics, the Sullys will sigh in their treasuries, he would have conjured louis d'or from stones. And Spiegelberg will be the name, in east and west, and into the mud with you, cowards and toads, as Spiegelberg spreads his wings and flies high into the temple of fame.[59]

Spiegelberg can imagine specific achievements only as things he *might* have done. He wants to be famous for being famous, and his fantasy of rising to world celebrity is based crucially on hatred and contempt for the rivals and inferiors whom he looks forward to crushing. In the play, Spiegelberg fades out as a character, but he does lead some of the robbers in attacking a convent and raping

---

[58] Friedrich Schleiermacher, *On Religion: Speeches to its Cultured Despisers*, tr. Richard Crouter (Cambridge, 1988), p. 211.

[59] Schiller, *The Robbers* and *Wallenstein*, tr. F. J. Lamport (Harmondsworth, 1979), pp. 40–1; Schiller, *Sämtliche Werke*, i. 507.

the nuns, a sign no doubt of his violent enmity to Christianity. Whether Spiegelberg is to be unambiguously understood as Jewish is still disputed, but his many references to Jerusalem, Josephus, and circumcision strongly suggest it. Philipp Veit has argued that his career is modelled on that of the adventurer Jacob Frank (1726–91), who, mingling Christian ideas with those of the pseudo-messiah Sabbatai Zvi, proclaimed himself the Messiah and induced his followers to maintain him in a castle at Offenbach am Main.[60] Through Spiegelberg, the frustrated young Schiller also projects his own ambitions, thus simultaneously expressing, disavowing, and caricaturing them: we shall find many Jewish figures serving similar functions in works by non-Jewish authors. At the same time, Spiegelberg conveys the desperate frustration of the excluded. In the twentieth century he was recognized by the Zionist Kurt Blumenfeld as 'an early form of the Jewish intellectual of later times'.[61]

For later generations, it was particularly important to know what the towering figure of Goethe thought about the Jews. Goethe's relation to the Enlightenment was mixed. His drama *Iphigenie auf Tauris* extends its universalist humanism to include not only Scythians but women.[62] He upheld deism, exalted morality over dogma, and affirmed the historical study of the Bible.[63] On the other hand, Goethe was critical of Newton, Voltaire, and D'Holbach.[64] He associated the Enlightenment especially with France, objected to its over-intellectualism and over-abstractness, and insisted on going back to direct, vital experience.

A similar ambivalence, tending towards disapproval, pervades Goethe's attitude towards the Jews. He spoke highly of such

[60] See Veit, 'The Strange Case of Moritz Spiegelberg', *Germanic Review*, 44 (1969), 171–85. Against Spiegelberg's Jewishness: Och, *Imago judaica*, pp. 214–19.

[61] Kurt Blumenfeld, *Erlebte Judenfrage: Ein Vierteljahrhundert deutscher Zionismus* (Stuttgart, 1962), p. 30.

[62] See T. J. Reed, 'Iphigenies Unmündigkeit: Zur weiblichen Aufklärung', in Georg Stötzel (ed.), *Germanistik — Forschungsstand und Perspektiven*, 2 vols. (Berlin, 1984), ii. 505–24.

[63] Deism: DKA I. xiv. 153; morality: 'Das Göttliche', I. i. 333–5; and Bible criticism: *Werke*, Hamburger Ausgabe, ed. Erich Trunz, 14 vols. (Hamburg, 1949–60), xii. 234. This edition is cited henceforth as HA. See Wolfdietrich Rasch, *Goethes 'Iphigenie auf Tauris' als Drama der Autonomie* (Munich, 1979).

[64] DKA I. xiv. 527–30, 535–6. See Dieter Borchmeyer, *Höfische Gesellschaft und französische Revolution bei Goethe* (Kronberg, 1977).

Jewish acquaintances as the salon hostess Rahel Levin and the composer Felix Mendelssohn-Bartholdy (both converts), the Kantian philosopher and physician Marcus Herz, the playwright Michael Beer (brother of the composer Meyerbeer), the composer Ferdinand Hiller, and the painter Moritz Oppenheim, whom he allowed to illustrate his small-town epic *Hermann und Dorothea*. On his holidays in Carlsbad Goethe made friends with cultivated Jewish ladies from Vienna, with whom he afterwards corresponded, notably Cäcilie von Eskeles (daughter of the Prussian Court Jew Daniel Itzig) and her sister-in-law Eleonore von Fliess, who was notorious for her many love-affairs.[65] Yet though there are no grounds for calling him an antisemite, his writings do contain numerous casual and clichéd disparagements of Jews, which were gleefully quoted, often out of context, in the antisemitic compendia of the nineteenth and twentieth centuries.[66] His visits to the Frankfurt ghetto enabled him to make fun of Judaism in his parody of a German-Jewish sermon, which came to light only in 1856.[67]

Goethe also upheld conventional prejudices against the admission of Jews to civil life. He thought that proposals for their emancipation would endanger social order (DKA I. xv. 615). He was annoyed by Duke Carl August's liberal ordinance of 1823 granting Jews freedom to practise their religion, marry non-Jews, attend grammar schools and universities, and practise trades. He deplored it as a 'scandalous law' which would 'undermine all moral feelings in families, which rested entirely on religious feelings' (strange sentiments from the author of *Elective Affinities*), and even wondered if it had been engineered by bribes from 'the almighty Rothschild'.[68] A similar conservatism seems to underlie the statement in *Wilhelm Meisters Wanderjahre* that the new society of emigrants, which is to teach the Christian religion for its ethical content, cannot admit any Jews because the latter, in rejecting Christianity, have rejected the highest achievements of

[65] See Florian Krobb, '"Überdies waren die Mädchen hübsch . . .": Goethes Jüdinnen', *Oxford German Studies*, 20–1 (1991–2), 33–45.

[66] See e.g. Theodor Fritsch, *Handbuch der Judenfrage* (Leipzig, 1942; 1st pub. in 1887 as *Antisemiten-Catechismus*), pp. 446–9, and the reply, restoring the quotations to their context, in *Antisemiten-Spiegel: Die Antisemiten im Lichte des Christenthums, des Rechtes und der Wissenschaft*, 2nd edn. (Danzig, 1900), pp. 344–9

[67] See Och, *Imago judaica*, p. 223.

[68] Conversation with Kanzler von Müller on 23 Sept. 1823, DKA II. x. 112.

culture (DKA I. x. 687). Goethe is prepared to be friendly with individual Jews, but shows a conventional disapproval of Jews in general. A judicious commentator concludes that in some ways 'he failed to soar beyond the prejudices of a courtier in a small eighteenth-century German princedom'.[69]

Some Enlightenment thinkers held a more positive view of Old Testament Jews and (less often) of their modern descendants. They were helped by the weakening of the theological outlook which required the Jews either to be revered as God's chosen people or deplored for rejecting the message of Christ. Instead, comparative and ethnographic perspectives made it possible to look at ancient and modern Jews in a cooler, less judgemental way. Thus Johann David Michaelis, a professor of Oriental languages at Göttingen, tried to examine the law of Moses by the philosophical method of Montesquieu, seeing it not as a divine system which was beyond criticism but as an attempt to regulate social life in particular historical and geographical circumstances.[70] In this light, Moses' legislation appears neither tyrannical nor absurd, but prudent and intelligent within its constraints. By comparing it with the customs of Bedouins, Michaelis strengthened the tendency to see the Jews not as unique but as similar to other peoples of the Middle East. This tendency was powerfully continued by Herder in his *Vom Geist der Ebräischen Poesie* (*The Spirit of Hebrew Poetry*, 1782). Against the charge of crudity, he defends the Hebrew language as primitive, sensuous, and energetic like the language of Homer. By treating the Old Testament not as theology but as poetry and fable, and comparing it with Arabic and other Oriental literatures, he liberates it from dogma and enriches the reader's appreciation. Against the charge that the Hebrews were narrow-minded, xenophobic, and frequently immoral, Herder palliates their misconduct by looking at its narrative context and defending their humanity. He particularly celebrates Moses as a wise

---

[69] William Rose, 'Goethe and the Jews', in his *Men, Myths and Movements in German Literature* (London, 1931), pp. 157–80 (p. 180). See also Mark Waldman, *Goethe and the Jews* (New York, 1934); Norbert Oellers, 'Goethe und Schiller in ihrem Verhältnis zum Judentum', in Hans Otto Horch and Horst Denkler (eds.), *Conditio Judaica: Judentum, Antisemitismus und deutschsprachige Literatur vom 18. Jahrhundert bis zum Ersten Weltkrieg*, part I (Tübingen, 1988), pp. 108–30; Günter Hartung, 'Goethe und die Juden', *Weimarer Beiträge*, 40 (1994), 398–416.

[70] Michaelis, *Mosaisches Recht*, 2nd edn., 6 vols. (Reutlingen, 1788–93).

legislator surpassing the Spartan Lycurgus: 'His legislation is the most ancient model we have, at least in writing, of how hygiene, morality, political order and the service of God are a single work.'[71] About modern Jews, however, Herder was more ambivalent, deploring their economic parasitism but blaming it on Christian oppression rather than intrinsic faults, and hoping that emancipation will turn the minority of wise and generous Jews into a majority.[72]

Among the many reasons for admitting the Jews to the society of the Enlightenment, three stood out: toleration, mercantilism, and rationality. First, given the wide acceptance that different branches of Christianity should be tolerated within the same state, it seemed logical to extend toleration also to practitioners of non-Christian religions, above all to the Jews. Second, mercantilists argued that the productive capacity of the state should be maximized by increasing the productivity and prosperity of its citizens; if Jews were to become useful members of the state, they had to be admitted to citizenship and drawn away from unproductive occupations like trading. Third, it was argued that far from being superstitious and backward, Judaism was a rational and moral religion, so that Jews were particularly well qualified to enter a society nominally based on deistic belief and rational morality. The foremost advocate of toleration was Lessing, especially in his play *Nathan der Weise* (*Nathan the Wise*, 1779); the mercantilist case for Jewish emancipation was put most forcefully by the Prussian civil servant Christian Wilhelm von Dohm; and the case for the rationality of Judaism was put from within Judaism by the philosopher Moses Mendelssohn, a friend of both Lessing and Dohm. Their arguments will be examined in the next three sections.

Given the context of Enlightened prejudice, the writings of Lessing, Dohm, and Mendelssohn introduce a remarkable change in outlook. But, as the following sections will argue, all three cases

---

[71] Johann Gottfried Herder, *Werke*, ed. Günter Arnold *et al.*, 10 vols. (Frankfurt, 1985–), v. 929.

[72] See Herder, *Ideen zur Philosophie der Geschichte der Menschheit* [1784–91], in *Werke*, vi. 491–2, 702; 'Bekehrung der Juden', in *Sämmtliche Werke*, ed. Bernhard Suphan, 33 vols. (Berlin, 1877–1913) xxiv. 64–75. For a recent, balanced study, see Karl Menges, 'Integration oder Assimilation: Herders Äußerungen über die Juden im Kontext der klassischen Emanzipationsdebatte', *Euphorion*, 90 (1996), 394–415.

contained weaknesses and contradictions which, in the long run, assisted the dissolution of traditional Judaism without affording Jews more than qualified acceptance in German society.

LESSING AND TOLERATION

In moving towards religious toleration, the Enlightenment transferred the emphasis from the community of faith to the individual believer.[73] The homogeneity of belief which the medieval Church had tried to impose was an ideal retained by the Reformers, especially Luther and Calvin, and the maxim of the Peace of Augsburg (1555), 'cuius regio eius religio', limited tolerance by letting princes dictate the religion of their subjects. After over a century of religious wars, however, toleration found its advocates, including Milton, Bayle, and Locke. Locke's *Letter on Toleration* assumes that the Church must be quite separate from civil society. Religion becomes a purely private, individual matter: 'the care of each man's salvation belongs only to himself'.[74] The ruler must not interfere with his subjects' religious beliefs and practices, unless they endanger the peace of society. Frederick the Great wrote in 1751 about the many sects tolerated in Prussia: 'All these sects live here in peace and contribute equally to the happiness of the state; no religion deviates much from the others on the subject of morals; hence they may all be equal in the sight of the government, which consequently leaves each man at liberty to go to heaven by whatever path he pleases; all that is asked of him is to be a good citizen.'[75]

Toleration seems to rest on a paradox. It requires us to tolerate offensive beliefs without being offended by them. For toleration

---

[73] See Klaus Schreiner, 'Toleranz', in Otto Brunner, Werner Conze, and Reinhart Koselleck (eds.), *Geschichtliche Grundbegriffe: Historisches Lexikon zur politisch-sozialen Sprache in Deutschland*, 8 vols. (Stuttgart, 1972–97), vi. 445–605; Harald Schultze, *Lessings Toleranzbegriff: Eine theologische Studie* (Göttingen, 1969). For an expansion of the present argument, see Ritchie Robertson, '"Dies hohe Lied der Duldung"? The ambiguities of toleration in Lessing's *Die Juden* and *Nathan der Weise*', MLR 93 (1998), 105–20.

[74] John Locke, *Epistola de Tolerantia/A Letter on Toleration*, ed. Raymond Klibansky, tr. J. W. Gough (Oxford, 1968), p. 125.

[75] [Frederick the Great], *Mémoires pour servir à l'histoire de la Maison de Brandenbourg* (Berlin, 1751), p. 396.

presupposes disapproval; otherwise there would be nothing to tolerate.[76] There are two ways to escape from this paradox. One is to refrain from claiming sole and entire possession of the truth, and to concede that those who disagree with us may have elements of truth within their differing traditions. This approach permits a productive exploration of different religious traditions. With its distrust of religion, however, the Enlightenment preferred the other approach, that of seeking a common ground on which proponents of different religions could agree. Enlightenment thinkers found this common ground in natural religion and natural morality. 'By *Natural Religion*,' wrote Matthew Tindal, 'I understand the Belief of the Existence of a God, and the Sense and Practice of those Duties, which result from the Knowledge, we, by our Reason, have of him, and his Perfections; and of ourselves, and or own Imperfections; and of the Relation we stand in to him, and to our Fellow-Creatures; so that the *Religion of Nature* takes in every Thing that is founded on the Reason and Nature of Things.'[77]

To resolve the conflict between anti-Jewish prejudice and the imperative of toleration, some mid-century writers argued that Jews too, being human, possessed natural morality and were capable of virtue. The pathbreaker was Christian Fürchtegott Gellert, a popular author of fables, hymns, and moral essays, and one of the most influential writers in mid-eighteenth-century Germany. Till Gellert, German novels had portrayed Jewish figures as malicious and deceitful, unwilling to help Christians except for money.[78] Gellert's novel *Leben der schwedischen Gräfin von G**** (*Life of the Swedish Countess of G——*, 1747–8) contains a noble Polish Jew, who is saved from freezing to death in Siberia by the Count von G—— and later shows gratitude by having him released from captivity and giving him food, clothes, and money. Unlike the novel's central characters, however, the Jew

---

[76] See Ian C. Markham, *Plurality and Christian Ethics* (Cambridge, 1994).

[77] Tindal, *Christianity as Old as the Creation*, p. 13.

[78] See Wolfgang Martens, 'Zur Figur eines edlen Juden im Aufklärungsroman vor Gotthold Ephraim Lessing', *Der Deutschunterricht*, 36 (1984), iv. 48–58; Jürgen Stenzel, 'Idealisierung und Vorurteil'. Zur Figur des "edlen Juden" in der deutschen Literatur des 18. Jahrhunderts', in Stéphane Mosès and Albrecht Schöne (eds.), *Juden in der deutschen Literatur* (Frankfurt, 1986), pp. 114–26; Charlene A. Lea, 'Tolerance Unlimited: "the Noble Jew" on the German and Austrian stage (1750–1805)', *German Quarterly*, 64 (1991), 166–77.

has no name, and indeed his Jewish features, apart from his grey beard and long fur coat, are played down. His piety is illustrated when he is found praying on his knees, in a posture that seems more Christian than Jewish. And he represents a questionable dialectic of philosemitism, for he is held up as an exception, proof that there *can* be good Jews: 'This man displayed the noblest gratitude and proved to me that there are good hearts even among the nation that seems to have them the least.'[79] Thus Gellert's philosemitism actually confirms anti-Jewish prejudice by conveying that good Jews, though they exist, are exceptional.

A similar dialectic qualifies Lessing's philosemitic plays *Die Juden* (*The Jews*, 1754) and *Nathan der Weise*. Lessing supported Jewish emancipation long before it seemed a practical possibility. He described the play *Die Juden*, which he originally wrote in 1749, as 'the outcome of serious reflection on the shameful oppression endured by a nation which, I should have thought, a Christian cannot contemplate without a kind of reverence' (L i. 645; cf. L iii. 175). Lessing's reputation as a militant supporter of toleration is based largely on these two plays, especially *Nathan*, which long enjoyed a cult status among emancipated Jews. On the play's centenary, Emil Lehmann declared: 'For the Jews *Nathan* marked the beginning of a new era, it was the pillar of fire that led them out of the desert life of the ghettos into the promised land of legal equality.'[80] It seemed that the tolerance preached in the play had now been turned into reality by legislation. A number of German Jews, including the grandfather of the historian and polemicist Theodor Lessing, adopted the surname Lessing out of gratitude for 'this Song of Songs of toleration' ('dies hohe Lied der Duldung').[81] But what kind of tolerance do Lessing's plays represent?

Die Juden exhibits, more interestingly and wittily than Gellert, a philosemitism that is ultimately subject to the same restrictions. A traveller saves a Baron from two highway robbers who are in

---

[79] Gellert, *Leben der schwedischen Gräfin von G**** (Stuttgart, 1968), p. 79. Och (*Imago judaica*, p. 123) denies that the Jew is presented as exceptional, but overlooks this passage.

[80] Lehmann, 'Lessing. Mendelssohn. Nathan', in *Lessing-Mendelssohn-Gedenkbuch. Zur hundertfünfzigjährigen Geburtsfeier von Gotthold Ephraim Lessing und Moses Mendelssohn, sowie zur Säcularfeier von Lessing's 'Nathan'*, herausgegeben vom Deutsch-Israelitischen Gemeindebunde (Leipzig, 1879), pp. 3–26 (p. 4).

[81] Theodor Lessing, *Einmal und nie wieder* ([1935] Gütersloh, 1969), p. 34.

fact the Baron's own servants, disguised as Jews. To protect themselves, the servants hold forth about godless, thieving Jews, while the Baron remarks that the Jews' deceitful character is apparent from their faces. He does not yet know that the traveller he is addressing is himself a Jew. The Baron offers the traveller, out of gratitude, his daughter's hand in marriage, but the traveller replies that he cannot marry his daughter because he is a Jew. Hence the standard happy ending of comedy is frustrated. The traveller's religion excludes him from the real integration represented by intermarriage, and his acceptance in Gentile society is confined to social and intellectual intercourse.

Since Lessing clearly intended to combat prejudice against the Jews, *Die Juden* is not so much philosemitic as anti-antisemitic.[82] The hypocritical antisemitic highwayman, who alarmingly declares that if he had the power he would poison every single Jew, exhibits not only the xenophobia of the rabble but also, since he cites the clergyman in his support, the influence of orthodox Lutheranism. Popular antisemitism is further illustrated by the traveller's own servant, who, on learning his master's identity, declares himself insulted through being employed by a Jew. The Baron, in recounting how a Jew insisted on the full repayment of a debt, undermines his own antisemitism in seeking to justify it; and he also undermines himself dramatically by delivering this tirade to the Jewish traveller, who replies with the gentle rebuke: 'I am no friend to general judgements about entire nations' (L i. 389). In reply to the Baron's words—'O how admirable the Jews would be if they were all like you!' (L i. 414)—the traveller turns the tables by wishing that all Christians possessed the Baron's amiable qualities. In the closing scene, the traveller acts as a spokesman of his people: 'In return I ask nothing more than that in future you judge of my people more mildly and less sweepingly' (L i. 413). Yet the play's philosemitism is limited by its presentation of the Jew as good because exceptional.[83] The Baron's words just quoted suggest that the Jew is an admirable Jew because he is untypical, both in his goodness, and in having no readily perceptible Jewish

---

[82] See Wilfried Barner, 'Vorurteil, Empirie, Rettung. Der junge Lessing und die Juden', in Herbert A. Strauss and Christhard Hoffmann (eds.), *Juden und Judentum in der Literatur* (Munich, 1985), pp. 52–77 (p. 68).

[83] See the sceptical examination by Hans Mayer, *Außenseiter* (Frankfurt, 1975), pp. 334–9.

qualities. We learn that he avoids eating pork and follows Jewish religious practice; but none of this is visible on stage. Despite Lessing's efforts to be even-handed, Jews and Christians are not subject to the same criteria. Both groups are judged by the standard of natural morality, but the Jew is further obliged to dress and talk like a Gentile. Religious toleration is mixed with social presentability.

In this moral comedy, Lessing is adumbrating a utopia in which people, whether Jews or Christians, are judged by the standard of universal morality: the traveller says that 'die allgemeine Menschenliebe' obliged him to save the Baron (L i. 378). But this is not a utopia in which difference is acknowledged, rather one to which people are admitted in so far as they erase their difference and conform to a common model, that of the universal, rational, enlightened human being. The traveller's comically stupid Christian servant exclaims: 'so there are also Jews who aren't Jews' ('es gibt doch wohl auch Juden, die keine Juden sind)' (L i. 414). He means that there are Jews who do not match his negative stereotype of the Jew. But, on a sceptical reading, he has unwittingly blurted out the truth: Jews can only be admitted to the society of the Enlightenment if they are not Jews, that is, if they have no distinctively Jewish features.

When Michaelis, whose study of the Mosaic law we have already encountered, complained that such a noble and cultivated Jew was very unlikely to exist in reality, as most Jews lived by trade, Lessing replied that the traveller was an unusual but possible figure, in contrast to the common run of Jews: 'To believe this, of course, you must know more about the Jews than the dissolute riff-raff that roams about at fairs' (L i. 418). This statement is unlikely to rest on much actual experience of Jews, since Saxony, where Lessing was brought up, prohibited them from residing. Wealthy Jewish merchants were allowed to visit the annual fairs, but swarms of Jewish pedlars were certainly not permitted. Lessing seems to be relying on familiar clichés.[84] Hence in Lessing's reply to Michaelis the individual Jew is presented as good by contrast with an anonymous and faceless swarm of bad Jews.

---

[84] See Stefan Rohrbacher and Michael Schmidt, *Judenbilder: Kulturgeschichte anti-jüdischer Mythen und antisemitischer Vorurteile* (Reinbek, 1991), pp. 23–5.

Nathan der Weise, written in the winter of 1778–9, not only represents a move in Lessing's theological controversy with Hauptpastor Goeze of Hamburg but follows a prolonged pre-occupation with theological questions that intensified in the 1770s. Lessing's religious thought is difficult to describe because he never expounded it systematically but expressed it in controversies, where prudent evasions and polemical point-scoring obscure what may have been his real opinions. It is likely that his beliefs, opinions, or attitudes were always mobile and inconsistent. Nevertheless, at least one constant can be identified: an appeal to reason and morality rather than faith or revelation as the criteria of religious truth. For Lessing, it was an insoluble problem that Christianity made historical claims—namely, that God's revelation occurred at a particular time and place in history—instead of being based on the universal claims of reason. The resurrection of Christ was a contingent historical fact, based on historical testimony but not underwritten by reason. Reason and revelation were disjoined, he said in 1755, by an 'ugly, broad ditch' over which he could not leap.[85] The image of the ditch expresses at least two aporias. First, the evidence for a historical event can never be completely reliable; falsification must always be possible in principle. Second, even an eyewitness to the events recorded in the Gospels could not know, simply from observation, that these were *religious* events. There is, then, no cognitive access to religious truth, the only kind of access that the rationalist Lessing is prepared to consider.

Unwilling to discard the concept of revelation, Lessing interprets it as moral instruction, and describes its gradual transmission to humankind in *Die Erziehung des Menschengeschlechts* (*The Education of the Human Race*, 1780), a speculative history of human development which relativizes Christianity by setting forth a doctrine of progressive revelation. Lessing supposes that the revelations of Moses and Christ are God's (or Providence's) way of gradually educating humankind; their content could have been discovered by unaided human reason, but the providential process of education speeds things up. Thus the revelation of

---

[85] 'On the Proof of the Spirit and of Power', in *Lessing's Theological Writings*, p. 55 (= L ii. 13). See Gordon E. Michalson, Jr., *Lessing's 'Ugly Ditch': A Study of Theology and History* (University Park, Pa., and London, 1985).

Moses was made to a savage and childlike people in the appropriately crude language of rewards and punishments; but when these moral lessons were in danger of being obscured by rabbinical over-ingenuity, a better instructor came in the person of Christ with a new school-book. Humanity will become mature when we no longer need such artificial inducements to morality and are able to do good because it is good, as Lessing foresees in paragraph 85 of *Die Erziehung*:

No! It will come! it will assuredly come! the time of the perfecting, when man, the more convinced his understanding feels about an ever better future, will nevertheless not need to borrow motives for his actions from this future; for he will do right because it *is* right, not because arbitrary rewards are set on it, which formerly were intended simply to fix and strengthen his unsteady gaze in recognizing the inner, better, rewards of well-doing.[86]

Lessing's historical account of religion both promotes and limits tolerance. It promotes tolerance by offering a perspective in which even the most barbarous beliefs disclose a measure of truth appropriate to their time. But it limits tolerance by removing any need to tolerate a belief that has outlived its usefulness. Thus in *Nathan* the belief of the Christian Daja, that Recha was saved from the fire by an angel, is dismissed by Nathan as illogical in itself and as belittling the human capacity for good action. Catholic Christianity evidently belongs to an early stage in human development. Judaism, on the other hand, is allotted a dual role in Lessing's historical scheme. On the one hand, the ancient Israelites are depicted in unflattering terms, in keeping with the common Enlightenment view of them. On the other hand, Nathan's Judaism represents a humane and enlightened outlook free from superstition. Thus, in Lessing's scheme, versions of Judaism both precede and follow Christianity on the way to the pure morality of the future.

Set in the Jerusalem of the Second Crusade, *Nathan* brings Christians, Jews, and Muslims together with unabashed artificiality. The wealthy Jew Nathan, returning from a business trip, learns from his servant Daja that there has been a fire in his house,

---

[86] *Lessing's Theological Writings*, p. 96 (= L viii. 508).

from which his adopted daughter Recha has been saved by a Knight Templar. The Templar, whose life has in turn been inexplicably spared by his captor Saladin, at first brusquely rejects the gratitude of a mere Jew, but eventually comes to appreciate Nathan's humanity. When the bigoted Patriarch of Jerusalem learns that a Jew has adopted a Christian child, the Templar, putting humanity before religious allegiance, refrains from disclosing that the people concerned are Nathan and Recha; he is already falling in love with the latter. Finally, an elaborate recognition scene discloses that the Templar and Recha are brother and sister, the children of Saladin's brother. As in *Die Juden*, the conventional happy ending of marriage is prevented, but without diminishing the general benevolence on which the curtain falls.

The play's message about human kinship transcending religious boundaries is not as straightforward as one might think. In *Nathan*, dogmatic religious belief is set in opposition to natural human affection and honesty; and the play's great strengths include its warm and attractive portrayal of flawed but convincingly and profoundly decent people. Such natural morality made the Templar save Recha's life and makes him, despite the contempt for Jews that he owes to his upbringing, warm to Nathan's palpable sincerity; it makes him unwilling to obey the Patriarch, who wants him to assassinate his benefactor, Saladin, and restrains him from revealing to the Patriarch the identity of the Jew who has brought up a Christian child. By contrast, Christian dogma encourages inhumanity. Daja, shown as a superstitious believer in miracles, thinks it wrong for Recha to be brought up in a non-Christian faith. The Patriarch, the only evil figure in the play, denies that there are any moral obligations towards non-Christians, or any moral commands that cannot be overridden by the (supposed) divine imperative. This intolerance is in turn based on the illusion that one's own religious belief is the one true faith and that one is therefore entitled to criticize members of other faiths. As the Templar points out, this exclusivism originates from the Jews, who first called themselves the chosen people, but has been bequeathed both to Christians and Muslims, and is at present showing its pernicious character in the Crusades:

You are surprised that I,
A Christian and a Templar, speak like this?
The pious frenzy whereby men believe
They have the better God, and are entitled
To force him on the whole world as the best,
Has never shown itself in darker hue
Than here, than now!   (L ii. 253)

However, although the Second Crusade allows Lessing to juxta-
pose the three religions, he shows little interest in their specific
character. The representation of Christianity is primarily polemical. With the few decent Christian characters—the Templar and
the Lay-Brother—their decency is shown as conflicting with the
obligations of their religion; Daja illustrates naïve superstition,
the Patriarch amoral bigotry. Neither Judaism nor Islam is represented in any detail. Nathan is never shown as engaging in any
specifically Jewish religious practices. He stands for a universal,
humane benevolence, as do the Muslims Saladin and Sittah.[87] To
typify Islam, Lessing introduces a dervish, or pious mendicant,
who intends to join the Ghebers (Parsees or Zoroastrians from
Persia) and do penance with them on the banks of the Ganges. It
seems that for Lessing, Islam was not distinct from Zoroastrian-
ism or Hinduism. Instead of anticipating Herder's sympathetic
interest in other cultures, Lessing shares the ahistorical outlook of
Voltaire. One of his sources, Voltaire's tragedy *Les Guèbres, ou la
Tolérance* (1769), which, like *Nathan*, culminates in the discovery
that practitioners of different religions are long-lost relatives,
similarly represents the Ghebers as exponents of pure morality;
their apparent sun-worship, which enrages the bloodthirsty priests
of Pluto, merely symbolizes a rational deism. Lessing likewise uses
Judaism and Islam, not as distinctive historical religions, but as
codes of pure morality serving as foils to Christianity.

In portraying Nathan, Lessing challenges antisemitism by giving
his protagonist some characteristics commonly thought Jewish,
such as his liking for disputation.[88] A sympathetic nineteenth-
century reader, David Strauss, thought Nathan displayed 'truly
Oriental Jewish qualities' in his artful and conciliatory dealings

---

[87] See Andrea Fuchs-Sumiyoshi, *Orientalismus in der deutschen Literatur*
(Hildesheim, 1984), pp. 35–41 (esp. p. 39).

[88] F. J. Lamport, *Lessing and the Drama* (Oxford, 1981), p. 205.

with other people and in his use of imagery and parable.[89] However, the other characters remark more than once how different he is from most Jews. His friend the dervish praises his love of civilized pleasures: 'Such a Jew as he, | It's true, is seldom found. He has good sense, | Lives well, is good at chess' (L ii. 245). The antisemitic prejudices voiced by Sittah and the Templar concern the Jews' supposed avarice and cowardice.[90] Nathan is unusual in not lending money: he is a merchant, not a usurer. Like the traveller in *Die Juden*, Nathan is presented as exceptional.[91]

Accordingly, Nathan refuses to identify himself with his people. He tells the Templar:

> Despise
> My nation as you please. We did not choose
> Our nations, either you or I. Are *we*
> Our nations? What does 'nation' mean? Are Jews
> And Christians first and foremost Jews and Christians,
> And human only second? Would that I
> Had found in you another person who
> Is happy to be human (*ein Mensch*)! (L ii. 253)

In preferring the term 'Mensch', Nathan shows that he and the Templar have transcended the restrictions of religion and nationality and joined a society of pure humanity. A 'Mensch'—a human being, independent of nationality, religion, or indeed gender—is presented as the ideal norm, just as it is in that other Enlightenment masterpiece, *The Magic Flute*:

SPEAKER: [. . .] He is a Prince!
SARASTRO: Yet more—he is a human being (*er ist Mensch*)![92]

The bearers of Lessing's ethical humanism are human beings independent of nationality or religion. Similarly, in his dialogues on Freemasonry, *Ernst und Falk* (written probably in 1777), Lessing describes the division of humanity into different nations

---

[89] Strauss, 'Über Lessing's *Nathan*' [1863], in *Lessings 'Nathan der Weise'*, ed. Klaus Bohnen (Darmstadt, 1984), pp. 11–45 (p. 32).

[90] On the play's treatment of anti-Jewish stereotypes, see Och, *Imago judaica*, pp. 149–62.

[91] As Victor Klemperer noted when rereading *Nathan* in the Third Reich: see his diary for 28 Jan. 1943 in *Ich will Zeugnis ablegen bis zum letzten. Tagebücher 1933–1941, 1942–1945*, ed. Walter Nowojski, 2 vols. (Berlin, 1995), ii. 320.

[92] Wolfgang Amadeus Mozart, *Die Zauberflöte*, ed. Hans-Albrecht Koch (Stuttgart, 1991), p. 37.

and classes as an evil which Freemasonry exists to alleviate. Freemasonry should be a network of men who have transcended nationality: 'men who have left behind the prejudices of their nation and know precisely the point at which patriotism ceases to be a virtue' (L viii. 465). In practice, Freemasonry does not live up to this ideal: Ernst finds that only educated Christians are admitted, and a Jew or a shoemaker would be unacceptable. The ideal of pure humanity in *Nathan*, however valuable as a regulative idea, is equally remote from experience, and to give it dramatic form Lessing has to dilute the specific national identities of his characters. As early as 1843 Fanny Lewald made a character in her novel *Jenny* complain that Nathan, Saladin, and the Templar all sounded like Protestants.[93] A commentator complained in 1909: 'His Nathan is no longer a Jew, nor his Saladin a Muslim, nor his Lay-Brother a Christian—if they ever were; for nothing but their name and status recalls their religion. [. . .] Their toleration cannot make a strong impression: what they have to tolerate in one another amounts to nothing at all.'[94] Rather, Lessing represents humanity as uniform: good people, followers of natural morality, may be found in every country. He is not interested in exploring cultural diversity, but in bypassing it.

The centre of *Nathan der Weise* is commonly taken to be the parable of the three rings. Thanks to his reputation for wisdom, Nathan is summoned before Saladin and asked which of the three religions is the true one. Nathan sidesteps this embarrassing conundrum by telling how a ring that made its possessor pleasing to God and man was handed down through the generations till it came to a father with three sons. He had two externally similar rings made, so that each son received one. Wondering which was the true ring, they took their problem to a judge, who told them that the authenticity of the ring could only be demonstrated by the upright conduct of its owner, and advised each to assist the ring's power by his benevolence, peacefulness, and devotion. Thus moral action becomes the test of a religion's truth. It is important to note that the parable is not saying that the other two rings are as good as the true one. Rather, as the Jewish novelist Berthold Auerbach

---

[93] Lewald, *Jenny* (1872 edn.), ed. Ulrike Helmer (Frankfurt, 1988), p. 233.
[94] Christoph Schrempf, *Lessing als Philosoph* ([1909] Stuttgart, 1921), p. 165.

noted in 1879, all three rings must be false.[95] For all three sons behaved equally badly in their dispute: 'each wants to be | The house's head and ruler' (L ii. 277), though the owner of the true ring ought to have behaved more magnanimously than the other two. Indeed the judge speculates that the true ring may have got lost and that each facsimile will serve provided its possessor lives up to it. The inner truth of each religion is its incitement to moral action. Tradition (the historical content of religion) cannot establish any absolute religious truth, because everyone believes the traditions in which he was brought up; rather, the historical element of religion is a fiction, and the only proof of any religious pudding is in the eating.

What does this parable contribute to religious toleration? With regard to the truth-claims of different religions, Lessing does seems to imply, as Nicholas Boyle says, an agnosticism which regards the cognitive element in religion as a fiction: 'The representatives of the three major religions, Judaism, Christianity, and Islam, are not here shown to tolerate one another's differences, for it is only temporary misunderstanding that prevents them from recognizing that they all think alike: they are shown rather to be agreed in a fourth, secret, religion of agnostic humanism.'[96] Revelation does not survive sceptical examination, just as the ring fails of its effect when put to the test. The historical and traditional basis of religion is revealed as simply a fairy-story, no different in principle from the 'Märchen' with which Nathan fobs off Saladin, and serving only to preserve the inner truth of religion, that is, its efficacy in promoting rational morality.

Although this conception of religion may sound somewhat arid, the text of *Nathan* continues to use familiar terms of religious emotion such as 'devotion to God' (L ii. 280). This devotion cannot be directed towards a transcendent or absolute source of good, for such a source would need to be located on the other side of the 'ugly, broad ditch' which Lessing could not cross. Nathan speaks in personal terms of God, but he also personifies Providence (L ii. 317). Lessing seems still to assume a Leibnizian providentialism, finding in the structure of the world an intrinsic

---

[95] Berthold Auerbach, 'Gedanken über Lessing's "Nathan"', in *Lessing-Mendelssohn-Gedenkbuch*, pp. 321–8 (p. 324).

[96] Boyle, *Goethe: The Poet and the Age*, i: *The Poetry of Desire* (Oxford, 1991), p. 33; cf. p. 273.

order which makes it ultimately unnecessary to imagine any creator outside the world. His emotional rhetoric suggests that, with the gradual education of the human race, the devotion which was misdirected in conventional religion will be transferred to the providential structure of reality which was all along its true though unrecognized object. This bold suggestion becomes most nearly explicit when Nathan tells the Lay-Brother how, long before, his wife and seven sons were burnt in a pogrom by Christians, and that he accepted this as God's will and took the infant Recha as compensation for his loss. Dramatically, it feels right that Nathan's goodness should rest on inner strength acquired by the acceptance of suffering. There is less psychological plausibility in his adoption of Recha as a providential substitute for his wife and sons.[97] Lessing's providentialism comes under most strain when Nathan says that after lying in dust and ashes, weeping, protesting against God, and cursing Christians, he gradually yielded to the voice of reason, which told him that the death of his wife and sons resulted from God's decree. This submission to the divine will recalls the Book of Job and Job's affirmation: 'Though he slay me, yet will I trust in him' (Job 13: 15).[98] Such submission is perhaps the most difficult thing that can be required of the believer. It is hard to believe that grief and bereavement can be accepted as part of the divine will simply through rational persuasion. By a contradiction which is to be welcomed, Lessing *shows* us a saintly submission to the divine will which is hard to reconcile with the agnosticism for which he implicitly *argues*.

Nathan is rightly accounted a masterpiece, not only for its restless intelligence but, above all perhaps, for the warmth and humanity of its characters. Gabriel Riesser may have been right in saying that the play's didactic effect came from its characters rather than from its explicit lesson: 'Anyone in whom the characters in Lessing's *Nathan* do not arouse warm sympathy, from whom the representatives of the three religions have not

---

[97] On the relation between this episode and Lessing's personal experience of bereavement, see Jill Anne Kowalik, '*Nathan der Weise* as Lessing's Work of Mourning', *Lessing Yearbook*, 21 (1989), 1–17 (esp. p. 7).

[98] On Nathan's resemblance to Job, as the latter was understood by 18th-cent. commentators, see Ingrid Strohschneider-Kohrs, *Vernunft als Weisheit: Studien zum späten Lessing* (Tübingen, 1991), pp. 90–101.

already gained by their personalities the tolerance and love they teach, such a person is entirely incapable of poetic sympathy.'[99] But even here there is a difficulty. The final revelation, of blood-relationships across religious divisions, is supposed to show how illusory are religious and national differences. Blood-relationships are being used only metaphorically to signify a *real* relatedness that is based on shared humanity, friendship, and love. Contingent physical bonds are merely symbolic of the bonds that are created by choosing and actively caring for other people. Nathan, however, is not related by blood to any of the characters. Granted, his adoption of Recha makes him her father in every sense that matters. But since he is not a blood-relative of anyone else, his membership of the human family is only a matter of choice; it is not underwritten by a symbolic blood-relationship. Thus he remains a lonely figure (like the bereaved Lessing) and one who must earn his membership of a community of which the others, as their blood-relationship signifies, are already members: in this respect his admission is analogous to the admission of Jews to German society. Instead of being declared to be already full members of society by virtue of their natural rights, they had to earn their membership by demonstrating their fitness to be citizens. Read thus against the grain, *Nathan* turns out to prophesy not the integration of Jews into German society but the precarious nature of the position which they held ultimately on sufferance.

EMANCIPATION: DOHM VERSUS HUMBOLDT

Religious toleration provided one set of arguments for Jewish emancipation. Other arguments proceeded from the gradually developing conception of the secular liberal state in which religion should be a private matter and all citizens should enjoy equal rights and equal duties. A third group of arguments, particularly powerful in the late eighteenth century, arose from mercantilism, with its principle that human resources should be put to

---

[99] Riesser, *Einige Worte über Lessing's Denkmal an die Israeliten Deutschlands gerichtet* (1838), in his *Gesammelte Schriften*, ed. M. Isler, 4 vols. (Frankfurt and Leipzig, 1867–8), iv. 30–1.

maximum use instead of confining one segment of the population to a narrow and unproductive range of occupations. The latter arguments are increasingly audible in the calls for Jewish emancipation that we hear in the 1770s. Thus an anonymous writer in *Der teutsche Merkur*, conceding the theological charges against the Jews, nevertheless urged that it was inhumane to saddle them with civil disabilities and drive them to usury, praised their domestic morality by contrast with Christian vices, and called for their admission to civil rights and professions.[100]

Mercantilism was a major motive behind the first practical steps taken at the start of the new decade. The Patents of Toleration issued by Joseph II from 1781 onwards (for Bohemia on 19 October 1781, for Vienna and Lower Austria on 2 January 1782) did not give Jews citizenship or equal legal rights, but did promote their 'civic betterment' by allowing them to practise agriculture, trades, and professions, to set up factories and large businesses, and to attend schools and universities.[101] This was part of the programme of toleration that also released Protestants and Greek Orthodox Christians in the Habsburg realms from discrimination. Joseph's toleration was based on belief in liberty of conscience and on the mercantilist desire to make all his subjects useful and productive for the state: 'For me', he assured his mother, Maria Theresia, in 1777, 'tolerance means only that in purely temporal matters, without regard to religion, I would employ, allow to own lands, practise trades and become citizens those who are competent and would bring advantage and industry to the State.'[102]

In the subsequent legal history of Jewish emancipation in Germany and Austria, four phases can be distinguished.[103] The period from 1781 to 1815 saw the Patents of Toleration in Austria, the influence of the French Revolution and Napoleon, and finally the emancipatory legislation of the Prussian reform period.

---

[100] Anon., 'Gedanken über das Schicksal der Juden', *Der teutsche Merkur*, 11 (July 1775), 213–20.
[101] For more detail, see Robert S. Wistrich, *The Jews of Vienna in the Age of Franz Joseph* (Oxford, 1989), pp. 16–22.
[102] *Maria Theresia und Joseph II. Ihre Correspondenz*, ed. Alfred Ritter von Arneth, 3 vols. (Vienna, 1867), ii. 152.
[103] See the invaluable article by Reinhard Rürup, 'The Tortuous and Thorny Path to Legal Equality: "Jew laws" and Emancipatory Legislation in Germany from the Late Eighteenth Century', *LBY* 31 (1986), 3–33.

During the period from 1815 to 1848 there were contradictory developments in which nearly all the (now 39) German states made progress towards emancipation but some revoked concessions already made. Some attempts were even made in 1840s Prussia to reorganize the Jews as *Judenschaften*, distinct entities within a Christian state. In 1848 the revolutionary movements led to the enactment of emancipatory legislation which was subsequently revoked in many German states. Between 1850 and the unification of Germany in 1871, Jews at last attained equal legal status in all German states.

Rather than pursue this history through its constitutional details, I want to look at two texts on emancipation which illustrate the two possible approaches to it. Christian Wilhelm von Dohm, in his book *Über die bürgerliche Verbesserung der Juden* (*On the Civil Improvement of the Jews*, 1781), argued for a form of emancipation which should be gradual and dependent on the Jews' increasing acculturation. Wilhelm von Humboldt in 1809 argued against such a policy and instead advocated granting Jews full civil rights at a stroke. Although Dohm's proposals had no immediate effect, emancipation was eventually carried out in the gradualist and conditional manner he suggested, and the consequences of this approach will deserve consideration.

Dohm, son of a clergyman at Lemgo in Westphalia, moved in Berlin Enlightenment circles from 1773 on. Having been a professor of economics, he entered the Prussian state service in 1779, where he had a distinguished career as an educational and constitutional reformer, and was a prolific writer on political, economic, and literary subjects.[104]

In his treatise on the Jews, Dohm starts from the mercantilist principle that a country's well-being depends on the growth of its population and remarks how odd it is that in most European countries the laws try to limit the numbers of the Jews. Excluded from agriculture, crafts, and most professions, and compelled to pay large sums annually for permission to reside in cities, Jews are obliged to make their living from commerce. Yet they are excluded too from many branches of commerce, and largely confined to

---

[104] See Heinrich Detering, 'Christian Wilhelm von Dohm und die Idee der Toleranz', in Peter Freimark *et al.* (eds.), *Lessing und die Toleranz* (Detroit and Munich, 1986), pp. 174–85; Robert Liberles, 'Dohm's Treatise on the Jews: A Defence of the Enlightenment', *LBY* 33 (1988), 29–42.

small-scale retail trade, or moneylending. This seems unjustifiable. 'Are many hard-working and good citizens less useful to the state because they originate from Asia and are distinguished by beards, circumcision, and a particular way of revering the Supreme Being which their most ancient ancestors have bequeathed to them?'[105]

Dohm's argument for Jewish integration is humane as well as pragmatic. Admittedly, as he later stressed in a history of his own time, he was not in the slightest an apologist for the Jews in their current condition.[106] He assumes that human beings are essentially uniform, but shaped in different ways by their environment. Hence he maintains that the Jews are not intrinsically bad, but have only been corrupted by centuries of oppression. If the oppression is removed, they will respond with gratitude. 'The Jew is still more a human being than a Jew (*Der Jude ist noch mehr Mensch als Jude*), and how is it possible for him not to love a state in which he could acquire his own property and enjoy it freely, in which he paid no higher taxes than other citizens, and where he too could attain honour and respect? [. . .] These human feelings would speak more loudly in his heart than the sophistical deductions of his rabbis.'[107] Jews are indeed morally corrupt, inclined to usury and commercial dishonesty, but these qualities result from their confinement to a despised branch of commerce which made them despise themselves, and will vanish when they are admitted to a full range of occupations. A frequent objection to the emancipation of Jews, namely that they were too unwarlike to fight for their country, is dismissed with reference to their military prowess, not only in Old Testament times, but in the armies of the Roman Empire. The pedantic excesses of talmudic Judaism are ascribed to oppression: their exclusion from political society gave them too much leisure for idle speculation. In any case they also have many virtues: they take care of their poor, enjoy a peaceful domestic life, are good husbands and fathers, and avoid sexual crimes. Their loyalty to their own religion is a sign of virtue rather than of reprehensible obduracy:

[105] Dohm, *Über die bürgerliche Verbesserung der Juden*, p. 16.

[106] Dohm, *Denkwürdigkeiten meiner Zeit oder Beiträge zur Geschichte vom lezten Viertel des achtzehnten und vom Anfang des neunzehnten Jahrhunderts 1778 bis 1806*, vol. iii (Lemgo and Hanover, 1815), p. 284.

[107] Dohm, *Über die bürgerliche Verbesserung der Juden*, p. 28.

Even this loyalty to their fathers' ancient faith gives the Jews' character a firmness which is advantageous to the development of their morality in general. On the one hand, the strict observance of many burdensome duties and customs does nourish among them a certain spirit of pettiness and makes them attach too much value to the observance of ceremonies, etc., [. . .] but on the other hand it restrains them from many transgressions and encourages them to fulfil their duties in general more minutely.[108]

Ironically, the effect of the Jews' integration would in fact be to loosen the hold of their religion and therefore to dissipate its putative advantages.

Dohm's recommendations were that the Jews should be given the same rights as all other subjects; they should be encouraged to adopt trades and professions other than commerce, especially artisan crafts and agriculture; they should keep their accounts and records in the language of the country, not in Hebrew; they should be allowed to study any subject, and their secular education should be directed by the state, while leaving their religious education intact; they should have complete freedom to practise their own religion; and they should be allowed to keep their own legal system to regulate private disputes among themselves. This last concession was unusual. Subsequent legislators insisted that the Jews must not form a state within the state, and that all their legal disputes should be handed over to the state legal system. At the session of the French National Assembly of 23 December 1789, the deputy Stanislas comte de Clermont-Tonnerre famously declared that nothing should be granted to the Jews as a nation, everything to the Jews as individuals: their corporate structure must be abandoned.[109]

The effect of Dohm's arguments was to associate Jewish emancipation with the reform of the Jews' character. Emancipation was interpreted as a contract, 'a quid pro quo in which the Jews were to be regenerated in exchange for rights'.[110] In return for civil

---

[108] Dohm, p. 94.
[109] Wanda Kampmann, *Deutsche und Juden: Die Geschichte der Juden in Deutschland vom Mittelalter bis zum Beginn des Ersten Weltkrieges* (Frankfurt, 1979), pp. 122–3; Phyllis Cohen Albert, 'Israelite and Jew: How did Nineteenth-Century French Jews Understand Assimilation?', in Jonathan Frankel and Steven J. Zipperstein (eds.), *Assimilation and Community: The Jews in Nineteenth-Century Europe* (Cambridge, 1992), pp. 88–109.   [110] Sorkin, *The Transformation of German Jewry*, p. 20.

liberties, the Jews had to demonstrate their success in acquiring German culture.

When Dohm was writing, there was little practical prospect of Jewish emancipation in Prussia, for Frederick the Great was opposed to it. Two decades after Frederick's death in 1786, however, the defeat of Prussia by France at the Battle of Jena in October 1806, and the resulting Peace of Tilsit which obliged Prussia to pay indemnities and supply soldiers to Napoleon, gave a loose-knit group of reformers in Berlin the opportunity to formulate and enact some innovatory legislation, beginning with the abolition of serfdom in 1807. The reformers then considered the legal status of Jews, producing an elaborate draft which acknowledged the arguments of Dohm and others that the 'corruption' of the Jews resulted only from their confinement to commerce. It was assumed, however, that to grant Jews full legal rights would be too sudden a reform, and that their emancipation should occur step by step. This draft was submitted to Wilhelm von Humboldt, who in the spring of 1809 had become Minister of Education in the new Prussian government. Humboldt's comments form a devastating critique of the project of gradual emancipation, and although gradualism was the policy adopted, Humboldt's counter-arguments deserve to be recorded as an exposure of its weaknesses.

Humboldt agrees that the Jews need to give up the self-government which makes them a state within the state and to become absorbed into the general population. To make this possible, they needed legal emancipation, not gradually, but at a stroke. Such a policy would be just, because Jews who shared the duties of other citizens should also enjoy the same rights; it would be logical, because if Jews were treated differently from others, their singularity would become more, not less, visible; and politically right, because gradualism implied treating Jews as a distinct race which deserved civil rights only in exceptional cases:

However many upright Jews the population may see, it will not readily change its opinion of the Jews as such, but will always regard these individuals merely as exceptions. Besides, the state should explicitly not teach people to respect the Jews, but it should remove the inhumane and prejudiced outlook that judges a person not by his specific qualities but by his descent and religion, and regards him, contrary to all true conceptions of human dignity, not as an individual but as a member of a race (*Race*) and as necessarily sharing certain qualities with his race. The state can only remove this outlook, however, by declaring loudly and clearly that it no longer recognizes any distinction between Jews and Christians.[111]

Instead of dispelling antisemitic prejudice, gradual emancipation would confirm it by supporting the popular belief that virtuous and civilized Jews were exceptional and that the mass of Jews did not deserve equal rights. It would confirm, in other words, the exceptionalism which, as we have seen, underlies the presentation of virtuous Jews by the philosemites Gellert and Lessing.

Humboldt went on to make further objections to the conception of the state as responsible for improving people's character. In keeping with the liberal view of the 'nightwatchman state' which he had set out in his essay on *The Limits of State Action* (1792), he maintained that the state should concentrate on removing restrictions to people's free self-development, not tell them what form their development should take: 'the state is not an educational, but a legal institution'.[112] In any case, if Jews were to have their civil rights progressively increased as their morals improved, how was such improvement to be measured? Was the state to compile statistics showing how many Jews had become farmers or soldiers, and award civil rights accordingly? The only way to avoid such undignified absurdities was to award civil rights at a stroke and ensure that Jews like all other citizens were subject to the laws of the land.

Since both Dohm's and Humboldt's approaches to emancipation see it as making possible a transformation, whether gradual or swift, in the character of the Jews, one might be tempted to call them philosemites only in a qualified sense. Humboldt hoped that equality would produce complete assimilation and thus end the specific existence of Jews as Jews. Similarly, in France, where such legislation was adopted, the Abbé Grégoire, in his essay on the regeneration of the Jews, argued that the improvement in the Jews' character would take place rapidly, in two generations at most,

---

[111] Humboldt, 'Über den Entwurf zu einer neuen Konstitution für die Juden', in his *Werke*, ed. Andreas Flitner and Klaus Giel, 5 vols. (Darmstadt, 1964), iv. 95–112 (p. 97).
[112] Ibid. 98. See Humboldt, *The Limits of State Action*, ed. J. W. Burrow (Cambridge, 1969).

provided they were given unconditional emancipation.[113] The emancipation of the French Jews was based on politics, that of the German Jews on culture, but in neither case were they encouraged or expected to retain their specific identity as Jews.

Indeed, the demand for radical emancipation could be based on acknowledged dislike of Jews or even on principled antisemitism. Although Humboldt mixed socially with the Jewish salon hostesses of 1790s Berlin, he found them personally irritating and wrote to his wife: 'I really only like the Jews en masse, en détail I take pains to avoid them.'[114] Radical emancipation is proposed also by the declared antisemite Christian Ludwig Paalzow, a Berlin lawyer and prolific writer on legal and religious subjects, who opposes Dohm's arguments by reviving the Voltairean view of the Jews as superstitious, obdurate, and xenophobic. He thinks that if emancipated, the Jews, through their solidarity, would obtain a monopoly on all commerce and reduce their fellow-citizens to slavery. This can only be avoided if the Jews cease to be Jews. They must cease to be a distinct social group; they must abandon the ceremonial law and indeed the practice of their religion; they must relinquish their self-government and their own schools; they must mingle and intermarry with their fellow-citizens, and assume all the citizen's duties.[115] This goes further than Dohm, but in the same direction; and it goes only a little further than the proposals made by Humboldt or the Abbé Grégoire.

While the protean persistence of antisemitism (to be explored in Chapter 3) would scarcely have been defeated by the radical emancipation Humboldt proposed, such measures might at least have made Jews as Jews less visible and deprived antisemitism of an obvious target. As it was, the gradual emancipation conducted in nineteenth-century Germany and Austria, with a number of

---

[113] Grégoire, *Essai sur la régénération physique, morale et politique des juifs* (Metz, 1789; repr. Paris, 1968), pp. 189–90.

[114] Letter of 30 Apr. 1816, quoted in Peter Honigmann, 'Über den Unterschied zwischen Alexander und Wilhelm von Humboldt in ihrem Verhältnis zum Judentum', in Renate Heuer and Ralph-Rainer Wuthenow (eds.), *Konfrontation und Koexistenz: Zur Geschichte des deutsche Judentums* (Frankfurt and New York, 1996), pp. 46–81 (p. 62).

[115] Paalzow, *Die Juden. Nebst einigen Bemerkungen über das Sendschreiben an Herrn Oberconsistorialrath und Probst Teller zu Berlin von einigen Hausvätern jüdischer Religion und die darauf erfolgte Tellersche Antwort* (Berlin, 1799).

retractions and regressions, continued, as Humboldt had warned, to draw attention to the Jews and their supposedly distinctive qualities. Prejudices against Jews easily regained respectability. In Prussia, there was discussion whether Jewish volunteers who had served in the campaigns of 1813–15 should be given the same right as other volunteers to enter the civil service, but the Government Council (*Staatsministerium*) thought not, even if they had won the Iron Cross: 'Apart from other reasons, the presumption of *lesser morality* is not invalidated by temporary bravery', wrote the Minister of Justice, von Kircheisen, in December 1815.[116] Restrictions on Jews' professional life, such as their exclusion in 1822 from teaching posts in Prussian schools and universities, could be evaded by conversion to Christianity, which, however, often seemed a shameful and opportunistic step. Heine's friend the legal philosopher Eduard Gans applied in 1822 for a Chair at Berlin; debarred by a hasty change in the law, Gans converted in 1825, and was appointed to the Chair in 1828. Heine denounced his conversion in a poem—'Once you did a hero's work, | Now you're nothing but a rogue'—but by the time he wrote this, Heine himself had secretly converted.[117] Jewish spokesmen like Gabriel Riesser protested against the unfairness of these pressures:

It might well be an impracticable project to classify Jews by the degree of their enlightenment (*nach ihrer Aufklärung*); but it is certainly a scandalous injustice to seek to criticize the religious views of an oppressed minority by a standard that is not and cannot be applied to the views of those confessing the state religion.[118]

By the 1860s, however, legal disabilities for Jews seemed anachronistic and absurd. In Austria, meanwhile, the process of Jewish emancipation was formally completed by the liberal *Staatsgrundgesetz* of 21 December 1867, which made all citizens equal before the law, gave them all access to public office, guaranteed freedom of faith and conscience, and rendered civic and political rights independent of religious belief. The Diet of the North

---

[116] Quoted in Rürup, 'The Tortuous and Thorny Path', p. 17; also in Kampmann, *Deutsche und Juden*, p. 164.

[117] 'To an Apostate', in *The Complete Poems of Heinrich Heine*, tr. Hal Draper (Oxford, 1982), p. 286. On Heine and Gans, see S. S. Prawer, *Heine's Jewish Comedy: A Study of his Portraits of Jews and Judaism* (Oxford, 1983), pp. 10–43.

[118] Riesser, 'Vorrede', *Über die Stellung der Bekenner des Mosaischen Glaubens in Deutschland*, in *Gesammelte Schriften*, ii. 13–14.

German Confederation (founded in 1866 after Prussia's victory over Austria and its South German allies) passed an Emancipation Act on 3 July 1869, stating: 'All remaining restrictions of civic and citizenhood rights imposed on the grounds of differences of religious confession are herewith abolished.'[119] With the unification of Germany in 1871, this law was extended to the whole of the new German Reich.

However, the presence of Jewish emancipation on the political agenda for so long served to accentuate Jewish difference. It was discussed in all State diets, and some 2,500 books, pamphlets, and periodical essays on the subject appeared between 1815 and 1850. 'What emerges clearly', writes Rürup about this material, 'is how remote Jews and Judaism still were to the eyes of most non-Jews. Even among Liberals good will went often hand in hand with incomprehension of the Jewish situation and Jewish life style, while in large sections of the population the otherness of the Jews—which took a long time to overcome in spite of the tendencies towards assimilation—continued to inspire suspicion, dislike or even hatred.'[120] Whatever the feelings they aroused, Jews remained highly visible, and their visibility is very apparent, as we shall see in Chapter 3, in nineteenth-century fiction, where a character's Jewishness is never an incidental feature—as Humboldt hoped it would become—but always central to his or her presentation. The triumph of liberal principles in the legislation of 1867 and 1871 was real, but not conclusive; as we shall see, people continued to envisage a 'Jewish question' which was simply more elusive and intractable.

MOSES MENDELSSOHN AND THE RATIONAL JEW

Dohm wrote his treatise at the request of Moses Mendelssohn, who was the great exemplar of a Jew suited to enter the society of the Enlightenment. 'Certainly', wrote the Abbé Grégoire, 'a nation which has the honour to have possessed Mendelssohn is at least at the dawn of reason.'[121] Gentiles were impressed by Mendelssohn's urbanity. Thus Gellert reported after a visit from

[119] Quoted in Rürup, 'The Tortuous and Thorny Path', p. 32.
[120] Ibid. 22.   [121] Grégoire, *Essai*, p. 106.

Mendelssohn: 'He lacks the awkwardness of his nation and talks with great good sense.'[122] For later generations of German Jews Mendelssohn exemplified the ability of Jews to enter a German culture defined by enlightened and humane ideals. Thus the liberal rabbi Ludwig Philippson wrote in 1879:

All the bad qualities imputed to Jews were disproved by Mendelssohn's personality and impact. Servility, impertinence, presumption, ignorance, eccentricity, lack of taste—qualities which were considered inseparable from the Jews—were entirely rebutted by Mendelssohn. He proved himself at once a citizen of the world, a German, and a Jew, and so harmoniously and yet so energetically that such a combination, previously thought impossible, seemed to spring from his very nature.[123]

Yet twentieth-century Jews who explored new forms of Jewish consciousness have been sharply critical of Mendelssohn and his legacy. The theologian Franz Rosenzweig regretted that Mendelssohn, sheltered by the universalist spirit of the Enlightenment, had left future generations defenceless against the dangers to Jewish identity arising from an age of intolerance.[124] And the Nietzsche-inspired Zionist Daniel Pasmanik, writing in a very different intellectual climate, denounced him for crippling the self-assurance which enabled the Jews to survive two thousand years of exile:

Mendelssohn was one of the first 'enlightened Jews' who wanted to erase the essential character of the Jewish soul, and to replace the Jews' powerful and vital efforts to attain *full* independence by legal equality and Jewish ethics.[125]

Mendelssohn's father was a Torah scribe in Dessau, a centre of the early Haskala. Many Hebrew grammars and Hebrew

---

[122] Letter quoted in Stenzel, 'Idealisierung und Vorurteil', p. 119; cf. Christopher M. Clark, *The Politics of Conversion: Missionary Protestantism and the Jews in Prussia 1728–1941* (Oxford, 1995), p. 80.

[123] Philippson, 'Moses Mendelssohns providentielle Sendung', in *Lessing-Mendelssohn-Gedenkbuch*, pp. 84–100 (p. 92).

[124] Rosenzweig, 'Vorspruch zu einer Mendelssohnfeier' (1929), in *Gesammelte Schriften*, iii: *Zweistromland*, ed. Reinhold and Annemarie Mayer (Dordrecht, 1984), p. 457.

[125] Pasmanik, *Die Seele Israels: Zur Psychologie des Diasporajudentums* (Cologne and Leipzig, 1911), pp. 68–9. In his diary for 1915, Gershom Scholem listed this little-known book among the dozen essential works of Zionism: Scholem, *Tagebücher, 1913–1917*, ed. Karlfried Gründer and Friedrich Niewöhner (Frankfurt, 1995), pp. 189–90.

philosophical texts were produced by the nearby Wulff printing-house. This helped Mendelssohn to study not only the Talmud but also medieval Jewish philosophy, especially that of Maimonides, whose *Guide for the Perplexed* was reprinted by Wulff in 1742. His teacher, David Fränkel, was a serious textual scholar, whose influence helped to detach Mendelssohn from the 'baroque Judaism' of his time. In 1743, when Fränkel moved to Berlin as chief rabbi, Mendelssohn followed him, and was allowed to continue his studies there at a time when the Jewish population of Berlin was officially restricted to 120 families (though 333 families were actually resident). There he met other Jews who were exploring secular knowledge; learnt standard German, besides French and Latin; studied Enlightenment thinkers, especially Leibniz, Locke, and Wolff; became friends with Lessing and the bookseller Friedrich Nicolai; moved freely in literary circles; and in 1755 published his first philosophical writings. His career as a factory manager enabled him to marry in 1762 and support a large family, but was a burdensome distraction from his literary activities.

Mendelssohn's philosophical ability was first publicly acknowledged when, in 1763, he was awarded a prize by the Berlin Royal Academy for his essay about the kind of certainty possible for metaphysical truths, narrowly beating an entry by Kant. In 1771 the Berlin Royal Academy decided to propose to Frederick the Great that Mendelssohn should be elected a member; but the King did not approve the proposal. Thus Mendelssohn came up against the limits of Enlightenment. His efforts to prove that a faithful Jew could be an enlightened human being were acknowledged by fellow-intellectuals, but did not receive the institutional recognition that would have been truly valuable.

Unfortunately Mendelssohn's fame made the excitable Swiss clergyman Johann Caspar Lavater think that he was ready to adopt Christianity and lead a mass conversion of the Jews that would herald the millennium. Lavater challenged Mendelssohn either to refute the proofs of Christianity supposedly advanced by Charles Bonnet (whose *Palingénésie philosophique* tries to resolve theological problems by a theory of reincarnation), or to accept Christianity. How was Mendelssohn to respond? There was no question of his abandoning his own religion. He told Lavater: 'I cannot see what would attach me to a religion which appears so strict and is so generally despised, unless I were convinced in my heart of its truth.'[126] But neither did he want to engage in public controversy. Had he done so, he would have risked appearing like the familiar disputatious Jew, the practitioner of *pilpul*, which he so much disliked.[127] Instead, it was important to maintain the civilized urbanity of a man of the Enlightenment. The first draft of his reply to Lavater contains bitter reflections on the state of the Jews: 'Why so many refutations of Judaism, when, as every schoolboy knows, we are completely helpless?'[128] These reflections are absent from his published reply, a restrained and digni-fied response which won the admiration of Lichtenberg, Michaelis, Herder, and many others.[129] His peaceful character casts doubt on the common assumption that Mendelssohn was the direct model for Lessing's highly argumentative Nathan.[130] Mendelssohn objected to Lessing's controversy with Goeze as being 'squabbles' (*Zänkereien*).[131]

Mendelssohn's reply to Lavater is interesting not least for its reflections on toleration. He did not share the vulgar-Enlightenment disapproval (still found at the present day) of all prejudices for lacking a clear rational foundation.[132] Instead, he points out that while everyone should combat harmful prejudices, such as fanati-cism, frivolity, and cynicism, there are other prejudices, based on tradition, that do no harm and indeed help to sustain morality. Rash attempts to demolish these are intolerant, and will merely be destructive:

To oppose such doctrines in public, because we consider them prejudices, is to dig up the ground to see whether it is solid and secure, without providing any other support for the building that stands on it. Anyone who cares more for the good of humanity than for his own fame will be

---

[126] Mendelssohn, 'Schreiben an den Herrn Diaconus Lavater zu Zürich' (1770), in *Gesammelte Schriften*, vii: *Schriften zum Judentum I*, ed. Simon Rawidowicz (Berlin, 1930), p. 9.

[127] See Sander L. Gilman, *Jewish Self-Hatred: Anti-Semitism and the Hidden Language of the Jews* (Baltimore and London, 1986), pp. 92–4.

[128] 'Was ihn zu diesem Schritte bewogen?', in *Gesammelte Schriften*, vii. 64.

[129] See Altmann, *Moses Mendelssohn*, p. 225.

[130] M. Kayserling, *Moses Mendelssohn: Sein Leben und seine Werke* (Leipzig, 1862), p. 330. Kayserling undertakes to identify the originals of several other characters in *Nathan*.

[131] Letter to Herder, 24 Sept. 1781, quoted in Kayserling, *Moses Mendelssohn*, p. 550.

[132] See Christopher Ricks, *T. S. Eliot and Prejudice* (London, 1988), ch. 3.

slow to voice his opinion about such prejudices, and will take care not to attack them outright without extreme caution, for fear of overturning a moral principle that he finds dubious before his fellow-men have *adopted the true principle* that he wishes to put in its place.[133]

Elsewhere Mendelssohn went further. Although polemics against prejudice might well have served him in his conflicts with conservative rabbis, he shocked some of his enlightened friends by warning them about 'prejudice against prejudices'.[134] And in *Jerusalem* he warns against the ideal of religious unity. A union of faiths is unrealistic, for since human nature is bound to bring forth a diversity of opinions, unity could only be imposed by tyranny and sustained by hypocrisy. 'For the sake of your felicity and ours, *a union of faiths is not tolerance*; it is diametrically opposed to true tolerance!'[135] Here we have an ideal of toleration based on respect for difference.[136]

Mendelssohn not only wanted to contribute to Enlightenment thought; he also wanted to improve the position of his fellow-Jews. First, he thought that their degradation was in large part linguistic. Language was a means of self-improvement. Mendelssohn shared the disapproval of Jewish-German felt by Gentiles such as his admirer, the novelist and psychologist Karl Philipp Moritz, who wrote of him that he 'was brought up amid the noise and confusion of a common Jewish school, where his ear could pick up nothing but discord and cacophony in the language'.[137] The Jewish-German language was widely thought to be a secret tongue in which Jewish thieves communicated; the Abbé Grégoire looked forward to its extirpation, claiming that it served only to increase ignorance or mask criminality.[138] Mendelssohn made his own attitude clear when the administrator Ernst Ferdinand Klein

---

[133] Mendelssohn, 'Schreiben an Lavater', pp. 13–14. See David Sorkin, *Moses Mendelssohn* (London, 1996), pp. 25–9.

[134] Letter to August Hennings, 20 Sept. 1779, quoted in Altmann, *Moses Mendelssohn*, p. 391; for his friends' reaction, see ibid., p. 393.

[135] Mendelssohn, *Jerusalem, or On Religious Power and Judaism*, tr. Allan Arkush (Hanover, NH, and London, 1983), p. 138.

[136] For further illustrations of Mendelssohn's toleration, see Willi Goetschel, 'Moses Mendelssohn und das Projekt der Aufklärung', *Germanic Review*, 71 (1996), 163–76 (p. 169); Sorkin, *Moses Mendelssohn*, p. 140.

[137] Moritz, 'Denkwürdigkeiten, aufgezeichnet zur Beförderung des Edlen und Schönen', in his *Werke*, ed. Horst Günther, 3 vols. (Frankfurt, 1981), iii. 190.

[138] Grégoire, *Essai*, p. 160.

consulted him about revising the oath required of a Jew in a non-Jewish court. An edict of 1757 had reaffirmed that the oath should be taken in the synagogue in the presence of ten adult Jews, and on particularly important occasions one had to swear sitting on a coffin and with a butcher's knife in one hand; the oath itself called down terrible curses on one's own head and on one's family if one swore falsely.[139] Mendelssohn thought that Jews should take the oath in German or Hebrew, but not in a mixed language; he wrote to Klein:

On the other hand, I should be sorry if the Jewish-German dialect and the mixture of Hebrew with German had to be authorized by the law.—I fear this jargon has contributed not a little to the immorality of the common man, and I look for excellent results from the recent increase among my brothers of the use of the pure German dialect.[140]

To Mendelssohn the bad Jew is the one who has not achieved linguistic acculturation.[141] But in his domestic life Mendelssohn himself used the Jewish-German language that he considered unfit for official use. He and Fromet Gugenheim, his future wife, corresponded in a language between standard German and Yiddish, written in Hebrew characters, with many Hebrew expressions and occasional French passages.[142] His friend the Enlightener Friedrich Nicolai reports that his mastery of German cost Mendelssohn great effort, and he was clearly self-conscious about his German style.[143] Thus he discloses a linguistic split between the private, domestic, emotional, Jewish identity and the public, official, impersonal German identity of the acculturated Jew.

In order to save his fellow-Jews from linguistic degradation,

---

[139] Geiger, *Geschichte der Juden in Berlin*, i. 72–3.

[140] Letter to Klein, 29 Aug. 1782, in Mendelssohn, *Gesammelte Schriften*, vii. 279. This seems to be a considered condemnation of the use of Yiddish on public occasions, and not a mere 'momentary outburst' as is argued by Werner Weinberg, 'Language Questions relating to Moses Mendelssohn's Pentateuch Translation', *Hebrew Union College Annual*, 55 (1984), 197–242 (p. 237). Cf. the association of language and morality in the attitude of the Scottish Enlightenment to what the historian William Robertson called 'those vicious forms of speech which are denominated Scotticisms' (quoted in Robert Crawford, *Devolving English Literature* (Oxford, 1992), p. 24). [141] See Gilman, *Jewish Self-Hatred*, pp. 102–3.

[142] See Altmann, *Moses Mendelssohn*, pp. 94–5; Reuven Michael, 'Vorwort' to his edition of Mendelssohn, *Briefwechsel (1761–1785) in deutscher Umschrift und in Übersetzung aus dem Hebräischen* (Stuttgart and Bad Cannstatt, 1994), p. VII.

[143] Altmann, *Moses Mendelssohn*, p. 39.

Mendelssohn undertook a translation of the Pentateuch into German. Yiddish translations of the Bible, first published in Amsterdam in the 1670s, were still widely used, especially by the Jews from Poland who were often employed as teachers by German Jews. Mendelssohn wanted to counteract their influence and that of their language, which he called (referring to an earlier translation) 'a stammering, distorted and corrupt language, loathsome to the soul of the reader who knows how to speak correctly'.[144] Since many educated Jews were familiar with German but did not know Hebrew well, Mendelssohn wanted to ensure that they could study the Pentateuch with the help of a good German translation. He had it printed in Hebrew characters, and in the prospectus insisted that Hebrew was the only authentic language for the Jewish people. The *maskilim* welcomed it and traditional rabbis disapproved of it, for the same reason—that it would encourage Jews to improve their German. Hartwig Wessely said that it would counteract the tendency in Jewish education to treat the study of Hebrew as unimportant compared to the Talmud, and also that it would improve the imperfect German spoken by the Jews in Germany and Poland.[145] Ezekiel Landau, Chief Rabbi of Prague, complained that it would mainly induce Jews to read more German books in order to understand the translation: 'Our Tora is thereby reduced to the role of a maidservant to the German tongue.'[146] Landau rightly saw that Mendelssohn was making it less necessary for German Jews to know Hebrew.

Secondly, Mendelssohn assisted assimilation by his interpretation of Judaism. He wanted to support Dohm's view that the ceremonial law did not prevent Jews from being good citizens. More abstractly, he wanted to confute the early Enlightenment's hostile view of Judaism as superstitious, by showing that it was compatible with reason. He therefore had to consider how far Judaism depended on revelation, and, if it did, how to bridge the 'ugly, broad ditch' that Lessing had found between truths of reason and historical facts. But if Judaism turned out not to depend on divine revelation but to be identifiable with the religion

---

[144] Quoted in Weinberg, 'Language Questions', p. 229.
[145] Altmann, *Moses Mendelssohn*, p. 378.
[146] Quoted in Altmann, *Moses Mendelssohn*, p. 383.

taught by reason and nature, what was the distinctive character of Judaism? Why should one not abandon it and adopt a nominally Christian deism, especially given the material advantages of such a conversion? The distinctiveness of Judaism must reside in the ceremonial law; but how could this elaborate code of everyday conduct be justified before the bar of reason?

The catalyst for Mendelssohn's treatise *Jerusalem* (1783) was an anonymous pamphlet by one August Cranz, *Das Forschen nach Licht und Recht* (*The Search for Light and Right*), published in 1782, which urged him to adopt Christianity, on the grounds that it had absorbed the religious essence of Judaism, and that the ceremonial law, originally intended to separate the Jews from idolaters, was now obsolete and harmful in making an unnecessary barrier between them and non-Jewish fellow-citizens. Part of Mendelssohn's reply was that neither Judaism nor any other organized religious body could be in conflict with the state, because all social obligations are also religious obligations. Neither State nor Church can exercise any power over sentiments and beliefs, therefore all religions have an equal right to toleration. Thus, in keeping with Enlightenment thought, Mendelssohn downplays the doctrinal element of religion, making it a private and individual matter, and stresses the moral, practical element. His redescription of Judaism as a religion, analogous in function to the Christian denominations, entails that it can no longer govern the entire life of a community through the normative political structure embodied in the *kehilla*. It becomes a personal and voluntary matter.[147] Mendelssohn is thus responding to the actual decline in the authority of the *kehilla* and in the communal solidarity of German Jews. He is among the founders of modern pluralism, helping, as David Sorkin points out, to create the philosophical foundations for a secular state which could accommodate numerous religions.[148]

The price to be paid, however, was a transformation in the character of Judaism. Michaelis had interpreted the Mosaic law as the political constitution of the community. Mendelssohn reinterprets it as giving moral guidance for the life of the individual. In his account, Judaism is indeed a revealed religion. But what was

---

[147] See Kochan, *Jews, Idols and Messiahs*, pp. 70–1.
[148] Sorkin, *The Transformation of German Jewry*, p. 69.

revealed to Moses on Sinai was not a religious doctrine. The Lord told Moses nothing that Moses did not know already.

Judaism boasts of no *exclusive* revelation of eternal truths that are indispensable to salvation, of no revealed religion in the sense in which that term is usually understood. Revealed *religion* is one thing, revealed *legislation*, another. The voice which let itself be heard on Sinai on that great day did not proclaim, 'I am the Eternal, your God, the necessary, independent being, omnipotent and omniscient, that recompenses men in a future life according to their deeds.' This is the universal *religion of mankind*, not Judaism; and the universal *religion of mankind*, without which men are neither virtuous nor capable of felicity, was not to be revealed there. In reality, it could not have been revealed there, for who was to be convinced of these eternal doctrines of salvation by the voice of thunder and the sound of trumpets.[149]

Humankind already possessed the universal religion: all that was revealed on Sinai was a particular way of putting it into practice. 'The Israelites possess a divine *legislation*—laws, command-ments, ordinances, rules of life, instruction in the will of God as to how they should conduct themselves in order to attain temporal and eternal felicity.'[150]

This leads on to Mendelssohn's attempt to justify the ceremonial law as a vehicle for morality. Spinoza and many other Enlightenment thinkers maintained that the ceremonial law existed in order to support the Jewish state, and that since the fall of Jerusalem in AD 71 and the dispersion of the Jews the law was obsolete.[151] They thus rejected Maimonides' assertion that 'every one of the six hundred and thirteen precepts serves to inculcate some truth, to remove some erroneous opinion, to estab-lish proper relations in society, to diminish evil, to train in good manners, or to warn against bad habits'.[152] Mendelssohn follows Maimonides, but with a difference. He replies, first, that the laws, however odd some of them may seem, share in the rationality of Judaism: 'All laws refer to, or are based on, eternal truths of reason, or remind us of them, and rouse us to ponder them. Hence, our rabbis rightly say: the laws and doctrines are related to each other, like body and soul.'[153] Ancient Judaism has no

---

[149] Mendelssohn, *Jerusalem*, p. 97.   [150] Ibid. 90.
[151] Spinoza, *Theologico-Political Treatise*, pp. 69–76.
[152] Moses Maimonides, *The Guide for the Perplexed*, tr. M. Friedländer (New York, 1956), p. 322.   [153] Mendelssohn, *Jerusalem*, p. 99.

articles of faith, but only a small number of fundamental principles. In order not to remain abstract and dead, these principles are embodied in the ceremonial practices enjoined on Jews. Mendelssohn supports this with semiotic arguments: ideas must be communicated by signs; but images and hieroglyphs promote confusion and idolatry; arbitrary signs like those of the alphabet generate excessive abstraction. The ceremonial law is a sign-system free from these defects. It is a living script which attaches humanity to reason, not by abstract contemplation or sterile disputation, but by encouraging people to enact the truths of reason in the details of their daily lives.[154]

Although both Maimonides and Mendelssohn ground the law on reason, the former discusses various justifications for particular ceremonial laws, while Mendelssohn avoids such debates and stresses the general relation between rational morality and its practical enactment in the law. He thus sidesteps the question why the universal truths of reason should be embodied in *these* particular practices. What truths of reason does one enact by attaching fringes to one's garments (Deut. 22: 12)? Why does rationality proscribe boiling a kid-goat in its mother's milk (Deut. 14: 21) or wearing wool mingled with linen (Deut. 22: 11)?[155] An anthropological approach (not available to Mendelssohn) would explain many of these prohibitions and injunctions by tracing them to systems of classification which transcend the opposition 'rational/irrational'.[156] But even in the eighteenth-century context, Mendelssohn's arguments invite the reply that the authority of these particular practices comes not from universal reason but from historical contingency. They form part of a time-honoured tradition that should be treated with pious obedience. If so, however, we are back at the 'ugly, broad ditch' that separates reason from history. Mendelssohn thought he had bridged this gap by denying that Judaism had any doctrines and defining it as a religion of practice; but as soon as we ask about the authority on which these practices are based, the gap opens up again.

[154] On this theory and modern responses to it, see Allan Arkush, *Moses Mendelssohn and the Enlightenment* (Albany, NY, 1994), pp. 212–18.
[155] Maimonides admits uncertainty about the former injunction (*Guide*, p. 371), and confesses his perplexity about others (p. 370).
[156] See Howard Eilberg-Schwartz, *The Savage in Judaism: An Anthropology of Israelite Religion and Ancient Judaism* (Bloomington and Indianapolis, 1990).

This problem was not apparent to most of Mendelssohn's admirers. To his nineteenth-century biographer Kayserling, his views on the ceremonial law seemed in perfect harmony with his theological rationalism. His religion was understood as religiosity: 'He and his friend Lessing had grasped not only rationalism but the fruitful idea that reason is a matter not of the intellect but of the heart and the emotions; he paid homage to the religion of reason, was a philosopher with his intellect, but in his heart and his life he was a strictly religious Jew.'[157] Kayserling thus involuntarily acknowledges that Mendelssohn's Judaism was not founded on his much-lauded reason but on the emotional and traditional loyalties which, in his letter to Lavater, he had defended so powerfully against the imputation of mere prejudice. Mendelssohn's loyalty to the ceremonial law seems humanly admirable but indefensible by the standards of his own rationalism. 'I cannot see', he wrote, 'how those born into the House of Jacob can in any conscientious manner disencumber themselves of the law.'[158] In his own life he observed the law: he wore a beard (albeit a small one), kept the dietary laws, and would not ride or write on the Sabbath.[159] His summons to Potsdam in 1771 to meet the Saxon ambassador coincided with the festival of Shemini Atzeret (the eighth day of the harvest festival of Sukkoth or Tabernacles), on which travel is not permitted; a meeting of rabbis dispensed Mendelssohn from this prohibition, but, in order not to scandalize Jewish onlookers, asked him to walk through the gate of Berlin and to alight from the carriage before it entered Potsdam.[160] But the next generation, more affected by the secular world and less attached to tradition, would often be reluctant to make even these concessions to the practice of Judaism. In retrospect, at least, it is clear that Mendelssohn was over-optimistic in assuming that other Jews would be equally scrupulous when confronted with the challenges and opportunities of the secular world.[161]

---

[157] Kayserling, *Moses Mendelssohn*, p. 373.

[158] Mendelssohn, *Jerusalem*, p. 133.

[159] Michael A. Meyer, *The Origins of the Modern Jew: Jewish Identity and European Culture in Germany, 1749–1824* (Detroit, 1967), p. 51.

[160] Altmann, *Moses Mendelssohn*, p. 276.

[161] See Lionel Kochan, *The Jewish Renaissance and Some of its Discontents* (Manchester, 1992), pp. 68–72.

MENDELSSOHN'S LEGACY

After Mendelssohn's death, his own children were prompt to abandon Judaism. Of his three sons, only Joseph, the eldest, remained a Jew, and a lukewarm one at that. Joseph's younger brother Abraham had his four children baptized, adding the name Bartholdy, to distinguish his branch of the family, and was later baptized himself along with his wife Leah Salomon. An agnostic, he adopted Christianity only for convenience. When his daughter Fanny was confirmed, he wrote to her that he practised a religion of morality which could have either a Jewish or a Christian form. He adds: 'We have brought you and your brothers and sisters up in Christianity because it is the form of belief held by most civilized people (*gesitteten Menschen*) and contains nothing that could distract you from the good.'[162] The third son, Nathan, also converted.

More spectacular, though, was the religious development of Mendelssohn's daughters Brendel (who soon changed her name to Dorothea) and Henriette. Much to her father's pleasure, the twenty-year-old Brendel married Simon Veit, a young banker, in 1783. She bore him four children, of whom two sons survived. Finding Veit uninspiring and uninterested in her, however, she was attracted by the intellectual young men whom she encountered in the Berlin salon kept by her friend Henriette Herz (wife of the doctor Marcus Herz), above all by the Romantic critic Friedrich Schlegel. Having obtained a divorce from Veit, she went to live with Schlegel in Jena in 1799. She was converted to Protestantism and married to Schlegel on 6 April 1804. Like many other Romantics, however, the Schlegels felt the pull of Roman Catholicism, and were received into the Church in 1808. Contemporaries admired Dorothea's devotion but noted that the zeal of the convert sometimes led her into 'hyper-Catholicism'.[163] Her sons Jonas and Philipp likewise became Catholics in Vienna in 1810. Her sister Henriette, an unmarried governess, became a Catholic in 1812. Only the third sister, Recha, remained a Jew.

The discomfort that being Jewish could entail is expressed most forcefully, however, by a friend of the Mendelssohn daughters whose

[162] Hensel, *Die Familie Mendelssohn*, p. 121.
[163] Caroline Pichler, *Denkwürdigkeiten aus meinem Leben*, ed. Emil Karl Blümml, 2 vols. (Munich, 1914), ii. 183.

reputation now stands high: Rahel Levin, known as Rahel Varnhagen from her marriage in 1814 to the diplomat Karl August Varnhagen von Ense. Contemporaries knew her best as the hostess of one of Berlin's most successful salons.[164] Founded after her father's death in 1790, and meeting in her attic apartment in her family mansion, it brought aristocrats, academics, writers, and cultivated women together for conversation about topics like the Berlin theatre, the latest works of Goethe, and the development of the French Revolution. The Berlin salons, and their offshoots in Vienna, temporarily raised the barriers separating aristocrats from commoners, men from women, Gentiles from Jews; though they were not free of tension, for Rahel's intellectuality and vivacity caused her to be cruelly satirized by the dramatist Julius von Voss and aroused the antipathy of Wilhelm von Humboldt, who wrote to his wife about 'little Levy' (*sic*, meaning Levin): 'She irritated me very much, but what can one do with the Jewish miss (*Judenmamsell*)? Gentz keeps saying she's the wittiest woman on earth. One must be able to do without wit.'[165]

During her lifetime Rahel published very little, and that little was anonymous: some comments on Goethe, extracted from letters to her husband, and some theatre reviews, which appeared in the journal *Morgenblatt für gebildete Stände* (*Morning Paper for the Cultivated Classes*). Before her death in 1833, however, she and her husband were already preparing a selection from her letters, which appeared that year as *Rahel: Ein Buch des Andenkens für ihre Freunde* (*Rahel: A Memorial Book for her Friends*) and was reissued by Varnhagen in an enlarged three-volume edition in 1834. Many volumes of Rahel's letters to various male and female correspondents are now available. As was common in the eighteenth century, they are works of self-exploration; Rahel's emotions are recorded with a raw, painful sincerity which is still astonishing to read.[166]

[164] See Deborah Hertz, *Jewish High Society in Old Regime Berlin* (New Haven and London, 1988).

[165] See Voss, *Die Griechheit: Original-Lustspiel in fünf Aufzügen* (Berlin, 1807); Honigmann, 'Über den Unterschied zwischen Alexander und Wilhelm von Humboldt', p. 63. Friedrich von Gentz, another frequenter of Rahel's salon, was a diplomat, first in Prussian, later in Austrian service.

[166] See Barbara Breysach, '*Die Persönlichkeit ist uns nur geliehen*': Zu Briefwechseln *Rahel Levin Varnhagens* (Würzburg, 1989).

In some famous letters to an early confidant, David Veit (nephew of Simon Veit, Dorothea Mendelssohn's first husband, and himself a medical student), Rahel reflects on the suffering that results from being 'a Jewess'. Not only is she a Jew, a member of a tiny minority, without immediate access to European culture, and subjected to social slights which continued to distress her throughout her life; but she is a woman, denied an education, unable to travel as Veit can, confined to domestic tasks and an empty social round, and still, in her twenties, under the thumb of her family who pounce on her slightest departure from good behaviour. In March 1795, she writes at length to Veit, describing her ill-health but insisting that her malaise is far more deep-seated:

Believe me—I'm not mad—there's *nothing wrong* with me in an ordinary way; the cause is always an immovable mountain, even if it can't be seen: *there's nothing wrong with me in an ordinary way.* I have such fantasies: as though, when I was driven into this world, a supernatural being had thrust these words with a dagger into my heart: 'Yes, have emotions, see the world as few see it, be great and noble, nor can I prevent you from constantly thinking, but *one* thing has been forgotten: be a Jewess!' And now my whole life is a process of bleeding to death; by keeping still, I can spin it out; every attempt to quench it is a new death; and immobility is possible only in death itself. These ravings are true, they can be translated. You may smile, or weep from compassion, I can trace every evil, every misfortune, every annoyance back to *that*; and I don't care if I look ridiculous in someone else's eyes. This opinion is my essence, and I must give you clear proof of it before I die.[167]

Here Rahel envisages her life as passive. She was not born but 'driven into this world' like a terrified animal. A supernatural being, a kind of bad fairy, decreed that her life should be a state of enforced immobility as the vitality she was born with gradually bleeds away; she is a patient who can only get worse. Similarly, the dreams recorded in Rahel's diaries, as Ursula Isselstein notes, all oppose rigidity to movement, and she had a lifelong phobic hatred of clocks and stagnant water, where energies are controlled or paralysed.[168] But Rahel responds to her situation with characteristic integrity. All she can do is form her opinion

---

[167] Rahel Varnhagen, *Briefwechsel*, ed. Friedhelm Kemp, 4 vols. (Munich, 1966–7), iii. 54.

[168] Isselstein, *Der Text aus meinem beleidigten Herzen: Studien zu Rahel Varnhagen* (Turin, 1993), pp. 126–7.

about her situation, and that opinion is her 'essence' (*Wesen*), her genuine and individual product. She is resolved to tell the truth about her feelings. In the letter she goes on to draw an alarming comparison between herself and a cripple who feels pain with every step he takes and receives no sympathy from the world, for which his misfortune is merely disgusting.

Later in this study, we shall encounter several Jews who profess a dislike of Jewishness that has been termed 'Jewish self-hatred'. In these cases, however, the dislike is usually projected onto other groups of Jews, and sometimes identified with racial qualities. By contrast, Rahel speaks only of herself; the fault lies with her social situation; and the beginnings of an answer to it are to be found in personal sincerity. This remained her ideal. Many years later she wrote to Pauline Wiesel, an unconventional woman whose combinations of marriage and love-affairs had placed her on the margins of respectable society:

The only difference between us is that you *live* everything, because you have courage, and had good fortune; I *think* most of it; because I didn't have good fortune, and gained no courage; not the kind that wrests happiness from the hands of fortune; I only learnt the courage to bear things; but nature shaped us both magnificently. And we are made to live the truth in this world. We've reached the same point by different routes. We are *alongside* human society. There is no place, no post, no empty title for us! *All* lies have one; eternal truth, right living and feeling, that springs undamaged from simple, deep characters, from the nature we can grasp, *has* none! And hence we are excluded from society. You, because you offended it. (Congratulations! at least you got something; many days of pleasure!) I, because I can't sin and lie with it.[169]

While Rahel cannot emulate the mobility of her Gentile friend, her situation as a Jew becomes the basis for her commitment to truthfulness. She turns to positive account the 'pariah' status described in her biography by Hannah Arendt, who took Rahel as a model for telling the truth, however uncomfortable and controversial it might be.[170]

---

[169] Letter to Wiesel, 12 Mar. 1810, in *Briefwechsel*, iii. 229.

[170] See Arendt, *Rahel Varnhagen: The Life of a Jewess*, tr. Richard and Clara Winston (London, 1957), and the sympathetic study by Ingeborg Nordmann, '"Fremdsein ist gut." Hannah Arendt über Rahel Varnhagen', in Barbara Hahn and Ursula Isselstein (eds.), *Rahel Levin Varnhagen: Die Wiederentdeckung einer Schriftstellerin* (Göttingen, 1987), pp. 196–207.

In practical terms, Rahel contradicted her own stress on passivity by responding realistically and actively to her situation, first by opening a salon which attracted many of the most interesting people in Berlin, then by looking for a marriage, not to a narrow-minded Jewish businessman such as Dorothea Mendelssohn had run away from, but to a Gentile. In 1814 she converted in order to marry Varnhagen, who as a Prussian diplomat and secretary to the Congress of Vienna gave her access to international society and enabled her in the 1820s again to host a Berlin salon frequented by the rising generation of intellectuals including the explorer Alexander von Humboldt, the historian Ranke, and the young Heine—who in turn, though more reluctantly, was to undergo a nominal conversion as the unavoidable 'entry-ticket to European culture' (H vi. 622).

While Mendelssohn's children and their friends were thus discarding Judaism, his followers were providing theoretical justifications for doing so. One of these was the philosopher Salomon Maimon, brought up in what is now Belarus, who distinguished himself as a young Talmud student, but, as he recounts in his autobiography, broke with his community and eventually set off for Berlin.[171] After many hardships he was taken up by Mendelssohn and enabled to study philosophy. His first publication, in 1790, was a critique of Kant. Having read the manuscript, Kant said that 'a glance at its contents enabled me to appreciate its excellence at once and to recognize that none of my opponents have understood me and my essential meaning so well as Maimon'.[172] His later works included a Hebrew commentary on Maimonides' *Guide to the Perplexed*; it was in honour of Maimonides that he had changed his name from Shlomo ben Yehoshua. Maimon was not only more advanced philosophically than Mendelssohn, but also more inclined to discard rather than revise traditional Judaism. Resenting what he considered the theocracy of the rabbinate, Maimon went out of his way to affront the orthodox. For example, in the wall of the synagogue at Posen there was a stag's horn which, it was believed, would cause the

---

[171] See Ritchie Robertson, 'From the Ghetto to Modern Culture: The Autobiographies of Salomon Maimon and Jakob Fromer', *Polin: A Yearbook of Polish-Jewish Studies*, 7 (1992), 12–30.

[172] Quoted in Samuel Hugo Bergman, *The Philosophy of Salomon Maimon*, tr. Noah J. Jacobs (Jerusalem, 1967), p. 5

instant death of anyone who touched it; Maimon touched it and made himself highly unpopular by remaining alive.[173] On another occasion, a rabbi showed Maimon a *shofar* and asked him: 'Do you know what that is?' to which Maimon boldly replied: 'Yes! It is the horn of a goat.'[174] His principle, he tells us, was to 'think about everything for himself'.[175] This ideal echoes Kant's famous exhortation: '*Sapere aude!* Have the courage to use your own intellect! is the watchword of Enlightenment.'[176] Maimon's individualism left him voluntarily isolated from the Jewish community.

Another Jewish Kantian, Lazarus Bendavid, had already abandoned the ceremonial law in his youth, when he went to the synagogue only to please his parents. While in Vienna, where he worked as a private tutor and gave lectures on Kant, Bendavid wrote a pamphlet on the faults of the contemporary Jews. Oppression, he argues, has made the Jews into a nation of slaves. The slave despises himself and his fellow-slaves. The Jews, accordingly, are egoistic and misanthropic. They suffer from self-contempt: the desire to have someone to look up to explains why Jews respect their rabbis; the desire to feel superior to the less fortunate explains why Jews are charitable to the poor. This is practically a theory of Jewish self-hatred; and it also illustrates self-hatred by denying the Jews any credit for good qualities. Like Mendelssohn, Bendavid thinks that the Jews' language is corrupt, and he blames their language for the intellectual corruption shown in their over-ingenuity: 'Lacking a correct language, the Jew also forgot how to think correctly; his thoughts became incoherent, his words were accompanied by gestures, his conclusions were all sorites lacking the middle term, his thinking resembled the quibbling of a child or the delirium of the fever patient rather than the deductions of a healthy adult man; his spirit became one-sided, his feelings eccentric.'[177]

Bendavid describes how the rapid progress of enlightenment is

---

[173] Maimon, *Lebensgeschichte*, p. 233.   [174] Ibid. 295.

[175] Ibid. 173; cf. pp. 230, 265.

[176] Kant, 'An Answer to the Question: What is Enlightenment?', in *Political Writings*, ed. Hans Reiss, tr. H. B. Nisbet, 2nd edn. (Cambridge, 1991), pp. 54–60 (p. 54).

[177] Bendavid, *Etwas zur Charackteristick der Juden* (Leipzig, 1793), p. 28. On him, see Dominique Bourel, 'Eine Generation später: Lazarus Bendavid (1762–1832)', *Wolfenbütteler Studien zur Aufklärung*, 19 (1994), 363–80.

dissolving the Jewish community. The majority are still blindly devoted to traditional Judaism, but, if they are wealthy, their children pretend to be enlightened but in fact neglect the ceremonial law because it would interfere with their dissipation.[178] Since the ceremonial law equates ritual with moral offences, those who abandon it can easily become completely amoral. Nevertheless, in contrast to Mendelssohn, Bendavid wants the 'shameful, senseless ceremonial law' to be completely abandoned: 'It is the hydra whose heads must all be cut off at once, if for each one that is cut off two more are not to grow in its place.'[179] He sees hope only in the small group who have broken away from Judaism without becoming irreligious, and who have transmuted its moral essence into natural religion.

A similar attitude was adopted by Mendelssohn's close friend David Friedländer, a leading figure in the Berlin Jewish community. Unlike Mendelssohn, Friedländer accepted without reserve Dohm's thesis that Jews had been corrupted by oppression and would become civilized if emancipated, and shared his hostility to the traditionally-minded rabbinate. He was less willing than Mendelssohn to endure the civil disabilities imposed on Jews. Although he himself had rights of citizenship, by virtue of the patent of naturalization granted to his father-in-law Daniel Itzig, he was unable to obtain the same rights for his family. In 1799, therefore, he and some other Berlin Jews sent an anonymous open letter to Provost Wilhelm Abraham Teller, a leading Lutheran theologian well known for his rationalism, saying that they were willing to adopt Christianity if they did not have to affirm its irrational and inessential dogmas. In this pamphlet Friedländer agrees with the Enlightenment that since the talmudic period Judaism has been a mere lifeless husk, its practices consisting of 'sanctity of works, verbiage, and empty trifling (*Werkheiligkeit, Wortkram, und leeren Tand*)'.[180] He suggests that Judaism and Protestantism are converging; the superstitions of traditional

---

[178] Precisely the same picture, from an anti-Jewish standpoint, is given by Adolph Freiherr von Knigge, *Über den Umgang mit Menschen*, 5th edn. (Frankfurt and Leipzig, 1808), p. 116.   [179] Bendavid, *Charackteristick*, pp. 54, 55.

[180] *Sendschreiben an Seine Hochwürden, Herrn Oberconsistorialrath und Probst Teller zu Berlin, von einigen Hausvätern jüdischer Religion* (Berlin, 1799), p. 34. On this publication and the resulting controversy, see Martin L. Davies, *Identity or History? Marcus Herz and the End of the Enlightenment* (Detroit, 1995), pp. 206–15.

Judaism, like those of Roman Catholicism, are being discarded, and both religions agree on the eternal truths of natural religion; revelation serves only to imprint them more forcibly on people's minds, but adds nothing substantial to them. The supernaturalism of the Old Testament is merely metaphorical, and Friedländer hints that such New Testament expressions as 'Son of God' may likewise be mere poetic imagery. He complains bitterly about the ceremonial law as an obsolete, expensive, and time-consuming nuisance which interferes with every aspect of the Jew's life, obstructs his dealings with non-Jews, and keeps him in a state of immaturity: 'For a thinking being there is nothing more humiliating than this perpetual state of immaturity: instead of giving rational grounds for one's conduct, perpetually having to appeal to legal authorities.'[181] 'Immaturity' (*Unmündigkeit*) is an important word. In Kant's famous essay 'What is Enlightenment?' it denotes the state from which the enlightened man should free himself in order to attain autonomy.[182] Combining this key term with the pamphlet's epigraph from I Corinthians 13 ('When I became a man, I put away childish things'), Friedländer's complaint implies that traditional Judaism is something childish which adult humanity will discard.

According to Friedländer, Judaism was already dissolving. 'The study of the basic language and the Talmud is declining among us from day to day; respect for the rabbis has sunk, and must continue to sink along with the neglect of ceremonial and ritual laws.'[183] Like Bendavid, Friedländer was worried that the decline of Judaism would mean a growth in immorality. He therefore wanted Jews to be able to abandon the day-to-day restrictions of the ceremonial law, and the civil restrictions imposed on non-Christians, by adopting Christianity, provided that Christianity meant no more than natural religion. The purpose of the open letter was therefore to ask Teller what confession of faith he and his colleagues would require from Jewish converts.

Though this request was extraordinary, Teller had in a sense invited it. He was not only prominent among the Neologists, who subjected revealed religion to rational and historical criticism, but also advocated the transmutation of Christianity into pure

---

[181] *Sendschreiben*, p. 10.   [182] Kant, *Political Writings*, p. 54.
[183] *Sendschreiben*, p. 79.

morality.[184] Nevertheless, he could not accept Friedländer's reduction of Christianity to deism. He replied that they would have to accept the basic truth 'that Christ, chosen and sent by God, was the founder of a better religion than all of your erstwhile service through ceremonials was or could be; that he is the lord and head of all who choose him as their model in the true worship of God and who follow his instruction'.[185] Friedländer could not accept conversion on these terms and withdrew into Judaism, later becoming a proponent of the Reform movement.

Friedländer was drawing the logical consequences of emancipation. Once Jews began mixing in the wider society, they could no longer follow the ceremonial law which was intended to govern their entire lives and to keep them separate from others. Judaism had either to be abandoned or to be reinvented. But there were grounds for the scepticism wittily expressed by Heine in a letter of 1823 to a Jewish friend:

Some corn-cutters (Friedländer & Co.) have sought to cure the body of Judaism from its wretched skin-disease by blood-letting, and thanks to their clumsiness and cobwebby bandages of reason Israel must bleed to death. [. . .] We no longer have the strength to wear beards, to hate, and to be tolerant out of hatred; that is the motive for our reformation. [. . .] Others want a miniature version of Protestant Christianity under Jewish management, and they make a *talles* [prayer-shawl] from the wool of the Lamb of God, and a jerkin from the feathers of the Holy Ghost's dove and underpants from Christian love, and they will go bankrupt and their successors will call themselves 'God, Christ & Co.'[186]

Without foreseeing the opportunism that Heine here attacks, Mendelssohn had begun the process of reinventing Judaism by identifying it with natural religion and universal humanity.

Meanwhile, in order to shore up traditional Judaism, it was being reshaped as orthodoxy by such figures as Rabbi Moses Sofer of Pressburg (Bratislava), whose motto was: 'Anything new is forbidden by the Torah.'[187] Sofer did not want Judaism to be picked apart by rational analysis, but to be preserved intact,

---

[184] See Karl Aner, *Die Theologie der Lessingzeit* (Halle, 1929), pp. 86–7.
[185] Quoted in Meyer, *The Origins of the Modern Jew*, p. 76.
[186] Letter to Immanuel Wohlwill, 1 Apr. 1823, in Heine, *Werke, Briefwechsel, Lebenszeugnisse*, Säkularausgabe, 27 vols. (Berlin, 1970–), xx. 71–2.
[187] Quoted in Mordechai Breuer, *Jüdische Orthodoxie im Deutschen Reich 1871–1918: Sozialgeschichte einer religiösen Minderheit* (Frankfurt, 1986), p. 33.

even at the price of isolating Jewish communities from the outside world.[188] Sofer's legacy to the present has been a powerful secessionist Judaism, highly visible in Israel and also, for British and American observers, in such phenomena as the rise of Lubavitcher Hasidism. Yet in so far as these forms of orthodoxy isolate themselves, not only socially, but also intellectually through their refusal to confront the questions posed to a traditional understanding of the Bible by scientific, historical, and archaeological discoveries, they revert to the mental narrowness from which Mendelssohn sought to free his Jewish contemporaries.[189]

The conflict between enlightenment and orthodoxy divided the Jewish world. Traditional-minded Jews tried to barricade themselves against modernity; enlightened Jews regarded the traditionalists as their enemy. Thus in a pamphlet in dialogue form, written in response to Friedländer's *Sendschreiben*, the ethical religion of the enlightened Jew is contrasted with the allegedly hypocritical traditionalism of the orthodox Jew: 'The former loves his religion because it leads him with secure steps to the source of virtue and happiness; the latter does not love it, he uses it only as a convenient instrument to conceal his base intentions and his selfishness.'[190] Bendavid is equally disparaging about the orthodox: 'They will forever remain incorrigible, and their extinction is the only hope for posterity.'[191] The obduracy and irrationality formerly attributed by Christians to Jews who rejected Christianity could now be ascribed by enlightened Jews to orthodox Jews who opposed the reduction of their faith to natural religion.

The implications of Mendelssohn's reformulations were explored by various nineteenth-century movements, originating in Germany, that sought to reconcile Judaism with modernity. The Reform movement sought to adjust Judaism to modern European civilization without infringing its basic principles.[192] It began with practice. Laymen in several German cities wanted

---

[188] See Jacob Katz, *Out of the Ghetto: The Social Background of Jewish Emancipation, 1770–1870* ([1973] New York, 1978), pp. 157–60.
[189] See Kochan, *The Jewish Renaissance*, ch. 3.
[190] *Gespräch über das Sendschreiben von einigen jüdischen Hausvätern an den Probst Teller, zwischen einem christlichen Theologen und einem alten Juden* (Berlin, 1799), p. 13.   [191] Bendavid, *Charackteristick*, pp. 46–7.
[192] See Michael A. Meyer, *Response to Modernity: A History of the Reform Movement in Judaism* (New York and Oxford, 1988).

to make their worship in the synagogue—or, as they preferred to call it, the temple—more like the dignified services of their Protestant neighbours. The first Reform congregation was established in 1818 in the Hamburg Temple, with sermons and prayers in German and an organ to accompany the prayers. The bar mitzvah was increasingly replaced by confirmation modelled on Christian catechisms and extended also to girls, while women and men ceased to be separated at services. In the 1840s Reform rabbis like Abraham Geiger and Samuel Holdheim began developing a Jewish theology in line with modern enlightened thought, abandoning claims that the Jews were specially elected by God and would ultimately be restored by the Messiah to the Promised Land. They were uncomfortable with specific Jewish practices such as the dietary laws, conceiving Judaism rather as a universalist religion which required Jews simply to set a good example in such universally binding requirements as justice, mercy, humility, and devotion. Judaism was no longer an all-encompassing way of life but another religion which could find its place in a pluralist society. It was a compromise, and thus vulnerable to Moses Hess's charge that the reformers had eviscerated Judaism. 'They fancy', wrote Hess in *Rome and Jerusalem* (1862),

that a recently manufactured prayer or hymn book, wherein a philosophical theism is put into rhyme and accompanied by music, is more elevating and soul-stirring than the fervent Hebrew prayers which express the pain and sorrow of a nation at the loss of its fatherland. They forget that these prayers, which not only created, but preserved for millenniums, the unity of Jewish worship, are even to-day the tie which binds into one people all the Jews scattered around the globe.[193]

Reform Judaism called forth a reaction in the Neo-Orthodoxy of Samson Raphael Hirsch, who became rabbi to a community of alarmed orthodox Jews in Frankfurt in 1851. Hirsch described his conception of Judaism in *Neunzehn Briefe über das Judentum* (*Nineteen Letters on Judaism*, 1836).[194] The central principle of the Torah is mutual service through observance of the Law, not through doctrines or dogmas; hence Judaism is not a religion

---

[193] Hess, *The Revival of Israel: Rome and Jerusalem, the Last Nationalist Question*, tr. Meyer Waxman (Lincoln, Nebr., and London, 1995), p. 95.

[194] See Hirsch, *The Nineteen Letters on Judaism*, ed. Jacob Breuer (Jerusalem and New York, 1969); Breuer, *Jüdische Orthodoxie*, pp. 30–4.

but an all-encompassing way of life. This life, however, need not be led in physical segregation from non-Jews, for Israel's unity is spiritual, not political, and a Jew can therefore be a full citizen of a modern state. Through the Torah, Jews were to set an example to the rest of humanity, and they should do so by mingling with humanity. But Reform Judaism, he thought, misunderstood Judaism by falsely comparing it to the Christian denominations and seeking to be just another religion. He thought it shameful to try to accommodate Judaism to the passing spirit of the age. He allowed change in externals, preaching in German and including a choir in his synagogue, in order to safeguard the essentials of Judaism. But what were the essentials of Judaism and what were the externals? Lacking any firm definition of these, Hirsch's Neo-Orthodoxy might be only, as Moses Hess called it, a 'desperate reaction';[195] it might differ only in degree, not in kind, from Reform Judaism.

Ironically, the Reformers accepted much of the Enlightenment case against Judaism. Unlike Mendelssohn, they accepted Spinoza's view that the ceremonial law was not binding on Diaspora Jewry. And they agreed with Kant and other Enlighteners that the highest expression of religion was morality. Thus the particular observances and traditions for which the Enlightenment had condemned Judaism were discarded; and the universal conception of morality by which the Enlightenment had condemned Judaism was now said to be its very essence.[196] But would Judaism, so conceived, retain any distinctive character of its own? The Reformers understandably wanted to reach a compromise between the traditions of Judaism and the values of the Enlightenment; but was that compromise likely to be stable? Both Reform and Neo-Orthodoxy found themselves in the same position as other religious groups: accepting the advantages of a pluralist and tolerant society, while trying to preserve their values against the secularizing pressures inherent in pluralism.

[195] Hess, *The Revival of Israel*, p. 113.
[196] This irony is brought out by Meyer, *Response to Modernity*, p. 65.

2

Liberalism

JEWS AND LIBERALISM IN THE NINETEENTH CENTURY

Throughout the nineteenth century Jews were conspicuously associated with liberalism, the political expression of the aspirations of the Enlightenment.[1] However, liberalism, a notoriously difficult term to define, had two main meanings. Earlier in the century it implied especially the search for universal human rights. Despite much diversity, liberals broadly agreed in desiring constitutional government with a large measure of popular participation; freedom of expression and abolition of censorship; and national unity as a means of evading the oppressive power of the German princes. Unlike their British counterparts, they were sympathetic to the power of the state. After all, in Austria and Prussia, enlightened ideals of a practical kind had been adopted and realized by the state bureaucracy; and while liberals deplored the petty abuse of bureaucratic power, they also considered that only the state could institute and enforce emancipatory legislation. They had less confidence in the wisdom of the masses, fearing that too great an extension of the suffrage would give power to the irresponsible mob. They saw political participation less as a means of social reform than as an instrument of enlightenment which should spread education and cultivation, summarized in the word *Bildung*, among the populace.

In both Germany and Austria the era of liberal ascendancy was the 1860s and 1870s.[2] The liberalism that enjoyed power, though, differed from its pre-1848 counterpart in representing especially

---

[1] See Kampmann, *Deutsche und Juden*; James J. Sheehan, *German Liberalism in the Nineteenth Century* (Chicago, 1978); Peter Pulzer, *Jews and the German State* (Oxford, 1992).

[2] See Albert Fuchs, *Geistige Strömungen in Österreich 1867–1918* ([1948] Vienna, 1984); Karlheinz Rossbacher, *Literatur und Liberalismus: Zur Kultur der Ringstraßenzeit in Wien* (Vienna, 1992).

the educated and wealthy middle class and the higher bureaucrats and supporting centralized and constitutional government, free enterprise, secularization, and material progress. Increasing stress was placed on the economics of the free market, on nationalism, and on strengthening the position of the bourgeoisie against those social groups—the Socialist working class, the women's movement, and, in the Habsburg monarchy, the non-German nationalities—that were struggling for emancipation in their turn.

Both the earlier emancipatory liberalism and the later free-market liberalism were prominently represented by Jews. Jews played a conspicuous part in the revolutions of 1848.[3] Of the delegates to the Frankfurt Parliament, seven were Jews: Johann Jacoby, Ignaz Kuranda, Gabriel Riesser, Moritz Veit, Ludwig Bamberger, Moritz Hartmann, and Friedrich Wilhelm Levysohn. Jews also fought on the barricades. There were at least ten Jews among the 'March victims' in Berlin. In many other German cities there were numerous Jews among the active revolutionaries. But Jews were particularly prominent among the revolutionaries in Vienna. Adolf Fischhof represented the masses on 13 March when he made an impromptu speech spelling out the demands of the Revolution. Of the sixteen revolutionaries buried in the University Church in Vienna on Friday 17 March, two were Jews. It was an ecumenical occasion: Rabbi Isak Noa Mannheimer took part in the ceremony and gave one of the funeral addresses, in which he pleaded for Jews, since they had suffered and been buried alongside Christians, to enjoy the same freedom.[4] Jews were also prominent on the Security Committee, to which Fischhof was elected Chairman; on the very active Student Committee, chaired by Josef Goldmark; and in the newly-constituted Reichstag which met in July 1848, its four Jewish deputies were Fischhof, Mannheimer, Goldmark, and the Cracow rabbi Berusch Meisels. A number of Jews were killed or forced to emigrate by the revolutionary fighting in October 1848, and Dr Hermann Jellinek, also a Jew, was among the nine revolutionaries executed by firing squad

---

[3] See Reinhard Rürup, 'The European Revolutions of 1848 and Jewish Emancipation', in Werner E. Mosse, Arnold Paucker, and Reinhard Rürup (eds.), *Revolution and Evolution: 1848 in German-Jewish History* (Tübingen, 1981), pp. 1–53.

[4] Mannheimer, 'Am Grabe der Gefallenen', *Wiener Sonntagsblätter*, 7, xii (19 Mar. 1848), 137–8.

in November 1848 after the city had been stormed by counter-revolutionary troops.

Two famous Jewish 1848ers, Gabriel Riesser and Johann Jacoby, serve to illustrate the different political paths that liberals could take. Riesser, a brilliant lawyer denied an academic career, refused to convert and sought to combine loyalty to Germany with an attachment to Jewish moral and domestic values. He began campaigning for emancipation by publishing pamphlets and by founding the newspaper *Der Jude* (*The Jew*) in 1832. In autumn 1848 he was elected one of the vice-presidents of the German National Assembly in Frankfurt. In 1861 he became the first Jewish judge in the High Court of his home town, Hamburg. He represented a new type of German-Jewish identity. He was deeply indebted to the supranational values of the Enlightenment, which he summed up in a eulogy on Lessing as 'the cultivation of humanity, human affection, enlightenment, freedom of conscience, and the struggle against intolerance, religious hatred, intellectual repression'.[5] But he was convinced that these values, including Jewish emancipation, could only be sustained within a united Germany. In Frankfurt he urged that Friedrich Wilhelm IV of Prussia should be invited to become Emperor of a united Germany, and was part of the deputation which unsuccessfully brought this invitation to the King.

If Riesser represents a Jew's successful entry into mainstream politics, Jacoby shows how consistent radicalism could lead to the political margins. A physician from Königsberg, Jacoby described vividly how the lives of Jews were damaged by Gentile contempt and their own insecurity:

The thought, 'You're a Jew!', is the spirit of torture that paralyses all true joy and forcibly suppresses all carefree relaxation. Excluded by the laws of the state from outward honours and from so many rights, held in low esteem by his Christian fellow-citizens or at least always suspecting this (and who can blame him?), the Jews feels humiliated by others' arrogance and is thus only too inclined to fear that every innocent remark may contain a slight.[6]

---

[5] Riesser, *Einige Worte über Lessing's Denkmal* (1838), *Gesammelte Schriften*, iv. 4.
[6] Letter of July 1832, quoted in Rolf Weber, *Johann Jacoby: Eine Biographie* (Cologne, 1988), p. 35.

In 1841 Jacoby created a sensation by publishing a pamphlet, *Vier Fragen beantwortet von einem Ostpreußen* (*Four Questions answered by an East Prussian*), which demanded popular participation in politics as a legal right, not a privilege, and as the acknowledgement of the people's maturity (*Mündigkeit*), a key term of Enlightenment discourse.[7] As a parliamentarian in 1848, he favoured a German republic (in contrast to Riesser's desire for a constitutional empire), but had to recognize that this ideal had little popular support. His consistent radicalism subsequently separated him from the liberal mainstream through his opposition to Bismarck's imperialist and militarist policies, and finally led him in 1872 to join the Social Democratic Party under Bebel. Karl Marx, who seldom praised contemporaries, acknowledged Jacoby as a courageous and honourable 'old radical' (*sic*) who was exceptional in taking the side of the proletariat.[8]

It was not only in radical politics that Jews were visible out of all proportion to their numbers. They were equally conspicuous in banking and finance. The old function of the Court Jews, that of financing the wars and provisioning the armies of eighteenth-century rulers, was required on a far larger scale during the Napoleonic Wars. International financial houses, like those of Baring and Rothschild, acted as intermediaries helping governments to finance their own and their allies' campaigns. Such financial operations could only be undertaken on an international scale. Meyer Amschel Rothschild, the founder of his House, established his five sons in the five financial centres of Europe: Frankfurt, London, Paris, Naples, and Vienna. After 1815 it was pre-eminently the Rothschilds who financed the major loans which helped old regimes to recover from the wars and new ones to become stable.[9] Their help was publicly acknowledged when in 1823 they were made hereditary Habsburg barons. Their international ties powerfully encouraged the conception of Jews as a close-knit body who placed family connections above national loyalties. And their power to influence the conduct of politics was enormously overestimated. Thus Heine, who was fascinated by the Rothschilds, describes James de Rothschild, in Paris, with

---

[7] Weber, *Jacoby*, p. 56.   [8] Ibid. 290.
[9] See E. J. Hobsbawm, *The Age of Revolution: Europe 1789–1848* (London, 1962), p. 96.

all the world's money in his pocket, symbolically overcoming Rome by receiving interest on a loan taken out by the Vatican.[10] In place of the military glory of Alexander or Napoleon, the modern world is ruled by 'Rothschild the Great' (H ii. 431); 'Money is the god of our age, and Rothschild is its prophet' (H v. 355).[11] But while the Rothschilds, or Bismarck's banker Bleichröder, were indispensable to modern politicians, they had no political agenda of their own, at least until after 1882, when Baron Edmond de Rothschild began supporting the Zionist settlements in Palestine.[12] Hannah Arendt speaks of their innocence in trusting in the continuity of government and in failing even to imagine what political power they could have wielded.[13]

The Rothschilds may have shaped the popular image of Jewish finance, but they were far from typical. Only a few of the nineteenth-century German-Jewish economic elite were descended from Court Jews.[14] It was more typical for a member of the Jewish petty bourgeoisie to attain business success, perhaps with the aid of a dowry and a well-timed move to a commercial city; he would then bequeath the management of the firm to his sons and/ or nephews, who would raise it to wealth and fame; in the third or subsequent generations those family members disinclined for business might branch out into cultural pursuits. A well-known example is the Warburg family: the Hamburg banker Moritz Warburg was the father both of Max Warburg, who continued the family business but refused all invitations to hold political office, and of the art historian Aby Warburg, founder of the Warburg Library, later the Warburg Institute, which was transferred from Hamburg to London in 1933. Jewish commercial and financial families often strengthened their position by marriage alliances. Thus to some extent they did form a network of interlinked dynasties. Many of these dynasties, however, were shortlived: sons often proved unable or unwilling to maintain their parents' business and were defeated by, or sold out to, new

---

[10] Heine, *Selected Prose*, tr. Ritchie Robertson (London, 1993), pp. 260–1.

[11] References in this form are to Heine, *Sämtliche Schriften*, ed. Klaus Briegleb, 6 vols. (Munich, 1968–76).

[12] See Simon Schama, *Two Rothschilds and the Land of Israel* (London, 1978).

[13] Arendt, *The Origins of Totalitarianism*, 3rd edn. (London, 1967), pp. 24–5.

[14] See W. E. Mosse, *The German-Jewish Economic Élite 1820–1935* (Oxford, 1989).

aspirants, often from small towns in the German provinces or in eastern Europe. There is nothing distinctively Jewish about this familiar sociological pattern: it is also followed by Thomas Mann's fictional Buddenbrooks (modelled on the history of his own family) who rise to wealth as army contractors in the Napoleonic Wars but come under the reluctant and unskilful leadership of Thomas Buddenbrook and peter out in his sensitive, musical, short-lived son Hanno. Nevertheless, the inaccurate notion that Jewish financiers and businessmen formed a close-knit international network was firmly imprinted on the popular mind. Hence 'the Jews' could be imagined as political radicals busy subverting the social order and simultaneously as self-interested plutocrats intent on exploiting it.

The prominence of Jewish financiers was misleading, both because their importance was gradually reduced by the rise of large corporate banks, and because it overshadowed the steady rise of most German Jews to middle-class status. By 1847, only half the Jewish population of Germany still consisted of small tradesmen and moneylenders; some businessmen and industrialists on a large scale were emerging. The Tietz family opened the first department store; the Aron Hirsch dynasty dominated the German metal trade; Jews established the coal and iron industry in Upper Silesia. Since Jews were excluded from the bureaucracy which traditionally absorbed large numbers of educated middle-class Germans, they were all the more numerous in professions like law and medicine, and in professions associated with modernization. They were heavily concentrated in commerce, transport, and industry. In a period when the German universities were overproducing graduates, many Jews were among those who entered the new, poorly paid profession of journalism.[15] Journalists who rose from the crowd of hacks included not only Heine and his opponent Ludwig Börne, but Karl Marx, editor of the *Rheinische Zeitung* in the early 1840s, and his collaborator Moses Hess. Hence Jews were marked out by 'occupational asymmetry'.[16] They also tended to be city-dwellers: in

---

[15] See Lenore O'Boyle, 'The Image of the Journalist in France, Germany, and England, 1815–1848', *Comparative Studies in Society and History*, 10 (1968), 290–317.　　　　　　　　　　　　[16] Pulzer, *Jews and the German State*, p. 23.

1800 90 per cent of German Jews had been country or small town dwellers, but by 1900 half of them lived in cities with populations of over 100,000.

German Jews readily identified with a united Germany as a means of transcending the local loyalties from which they felt themselves excluded and as a means of promoting emancipatory legislation. The National Liberal party, founded by Rudolf von Bennigsen in 1866, was able to dominate the Reichstag of 1871, and to co-operate with Bismarck in constructing many of the basic institutions of the new Empire. The party's parliamentary leaders included Ludwig Bamberger, Eduard Lasker, and Heinrich Oppenheim, though none of these identified themselves with the Jewish community. Some moderate liberals, like Bamberger, disliked Bismarck's methods but thought that national unity, however achieved, would lead to liberal reforms. Being determined to limit the influence of parliament, however, Bismarck allowed the liberals much more leeway in economic than in directly political matters. The financial boom of 1870–3 (*Gründerzeit*), with its speculative mania, collapsed in 1873, and many small investors lost their life savings in the crash. Although it was Lasker who had exposed the 'Strousberg system', in which unscrupulous financiers like the Jewish railway entrepreneur Baron Bethel Strousberg colluded with civil servants to set up fraudulent businesses, the liberals in general, and Jews in particular, were blamed for the crash, especially by the journalist Otto Glagau in his series of articles in *Die Gartenlaube* (1874–6). Glagau's articles opened the period in which the public avowal of antisemitism became respectable in Germany.

In the Austro-Hungarian Empire, liberalism dominated politics in the 'Austrian' section from 1867 to the fall of the liberal government in 1879. However, the liberals were discredited by the Austrian counterpart of the German economic boom which was likewise followed by a Stock Exchange collapse in 1873 and by a series of public scandals. After fourteen years of opposition, they were represented in government between 1893 and 1897, after which they split into several contending and ineffectual groups. Although Austrian history has sometimes been written as the supersession of a benign liberalism by populist mass parties, it would seem that non-Jewish liberals at least retained considerable political influence by adapting to the new climate with an admixture of German nationalism.[17] The new atmosphere can be illustrated by the parliamentary deputy Georg Ritter von Schönerer, who in 1879 formed the Volkspartei in order to combat 'Jewish' free-market capitalism and to support the German-speaking population of the multinational Empire. When refounded in 1882 as the Deutschnationale Partei, Schönerer's group issued a nationalist and democratic manifesto known as the Linz Programme, which included a demand (added in 1885) for 'the removal of Jewish influence from all sections of public life'.[18] Schönerer was soon eclipsed, however, by the charismatic Dr Karl Lueger, the Christian Social leader who became Mayor of Vienna in 1897 and remained in office until his death in 1910. Though Lueger, building on the liberals' foundations, had many municipal achievements to his credit, such as the improvement of gas and water supplies, the electrification of the tramway system, and the creation of parks, he owed some of his popularity to his repulsive antisemitic rhetoric.[19] Although Lueger did Jews no direct harm, he decisively lowered the quality of political discourse, helped to make antisemitism reputable, and encouraged an obsessive concern with the 'Jewish question'.

Despite the decline in their political dominance, Austrian liberals retained real influence in the civil service, banking and industry, the universities, and the press (whose leading liberal organs were the *Neue Freie Presse* and the *Neues Wiener Tagblatt*). Above all, liberalism meant for Austrian Jews an identification with the central Imperial power. Unlike Czechs, Poles, or Magyars, they had no other political identity available. A writer in the *Österreichische Wochenschrift*, the Viennese liberal Jewish newspaper, insisted in June 1917: 'In fact the Jews are not only the most loyal citizens of the Monarchy, but are also the only unconditional Austrians in this state.'[20] The

---

[17] See Pieter M. Judson, '"Whether Race or Conviction should be the Standard": National Identity and Liberal Politics in Nineteenth-Century Austria', *Austrian History Yearbook*, 22 (1991), 76–95; contrast Carl E. Schorske, *Fin de Siècle Vienna: Politics and Culture* (Cambridge, 1981).

[18] See Peter Pulzer, *The Rise of Political Anti-Semitism in Germany and Austria*, 2nd edn. (London, 1988), p. 147.

[19] See Richard S. Geehr, *Karl Lueger, Mayor of Fin de Siècle Vienna* (Detroit, 1990), ch. 5.

[20] Quoted by Marsha L. Rozenblit, 'The Dilemma of Identity: the Impact of the First World War on Habsburg Jewry', *Austrian Studies*, 5 (1994), 144–57 (pp. 149–50).

best-known literary depiction of this attitude occurs in Franz Theodor Csokor's play about the dissolution of the Habsburg Monarchy, *3. November 1918* (1936), in which a number of officers of different nationalities declare their new national loyalties as they throw earth into a grave, while it is left to the Jewish army doctor to say: 'Earth from Austria'.[21]

Broadly, then, we have a development in which emancipatory liberalism gradually loses out to free-market liberalism and Jews are gradually excluded from the political process. Their entry into German and Austrian society, outwardly successful, gave them limited and decreasing access to real political power, while they continued, even after full formal emancipation, to be identified as Jews. An analogous conflict can be found in literature, where writers upholding various types of liberalism nevertheless disclose in their fiction the seemingly insoluble problems of Jewish emancipation. Three texts from the early nineteenth century—Heine's *Die Bäder von Lucca* (1829), Berthold Auerbach's *Spinoza* (1837), and Fanny Lewald's *Jenny* (1843)—will illustrate the aporias which were masked in public pronouncements but disclosed in fiction.

As we have seen, religious observance in Heine's family was casual if it existed.[22] He was educated at a Catholic school and knew more about Christianity than about Judaism. Claims that his works are full of talmudic references are nearly as implausible as Max Brod's efforts to find a primordial Jewishness linking Heine with the medieval Jewish poet Süsskind von Trimberg.[23] Despite his support for Jewish emancipation and his interest in Jewish history (apparent from his unfinished novel *Der Rabbi von Bacherach*, an attempt to apply Walter Scott's historicism to the Jews of the medieval Rhineland), Heine converted in 1825 for frankly opportunistic reasons. His ambivalence towards actual Jews and to Jewish instruction emerges from his recollections:

---

[21] Csokor, *Europäische Trilogie* (Vienna, 1952), p. 57.

[22] For an introduction to the complex topic of Heine and Judaism, see Ritchie Robertson, *Heine* (London, 1988), ch. 4; for encyclopaedic detail, Prawer, *Heine's Jewish Comedy*.

[23] Israel Tabak, *Judaic Lore in Heine* (Baltimore, 1948); Brod, *Heinrich Heine* (Amsterdam, 1935), pp. 323–33. See appendix 2, 'The Jewish Image: Max Brod', in Jeffrey L. Sammons, *Heinrich Heine, the Elusive Poet* (New Haven, 1969), pp. 446–65.

Hebrew was easier [than Greek], for I always had a soft spot for the Jews, even though they crucify my good name to this day; but I could not learn as much Hebrew as my pocket-watch, which had much intimate contact with pawnbrokers, and thus acquired many Jewish habits—for example, it wouldn't go on Saturdays—and learnt the sacred language, and practised its grammar afterwards; for in sleepless nights I would often be astonished to hear it ticking to itself: *katal, katalta, katalti—kittel, kittalta, kittalti—pokat, pokadeti—pikat—pik—pik—*[24]

The most memorable characters in Heine's comedy of manners, *Die Bäder von Lucca* (*The Baths of Lucca*, 1829), are the complementary Jewish pair: the Marchese Christophoro di Gumpelino and his servant Hyazinth. Gumpelino, formerly the banker Christian Gumpel of Hamburg, has now acquired a title of nobility, the Catholic religion, and a great display of European culture (*Bildung*); he has retained his loyal servant Hirsch but changed the latter's name to match that of his dog, Apollo. With this pair Heine has revived a long-established comic formula, that of the idealist versus the practical man, as with Don Quixote and Sancho Panza. Gumpelino seeks to escape from Jewishness: he displays his culture by claiming to identify paintings blindfold, boasts of the literary connoisseurship shown by his knowledge of actresses, and according to his servant, spends two hours every evening kneeling before the 'Prima Donna' (H ii. 427). By contrast, Hirsch is down-to-earth and unsentimental. His double profession as a collector of lottery-tickets and cutter of corns expresses two aspects of Jewishness: a concern with money, which after all requires practical good sense, and an awareness of the body, the undignified physical being that we all share. Not only did he cut his lovers' corns, but he even cut those of the great Nathan Rothschild. This bodily awareness establishes a solidarity among all Jews. Hirsch tells how another Rothschild, Salomon, entertained him to dinner 'ganz famillionär' ('quite famillionairely', H ii. 425). Similarly, recognizing the narrator as an old acquaintance from Hamburg, Hirsch drops all pretensions to culture, much to Gumpelino's embarrassment, on the grounds that Jews can relax among themselves.

Gumpelino's pretensions are betrayed by his body. Not only do

---

[24] 'Ideas. The Book of Le Grand', in Heine, *Selected Prose*, p. 108; H ii. 268. The Hebrew words come from the paradigms of the verbs for 'kill' and 'seek'.

we hear much about his nose, which is compared to the Leaning Tower of Pisa, and about his fatness, but he is also in love with an English aristocrat, Lady Julia Maxfield. The story suggests that an English noblewoman is at the furthest remove from Jewishness and hence the most desirable sexual object. When the lovesick Gumpelino declaims passages from *Romeo and Juliet*, Hirsch reduces his passion to a medical problem and recommends a laxative passed on by *his* lover, 'fat Gudel from the Rubbish-Dump' (the Dreckwall or Jewish quarter in Hamburg). Having swallowed the laxative, the unfortunate Gumpelino receives a summons from his beloved to which he cannot respond. But this is poetic justice for his efforts to sublimate his physical desires through poetry and religion. His efforts at acculturation have weakened his contact with the basic realities of life. For Hirsch, on the other hand, the smells and bells of Gumpelino's Catholicism are a luxury unavailable to practical people who need to add up figures. Thus Heine vindicates the unromantic ordinariness of Hirsch by contrast with the artificial affectations of Gumpelino.

Traditional Judaism appeals no more to Hirsch than to Gumpelino, but it does feature in the nostalgic sketch of the pedlar Moses Lump. After running through the streets all week with his pack, Moses Lump finds fulfilment on the Sabbath, when, presiding over the Friday evening meal with his family, he feels like a king. This famous passage represents a traditional Judaism which is not available to any of the characters in the text.

A contrasting image of Judaism is personified by the narrator. Ostensibly identical with Heine, he is in fact a shifting, fluid presence. For not only is he on familiar terms with the incorrigibly Jewish Hirsch, free from Gumpelino's embarrassment at his servant's gaffes; but Gentiles accept him as a German, so that he is also the ex-lover of a British aristocrat, Lady Mathilde, and clearly the future lover of the beautiful Italian singer Francesca. Thus the narrator embodies a relaxed, sophisticated sexuality which easily achieves the conquests denied to Gumpelino. Gumpelino pays court to his lady-love, presenting her with flowers and ridiculous verses, in an outmoded, quasi-feudal fashion; the narrator talks with his ex-lover in an adult, worldly, teasing manner. When the narrator smiles mockingly at Gumpelino's rhapsodies, the latter accuses him of being a cynical, self-divided character, a Byron; but of course Gumpelino's pretensions to heartfelt emotion are ridiculed, and Heine is implying that irony like his is the only way in which a modern Jew can be authentic.

The text has a further, distasteful twist. Prevented by diarrhoea from enjoying Lady Maxfield, Gumpelino solaces himself with the poetry of Count August von Platen. Platen is a great poet of homosexual love; but he had launched a petty attack on Heine in one of his plays, calling him 'pride of the synagogue', and Heine took his revenge with an all-out homophobic assault.[25] The elaborate metrical forms of Platen's poetry are made to correspond to Gumpelino's cultural affectation, while Platen's homosexuality is aligned with the physical failure that keeps Gumpelino from erotic fulfilment (the common motif of anality need not be underlined). Thus, Heine is saying, the quasi-acculturated Jew, in escaping from the Jewish awareness of physicality into a merely verbal culture, has also lost his manhood; while the narrator embodies a form of Jewishness which combines an unembarrassed acknowledgement of one's Jewish roots, a sophisticated intimacy with European culture, and sexual success with a variety of desirable Gentile women. Homophobia and sexual bragging (the latter seen most unattractively in the poems headed 'Verschiedene' or 'Sundry Women') are unfortunately recurrent in Heine's work; but the important point here is that the Jewishness of the narrator in *Die Bäder von Lucca* is a purely literary construct, incapable of being lived. Heine is using fiction to compensate for the unsatisfactoriness of actual emancipation.

Berthold Auerbach (originally Moyses Baruch; 1812–82) was, after Heine, the most important German-Jewish creative writer of the nineteenth century. His international reputation rested above all on his tales of peasant life in his home region of south-western Germany, the *Schwarzwälder Dorfgeschichten* (*Black Forest Village Tales*, 1843–53). He received both a traditional *heder* education and a secular German education, and intended to become a rabbi, but doubted his vocation and studied law at Tübingen. He proved his liberal nationalism by displaying the German national colours, for which he was expelled from university and imprisoned for two months, whereupon he was obliged to

---

[25] See H ii. 832. On the Heine–Platen dispute, see Paul Derks, *Die Schande der heiligen Päderastie: Homosexualität und Öffentlichkeit in der deutschen Literatur 1750–1850* (Berlin, 1990).

adopt a literary career. His friends included the politician Eduard Lasker and the leading Reform rabbi Abraham Geiger, figures who seemed to embody the acceptance of Jews at the centre of German society. He believed that since Jews were not a distinct people (*Volk*) but a religious confession, there was no obstacle to their assimilation into the German nation, provided they earned emancipation through immersion in German culture. He hated the radicals Heine and Börne as traitors both to Germany and to Jewish integration.

Auerbach's fiction, however, undermines the naïve optimism of his public pronouncements. His village tales are an idealized picture of the German peasantry as both rooted in the soil and hospitable to liberalism—an ideal Germany in which Jewish assimilation would present no problem.[26] The potential difficulties of emancipation are projected into the Jewish past in his two historical novels, *Spinoza* (1837) and *Dichter und Kaufmann* (*Poet and Merchant*, 1840). The latter depicts the eighteenth-century writer Moses Ephraim Kuh, who acquired Western languages in Breslau, joined Mendelssohn's circle in Berlin in 1763, but was unable to establish himself either there or at home: back in Breslau, he felt persecuted as a freethinker by the orthodox community and lived out his Western identity in the only way permitted—on paper, by writing epigrams.[27] In portraying Kuh's slow descent into madness, Auerbach may well be projecting and thus exorcizing his own anxieties about unsuccessful integration.[28]

The earlier novel, *Spinoza*, is ostensibly more hopeful. Spinoza, a famous victim of the intolerance of orthodox Judaism, appears as the forerunner of a modern enlightened religiosity. He encounters not only the bigotry which demands that a renegade from Judaism must be stoned to death, but the arid subtlety and deep immorality of Talmud study and the obscurantism of Kabbalistic mysticism. Yet the rejection of religion by van den Emde, his prospective father-in-law, a cynical materialist and hedonist, is no more attractive. Spinoza arrives at a pantheistic

[26] See Sorkin, *The Transformation of German Jewry*, p. 154.

[27] A selection from Kuh's epigrams is quoted in Och, *Imago judaica*, pp. 236–7.

[28] See Jeffrey L. Sammons, 'Observations on Berthold Auerbach's Jewish Novels', in his *Imagination and History: Selected Papers on Nineteenth-Century German Literature* (New York, 1988), pp. 177–91 (p. 188).

sense of oneness with the universe which leads to his excommunication. Auerbach makes him an honorary Protestant by comparing him to the embattled Luther at the Diet of Worms. Spinoza similarly refuses to recant his faith, which finds God present, not in any scriptures, but in nature and the human heart. He explains the Bible rationalistically: 'In our reason, on the height of the pure idea of God, here is Sinai.'[29] The same problem thus arises as with Mendelssohn: relying on universal reason, why does Spinoza insist on remaining a Jew, when he has denuded his Judaism of all its particular content? Moreover, the novel ends by showing Spinoza living as a free man: 'his own existence with its sufferings was surrendered to the universe, and in the enjoyment of perceiving the divine truth he led eternal life.'[30] Yet this rational mysticism, this *amor Dei intellectualis*, is evidently a compensation for the complete isolation in which Spinoza ends his life. It is not a model for Jewish integration into society, but a means of enduring exclusion from society.

Fanny Lewald (1811–89) was brought up in an enlightened, liberal Jewish family in Königsberg. Her grandfather attended synagogue only as a social convention; his favourite reading was the works of the French Encyclopaedists. Her parents would gladly have converted but for family pressure; her mother, who felt strongly drawn towards Christianity, considered it 'a misfortune to be a Jewess'.[31] They ignored Jewish matters and allowed their children to receive Christian instruction at school. It was only from a pious Jewish neighbour that Fanny, at the age of 5, first learnt that she was a Jew. She converted in 1830 to a merely nominal Christianity. In 1845 she met the unhappily married teacher Adolf Stahr, and maintained a relationship with him till his divorce permitted them to marry in 1855. They were friendly with the similarly unconventional couple G. H. Lewes and Marian Evans (George Eliot).[32] Fanny Lewald's energies were dedicated to progressive social causes, above all to the emancipation of women, including the poor, so that they might have professional careers and economic independence; her treatise *Für und wider die*

---

[29] Auerbach, *Gesammelte Schriften*, 20 vols. (Stuttgart and Augsburg, 1858), xi. 194. [30] Ibid. xi. 227.
[31] Fanny Lewald, *Meine Lebensgeschichte*, ed. Gisela Brinker-Gabler (Frankfurt, 1980), p. 37. See Gabriele Schneider, *Fanny Lewald* (Reinbek, 1996).
[32] See Rosemary Ashton, *George Eliot: A Life* (London, 1996), p. 129.

Frauen. Vierzehn Briefe (*For and Against Women: Fourteen Letters*, 1870) elicited a letter of admiration from John Stuart Mill.

Lewald's accomplished early novel *Jenny* (1843) is a reply to Lessing's *Nathan der Weise* which undertakes to display the real hindrances to interconfessional marriage and to illustrate how these obstacles are founded in the psychologies of Jews and Christians. Her novel opens in 1832 and ends in the early 1840s. The two children of the wealthy banker Meier are both in love with Christians. Eduard, a doctor and committed liberal, is eventually denied official permission to marry a Christian, so renounces his sweetheart rather than be disloyal to his nation. Jenny is less steadfast. She is in love with Reinhard, a candidate for the Lutheran ministry. In order to become his wife, she receives instruction in Christianity, but having adopted her father's Spinozistic identification of God with Nature and of religion with morality, she finds the Christian doctrines of the Trinity and the Incarnation unintelligible except as poetic imagery, while the teaching of Christ seems to her to add nothing to the laws of Moses. Her intellectual conflicts, recounted in strikingly sharp and intelligent prose, lead to self-deception which she cannot sustain. After her baptism, she writes Reinhard a letter, admitting that she cannot believe in Christianity, which ends their relationship.

In Jenny and Eduard, the qualities defined as Jewish are steadfastness, loyalty, and rationality (*Verstand* and *Vernunft*), which preclude the acceptance of any positive religion and allow them only to anticipate a future religion based on morality and truth. The Christians shown in the novel have not attained this religion of rational morality. Their devotion is represented, through the Jewish figures, as over-emotional, idealistic, and compatible with dishonesty and selfishness. Jenny's friend Therese, who is herself in love with Reinhard, overhears another character confessing his love for Jenny, and from confused (but easily imaginable) motives passes this information on to Reinhard's mother, who in turn conveys it to her son, thus ensuring that he rejects Jenny with the utmost bitterness and marries Therese instead.

Even without religious prejudice, intermarriage is shown to be ruled out by social prejudice. Eight years after her breach with Reinhard, Jenny attracts the love of another and more enlightened

Gentile, Graf Walter, and they are about to marry, when Walter finds himself obliged to avenge an antisemitic insult by fighting a duel in which he is killed, whereupon Jenny dies of grief. Though hasty and contrived, this ending does convey that, even if one's immediate circle agrees to a mixed marriage, the world at large will never accept it. The survivors of Jenny's family are close to despair, but Eduard reassures them:

'We live', he said, with the enthusiasm of a seer, 'in order to see a time when no such victims will bleed on the altar of prejudices! Let us live to see a free future, the emancipation of our people!'[33]

This conclusion evades the aporia to which the novel points: the attainment of legal emancipation might well leave intact the social prejudices to which Jenny and Walter fall victim; a better solution might be for individuals to defy such prejudices and illustrate in their own lives the possibility of harmonious intermarriage, rather than transferring, as Eduard does, the fight against prejudice from the personal to the abstractly political level. Eduard, presented as exemplary, is modelled on Lewald's friend and fellow-townsman Johann Jacoby.[34] His sonorous idealism seems fated, like Jacoby's, to lead to the political sidelines.

Alongside Eduard's abstract idealism, the novel offers other examples of true and false emancipation. The latter is represented by the semi-comic figure of Dr Steinheim, whose dark curly hair and awkward posture give him a 'Jewish' appearance insufficiently disguised by his careful yet tasteless clothes. Linguistically he is equally awkward. He converses almost entirely in quotations from Goethe and Schiller, while his unacculturated mother talks embarrassingly in 'Jargon'.[35] Hence Steinheim, like Heine's Gumpelino, has failed to find a language of his own or to absorb the German culture he flaunts. It is not surprising that at the end of the novel he has degenerated into a self-important hypochondriac, a domestic tyrant, and a selfish reactionary. Here, as in much German-Jewish fiction, an inauthentic language corresponds to an inauthentic morality. Jenny and Eduard, by contrast, talk an unaffected language which is the key to their moral integrity.

---

[33] Lewald, *Jenny*, p. 253.
[34] See Gabriele Schneider, 'Unbekannte Briefe Fanny Lewalds an Johann Jacoby aus den Jahren 1865 und 1866', *Menora*, 6 (1995), 137–60 (p. 150).
[35] Lewald, *Jenny*, p. 74.

The novel also illustrates Jenny's gradual emancipation from womanly subordination. Her capacity for emancipation is presented as Jewish. In contrast to the stolid Therese, Jenny is a lively, witty young woman who arouses Gentile disapproval of forward Jewish girls. Reinhard's mother warns him that girls like Jenny are spoiled by male company which promotes their intellect and their enlightenment ('ihr Geist und ihre Aufklärung') and makes them too ready to cast away prejudices and, with the light of reason, to banish the semi-darkness in which piety can flourish.[36] In adopting Christianity for Reinhard's sake, she is committing an act of bad faith against which her better self revolts. Her renunciation of Reinhard marks her step into maturity. While Lewald as narrator assures us that women's love requires submission to men, she also shows us Jenny sketching out a relationship of equals which comes close to being realized in her marriage to Walter. When Walter rejects the familiar emblem of the feminine ivy tenderly entwining the masculine oak, Jenny instead proposes the image of two equally flourishing trees with their branches interlinked.[37] Her self-affirmation as equal to men coincides with her self-affirmation as a Jew: after overhearing some antisemitic gossip, she gives a public performance of one of Byron's *Hebrew Melodies* in which a Jewish girl calls down Jehovah's vengeance on her people's oppressors. Unlike Eduard, Jenny illustrates possibilities of emancipation in personal life. Her mature devotion to Walter ensures a tragic ending by making her unable to survive his death.

SCHNITZLER: LIBERALISM AND IRONY

To pursue the development of liberal and enlightened ideals among emancipated Jews, we now move forward to early twentieth-century Vienna and to three writers—Arthur Schnitzler, Stefan Zweig, and Sigmund Freud—who remained loyal to the values of liberalism and understood them as a Jewish contribution to wider European culture. All three shared an Enlightenment commitment to rational inquiry. In all three, this commitments leads to aporias: in Schnitzler, to an ironic acknowledgement of the self-defeating

---

[36] Lewald, *Jenny*, p. 70.   [37] Ibid. 136, 207.

character of honest inquiry; in Zweig, to depicting the defence-lessness of the humane, rational humanist; and in Freud, to an investigation of the irrational depths of the psyche which culmin-ates in the construction of new myths, including the strange myth of the origin of the Jews which he sets out in his last major work, *Moses and Monotheism.*

Schnitzler, born in Vienna in 1862 as the son of a successful doctor who had immigrated there from his Hungarian birthplace Nagykanizsa, would seem to typify Jewish assimilation to a society shaped by the values of liberalism and the Enlightenment. A trained doctor, as well as a leading member of the *fin-de-siècle* literary generation called Young Vienna, Schnitzler, in his plays, short stories, and novels, combines humane tolerance with psycho-logical insight. In the last two decades, the publication of his diaries has deepened our understanding of him by showing how, despite the frequent sadness of his life, he maintained a humane and rational outlook in an age of competing ideologies, national-isms, and pseudo-religions. Few contemporaries matched the sanity and prescience of his response to the outbreak of the First World War: 'World war. World ruin. Monstrous and appalling news' (*T* 4 August 1914).[38]

Yet Schnitzler's work seethes with problems. For, first, his Jewishness lacks any distinctively Jewish content. He increasingly found liberalism yielding to official antisemitism. In 1912 he wrote: 'when these pages may be read, it will perhaps no longer be possible to gain a correct impression (at least I hope so) of the importance, spiritually almost more than politically or socially, that was assigned to the so-called Jewish question when these lines were written. It was not possible, especially not for a Jew in public life, to ignore the fact that he was a Jew; nobody else was doing so, not the Gentiles and even less the Jews' (*J* 328).[39] Yet he could not

---

[38] Schnitzler's works, letters, and diaries are referred to by the following abbreviations:

A   *Aphorismen und Betrachtungen*, ed. Robert O. Weiss (Frankfurt, 1967);
D   *Die Dramatischen Werke*, 2 vols. (Frankfurt, 1962);
E   *Die Erzählenden Schriften*, 2 vols. (Frankfurt, 1961);
J   *Jugend in Wien*, ed. Therese Nickl and Heinrich Schnitzler (Vienna, 1968);
Br i   *Briefe 1875–1912*, ed. Therese Nickl and Heinrich Schnitzler (Frankfurt, 1981);
Br ii *Briefe 1913–1931*, ed. Peter Michael Braunwarth *et al.* (Frankfurt, 1984);
T   *Tagebuch* (Vienna, 1981–).

[39] Schnitzler, *My Youth in Vienna*, tr. Catherine Hutter (London, 1971), pp. 6–7.

oppose antisemitism with any positive conception of Jewishness, only with a generalized humanitarianism; and his humane values could not be held with the same fervour as the racism of the antisemites, because that very fervour was something Schnitzler disavowed. Under these circumstances it says much for Schnitzler that he avoided the temptation to reshape his Jewish identity in the image of the bad Jew projected by antisemitism, a reaction-formation examined in Chapter 4 below under the heading 'Self-Hatred'. Second, Schnitzler adheres to liberal values with an honesty that eventually exposes the very limitations of liberalism. While celebrating these values nostalgically, he also criticizes them unsparingly from within, though with no other values to replace them. The diaries which he kept from 1879 till near his death in 1931 are not only a rich, virtually untapped source for biography and cultural history; they illustrate the difficulties of being honest in everyday life and let us see the values of the Enlightenment as a matter of day-to-day praxis. Both Schnitzler's personal and public writings reveal the ironic aporias to which his rationalism led.

Judaism featured in Schnitzler's upbringing only as a fading family memory and as an unwelcome school subject. In his post-humously published autobiography he tells us: 'I was repelled by all dogma, from whichever pulpit it was preached or at whatever school it was taught. I found the subject, in the true sense of the word, undiscussable. I had as little relation to the so-called beliefs of my fathers—to that which was *truly* belief and not merely memory, tradition and atmosphere—as to any other religion' (*J* 96–7).[40] His thirteenth birthday, nominally his bar mitzvah, was celebrated in a thoroughly secular and assimilationist way, by giving him handsome editions of the German classics. The religious instruction imparted by rabbis at school met with a rationalist response: asked why it was not blasphemous for Job to curse the day he was born, young Schnitzler replied that Job's birth was not due to God (*J* 81). In adult life he described himself as 'an Austrian citizen of the Jewish race acknowledging German culture' (*T* 1 Nov. 1918). Yet he had his son Heinrich taught Hebrew (*T* 27 Dec. 1913).

In opposing dogmatic religion, Schnitzler's main target was not Judaism but the Roman Catholic Church, whose massive moral

[40] Schnitzler, 77 (trans. modified).

and political influence had been attacked by a succession of anti-clerical writers from the Austrian Enlightenment onwards.[41] He describes how, while still at school, he baited a preacher in the Viennese church of Maria am Gestade: 'I happened to be facing the priest as he expounded things which I considered exceptional nonsense, and I stared at him with deliberate scorn, whereupon he looked straight back at me, his eyes filled with a fury that couldn't fail to attract the attention of those around me' (*J* 98).[42] His anticlericalism could not but be strengthened by the antisemitic agitation later carried out, against their superiors' disapproval, by the notorious priests Deckert and Abel.[43] He reserves particular scorn for Jews who convert to Catholicism. Hans Schlesinger, the brother-in-law of Hugo von Hofmannsthal, did so and inspired the following comment from Schnitzler: 'Already believes in Purgatory, and in everything else in the catechism. Is now happy and content. May even become a priest.—A Jew ought either to be intelligent or never be born at all' (*T* 10 Jan. 1911). An article published on Christmas Day 1909 in the *Neue Freie Presse* by the evidently Jewish journalist Julian Sternberg, who had claimed to feel profoundly Christian emotions in St Stephen's Cathedral, causes Schnitzler and his fellow-writer Richard Beer-Hofmann to agree 'that the Jews are the Jews' misfortune' (*T* 25 Dec. 1909).

Schnitzler's own beliefs are indebted to the Enlightenment, but only diffusely. Specific links with Enlightenment are difficult to establish, though he enjoyed reading Gibbon (letter to Georg Brandes, *Br* i, 3 May 1900).[44] An early diary entry wishes that 'correct views' instead of 'mystical, unscientific notions' could be implanted in all schoolchildren as a means of enlightening them (*T* 31 May 1880). These 'correct views' would have been primarily those of scientific materialism. Like Freud, Schnitzler received his medical training from Theodor Meynert and Ernst von Brücke. He acquired from them a materialist and determinist outlook, which he later had difficulty in reconciling with his desire to believe in a modest measure of free will. Even as a young man

---

[41] See Peter Horwath, *Der Kampf gegen die religiöse Tradition: Die Kulturkampfliteratur Österreichs, 1780–1918* (Berne, 1978).

[42] Schnitzler, *My Youth in Vienna*, p. 98.

[43] See Norbert Abels, *Sicherheit ist nirgends: Judentum und Aufklärung bei Arthur Schnitzler* (Königstein, 1982), p. 20.

[44] See Hartmut Scheible, *Arthur Schnitzler und die Aufklärung* (Munich, 1977).

he expresses not missionary enthusiasm but regret: 'To my own regret, the materialists' outlook is becoming increasingly plausible and probable' (*T* 28 Apr. 1880). The later Schnitzler, however, is less inclined to advance positive beliefs of his own than to undermine other beliefs with ironic scepticism. In his diary for 25 December 1914 he calls for the rehabilitation of the much-abused words 'scepticism, liberalism, psychology'. In his autobiography, written mainly between 1915 and 1918, he looks back patronizingly on his youthful atheism and materialism, assuming instead an agnostic standpoint.

An attachment to scientific determinism, however, underlies Schnitzler's ethic of honesty. Determinism seemed to rule out ethical action; all one could do was to face the facts. Hence the ethical imperative shifted from action to knowledge. Ruthless honesty became a prime duty, not only for Schnitzler, but for rationalist and progressivist intellectuals of his generation. They thought themselves morally obliged to sweep away lies and illusions, and to face the truth revealed, however dismal it might be. In this spirit, Max Nordau undertook to dismantle bourgeois morality in *Die conventionellen Lügen der Kulturmenschheit* (*The Conventional Lies of Civilized Humanity*, 1883), while Freud tried to do the same for religion in *The Future of an Illusion* (1927). The chief exemplars of this destructive honesty were Nietzsche and Ibsen. Their names were habitually joined in *fin-de-siècle* writing, whether as inspiring representatives of individualism or as degenerate representatives of ego-mania.[45] Schnitzler admired both: in a letter to an unknown correspondent he ranks them together with Goethe, Beethoven, and Maupassant (!—*Br* i, 21 June 1895), and they are linked as emancipatory writers in his novel *Der Weg ins Freie* (*E* i. 775).[46] Born in 1862, however, Schnitzler was just too old, as well as too clear-headed, to undergo the 'Nietzsche experience' of so many modern writers, though there may be an echo of Nietzsche's mountain imagery when

---

[45] Contrast Otto Weininger, 'Über Henrik Ibsen und seine Dichtung "Peer Gynt"', in his *Über die letzten Dinge* (Munich, 1980), p. 19, with Max Nordau, *Degeneration* (London, 1898), p. 415.

[46] See Herbert W. Reichert, 'Nietzsche and Schnitzler', in Reichert and Herman Salinger (eds.), *Studies in Arthur Schnitzler* (Chapel Hill, NC, 1963), pp. 95–107; contrast J. M. Hawes, 'The Secret Life of Georg von Wergenthin: Nietzschean Analysis and Narrative Authority in Arthur Schnitzler's *Der Weg ins Freie*', MLR 90 (1995), 377–87.

Schnitzler describes himself as 'a writer for people with a head for heights' ('ein Dichter für Schwindelfreie', *T* 23 Dec. 1917).

Ibsen was at least equally important for Schnitzler, both as moralist and as dramatist. His influence is apparent both in Schnitzler's diaries and in his ironic drama *Professor Bernhardi* (1912). Enthusiasm for Ibsen—who was seen as a thoroughly modern writer, opposed to mere conventions and demanding a break with the past—was common in Schnitzler's circle. Hermann Bahr, who had published a major critical essay on Ibsen in 1887, later wrote that Ibsen had stood godfather to Young Vienna.[47] In 1896 Schnitzler visited Ibsen in Christiania (now Oslo) and had an amicable conversation, in which Ibsen praised his domestic tragedy *Liebelei* (*T* 25–6 July 1896). In 1917 he dreamt that he was acting the part of Relling in *The Wild Duck* (*T* 22 May 1917). No Ibsen role could have been more suitable: Relling is the doctor who sees through the delusions and deceptions in which the Ekdal family are trapped, and who sustains the family, not by undeceiving them, but by encouraging their 'life-lies'. He is contrasted with Molvik, the drunken clergyman who can no longer help anyone (representing the perceived futility of religion) and needs his sense of self-esteem supported by the illusion that he is a demoniac; and with Werle, the inept idealist, whose attempts to enlighten the family merely lead to the death of its most vulnerable member, the child Hedvik. Relling thus embodies honesty, but the despairing honesty of a perceptive onlooker who cannot improve the world. Honesty as Ibsen conceives it must be directed first and foremost at oneself.

Schnitzler's honesty, likewise, is first and foremost relentless self-knowledge. His first notes on autobiography emphasize this. In 1901 he resolves to be as truthful as his memory permits. 'I don't know,' he continues, 'if the inclination to be truthful toward myself was a part of me from the beginning. One thing is certain—in the course of years it has increased, in fact today the tendency seems to me to be my liveliest and most steadfast impulse' (*J* 324).[48] However, although in his autobiography Schnitzler prides himself on his lack of illusions (*J* 83), in his

[47] Bahr, *Selbstbildnis* (Berlin, 1923), p. 278. See 'Ibsen in Wien' in *Das Junge Wien: Österreichische Literatur- und Kunstkritik 1887–1904*, ed. Gotthart Wunberg, 2 vols. (Tübingen, 1976), pp. LXII–LXVI.   [48] Schnitzler, *My Youth in Vienna*, p. 2.

Buch der Sprüche und Bedenken (*Book of Sayings and Misgivings*, 1927) he is more searching:

It is quite easy to talk in all honesty (*Aufrichtigkeit*) about one's weaknesses, one's vices, even about one's crimes. But to avoid talking about them as though these weaknesses were extremely charming, these vices unusually interesting or even, at bottom, disguised virtues—and as though these crimes were the boldest and most grandiose ever committed—*that* takes art, and this is where real truthfulness would have to begin. It is seldom to be found in autobiographies. (*A* 110)

In the diaries, truthfulness likewise requires an effort, especially amid the emotional and sexual entanglements recorded in the 1890s. One example of difficult honesty occurs when he is in love with Mizi Glümer and at last has, but does not take, the chance to sleep with the long-desired Olga Waissnix: 'Yes, if Olga were already mine, I would hardly have any distinct awareness of being unfaithful to Mz.—yes, that is how I feel today—to write it down quite honestly (*ganz aufrichtig*): if Olga were to die today, I would feel less stirred than if Mz. failed to turn up for a rendezvous' (*T* 10 Aug. 1890). A slight disagreement with a later lover, Marie Reinhart, causes Schnitzler to foresee the end of their relationship and to reflect: 'Relationships, like people, are born with their deaths already predestined' (*T* 24 Mar. 1895). After a 'frank' conversation with Marie Reinhart, in which they agree that it would be absurd to swear undying love, Schnitzler remarks: 'There is something sad about this honesty (*Aufrichtigkeit*)' (*T* 13 May 1895). And after another: 'Our love will perish of this honesty' (*T* 12 Sept. 1895). These reflections recall how Anatol, the man-about-town whose dramatic adventures first made Schnitzler famous, anticipates the end of a new love affair even as it begins:

ANATOL: I told Annie honestly (*aufrichtig*), right at the start . . . as we were swearing undying love: 'You know, Annie dear—whichever of us feels one day that things are ending—will say so frankly. . .'
MAX: Ah, you agreed on that in the very moment when you were swearing undying love . . . excellent! (*D* i. 71)

In the play, the role of Anatol, sustaining his life by keeping up the necessary minimum of self-deception, is complemented by that of Max, the *raisonneur* and onlooker who plays no active part in life but comments on Anatol's delusions. A similar disjunction between insight and delusion structures *The Wild Duck*: the Ekdal family lead their deluded life while Relling plays the inactive observer. In his diaries, however, Schnitzler has both to live and observe, and each activity interferes with the other.

The diaries continually reveal the problems arising from Schnitzler's ethic of truthfulness.[49] One is that self-knowledge is not enough. Emotions need not only to be identified but to be confronted and worked through. Thus in 1893 Schnitzler records the agonizing break-up of his relationship with Mizi Glümer. He is clear-sighted about their feelings, including at various times his pity as well as disgust for her, his wish at some moments to find an excuse for resuming the relationship, and the pleasure he takes in tormenting her by denunciations. Eventually things become too appalling, for while this is going on Schnitzler's father dies, and grief for him and for the relationship cause Schnitzler's self-analytic language to collapse into incoherence and yield to religious language:

Poor dead Mizi! Of course love has gone, consumed by disgust; but where it burned and caused such happiness, this infinite heartfelt love—there's something there, and at times it gnaws cruelly—I feel the place where it was—truly, the superstitious cliché and question forces its way to my lips: My God, my God, whatever have I done? (*T* 16 May 1893)

Similar religious vocabulary appears in a passage from *Jugend in Wien* where Schnitzler remarks that attempts at truthfulness are usually intended to give oneself a kind of absolution (*J* 126). Schnitzler's irony here shows his uneasy awareness that painful emotional material cannot be dealt with simply by intellectual analysis, but requires some kind of catharsis, one version of which is the confession and absolution that were unavailable to him.

Since psychoanalysis has often been seen as a secular substitute for the confessional, one might have thought it suitable for Schnitzler. However, he conceives self-knowledge mainly as introspection in which one is oneself the final authority. He does not adopt the psychoanalytic model of self-knowledge, in which the self's true motives are occluded behind verbal and other parapraxes, and can be brought to light only through the drama

---

[49] For a fuller account, see Ritchie Robertson, 'Schnitzler's Honesty', in Alan Deighton (ed.), *Order from Confusion: Essays presented to Edward McInnes on the Occasion of his Sixtieth Birthday* (Hull, 1995), pp. 162–85.

of transference and counter-transference; though he comes close to it in the play *Paracelsus* (1899), where emotional truth is brought to the surface by hypnosis, displacement, and confession. Generally, however, he thinks of personal truth as private and incommunicable: 'after all, one can only ever utter half-truths, except to oneself, and that only in dreams' (*T* 19 Jan. 1905).

Schnitzler's acquaintance with Freud was cordial though rather distant.[50] He read Freud's *Interpretation of Dreams* as soon as it came out (*T* 26 Mar. 1900), but found much in Freud unacceptable, particularly the assumption of psychic determinism and the theory of infantile sexuality.[51] Although Freud called him his 'double', Schnitzler's psychological fictions emphasize the interplay of individuals with their social setting instead of the supposed childhood origins of their neuroses.[52] On 16 August 1922 Schnitzler spent a pleasant morning with Freud; they talked about Freud's analysis of Mahler, and Schnitzler confirmed that it had made Mahler much happier; when Freud began offering interpretations of the symbols in his plays, however, Schnitzler was both intrigued and repelled:

His whole character attracted me, and I sense a certain desire to talk with him about all the abysses of my work (and my existence)—but I don't think I will. (*T* 16 Aug. 1922)

The previous night he had a significant dream in which, having talked of meeting Freud, he saw Freud moving away from him. He received Theodor Reik's psychoanalytic study of his work with cautious praise, but added: 'I feel more and more strongly that there are more paths into the darkness of the soul than psychoanalysts allow themselves to dream (and dream-interpret)' (*Br* ii, 31 Dec. 1913); to his ex-wife he wrote concerning Reik: 'unfortunately, like all psychoanalysts, he has a complex about complexes' ('den Complexen-Complex', *Br* ii, 9 Dec. 1923).

Although many psychic forces in Schnitzler's life seem to call for psychoanalysis, he can do no more than record them. For example,

[50] See Freud, 'Briefe an Arthur Schnitzler', *Neue Rundschau*, 66 (1955), 95–106; for studies of their relationship, Michael Worbs, *Nervenkunst: Literatur und Psychoanalyse im Wien der Jahrhundertwende* (Frankfurt, 1983); Ulrich Weinzierl, *Arthur Schnitzler: Lieben Träumen Sterben* (Frankfurt, 1994), pp. 63–79.
[51] Ernest Jones, *Sigmund Freud: Life and Work*, 3 vols. (London, 1953–7), iii. 88–9.
[52] See Wolfgang Nehring, 'Schnitzler, Freud's alter ego?', *MAL* 10 (1977), iii/iv. 179–94.

he got on badly with his father. Johann Schnitzler was disappointed that his elder son, instead of applying himself to medicine, spent much time on literature, gadding about town, running up debts and consorting with unsuitable women. The year after his father's death, Schnitzler experienced auditory hallucinations in which voices uttered meaningless sentences, the only distinct voice being that of his father (*T* 24 Oct. 1894). Two years later, in November 1896, he began to suffer from tinnitus (*T* 24 Nov. 1896), and it may not be extravagant to suspect a psychosomatic connection: having refused to listen to his father's voice during his lifetime, Schnitzler was condemned to hear it incessantly after his death. More generally, after the age of 30 the life recorded in his diaries becomes increasingly frustrated and unhappy. He suffers major bereavements: not only the death of his father, but the stillbirth of his and Marie Reinhart's child, and the unexpected death of Marie herself. Add to that the emotional wear and tear of the slow-dying (and never quite dead) relationship with Mizi Glümer; his hypochondria, nourished by medical knowledge, his anxiety attacks, his tinnitus, and his increasing weariness of other people's company; and we have a state of mind in which truthfulness is of little use. Similarly, the torment Schnitzler underwent when his marriage to Olga Gussmann broke up in the early 1920s—almost every morning began with an outburst of weeping (*T* 19 Nov. 1920)—could not be alleviated by honesty or self-knowledge. Insight into Olga's shortcomings only deepened his sadness, and a self-analytic conversation, reported with a revealing lack of self-irony, only widened the gulf between them: 'To my clear, but somewhat forceful deductions she replied illogically and crossly' (*T* 10 Oct. 1921).

In the end, Schnitzler's ideal of self-knowledge proved self-defeating. Truthfulness is bound eventually to be turned against the ideal of truthfulness, as when Nietzsche 'unmasks' the search for truth as a mere disguise for the will to power. In 1901, having formulated his ideal of truthfulness, Schnitzler wonders if it is anything more than a pathological compulsion (*Zwangsvorstellung*) that he has developed to compensate for his disorderly emotional life (*J* 324). Thus the ethical urge towards truthfulness leads Schnitzler to explore the psychological motives for truthfulness and thence to the reductionist fallacy that truthfulness has no motives other than psychological ones.

Schnitzler's ethic of truthfulness does not mean not lying; it means not being taken in by his own lies. He resolves to be truthful with himself about even trivial basenesses, and so records the slight twinge of satisfaction he feels on telling the cabman to drive to the Catholic cemetery (where Marie Reinhart's grave is):

Since I have decided to conceal none of my meannesses and stupidities from myself, [I] mention this too. The only thing that excuses it in my own eyes is that I recognize everything. But the faint satisfaction in this self-knowledge paralyses what is good about it. (*T* 13 Mar. 1900)

Here Schnitzler notes the futility of self-knowledge. It should make one improve one's conduct. But the satisfaction it gives renders it ineffectual, and one is no better than before. Indeed, Schnitzler's freedom from illusions, his ethic of truthfulness, seem to have no influence on his conduct, as he admits in his memoirs: 'the fact that I have never tried to deceive myself about the nature of my feelings nor the quality of those people to whom I felt close, has not saved me from suffering injustices nor from inflicting them' (*J* 83).[53] Subtract the self-congratulation from this statement, and it becomes a confession of despair. Such merely intellectual honesty makes one a paralysed spectator, observing events but unable to affect them.

The negative side of truthfulness is apparent in Schnitzler's plays and stories. Many of them deal with disillusionment. An obvious example is *Liebelei* (1895), where we are to assume that Christine kills herself on learning that her lover has been unfaithful to her. Another is *Frau Berta Garlan* (1901), where an innocent young widow learns of sordid affairs going on among her friends, and re-establishes contact with a former lover only to learn that he wants her as his mistress every four to six weeks. On the more positive side, *Die Toten schweigen* (1897) ends with the wife about to come clean to her husband about her relationship with another man, now dead; her husband, in perceiving that she has a secret, seems more observant than the story has hitherto suggested, and one can imagine that she will find relief in confessing to him. The cynical observation that 'dead men tell no tales'

53 Schnitzler, *My Youth in Vienna*, p. 68.

is only part of the story's message. The value of confession is implied more strongly in *Paracelsus* (1899), where Justina acts out her earlier attraction to Paracelsus by projecting it on to Junker Anselm and thus reaffirms her commitment to marriage with Cyprian, who himself learns from the experience. Paracelsus' affirmation that all human activity is play is not the drama's final message, and not even its last word.[54]

The futility of intellectual subtlety is best illustrated by Heinrich Bermann, the Jewish intellectual in *Der Weg ins Freie*, who comes close to Schnitzler's own scepticism. Understanding other people, Heinrich assures Georg, is merely a sport: 'Understanding has nothing whatever to do with our feelings—almost as little as with our actions. It does not protect us from suffering, nor from disgust, nor from destruction. It leads nowhere' (*E* i. 842). This scepticism is hard to reconcile with Bermann's individualist view that liberation cannot come through joining a cause, like the Zionists and Socialists by whom he is surrounded, but only, through self-exploration:

I do not believe that such journeys into the open can be undertaken communally . . . for the roads there are not outside in the country, but in ourselves. It is important for each person to find his own inner path. For that it is of course necessary to see as clearly as possible into oneself, to illuminate one's remotest corners.   (*E* i. 833)

At the end of the novel Heinrich's ex-lover commits suicide and Heinrich is left analysing his feelings, which leads him merely into labyrinths of futile ingenuity and does not palliate his pain. It seems that honesty is futile when applied to psychology: 'It always depends how deep we look into ourselves. And when the lights are on in every storey, we are everything at once: guilty and innocent, cowards and heroes, fools and sages' (*E* i. 957). The image of artificial light questions the pretensions of the Enlightenment by underlining how useless mere knowledge is when it cannot issue in action. Georg goes on living; Heinrich is left to confront his pain and guilt, but his very commitment to intellectual understanding denies him any means of absorbing and transmuting these feelings.

[54] See Martin Swales, *Arthur Schnitzler: A Critical Study* (Oxford, 1971), pp. 133–8; Scheible, *Schnitzler und die Aufklärung*, p. 56.

In this novel Schnitzler presents the problem of self-defeating truthfulness as a Jewish problem. The contrast between Heinrich and Georg is a contrast between Jew and Gentile, between the rational heir of the Enlightenment and the man driven by irrational energies. Georg and Heinrich are similar, however, in that their emotional entanglements both end in somebody else's death. Georg has been uncertain whether or not to marry his lover Anna Rosner, who is pregnant with his child. He insists, despite Anna's reluctance, that the child shall be given to foster-parents. Conveniently (as Georg's acquaintance Nürnberger hints, *E* i. 932) the child dies, and even better, Anna terminates the relationship. Georg is thus able to find a 'road to the open' by starting a career as an orchestral conductor in Germany. Psychologically, it is plain that Georg regards Anna as a mother-substitute (*E* i. 868, 901): a typical Don Juan figure, he is promiscuous because he is always seeking to recapture maternal love, the only satisfying kind. Narrative logic therefore requires the child to die (being as it were incestuous), and forbids Georg to marry Anna. But this psychological reading in turn points to a subtext in which Georg, the nominal Christian, is saved by his devotion to an inaccessible mother-figure and by another person's sacrificial death. A viewpoint is conceivable from which this could appear as a selfish and over-comfortable way of escaping from guilt; while Heinrich, the Jewish intellectual, has no access to absolution, but could be seen as tragically courageous in bearing his guilt unaided. Schnitzler juxtaposes both their fates without endorsing either.

While in *Der Weg ins Freie* Schnitzler concentrates on honesty and its limitations in a private context, his play *Professor Bernhardi* sets personal integrity in a political arena. Schnitzler's political loyalties were to the Austrian liberal era, though in retrospect he was ironic about liberals' naïve confidence in the stability of their world:

The circumstance that I spent my childhood and adolescence in an atmosphere that was determined by the so-called liberalism of the 1860s and 1870s did not leave me unscathed. The basic error of this outlook (*Weltanschauung*) seems to me to have been the fact that certain idealized values were taken for granted from the start as fixed and incontestable; that a false belief was aroused in young people, who were supposed to strive on a prescribed way toward clearly defined goals, and then forthwith be able to build their house and their world on a stable foundation.

In those days we thought we knew what was true, good and beautiful; and all life lay ahead of us in grandiose simplicity. Thus the thought was far from my mind that every one of us was, so to speak, living in a new world at every moment; and that, just as God had made the world, every man had to build his house anew each day.   (*J* 325)[55]

By the time he wrote *Bernhardi*, premiered in 1912, Schnitzler felt that this liberal world had succumbed to the influence of new and illiberal mass parties, especially the Christian Social Party of which the antisemitic Karl Lueger (1844–1910) had been a highly audible spokesman, and behind which Schnitzler feared the baleful power of the Catholic Church. His Bernhardi, a distinguished Jewish doctor, tries to uphold enlightened values after the tide has turned against them, and the result is an ironic comedy which owes much to Ibsen.

Following Ibsen, Schnitzler conceives enlightenment as an agnostic humanism using science to improve people's material lives and to dispel irrational beliefs. It is in *A Public Enemy* that Ibsen displays these values most emphatically while also satirizing the idealist who upholds them, in a strange double perspective.[56] In this play, the idealistic scientist Dr Stockmann finds that the water feeding the new and profitable Baths in his home town are polluted. Contrary to his ingenuous expectations, this discovery annoys his brother the Mayor, who threatens him with dismissal from his post as medical officer to the Baths; while the ostensibly liberal and progressive journalists, who initially offer him the support of the 'compact majority' because they think his discovery may serve their campaign against the town's oligarchy, soon transfer their support when they find that he is a dangerous ally and the oligarchy a promising source of patronage. In a public meeting, Stockmann strays from revealing biological pollution into denouncing moral corruption and the stupidity of the majority with its credulous attachment to outworn ideas. Only the progressive, intelligent vanguard like himself, he maintains, should have any authority. Not surprisingly, these sentiments lead to his denunciation as a public enemy, to which he replies: 'You shall hear from your Public Enemy before he shakes the dust of

[55] Schnitzler, *My Youth in Vienna*, p. 3 (trans. modified).
[56] Contemporaries compared the two plays: see W. E. Yates, *Schnitzler, Hofmannsthal and the Austrian Theatre* (New Haven and London, 1992), pp. 97–8.

this place off his feet! I'm not as forbearing as a certain person was
. . . I don't say "I forgive you, for you know not what you do."'[57]
At the end of the play, Stockmann declares that he is the strongest
man in the world because he is alone.

From this final declaration, the whole play begins to unravel. For
Stockmann is not alone. He has a wife and three children. He
belongs in a network of social relationships which he does not
understand. His futile denunciation of stupidity entirely frustrates
his original task of getting the Baths cleaned up. He is a great self-
centred child, a monologist who never listens to others. His social
doctrine turns out to be a pseudo-Darwinian call for a dictatorship of the progressive intelligentsia. Yet his opponents, the
unprincipled politicians and journalists, are deeply unattractive
people who represent no cause larger than self-interest. Hence the
play does ask to be read as presenting a lonely idealist confronting
a corrupt and philistine society; yet, with the truth of literature, it
also exposes the self-deceived egotism of the idealist. It founds a
series of ostensibly progressive plays featuring social reformers or
revolutionaries whose idealism is exposed as naïvety or worse:
Gregers Werle in *The Wild Duck*, Alfred Loth in Hauptmann's
Vor Sonnenaufgang, and, as we shall see in Chapter 5, Friedrich in
Toller's *Die Wandlung*.

Professor Bernhardi belongs to this group. As in *A Public
Enemy*, we have a central issue which is supposed to be morally
unambiguous, like the need to clean up the Baths; around it there
grows up a vast tangle of political complications with which the
idealistic hero is ill-equipped to cope. Schnitzler takes on a larger
task, however, by putting his secular scientist in confrontation
with the values and power of the Church. Although Schnitzler
insisted that the play was a comedy of character without a
message or 'Tendenz', it is more tendentious than he acknowledges
(*Br* ii. 1–6, 99–100).

The central issue occupies the first Act of the play. In the
Elisabethinum, the hospital founded and run by Bernhardi, a
young woman is dying of a miscarriage. She has no emotional
support; her lover has disappeared. She cannot live more than
another hour, but has no idea that she is dying, for a camphor

---

[57] *A Public Enemy* in Ibsen, *Ghosts and Other Plays*, tr. Peter Watts (Harmondsworth, 1964), p. 195. Cf. Matt. 10: 14; Luke 23: 34.

injection has put her in a state of euphoria. A nurse who belongs to a Catholic lay sisterhood fetches a priest to give the young woman the last rites. Bernhardi thinks it cruel to take her out of her euphoria and frighten her; he asserts that it is his duty as a doctor to give his patients a happy death, and he therefore explicitly forbids the priest to enter the sick-room, touching him lightly on the shoulder to deter him. What further means of deterrence Bernhardi might have used we never learn, for at that point the nurse reports that the young woman is dead. Neither Bernhardi nor the priest has attained his object: the woman died in fear but without receiving the sacrament. Nevertheless, this confrontation between a Jewish doctor and a priest is blown up into a huge scandal, with a question asked in Parliament, an official inquiry, and a court case in which Bernhardi is sentenced to two months' imprisonment and forbidden to practise medicine.

Schnitzler's presentation of this issue is slanted in Bernhardi's favour.[58] His closest medical colleagues, who come across as people of extreme integrity, declare that he only 'asked the priest to let a poor, sick child of humanity die in peace' (*D* ii. 397) and that the Church's solicitude went beyond justifiable bounds (*D* ii. 405). After Bernhardi's condemnation, the priest pays him an unexpected visit to affirm that he acted correctly (*D* ii. 430). However, Bernhardi did not merely *ask* the priest to leave the woman alone; he explicitly *forbade* him to approach her. Since she was about to die anyway, the priest's appearance could not affect her medical condition, only (from Bernhardi's viewpoint) her emotional state, and to bar the priest's entry therefore went beyond Bernhardi's duty as a doctor.

Bernhardi also ignores the priest's reply: 'A happy death.—It is likely, Professor, that that means something different to each of us' (*D* ii. 357). 'Glück' (happiness) is an important word for Bernhardi. Rather than condemning the young woman for getting pregnant, he reflects sadly and enigmatically that her death results from former 'Liebesglück' (happiness in love; *D* ii. 345). He sees happiness only as emotion and sensation. The priest, however, does not come to condemn her but to give her absolution and to help her passage into the next world by the sacrament. It was for

---

[58] See the sceptical reading in Yates, *Schnitzler, Hofmannsthal, and the Austrian Theatre*, pp. 91–2.

him, not for Bernhardi, to decide whether her emotional state justified withholding the sacrament. In bringing her the sacrament, he was treating her, not as a creature of emotion, but as a responsible person equipped with intellect and will and able to face the prospect of death with spiritual help. By a supreme irony, the priest was acting in the spirit of the Enlightenment by treating his charge as an autonomous human being; while Bernhardi, in leaving her under an illusion, was acting in the paternalistic manner supposed by Enlighteners to be characteristic of a clerical elite. Schnitzler is depicting a situation in which the doctor seeks to take over the authority formerly held by the priest, and is at least as likely to misuse his power over his patients as priests were to domineer over their flock.

The play then presents an irreconcilable conflict between two incompatible views of the world. In his conversation with the priest in Act 4, Bernhardi says that his religion, or whatever substitute he possesses, obliges him to understand even where he is not understood (*D* ii. 435); but neither he nor Schnitzler makes good this claim. Bernhardi's standpoint is presented as a basic humanity which can be questioned only by the bigoted or the malicious; while, with the partial exception of the priest, the professed Christians in the play are all depicted as hypocritical and as representatives of a politicized and antisemitic Catholic Church which is hostile to enlightenment. Even the priest, though fundamentally decent and intelligent, justifies himself for telling less than the whole truth in court in a manner that invites the term Jesuitical; is quick to make the infamous suggestion that Bernhardi acted from a Jewish antipathy to Christianity; and avers that his Church's supreme value is discipline and obedience. His truthful testimony earns him the displeasure of his superiors and he is transferred from a parish in central Vienna to a remote spot on the Polish frontier. His name, Franz Reder, is only mentioned once, when a newspaper report is read aloud; otherwise he is always 'the priest', implying that he is less an individual than a member of an organization. We hear much about the clerical parties in Parliament (that is, Christian Socials) which are in an unholy alliance with the German nationalists and deeply tainted by antisemitism.

Against such antagonists, it is easy for Bernhardi to cut a good figure. His only fault is the excessive good nature which makes him underestimate the wiliness of Flint, the Minister in charge of universities (to which the Elisabethinum, as a teaching hospital, belongs). Schnitzler copies Ibsen's device of letting his idealist hero quote the Bible against Christian opponents. Foreseeing that his enemies will make political capital out of his actions, Bernhardi says: 'The Lord pardon them—they know damned well what they're doing' (D ii. 359). After resigning his post, he tells the other doctors: 'Whoever is not for me is against me' (D ii. 416); to an opponent who has testified in his favour, he says: 'A penitent sinner is more pleasing in my sight than ten just men' (D ii. 424, cf. Luke 15: 7); and in his conversation with the priest he sanctimoniously insists that he is 'pure in heart' (D ii. 434), echoing the Sermon on the Mount (Matt. 5: 8).[59] Schnitzler also seeks to give Bernhardi's embattled stance more credibility by evoking the intolerance of the past: Bernhardi's princely patron tells him that two hundred years earlier he would have been burnt alive, and the Minister doubts whether he would be so stubborn if such a prospect still existed (D ii. 369–70, 456). The isolated Bernhardi strongly recalls the protagonist of Lessing's *Nathan der Weise*, who really did risk being burnt at the stake by the menacing Patriarch of Jerusalem.

Compared to *Nathan*, however, *Professor Bernhardi* is a less inspiring, more sourly ironic play. Bernhardi is neither a crusader nor a martyr: released from prison, he wants only to return to private life, though his associates want him to use media opportunities to promote his beliefs. Politics are seen as inherently corrupting, the domain of the eel-like Flint, while the staunch old liberal Pflugfelder is a forlorn and ineffectual figure. Flint is a powerful rhetorician, able to command attention in Parliament; but instead of adhering to principles, he keeps twisting and turning in pursuit of political advantage. While the ideal politician might be a person of principle with enough rhetorical power to persuade others and enough constancy to make only tactical concessions, Schnitzler shows us a situation in which principles exist only in personal life and the public world is dominated by rhetoricians without inner substance. His depiction reflects his

---

[59] On these quotations, see Heinrich Kaulen, 'Antisemitismus und Aufklärung. Zum Verständnis von Arthur Schnitzlers *Professor Bernhardi*', ZfdP 100 (1981), 177–98 (pp. 183–4).

long-felt contempt for politics as such: 'It is the lowest thing and has the least to do with the *essence* of humanity' (*T* 10 May 1896). Above all, professional and public life in the play are dominated by the Jewish question. Even a disagreement between two doctors about a patient's diagnosis turns into a Jewish–Gentile dispute. Here the detailed stage directions which Schnitzler, like his contemporaries Shaw and Hauptmann, provides, enable us to recognize degrees of 'Jewishness', assimilation, or 'Austrianness', from the shambling posture of Dr Löwenstein or the 'Bierdeutsch' (beery German) with occasional Jewish tones uttered by the convert Dr Schreimann to the exaggerated Austrian accent of Dr Ebenwald. Curiously enough, Bernhardi himself cannot be located on this scale. His introductory stage direction describes him as over 50 with a greying beard, shortish hair, and the bearing of a man of the world rather than a scholar (*D* ii. 340–1). We are not told what his voice sounds like: an important omission, since Schnitzler, whom his creation otherwise resembles, was self-conscious about his 'nasal, Jewish' voice (*T* 19 Mar. 1907). Bernhardi, the enlightened Jewish scientist, is not recognizable as a Jew (except by his ironic remarks towards ostentatious Christians). Like the bearers of Lessing's ethical humanism, he is a human being outwardly independent of nationality.[60]

As these examples suggest, public self-presentation is all-important in this play, which is set very much in the public world. We do not find the alternation between public and domestic scenes characteristic of German historical drama. Bernhardi (again like Lessing's Nathan) appears to be a widower. There are a few semi-surreptitious signs of affection between himself and his son Oskar, who is a doctor in the hospital. Otherwise, the characters all appear in public roles, speaking in more or less artificial public voices (which Schnitzler catches with a fine ear), and correspondingly wary and watchful. The tête-à-têtes—between Bernhardi and Flint, the priest, and his rival Dr Ebenwald—are all tense scenes in which the characters are sounding each other out or sparring. There are no women on stage except for the nurse; the young woman whose death precipitates the scandal is never seen; we do not even learn her name.

---

[60] See Peter Horwath, 'Arthur Schnitzlers *Professor Bernhardi*. Eine Studie über Person und Tendenz. I', *Literatur und Kritik*, 12 (Mar. 1967), 88–104 (p. 91).

The play's tone is set by a minor character, Kurt Pflugfelder, who says early on that he has not renounced his earlier antisemitism but has become an anti-Aryan as well: 'I think people in general are a pretty inadequate bunch, and I hold on to the few exceptions here and there' (D ii. 352). Providence is referred to only ironically, when Bernhardi remarks that diseases are so complicated as to make one lose one's faith in Providence (D ii. 350), implying that only a simple-minded person can have such faith. Religion is seen as intellectual immaturity: Flint, alone with his under-secretary, drops the public mask and questions whether 'the people are, or ever will be, mature enough to exist without religion' (D ii. 446). Yet the maturity displayed by Bernhardi is bleak, while, as we have seen, the would-be humane belief in the pursuit of happiness, understood as emotion, proves on close scrutiny to be an abandonment of the ideals of the Enlightenment.

THE EUROPEAN HUMANISM OF STEFAN ZWEIG

Stefan Zweig (1881–1942), the prolific author of best-selling biographies and Novellen, typifies writers of Jewish descent for whom emancipation provided the entry ticket to European culture. Though Zweig did not convert, his links with Judaism were tenuous. He was brought up in a highly assimilated home, the son of a successful textile manufacturer who had moved to Vienna from the Bohemian provinces, and received no religious training. He said in a 1931 interview: 'my mother and father were Jewish only through accident of birth'.[61] In 1941 he refused an invitation to give the reading at the Yom Kippur service in the synagogue at Rio de Janeiro because 'like most Austrians I was brought up in the most lax fashion in matters of faith and would not be able to overcome a feeling of uncertainty in an assembly of real believers'.[62] He was not attracted to Herzl's Jewish nationalism, and regarded many expressions of Jewish pride as mere disguised insecurity, yet he felt at ease as a Jew and equated conversion with disloyalty.[63] Unlike Schnitzler in *Der Weg ins*

---

[61] D. A. Prater, *European of Yesterday: A Biography of Stefan Zweig* (Oxford, 1972), p. 190. [62] Ibid. 315–16.

[63] Zweig, letter of 8 May 1916, in Martin Buber, *Briefwechsel aus sieben Jahrzehnten*, ed. Grete Schaeder, 3 vols. (Heidelberg, 1972–5), i. 431.

Freie and *Professor Bernhardi*, Zweig did not directly address the 'Jewish question', but his major works on Jewish themes, the biblical drama *Jeremias* and the Novelle *Buchmendel*, reveal much about his assimilation.

In his autobiography, *Die Welt von Gestern* (*The World of Yesterday*, 1942), Zweig interprets assimilation as the attainment of European culture. The acquisition of wealth is merely a means to this end. By acquiring it and becoming consumers of culture, he tells us, they were fulfilling the immanent will of the Jew, which is to rise from the base necessities of commerce to the world of the spirit.

Subconsciously something in the Jew seeks to escape the morally dubious, the distasteful, the petty, the unspiritual, which is attached to all trade, and all that is purely business, and to lift himself up to the moneyless sphere of the intellectual (*des Geistigen*), as if—in the Wagnerian sense—he wished to redeem himself and his whole race from the curse of money. And that is why among Jews the impulse to wealth is exhausted in two, or at most three, generations within one family, and the mightiest dynasties find their sons unwilling to take over the banks, the factories, the established and secure businesses of their fathers. It is not chance that a Lord Rothschild became an ornithologist, a Warburg an art historian, a Cassirer a philosopher, a Sassoon a poet. They all obey the same subconscious impulse, to free themselves of cold money-making, that thing that confines Jewry; and perhaps it expresses a secret longing to resolve the merely Jewish—through flight into the intellectual—into humanity at large (*ins allgemein Menschliche*).[64]

Zweig's presentation of the Jewish character here is highly ambivalent. His first move, implicitly relying on the antisemitic association of Jews with money-grubbing, is to claim that Jews are in fact driven by powerful unconscious forces to free themselves from commerce, as though commerce were alien to their true nature. Zweig's second move, however, undoes his first by implying that the intellectual world is important for Jews not for its own sake but as an escape from the unwanted yet barely resistible attraction of commerce, described melodramatically as a curse. Apparently it does not matter which intellectual pursuits the Jew adopts—ornithology, art history, philosophy, or poetry—so long as they serve as a talisman to ward off this curse. And in Zweig's

[64] Zweig, *The World of Yesterday* (London, 1943), pp. 20–1.

third move, the intellectual world permits an escape from Jewishness altogether. We are left with an opposition between Jewishness, which seems irremediably tainted by the curse of commerce, and a universal humanism which seems strangely colourless and directionless: a world of the spirit (anticipating Hermann Hesse's glass bead game) in which ornithology and poetry have equal value. In short: while Judaism is valuable as giving access to humanism, humanism is valuable as affording an escape from Judaism.

Zweig's international humanism does, however, have substantive values, which have been summed up by David Turner: 'first, an emphasis on personal freedom together with a condemnation of those forces which restrict or destroy it; second, a high regard for intensity of experience and passionate commitment as opposed to emotional indifference; third, an ideal of the rounded personality, of wide human and cultural interests, in contradistinction to narrow-mindedness of any kind; fourth, an affirmation of human brotherhood across all man-made barriers of race, creed or class'.[65] To this Turner adds compassion for individuals, a virtue that Zweig also praised in his friends Romain Rolland and Joseph Roth. And one must add, emphatically, Zweig's commitment to a European ideal of culture, evident in his many studies of artistic and historical figures from Erasmus and Montaigne to Tolstoy and Freud. The English-speaking reader may think of the European ideal represented by T. S. Eliot and his journal *The Criterion*.

It is easy to criticize this humanism in retrospect and from the outside. Zweig's humanism, like Schnitzler's, is based on the values of late nineteenth-century Viennese liberalism. Although in his essay on Freud he criticizes the 'Vernunftrausch' ('rational intoxication') into which liberalism was led by scientific progress, and here and in *The World of Yesterday* he condemns the oppressive sexual hypocrisy of pre-Freudian civilization, his nostalgic portrayal of 'the golden age of security' ignores the widespread poverty of the *fin de siècle* and the rise of illiberal mass politics.[66]

---

[65] Turner, *Moral Values and the Human Zoo: The 'Novellen' of Stefan Zweig* (Hull, 1988), p. 126.

[66] See the critical articles by Georg Iggers, 'Some Introductory Observations on Stefan Zweig's *World of Yesterday*', in Marion Sonnenfeld (ed.), *Stefan Zweig: The World of Yesterday's Humanist Today* (Albany, NY, 1983), pp. 1–9, and Leon Botstein, 'Stefan Zweig and the illusion of the Jewish European', ibid. 82–110.

His humanism seems designed for cultured, leisured, and moneyed individuals; he shows little concern to diffuse cultural values among the masses, as the Viennese Social Democrats tried to do after the First World War. In his literary judgements, Zweig displays a pre-modern sensibility. Unlike Karl Kraus, who unerringly perceived the genius of Peter Altenberg, Else Lasker-Schüler, and Brecht, and unlike Hofmannsthal, who for all his conservatism recognized an epochal shift of consciousness in Brecht's *Baal*, Zweig remains attached to pre-1914 writers who share his values: Barbusse, Duhamel, Rolland, Gorky, Yeats, and Shaw. Yet, on the credit side, he was not attracted by the disturbingly anti-humane tendency in much modernist art which enabled some of its practitioners (Pound, Benn, Jünger) to welcome fascism, nor by the irrationalism of a Spengler, nor by the Habsburg legitimist fantasies of his friend Joseph Roth. The limitations of his humanism at least excluded many modern manias.

Nowadays Zweig's most-read work is probably his autobiography, written in New York and Rio de Janeiro in 1941. Inevitably, it reshapes his life from the perspective of old age, disillusionment, and exile, recounting his efforts to regain the lost security of his upbringing.[67] Like Roth in *Radetzkymarsch*, however, Zweig combines nostalgia with criticism. He unmasks the late nineteenth century as a period of intense though peaceful repression: sexuality (at least that of middle-class women) is repressed through over-elaborate clothing, individuality is repressed through an unimaginative educational system, youth in general is repressed by an emphasis on age and respectability. The First World War reveals how ill-founded this apparent security was. However, after the war Zweig becomes a successful writer and recreates his secure environment through his books. On his fiftieth birthday, he tells us, his reflections went thus: 'It seemed as if there were nothing further to be achieved, destiny seemed to be tamed. The security which I had known of old in my parents' home, and which had disappeared during the war, had been recaptured by my own efforts.'[68] At the same time he felt uneasy

[67] On its structure, and its significant omissions, see Mark H. Gelber, '*Die Welt von Gestern* als Exilliteratur', in id. and Klaus Zelewitz (eds.), *Stefan Zweig: Exil und Suche nach dem Weltfrieden* (Riverside, Calif., 1995), pp. 148–63.

[68] Zweig, *The World of Yesterday*, pp. 269–70.

about his too comfortable life. The rise of Hitler answered his
unease by destroying this security as well and driving Zweig into
exile.

Counterpointed with this narrative is another that concerns
Zweig's Jewish identity. Nine-tenths of his Viennese friends were
Jews. Despite their identification with liberalism, they felt no
discomfort, even after Lueger's appointment as mayor, for his
rhetoric had no effect on their lives. Zweig describes his early
life as solely devoted to aesthetic matters. He published poems,
and wrote for the *Neue Freie Presse* and other leading newspapers
and journals; he travelled as far as India and America; and he
began an unrivalled collection of manuscripts. Yet in retrospect
this comfortable devotion to aesthetic matters feels empty. Its
hollowness becomes explicit in Zweig's description of the industrialist and intellectual Walther Rathenau:

His mind had the effect of an ingeniously contrived apparatus, his home
that of a museum. One could never really get warm in his feudal Queen
Louise palace in Brandenburg: its order was too obvious, its arrangement
too studied, its cleanliness too clean. His thinking had the transparency
of glass, hence seemed unsubstantial; rarely have I sensed the tragedy of
the Jew more strongly than in his personality which, with all of its
apparent superiority, was full of a deep unrest and uncertainty. [. . .] In
Rathenau's case I always felt that, in spite of his immeasurable cleverness,
his feet were not firmly on the ground.[69]

The Prussian palace which lacks homely warmth symbolizes an
acculturation which is never quite natural. But is Rathenau here
serving as a figure onto whom Zweig projects his own self-doubt?

In Zweig's account, his development from an aesthete into a
serious writer was bound up with his rediscovery of his Jewish
identity, and both these changes were occasioned by the War. In
writing his play *Jeremias*, which had its première in Zurich in
1917, Zweig issued a protest against war, and, by identifying with
the prophet Jeremiah, gained an understanding of the fate of the
Jews: 'in choosing a biblical theme I had unknowingly touched
upon something that had remained unused in me up to that time:
that community with the Jewish destiny whether in my blood or
darkly founded in tradition'.[70] Zweig's adoption of pacifism
during the First World War was considerably more hesitant than

[69] Zweig, 143.   [70] Ibid. 195.

his retrospective self-justification implies. By making the War and *Jeremias* central to his autobiography, however, he gives his narrative a double movement. The catastrophe that destroys Zweig's initial security gives him a purpose in life by enabling him to identify with the Jewish people.

Zweig's autobiography clearly imposes an enormous simplification on the disturbing complexities of experience. His devotion to books and writers—above all, perhaps, to the French pacifist and humanist Romain Rolland—accompanies a determination to avoid ordinary commitments. *The World of Yesterday* is silent both about the compulsive womanizing recorded in his early diaries and about his long relationship with Friderike von Winternitz. It says much about the house on the Kapuzinerberg outside Salzburg which he bought in 1917, but does not convey that Friderike was largely responsible for its upkeep while her husband stayed there only intermittently, leading otherwise a nomadic life in hotel rooms. Europe represented an ideal, imaginary home for someone like Zweig who was reluctant to settle firmly in an actual home. Exile—in London, the USA, and Brazil—did not radically change his way of life, though it remains ironic that, as his biographer says, 'The citizen of the world had become the wandering Jew.'[71]

Doubts about Zweig's humanism may be strengthened by considering the collection of manuscripts which he began in his teens. Its prize pieces were the manuscript of Goethe's ecstatic poem 'Mailied' and Blake's visionary portrait of King John, which were displayed under glass on opposite walls of his flat. The museum-like character of his humanism seems analogous to the artificiality he recognized in Rathenau. So does its remoteness from the creative genius it celebrates. The manuscripts seem like fetishistic mementoes of a creative power to which Zweig himself could not aspire. Leon Botstein has argued that Zweig's collection of manuscripts served a vacuous notion of genius transcending history, whereas Freud's collection of antiquities and Walter Benjamin's collection of books expressed an enjoyment of the unique.[72] In so far as Zweig's humanism rests on familiar truisms,

---

[71] Prater, *European of Yesterday*, p. 352.

[72] Botstein, 'Stefan Zweig and the Illusion of the Jewish European', pp. 92–3. See Benjamin, 'Unpacking my Library', in *Illuminations*, tr. Harry Zohn (London, 1970), pp. 61–9.

it certainly seems less appealing in the postmodern era than Benjamin's interest in the unique particular. Similarly, the groups of biographical sketches that Zweig published tend to erode the individuality of their sometimes ill-assorted subjects and reduce them to the lowest common denominator (e.g. Mesmer, Mary Baker Eddy, and Freud in *Die Heilung durch den Geist*). These bland sketches, according to Karl Kraus, gave Zweig's readers the illusion of easy access to high culture, as though they needed only to enter a lift to be transported to lofty heights.[73]

The greatest weakness of Zweig's European humanism seems to be its remoteness from politics. Not that art should become a political instrument, as Benjamin demanded; but a humanism worthy of the name needs. proponents who defend it publicly against competing ideologies, and who draw its practical consequences by combating inhuman policies whenever they can. Zweig's retiring temperament made him reluctant to take a public stand, and his subsequent self-justifications are not always truthful. Although in *The World of Yesterday* he claims always to have been a pacifist, it is clear from letters and diaries that when the First World War broke out he shared the patriotic enthusiasm and the naïve clichés of the time.[74] His horror at the suffering the War produced did not stop him from writing military propaganda. He expected to be called up, but was spared active service by being employed in the Austrian Kriegsarchiv, along with many other writers (among them Hofmannsthal, Rilke, Bahr, and Bartsch), to write patriotic publicity material. The pacifism which finds expression in *Jeremias* took time to develop. Zweig's waverings have been sufficiently censured by commentators who measure him against the standard set by Kraus.[75] And while the comparison may seem unfair, since Kraus had been a public voice since the 1890s, Zweig himself injudiciously invited such comparisons by entering the public arena with *Jeremias*.

Jeremias, however, is a better, more complex, and more personal work than its detractors admit. Its hero is the prophet who warned accurately but in vain that the kingdom of Judah would fall to the

---

[73] Kraus, 'Pretiosen', *Die Fackel*, 726–9 (May–June 1926), 55–6.

[74] See Prater, *European of Yesterday*, pp. 71–3.

[75] See the chapter on Zweig in C. E. Williams, *The Broken Eagle: The Politics of Austrian Literature from Empire to Anschluss* (London, 1974); Edward Timms, *Karl Kraus, Apocalyptic Satirist* (New Haven and London, 1986), p. 299.

Babylonians. After a two-year siege, Jerusalem was captured in
587 BC, and King Zedekiah, having witnessed the deaths of his
children, was blinded and transported to Babylon along with part
of the population. During the siege, Jeremiah was imprisoned for
defeatism, but was secretly consulted by Zedekiah (Jer. 38). After
the city's fall, Jeremiah was offered a place at the Babylonian
court, but decided to stay behind in Judah (Jer. 40: 1–6).

The impetus behind the play is moral and psychological rather
than political. Its psychological dimension concerns the relationship between Jeremias, his prophetic gift, and his mother. The
biblical Jeremiah remained unmarried at the Lord's command
(Jer. 16: 2); this may have encouraged Zweig to explore his
difficult relationship with his own mother, a strong-willed
character who brought him up strictly. In adult life, he did not
tell her about his relationship with Friderike von Winternitz for
over six years, and he clashed with her immediately after his
father's death in 1926, when he described her in a letter to a
friend as showing 'complete helplessness combined with selfishness, incredible lack of independence with ungovernable
obstinacy'.[76] It is tempting to relate this difficult relationship to
the compulsive womanizing recorded as 'episodes' or 'adventures'
in Zweig's early diaries and to the lack of commitment shown by
the intensity of what could only be a short-lived relationship with
'Marcelle' during his six-week stay in Paris in 1913 and by his
discomfort with Friderike's sexuality: his diary notes: 'She is
loving and tender. I wish her sensuality would disappear.'[77] The
opening scene shows how close Jeremias is to his mother and
implies that he identifies her voice with the voice of God. Rather
than undermining his prophetic mission, this shows him as the
mouthpiece of caring, maternal humanity that is suppressed by
militarism. Though he could easily have been depicted as a self-
righteous, rancorous figure, Zweig emphasizes his loving concern
for Jerusalem: far from exulting when his prophecies are vindi-
cated, he wishes he could be proved a liar and Jerusalem remain
unharmed. We learn that Jeremias was consecrated by his mother
as a priest in God's service, but his prophetic calling makes him
resolve to be a victim rather than a sacrificer: 'No, mother, I have

[76] Prater, *European of Yesterday*, p. 161.
[77] Zweig, *Tagebücher*, ed. Knut Beck (Frankfurt, 1984), p. 71.

not taken service as a sacrificer; I myself want to be the sacrifice.'[78] Yet his mother threatens to curse him if he spreads alarm. Thus his mission, while embodying his mother's values, also estranges him from her.

The relationship between Jeremias and his mother reaches a crisis in the scene entitled 'The Testing of the Prophet' which recalls Ibsen's portrayal of Peer Gynt at his mother's deathbed. In a lyrical dialogue with his dying mother, Jeremias tries to soothe her by telling her that Jerusalem is not in danger; she disbelieves him, and finally he feels compelled to tell her the truth, whereupon she dies, and his relatives accuse him of killing her. At this moment of utter abandonment, 'cast out from my mother's womb into the world', Jeremias is assailed by the priests and people who accuse him of spreading alarm and despondency.[79] Paralysed by grief and feeling abandoned by God, he is led away to imprisonment.

Eventually, Jeremias' prophetic calling enables him to form a bond with his people that replaces his bond with his mother. During the siege, the official prophets and military leaders stir up war-fever among a populace as fickle as the wartime Viennese public whose gullibility Zweig noted in his diary.[80] Jeremias secretly urges Zedekia to negotiate for peace, but in the great council scene 'Voices at Midnight' Zedekia rejects the humiliating terms offered by the Babylonians, who require him to wear a wooden yoke in token of submission and receive his crown from Nebuchadnezzar. Like the refractory hero of an earlier Austrian play, Grillparzer's *König Ottokars Glück und Ende* (1823), Zedekia, through his pride, ends up suffering a worse fate but undergoing a spiritual rebirth.

The play's appeal is widened by Jeremias' strangely insistent Christian imagery. As Jerusalem falls, Jeremias submits to God's will, offering even to be scourged, pierced, and crucified as a 'Sühnopfer' (expiatory sacrifice) to save Jerusalem.[81] Anyone who dies on the cross, he continues, will be able to mediate between God and man and bring about love and peace on earth. The fall of the city provokes him into a brief revolt against God for

---

[78] Zweig, *Die Dramen*, ed. Richard Friedenthal (Frankfurt, 1964), p. 372.
[79] Ibid. 431.　　　[80] See Zweig, *Tagebücher*, pp. 180, 182.
[81] Zweig, *Die Dramen*, p. 468.

subjecting him to futile sufferings; but he is restored to harmony with God after refusing the Babylonians' invitation to become a royal Magus. His wrangling with God recalls not only the complaints of the biblical Jeremiah (e.g. Jer. 15) but also those of Job. The imagery of the Crucifixion is to some degree harmonized with the Old Testament ambience when, as the survivors prepare to go into exile, Jeremias acclaims the blinded Zedekia as their proper leader:

> Behold, behold,
> People of suffering, people of God,
> God heard your prayer,
> He sent you a leader!
> Crowned with pain,
> Scorned by men,
> Who like he
> Can be king of the blest who go down to defeat?
> God has closed his earthly sight
> To let him behold the heavenly realm:
> Oh, brother, was any of David's line
> A king of sufferers like unto him?[82]

The allusion to David's line further associates Zedekia with Christ, and he is also linked with the suffering servant in Isaiah 53 who is a type of Christ. Leon Botstein calls this 'a Judeo-Christian-pagan synthesis, with elements visible in it from all three cultures'.[83] Yet the pagan element seems confined to the Babylonians' respect for Jeremias; we have rather a synthesis of Judaism and Christianity in which Zweig seeks to transfer the moral force of the Crucifixion to Judaism, while, no doubt, appealing to an Austrian Catholic readership. Appropriately, the play was much admired by Heinrich Lammasch, the Catholic international lawyer who in 1917–18 led a small group of anti-militarist Austrians who aimed at making peace separately from Germany.[84]

Finally, Jeremias leads the exiled Jewish people into its historical destiny, accompanied by tremendous choruses. He prophesies that the earthly Jerusalem they are leaving will be replaced in their

---

[82] Zweig, 501.

[83] Botstein, 'Stefan Zweig and the Illusion of the Jewish European', p. 94.

[84] See Prater, *European of Yesterday*, p. 94.

hearts by a spiritual Jerusalem, and in this sense Jerusalem will be everlasting. At the end of the play, Jeremias merges unobtrusively into his nation, which collectively declares its destiny. The solidarity of people, prophet, and king is established by the experience of exile:

> We wander through nations, we wander through ages
> Along the unending pathways of pain,
> Forever vanquished for everlasting,
> Slaves to the hearth where we rest on our travels,
> Lowly bondsmen to lowly toil,
> Yet the cities crumble, the nations slide
> Into the darkness like plunging stars,
> And those who covered our backs with blows,
> Their children's children shall come to naught.
> But we keep on striding, striding, striding
> Into the strength that is all our own,
> Amid earth's phantoms alone abiding,
> And out of our sorrows we build God's throne.[85]

Thus the play defines the Jewish people as quintessential exiles while depicting with psychological finesse the relation established between the outsider Jeremias and the nation which serves as a mother-substitute. The father-figures are discredited (the generals and false prophets) or brought low by suffering (Zedekia). Altogether the play can bear comparison with the best anti-War dramas such as Hasenclever's *Antigone* and Kaiser's *Die Bürger von Calais*.

The European crisis of the 1930s put Zweig's fortitude under unbearable strain. In 1932 he successfully appealed to Mussolini to release a political prisoner, Dr Germani, who had been imprisoned for trying to get the children of Matteotti, Mussolini's Socialist opponent and victim, out of Italy.[86] When living in London in the 1930s, he helped refugees, but felt unable to cope with all the appeals made to him. Still, his letters of the time at least show an agonized awareness of human misery, in contrast to the surprising callousness with which his correspondent Arnold Zweig is prepared to 'write off' the German Jews.[87]

---

[85] Zweig, *Die Dramen*, p. 507.   [86] See Prater, *European of Yesterday*, p. 205.
[87] Jeffrey B. Berlin, 'The Austrian Catastrophe: Political Reflections in the Unpublished Correspondence of Stefan Zweig and Arnold Zweig', *Austrian Studies*, 6 (1995), 3–21 (p. 10).

And he was willing to criticize the Soviet Union for failing to help refugees from Fascism, at a time when his friend Romain Rolland was publicly supporting the Soviet Union while privately well aware of the horrors of Stalinism.[88]

Deep doubts pervade a book that is often understood as Zweig's manifesto of European humanism, the study of Erasmus which he published when Nazism was already established in Germany and threatening Austria. *Erasmus von Rotterdam* (1935) is really an inquiry into the strengths and limitations of humanism, attached to a biographical sketch of a great humanist who tried to reconcile the warring camps of the Reformation but ended up trapped between them.

Erasmus is seen, with some anachronism, as anticipating and symbolizing Zweig's own humanism. Zweig conflates two senses of 'humanism': the study of classical texts and the espousal of humane values. He celebrates Erasmus as the first conscious European, as a militant pacifist, and as 'the most eloquent advocate of the humanist ideal of friendship towards the world and the spirit'.[89] Neither a rebel nor a revolutionary, he preferred to make compromises in order to preserve his independence. Hence, like Zweig, he led a nomadic life, always travelling between Holland, England, Italy, Germany, and Switzerland. Like Zweig, too, he was a bibliophile, raising money to buy books and delighting in their physical character as well as their contents. He figures as the opponent of fanaticism, seeing in such irrationality 'the inherited evil of our world' (p. 10). His error, Zweig says with sad irony, was to believe in enlightenment:

For this was the deepest belief (and the beautiful, the tragic error) of this early humanism: Erasmus and his associates thought that mankind could progress through enlightenment and hoped that both the individual and the community could be educated by a wider diffusion of culture, writing, study and books.   (p. 14)

Zweig makes a few gentle criticisms. Erasmus' tolerance, which interpreted Christianity as humane morality, may seem somewhat reductive and general. His humanism was too elitist. Some of his colleagues now seem bookish pedants. More seriously, the reason in which Erasmus so firmly believed cannot create anything:

Reason can never be more than a regulative force, it cannot by itself be a creative one; but in fact the truly productive force always requires an illusion. Being so wondrously free from illusion, Erasmus remained free from passion throughout his life, a great, cool-headed, fair-minded man, who never knew life's final happiness, entire devotion, the expenditure of one's energies on a sacred cause.   (p. 80)

Here Zweig's ambivalence becomes apparent. Erasmus was too rational to experience passion, and, like other humanists, he was too civilized to understand the irrational. Such optimism makes humanists imperfect guides to life, for they do not understand the irrational energies that make creativity possible.

Through Erasmus, Zweig explores the strengths and limitations of the ideal of the civilized human being. The most intense feeling available to Erasmus, an intellectual devotion, is evoked in Zweig's fine commentary on the famous painting by Holbein that shows Erasmus writing at his desk:

Erasmus is standing at his desk, and one involuntarily feels in one's very nerves that he is alone. Absolute silence prevails in this room, the door must be closed behind him as he works, no-one comes or goes, nothing moves in this narrow cell; but whatever were going on around him, this man, absorbed in himself, spell-bound by the trance of activity, would not notice it. His motionlessness seems like stony stillness, yet if one looks at him more closely, this state is not stillness but entire self-absorption, a mysterious, wholly inward form of life. For it is with the tautest concentration, as though his pupil were casting a beam of light onto the word, that the blue blaze of his eye follows the writing on the white page, where his slender, thin, almost feminine hand traces its characters in obedience to a higher command.   (pp. 60–1)

This evocation of intellectual absorption, a worthy counterpart to Rilke's poem 'Der Leser' ('The Reader'), makes its subject obedient to a command from above, implying that writing is an act of devotion and the concentration that of prayer. By mentioning Erasmus' delicate, 'almost feminine' hand, Zweig implies that the civilized person transcends the opposition of feminine and masculine; but he also implies that such a figure is vulnerable and defenceless. The silence surrounding Erasmus betokens a privileged atmosphere of wealth and comfort. Thus this intellectual concentration is a rare and fragile possibility. It is threatened, as Zweig goes on to say, by the living conditions of the sixteenth century and by the hypersensitivity and frailty of Erasmus' body, 'which this spiritual man dragged along with him like the burdensome and fragile shell of a snail' (p. 62).

The opposite of Erasmus is Martin Luther. If Erasmus is the man of reason, Luther—for better and, mostly, for worse—embodies passion. If Erasmus hates fanaticism, Luther is the fanatical man of action par excellence, his passionate rage contrasting with Erasmus' colourless abstract reason. In opposition to the delicate valetudinarian Erasmus with his reedy voice, Zweig depicts Luther as an energetic, coarse, bull-like, beer-swilling embodiment of brute vitality, an expression of Germany's elemental forces. He represents 'the revolutionary, driven by the demonic energies lurking in the German people' (p. 20). While Erasmus was a cosmopolitan figure, Luther aroused the narrow, xenophobic feeling of German nationhood.

It is not difficult to discern here a symbolic opposition of Jew and German. Of course Erasmus was not a Jew, nor does Zweig represent him as one. But in transcending nationality, in his commitment to the spirit, in his physical vulnerability, he shares the features that Zweig thought Jewish in his own humanism. Luther, by contrast, appears as an ultra-German figure, and in 1935 it would be easy to associate him with the revolution that the Nazis were carrying out in Germany, especially since National Socialist propaganda claimed Luther as a forerunner.[90]

This opposition also concedes the weakness of Zweig's own politics. Modern humanists find themselves helpless before the irrationality of fascism, which they cannot understand, still less control. Erasmus also illustrates Zweig's belief that those dedicated to the life of the spirit should avoid political commitment, as Goethe did during the Napoleonic Wars. 'The man of the spirit must not take sides; his realm is that of justice, which transcends all divisions' (p. 134). The conflicts of the Reformation, however, formed one of the rare occasions when detachment was impossible, and thus put Erasmus in a painful position, for he knew (as Zweig did of himself) that he was not the stuff of which martyrs or

[90] See Johannes Brosseder, *Luthers Stellung zu den Juden im Spiegel seiner Interpreten* (Munich, 1972).

heroes are made. When everyone appealed to him to take a public stand, he temporized for years, and even Zweig criticizes him for avoiding a meeting with the sick fanatic Ulrich von Hutten on the feeble pretext that his health would not allow him to meet Hutten in a warm room. Yet Luther's fanatical commitment brought its own penalties. The irrational forces he had roused soon turned against him, and he found himself assailed by extremists on his left: 'He was beginning to undergo the eternal fate of every revolutionary: he too, having wished to replace the old order with a new one, had unleashed the forces of chaos and was in danger of having his radicalism trampled down by those who were still more radical' (p. 191).

Finally, the opposition between Erasmus and Luther expresses the doubts about the value of civilization that Zweig had elaborated a few years earlier in his essay on Freud. He interprets *Civilization and its Discontents* as showing how mankind overcomes primitive drives to become civilized, and yet does not become happier. Civilized humanity seems to lead a bloodless, etiolated existence, estranged from its animal instincts. 'As our emotional life flows into narrower, more ramified channels, it ceases to be an elemental flood [. . .] and the individual soul comes to suspect that progress has impoverished it and, by socializing the self, robbed it of its inmost self.'[91] The intellectual absorption of Erasmus may seem a thin and fragile substitute for the intense, animal-like, passionate existence represented by Luther.

In *Erasmus*, the Jewish character of Zweig's humanism is only faintly intimated in the references to Erasmus' cosmopolitan life. Jewish humanism is examined, more explicitly and ambivalently, in one of Zweig's best Novellen, *Buchmendel* (Book-Mendel, 1929). *Buchmendel* is an affectionate though very distanced portrait of a Galician bookseller in Vienna. The narrator, sheltering from the rain in a Vienna coffee-house, recollects Jakob Mendel, who twenty years earlier was one of its invariable customers. Mendel's powers of concentration, accompanied by swaying his body as if in prayer, enabled him to develop an astounding memory for the titles of books:

---

[91] Zweig, *Die Heilung durch den Geist* (Leipzig, 1932), pp. 434–5.

Apart from books, this extraordinary person knew nothing about the world; for all the phenomena of existence only began to be real for him when they were moulded into letters, gathered in a book and, as it were, sterilized. He did not read even these books, however, for their meaning, for their intellectual and narrative content: it was only their names, their prices, their physical appearance, and their title-pages, that attracted his passion. Ultimately unproductive and uncreative, a mere index to a hundred thousand names and titles, stamped into the soft brain-tissue of a mammal instead of being inscribed in a book catalogue, this specifically book-selling memory possessed by Jacob Mendel was nonetheless, in its unique perfection, no less a phenomenon than Napoleon's memory for faces, Mezzofanti's for languages, Lasker's for chess openings, Busoni's for music.[92]

This passage begins to disclose the narrator's ambivalence towards Mendel. On the one hand, he celebrates Mendel as a true and selfless devotee of the world of the spirit, who has applied the gift of concentration to one area of intellectual activity and brought it to perfection. It is flattering to associate Mendel with Napoleon, with the Vatican librarian Cardinal Mezzofanti, who is said to have known over fifty languages with many of their dialects, with the erudite composer Busoni, and with the chess grandmaster Lasker. On the other hand, these are narrowly specialized abilities. This conception of intellectual life recalls Zweig's tendency to conceive culture as a glass bead game of the spirit. Mendel's mental book-catalogue resembles Zweig's collection of books and manuscripts, both testifying to their owners' remoteness from the creativity whose products they can only possess.

It is significant, too, that Mendel is an Eastern Jew. Born just across the Russian frontier, he went to Vienna to study for the rabbinate, but transferred his attention to book-dealing. Small and hunchbacked with a huge beard and Yiddish-tinged German, he corresponds to familiar models of the 'Ostjude'. He is described with implied disparagement as a book-hawker ('Buchtrödler', p. 98; 'Buchschacherer', p. 99). His powers of concentration and memory have evidently been transferred from Talmud study, which, it is implied, equipped him for the merely external intellectual activity he now practises. Thus the story presupposes the Enlightenment's conception of Talmud study as mere futile

[92] Zweig, *Novellen*, 2 vols. (Berlin and Weimar, 1980), i. 97–8.

ratiocination. Transposing these mental habits to Western culture, and learning only the exterior details of books, Mendel becomes an extreme instance of the uncreative Jew, cut off not only from reality but even from the contents of books.

Throughout the story the narrator is uneasy about the similarities between himself and Mendel. As David Turner notes, Zweig's story bears a striking resemblance to Grillparzer's tale about an eccentric musician, *Der arme Spielmann* (*The Poor Minstrel*, 1848).[93] In both, the central character is contrasted with the narrator. Grillparzer's narrator, a successful dramatist animated by anthropological curiosity rather than human sympathy, differs from Zweig's humane narrator, but the latter is distinguished from Mendel by having a memory which functions erratically but vividly, whereas Mendel's memory for books is unaffected by experience. The narrator reflects on how his own memory works: it is 'strangely fashioned, at once good and bad, defiant and self-willed, yet also indescribably faithful' (p. 91); it does not obey his will, yet seemingly trivial associations can call up minutely precise visions from the remote past. His procedure of casting hooks into the depths of memory and eventually fishing up his prey recalls Proust's description of the workings of involuntary memory and, even more closely, the mysterious operation of Coleridge's 'tenacious and systematizing memory' which produced 'Kubla Khan'.[94] But he also comes closer to Mendel when he describes his mind as a 'memory-machine', albeit one which functions far less efficiently than Mendel's.

The narrator's identification with Mendel also appears when he lets Mendel illustrate how vulnerable the life of the spirit is to the brutality of politics and warfare. In seeing the world through a library catalogue, Mendel represents a version of Zweig's own international humanism. His remoteness from day-to-day events brings about Mendel's downfall. Ignoring the First World War, he writes to booksellers in Paris and London to ask why they have stopped sending him bibliographical periodicals; this correspondence with enemy countries leads to his arrest; he is discovered still to be a Russian citizen, and is imprisoned in a concentration

---

[93] Turner, *Moral Values*, pp. 93–4, 226.
[94] John Livingston Lowes, *The Road to Xanadu: A Study in the Ways of the Imagination* (London, 1927), p. 54.

camp, among illiterates and without books. Though he is released, his memory has been lost. The internment of harmless civilians is rightly denounced as 'a crime against civilization' (p. 111). This theme puts the story in the same genre as other stories of inoffensive little Jews who get caught up in the bureaucratic machinery of the Habsburg Empire.[95]

By contrast with this story, Zweig's autobiography is an impersonal, self-concealing book. Zweig writes best and most personally when he finds objective correlatives—Jeremias, Erasmus, Mendel—to express his feelings of self-doubt. And he writes best about his humanism when acknowledging how seriously it is threatened by modern and older barbarisms.

FREUD: SCIENCE VERSUS RELIGION

Freud's Jewish identity has recently received minute scrutiny.[96] He himself provided some important statements which stress his remoteness from religious Judaism and his association of Jewishness with scientific rationality. This understanding goes back to Mendelssohn's image of the rational, unsuperstitious Jew, combining it, as Schnitzler also did, with a partisan stance in the nineteenth-century conflict between science and religion, and toning down its ethical idealism by an increasing emphasis on materialism.

In his 1930 preface to the Hebrew translation of *Totem and Taboo* Freud described himself as 'an author who is ignorant of the language of holy writ, who is completely estranged from the religion of his fathers—as well as from every other religion—and who cannot take a share in nationalist ideals, but who has yet

---

[95] Cf. the fate of Jossel in H. W. Katz, *Die Fischmanns* ([1938] Weinheim, 1994); Albert Drach, *Das große Protokoll gegen Zwetschkenbaum* (Munich and Vienna, 1964); other examples in Claudio Magris, *Weit von wo: Verlorene Welt des Ostjudentums*, tr. Jutta Prasse (Vienna, 1974), p. 56.

[96] For a lucid survey, see Robert S. Wistrich, 'The Jewish Identity of Sigmund Freud', in his *The Jews of Vienna in the Age of Franz Joseph* (Oxford, 1989), pp. 537–82. A full bibliography up to 1992 may be found in Sander L. Gilman, *Freud, Race and Gender* (Princeton, 1993), pp. 201–4, and id., *The Case of Sigmund Freud: Medicine and Identity at the Fin de Siècle* (Baltimore and London, 1993), pp. 229–32; both books are themselves major contributions. An important overview, to which I am much indebted despite frequent disagreement, is Moshe Gresser, *Dual Allegiance: Freud as a Modern Jew* (Albany, NY, 1994).

never repudiated his people, who feels that he is in his essential nature a Jew and who has no desire to alter that nature' (*SE* xiii. xv). And in 1926 he told the Viennese fraternity B'nai B'rith, to which he had belonged since 1897:

That you are Jews could only be welcome to me, for I was myself a Jew, and it has always appeared to me not only undignified, but outright foolish to deny it. What tied me to Jewry was—I have to admit it—not the faith, not even the national pride, for I was always an unbeliever, have been brought up without religion, but not without respect for the so-called 'ethical' demands of human civilization. Whenever I have experienced feelings of national exaltation, I have tried to suppress them as disastrous and unfair, frightened by the warning example of those nations among which we Jews live. But there remained enough to make the attraction of Jews and Judaism irresistible, many dark emotional powers all the stronger the less they could be expressed in words, as well as the clear consciousness of an inner identity, the familiarity of the same psychological structure (*der gleichen seelischen Identität*).[97]

The Jewish elements in Freud's upbringing have often been scrutinized with an understandable zeal that leads to exaggeration. His grandfather was a Hasidic rabbi in Galicia; his father, Jakob Freud, emigrated first to Freiberg (Příbor) in Moravia, where Freud was born in 1856, and then to Vienna; his mother came originally from Brody in Galicia.[98] Jakob Freud was familiar with Jewish learning and rituals, but had abandoned much of his religious practice by the time of his son's birth, and seemed to his grandchildren to have become a complete free-thinker.[99] His father, Freud later said, 'let me grow up in complete ignorance of everything that concerned Judaism'.[100] We do not actually know if his family attended synagogue or if he had a bar mitzvah; the only evidence for the latter is that when he was 13 Freud was given Börne's collected works, possibly as a bar mitzvah present.[101] For

[97] *Letters 1873–1939*, ed. by Ernst L. Freud (London, 1961), pp. 366–7 (6 May 1926).

[98] For detailed accounts of Freud's family background and upbringing, see Marianne Krüll, *Freud and his Father* (London, 1987); Jerry Victor Diller, *Freud's Jewish Identity: A Case Study in the Impact of Ethnicity* (London and Toronto, 1991).

[99] Jones, *Freud*, i. 21.

[100] Letter to Yehuda Dvosis-Dvir, 15 Dec. 1928, quoted in Emanuel Rice, *Freud and Moses* (Albany, NY, 1990), p. 44.

[101] Y. H. Yerushalmi, *Freud's Moses: Judaism Terminable and Interminable* (New Haven and London, 1991), p. 132.

his thirty-fifth birthday his father gave him a copy of Ludwig Phillipson's three-volume edition of the Bible in parallel columns of Hebrew and German with extensive commentaries; Jakob Freud inserted an affectionate Hebrew inscription, but there is no evidence that Freud could read it, let alone that this inscription 'left a deep imprint on his identity'.[102] Although Freud obtained high marks for Hebrew at school, he said as an adult that he could no longer read Hebrew, which suggests that the standard of instruction was not exacting.[103] His early letters quote familiar biblical passages and show some elementary knowledge, treated sarcastically, about Jewish festivals and the Passover formulae.[104] In 1877 Freud talks scornfully about the celebration of the Jewish New Year ('Spektakel' and 'massenhaftes Fressen').[105] His indifference to Jewish traditions is shown by his referring to Passover as 'Easter', whereas his wife Martha called it 'Pessach'.[106] In 1886 he considered converting to Protestantism, but instead agreed to an orthodox Jewish wedding ceremony, though he stubbornly opposed as superstitious even such ritual actions as lighting candles on Friday evening.[107] Although Martha Freud kept kosher and fasted on Yom Kippur, the children were brought up without any traces of Jewish ritual: they celebrated Christmas and Easter, with a Christmas tree and Easter eggs.[108]

In estimating the relative importance of the Jewish elements in Freud's education, one should remember that he had a sound classical education and throughout his life astonished people by his familiarity with the classics and classical philology.[109] He

---

[102] Gresser, *Dual Allegiance*, p. 28. The inscription is interpreted in great detail by Rice, *Freud and Moses*, pp. 62–84.

[103] Cf. Peter Gay, *Freud: A Life for our Time* (London, 1988), p. 599.

[104] Freud, *Jugendbriefe an Eduard Silberstein 1871–1881*, ed. Walter Boehlich (Frankfurt, 1989), p. 74 (18 Sept. 1874); cf. p. 103 (21 Feb. 1875), and Gresser, *Dual Allegiance*, pp. 49–53.

[105] Freud, *Jugendbriefe an Silberstein*, p. 191 (7 Sept. 1877).

[106] Ibid. 74 (18 Sept. 1874); *SE* iv. 443; letter from Martha Freud quoted in Gresser, *Dual Allegiance*, p. 230.

[107] See Paul Roazen, *Freud and his Followers* (Harmondsworth, 1979), p. 71.

[108] Gay, *Freud: A Life for our Time*, p. 600.

[109] See Ernest Jones, *Free Associations: Memories of a Psycho-Analyst* (London, 1959), p. 35; Worbs, *Nervenkunst*; Peter L. Rudnytsky, *Freud and Oedipus* (New York, 1987); Robin N. Mitchell-Boyask, 'Freud's Reading of Classical Literature and Classical Philology', in Sander L. Gilman *et al.* (eds.), *Reading Freud's Reading* (New York, 1993), pp. 23–46; Peter Loewenberg, 'The Pagan Freud', in his *Fantasy and Reality in History* (New York and Oxford, 1995), pp. 16–32.

wrote that his classical learning had brought him 'as much consolation as anything else in the struggle of life' (*SE* xiii. 241). The classics pervade his writings far more thoroughly than Jewish scripture and tradition. He told a correspondent that his dream interpretation was much more similar to 'the understanding of dreams among the ancient Greeks' than to talmudic dream interpretation.[110] The study of parapraxes has much in common with textual scholarship, which is why Freud's methods have been criticized most effectively by a philologist.[111] His comparison of psychoanalysis to archaeology was inspired by such classical investigations as Schliemann's excavation of Troy. Above all, by naming his central discovery after Oedipus, he implied that the Greeks were the paradigm of humanity.

Freud was also the product of Christian culture, and regarded it with extreme ambivalence. He was so anticlerical that in 1937, a few months before the absorption of Austria into Greater Germany, he told a visitor, René Laforgue, that he was not afraid of the Nazis but wanted help against his 'true enemy', which was 'religion, the Roman Catholic Church'.[112] But there was also a deep attraction. Many Jewish children had Christian nursemaids whose influence could be lasting, as Franz Werfel records in his novel *Barbara oder die Frömmigkeit* (*Barbara or Piety*, 1929). Freud's nurse, Resi Wittek, often took him to Catholic churches.[113] When he was 3 Resi was dismissed for stealing, and Paul Vitz argues that his sudden separation from her induced anxiety and made him associate Catholic ceremonial with his lost world of security.[114] Although Freud had an initial block about visiting Rome, he was very anxious to do so, preferably at Easter; his many visits were clearly relaxed and joyful experiences; and despite his claim to prefer classical to Christian Rome, he kept

---

[110] Letter to A. Drujanow, 3 Mar. 1910, quoted in Peter Gay, *A Godless Jew: Freud, Atheism, and the Making of Psychoanalysis* (New Haven and London, 1987), pp. 32–3. See S. R. F. Price, 'The Future of Dreams: From Freud to Artemidorus', *Past and Present*, 113 (Nov. 1986), 3–37.

[111] See Sebastiano Timpanaro, *The Freudian Slip*, tr. Kate Soper (London, 1974).

[112] Laforgue, 'Personal Memories of Freud', in *Freud as we knew him*, ed. Hendrik M. Ruitenbeek (Detroit, 1973), pp. 341–9 (p. 344).

[113] See letter of 3 Oct. 1897 in *The Complete Letters of Sigmund Freud to Wilhelm Fliess, 1887–1904*, tr. and ed. J. M. Masson (Cambridge, Mass., and London, 1985), p. 268.

[114] Vitz, *Sigmund Freud's Christian Unconscious* (New York, 1988), p. 22.

revisiting Christian monuments like the Sistine Chapel, the catacombs, and of course Michelangelo's statue of Moses in the church of San Pietro in Vincoli.

Freud also acquired fantasies about hell which seem incongruous in a Jew. He recalled that when he passed through Breslau station at the age of 3, 'the gas flames which I saw for the first time reminded me of spirits burning in hell'.[115] And he evoked the unconscious as 'an intellectual hell, with layer upon layer; in the darkest core, glimpses of the contours of Lucifer-Amor'.[116] His identification with this hell and his opposition to spiritual and moral authorities are registered in the Virgilian epigraph to *The Interpretation of Dreams*: 'flectere si nequeo superos, Acheronta movebo'.[117] He tells Fliess pompously that he could not fully enjoy Rome because 'I found it difficult to tolerate the lie concerning man's redemption, which raises its head to high heaven'.[118] He presents himself as facing the harsh psychological realities which undermine any belief in divine or providential benevolence, and which the pious, in his view, have projected onto the Devil, who, as a metaphysical scapegoat, 'play[s] the same part as an agent of economic discharge as the Jew does in the world of the Aryan ideal' (*SE* xxi. 120). His many quotations from Goethe's *Faust* imply identification not only with the ambitious Faust but also with the cynical Mephistopheles, who sees the seamy and earthy side of humanity, and who is invoked as witness to the destructive instinct (*SE* xxi. 120–1). Discussing with his followers a painting by Moritz von Schwind that showed the Devil building a cathedral at the command of St Wolfgang, Freud declared that he was himself the Devil, quarrying in the unconscious that underlay the apparently effortless achievements of culture.[119] The Devil was Freud's metaphor for his own stance as antagonist to a self-deluding optimism that he identified particularly with official Christianity.

Hence Freud's scientific career was also a subversive campaign

[115] *Letters of Freud to Fliess*, p. 285 (3 Dec. 1897).

[116] Ibid. 421 (10 July 1900).

[117] *Aeneid*, vii. 313: 'If Heaven I cannot bend, then Hell I will arouse.' See Walter Schönau, *Sigmund Freuds Prosa: Literarische Elemente seines Stils* (Stuttgart, 1968), pp. 61–73.   [118] *Letters of Freud to Fliess*, p. 449 (19 Sept. 1901).

[119] This anecdote exists in several versions: two are given in Roazen, *Freud and his Followers*, pp. 331–2.

against religion. 'Confronting religion,' writes Philip Rieff, 'psychoanalysis shows itself for what it is: the last great formulation of nineteenth-century secularism, complete with substitute doctrine and cult.'[120] Freud's scepticism is already clear from his early letters to Silberstein. He recounts with surprise how he, 'a godless medical man and empiricist', has been attending lectures on the existence of God by Franz Brentano, but has also been reading the atheist philosophers David Friedrich Strauss and especially Ludwig Feuerbach, 'whom of all philosophers I revere and admire most highly'.[121] His youthful heroes also included scientists like Darwin, Huxley, and Tyndall. He first declared his open opposition to religion in 'Obsessive Acts and Religious Practices' (1907), where compulsive actions and religious rituals are equated and ascribed to guilt resulting from repression, so that religion is called 'a universal obsessional neurosis' (*SE* ix. 126–7). In *Totem and Taboo* (1911) religion is explained as originating, along with all other cultural achievements, in the Oedipus complex. In *Group Psychology and the Analysis of the Ego* (1921) Freud describes the Church, inappropriately, as a crowd modelled on the primal horde and united by fixation on a leader.[122] In his most direct polemic against religion, *The Future of an Illusion*, Freud describes religious doctrines as 'neurotic relics' surviving from primitive times when people tried to make the unfriendly universe seem intelligible by ascribing its operations to a loved and dreaded God, and argues that now, like the patient in analytic treatment, humankind should abandon its collective neurosis and maturely face the bleakness of reality. He ends his peroration with a dismissive quotation from 'one of our fellow-unbelievers' (*Unglaubensgenossen*), Heine:

> The heavens we can safely leave
> To the angels and the sparrows.[123]

[120] Rieff, *Freud: The Mind of the Moralist*, 3rd edn. (Chicago, 1979), p. 257.

[121] Freud, *Jugendbriefe an Silberstein*, pp. 82, 111; see William J. McGrath, *Freud's Discovery of Psychoanalysis: The Politics of Hysteria* (Ithaca, NY, and London, 1986), pp. 105–7.

[122] See Paul Connerton, 'Freud and the Crowd', in Edward Timms and Peter Collier (eds.), *Visions and Blueprints: Avant-garde Culture and Radical Politics in Early Twentieth-Century Europe* (Manchester, 1988), pp. 194–207.

[123] *Complete Poems of Heine*, p. 484.

In 1932, in the last of Freud's second series of *New Introductory Lectures on Psychoanalysis*, he sums up the scientific world-view, including psychoanalysis, as a programme of rigorous scepticism which dismisses revelation or intuition as sources of knowledge. Religion, by contrast, is based on wishful thinking: '[i]ts doctrines bear the imprint of the times in which they arose, the ignorant times of the childhood of humanity' (*SE* xxii. 168). Thus Freud represents religious belief as a childish delusion which must yield to adult insight, and as a neurosis which can be cured by psychoanalysis. Both models recall Kant's famous account of enlightenment as the process of attaining maturity and learning to think for oneself.

Freud saw history as an ascent from religion to science. His anthropological writings presuppose a sequence of 'three great pictures of the universe: animistic (or mythological), religious and scientific' (*SE* xiii. 77). In his teens he acquired from the historians Buckle and Lecky a conception of history as a narrative of individuation and secularization.[124] Buckle's *Introduction to the History of Civilization in England* is an essay in comparative intellectual sociology, whose pioneering ambition does much to compensate for its occasional crudity. Buckle sees history as the ascent of 'that bold, inquisitive, and scientific spirit, which is constantly advancing, and on which all future progress must depend'.[125] He intends to contribute to this process by extending positivistic science to discover regular laws in history. In opposition to the pieties of Victorian England, he insists that civilization depends not on moral progress but on intellectual progress; it is the latter, not the former, which has swept away one of the two greatest evils, religious persecution, and promises to abolish the other, namely war. The book by Lecky that Freud read was most probably *History of the Rise and Influence of the Spirit of Rationalism in Europe*, in which rationalism is defined as the antithesis of dogmatic theology. Lecky recounts three associated narratives: the intellectual development away from belief in miracles and anthropomorphic conceptions of God and towards reliance on empirical

[124] Freud, letter of 30 Oct. 1927 to Julie Braun-Vogelstein, in *Letters 1873–1939*, p. 379.
[125] Henry Thomas Buckle, *Introduction to the History of Civilization in England*, ed. John M. Robertson (London, 1904), p. 75. Originally published in two volumes as *History of Civilization in England* (1857–61).

evidence; the moral development away from rule by fear and towards the authority of the individual conscience; and the political development of secularization and democracy. These narratives are propelled by enlightened individuals such as Montaigne, 'the first great representative of the modern secular and rationalistic spirit', who, by an unexplained process, succeeded in 'extricating his mind from the trammels of the past'.[126] In this model of intellectual history, pioneering thinkers repeatedly enter into conflict with traditional and dogmatic authority and ultimately succeed because their views correspond to empirical reality. The importance of individuals in Freud's historical narrative will become fully apparent when we examine his interest in great men like the protagonist of *Moses and Monotheism*.

The meaning of 'science' for Freud is complex. The early Freud considered medical science an exact and objective procedure operating with mechanistic models. His teacher Ernst von Brücke, in whose laboratory Freud worked from 1876 to 1882, was Vienna's leading adherent to the physicalist school of Helmholtz. Brücke maintained that the only forces active in the organism were physical and chemical ones, that the conservation of matter held in biology as much as in physics, and that mental phenomena could be understood strictly as cause and effect.[127] Freud's later teacher Jean-Martin Charcot not only identified hysteria as a medical condition, but managed to explain historical cases of demonic possession in medical terms, as part of the enlightened and secularizing approach that deeply impressed Freud. Moreover, Freud's conception of the scientist fitted in with a widespread late nineteenth-century attitude of militant agnosticism which assumed that the truth about humanity's position in a godless universe would necessarily be unpleasant and stressed the masculine strength required to face the truth without recourse to consolation.[128] The dogged, embattled posture in the face of an

---

[126] W. E. H. Lecky, *History of the Rise and Influence of the Spirit of Rationalism in Europe*, 2 vols. (London, 1865), i. 103.

[127] See Ronald W. Clark, *Freud: The Man and the Cause* (London, 1980), p. 41; Frank J. Sulloway, *Freud, Biologist of the Mind: Beyond the Psychoanalytic Legend*, 2nd edn. (Cambridge, Mass., and London, 1992).

[128] See Charles Taylor, *Sources of the Self: The Making of the Modern Identity* (Cambridge, 1989), pp. 404–5.

indifferent universe is familiar from Nietzsche ('What does not kill me strengthens me'), from Joseph Conrad ('In the destructive element immerse'), and from the bombast (admired by Conrad) of Bertrand Russell's essay 'A Free Man's Worship'.[129] In Freud's case it matched the 'militant puritanism' which led him to name a son after Oliver Cromwell.[130]

Freud felt that his Jewishness enabled him to contribute to the enlightenment of humankind through science in indirect and complex ways. There was nothing specifically Jewish about psycho-analysis; rather, the universalist, rationalist claims of science enabled Freud to escape from a specifically Jewish identity: 'that psychoanalysis itself is a Jewish product seems to me nonsense. As a scientific work, it is neither Jewish nor Catholic nor Gentile.'[131] But he was sufficiently attached to the Mendelssohnian image of the rational Jew, to think his scientific advances were assisted by his Jewish freedom from prejudices and affinity with rationalism. As a Jew, Freud thought of himself as being in permanent opposi-tion against established prejudices. 'Because I was a Jew, I found myself free from many prejudices which restricted others in the use of their intellect; and as a Jew I was prepared to join the Opposi-tion and to do without agreement with the "compact majority"' (*SE* xx. 274). By quoting the phrase 'compact majority' he associated himself with Ibsen's Dr Stockmann, revealing the plague-infested sewers on which the town's prosperity rests. This liking for a solitary, embattled stance appears in his early identi-fication with Hannibal, whose conflict with Rome 'symbolized the conflict between the tenacity of Jewry and the organization of the Catholic Church' (*SE* iv. 196).

By his 'discovery of psychoanalysis', the supposed revelation that reports of infant abuse were largely endogenic fantasies, Freud moved away from his positivistic conception of science. Mechan-istic models of the psyche, like the hydraulic model that Freud keeps modifying, are only of heuristic help. Many familiar polemics have established that psychoanalysis cannot claim to be an experimental science.[132] Far from being objective or repeatable,

---

[129] See Ray Monk, *Bertrand Russell: The Spirit of Solitude* (London, 1996), pp. 333–4.   [130] Rieff, *Freud*, p. 260.
[131] Quoted in Gilman, *Freud, Race, and Gender*, p. 29, from Smiley Blanton, *Diary of my Analysis with Sigmund Freud* (New York, 1971), p. 43.
[132] See e.g. Ernest Gellner, *The Psychoanalytic Movement* (London, 1985).

it depends on empathy and interpretation. As a technique of interpreting character, it belongs to a model of research opposed to that of mechanistic science and closer to the activity of the hunter who interprets clues.[133] Not surprisingly, therefore, psychoanalysis has been largely ignored by subsequent scientists but has borne fruit in the humanities. Nor is it surprising that Freud himself increasingly studied cultural subjects: dreams, parapraxes, jokes, literature, art history, religion, ritual, crowds, and myth. His boldest hypotheses, like those of the instincts or drives (*Triebe*), develop into grandiose myths, for which Freud seeks support in Plato and Schopenhauer (e.g. *SE* xxii. 107, 209). 'Instincts are mythical entities, magnificent in their indefiniteness', he declared in 1932 (*SE* xxii. 95). 'Does not every science come in the end to a kind of mythology like this? Cannot the same be said to-day of your own Physics?' he rather lamely asked Einstein (*SE* xxii. 211). But while Freud unleashes his imagination in developing his own theories, he retains the pose of the scientist in his opposition to religion, especially in *The Future of an Illusion*, where religion is judged without empathy and by the rationalistic standards that Freud had effectively discarded in his creative work.

The embattled isolation of the scientific rationalist was tempered by the 'psychological structure' that Freud felt linking him to other Jews. Thus he and Karl Abraham agree on the 'racial kinship' ('Rassenverwandtschaft') separating them as Jews from the Christian Jung, and on the durability of their 'talmudic way of thinking'.[134] They seem strangely to conflate racial with cultural differences. The notion that a 'talmudic way of thinking' or similar mental disposition could be preserved in the psyche without being transmitted through education probably derives from the 'national psychology' (*Völkerpsychologie*) elaborated by the Jewish psychologist Moritz Lazarus and his brother-in-law

---

[133] See Carlo Ginzburg, 'Clues: Roots of an Evidential Paradigm', in his *Myths, Emblems, Clues*, tr. John and Anne C. Tedeschi (London, 1990), pp. 96–125. Cf. Jonathan Lear, *Love and its Place in Nature: A Philosophical Interpretation of Freudian Psychoanalysis* (London, 1990).

[134] *A Psycho-Analytic Dialogue: The Letters of Sigmund Freud and Karl Abraham, 1907–1926*, ed. Hilda C. Abraham and Ernst L. Freud, tr. Bernard Marsh and Hilda C. Abraham (London, 1965), p. 34 (3 May 1908); p. 36 (11 May 1908).

the philologist Heymann Steinthal.[135] Lazarus and Steinthal were interested not in races (biological groups with immutable characteristics) but in 'nations' moulded by history into a common psychological structure (*Volksgeist*), manifested in cultural phenomena such as language, religion, art, customs, institutions, and laws. In accordance with Lamarck's evolutionism, these structures could be modified by historical accretions, so that Jews steeped in the Talmud could bequeath the resulting mind-set to remote descendants.

For Freud, the Jewish 'psychological structure' includes a down-to-earth, deflating, materialist outlook which stresses such basic realities as the body, sex, and food. Here he finds support in Heine. Both associate Judaism with eating: Freud, referring to Passover food, asserts that 'religion is directed exclusively to the senses'; Heine repeatedly praises the stew called 'Schalet'.[136] More generally, Freud loves to quote the humorously or brutally physical moments in Heine, above all when he lets his essay 'The Acquisition and Control of Fire' culminate in the devastating couplet from 'Zur Teleologie':

> Was dem Menschen dient zum Seichen,
> Damit schafft er seinesgleichen.
>
> What one needs to piss, thereby
> Also serves to multiply.[137]

Moreover, Heine seems not just to have confirmed but even inspired some of Freud's ideas. He illustrates the relation between illness and creativity from some lines by Heine (*SE* xiv. 85) and quotes in *Moses and Monotheism* Heine's sombre description of Judaism as a sickness originating in Egypt, 'the plague they carried from the grim Nile valley' (*SE* xxiii. 31).[138]

Freud's taste for deflation shows itself also in his liking for Galician Jewish anecdotes, many of which he discussed in *Jokes and their Relation to the Unconscious* (1905). He liked such jokes

---

[135] See Gilman, *Freud, Race, and Gender*, pp. 27–8, and the introduction to Moritz Lazarus and Heymann Steinthal, *Die Begründer der Völkerpsychologie in ihren Briefen*, ed. Ingrid Belke (Tübingen, 1971).

[136] Freud, *Jugendbriefe an Silberstein*, p. 74 (18 Sept. 1874); Heine, H i. 499; vi. 128; *Begegnungen mit Heine*, ed. Michael Werner, 2 vols. (Hamburg, 1973), i. 225. See Sander L. Gilman, 'Freud reads Heine reads Freud', in Mark H. Gelber (ed.), *The Jewish Reception of Heinrich Heine* (Tübingen, 1992), pp. 77–94.

[137] *Complete Poems of Heine*, p. 802.   [138] Ibid. 399.

as evidence of Jews' ability to appreciate their own good and bad qualities, as expressions of their democratic spirit, and as a controlled rebellion against the restrictions of the Jewish law (*SE* viii. 111–12). Freud's use of them illustrates his own theory of jokes.[139] The joke permits the expression of material that is normally repressed. The momentary relief from the effort of repression produces laughter. Moreover, the joke establishes a relationship between the teller and the hearer at the expense of the object. Hence Freud, retelling jokes in German for a German-speaking readership, both expresses his own Jewish difference and overcomes it. He transfers his physical Jewishness to the subject of the joke while expressing his Jewish intellectuality by telling and analysing the joke. The jokes formed a body of allusions that helped him to feel at home with fellow-Jews like Fliess. These jokes tend to be about deflating pretensions, like the story of Itzig the Sunday horseman whose horse is in charge, or compensating for wretchedness, like the story of two beggars (*Schnorrer*) who divide up their territory so that one gets the province of Posen.[140] Indeed his theory that Moses was an Egyptian derives support from a Jewish joke in which a little boy, told that the Princess was not Moses' mother but merely found him among the bulrushes, replies: 'Says she!' (*SE* xv. 161).

On the one hand, therefore, Freud's Jewish identity, formed in Mendelssohn's rationalist mould, enabled him paradoxically to escape from Jewishness into the universalist, rationalist world of science. On the other, his very Jewishness enabled him to devise psychoanalysis, by accepting the basic physical realities of life and developing a disrespectful, probing, subversive, and aggressive attitude towards the taboos with which Christian culture sought to surround them. His scientific stance is implicitly masculine, that of an aggressor, a hero, a conquistador.[141] But to see Freud's opposition to religion in general, and the Catholic Church in particular, as an Oedipal conflict with a paternal authority would be misleading. It should be related rather to his complex feelings about his mother: her demanding love spurred on his creativity, and he suppressed his hostility by idealizing her. Part of this

[139] See Gilman, *Jewish Self-Hatred*, pp. 262–7.
[140] See *Letters of Freud to Fliess*, pp. 254 (Posen), 319 (Itzig); cf. 87, 148, 266, 353.
[141] See Sulloway, *Freud, Biologist of the Mind*, pp. 476–84.

idealization is his conception of femininity as based on masochistic submission, something hardly exhibited by the redoubtable
Amalie Freud.[142] His opposition to religion may be interpreted as
resentment against his mother and also against the mother-
substitute (his Catholic nurse) who had rejected him and deprived
him not only of her love but of access to an enticing 'feminine'
world of religious symbolism. Excluded from this maternal world,
Freud adopts a 'masculine' posture of lonely, embattled rationality,
supported by the followers who form his 'band of brothers'. He
avenges himself on the lost world of symbolism by subjecting it to
reductive psychoanalytic interpretations, but he also regains it by
covertly making his 'science' into a technique of imaginative
empathy and appropriation while maintaining the pose of the
aggressive rationalist.

As his scientific pretensions wear thin, Freud's scientific project
becomes increasingly self-defeating. A gulf opens up between the
professed rationality of his method and the primitive irrationality
of human culture. Regression to the primitive is repeatedly
invoked to explain the reappearance of barbarism within civilization. Human nature now appears essentially irrational. *Totem and
Taboo* (1913) already sought to show how much civilized humanity shared with the mental life of primitive peoples. The First
World War, which shockingly confirmed the power of primitive
feeling, elicited Freud's pessimistic *Thoughts for the Times on War
and Death* (1915). After the War his thinking comes to centre on
aggression, the destructive impulse postulated in *Beyond the
Pleasure Principle* (1920). In *Civilization and its Discontents*
(1930) Freud's progressive conception of history becomes bitterly
ironic. For civilization is built on the renunciation of instincts. The
lower bodily functions have to be controlled and disguised by
practices of cleanliness. Sexual desire has to be restrained and
channelled. Man's powerful aggressive instincts must be controlled
by promoting social affection. And the only way to control aggression is to internalize it as the super-ego which turns one's
aggression against oneself, so that, the more one practises civilized
restraint, the more guilty and miserable one feels: 'the price we pay

---

[142] See 'The Economic Problem in Masochism' (1924), *SE* xix. 159–70; Estelle
Roith, *The Riddle of Freud: Jewish Influences on his Theory of Female Sexuality*
(London, 1987); Deborah P. Margolis, *Freud and his Mother* (Northvale, NJ, 1996).

for our advance in civilization is a loss of happiness through the heightening of our sense of guilt' (*SE* xxi. 134).

How can this sense of guilt be overcome? Does the self-knowledge derived from rational insight give any feeling of relief, release, or absolution? The psychoanalytic understanding of the super-ego does not liberate one from its effects, since the super-ego is needed for civilization to continue. At best, psychoanalysis enables one to endure the pressure of the super-ego; at worst, it can make one a spectator, like the Schnitzler of the diaries, endowed with a self-knowledge that cannot substantially affect one's life. When Freud mentions the idea of release, he ascribes it to religions, which 'claim to redeem mankind from this sense of guilt, which they call sin'; Christianity does this by 'the sacrificial death of a single person' (*SE* xxi. 136), but since Freud refers to his theory of the origins of redemptive sacrifice put forward in *Totem and Taboo*, it is evident that Christianity offers, in his eyes, only a continuing illusion.

Unable to escape from this impasse, Freud transfers his attention from the individual to the cultural super-ego. He thinks that an epoch of civilization, like an individual, has a super-ego, 'based on the impression left behind by the personalities of great leaders—men of overwhelming force of mind in whom one of the human impulsions has found its strongest and purest, and therefore often its most one-sided, expression' (*SE* xxi. 141). It seems therefore that reason cannot by itself act like a secularized providence, guiding humankind to ever greater enlightenment. Enlightenment must be imposed through irrational means by the authority of great men (like Montaigne as envisaged by Lecky in Freud's schoolboy reading). In the age of the dictators, metaphors of irrational authority pervade Freud's language. He writes in 1932: 'Our best hope for the future is that the intellect—the scientific spirit, reason—will in time establish a dictatorship in man's psychic life' (*SE* xxii. 171). Reason, it seems, must work through irrational means. The propagation of enlightenment by the cultural super-ego forms an important theme of Freud's last major book, *Moses and Monotheism*.

Moses and Monotheism was published, and indeed partially written, during Freud's exile in London, but its genesis goes back to 1934. The rise of Hitler and the ill-treatment of the German Jews impelled Freud to seek the causes of antisemitism in the distinctive character of the Jewish people, and to investigate their origins. As early as 1934 he told Arnold Zweig that he had found the formula: 'Moses created the Jews.'[143] In the text, however, Freud acknowledges that his dealings with biblical tradition are autocratic and arbitrary, and that his structure has weak as well as strong points; while in his letters to Zweig he admits 'the weakness of my historical construction' and also seems uncertain about the genre of the work. He first refers to it as *The Man Moses, a Historical Novel*. Later he admits that 'this historical novel won't stand up to my own criticism'.[144] His doubts are reflected in the book's formal and generic uncertainties. Its repetitious and confusing form makes it seem a display of work in progress rather than a finished treatise. Nor can it be taken seriously as a work of biblical scholarship.[145] Rather, the illusion of scholarship released Freud's imagination to explore the themes which he formulates as follows: 'what the real nature of a tradition resides in, and what its special power rests on, how impossible it is to dispute the personal influence upon world-history of individual great men' (*SE* xxiii. 52).

National and international politics affected the book in other ways. As Freud admits in the first prefatory note, some modern states reveal an alliance of progress with barbarism: above all the Soviet Union, where religion has been banished and sexuality liberated, and where people's living conditions are being improved with the aid of brutal coercion and intellectual repression (*SE* xxiii. 54). Enlightenment has triumphed, but at the cost of its own corruption by its opposite. Hence *Moses and Monotheism* reflects on the very possibility of progress through enlightenment.

Even more ironically, Freud, still living in Austria, finds his liberty of expression protected by his old enemy, the Catholic Church. The Austrian corporate state, set up by Engelbert Dollfuss in 1933, represented an extreme reaction against the liberal era in which Freud had grown up. It was dominated by the Catholic Church and drew on long-established conservative and antisemitic traditions. Its corporatist programme was an

---

[143] *The Letters of Sigmund Freud and Arnold Zweig*, ed. Ernst L. Freud, tr. W. and E. Robson-Scott (London, 1970), p. 91 (30 Sept. 1934).

[144] Ibid. 104 (14 Mar. 1935), 91 (30 Sept. 1934), 97 (6 Nov. 1934).

[145] The pertinent criticisms are succinctly made in the review by Salo W. Baron, *American Journal of Sociology*, 45 (1939), 471–7.

amalgam of traditions of Catholic and conservative political thought, opposed to the atomizing and secularizing influence of liberal capitalism. Living in such relative security, Freud thought it better not to publish *Moses and Monotheism* in Austria for fear of arousing Catholic enmity.

The book's main theses certainly make it a major offensive in Freud's lifelong anti-religious campaign. Freud contends that Moses was an Egyptian, pointing out that Moses is part of an Egyptian name, meaning 'son', and arguing that the biblical story of Moses' being discovered among the bulrushes is essentially a 'family romance' distorted by Jewish chroniclers to conceal that he was an Egyptian.

Freud then tries to explain the origins of Jewish monotheism. He points out its similarities to the monotheistic worship of the sun-god Aten introduced by a Pharaoh of the Eighteenth Dynasty, Amenophis IV, who took the name Akhenaten. This monarch forbade any statue of Aten to be made, just as Moses' commandments later forbade the making of a graven image of God. His inscriptions emphasize the ethical values of truth and justice, which were later to be upheld by Moses' commandments and the prophets. Freud was not the first person to point out this resemblance and suggest a debt; his associate Karl Abraham had done so in 1912, in an article published in *Imago*, to which Freud, curiously enough, makes no reference.[146] And the connection is also made in one of the books he does quote, J. H. Breasted's *The Dawn of Conscience*. Freud's own contribution is his account of the part played by Moses in bringing monotheism to the Hebrews.

Freud maintains that Akhenaten's adherents included a nobleman probably called Tuthmosis, a name later shortened to Moses. After Akhenaten's death and the restoration of polytheism by the priesthood, Moses preserved monotheism and satisfied his own ambition by imposing the doctrine on the Hebrews, whom he then led out of Egypt to the land of Canaan. Freud also adopts a theory put forward in 1922 by the biblical scholar Eduard Sellin, who interpreted some passages in Hosea as meaning that Moses was

---

[146] Abraham, 'Amenhotep IV. (Echnaton). Psychoanalytische Beiträge zum Verständnis seiner Persönlichkeit und des monotheistischen Aton-Kultes', *Imago*, 1 (1912), 334–60.

killed by his people just before entering the Promised Land.[147] In order to relieve their guilt, the Hebrews not only exalted Moses' memory, but went even further. As their conception of God developed, they formed him in the image of Moses. In affirming that their God had singled them out as his chosen people, they were really referring to the fact that Moses, the Egyptian prince, had condescended to choose them as the inheritors of monotheism.

Freud's next problem is to explain how the elevated doctrine that Moses had brought from Egypt managed to survive. For many generations it was submerged by the crude sacrificial cult of Yahweh, 'a coarse, narrow-minded local god, violent and blood-thirsty' (*SE* xxiii. 50), but resurfaced as the accepted religion of the Jews. It could not survive merely in oral tradition, for that would not give it the aura of unquestionable authority that a religious doctrine needs. Freud's answer depends on the biological dictum that ontogeny repeats phylogeny—the development of the individual repeats that of the species. Transferring this principle from biology to psychology, he assumes that a nation has a collective mind in which great events affecting the nation as a whole are not forgotten but repressed. This process is analogous to the formation of a traumatic neurosis in the individual. The trauma is acquired in early childhood, is repressed during the latency period, and resurfaces after puberty as an obsessional neurosis, a compulsion to re-experience the original traumatic event. With the Israelites, the traumatic event was the killing of Moses. After a latency period in which they worshipped Yahweh, the memory of Moses and his doctrines resurfaced, so that the dead Moses was incomparably more powerful than the living one had been. These events are themselves made possible by the event which, in Freud's view, founded human society, the killing of the primal father by his sons who afterwards bore the burden of guilt. Thus monotheism survived by its association with the murder of its proponent.

If we regard *Moses and Monotheism* as an imaginative work, we will recall that for many years past Freud's interest in Moses

---

[147] Sellin, *Mose und seine Bedeutung für die israelitisch-jüdische Religions-geschichte* (Leipzig, 1922), esp. p. 43. The crucial passages are Hosea 5: 1, which Sellin (unlike most translators) interprets as referring to Shittim, the scene of idolatry and violence in Num. 25, and Hosea 9: 7–14.

had amounted to an identification. This is clear from the paper on the Moses of Michelangelo, which concludes that the statue depicts Moses just after he has glimpsed the Israelites worshipping the golden calf. Freud wrote this paper shortly after the Psychoanalytic Congress at Munich in 1913, at which it became clear that Jung was following Adler and Stekel into what Freud saw as apostasy.[148] In it Freud disputes the traditional view that Michelangelo depicts Moses dropping the tablets. Instead, in Freud's interpretation, Moses is clutching them to prevent them from falling to the ground. Thus he begins rehabilitating Moses from his biblical reputation of being impulsive and hot-tempered. Moses is a great man who can control his emotions in order to preserve the truth.

In this narrative, monotheism is not a divine revelation but a human invention. Not that Freud, in the manner of the notorious *Traité des trois imposteurs*, makes Moses a deliberate fraud; but Moses' personality stamps itself on the unconscious minds of his followers. In proposing a human origin for monotheism, Freud is opposing not only the official doctrines of the Catholic Church but also the peculiar theory of monotheism put forward by Father Wilhelm Schmidt, SVD, whom Freud mentions in his letters to Zweig as a student of comparative religion, an enemy of psychoanalysis, a confidant of the Pope, and a grey eminence behind the Austrian corporate state.[149] Father Schmidt, in his day a world-famous anthropologist, taught at the seminary of the missionary society Societas Verbi Divini in St Gabriel, outside Vienna. From 1925 to 1938 he was also professor of anthropology at Vienna University. He was also a leading representative of antisemitic racial theory, though he was a firm anti-Nazi who went into exile in Switzerland after the annexation of Austria in 1938. His theory of monotheism, expounded in his huge twelve-volume work *Der Ursprung der Gottesidee* (*The Origin of the Idea of God*, 1926–55), supposes that in primeval times the Supreme Being literally descended to earth and made himself known to humanity, but that now the original purity of monotheism survived only among remote peoples like the Congolese Pygmies, the Australian

---

[148] Jones, *Freud*, ii. 411; Martin S. Bergmann, 'Moses and the Evolution of Freud's Jewish Identity', in Mortimer Ostow (ed.), *Judaism and Psychoanalysis* (New York, 1982), pp. 111–41.

[149] *Letters of Freud and Zweig*, p. 92 (30 Oct. 1934); pp. 130–1 (17 June 1936).

Aborigines, the Tierra del Fuegans and the Andaman Islanders, in whom Schmidt as an anthropologist was especially interested. Freud's human-centred theory of monotheism is a surreptitious riposte to Schmidt, intended to show that monotheism is really homage to a great man.[150]

In *Moses and Monotheism* Freud complicates his narrative by surmising that Moses was killed by his followers. Freud gives credit for this idea to Eduard Sellin. But Sellin's suggestion rests on a flimsy basis and has never been accepted by other biblical scholars. However, as Freud later points out, the murder of Moses was also suggested by Goethe. It is put forward as a semi-serious speculation in Goethe's ironic retelling of the story of Moses in 'Israel in der Wüste' ('Israel in the Wilderness') which forms part of the notes appended to his collection of Orientalizing poetry, the *West-Östlicher Divan* (*West-Eastern Divan*).[151] We can safely assume that Freud had been familiar with this idea for many years and that it formed part of the original imaginative core around which *Moses and Monotheism* gradually took shape. But while Goethe supposes that Moses' followers killed him because they were tired of his ill-temper and incompetent leadership, Freud has Moses killed by people unable to endure the elevated doctrines he has taught them. He suffers, Freud says, the fate of all enlightened despots. Hence Moses is now the primal father killed by his sons, the figure whom Freud places at the origin of religion; and also the enlightened leader who offers his followers new truths which they are too blinkered to accept.

The truths offered by this enlightened despot, the Jewish identity created by Moses, correspond to Freud's conception of the rational Jew. Yet the truth preserved by Moses is the mono-theism of Akhenaten. In studies of the origins of religion written in Freud's lifetime, Akhenaten held an honoured place, for his monotheism and his ethics were seen as anticipating those of Christianity, and hence the elements within Christianity which could be preserved in a secular and rationalist age. The account of Akhenaten by J. H. Breasted, on which Freud chiefly relied, is in

---

[150] For fuller accounts of Schmidt in relation to Freud, see Ritchie Robertson, '"My true enemy": Freud and the Catholic Church 1927–1939', in Kenneth Segar and John Warren (eds.), *Austria in the Thirties: Culture and Politics* (Riverside, Calif., 1991), pp. 328–44; Yerushalmi, *Freud's Moses*, pp. 27–9.

[151] Goethe, HA ii. 207–25, esp. pp. 216–17.

this tradition. After describing Akhenaten's enlightened and universalist ideals, Breasted brushes aside the intervening millennia and identifies these ideals with 'the fundamental conclusions that form the basis of moral convictions, and continue to do so in civilised life'.[152] Hence the monotheism of Akhenaten and Moses fits neatly into Freud's conception of intellectual development towards scientific rationality.

If we ask how Judaism fits into this picture, the answer is dialectical. Freud regards Judaism as a traumatic neurosis, like other religions. But it is more advanced than other religions: ethically, because of its stress on truth and justice; and intellectually, because its prohibition of image-making trains its devotees in abstract thought. By comparison, Christianity represents a regression to a more emotional form of religion, in which the pleasure principle has more power, and where intellectual development is inhibited by 'superstitious, magical and mystical elements' (*SE* xxiii. 88). Judaism therefore offers a better starting-point from which to advance into the scientific age. This is why Jews seem better equipped than Christians for the science known as psychoanalysis, and why Freud thought that Jung, as a Christian and a pastor's son, could only accept psychoanalysis after combating inner resistances from which Jews like himself were free. Freud wrote to Abraham: 'On the whole it is easier for us Jews, as we lack the mystical element.'[153]

Yet the book also undermines Freud's rationalism by supporting his doubts about reason and implicitly denying his lingering belief in the perfectibility of man through reason. For in maintaining that monotheism survived in the Jews' collective unconscious by its association with the killing of Moses, Freud is arguing that ethical and intellectual doctrines are transmitted by irrational means. We no longer have the Enlightenment assumption that truth is discovered by a rational process of inquiry, consisting of examination of empirical evidence and open discussion in which the more reasonable side eventually wins. Instead, we learn that doctrines are transmitted by a 'great man' whose traits are those of

---

[152] Breasted, *The Dawn of Conscience* (New York, 1934), p. 384. On Breasted's humanism, see W. F. Albright, *History, Archaeology and Christian Humanism* (London, 1965), pp. 217–28; and for sceptical comment on his appropriation of Akhenaten, see Cyril Aldred, *Akhenaten* (London, 1968), p. 257.

[153] *A Psycho-Analytic Dialogue*, p. 46 (20 July 1908).

the primal father. His authority imprints his teachings on his followers' minds. Only thus can his doctrines acquire the unquestionable certainty that they need in order to survive. Recalling Nietzsche's account of the imposition of memory by violence in *The Genealogy of Morals*, one could perhaps say that *Moses and Monotheism* is Freud's most Nietzschean book.

In describing how the leader's doctrines are rejected by his disloyal followers, the text contains an element of personal fantasy. Freud knew that the psychoanalytic movement itself was dismayingly fissile. He had already seen how liable psychoanalysis was to regress into a pseudo-religion, and had witnessed the defections of Adler, Stekel, Jung, Rank, and Ferenczi. Yet the paradoxical implication concealed in *Moses and Monotheism* is that the disloyal followers are better guardians of the founder's doctrines than the loyal ones. The loyal followers will transmit his doctrines faithfully, but, lacking the stamp of irrational authority, these doctrines will eventually be forgotten. The disloyal followers will repress these doctrines, but eventually they will resurface, carrying a powerful emotional charge which will ensure their survival.

A further complication is that in Freud's myth, Moses creates the Jews but is not himself a Jew. And in so far as Freud identified with Moses, that must imply a fantasy in which Freud himself was not a Jew.[154] When rebuked for depriving the Jews of their leader Moses at a time of crisis, Freud appealed to the stern demands of scientific truth and to the tradition of Jewish courage:

Needless to say, I don't like offending my own people, either. But what can I do about it? I have spent my whole life standing up for what I have considered to be the scientific truth, even when it was uncomfortable and unpleasant for my fellowmen. I cannot end up with an act of disavowal. [. . .] Well, we Jews have been reproached for growing cowardly in the course of the centuries. (Once upon a time we were a valiant nation.) In this transformation I had no share.[155]

---

[154] See Marthe Robert, *From Oedipus to Moses: Freud's Jewish Identity* (London, 1977), esp. p. 167; Daniel Boyarin, ' "An Imaginary and Desirable Converse": *Moses and Monotheism* as Family Romance', in Timothy K. Beal and David M. Gunn (eds.), *Reading Bibles, Writing Bodies* (London, 1997), pp. 184–204.

[155] Freud, *Letters 1873–1939*, pp. 448, 450 (31 Oct. 1938).

Thus *Moses and Monotheism* is intended, by the supposed rigour of its arguments, to illustrate Jewish rationality, even when denying the Jewishness of a national hero.

These contradictions begin to make sense, however, if we see that Freud has superimposed onto the story of Moses another myth, that of Prometheus. Prometheus was the Titan of Greek legend who defied the gods, first by making human beings out of clay, and secondly by stealing fire from heaven in order to benefit humanity. The story of Prometheus gained cultural authority from forming part of the classical learning that Freud so much valued and from being the subject of a famous poem by the young Goethe, in which Prometheus derides the impotent thunderings of Zeus and calmly continues forming human beings in his own image (the subversive allusion to Gen. 1: 26 expresses the young Goethe's opposition to official Christianity):

Here I sit, making men in my own image, a race that shall resemble me, a race that shall suffer and weep, and know joy and delight, and be heedless of you, as I am.[156]

In identifying not only with Moses but also with the Titan Prometheus, Freud satisfies his fantasy of himself as a conquistador. He imagines himself as a superhuman being, between the gods and humanity, who defies the former—as in the epigraph to *The Interpretation of Dreams*—and benefits the latter by the gift of fire. If fire suggests the enlightenment with which Freud associated Jewish rationality, the clay from which Prometheus moulds humanity suggests the down-to-earth materialism which Freud also thought characteristic of his innately Jewish outlook.

Moses and Monotheism, then, is an intricate, self-contradicting work, in which Freud affirms rationality while undermining it with the image of the charismatic leader. Instead of a progression from primitive ignorance through enlightenment to scientific rationality, we now have a scheme in which violence and repression are the most effective means of transmitting enlightened doctrines. Alarmed by the modern alliance between progress and barbarism, Freud has constructed his own version of such an alliance, and in trying to support the association of Jewish identity with enlightenment he has put at risk his own lifelong ideals.

---

[156] *Goethe*, tr. David Luke (Harmondsworth, 1964), p. 19; see DKA I. i. 203–4.

3

Antisemitism

VARIETIES OF ANTISEMITISM

Is antisemitism a single phenomenon? Can a term coined in the 1870s be applied retrospectively to the hostility to Jews found in the Roman Empire, in Europe in the High Middle Ages, and in Europe since the Enlightenment, without imposing a spurious unity upon diverse phenomena?[1] Recalling Lovejoy's famous paper 'On the Discrimination of Romanticisms', one may be tempted to propose a discrimination of antisemitisms that would dissolve the unity of the concept.[2] Under the impact of the Holocaust, however, and feeling that such an immense catastrophe must have correspondingly tenacious historical roots, attempts have been made to write a continuous history of antisemitism from the ancient world till the twentieth century.[3] Some writers have insisted on particular continuities. Holocaust theologians try to trace modern antisemitism back to the Church Fathers' denunciations of 'Old Israel' and its obdurate rejection of the Christian message.[4] Others trace it back to the anti-Jewish superstitions— the charges of worshipping the Devil and carrying out ritual murders of Christian children—that arose in the Middle Ages.[5]

---

[1] On the origin of the term 'antisemitism', see Moshe Zimmermann, *Wilhelm Marr: The Patriarch of Anti-Semitism* (New York, 1986).

[2] Arthur O. Lovejoy, 'On the Discrimination of Romanticisms', *Publications of the Modern Language Association*, 29 (1924), 229–53.

[3] See e.g. Léon Poliakov, *The History of Antisemitism*, 4 vols. (London, 1974–86); Sander L. Gilman and Steven T. Katz (eds.), *Anti-Semitism in Times of Crisis* (New York and London, 1991); Robert S. Wistrich, *Antisemitism: The Longest Hatred* (London, 1991).

[4] See Rosemary Radford Ruether, *Faith and Fratricide: The Theological Roots of Anti-Semitism* (New York, 1974), and for comment, Clemens Thoma, *A Christian Theology of Judaism*, tr. Helga Croner (New York, 1980), pp. 152–61.

[5] Joshua Trachtenberg, *The Devil and the Jews: The Medieval Conception of the Jew and its Relation to Modern Antisemitism* (New Haven, 1943), esp. p. 219. On

This, however, is broad-brush history, and on closer examination the continuities tend to dissolve. Certainly passages in the
Gospels, especially John 8: 14–56, embarrassingly use the blanket
term 'the Jews' for Jesus' opponents, thereby expressing, not the
situation during Jesus' ministry, but the tensions between the
Jewish and Christian communities at the end of the first century;
and, beyond that, there has been a long-standing tension between
Christianity and the older religion from which it grew and whose
proponents have often perplexed Christians by persisting in their
traditional devotion without accepting the Christian message.
Nevertheless, antisemitism does not seem as intimately connected
to Christianity as Holocaust theologians maintain. Roman writers
like Cicero and Tacitus show animus against Jews in the Empire.[6]
In the early Middle Ages Jews lived peacefully in the Christian
world. The legend of ritual murder arose in the 1150s and
accompanied the western European social revolution, the transition from segmentary society to the state, which gave administrators the power not just to settle particular disputes but to
persecute those who seemed to threaten the new order; to this
end society was reclassified and outsiders created as objects of
persecution—not only Jews but heretics, lepers, and homosexuals.[7] Continuities between the antisemitism of Christendom
and that of the post-Enlightenment world are weakened above all
by the fact, emphasized in Steven Katz's massively documented
study of early antisemitism, that despite the physical and
economic oppression of Jews, Christendom never promoted
genocide; indeed, the Popes and many secular potentates tried to
protect Jews from popular violence.[8] The preservation of the Jews
was dictated both by humanity and by theology: according to St
Augustine, they were needed as a 'witness-people' whose ultimate
conversion would confirm the Christian revelation.[9]

In the 'post-Christian' modernity inaugurated by the Enlighten-

these superstitions, see Alan Dundes (ed.), *The Blood Libel Legend: A Casebook in
Anti-Semitic Folklore* (Madison, 1991); Rohrbacher and Schmidt, *Judenbilder*.

[6] See Sevenster, *The Roots of Pagan Anti-Semitism*.

[7] See R. I. Moore, *The Formation of a Persecuting Society* (Oxford, 1987).

[8] Katz, *The Holocaust in Historical Context*, i: *The Holocaust and Mass Death
before the Modern Age* (New York and Oxford, 1994), esp. pp. 173–4.

[9] See Stephen R. Haynes, *Jews and the Christian Imagination: Reluctant Witnesses*
(London, 1995).

ment, however, new possibilities of reforming and purifying society by rational and technical means accompanied a diminution in the moral inhibitions on maltreating fellow-humans. The modern recrudescence of antisemitic rhetoric with a Christian flavour, and of the blood libel, disguises a deeper discontinuity between Christian and post-Christian antisemitisms. For modern antisemitism has licensed genocide. For the first time in history, a concerted attempt was made to massacre all Jews. One might wish to agree with Freud that the alliance between progress and barbarism, visible in the Soviet Union, differed from the undiluted barbarism of National Socialism: 'We feel it as a relief from an oppressive apprehension when we see in the case of the German people that a relapse into almost prehistoric barbarism can occur as well without being attached to any progressive ideas' (*SE* xxiii. 54). But Horkheimer and Adorno, and more recently Zygmunt Bauman, have argued in effect that Freud's apprehension was well founded: that the Holocaust, the culminating atrocity of Nazism, was not a strange aberration in an enlightened modern world; rather, genocide is something made possible by the Enlightenment and by modernity.[10]

Modernity sees in society not a God-given order, as in pre-Enlightenment centuries, or an organic growth, as the Romantics thought, but a man-made construct that can, however arduously, be reshaped in accordance with human desires and rational goals. Such reshaping may occur through revolution and upheaval, or more peacefully through social engineering. The goals of social engineering may vary from the improvement of health care to the sterilization of the sick, but they subordinate the well-being of the individual to the greatest good of the greatest number. Such premises may license the decision to exterminate a social group that has been deemed unhealthy, incurable and unassimilable. The Holocaust was a horrendously efficient way of achieving this end:

[T]he Holocaust was as much a product, as it was a failure, of modern civilization. Like everything else done in the modern—rational, planned, scientifically informed, expert, efficiently managed, co-ordinated—way, the Holocaust left behind and put to shame all its alleged pre-modern

[10] See Max Horkheimer and T. W. Adorno, *Dialectic of Enlightenment*, tr. John Cumming (New York, 1972); Zygmunt Bauman, *Modernity and the Holocaust* (Cambridge, 1989).

equivalents, exposing them as primitive, wasteful and ineffective by comparison. [. . .] It towers high above the past genocidal episodes in the same way as the modern industrial plant towers above the craftsman's cottage workshop, or the modern industrial farm, with its tractors, combines and pesticides, towers above the peasant farmstead with its horse, hoe and hand-weeding.[11]

Such a project of social engineering depends on two pillars of the Enlightenment: bureaucracy and science. The Enlightenment is no longer seen primarily as a movement of ideas, as it was by Ernst Cassirer, but rather as conducted by the vast numbers of bureaucrats who ran the eighteenth-century 'police states' on the mercantilist principles outlined in Chapter 1. The importance of these university-trained and reform-minded administrators as bearers of the Enlightenment has been demonstrated above all by the historian Franco Venturi.[12] It was possible, as we shall see in Chapter 5, for well-intentioned bureaucrats to put forward the most inhumane proposals. For bureaucracy depends on indirect action. Bureaucrats are separated by many partitions from the human beings whose lives they administer. Bureaucracy works by turning messy human problems into standard administrative tasks. Hence bureaucratic rationality tends to become independent of ethical norms. And a bureaucratic apparatus readily becomes self-propelled, losing sight of its purpose while enthusiastically elaborating its means. The present-day visitor to Auschwitz may see, from the meticulous lists and photographs of victims, what bureaucratic assiduity went into the mass production of death, even while troops and rolling stock were urgently required on the Russian front. The Holocaust, in representing the extreme application of technical rationality to barbaric and insane ends, was part of that transformation of the world to which the Enlightenment attached such utopian expectations.

While National Socialism certainly institutionalized barbarism for racist and genocidal purposes, its institutions carried the modern authority of science.[13] As far as biology, genetics, and psychology are concerned, the enthusiastic participation of

[11] Bauman, *Modernity*, p. 89.

[12] See Franco Venturi, *Utopia and Reform in the Enlightenment* (Cambridge, 1971), and contrast Ernst Cassirer, *Die Philosophie der Aufklärung* (Tübingen, 1932).

[13] See Michael Burleigh and Wolfgang Wippermann, *The Racial State: Germany 1933–1945* (Cambridge, 1991), pp. 44–73.

scientists in Nazi racial policies disproves the myth of science, so dear to Freud, as a pure pursuit of knowledge unencumbered by social concerns.[14] For, first, scientific research rests on hypotheses, assumptions, and metaphors which are drawn from the wider social world and may either stimulate or misdirect research. The concept of racial hygiene rested on the assumption, widely shared by Right and Left in Britain as well as Germany, that the hereditary qualities of the population could be improved by the eugenic control of procreation. Eugenics seemed both reputable and socially responsible. And hence, secondly, it is difficult to draw a line between 'normal science' and corrupt Nazi science.[15] The Kaiser Wilhelm Institute for Anthropology, Human Heredity and Eugenics, established in 1927, responded first to the social anxieties of the Weimar Republic and later to the racial demands of National Socialism; its director, Eugen Fischer, continued as a researcher after the Second World War. Josef Mengele was assistant to one of Fischer's colleagues while working as camp doctor at Auschwitz, from which he supplied the KWI with the eyes of murdered gypsies and the internal organs of murdered children for analysis. Konrad Lorenz, awarded the Nobel Prize for Medicine in 1973, conducted his research on animal instinct in the 1930s while arguing that the decline of civilization should be reversed by the elimination of inferior (*minderwertig*) persons under a scientifically founded racial policy.[16] Lorenz's casual references to elimination confirm that, thirdly, science has no built-in moral constraints. Even in 1973 he expressed regret that humane compassion for individuals conflicted with the wider interests of humankind.

Bauman's analysis invites us to understand the Holocaust as an aberration, certainly, but one made possible by essentially modern preconditions: by the conjunction of a programme of social engineering with the bureaucratic resources required to execute it. This is consistent with recent functionalist explanations which

[14] See Paul Weindling, *Health, Race and German Politics between National Unification and Nazism, 1870–1945* (Cambridge, 1989).
[15] See Mario Biagoli, 'Science, Modernity, and the "Final Solution"', in Saul Friedlander (ed.), *Probing the Limits of Representation: Nazism and the 'Final Solution'* (Cambridge, Mass., 1992), pp. 185–205.
[16] See Ute Deichmann, *Biologen unter Hitler: Vertreibung, Karriere, Forschung* (Frankfurt and New York, 1992), pp. 247–66.

see the Holocaust not as the result of Hitler's long-meditated strategy but as the solution found by bureaucrats to the problem of dealing with vast numbers of Jews in occupied territories.[17] It transfers the emphasis from Hitler's personal antisemitism, extreme and obsessive though that was, to the bureaucratic outlook which reduces human misery to an administrative challenge.

Undoubtedly, as Daniel Goldhagen has recently insisted, the bureaucracy of the Holocaust was assisted by a predisposition to regard the Jews as an alien population that needed special treatment.[18] But, in contrast to Goldhagen's sweeping generalizations, this predisposition can be traced through numerous varieties of antisemitism, which did not exist in isolation but as components of a larger conception of society and the world. Antisemitism may claim a religious, an economic, a racial, or a cultural basis; it may combine several of these in differing proportions. Such distinctions indicate that antisemitism is protean. When some antisemitic claims are refuted, antisemites do not admit defeat but regroup around other claims that are less susceptible to empirical disproof. In what follows, I want to distinguish an antisemitism based on the nationalistic concept of the 'Volk' from a subsequent antisemitism based on the quasi-scientific concept of 'race'; to sketch an 'anti-modern mentality' in which antisemitism was one component; and to draw attention to a little-noticed variety of antisemitism, the 'cultural antisemitism' of the 1920s.

From Language to Race

In the eighteenth century, a conception of 'Germany' founded on dynastic and territorial bases was gradually replaced by a new and more specific cultural identity. The great writers of the late Enlightenment—Lessing, Goethe, Schiller, Kant—felt themselves to be cosmopolitans or citizens of the world rather than local patriots. Nevertheless, Lessing opposed the influence of French

[17] See Tim Mason, 'Intention and Explanation: A Current Controversy about the Interpretation of National Socialism', in his *Nazism, Fascism and the Working Class* (Cambridge, 1995), pp. 212–30; Christopher R. Browning, *The Path to Genocide: Essays on Launching the Final Solution* (Cambridge, 1992).
[18] See Goldhagen, *Hitler's Willing Executioners: Ordinary Germans and the Holocaust* (London, 1996). For criticism of Goldhagen, see especially Ruth Bettina Birn, 'Revising the Holocaust', *Historical Journal*, 40 (1997), 195–215. A range of reactions is given in *Ein Volk von Mördern?*, ed. Julius H. Schoeps (Hamburg, 1996).

theatrical models and called for an authentically German drama using materials like the Faust legend. In his comedy *Minna von Barnhelm* (1767) he introduced the dishonest Frenchman Riccaut de la Marlinière whose immorality seems confirmed by his caricaturally bad German. Goethe praised Lessing for presenting in this play a subject that was distinctively German and contemporary—the reconciliation of Saxony and Prussia after the Seven Years War (DKA I xv. 307–8). The young Goethe himself sought German or Germanic art in folk-song, in Shakespeare, and in the Gothic architecture which, in his essay on Strasbourg Cathedral, he described as an organic and individual art producing a 'tree of God'.[19] French and Italian architecture, by contrast, have no organic life but depend on the heritage of classicism. These images—the dishonest foreigner from a superficial culture— would presently be transferred to the Jews.

Goethe wrote his essay under the influence of Herder, who questioned the cosmopolitanism of the Enlightenment. Herder feared a state of tedious uniformity in which everyone would speak French, adopt French manners, and become 'philanthropic citizens of the world'. 'The princes speak French, and soon everybody will follow their example; and then, behold, perfect bliss: the golden age, when all the world will speak one tongue, one universal language, is dawning again! There will be one flock and one shepherd! National cultures, where are you?'[20] Instead, Herder insisted on the importance of individual cultures. Each culture is unique, and its unique character is expressed first and foremost in its language: not in the language of the educated, but in that of the people, the *Volk*, with its folk-songs and folk-tales. By a linguistic slippage, *Volk* can also mean the nation as a whole. Thus the spirit of a nation (*Volksgeist*) is best expressed in its popular culture, a conviction that was to inspire innumerable Romantic nationalists, scholars and ethnographers.[21]

Herder's conception of the *Volk* was developed by the German Romantics and particularly by Johann Gottlieb Fichte in his

---

[19] Herder *et al.*, *Von deutscher Art und Kunst*, ed. Edna Purdie (Oxford, 1924), p. 125.
[20] J. G. *Herder on Social and Political Culture*, ed. and tr. F. M. Barnard (Cambridge, 1969), p. 209.
[21] See Peter Burke, *Popular Culture in Early Modern Europe* (London, 1978), esp. ch. 1: 'The Discovery of the People'.

patriotic *Reden an die deutsche Nation* (*Addresses to the German Nation*), delivered in Berlin in 1807–8 when Prussia, after its defeat at Jena, was occupied by Napoleon's troops. Hence Fichte defines the German nation by contrast with an other which, as in Goethe and Lessing, is the French; and he makes the difference primarily a linguistic one. Although Fichte says little about the Jews, later writers would soon transform his contrast between the Germans and the French into a contrast between Germans and Jews.

Fichte's account of the German character bases it on the German language. Language, for Fichte, is crucial in defining nationhood. Language determines consciousness, not the other way round. Although a language undergoes superficial changes, it always remains 'the same living linguistic force of nature', original and irrepressible.[22] The key words here, 'ursprünglich' (original), 'Kraft' (force), and 'Natur' (nature), exercise tremendous rhetorical power. They enable Fichte to dignify German by associating it with Greek, another 'original' language, and thus placing the Germans on a par with classical antiquity. By contrast, the Romance languages are spoken by the descendants of those Germanic tribes which, instead of staying in their northern European homeland, migrated south, came under Roman influence, and lost their original language. The language they adopted, Latin, was not for them an original language, but a superficial and artificial acquisition. Hence the Romance languages are not really alive, but cut off from the primal energies of German. Only an 'Ursprache' or 'primal language', like German (or Greek), can give rise to true philosophy and literature, or as Fichte prefers to call them, 'Denken' and 'Dichtung'.

For the nineteenth century, Fichte provided an especially trenchant formulation of the myth of the *Volk* as a transpersonal continuity constituted through language. Membership of the *Volk*, thus understood, required an intimacy with its language which the outsider could never attain. While Fichte's outsiders were the French, for later generations they were the Jews. Fichte's linguistic mysticism powerfully supported the notion of the 'hidden language of the Jew'—the idea that, no matter how

---

[22] Fichte, *Reden an die deutsche Nation*, ed. Reinhard Lauth (Hamburg, 1978), p. 62.

impeccably the Jew speaks and writes German, it is not his true language and serves merely to conceal his true identity, which will always be revealed as Jewish through verbal peculiarities, tones of voice, or body-language.

The 'hidden language' which debarred the Jew from joining the German *Volk* was most influentially described by Wagner in his essay 'Das Judenthum in der Musik' ('Judaism in Music', 1850). While this essay gave impetus to the pseudo-scientific racial anti-semitism that developed later in the century, its own arguments are based on a conflict between modern capitalism and the integrity of the German *Volk*. It presents a concentrated catalogue of 'Jewish' images which in the following hundred years would become standard in antisemitic polemic.

Wagner's essay starts from the assumption that Germans have an instinctive antipathy towards Jews, and that liberals, in pursuit of an abstract principle, have tried to ignore this antipathy and thus brought about the emancipation of the Jews; the Jews, however, in reality as opposed to abstract principle, possess economic power; in art this takes the form of 'die Verjüdung [*sic*] der modernen Kunst', the Judaization of modern art, which is so obvious as to need no evidence: Jews turn the sacred products of genius into marketable commodities.[23]

The Jew's physical appearance is repulsive to all Europeans, and therefore a Jew cannot be represented in painting or on the stage unless he is completely idealized. But, above all, the language of the Jew is crucial. Jews speak European languages only as foreigners. They are not members of a linguistic community (a 'Volk'). Hence, lacking an immediate relation to language, the Jew cannot express himself naturally and idiomatically. The true language of the Jews is Hebrew, though it survives only as a dead language. The Jews thus cannot be creative; they can only mimic the authentic linguistic creations of others.

Moreover, the Jew's manner of speaking is alien and unpleasant: Wagner describes it by near-untranslatable onomatopoeia as 'ein zischender, schrillender, summsender und murksender Lautausdruck', a hissing, squealing, buzzing snuffle, combined with offensive departures from German idiom. And this noise does not

---

[23] Wagner, *Gesammelte Schriften und Dichtungen* (Leipzig, 1887; repr. Hildesheim, 1976), v. 66–85 (p. 68). The essay was reissued with additions in 1869.

express any strong feelings, for Jews in contact with non-Jews are cold and unemotional, except when their own egoistic interests are at stake; and when they do express emotion, that appears ridiculous. Jews therefore are even less capable of song than of speech, for song is passionate speech, the language of emotions. Jews' attempts to sing are therefore utterly repulsive.

How then have Jews managed to enter the musical world? Modern society is increasingly dominated by money. Culture ('Bildung') has increasingly become a purchasable commodity. It has therefore been possible for Jews to acquire culture of a sort:

The cultured Jew has taken the most unspeakable pains to strip off all the obvious tokens of his lower co-religionists: in many a case he has even held it wise to make a Christian baptism wash away the traces of his origin. This zeal, however, has never got so far as to let him reap the hoped-for fruits: it has conducted only to his utter isolation, and to making him the most heartless of all human beings; to such a pitch, that we have been bound to lose even our earlier sympathy for the tragic history of his stock. He arrogantly tore asunder his connexion with the former comrades in his suffering, but he has remained unable to replace it by a new connexion with that society in which he has soared up. He stands in correlation with none but those who need his money: and never yet has money thriven to the point of knitting a goodly bond betwixt man and man. Alien and apathetic stands the educated Jew in midst of a society he does not understand, with whose tastes and aspirations he does not sympathise, whose history and evolution have always been indifferent to him.[24]

Cut off from a community, the Jew is incapable of love and of creation, for the latter requires some residual contact with what Wagner, in organic imagery that echoes both Herder and Fichte, calls the soil of the national spirit ('mit ihrem natürlichen Boden, dem wirklichen Volksgeiste').[25] The isolated Jew has nothing to express; and if he learns the means of expression, he can merely imitate, like a parrot. In music, the Jew is thrown back on the music of the synagogue, which is fossilized, like the whole of Jewish cultural life. Synagogue music is as disgusting as the Jews' language: 'Who has not been seized with a feeling of the greatest revulsion, of horror mingled with the absurd, at hearing

---

[24] Wagner, *Judaism in Music and Other Essays*, tr. W. A. Ellis (Lincoln, Nebr., and London, 1995), pp. 77–8 (trans. modified).

[25] 'Das Judenthum in der Musik', p. 75.

that sense-and-sound confounding gurgling, yodelling and cackling, which no intentional caricature can make more repugnant than as offered here in full, in naive seriousness?'[26] When the Jew tries to compose music, what he produces is ultimately inspired by synagogue music, just as German compositions are ultimately inspired by German folk-songs, and he can only imitate superficial features of German music. This licenses Wagner's attack on Meyerbeer and Mendelssohn. Heine and Börne are mentioned, the former as a pseudo-poet who at least exposed, through his satires, the dishonesty of his fellow-Jews, the latter as a pitiable being who sought redemption from Jewishness. There is only one way, however—Wagner concludes—that Jews can be redeemed from the curse of Jewishness: 'the redemption of Ahasuerus—perishing (der *Untergang*)!'[27] Although, with hindsight, this may sound ominously like a call for the physical extermination of the Jews, Wagner appears to mean their complete assimilation.[28] He does not believe in immutable racial differences but in *völkisch* characteristics which, though tenacious, can be changed by effort. Like Herder, he is insisting that Jews must discard their distinctive qualities to become integrated into humanity.

The hidden language of the Jew appears also in Wagner's music-dramas. Many of their characters can be identified with some confidence as 'Jewish'. Beckmesser in *Die Meistersinger von Nürnberg* represents the philistine, uncreative Jew, the castrated Klingsor in *Parsifal* represents the unmanly Jew, Kundry the sensual and Oriental Jewish woman, Alberich in the *Ring* the Jewish capitalist.[29] The clearest case is Alberich's brother Mime. Mime's very name (adapted from Wagner's Scandinavian source) implies the imitativeness of the Jew, and he was recognized by contemporaries as a Jewish figure. Gustav Mahler complained of the tenor Julius Spielmann, who introduced 'unforgivable clowning' and 'Jewish jargon' to the role of Mime at the Vienna

---

[26] Wagner, *Judaism in Music*, p. 91 (trans. modified).

[27] Ibid. 100 (trans. modified). Ahasuerus is the Wandering Jew.

[28] See Dieter Borchmeyer, 'The Question of Anti-Semitism', in Ulrich Müller and Peter Wapnewski (eds.), *Wagner Handbook* (Cambridge, Mass., 1992), pp. 166–85 (p. 174).

[29] See Paul Lawrence Rose, *Wagner: Race and Revolution* (London, 1992), pp. 66–72, 111–12; Marc A. Weiner, *Richard Wagner and the Anti-Semitic Imagination* (Lincoln, Nebr., and London, 1995).

Hofoper in September 1898: 'No doubt, with Mime, Wagner intended to ridicule the Jews (with all the traits he bestowed on them—excessive humility and greed—the jargon is textually and musically so cleverly suggested) but for God's sake, it must not be exaggerated and overdone, as Spielmann does it.[30] Through Mime Wagner dramatizes the hidden language of the Jew. In Act 2 of *Siegfried*, the hero returns to the cave where he was brought up by the hateful, alien Mime. Siegfried has killed the dragon Fafner and gained the Nibelungs' treasure. Having swallowed some of the dragon's blood, he is able to understand the language of animals, including that of the Forest Bird who advises him; he is also able to understand the hidden language of the Jew. So when Mime creeps up to him, rubbing his hands and making 'flattering gestures', Siegfried is not taken in.[31] In an incongruously tender and coaxing voice, Mime explicitly declares his intention of drugging Siegfried, murdering him in his sleep, and keeping the treasure for himself. Thus, thanks to the dragon's blood (Siegfried's contact with nature), Siegfried is enabled to perceive the duplicity of the Jew and to respond by killing him.

Wagner thus founded a lasting myth of the loveless, rational Jew cut off from the warm, intuitive German folk-community and seeking vengefully to destroy it through money and the intellect. But the myth was still to be reinforced by the seeming authority of science, which lent ominous power to the concept of race. Race provided a narrower criterion than language for membership of the *Volk*. A language, after all, can be learnt, along with a way of life and a set of values. Even the Prussian historian Heinrich von Treitschke admitted that several Jews, including Felix Mendelssohn and Gabriel Riesser, had become 'deutsche Männer' imbued with the German spirit.[32] For some antisemites, language was not exclusive enough. They sought more subtle distinguishing marks. The Romantic novelist Achim von Arnim warned in 1811 against 'hidden' Jews, asserting that Jews no longer observe their own religious laws and thus infiltrate society all the more effectively. His main example of the ineradic-

[30] Henry-Louis de La Grange, *Gustav Mahler*, ii: *Vienna: The Years of Challenge (1897–1904)* (Oxford, 1995), p. 113.

[31] See Wagner, *Die Musikdramen* (Munich, 1978), p. 710.

[32] Treitschke, 'Unsere Aussichten', *Preußische Jahrbücher*, 44 (1879), 559–76 (p. 573).

able nature of the Jew is the ancient libel of the Jewish smell or *foetor judaicus*, on which he spends some time, speculating on whether it comes from eating garlic or is an acid or alkaline effluxion.[33] Later in the century, such conceptions were built into a quasi-scientific racialism which located 'Jewishness' in ineradicable physical traits that made it impossible for Jews to mix with Germans.

First the discourse and then the 'science' of race were emerging by mid-century, and not only in Germany.[34] 'Race is everything: literature, science, art—in a word, civilization, depends on it', wrote the Scottish anatomist Robert Knox in 1850.[35] And: 'the racial question overshadows all other problems of history', claimed Comte Arthur de Gobineau (1816–82) in his *Essai sur l'inégalité des races humaines* (1853–5), a book more influential in Germany than in France.[36] Assumptions about race were all-pervasive. They drew partly on physiology, with its attempts to classify humanity into different types, and partly on the new science of comparative philology, which, on assumptions going back to Herder, suggested that a language could provide evidence about the cultural and even physical character of its speakers, and thus suggested an easy move from language to race. Hence the derivation of Indo-European languages from a common ancestor, one of whose descendants was Sanskrit, became confused with the supposed origin of civilization from ancient India. Speakers of Indo-European languages were imagined as racially akin (sometimes as 'Aryans'), and as radically different from speakers of Semitic languages.

Although racial science now seems dated, objectionable, and often cranky, it was part of the normal science of its day, and it would be hard to draw a division on the spectrum that connects reputable studies in physical anthropology with those which harness anthropology to familiar stereotypes. Thus the Franco-Russian anthropologist Deniker put forward a classification of

---

[33] Arnim, 'Über die Kennzeichen des Judentums', in *Schriften*, ed. Roswitha Burwick *et al.*, 6 vols. (Frankfurt, 1990–2), vi. 362–87.

[34] See George L. Mosse, *Toward the Final Solution: A History of European Racism* (London, 1978); Robert J. C. Young, *Colonial Desire: Hybridity in Theory, Culture and Race* (London, 1995).

[35] Knox, *The Races of Men: A Fragment* (London, 1850), p. v.

[36] Quoted in Michael D. Biddiss, *Father of Racist Ideology: The Social and Political Thought of Count Gobineau* (London, 1970), pp. 112–13.

the six principal European races that was widely accepted as standard, though with variations of terminology: they were Northern, Eastern, Western (later 'Alpine'), Ibero-insular, Littoral (later 'Mediterranean'), and Adriatic (or 'Dinaric'). What the English translation calls the Northern type became in German 'nordisch' and returned to English as 'Nordic man'. Deniker's account of this type, illustrated by a photograph of a young Sussex farmer, is severely factual: '*Fair, dolichocephalic race of very high stature*, which may be called the *Northern Race*, because its representatives are grouped together almost exclusively in the north of Europe.[37] Deniker was hardly to blame for the insouciant enthusiasm with which racial ideologists seized on this description and endowed it with moral qualities. Thus a few years later Ludwig Woltmann gives Nordic man the Linnaean and therefore more scientific-sounding name 'homo europaeus flavus', contrasted with 'homo mediterraneus' (Mediterranean) and 'homo brachycephalus' (Alpine), and credits him with the greatest cultural achievements thanks to his larger brain and slow sexual maturation.[38] Woltmann goes on to argue that all the great men of the Italian Renaissance were of Nordic descent. Others make yet more absurd claims: the mummy of Rameses II of Egypt, already a popular candidate for honorary European or Jewish status in the 1860s, was later claimed as a descendant of the Nordic race.[39]

Against this background, an intense debate was conducted in academic and semi-academic publications, some of it by Jewish thinkers, about the nature of the Jewish race.[40] Often the authority

[37] J. Deniker, *The Races of Man: An Outline of Anthropology and Ethnography* (London, 1900), pp. 326, 328. 'Dolichocephalic' means long-headed, in contrast to 'brachycephalic'.

[38] Ludwig Woltmann, *Die Germanen und die Renaissance in Italien* (Leipzig, 1905), pp. 10, 13. Cf. Hilaire Belloc: 'Behold, my child, the Nordic Man | And be as like him as you can. | His legs are long; | his mind is slow; his hair is lank and made of tow' (*Complete Verse* (London, 1970), p. 221).

[39] A complete difference of opinion on whether Rameses II looked European or Jewish is pointed out by Charles Darwin, *The Descent of Man, and Selection in Relation to Sex*, 2 vols. ([1871] Princeton, 1981), i. 217. For his Nordic character, see Ignaz Zollschan, *Das Rassenproblem unter besonderer Berücksichtigung der theoretischen Grundlagen der jüdischen Rassenfrage* (Vienna and Leipzig, 1910), p. 21.

[40] Useful surveys of this debate are J. M. Judt, *Die Juden als Rasse: Eine Analyse aus dem Gebiete der Anthropologie* (Berlin, n.d. [1903?]), and Elias Auerbach, 'Rassenkunde', *Der Jude*, 5 (1920–1), i. 49–57. See also John M. Efron, *Defenders of the Race: Jewish Doctors and Race Science in Fin-de-Siècle Europe* (New Haven and London, 1994).

of science was invoked not to question a conventional assumption but to seek a solid basis for it. Most agreed with Richard Andree's assertion, in a widely-read work of popular ethnography, that there was a recognizable Jewish type:

We all know the 'Jewish type', we immediately distinguish the Jew by his face, his entire bearing, the way he holds his head, his gesticulation, and even the most assimilated Jew, if the expression may be permitted, can still be recognized by some feature of his race. [. . .] But if we are required to define this type and provide any general formula for it, we find ourselves at a loss, for our terminology and our powers of definition lag behind, unable to keep pace with our emotion and our intuition.[41]

It was, however, difficult for racial science to anchor this vague perception in demonstrable traits, especially as, from the outset, physical traits were mingled with cultural and moral qualities. Thus Andree includes among racial traits the Jews' supposed fecundity, their disinclination for manual labour, and their inability to master languages perfectly.[42] Many traits ascribed to Jews are clearly environmental, especially within the elaborate pathology of European Jews. 'The European Jews are distinguished both from the people among whom they live and from the non-European Jews by a *greater* percentage of physically defective individuals. Along with bandy legs, flat feet, round backs, flat chests they are much more often afflicted by hereditary constitutional ailments, such as gout, diabetes, rheumatism.'[43] The nervousness, hysteria, and insanity engendered by modern urban life applied especially to the Jews. 'The Jew is the most nervous and, in so far, the most modern of men', wrote the anti-antisemite Anatole Leroy-Beaulieu.[44] Worse still, they were considered so prone to insanity that some doctors spoke of a specific 'psychosis judaica'.[45]

In trying to classify humanity, physical anthropology sought

---

[41] Andree, *Zur Volkskunde der Juden* (Bielefeld and Leipzig, 1881), p. 37.

[42] Ibid. 79, 116–17.

[43] C. H. Stratz, *Was sind Juden? Eine ethnographisch-anthropologische Studie* (Vienna and Leipzig, 1903), p. 19. On this vast subject, see Sander L. Gilman, *The Jew's Body* (London and New York, 1991).

[44] Leroy-Beaulieu, *Israel among the Nations: A Study of the Jews and Antisemitism*, tr. Frances Hellman (London, 1895), pp. 168–9.

[45] M. J. Gutmann, *Über den heutigen Stand der Rasse und Krankheitsfrage der Juden* (Munich, 1920), p. 42.

criteria that were unaffected by environment. A favourite was skull measurement. 'Aryans', and especially Germans, were dolichocephalic; Jews were predominantly brachycephalic, which was confusing for those who wanted to classify them as Semites and associate them with the long-headed Arabs of the present. Skulls of ancient inhabitants of Palestine were not available for comparison. Another popular criterion was the colour of hair and eyes, and here Jews showed a bewildering diversity. Although Jews were conventionally supposed to be dark-haired, visitors to Palestine remarked on the large number of fair-haired, blue-eyed, and fair-skinned children to be seen there, while in parts of eastern Europe fair-haired or red-haired Jews outnumbered dark ones.[46] The German biologist Rudolf Virchow in 1875–6 tested racial claims empirically by organizing a national survey of 6,758,827 German and Jewish schoolchildren to see what colours of hair, skin, and eyes predominated. He found that while the majority of Jewish schoolchildren had brown hair and brown eyes, 32 per cent of them had fair hair and 19 per cent had blue eyes.[47] This he attributed to large-scale intermarriage in the past. Maurice Fishberg's investigations among Jews in New York demolished the notion that Jews normally had hooked noses and showed that the predominant type of nose among Jews was the straight or Greek type.[48] The notion of a pure Jewish or a pure German race therefore seemed chimerical. Such inquiries may seem pedantic and distasteful, but they served a purpose in refuting those antisemitic arguments that claimed an empirical basis.

These investigations made it difficult to sustain the claim that the Jewish race was uniform and immutable, a view that pre-dates anthropology and is rooted in the conception of Jews as a fossil people frozen in a rigid and unchangeable religion. Such assumptions seemed to find support from archaeology. Modern Jews were supposed to resemble 'Semites' depicted on Egyptian tombs. The authors of a work on physical anthropology, published at

[46] A. H. Sayce, 'The White Race of Palestine', *Nature*, 38 (2 Aug. 1888), 321–3; M. J. bin Gorion, *Vom östlichen Judentum* (Berlin and Vienna, 1918), p. 12; Heinrich York-Steiner, *Die Kunst als Jude zu leben* (Leipzig, 1928), p. 349.

[47] Virchow, 'Gesammtbericht über die von der deutschen anthropologischen Gesellschaft veranlassten Erhebungen über die Farbe der Haut, der Haare und der Augen der Schulkinder in Deutschland', *Archiv für Anthropologie*, 16 (1886), 275–475 (statistics from pp. 298–9).

[48] Fishberg, *The Jews: A Study of Race and Environment* (London, 1911), p. 79.

Philadelphia in 1860, allege that a Hebrew on a Chaldean monument of the seventh century BC looks exactly like the leading Jewish citizen of Mobile, Alabama.[49] Yet the claim that Jews have always looked distinctive can be refuted by asking why, in the Middle Ages, they were obliged to wear yellow badges to identify themselves.[50] By the turn of the century, the better-informed racial anthropologists agreed that there was no homogeneous Jewish race. The features that had been thought characteristically Jewish could also be found elsewhere. Stratz quotes travellers to show that the 'Jewish type' can also be found among Japanese, Creek and Choctaw Indians, Indonesians and Papuans, and adds: 'I can testify from my own experience that I have encountered noble Jewish faces not only in Javanese princely families, but also in ancient German and French aristocratic families and likewise in old Dutch patrician families. Finally I may point out that among the numerous busts of Roman emperors there are not a few that show the Jewish type.'[51]

Faced with the palpable diversity of Jews, racial theorists tried to classify Jews into sub-groups. In 1863 Carl Vogt proposed a physical basis for the familiar cultural division of Jews into Sephardim (from the Mediterranean area) and Ashkenazim (from Germany and eastern Europe):

[W]e find chiefly in the North, in Russia and Poland, Germany and Bohemia, a tribe of Jews frequently with red hair, short beard, pug nose, small grey cunning eyes, massive trunk, round face and broad cheek bones, resembling many Sclavonian tribes of the North. In the East, on the contrary, and about the Mediterranean, as well as in Portugal and in Holland, we find the Semitic stock with long black hair and beard, large almond-shaped eyes with a melancholy expression, oval face and prominent nose; in short, that type represented in the portraits of Rembrandt.[52]

These categories seemed to offer a scientific distinction between the admirable, long-headed, Sephardic Jew and the repellent,

---

[49] J. C. Nott and A. R. Gliddon, *Types of Mankind* (Philadelphia, 1860), quoted in Fishberg, *The Jews*, pp. 90–2.   [50] Fishberg, *The Jews*, p. 92.

[51] Stratz, *Was sind Juden?*, p. 24.

[52] Vogt, *Lectures on Man* (London, 1864), p. 433. The distinction is developed by Fishberg, *The Jews*, pp. 108–11. On the well-established cultural distinction, see H. J. Zimmels, *Ashkenazim and Sephardim: Their Relations, Differences, and Problems as Reflected in the Rabbinical Responsa* (London, 1958).

short-headed Jew of Germany and Poland. This could easily be translated, as it was by the reactionary German nationalist Langbehn, into a distinction between the noble Jews of the past and the contemptible Jews of the present: 'It is a long way from Abraham, Job, Isaiah, the Psalmist to present-day Talmudists, stockjobbers, reporters; as far as from the noble to the vulgar.'[53] Though widely accepted for a time, the distinction between Sephardim and Ashkenazim was not supported by cranial measurements or examinations of hair and eye colour, and Zionist anthropologists, intent on establishing the unity of the Jewish race, roundly rejected it.[54]

Another possible explanation for Jewish diversity was that, contrary to popular belief, their apparent seclusion had been undermined by continual interbreeding, so that the very notion of a unified Jewish race became chimerical. Some ascribed diversity to the interbreeding in pre-Exilic times between the ancient Jews and the peoples they found in Palestine, so that the Jews were a mixed race which had acquired a certain uniformity in subsequent millennia. It remained in dispute whether the peoples they mixed with were Hittites, Central Asians, or negroes encountered in Africa.[55] Given antisemitic prejudice and Jewish prohibitions on exogamy, interbreeding in the Diaspora period seemed less likely, though Fishberg argues that the repeated prohibitions of intermarriage by Church Councils imply that it was common, and he also thinks that the adoption of Judaism by the Khazars in the eighth century caused much intermingling and probably produced the basis of the eastern European Jewish population.[56] These speculations derived their point from their social implications. For if Jews did not constitute a distinct race, then the barriers to their assimilation into European life were obviously absurd and should be dismantled.

In pursuit of this cause, investigators increasingly argued that many of the Jews' physical differences resulted from their

---

[53] [Julius Langbehn], *Rembrandt als Erzieher. Von einem Deutschen*, Illustrierte Volksausgabe (Weimar, 1922), p. 36; 1st pub. 1890.

[54] Accepted e.g. by Deniker, *The Races of Man*, p. 424, and Fishberg, *The Jews*, p. 106; rejected on craniometric grounds by Judt, *Die Juden als Rasse*, and Zollschan, *Das Rassenproblem*, pp. 36–42.

[55] See Moritz Alsberg, *Rassenmischung im Judenthum* (Hamburg, 1891) (Hittites); Judt, *Die Juden als Rasse* (Central Asians); Stratz, *Was sind Juden?* (negroes).

[56] Fishberg, *The Jews*, pp. 191–2.

environment. Some argued that the Jews assumed the physical character of the various peoples they lived among, so that the German Jew represented a markedly different type from the English, Russian, or American Jew.[57] The poor physique found among Jewish army recruits could not be a racial trait, since biblical Jews were successful warriors, but must be due to life in the European ghetto.[58] The Jew's slight build and his hasty and timorous movements were caused by undernourishment and oppression: both disappeared among immigrants who had left eastern Europe for the United States.[59]

The racial science pursued by liberals, whether Jewish like Fishberg or Gentile like Virchow, thus arrived at results unpleasing to antisemites. The latter were obliged to transfer their emphasis from physical qualities, which can be empirically examined, to emotional or spiritual qualities which, they claim, can be perceived intuitively.

An influential example of this strategy is Houston Stuart Chamberlain's *Die Grundlagen des 19. Jahrhunderts* (*The Foundations of the Nineteenth Century*, 1899), which develops Gobineau's ideas about racial decline. Chamberlain was an Englishman who became an adoptive German and an admirer of Wagner; his second wife was Wagner's daughter Eva. Ironically, he first heard about Wagner's music-dramas from two Jews whom he met in Interlaken in 1875. In the late 1880s he became a member of the inner circle around Cosima Wagner. Chamberlain was asked to write a popular survey of modern culture to be published in the year 1900. He intended a three-part study, but completed only the first, which examines earlier history as a prelude to the nineteenth century.

Chamberlain agrees that race is the key to history. Only a pure race is capable of great achievements. But unlike Gobineau, who thought that pure races were bound to become mixed with inferior ones, Chamberlain thinks that a pure race does not exist naturally but must be brought into being by deliberate breeding. When obliged to define a race, however, he drops his biological pretensions and falls back on intuitive conviction:

[57] Sigmund Feist, *Stammeskunde der Juden: Die jüdischen Stämme der Erde in alter und neuer Zeit* (Leipzig, 1925), p. 28.
[58] Alsberg, *Rassenmischung*, pp. 29–30.   [59] Fishberg, *The Jews*, p. 164.

Nothing is so convincing as the consciousness of the possession of Race. The man who belongs to a distinct, pure race, never loses the sense of it.[60]

The Aryan race, according to Chamberlain, is united not only by physical features but also by its racial soul, which is religious and mystical. The 'Germane' ('Teuton' in the English translation) is active and emotional, but not intellectual: 'he really thinks little in comparison with other Aryans; his gifts impel him to act and to feel.'[61] By contrast, the Jews are materialistic and legalistic; their religion consists merely of external laws and rules; they try to solve the riddle of existence by rational means, instead of the Aryan's intuition. Chamberlain insists that Christ was not a Jew. Besides advancing a pseudo-historical argument that the inhabitants of Galilee were not Jewish, he asserts with intuitive conviction that a Jew could not have founded a religion as Christ did. Christ must have been an Aryan. Similarly, the great figures of the Italian Renaissance must have been 'Germanen'. In Chamberlain's vision of the world, members of a pure race form a beleaguered minority, surrounded by swarms of mixed-race people whom he calls mongrels, mulattos, and mestizos. He illustrates this from the late Roman Empire, when people from all over the Mediterranean mingled in Rome, destroying classical culture and replacing it with a shallow and derivative pseudo-culture, and also from the nations of modern Latin America. Perhaps his imagery is most important: pure races form islands amid the swirling flood of the 'national chaos' ('Völkerchaos'). Such imagery gained resonance at a time when German-speaking communities in an increasingly nationalistic central Europe were said to form 'linguistic islands'.[62]

Chamberlain's book was widely sold, read, and discussed. Three impressions appeared within the first year of publication; a cheap popular edition brought out in 1906 sold over 10,000 copies within ten days and over 100,000 copies by 1915.[63] The Kaiser wrote Chamberlain a fan letter, calling him a liberator who

---

[60] H. S. Chamberlain, *The Foundations of the Nineteenth Century*, tr. John Lees, 2 vols. (London, 1911), i. 269. [61] Ibid. i. 576.

[62] On this concept, see Hartmut Binder, 'Entlarvung einer Chimäre: Die deutsche Sprachinsel Prag', in Maurice Godé *et al.* (eds.), *Allemands, juifs et tchèques à Prague* (Montpellier, 1996), pp. 183–209.

[63] On the reception of the *Foundations*, see Geoffrey G. Field, *Evangelist of Race: The Germanic Vision of Houston Stewart Chamberlain* (New York, 1981), ch. 6.

had aroused 'all the mighty Germanic Aryanism (*das Urarisch-Germanische*) that slumbered within me'.[64] When the English translation appeared in 1911, Bernard Shaw praised it for revealing religious fanaticism as the true enemy of Socialism: 'What Mr. Houston Chamberlain calls the Chaos (meaning the population of mongrels produced by the Roman Pontifical Empire and controlled by the real Judaic Ezekielite Jew who still believes in the dedication of the whole earth by Jehovah to the domination of his chosen people) is an accomplished fact.'[65] It was also one of the few books read by many leading Nazis: by Hitler, Goebbels, Himmler, Hess, Eckart, von Schirach, and Rosenberg. Chamberlain's attribution of historic achievements to 'Germanen' found enthusiastic support, as did his denial that Christ was a Jew. Artur Dinter, proponent of an eccentric 'spirit-Christianity', is certain that Jesus, far from being a 'race-Jew', was 'the greatest and mightiest antisemite of all time'.[66] The hero of Goebbels's novel *Michael* affirms: 'Christ cannot have been a Jew. I have no need to prove that scientifically. It's just so!'[67] Some go further and claim that the more attractive figures in the Old Testament must have been Aryans. Dinter, who in 1927 founded the German People's Church to promote an Aryan doctrine of salvation, asserts that Esau was plainly an Aryan, good-natured and trusting, Jacob a typical Jew who deceived him.[68]

Chamberlain's slippery concept of race reappears in the accredited racial science which flourished before and under Nazism, both in its more technical and its more popular versions. Thus the standard textbook, *Human Heredity*, whose authors later held high positions under the Third Reich, defines a 'race' vaguely as 'human beings with a like hereditary equipment';[69] one contributor confidently describes the Nordic,

[64] Field, *Evangelist of Race*, p. 252; cf. John C. G. Röhl, *The Kaiser and his Court: Wilhelm II and the Government of Germany*, tr. Terence F. Cole (Cambridge, 1994), p. 205.
[65] G.B.S., 'Our Book-shelf', *Fabian News*, 22 (June 1911), 52–3 (p. 53).
[66] Dinter, 'Die Rassen- und Judenfrage im Lichte des Geistchristentums'; *Der Jud ist schuld . . . ? Diskussionsbuch über die Judenfrage* (Basle, 1932), pp. 95–106 (p. 103).
[67] Joseph Goebbels, *Michael: Ein deutsches Schicksal in Tagebuchblättern* ([1929]; Munich, n.d.), p. 58.
[68] Dinter, *Die Sünde wider das Blut: Ein Zeitroman* (Leipzig, 1921), p. 133.
[69] Erwin Baur, Eugen Fischer, and Fritz Lenz, *Human Heredity*, tr. Eden and Cedar Paul (London, 1931), p. 178.

Mediterranean, Alpine, and Dinaric races of Europe, another questions the very existence of the last-named. The final chapter by Fritz Lenz, 'Psychological differences between the leading races of mankind', mainly describes familiar national characteristics; the term 'race' is merely decorative. It includes a familiar account of the Nordic type who owes his technical ability and his gift for mastery over nature to selection by the northern environment, and who, typified by the Vikings, is courageous, enterprising, violent, with a will to power and a talent for political organization, though little empathy with others. The Jew, by contrast, is intelligent and alert, though rarely a genius; good at abstract sciences like physics, gifted at music, with powers of empathy that produce many Jewish actors. Thus familiar stereotypes are lent the authority of science by appearing within the same covers as treatises on anthropology and genetics.

The most successful popularizer was Hans F. K. Günther, the chief racial ideologist associated with Nazism. In 1930 Wilhelm Frick, the Thuringian Nazi leader, established for Günther a Chair of racial hygiene at the University of Jena. Günther's most popular work was *Rassenkunde des deutschen Volkes* (*Racial Study of the German People*, 1922); by 1942 the original work and an abridgement had combined sales of more than 322,000 copies.[70] Günther professes to adhere to physical anthropology, but he slips from physical to spiritual qualities when he offers the following definition of 'race':

A race presents itself in a group of people which differs from all other human groups by its specific combination of physical features and spiritual qualities and repeatedly gives birth only to its like.[71]

The spiritual qualities of Nordic man include, not surprisingly, truthfulness, capacity for judgement, and energy; he is active and practical, daring but also cool and cautious, with a strong sense of duty and high demands from others; he is distant, cool, and reserved towards other people, but has particular emotional depth ('Gemütstiefe') and a strong feeling for freedom and nature. Thus

[70] Gary D. Stark, *Entrepreneurs of Ideology: Neoconservative Publishers in Germany, 1890–1933* (Chapel Hill, NC, 1981), p. 197.
[71] Günther, *Rassenkunde Europas*, 2nd edn. (Munich, 1926), p. 8, emphasis in original.

Günther too is dressing up national stereotypes in quasi-scientific garb.

In doing so, Günther does not reach the absurdity attained by his rival Ludwig Ferdinand Clauss, author of *Die nordische Seele* (*The Nordic Soul*, 1923). Indeed Günther denounced Clauss for adopting an idealistic approach which was based insufficiently on physical anthropology. For Clauss, 'race' is synonymous with the untranslatable term 'Artung', and this in turn with 'style of experience'. Clauss is really talking about familiar national stereotypes, as becomes clear when he illustrates styles of experience from everyday incidents like railway travel: the Nordic man ('der Norde') always looks for an empty compartment and maintains a distance from his fellow-travellers.[72]

Thus the seemingly enormous explanatory power offered by the concept of 'race' dissolves on being sceptically examined. The term resists definition; its function is to confer scientific authority on widely held assumptions about national character. Because these assumptions were familiar, racial theories built on them seemed immediately convincing.

It may seem surprising that such theories should flourish at the high tide of modernity in the early twentieth century. Yet, as we shall see in the next section, modernity was widely felt to be disturbing and destructive, and when, in Marx's words, 'all that is solid melts into air', people understandably look for something solid and unchangeable. Thus the concept of 'race' seemed reassuringly firm, even if it merely reified familiar notions about national character.

Cultural Antisemitism

Building on ideas from Fichte, Nietzsche, and Wagner, some thinkers of the 1920s tried to place antisemitism on a cultural instead of a pseudo-scientific basis. Besides Oswald Spengler, they included such lesser-known figures as Hans Blüher, Wilhelm Stapel, Gerhard Kittel, and Wilhelm Schmidt. Blüher was already a prominent figure in the Wandervogel movement and author of a book

---

[72] Clauss, *Die nordische Seele* (Munich, 1923), p. 27. On Günther and Clauss, see Hans-Jürgen Lutzhöft, *Der Nordische Gedanke in Deutschland 1920–1940* (Stuttgart, 1971).

on male homoeroticism whose many admirers included Kafka and Thomas Mann; Kafka also knew, and agonized over, his anti-semitic treatise *Secessio Judaica*.[73] Stapel was from 1918 onwards editor of *Deutsches Volkstum*, the representative journal for the right-wing intelligentsia. Professing an eccentric variant of Protestant theology, according to which no moral or political action could alleviate man's fallen state, Stapel nevertheless regarded liberal and democratic ideas as an absolute enemy, and considered his own opposition to the Weimar Republic as also a fight against anti-Christian forces. Though a supporter of Hitler as well as a prominent polemicist against Jews in literature, he never joined the National Socialist Party and fell from official favour in the late 1930s.[74] Kittel was a distinguished theologian, who as professor at Tübingen launched a theological dictionary of the New Testament.[75] We have already met Schmidt as professor of anthropology at Vienna University; as a racial theorist, he was indebted especially to Clauss.

These writers represent a tendency that was recognized at the time and defined as 'cultural antisemitism'.[76] They are distinctive in that, to avoid the naïve, discredited discourse of race, they locate difference in a cultural stratum denoted by the terms 'essence' or 'substance', but just as inaccessible to empirical inquiry as Chamberlain's or Günther's 'racial soul'. This cultural, non-racial antisemitism is illustrated in Spengler's *Decline of the West*. Spengler, though an extreme nationalist, is not himself an antisemitic writer, and opposes simple-minded racialism; but anti-semitism is implicit in his claim that cultures are entirely separate from one another. Thus the Renaissance was not a real rediscovery of the alien and inaccessible 'Apollonian' culture of antiquity, but merely a 'pseudomorphosis' within Faustian or Germanic culture. Similarly, the Jews, like the Arabs, belong to Magian culture and therefore cannot impinge on the Faustian or Germanic culture.

---

[73] Franz Kafka, *Tagebücher*, ed. Hans-Gerd Koch, Michael Müller and Malcolm Pasley (Frankfurt, 1990), Textband, pp. 923–4.

[74] See Helmut Thomke, *Politik und Christentum bei Wilhelm Stapel* (Diss., Mainz, 1973), esp. pp. 504–20 on Stapel's antisemitism.

[75] See Albright, *History, Archaeology and Christian Humanism*, ch. 10; Robert P. Ericksen, *Theologians under Hitler: Gerhard Kittel, Paul Althaus and Emanuel Hirsch* (New Haven and London, 1985).

[76] See Erik Nölting, *Das 'zersetzende' Judentum. Eine Auseinandersetzung mit dem kulturellen Antisemitismus* (Berlin, 1924).

Hence Jewish assimilation can only be illusory. According to Spengler's section on 'Jewry', the Jews are now a fossil people who cannot be more than superficially involved in the culture of the young and vigorous Germans.[77]

Spengler's organicism recurs in Stapel's claim that a *Volk* is a natural organism, like a tree or a swarm of bees. To enter another *Volk* would mean altering the roots of one's personality: 'Hence it is impossible for a Chinese to become essentially ('wesenhaft') an Englishman, an Italian essentially a Russian, a Jew essentially a German. He can learn and employ the language and all the remaining cultural forms of the other nation, but he will handle these cultural forms in his innate manner.'[78]

While Stapel tries to reach a national essence beyond language and *Volksgeist*, he also seeks to demonstrate the linguistic Jewishness of Jewish authors by literary analysis. He asserts that the Jew writing German is really writing Yiddish, and illustrates this by a comparison of Heine's folk-songs with those of Eichendorff: 'Heine's songs written in the manner of the German folk-song are without authentic emotion ('nachempfunden'); where he draws on his own depths, it surges forth from a Jewish soul.'[79] Besides some sharp observations, for example on how incongruous the verb 'funkeln' (sparkle) would be in a German folk-song, Stapel tries to discover in Heine's line 'Ich weiß nicht, was soll es bedeuten', with its non-standard inversion, the body-language of the Jew: 'the words enter into our arms and compel us to shrug our shoulders, while the palms of our hands are spread out: a typically Jewish gesture';[80] and in the poem's tentative conclusion Stapel finds 'a model example of Jewish sentimentality, the sentimentality of the head inclined sideways and slightly backward with the abstracted gaze, a posture from which the Jew can often jump with a witty word; for this sentimentality is akin to irony, and lacks the melancholy of German sentimentality'.[81]

These writers agree in giving their antisemitism a strong

---

[77] Spengler, *The Decline of the West*, tr. C. F. Atkinson, 2 vols. (London, 1929), ii. 315–23.

[78] Stapel, *Antisemitismus und Antigermanismus: Über das seelische Problem der Symbiose des deutschen und des jüdischen Volkes* (Hamburg, 1928), p. 17.

[79] Ibid. 31.

[80] For an example of this gesture, see the caricature of Kraus reproduced on the back of the dust jacket of Timms, *Karl Kraus*.   [81] Stapel, *Antisemitismus*, p. 57.

religious colouring which masks its real basis in notions of *Volk* and 'Volkstum' derived from Fichte. Thus Stapel cites Fichte in support of his claim that racial difference is divinely established. Schmidt explicitly rejects the pseudo-biological, materialist race theories of the National Socialists and insists that the crucial difference between Jews and Aryans lies in the 'psychic structure' of the Jews. Since rejecting the Messiah they have been 'a people who, in the deepest region of their souls, have lost contact with their national roots (*ein im tiefsten Seelengrunde ihrer Nation entwurzeltes Volk*)'.[82] Kittel similarly interprets the Jews' fate as tragic punishment for the disobedience of Israel; but his organic language goes back to Fichte when he asserts that the modern Jew is uprooted from his 'Volkstum':

But the poison that really eats into the nation's body (*Volkskörper*) like an uncanny sickness is rootless, homeless, decadent Jewry. It is *this* Jewry that must corrode all genuine religious, cultural, and national ideas that have grown from the people (*Volkstum*), because its rootlessness makes it essentially (*wesenhaft*) separate. It is *this* Jewry that means corrosion (*Zersetzung*). Corrosion can take very different forms. It can be a weary, subtle resignation which is still dangerous because it debilitates and infects others and devours the marrow of a people; it can be a cold, calculating, perhaps self-torturing and self-mutilating relativism; it can be wild agitation and demagogy to which nothing is sacred. It is always spiritual homelessness, and hence poison and dissolution.[83]

Here Kittel uses 'corrosion' to embrace many types of Jew: the *fin-de-siècle* aesthete, the intellectual, and the revolutionary. All are defined as antithetical to the supposedly rooted German, and to the Jews of the Old Testament who were still settled in Palestine.

Blüher continues the racist reinterpretation of religious history by maintaining that the Jews' historical mission was to produce Christ. The guilt of killing him has rendered them all incurably sick in their 'substance'.[84] They are now inwardly broken, no longer a nation, and destructive in their effect on real nations ('Völker'). However, Blüher's own relation to Christianity is unclear. His book on homoeroticism polemicizes against Christian

---

[82] Schmidt, 'Das Rassenprinzip des Nationalsozialismus', *Schönere Zukunft*, 7 (24 July 1932), 999–1000 (p. 999). See also his 'Zur Judenfrage', *Schönere Zukunft*, 9 (21 Jan. 1934), 408–9.   [83] Kittel, *Die Judenfrage* (Stuttgart, 1933), p. 25.
[84] Blüher, *Secessio Judaica. Philosophische Grundlegung der historischen Situation des Judentums und der antisemitischen Bewegung* (Berlin, 1922), p. 20.

disapproval of homosexuality; Blüher treats love and hatred as indispensable, inseparable psychic forces, and argues that it is absurd for Christianity to preach love; the Greeks were more sensible in adjuring people to hate their enemies.[85] Since he also confesses that the intellectual male type that most attracts him is commonly represented by Jews, especially of the noble kind painted by Rembrandt, one wonders about the private motives lying behind the coldly impassive style of *Secessio Judaica*.[86]

Despite the flimsy basis of their antisemitism, these writers maintain that Jews are absolutely alien and unassimilable. Kittel rejects extermination only because it would not work: 'A *violent extermination of Jewry* is not a serious option: if the Spanish Inquisitions and the Russian pogroms did not accomplish this, it will certainly not be possible in the twentieth century.'[87] Instead, he recommends that Jews should be accorded 'guest status' in Germany, with no attempt to assimilate them: they must be forbidden to hold public office; their books must be clearly marked as Jewish; they should not teach at German universities or practise German law; mixed marriages should be forbidden unless the non-Jewish partner becomes a Jew; 'Mischlinge' should suffer legal restrictions till the third or fourth generation. Kittel accepts that these measures will require severity, and that some sensitive people will be spiritually broken by losing their profession which gave their lives meaning, but he insists that, while Germans should appreciate their tragedy and alleviate their hardships, sentimental softness is out of place.

Blüher discusses the 'Jewish problem' from the viewpoint of a right-wing German nationalist who professes to be free from Jew-hatred but to be convinced that Jews and Germans were culturally unassimilable. He says that Jews disguise their lack of healthy substance by means of mimicry. By using this Darwinian image, Blüher translates Wagner's idea that the Jew is always a foreigner into biological language but bases it on a cultural difference. Under the Weimar Republic, according to Blüher, the difference between Jews and Germans is becoming unmistakable, as is shown by the visibility of Jews in public and cultural life, by

---

[85] Blüher, *Die Rolle der Erotik in der männlichen Gesellschaft. Eine Theorie der menschlichen Staatsbildung nach Wesen und Wert*, ed. Hans Joachim Schoeps (Stuttgart, 1962), pp. 192–3.   [86] Blüher, *Die Rolle der Erotik*, p. 189.

[87] Kittel, *Die Judenfrage*, p. 14. Emphasis in original.

the growth of antisemitism, and by the Zionist movement, which Blüher welcomes as a means of finally separating Jews and Germans.

By insisting that Jews and Germans are prevented from mixing by their deep-seated cultural and religious difference, Blüher is able to avoid the gross libels of earlier antisemitism. Instead of misrepresenting the Jews as cowardly, he admits that they fought bravely in the First World War. He admits that a Jewish judge may be unimpeachable in his justice, and that a Jewish man may sincerely love a German woman. Nevertheless, it is impermissible for a Jew to be a German officer or a German judge, or to marry a German woman. Thus all the evidence showing that Jews are suitable citizens of Germany is acknowledged, only to be swept aside. The ostensible absence of animus from Blüher's antisemitism makes it peculiarly chilling, and never more so than when he prophesies that the Jews will attract hostility all over the world and suffer a pogrom on a worldwide scale—except in Germany:

The global pogrom is coming, without a doubt. Germany will be the only country that draws back from murder. [. . .] It is ignoble to torment the disarmed enemy. The German is not a Frenchman.[88]

Under the dignified guise of 'culture', this variety of antisemitism relies on a biological discourse that is as dehumanizing as the racialism discussed earlier. In his rejoinder of 1924, Erik Nölting argues that the national culture is not an organism but an organization, resulting from centuries of shared experience, but able to absorb anybody, though not overnight; and thanks to the presence of Jews in Germany for two thousand years, a virtually unique 'cultural symbiosis' has indeed taken place. Nölting also, and equally plausibly, charges cultural antisemites with nostalgia for a pre-modern Romantic Germany in which the Jew could still be imagined as an alien predator; but this Germany has long since been superseded by the modern, capitalist world which needs to be accepted.

Nostalgia is apparent in the literary text that best illustrates cultural antisemitism, Hermann Bahr's novel *Die Rotte Korahs*

---

[88] Blüher, *Secessio Judaica*, p. 67. Cf. the predictions of the Prussian missionary E. Schaeffer in 1919, quoted in Clark, *The Politics of Conversion*, p. 282.

(*Korah's Rabble*, 1919). Throughout his career, Bahr's commitments were notoriously protean, and the novel represents the closing of a circle. As a young man Bahr was an extreme antisemite and German nationalist, anxious for the union of Austria with Germany, and closely associated with Georg von Schönerer. In 1883 an inflammatory speech at a dinner in memory of Richard Wagner got Bahr expelled from the University of Vienna. Since his outspoken political views made him unacceptable at any other Austrian university, he moved to Berlin, where his interests shifted from politics to new literary movements. Back in Vienna, he energized the 'Jung-Wien' group, whose members (Schnitzler, Hofmannsthal, Beer-Hofmann, etc.) were mainly Jews or of Jewish descent. In 1914 Bahr officially returned to the Catholic Church. He assumed the stance of an Austrian patriot, supported the War in the hope that it would unite Germany and Austria, and contributed, like Hofmannsthal and many others, to the construction of a nationalist Austrian myth. Although Bahr opposed racial antisemitism, he did not think that his ideal Austria could accommodate a population of unbaptized Jews.[89]

Die Rotte Korahs, like Spengler's *Decline*, was written during the War and published immediately afterwards. Its action is slight, serving mainly to allow various characters to deliver long and impassioned speeches on Austrian identity and the Jewish problem. Set in 1917, it celebrates Catholic Austria, typified by its central character, Ferdinand von Držić, who, having been wounded at the front, is now a diplomat. It is structured round a series of conversations: with Ferdinand's friend, a racist antisemite; with the self-hating Jew Dr Adolf Beer; with Ferdinand's lawyer, a Christian of Jewish descent; with Ferdinand's father, a 'good Austrian' and pious Catholic; and finally with the novel's supreme authority, the Canon (*Domherr*) whose attachment to St Stephen's Cathedral in Vienna also places him at the physical centre of Catholic Austria.

After the sudden death of a notoriously dishonest Jewish financier called Jason (originally Jakobsohn), Ferdinand discovers that he is Jason's natural son and heir to his huge fortune. At first, feeling that he has had a hateful new identity forced on him, he is

---

[89] See Donald G. Daviau, 'Hermann Bahr und der Antisemitismus, Zionismus und die Judenfrage', *Literatur und Kritik*, 221/222 (Feb.–Mar. 1988), 21–41.

inclined to reject the legacy. However, he learns from his advisers that Jewishness is a spiritual, not a physical quality: 'A Jew (*Ein Jud*) is anyone to whom money is more important than people.'[90] Jewishness therefore means the materialism characteristic of modernity. The Jewish 'poison' cannot be eradicated from Western society: even if all the Jews were killed, Jewish ancestry, however remote, is indelible. But Jews are separated from others by the crime of deicide, which, according to the Jewish Dr Beer, has made them the tragic nation. From the Christian viewpoint represented in the novel by the Canon, however, there is no longer a Jewish nation, nor has there been one since the Crucifixion: by their rejection of Christ the Jews forfeited their status as the chosen people and have been scattered over the earth by way of punishment. The Scriptures command the spirit to overcome the flesh, as illustrated by Jesus' rejection of his mother and brothers when they sought to dissuade him from his mission. Ferdinand is called upon to perform an analogous act by being placed in a position to choose between the Jewish identity resulting from his fleshly descent and his spiritual identity as an Austrian Catholic. Thus he is, however remotely, a type of Christ.

The novel sharply distinguishes cultural antisemitism, that is, opposition to the materialistic 'Jewishness' embodied in 'Jews of all races', from the common antisemitism that attacks Jews on racial grounds (p. 424). The Canon even condemns the latter as 'the racial madness' which is 'the curse of our time' (p. 419). However, materialism is particularly represented by the modern urbanized and westernized Jews. It is they, not the Jews in general, who are under a curse which condemns them to a nomadic existence and forbids them to take root in the soil. They are not a nation ('Volk') but merely a rootless horde. The Zionists may succeed in striking roots in Palestine: at the least, they are upright and dedicated Jews who aim to restore their nation's strength.

The case against modern Jews is delivered by one of them, Dr Beer, and underpinned by his own gifts. He is a doctor who has distinguished himself by bravery at the front, and would like to return, but is retained by his medical superior for his exceptional operating skill. His self-hating discourse is directed, not against talmudic Judaism, which he respects for its logical achievements,

---

[90] Bahr, *Die Rotte Korahs* (Berlin, 1919), p. 314. Future page references in text.

nor the still unassimilated Jews of eastern Europe, but against westernized Jews: 'the Jews of here and now, who have made the name Jew a horror to all nations' p. 102). Since he is himself one, he has to display a self-cancelling irony which is an extreme version of the over-intellectuality ascribed to Jews. To explain his desire to return to the front, he disclaims all higher motives by saying that he is acting from pure egoism, to prove that no action by Jews can alter Gentile's low opinion of them. He then launches into an amazing tirade against modern Jews, declaring that only a Jew can know enough about them to be a true antisemite. They are masters of modernity because they are never for an instant distracted by morality or conscience from the modern imperative of commerce. The Jews have had their hateful qualities developed by Gentile maltreatment (confining them in ghettos, restricting them to usury); Gentiles have thus bred the ultra-cynical Jewish type, the 'Epikores' (unbeliever), for whom everything is merely a source of profit. Thus Gentiles have made Jews scapegoats, training them to run the modern commercial world from which Gentiles too want to profit but are not quite unscrupulous or intelligent enough; and when Gentiles and Jews are involved in dishonesty, it is always the Jew who is left to bear the blame, as the current trial of the financier Jason demonstrates. At the end of the novel, however, Beer undermines his own irony and earns Ferdinand's respect by his commitment to Zionism. Exceptions like him, however, do nothing to exonerate the great mass of modern Jews, who are 'Korah's rabble'. In Numbers 16, Korah and his followers disputed the authority of Moses and Aaron; their rebellion was punished when they were swallowed up by the earth.

The novel is, however, ambiguous. Bahr's best biographer has described it as 'Bahr's strongest and most convincing rejoinder to racial antisemitism'.[91] However, it expresses a *cultural* anti-semitism in which anti-Jewish prejudices from several sources converge. It affirms (through the Canon) that the Jews are collectively accursed in the Christian era, and (through Beer, who as a self-hating Jew knows what he is talking about) that the westernized Jews are cynical materialists. Although it pretends

[91] Donald G. Daviau, *Der Mann von Übermorgen: Hermann Bahr 1863–1934* (Vienna, 1984), p. 187.

to decouple 'Jewishness' from actual Jews, the two remain closely linked. The Zionist solution is presented, even by Beer, as one in which even the Zionists do not really believe, and which can only succeed by divine intervention. They hope 'that such an enormous sacrifice, presented in such purity, cannot be futile but must be answered by a miracle' (p. 473). Thus Zionism is brought back within the novel's Christian framework. If the Jews perform a supreme act of sacrifice, entirely renouncing the westernized, materialistic character which is the ultimate result of their rejection of Christ, then God may reward them by a miracle. Bahr constructs an Austrian-Christian cosmos with Vienna at the centre, Palestine at the edge, and no scope for human activity without divine assistance.

We have then a succession of overlapping varieties of antisemitism: *völkisch*, racial, and cultural antisemitism. When one variety becomes untenable, another, more immune to disproof, takes its place.

The Anti-Modern Mentality

Are we, however, to see racial theory not merely as a reaction to modernity but as providing a new basis for antisemitism and thus leading to the Holocaust? The attempt has been made to chart a continuous growth of German antisemitism from Luther's anti-Jewish diatribes through nineteenth- and twentieth-century racism to the fantasies of Hitler;[92] and to postulate an 'eliminationist mind-set' shared by those who wanted the Jews to have their objectionable traits removed by European culture and by those who wanted them to be exterminated.[93] Historical research does not disclose a national obsession with antisemitism. While antisemitism undoubtedly developed in Germany from 1880 to 1930, historians have found that for most Germans, even at that period, antisemitism was not prominent as a distinct issue. No antisemitic political party under the Wilhelmine Empire lasted long, and antisemitism did not rank high among people's reasons for

---

[92] See e.g. the opening chapters of Lucy Dawidowicz, *The War Against the Jews* (London, 1975); P. L. Rose, *Revolutionary Antisemitism from Kant to Wagner* (Princeton, 1990). Such efforts are discussed critically in Katz, *The Holocaust in Historical Context*, i. 227–35.

[93] Goldhagen, *Hitler's Willing Executioners*, p. 69 and *passim*.

supporting Nazism.[94] We also need to distinguish casual from doctrinaire antisemitism.[95] There have certainly been numerous fanatics, like Grattenauer, Marr, and Dühring, for whom antisemitism was a major or even overriding part of their world-view. The scarcely believable trashiness of their writings, however, makes it hard to see such pamphleteers as pillars of modern antisemitism.[96] The responsibility for antisemitism cannot lie solely with such doctrinaire antisemites. But are we then to suppose, with Goldhagen, that most Germans were antisemitic, differing only in whether their antisemitism was latent or manifest? This might seem tempting when we find disparaging comments about Jews even in the letters of the humane novelist Theodor Fontane, who wrote in 1886 to his friend Georg Friedländer that 'the German spirit is infinitely superior to the Jewish one'.[97] Are we to lump Fontane together with Marr and Dühring? Rather, his example shows that antisemitism, whether casual or doctrinaire, rarely appears in isolation. Usually it forms part, and not necessarily a prominent part, of a wider world-view.

In order to explain the continuity of antisemitic beliefs in Imperial Germany despite the failure of antisemitism as a political force, the historian Shulamit Volkov has argued that antisemitism became firmly entrenched in a body of assumptions which identified 'the Jew' with the unacceptable aspects of capitalist modernity. This was 'a radical anti-modern mentality, rejecting liberalism, capitalism, socialism; in a nostalgic passion for a long-lost world. It implied a series of political views including an opposition to democracy and a call for the re-establishment of

[94] See Pulzer, *The Rise of Political Anti-Semitism in Germany and Austria*; Richard Levy, *The Downfall of the Anti-Semitic Political Parties in Imperial Germany* (New Haven and London, 1975); Ian Kershaw, 'The Persecution of the Jews and German Popular Opinion in the Third Reich', *LBY* 26 (1981), 261–89.

[95] See Sigurd Paul Scheichl, 'The Contexts and Nuances of Anti-Jewish Language: Were all the "Antisemites" Antisemites?', in Ivar Oxaal, Michael Pollak, and Gerhard Botz (eds.), *Jews, Antisemitism and Culture in Vienna* (London, 1987), pp. 89–110.

[96] See C. W. F. Grattenauer, *Wider die Juden. Ein Wort der Warnung an alle unsere christliche Mitbürger* (Berlin, 1803); W. Marr, *Der Sieg des Judenthums über das Germanenthum. Vom nicht confessionellen Standpunkt aus betrachtet* (Berne, 1879); E. Dühring, *Die Judenfrage als Racen-, Sitten- und Culturfrage. Mit einer weltgeschichtlichen Antwort*, 2nd edn. (Karlsruhe and Leipzig, 1881).

[97] Fontane, letter of 19 Sept. 1886, *Briefe an Georg Friedländer*, ed. Kurt Schreinert (Heidelberg, 1954), p. 55. See Wolfgang Paulsen, 'Theodor Fontane—the Philosemitic Antisemite', *LBY* 26 (1981), 303–22.

a national community of harmony and justice. It was associated with extreme nationalism, a colonial and imperial drive, an enthusiasm for war and an advocacy of a pre-industrial moral code, tinged with more than a trace of hypocrisy. In one way or another it was always combined with antisemitism.'[98] From the 1870s onward, antisemitism formed part of a system of beliefs which may be called a cultural code or a mentality. Since this system was coherent and self-confirming, it was able to survive even though it did not accord with empirical reality.

Volkov's 'anti-modern mentality', with antisemitism as part of the package, seems to me more plausible than Goldhagen's 'eliminationist mind-set'. The latter is a loose notion, comprehending those (including, as we have seen, many Jews) who wanted Jews' objectionable traits to be removed by European culture, as well as those who wanted the Jews to be exterminated. The problematic philosemitism of Dohm is thus levelled with the fanatical antisemitism of Dühring.[99] Volkov's concept accounts better for the persistence of antisemitism along with its initial failure to generate a durable political movement.

The anti-modern mentality relied heavily on national stereotypes. Stereotypes, as sets of initial expectations, are an indispensable means of ordering our knowledge of the world; but it is fatal to hold them so rigidly that they cannot be modified by encounter with individuals. Antisemitism talks not about individuals but about 'the Jews' or, still more darkly, about 'the Jew'. David Bankier has shown that ordinary people in Nazi Germany typically maintained that 'the Jews' were harmful but that their own Jewish neighbours were an exception.[100] Stereotypes are not only tenacious, but transferable. The eighteenth-century stereotype of the Frenchman, illustrated by Lessing's Riccaut, who is dishonest and talks bad German, easily developed into the stereotype of the Jew who was outwardly emancipated but inwardly adhered to his own clannish morality and his hidden language. As we have seen, Herder associated language and creativity; Fichte maintained that the French were

---

[98] Shulamit Volkov, 'Antisemitism as a Cultural Code: Reflections on the History and Historiography of Antisemitism in Imperial Germany', *LBY* 23 (1978), 25–46 (p. 31).　　　　[99] Goldhagen, *Hitler's Willing Executioners*, esp. pp. 56–7.
[100] Bankier, *The Germans and the Final Solution: Public Opinion under Nazism* (Oxford, 1992).

debarred from creativity by their superficial language; and Wagner transferred this stigma to the Jews.

Such a mentality is self-contradictory, but its contradictions need to be seen as part of its strength. Arnold Zweig points out the typical self-contradiction of the antisemite, who sees himself both as tragic hero and triumphant victor: 'For he is both hero and dragon-slayer, he enjoys seeing himself enshrouded by the tragedy of doomed nobility—and he is also, paradoxically, sure of his victory.'[101] Similarly, Chamberlain in *The Foundations of the Nineteenth Century* is ultimately issuing two contradictory messages. The Germanic race is triumphant; the Germanic race is in terrible danger. In parts of his book Chamberlain brags monstrously about the excellence of the Aryans, maintaining that the civilization created by the Germanic race is 'beyond question the greatest that has hitherto been accomplished by man'. Elsewhere, however, he laments that 'our governments, our law, our science, our commerce, our literature, our art . . . practically all branches of our life have become willing slaves of the Jews'.[102] Thus Chamberlain flatters his readers by telling them that as 'Germanen' they share the credit for modern civilization; but he also acknowledges their feelings of unease by saying that something is indeed wrong with modern civilization and blaming it on an external enemy, the Jew. The antisemitic fantasy thus satisfies two sets of desires simultaneously, and the emotional satisfaction thus generated sweeps one past the contradictions. Moreover, these very contradictions serve to protect the fantasy yet more securely against empirical disproof, because events that seem to threaten one part of the fantasy, such as Germany's defeat in 1918, can be taken to support the other part. Nationalists promptly blamed Germany's defeat on an imaginary Jewish conspiracy.

The anti-modern mentality was hostile to liberalism in two senses: to the emancipatory individualism that animated the revolutionaries of 1848, and to the free-market liberalism that triumphed in the *Gründerzeit* (1870–3). Imperial Germany, as Peter Pulzer has argued, retained a conservative tendency to regard individuals primarily as representatives of estates and corporations,

---

[101] Zweig, *Caliban oder Politik und Leidenschaft* (Potsdam, 1927), p. 45.
[102] Chamberlain, *Foundations*, ii. 228; i. 330.

such as religious denominations.[103] Somebody identifiable as a practising Jew might suffer antisemitic discrimination, but somebody who had left the Jewish community could easily appear an unclassifiable, mobile, untrustworthy, and threatening person. A formerly fixed society was becoming disturbingly fluid. Meanwhile, economic liberalism aroused understandable hostility from the *Mittelstand*, small and middling farmers, artisans, shopkeepers, white-collar workers in industry and the civil service, and the professional middle class. These people were alarmed by the rapid development of industrial capitalism and by its obverse, the rise of the organized working class. They saw their salvation in the concept of the *Volk*, implying a national unity that transcended class interests. After the economic depression that followed the stock-exchange crash of 1873, both in Germany and Austria, simple explanations, indeed scapegoats, were welcomed. The journalist Otto Glagau associated the liberal economic principles, which had so spectacularly failed, with the Jews. The impoverishment of the working classes, the 'social question', was identified by Glagau with the 'Jewish question' and attributed to the dominance of an alien race. This slogan ('Die soziale Frage ist die Judenfrage') caught on by its deceptive simplicity, its appeal to conservatism, and its offering an alternative to Socialism.[104]

In the late 1870s antisemitism became a subject of public discussion. Its best-known spokesmen were the Berlin Court preacher Adolf Stöcker and the historian Treitschke.[105] In 1878 Stöcker founded the Christian Social Workers' Party. His addresses to it increasingly blamed economic problems on Jews, notably his speech of 19 September 1879: 'Our Demands on Modern Jewry'. He was associated with Bernhard Förster, Nietzsche's brother-in-law, who helped to organize the Anti-Semitic Petition which was presented to Bismarck in 1882 with 225,000 signatures. Bismarck gave Stöcker only brief and tactical support. But the new antisemitism found a prominent supporter in Treitschke, who described the Jews as a danger to national life, especially in his much-read essay, 'Our Prospects', published in November 1879. Here he warned against Jewish immigration from eastern Europe,

---

[103] Pulzer, *Jews and the German State*, pp. 63–4.
[104] Volkov, 'Antisemitism as a Cultural Code', p. 40.
[105] See Pulzer, *The Rise of Political Anti-Semitism*, esp. ch. 10.

complaining that the media were already dominated by Jews unfamiliar with German values, and warning against the influx of 'ambitious trouser-selling youths [. . .] whose children and grandchildren will one day control Germany's stock-exchanges and newspapers'.[106] The alarm caused among the Jewish community can be traced from the vigorous debate that Treitschke's article initiated.[107] Thereafter, discussions of the Jews' place in Germany are haunted by a sense of insecurity that, as the next chapter will show, surfaces repeatedly in the literature of the time. In Austria, as we have seen, a still stronger insecurity was generated by the nationalist antisemitism of Schönerer and the populist rhetoric of Lueger.

Stöcker, Schönerer, and Lueger did not seek to reverse Jewish emancipation. Despite Hitler's admiration for their propaganda tactics, they are not to be seen as forerunners of the Nazis' antisemitic legislation.[108] They are important for promoting an anti-modern mentality of which antisemitism was a component. This mentality includes a stock of antisemitic images which will now be rapidly surveyed. We shall see in Chapter 4 that these images recur in the texts of Jewish writers who wish to dissociate themselves from aspects of Jewish influence.

Antisemitic Images

The antisemitic images that formed part of the anti-modern mentality were not primarily the traditional visual images of the evil Jew. The unpleasant images familiar from caricature are most handily listed in a French source, Edouard Drumont's immense diatribe against Jewish influence in the Third Republic:

The principal signs by which one can recognize the Jew are the notorious hooked nose, blinking eyes, clenched teeth, protruding ears, finger-nails that are square instead of almond-shaped, an excessively long torso, flat feet, bow legs, and the soft, greasy hand of the hypocrite and the traitor. They very often have one arm shorter than the other.[109]

[106] Treitschke, 'Unsere Aussichten', pp. 572–3.
[107] See *Der Berliner Antisemitismusstreit*, ed. Walter Boehlich (Frankfurt, 1965).
[108] See Hitler, *Mein Kampf* (Munich, 1943), pp. 107–10.
[109] Drumont, *La France juive*, 2 vols. (Paris, 1887), i. 35.

It was not the likely prospect of meeting such monsters that worried antisemites. Nor should excessive attention be paid to images of Jews as enemies to Christianity and ritual murderers of Christian children, though such images did survive and were evoked by antisemitic propaganda exploiting popular hysteria. In 1891, when a boy's corpse was discovered in a barn near Xanten in the Rhineland, charges of ritual murder were made against the local Jewish butcher and ex-slaughterer Adolf Büschhoff; and though Büschhoff was able to prove his innocence, his neighbours wrecked his house and obliged him to move to another district. Thereafter rumours of ritual murder arose somewhere in Germany almost annually.[110] Images of the Jew as murderer and bloodsucker were duly exploited by Nazi propaganda, notably in the May 1939 issue of *Der Stürmer* devoted to ritual murder.[111]

Although such revivals of pre-modern antisemitism were sensational, alarming, and pernicious, they were less pervasive than the specifically modern antisemitism in which 'the Jew' was dreaded because he was invisible. The influence of 'the Jew' was thought to permeate the modern society which was forcing unemployed farm-workers to move to mushroom cities and subjecting them to the unintelligible power of international capitalism and finance. A scapegoat was required to embody the hateful qualities of modernity.

Following Wagner, many claimed that the modern world was undergoing Judaization or *Verjudung*.[112] Eugen Dühring traces this process back to the French Revolution. The achievements of the middle classes, he complains, have been hijacked by the Jews, with Börne and Heine as their advance guard; the period 1860–80 is that of Jewish domination (*Judenherrschaft*).[113] As counter-

[110] See Rohrbacher and Schmidt, *Judenbilder*, esp. pp. 336–48. Such practices are widely attributed to unpopular out-groups: thus many 18th-cent. French Catholics believed that Protestants practised ritual murder. See David D. Bien, *The Calas Affair: Persecution, Toleration, and Heresy in Eighteenth-Century Toulouse* (Princeton, 1960), p. 118.

[111] The front page of the 'ritual murder' issue of *Der Stürmer* is reproduced in Ruth Gay, *The Jews of Germany: A Historical Portrait* (New Haven and London, 1992), p. 258.

[112] See Steven E. Aschheim, '"The Jew within": The Myth of "Judaization" in Germany', in Jehuda Reinharz and Walter Schatzberg (eds.), *The Jewish Response to German Culture from the Enlightenment to the Second World War* (Hanover, NH, and London, 1985), pp. 212–41.   [113] Dühring, *Die Judenfrage*, p. 11.

measures, Dühring proposes that the presence of Jews in politics
and the judiciary should be strictly proportional to their share in
the population; Germans should have the right to reject a Jew as
judge; Jewish companies above a certain size should be placed
under state supervision; Jewish immigration should be stopped;
Jews should not be allowed to teach in non-Jewish schools and
universities. Dühring and others, however, do not credit the Jews
with inventing liberalism: rather, they have exploited and
corrupted the emancipatory achievements of non-Jews. Ernst
Jünger maintains in 1930:

The Jew is not the father but the son of liberalism, just as he cannot play
a creative role, for good or ill, in anything connected with German life. In
order to be dangerous, infectious, destructive, he first needed a state of
affairs that enabled him to assume his new shape as the civilized Jew
(*Zivilisationsjuden*). The state of affairs was brought about by liberalism, by the spirit's great declaration of independence, and it cannot be
ended by any event save the complete bankruptcy of liberalism.[114]

As we have seen with Chamberlain, fear of Jewish influence
often amounted to paranoia. The founder of the Antisemitic
League, Wilhelm Marr, says that in his doom-laden treatise *Der
Sieg des Judenthums über das Germanenthum* (*The Victory of
Jewry over Germandom*, 1879), 'I recognized the *historical fact*
that, during the course of 2000 years, Israel in Germany had
succeeded in encircling the German world time and again, and
Protestant or Catholic *Christianity* are powerless against this
encirclement.'[115] After the First World War, resentment at defeat
could easily be displaced onto the Jews: hence the appeal of the
Protocols of the Elders of Zion which appeared in Germany in
1920, purporting to disclose a Jewish plot to take over the world
by finance and the press and install a despotic world government
which would destroy all religions but Judaism.[116] 'The Jew's
arrogance and presumption have increased along with his power

[114] Jünger, 'Über Nationalismus und Judenfrage', *Süddeutsche Monatshefte*, 27
(1930), 843–5 (pp. 844–5).
[115] Quoted in Zimmermann, *Wilhelm Marr*, p. 137; emphasis in original.
[116] [S. A. Nilus], *The Jewish Peril: Protocols of the Learned Elders of Zion* (London,
1920). See Norman Cohn, *Warrant for Genocide: The Myth of the Jewish World-
Conspiracy and the Protocols of the Elders of Zion* (London, 1967); and for a contemporary rebuttal, Binjamin Segel, *Die Protokolle der Weisen von Zion kritisch
beleuchtet* (Berlin, 1924).

in Germany and the entire world to an intolerable level',
complained Graf Ernst Reventlow in 1930; 'the Jewish people
regards it not only as its right but as its divine mission to rule
the nations.'[117] 'Since 1918 Jewish dominance has amounted
virtually to dictatorship,' agreed the veteran antisemite Theodor
Fritsch. 'Not only the whole of economic life, but also the political
measures taken by the government receive directions from high
finance.'[118] Such paranoia was not confined to Germany: Gerhard
Kittel declared in 1933 'that *throughout the world, in every
country on earth,* the Jews (*Judenschaft*) along with the world
opinion which they control, and the economic forces which they
likewise control, are standing behind the German Jews!'[119]

The association of Jews with finance had a specious justification
in the activities of international banking and commercial houses,
but it was generally based on attributing to the Jews a natural
affinity with capitalism. The most reputable proponent of this
view was the distinguished economic historian Werner Sombart
in *The Jews and Modern Capitalism* (1911). Sombart was stimulated by Max Weber's *The Protestant Ethic and the Spirit of
Capitalism* (1904–5) to argue that the Puritans' affinity for capitalism was fully shared by the Jews. Weber depicted Puritans as
rational, sober, goal-directed, with a belief in worldly prosperity
as the reward for hard work that encouraged a system of ethical
bookkeeping; Jews, Sombart argued, derived all these qualities
from their religion, which was legalistic and rational, devoid of
mystery or profound emotion, based on a contract between God
and Israel, and favourable to the profit motive. Here we recognize
the image of the rational Jew so assiduously promoted by Moses
Mendelssohn. It enables Sombart to maintain that the Jews'
rational, calculating character helped them to develop capitalism,
exploit the New World, and finance modern nation-states. Moreover, they were dispersed throughout the world, used to adapting
to different environments, and disinclined to feel moral obligations to the strangers with whom they dealt. They were the first
modern people: 'The Jewish outlook was the "modern" outlook;

[117] Reventlow, 'Deutsche—Juden', *Süddeutsche Monatshefte*, 27 (1930), 846–52
(pp. 848, 851).
[118] Fritsch, 'Zur Geschichte der antisemitischen Bewegung', *Süddeutsche Monatshefte*, 27 (1930), 852–6 (p. 855).
[119] Kittel, *Die Judenfrage*, p. 27. Emphasis in original.

the Jew was actuated in his economic activities in the same way as the modern man.'[120] Thus the Jews demolished the old, slow-moving world of feudal relations, in which wealth corresponded to need and usury was proscribed, and instituted the modern world of competition, individualism, and constant adaptation to new roles.

Sombart's arguments reappear, travestied, in antisemitic polemic. Since money is abstract, international, and rootless, there was scope for the facile identification of Jews, liberalism, and money that was made crassly by Goebbels in his novel *Michael*:

Money rules the world! A terrible saying when it comes true. Today we are perishing of its literal truth. Money—Jew, these are the thing and the person that belong together.

Money is rootless. It stands above the races. It eats its way slowly into the nations' healthy organism, gradually poisoning their creative strength.

We must free ourselves from money by struggle and work. Shatter the illusion within ourselves. Then at last the golden calf too will fall.

Liberalism is in its deepest significance the doctrine of money.[121]

Another antisemitic obsession was with Jewish domination of the press. Jews entered journalism in disproportionate numbers, because it offered a career to educated men debarred from other professions; several well-known papers, like the Mosse concern's *Berliner Tageblatt* and the Vienna *Neue Freie Presse*, had Jewish owners. As early as 1879 we find a pseudonymous pamphleteer complaining that the daily press in Berlin and Vienna is dominated by Jews, whose 'all-corroding poison' has rendered it incurably venal and corrupt.[122] In 1898 Fontane complained that the case for Alfred Dreyfus was being advanced by an international newspaper conspiracy: 'the European press is a great Jewish power which has tried to impose *its* opinion on the entire world'.[123] Those who thought modern journalism relied on vicious practices considered it a particularly suitable profession for Jews. In 1895 the young Thomas Mann dissuaded his friend Otto Grautoff from a journalistic career by telling him: 'The profession of a

---

[120] Sombart, *The Jews and Modern Capitalism*, tr. M. Epstein (London, 1913), p. 153.　　　　[121] Goebbels, *Michael*, pp. 138–9.
[122] 'Junius', *Das Judenthum und die Tagespresse: Ein Mahnwort in ernster Stunde* (Leipzig, 1879), p. 32.　　　　[123] Fontane, *Briefe an Georg Friedländer*, p. 320.

newspaperman requires pliancy, circumspection, slyness, dexterous impudence [. . .] vulgar qualities which, as we all know, make Jews so suitable for the press, and which you do not possess.'[124] A more sympathetic observer suggested in 1922 that Jews were fitted for journalism by the qualities implanted by their history of persecution, notably the empathy required to perceive danger, the capacity for disguise needed by the hunted, and the uncreative productivity that a journalist needs in order to meet deadlines.[125]

Denied access to state service, many Jews entered not only journalism but also private legal practice, medicine, and acting. To Gentiles, they often seemed to excel in these professions by virtue of a keen but superficial intellect devoid of creative power.[126] The Jewish mind could master any subject without real, intuitive understanding of its essence. This notion transposes to secular life the conception of Judaism as a fossil religion and the Talmud as a mere compilation of dead laws. 'The Jews' relation to Jehovah was unimaginative and heartless, expressed in treatises and business dealings, ossified in formalism', asserted Wilhelm Marr.[127] In secular life, added Dühring, the Jews could never produce a genius, but at most a talent for trading in other people's ideas and giving them a gloss of originality: thus Heine was an uncreative imitator of Byron.[128] Such polemics merely embroider the case proposed by Wagner in 'Das Judenthum in der Musik'.

Lacking the original creativity of which Fichte had spoken, the Jew had to resort to irony. Only Germans were capable of humour. Jews, like Frenchmen, could manage only intellectual wit. But since Jews were not only shallow but self-divided, their wit was turned against themselves as self-lacerating irony. Hence Treitschke deplores 'the bad Jewish habit of self-mockery' and ascribes it uncharitably to the painful contrast between the Jews' Oriental nature and the Western exterior which they were

---

[124] Mann, *Briefe an Otto Grautoff und Ida Boy-Ed*, ed. Peter de Mendelssohn (Frankfurt, 1975), p. 43.

[125] Paul Mayer, 'Maximilian Harden', in Gustav Krojanker (ed.), *Juden in der deutschen Literatur. Essays über zeitgenössische Schriftsteller* (Berlin, 1922), pp. 101–12.

[126] See Sander L. Gilman, *Smart Jews: The Construction of the Image of Jewish Superior Intelligence* (Lincoln, Nebr., and London, 1996).

[127] Marr, *Der Sieg des Judenthums*, p. 6.

[128] Dühring, *Die Judenfrage*, p. 48, 56.

obliged to adopt.[129] This Jewish irony was seen in Goethe's Mephisto, who in the nineteenth century had been imagined as French or Italian in contrast to the ultra-German Faust.[130] Hence both Dinter and Hitler take Mephisto to typify the ironic, impotent, and uncreative Jew.[131]

Devoid of creativity, and used to obeying an abstract law, the Jew was thought to lack any notion of the holy, any mysticism. Renan, in the preface to his study of Semitic languages, influentially described the Semites as an inferior race, who had given the world monotheism because their minds were too simple and self-centred to explore complex philosophical ideas, create civil society, or cultivate the arts.[132] In a qualified defence of the Semites, the Russian Orientalist Chwolson, himself a Jew, nevertheless acknowledges the Jews' spiritually down-to-earth character: 'The Semite possesses no such wealth and variety of ideas as the Aryan does, but he possesses a sound, practical, almost mathematical intellect, a gift for grasping ideas quickly and easily, and a sharp mind that often degenerates into logic-chopping.'[133] Drawing on such respectable sources, and on Reform Jews who insisted on the lack of mystery in their religion, Chamberlain could easily maintain that Judaism entirely lacked the imagination, mysticism, and profundity of the Aryan soul: 'Now consider what kind of religion men can have whose most outstanding characteristic is the absolute lack of every metaphysical emotion, every philosophical capacity!'[134] Graf Ernst Reventlow agreed: 'A people that has had no religious childhood and development of its own, no myth, no religious mysticism, but has never surmounted a pseudo-religious glorification of its own egoism, thus remains an alien and hostile element amid such a nation as the Germans.'[135]

---

[129] Treitschke, *Deutsche Geschichte im neunzehnten Jahrhundert*, 5 vols. (Leipzig, 1879–94), iii. 704.

[130] See G. von Loeper's edition of *Faust* (1871), quoted in Hans Schwerte, *Faust und das Faustische: Ein Kapitel deutscher Ideologie* (Stuttgart, 1962), p. 152; Cosima Wagner, *Diaries*, ed. Martin Gregor-Dellin and Dietrich Mack, tr. Geoffrey Skelton 2 vols., (London, 1978), i. 387 (8 July 1871).

[131] Dinter, 'Die Rassen- und Judenfrage', *Der Jud ist schuld . . . ?*, pp. 100–1; Hitler, *Mein Kampf*, p. 332.

[132] Ernest Renan, *Histoire générale et système comparé des langues sémitiques*, part 1 (Paris, 1855), pp. 1–16; see Edward Said, *Orientalism* (London, 1978), pp. 130–48.

[133] D. Chwolson, *Die semitischen Völker: Versuch einer Charakteristik* (Berlin, 1872), p. 27.   [134] Chamberlain, *Foundations*, i. 411.

[135] Reventlow, 'Was sind für uns die Juden?', in *Der Jud ist schuld . . . ?*, pp. 13–39 (p. 17).

Once again, by a cruel irony, this image of the rational Jew is a negative version of the image that Enlighteners like Mendelssohn had striven to present a century earlier, in order to free Judaism from the charge of superstition.

Along with his iron rationality, the Jew was credited with a powerful will that left the Aryan at his mercy, and a dangerous ability to adapt himself to all situations. 'What I called the Jews' historical instinct', says Chamberlain, 'rests ultimately upon an enormously developed *will*.'[136] Nietzsche calls the Jews 'the adaptable nation *par excellence*'.[137] The very success with which Jews entered European society was interpreted as proof of their infinitely protean nature:

That a Felix Mendelssohn should write German music, that a Jacques Offenbach [should write] French and a Souza Yankee-doodle, that Lord Beaconsfield should set up as an Englishman, Gambetta as a Frenchman, Lassalle as a German; in short, that talent should so often have nothing Jewish about it, but be in accord with its environment, has curiously enough again and again been urged as evidence that there are no specifically Jewish characteristics, whereas in truth it proves the very opposite in a striking fashion. It proves that Jews have the gift of adaptability in an eminently high degree.[138]

Jewish adaptability was often described by the Darwinian term 'mimicry', denoting the imitative technique by which some species disguise themselves from predators. Adolf Bartels credits Jews with an 'immense talent for mimicry'; Arthur Trebitsch charges them with obtaining legal equality through adaptive mimicry of clothing, language, customs, political outlook, and so forth.[139] Such adaptability was superficial only: the historian Theodor Mommsen speaks of the Jew 'who is as unwilling to discard the core of his national characteristics as he is ready to cloak it in whatever nationality happens to suit him and, up to a point, snuggles up to an alien popular character ('Volkstümlichkeit')'.[140]

[136] Chamberlain, *Foundations*, i. 238.

[137] Friedrich Nietzsche, *Die fröhliche Wissenschaft*, in *Werke*, ed. Giorgio Colli and Mazzino Montinari (Berlin and New York, 1972–), v. ii. 291.

[138] Sombart, *The Jews and Modern Capitalism*, pp. 270–1.

[139] Bartels, *Jüdische Herkunft und Literaturwissenschaft* (Leipzig, 1925), p. 37; Trebitsch, *Geist und Judentum: Eine grundlegende Untersuchung* (Vienna and Leipzig, 1919), p. 112. Cf. Darwin, *The Descent of Man*, i. 411–15.

[140] Mommsen, *Römische Geschichte*, iii: *Von Sullas Tode bis zur Schlacht von Thapsus*, 10th edn. (Berlin, 1909), p. 550.

Thus the very qualities that enabled Jews to enter Western culture—determination and adaptability—were now held against them. While the Enlightenment had complained of their rigid adherence to traditional beliefs, their opponents now denounced their willingness to adopt Western values.

The concept of the Jew as superficially adaptable generated frightening images of nomads who quartered themselves on settled nations or parasites who penetrated the host's body. Hermann Bahr invents a character of Jewish descent to proclaim that modern urbanized Jews are nomads without a fatherland, 'hordes, rabbles, nomads, gypsies, wandering, straying, on the run; no longer anything organic, but rootless outlaws and exiles!'[141] The typical Jew was the Wandering Jew. Sombart credits the Jews with 'inherent "Nomadism" or "Saharaism"', and argues that this quality equips them for the unsettled life characteristic of the desert-like modern city: the Jew flourishes in urban wastelands.[142] Jung combined both images when in 1934 he wrote of the 'Jew who is something of a nomad, has never yet created a cultural form of his own and as far as we can see never will, since all his instincts and talents require a more or less civilized nation to act as a host for their development'.[143] The parasite image was developed in gruesome biological detail.[144] Dühring says that, though deeply involved in political and financial corruption, Jews do not initiate it, but exploit it parasitically: 'The Jew is in his proper place where he can become the parasite on present or imminent corruption. Where he feels most comfortable in the nations' flesh, we must see if it is still healthy.'[145] The hero of Rudolf Hans Bartsch's violently antisemitic novel about a mixed marriage, *Seine Jüdin* (*His Jewess*, 1921), says plaintively: 'They also penetrate our Aryan soul and ravage it as parasitic wasps do a wretched worm; painfully, slowly and fatally!'[146] The clumsy, emotional, good-hearted German is represented as helpless before the cunning, unscrupulous Jew. Goebbels, as so often, presents the

[141] Bahr, *Die Rotte Korahs*, pp. 334–5.
[142] Sombart, *The Jews and Modern Capitalism*, p. 328.
[143] C. G. Jung, *The Collected Works*, tr. R. F. C. Hull, 2nd edn. (London and Princeton, 1970), x. 165–6.
[144] See Alex Bein, 'The Jewish Parasite: Notes on the Semantics of the Jewish Problem, with Special Reference to Germany', *LBY* 9 (1964), 3–40.
[145] Dühring, *Die Judenfrage*, p. 8.
[146] Bartsch, *Seine Jüdin* (Leipzig, 1921), pp. 81–2.

image most bluntly when he makes his hero say: '[The Jew] is the pus-filled ulcer in the body of our sick people (*unseres kranken Volkstums*). Peace? Can the lung keep peace with the tubercular bacillus?'[147]

These images drew on the assumption that Jews were themselves sick—weakly, deformed, hysterical, or mad—indeed, that Jewishness was itself the sickness with which the modern world was infected. 'Jewry is the disease of the nineteenth century', declared a pamphleteer. 'It is a plague that threatens to infect anyone who dares to enter public life.'[148] This rhetoric was dehumanizing and pseudo-scientific. It implied that to attack the source of modern corruption was an act of surgery, painful for the victim but beneficent for the organism as a whole. It helped to legitimate the murderous science that eventually sought to heal the body of the German people by surgically removing such foreign invaders as Jews, gypsies, and homosexuals.[149]

Anti-Antisemitism

Jews and their allies naturally fought back against antisemitism.[150] Both Jews and non-Jews were active in the Verein zur Abwehr des Antisemitismus (Society for Defence against Antisemitism), founded in 1891, while Jews founded the Centralverein deutscher Staatsbürger jüdischen Glaubens (Central Society of German Citizens of the Jewish Faith), usually abbreviated to CV, to assert themselves and resist antisemitic libels by legal challenges. Similar bodies were established in Austria. The CV, which had some 40,000 members by 1914, maintained that Jews were no longer a unified people or *Volk*. They were held together only by common descent and by an essentially religious self-definition, neither of which could be obstacles to their enjoying full German citizenship. The CV succeeded in obtaining prosecutions for antisemitic propaganda: between 1893 and 1915 at least

---

[147] Goebbels, *Michael*, p. 57.

[148] 'Junius', *Das Judenthum und die Tagespresse*, p. 7.

[149] See Benno Müller-Hill, *Murderous Science: Elimination by Scientific Selection of Jews, Gypsies, and Others, Germany 1933–1945*, tr. George R. Fraser (Oxford, 1988).

[150] See Ismar Schorsch, *Jewish Reactions to German Anti-Semitism, 1870–1914* (New York, 1972); Marjorie Lamberti, *Jewish Activism in Imperial Germany: The Struggle for Civil Equality* (New Haven and London, 1978).

537 persons of antisemitic affiliation stood trial, earning prison sentences that totalled 135 years; the CV continued this policy under the Weimar Republic, and succeeded in having the Nazi agitators Theodor Fritsch and Julius Streicher sent to prison.[151] Particularly notable was the 'Harand Movement', officially called the World Organization against Racial Hatred and Human Need, founded in Austria in 1933 by Irene Harand, a young Gentile woman whose ethical commitment made up for her political inexperience, and the Jewish lawyer Moritz Zalman; it soon acquired 40,000 members, mostly non-Jews. In many books and speeches, Harand rebutted the charges levelled against Jews in *Mein Kampf* and, all too often, Austrian Church publications.[152]

Anti-antisemitic movements have received thorough and affirmative study. It is not always clear how effective they were. They raised the morale of their supporters, and they scored many local successes in prosecuting antisemitic agitators. Despite these achievements, the CV at least could not take too bold a stand for fear of publicizing the antisemitism it sought to oppose and betraying that Jews were still a separate group. One of its leaders, Ludwig Holländer, revealed its precarious position by admitting: 'The German Jews are step-children, and step-children have to be on their best behaviour.'[153] In some ways non-Jews like Harand could attack antisemitism more credibly; yet as mature citizens Jews needed to fight their own battles.

Whether Gentile or Jewish, however, anti-antisemites were least effective in combating the mentality of their opponents. The weakness of the anti-antisemites emerges from their many well-intentioned publications. Anti-antisemites issued such handbooks as the *Antisemiten-Spiegel* (*Mirror for Antisemites*), a reversal of the long-standing antisemitic genre of the *Judenspiegel* or 'Mirror for Jews'; this systematically refuted the charges levelled by anti-semites, demonstrating, for example, that Jewish law forbade usury, that many Jews were tradesmen or farmers, that the Talmud was not hostile to Gentiles, and so on. This was a riposte also to

[151] See Pulzer, *Jews and the German State*, pp. 120, 284; Richard Levy, *The Downfall of the Antisemitic Political Parties*, p. 159.
[152] See Bruce Pauley, *From Prejudice to Persecution: A History of Austrian Anti-Semitism* (Chapel Hill, NC, 1992), pp. 253–8.
[153] Blumenfeld, *Erlebte Judenfrage*, p. 51.

the antisemitic lexica typified by Fritsch's popular *Handbuch der Judenfrage* and represented most extravagantly by the gigantic *Semi-Kürschner* (that is, a 'Semitic' counterpart to Kürschner's standard literary directory), originally subtitled *Literary lexicon of writers, poets, bankers, financiers, doctors, actors, artists, musicians, officers, lawyers, revolutionaries, feminists, Social Democrats, etc. of Jewish race or connection, who were active or known in Germany in 1813–1913*. It was later renamed *Sigilla Veri (Seal of Truth)* with the even more paranoid sub-title *Lexicon of the Jews, their friends and foes in all times and zones, especially Germany, the Jews' doctrines, customs, tricks and statistics along with their thieves' slang, false names, secret societies, etc.*[154]

The growth of antisemitism during and after the First World War provoked a flood of anti-antisemitic publications. The authors write in good faith from various standpoints. Heinrich Elchanan York-Steiner was a Zionist and former colleague of Theodor Herzl. Friedrich von Oppeln-Bronikowski defines himself as a German nationalist and convinced monarchist. Heinrich Coudenhove-Kalergi, a Roman Catholic with no Jewish blood, had a career in the Austrian diplomatic service which took him to Athens, Constantinople, Rio de Janeiro, and Tokyo, but he abandoned it prematurely to devote himself to study and writing. Without any political affiliation, he was devoted to liberal causes, and was such a fervent pacifist that he forbade his children to play with toy soldiers. His books included *Das Wesen des Anti-semitismus (The Essence of Antisemitism,* 1901), which was reissued in 1932 with a preface by his son. Though the anti-antisemites were transparently well-intentioned, the effectiveness of their writings and the soundness of their assumptions may be doubted.[155]

Anti-antisemites oppose the simplicities of racial theory, but

---

[154] Philipp Stauff (ed.), *Semi-Kürschner oder Literarisches Lexikon der Schriftstel-ler, Dichter, Bankiers, Geldleute, Ärzte, Schauspieler, Künstler, Musiker, Offiziere, Rechtsanwälte, Revolutionäre, Frauenrechtlerinnen, Sozialdemokraten usw., jüdischer Rasse und Versippung, die von 1813–1913 in Deutschland tätig oder bekannt waren* (Berlin, 1913). The later edition is E. Ekkehard, *Sigilla Veri (Ph. Stauff's Semi-Kürschner). Lexikon der Juden, -Genossen und -Gegner aller Zeiten und Zonen, insbesondere Deutschlands, der Lehren, Gebräuche, Kunstgriffe und Statistiken der Juden sowie ihrer Gaunersprache, Trugnamen, Geheimbünde, usw.* (Erfurt, 1929).

[155] For a sharp and disillusioned study, see Henryk M. Broder, *Der ewige Antisemit: Über Sinn und Funktion eines beständigen Gefühls* (Frankfurt, 1986), esp. ch. 6.

agree that Jews are racially distinct. Coudenhove-Kalergi equivo-
cates, pointing out that since 'Semitic' is a language family there is
no Semitic race, but also remarking that Renan could not have
charged that Semites are uncreative if he had known that the
Assyrians and Babylonians, who formed civilization, spoke
Semitic languages.[156] The philosopher Constantin Brunner,
having argued that no physical feature is exclusively Jewish,
restores racial difference by maintaining that Jews represent the
primal human race, from which other races have since become
differentiated. Hence Jews have some qualities of all other races,
but are essentially neutral: their specific character is the lack of a
racially specific character. Under the guise of acknowledging their
antiquity, this notion seems to rehabilitate the stereotype of Jews
as adaptable but inwardly unchangeable.[157] York-Steiner also
stresses Jewish difference, seeing it not as innate but as the result
of cultural pressures. It should be preserved, he thinks, on the
grounds that biological diversity and therefore cultural diversity is
a good thing.[158]

Anti-antisemites play down Jewish vices and stress their virtues.
Coudenhove-Kalergi admits that in some countries Jews are over-
represented among usurers, procurers, and swindlers, but only
because Christians forced them to concentrate on commerce and
hence on these corruptions of it.[159] It is not true that Jews shun
manual labour, for he has seen many Jewish craftsmen in the East
End of London, and Jewish porters and boatmen in Salonica.[160]
York-Steiner corroborates this by citing a Russian newspaper
which reported in 1901 that in Vilna many of the carters, most
of the road-menders, and all the chimney-sweeps were Jews.[161]
Nor are Jews cowardly: Coudenhove-Kalergi mentions three Jews
who were distinguished for their courage in the Franco-Prussian
War.[162] Such arguments suffer not only from triviality but from
emphasizing Jews' difference; from relying on generalizations
which are vulnerable to counter-examples; and from implying,

---

[156] Heinrich Graf Coudenhove-Kalergi, *Das Wesen des Antisemitismus*, reissued
with preface by R. N. Coudenhove-Kalergi (Leipzig and Vienna, 1932), pp. 60–2.
[157] Brunner, *Der Judenhaß und die Juden* (Berlin, 1918), pp. 56–7.
[158] York-Steiner, *Die Kunst als Jude zu leben*, pp. 187–8.
[159] Coudenhove-Kalergi, *Das Wesen des Antisemitismus*, p. 238.
[160] Ibid. 229.   [161] York-Steiner, *Die Kunst als Jude zu leben*, p. 229.
[162] Coudenhove-Kalergi, *Das Wesen des Antisemitismus*, p. 235.

by singling out individual Jews or Jewish groups for their courage or hard work, that these stand out as exceptions, like the Jewish traveller praised in Lessing's *Die Juden* as an unrepresentative because virtuous Jew.

Another tactic is to praise the Jews for their contribution to civilization. In sharp contrast to Chamberlain's denial that Christ was a Jew, the anti-antisemites give the Jews credit for Christianity: Brunner asserts that Christianity is Jewish, and that Christ was 'the most Jewish of all Jews'.[163] Oppeln-Bronikowski particularly argues that since Jesus a list of outstanding Jews have contributed to civilization. Unfortunately his candidates include not only Spinoza but Fritz Haber, who pioneered the use of poison gas in the First World War.[164] It might seem less controversial when Oppeln-Bronikowski praises the Jews' contribution to German culture by listing Jewish writers and actors. But this too could backfire, because the more he emphasizes the Jews' presence in cultural life, the more he confirms the antisemitic suspicion that German culture is Judaized (*verjudet*).

Although the works of anti-antisemites are full of good will and good sense, they unfortunately tend to be framed in assumptions about Jewish difference that come from the same mind-set as the libels of antisemitism. The conservative Oppeln-Bronikowski sees no difficulty in absorbing German Jews, provided that the frontier is firmly closed against 'the Eastern Jews with their bad instincts'.[165] He regards radicals like Kurt Tucholsky as poisonous, and merely parries the antisemitic charge that all Jews are poison by replying that in the cavalry he used to give a sick horse a small dose of arsenic to reanimate it: 'The Jew is such a poison. In large doses it may kill, in small doses it is stimulating and invigorating.'[166]

Anti-antisemites always remain one step behind their antagonists. They do not realize that antisemitism is not a mistake but a mentality. They see it as a survival from the religious past, not

---

[163] Brunner, *Der Judenhaß*, p. 186.

[164] Oppeln-Bronikowski, *Antisemitismus? Eine unparteiische Prüfung des Problems* (Charlottenburg, 1920), pp. 51–2.

[165] Oppeln-Bronikowski, *Gerechtigkeit! Zur Lösung der Judenfrage* (Berlin-Wilmersdorf, 1932), p. 64.

[166] Oppeln-Bronikowski, *Antisemitismus?*, p. 44; on Tucholsky, see *Gerechtigkeit!*, p. 63.

realizing that its protean character allows it to adjust to economic or racial antagonisms. They expect it to fade, and look forward to the increased integration of Jews into German society. Brunner advises Jews to assist this process by discarding conspicuously Jewish names which attracted hatred, thereby conceding that Jews can only be accepted if they remain inconspicuous.[167] According to the philologist Matthias Mieses, the only solution is 'Humanität': people must be taught that antisemitism is an archaic survival: 'When people learn to think more nobly, when the world of human emotion keeps pace with knowledge, then a new dawn of earthly happiness will gleam, and the torment of the Jews will disappear. Mankind must be taught humanity.'[168] By the 1920s, however, the slogans of the Enlightenment were sounding tinny.

Programmatic anti-antisemitism finds literary expression in the novel by Arthur Zapp, *Das neue Ghetto*, evidently written as a reply to such libels as the *Protocols of the Elders of Zion*. The central figure, and the unequivocal spokesman for the author's views, is Dr Siegfried Bornfeld, a lecturer in economics at the University of Berlin and a paragon of physical and moral courage. In the very first scene he displays his horsemanship and his presence of mind by saving the life of a young woman whose horse has run away with her. Siegfried's views are expressed in long tirades, perfunctorily worked into the narrative, which propose patriotic assimilation as the solution to the Jewish question and denounce Zionists for disloyalty to Germany. The antisemites, Siegfried proclaims, 'will not prevent us from fusing ever more closely with our German fatherland, with our German people, to form a single, strong German nation that is respected in the future family of peoples'.[169] But although Siegfried affirms his Jewishness, and marries a Gentile without converting, the content of his Jewishness is problematic. While the novel defines Jewishness ostensibly in religious terms, it depicts a decline in Jewish observance from the orthodoxy of Siegfried's grandfather, who dies early in the novel, via the liberalism of his father, who attends synagogue only on high holidays, to Siegfried's own reduction of

[167] Brunner, *Der Judenhaß*, p. 305.
[168] Mieses, *Der Ursprung des Judenhasses* (Berlin and Vienna, 1923), p. 578.
[169] Zapp, *Das neue Ghetto: Ein Roman aus der Zeit* (Berlin-Nowawes, n.d. [1922?]), p. 186.

Judaism to Moses' command 'Love your neighbour as yourself' and Hillel's injunction 'That which is hateful unto you, do not do to your neighbour'. This residual Judaism no longer contains anything distinctive.

Meanwhile, the novel makes massive concessions to antisemitism by using crude racial stereotypes. While Siegfried has nothing Jewish about his appearance and affirms his Jewish identity on principle, his brother Martin, who insists on calling himself a German despite his recognizably 'Jewish' appearance, represents a slavish dependence on the Gentile world, along with the cynical materialism ascribed to Jews by antisemites. Worse still is their Galician cousin, with his hooked nose, curly black hair, and thick lips; while a detestable Prussian aristocrat illustrates the absurdity of antisemitism by having 'features that might pass as Semitic: the hooked nose, the restless dark eyes, and the deep black curly hair'.[170] For this novel, the only good Jew is the invisible, merely nominal Jew. Its German patriotism, with the suppression of Jewish difference, is masked by the universalist slogans of the Enlightenment: Siegfried sees a solution to the Jewish question in a distant future 'when all will explain the world, its origin, its laws, its purpose, scientifically; when the needs of the heart will be satisfied, not by ecclesiastical institutions, by worshipping an imaginary divinity that human beings have themselves created, but in the love of humanity'.[171] By religious toleration, Siegfried really means the abolition of religion; and by the acceptance of Jews as Germans, he is really repeating Kant's assertion that 'the euthanasia of Judaism is the religion of pure morality'.[172]

It would be wrong to charge all anti-antisemites with such naïvety; but they fail to recognize that antisemitism is not a mistake which can be corrected but a mind-set whose assumptions influence the thinking even of its declared opponents.

LITERARY IMAGES OF THE JEW

Further insight into German mentalities comes from literature. Just as we have to approach reality via stereotypes, so literature

---

[170] Zapp, 91.　　　　[171] Ibid., 193.　　　　[172] Kant, *Werke*, vi. 517–18.

reports on reality, not by direct mimesis, but by adapting pre-formed models. These models can give insight into the assumptions of a given culture. Many writers whose attitudes to Jews are highly liberal resort, at least half unwittingly, to familiar stereotypes when representing Jews in literature. The familiarity of an image often seems to guarantee its faithfulness to reality. Given the need to be selective, I shall survey the representation of Jews in comedy, with its liking for familiar targets; in the realistic fiction of Wilhelm Raabe and Ferdinand von Saar; and in some major novels and short stories by Thomas Mann, in which deep ambivalences about the 'Jewish question' find expression.

The Comic Jew in Drama

Jews were popular as comic characters on the German stage from the early eighteenth century onwards. We find Jews who cheat at every turn, lament the loss of their money, and, above all, speak the 'Jewish' form of German known as *Jargon* or *Mauscheldeutsch*. 'Jewish' German is distinguished by vowel changes, incorrect case endings, Yiddish vocabulary (e.g. *Bocher*, young student; *Goi*, non-Jew; *Tineff*, dirt), and the inability to place the infinitive verb at the end of a main clause or the verb at the end of a subordinate clause: e.g. 'Ich will doch werden raich' where standard German requires 'Ich will doch reich werden'.[173] While 'Jewish' language may sometimes represent particular dialects accurately, it hardens, by the later nineteenth century, into a conventional sign of Jewishness, consisting only of misplaced verbs and Yiddish vocabulary.

In the theatre, standard Jewish roles soon developed: the greedy creditor, the lovelorn girl, the Yiddish-speaking father.[174] Thus Goethe, in *Wilhelm Meisters theatralische Sendung* (*Wilhelm Meister's Theatrical Mission*), describes how the actor Serlo could delight cultivated audiences by imitating a rabbi:

---

[173] [K. B. A. Sessa], *Unser Verkehr: Eine Posse in einem Akt*, in *Deutsche Schaubühne; oder dramatische Bibliothek der neuesten Lust- Schau- Sing- und Trauerspiele*, vol. xxx (Augsburg and Leipzig, n.d. [1815?]), p. 202. On 'Jewish' language, see Matthias Richter, *Die Sprache jüdischer Figuren in der deutschen Literatur (1750–1933): Studien zu Form und Funktion* (Göttingen, 1995).

[174] See Hans-Joachim Neubauer, *Judenfiguren: Drama und Theater im frühen 19. Jahrhundert* (Frankfurt and New York, 1994).

[. . .] probably nobody has performed the caricature of a Jewish rabbi better than he did. The contorted zeal, the loathsome sensual enthusiasm, the crazy gestures, the confused muttering, the harsh shrieking, the gentle movements punctuated by moments of intensity, the grotesque absurdity of outworn nonsense—he had grasped all this so admirably and could reproduce it in such concentration that such a disgusting display could make any person of taste happy for a quarter of an hour.[175]

This description may imply sexual as well as anti-religious satire. Gunnar Och suggests that the part Serlo plays here is that of the Rabbi in *Die Judenhochzeit* (*The Jew's Wedding*, 1771) by the Viennese dramatist and impresario Felix Kurz-Bernardon; in this play the Rabbi is the unwanted wooer of a young woman, and hence a figure to be ridiculed and abused.[176] Similar crude sexual comedy occurs in Lenz's *Die Soldaten* (*The Soldiers*, 1776), where one of the soldiers, as victim of a practical joke, is deluded into getting into bed with the old Jew Aaron and is then accused by his comrades of indecency. Little sympathy is invited for the Jew: he serves to illustrate the soldiers' horseplay. Likewise, in H. L. Wagner's *Die Reue nach der Tat* (*Repentance Too Late*, 1775), an unnamed Jew, bitten by a nobleman's dog, is introduced to bring out the humanity of the good characters and, by telling his life-story, to provide a thematic parallel to the main story: he is neither integrated with the others, nor an object of interest in his own right.

Theological aspersions on Jews also recur. Friedrich 'Maler' Müller, in *Fausts Leben* (*Faust's Life*, 1778), has Faust pursued by Jewish creditors called Mauschel and Itzick, who utter such Jewish expressions as 'Au wai!'[177] The devils who want Faust's soul have previously roused the Jews and entered into them in order to make them completely remorseless: thus Müller exploits the associations between the Devil and the Jews. Theology is central to Achim von Arnim's *Halle und Jerusalem* (1811). Originally an adaptation of Gryphius's Baroque morality-play *Cardenio und Celinde* (1657), this developed into a grandiose religious drama indebted to Calderón. It has two main Jewish

---

[175] Goethe, DKA I. ix. 344; the reference to the Jew was removed when Goethe revised this for the *Lehrjahre*, see ibid. 633, but cf. the brief allusion to a comic Jewish part, ibid. 472.   [176] Och, *Imago judaica*, p. 94.

[177] *Sturm und Drang: dramatische Schriften*, 2 vols. (Heidelberg, n.d.), ii. 375–7; for discussion, Och, *Imago judaica*, pp. 210–14.

figures. One is the Wandering Jew, Ahasuerus, who announces the impending arrival of the Messiah and conversion of the Jews, and seeks to recall Cardenio, now a Faustian figure, to the Christian life by telling him and his lover Celinde to make a pilgrimage to Jerusalem. The other is the comic Jew Nathan, who embodies the unscrupulous money-grubbing traditionally ascribed to Jews but also reveals the effects of emancipation: he neglects his own religion by doing business and getting drunk on the Sabbath; his grandchildren are baptized, but betray their unchangeable character by playing at being creditors collecting loans. He dies after a visit from the Wandering Jew, who has acknowledged the truth of Christianity and illustrates the true function of the Jews, namely to warn of the consequences of rejecting Christ.[178]

Reviving theological animus of the past was less profitable, however, than satirizing the cultured Jews of the present day. This was the aim of Julius von Voss's parody of *Nathan der Weise*, where Nathan figures as a rheumy-eyed miser who speaks in German full of Yiddishisms and fragments of Hebrew, and Recha as an affected bluestocking who, sharing Mendelssohn's view that Jews should speak either pure Hebrew or pure German, rebukes her father for his uncultured language:

> Vater weiset die Thorheit
> Des ekeln unästhetischen Jargons von euch,
> Dem was man Zeitgeist nennt, gar nicht mehr frommend.
> Nur eine Sprache sollt ihr reden, seys
> Die das levitische Gesetz verfaßt,
> Seys die man jetzt am Jordansstrande hört,
> Nur nicht geschmacklos untermischt, nur nicht
> Der Vorzeit Brauch er tippelt gar mir nicht,
> Ich schwebe schon auf des Jahrhunderts Höhe,
> Und will, daß ihr mitschreiten sollt, kein Gnom,
> Ein genialer Ries' glaubt mir, ich will
> Euch leiten, wie den Greis von Kolonos
> Die sanftere Hellenin.—Hört ich spreche,
> Schon keinen Dialekt mehr, weiß die Rede
> Der höhern Bildung wie mein Aschre—eh,

---

[178] Arnim, *Halle und Jerusalem: Studentenspiel und Pilgerabenteuer*, in his *Sämmtliche Werke* (Berlin, 1846); on this play, see Och, *Imago judaica*, pp. 275–80.

Will dibbern, wie mein Abc, man merkt
Mir nimmer noch die Jüdin an—[179]

          Father, don't be silly,
Give up the horrid unaesthetic jargon,
That ill beseems the spirit of the age.
You ought to speak a single language, be it
That of the lawcode of Leviticus,
Or what we hear today on Jordan's strand,
But not a tasteless mixture, as was wont
In former times, it really turns me up;
Aloft upon our century's giddy heights,
I want you to accompany me, not
A gnome—a giant in the realm of thought;
I'll guide you, as the mild Hellenic maid
Guided her sire of Colonus. How's that, then?
There ain't no trace of dialect, I know
Civilized language like my *ashre*—er—
My ABC, I meant to *dibber*; no-one
Would ever take me for a Jewess—

Admittedly, Voss's play is even more anti-Catholic, in presenting Daja as sex-crazed and the Patriarch as drunken, than it is anti-Jewish. A friend of Salomon Maimon and of Maimon's biographer Sabattia Joseph Wolff, Voss was at least not a conscious Jew-hater. Indeed he gives Nathan a serious speech in good German about Jewish piety and morality. Yet the linguistic change itself indicates that specifically Jewish language is false and immoral.

Even more ill-natured is the comedy *Unser Verkehr* (*The Company We Keep*) by Karl Borromäus Alexander Sessa. After its première at Breslau, the play was revived in Berlin in 1815 by the famous actors Ludwig Devrient and Albert Wurm. Initially the Jews of Berlin managed to persuade the liberal Prussian Chancellor Hardenberg to prohibit its performance, but in response to public demand the play was performed in September 1815 and soon played to packed houses throughout Germany.[180] The play

---

[179] Voss, *Der travestirte Nathan der Weise: Posse in zwey Akten*, ed. Leif Ludwig Albertsen (Berne, Frankfurt, New York, 1985), p. 29. Voss misinterprets *ashre* as 'ABC': see Richter, *Sprache*, pp. 174–5. On Nathan's language, see Gilman, *Jewish Self-Hatred*, p. 140.

[180] On the play and its reception, see Charlene A. Lea, *Emancipation, Assimilation and Stereotype: The Image of the Jew in German and Austrian Drama (1800–1850)* (Bonn, 1978), pp. 80–6; Neubauer, *Judenfiguren*, pp. 113–20.

satirizes Jewish emancipation by mocking Jews' attempts to acquire German language and culture. Jakob Hirsch, son of a pedlar, is sent out by his parents to earn his living, but, having elegant tastes, does not like the prospect. He makes up to several characters, who scorn and threaten him; when it is announced that he has won the lottery, everyone fawns on him; but when the news turns out to result from a clerical error, everyone deserts him, and he is left where he began. His first soliloquy reveals his cultural aspirations:

Was soll ich tun? Ich will doch werden raich—bald—in kurzer Zeit—(nachsinnend) Ä Kaufmann handelt mit seinen Wooren, ä Schenie mit seine Talente!—Ich hob doch Talente, ich bin ä Schenie—ich bin nich geboren sum Handel! [. . .] (er streicht sich die Haare und putzt an sich herum) Ich will werfen den Juden bei Seit, ich bin doch aufgeklärt—ich hob doch gar nix Jüdisches an mir!

What am I to do? I want to get rich—soon—quickly (*pondering*) A merchant deals in wares, a genius in talents!—I've got talents, I'm a genius—I wasn't born for trade! [. . .] (*he smoothes his hair and tidies himself*) I'll throw the Jew aside, after all, I'm enlightened—there ain't nothing Jewish about me!

Then he sums up his talents:

Wann ich wer kummen äsau—(er macht Bücklinge) Ich känn doch tanzen!—Wenn ich wer sprechen franzesch: bon jour, mademoiselle, a vos [*sic*] service, monsieur!—Ich känn doch franzesch!—Wenn ich wer deklämiren: 'Leonore fuhr ums Morgenroth empor aus schwere Träume'—ich kenn doch aach deklämiren!—Wenn ich wer singen: 'Bei Männern welche Liebe fühlen'—ich känn doch gor singen!—Ich wer doch noch auswendig lernen das Ästhaitisch—gor geschwind, und machen ä poor ländliche Sonnette und ä Bibliothek von Trauerspiele in Jamben—Wos ist der mehr?[181]

If I go like this—(*he bows*) why, I can dance!—If I speak French: 'bon jour, mademoiselle, a vos service, monsieur!'—why, I know French! If I recite: 'Lenore rose at dawn of day from 'ard and 'eavy dreams'—why, I can recite poetry too! If I sing: 'In men who feel the breath of love'—why, I can even sing!—I'll learn Aesthetic by heart, while I'm at it, quick as a flash, and make a couple of rural sonnets and a library of blank-verse tragedies—What can anyone do that I can't?

---

[181] *Unser Verkehr*, pp. 202–3.

Note that Jakob conceives assimilation as learning a series of languages, even 'aesthetic'. All the Jewish characters speak versions of Jewish-German, except the ex-student Isidorus Morgenländer (formerly Isachar) who speaks in bookish, stilted language: 'Yes, I have become a doctor! Why do you wonder? Darkness has grown light to me, and matters hidden are revealed. You are still held captive in the night of death, enveloped by the fog of reflection.'[182] This book-talk, we are to gather, is the only non-Jewish language a Jew can acquire.

The success of *Unser Verkehr* was following with disturbing speed by a series of anti-Jewish riots in Würzburg, Frankfurt, Hamburg, and other towns in August 1819. No Jews were killed, but many were assaulted in the streets and badly beaten up, and Jewish shops were looted to cries of 'Hep-Hep' (explained by false etymology as the Crusaders' slogan, 'Hierosolyma est perdita').[183] After the riots, Voss defended himself and Sessa, rather naïvely, against the charge of fostering anti-Jewish violence. He denies that caricatures of Jews in comedy can be applied to Jews as a whole, any more than the caricature of the soldier, the nobleman, the hypocrite, etc.[184] His Jewish friends did not accept this argument. Wolff replied that the play was so widely accepted as a satire on Jews in general that people even recited passages from it in the presence of Jews.[185] Börne, in his review, agreed that unlike social satire, the play was directed against an entire race, and added that there was nothing funny about someone's aspirations to self-improvement.[186]

The greatest centre of popular comedy in the German-speaking world was Vienna, where the theatre had been firmly established since 1710. When restrictions on immigration were lifted, following the 1848 revolution, Vienna's Jewish population rose sharply. By 1869 some thirty thousand Jews lived in the three central districts. Yet, in contrast to northern Germany, Jewish characters

---

[182] *Unser Verkehr*, pp. 217.

[183] See Jacob Katz, *Die Hep-Hep-Verfolgungen des Jahres 1819* (Berlin, 1994); the origin of the name is discussed on p. 29.

[184] Voss, *Die Hep Heps in Franken und anderer* [sic] *Orten* (Teutonien [i.e. Berlin], 1819), p. 7; cf. Johannes Hahn, *Julius von Voß* (Berlin, 1910).

[185] Wolff, *Wieder Juden: Sendschreiben an Herrn Julius v. Voß, veranlasst durch die, von ihm mir gewidmete, Schrift die Hep Heps, zur Vertheidigung der Christen* (Berlin, 1819), p. 43 n.

[186] Börne, '*Unser Verkehr*' [1818?] in *Sämtliche Schriften*, i. 415–21.

are rare on the Viennese stage, and its comedy lacks the standard Jewish roles familiar from German theatre. One of the major popular theatres was situated in the Leopoldstadt, the area where most Jews lived, and many of them attended performances. The only play that might be considered antisemitic is Nestroy's *Judith und Holofernes* (1849), a parody of Friedrich Hebbel's solemn tragedy *Judith* (1841). The Jews of Bethulien, besieged by Holofernes, plan to buy up provisions, complain about the fall in share prices, and make comically inept and insubordinate soldiers. These passages are tactless, given that Jews had distinguished themselves in the revolution of the previous year, but far from bitter. The anticlerical picture of the High Priest Jojakim ('I shall drop my words of comfort into the yearning soul. Woe! Woe! Thrice woe!')—an ideal part for the late Frankie Howerd—is milder than Lessing's caricature of the Patriarch or the antimonastic satire in Nestroy's *Freiheit in Krähwinkel* (*Liberty in Sleepy Hollow*, 1848).[187] Nothing suggests that Nestroy himself had any antisemitic feelings, any more than the partly Jewish audience that saw the play 67 times between 1849 and 1862. Neither Nestroy nor his audience objected to an easy source of humour.

Hebbel, who had settled in Vienna, wrote an extraordinary comedy, *Der Diamant* (*The Diamond*, 1847), centring on the Jew Benjamin who safeguards a stolen diamond by swallowing it. Other characters threaten to retrieve the diamond by cutting Benjamin open, either with medical instruments or with a butcher's knife. Finally Benjamin pretends to have excreted the diamond but in fact hands over a worthless stone which, implausibly, satisfies everyone. This grotesquely nasty play, which Hebbel considered a masterpiece, anticipates Freudian theories of anality by its association of wealth with excrement; when Benjamin suffers from stomach pains, we see the materialistic Jew being punished for his greed by the materiality of the wealth concealed in his intestines; and the threats to eviscerate him sound like

[187] Nestroy, *Sämtliche Werke*, ed. Fritz Brukner and Otto Rommel, 12 vols. (Vienna, 1924–30), iv. 174. See Colin Walker, 'Nestroy's *Judith und Holofernes* and Antisemitism in Vienna', *Oxford German Studies*, 12 (1981), 85–110; Jürgen Hein, 'Judenthematik im Wiener Volkstheater', in Hans Otto Horch and Horst Denkler (eds.), *Conditio Judaica: Judentum, Antisemitismus und deutschsprachige Literatur vom 18. Jahrhundert bis zum Ersten Weltkrieg*, part 1 (Tübingen, 1988), pp. 164–86.

retribution for the Jew's alleged cruelty as ritual slaughterer or as ritual murderer (associations already present in Shakespeare's Shylock).

In later nineteenth-century comedies the immoral, imperfectly acculturated Jew is often a journalist. An early example is Morgenroth in Eduard Bauernfeld's *Der literarische Salon* (*The Literary Salon*, 1836). He is based both on the Hungarian-Jewish satirist Moritz Saphir (who sat through the première in agony) and, since he comes from Hamburg and declares his allegiance to the recently banned Young German movement, on Heine. His name recalls Sessa's Morgenländer, his syntax is Jewish, his idleness and venality are obvious, and his ambitions are grandiose: 'I have come to enlighten the world' ('Ich bin gekommen, aufzuklären die Welt').[188] Many such figures stem from the Jewish journalist Schmock in Gustav Freytag's play *Die Journalisten* (1854) who betrays his linguistic corruption by speaking *Jargon* (indicated by misplaced verbs) and his pliability—admittedly under pressure from a tyrannical editor—by being willing to write on either the conservative or the liberal side. His name became a standard term for a hack writer or pushy journalist.[189] Arno Holz's play *Sozialaristokraten* (*Social Aristocrats*, 1896) includes an unscrupulous journalist, Dr Moritz Naphtali, who is about to found an antisemitic journal under the name Dr Moritz Wahrmann; he forms an alliance with the vain pseudo-radical Dr Gehrke, persuading him to stand as parliamentary candidate for an antisemitic party. Not only does Naphtali pass under a false name, but he falls into Jewish jargon for the corrupt language of intrigue ('Und wenn wir Ihn nu offerierten n goldsichren Wahlkreis?'—'And suppose we offered you a seat what's safe as houses?').[190] Bahr introduces into his comedy *Das Tschaperl* (*The Bird-Brain*, 1898) the unnecessary character of an unscrupulous journalist called Dackl (i.e. 'dachshund') who is unmistakably a Jew from Galicia and who defends his malpractices by his poverty, thus

[188] Bauernfeld, *Gesammelte Schriften*, 12 vols. (Vienna, 1871), iii. 253. See Lothar Kahn, 'Moritz Gottlieb Saphir', *LBY* 20 (1975), 247–57.

[189] See Freytag, *Die Journalisten* (Stuttgart, 1977), p. 46: 'ich kann schreiben nach jeder Richtung'; and the satire by Fritz Mauthner, *Schmock oder Die litterarische Karriere der Gegenwart* (Berlin, 1888).

[190] Holz, *Sozialaristokraten* (Stuttgart, 1980), p. 61.

proving his own venality.[191] But the best comedy about journalists is by a Jewish writer: Schnitzler's *Fink und Fliederbusch* (1917), where a journalist who, like Schmock, writes under two different names for different sides is committed to fighting a duel with his alter ego, and solemnly declares that he is doing so to defend his convictions.[192] This drastically illustrates Schnitzler's view that journalists defend opposed convictions with an equal show of certainty.

Hostile caricatures of the Jewish journalist turn up not only in drama but in the most unexpected places. In his Dada novel *Tenderenda der Phantast* Hugo Ball includes a character called Lilienstein who does not, as Ball's biographer thinks, represent 'the isolated poet';[193] rather he is a Jewish journalist who is tried for rationality and blasphemy ('having assumed a grey shape to ruin the mystics' grazing-grounds') and defended by the Devil; in his final speech he proclaims himself King of the Jews and recommends a laxative called 'Autolax' (the excremental imagery of medieval antisemitism is invoked to show that what Jews produce is worthless).[194]

Realism: Raabe and Saar

Realist literature depicts Jews with the aid of two linked conventions. First, Jews are recognizable through their language, especially when emotion or pain deprives them of control. This assumption is neatly captured in one of the many Jewish jokes Freud tells in *Jokes and their Relation to the Unconscious* (I have modified Strachey's translation to make clear when the character resorts to Yiddish):

The doctor, who had been asked to look after the Baroness at her confinement, pronounced that the moment had not come, and suggested to the Baron that in the meantime they should have a game of cards in the next room. After a while a cry of pain from the Baroness struck the ears of the two men: 'Ah, mon Dieu, que je souffre!' Her husband sprang up,

[191] Bahr, *Das Tschaperl* (Berlin, 1898), p. 27.
[192] Schnitzler, D ii. 629. On the play's relation to Freytag, see Hartmut Scheible, *Liebe und Liberalismus: über Arthur Schnitzler* (Bielefeld, 1996), ch. 1.
[193] Philip Mann, *Hugo Ball: An Intellectual Biography* (London, 1987), p. 101.
[194] Ball, *Tenderenda der Phantast* (Zurich, 1967), pp. 47–8. Note also the evidently Jewish 'Modegötzen' on p. 59.

but the doctor signed to him to sit down: 'It's nothing. Let's go on with the game!' A little later there were again sounds from the pregnant woman: 'Mein Gott, mein Gott, what terrible pains!' — 'Aren't you going in, Professor?' asked the Baron. — 'No, no. It's not time yet.' — At last there came from next door an unmistakable cry of 'Oi, vay, vay!' The doctor threw down his cards and exclaimed: '*Now* it's time.'[195]

The Baroness's French is that of the rootless, cosmopolitan Jew; her German is that of the culture she inhabits but has not internalized; but Yiddish is her real language, that of the body and of spontaneous feeling. In Freytag's *Soll und Haben* (*Debit and Credit*, 1855), a best-seller which depicted an idealized German bourgeoisie threatened by the disorderly Poles and the active, malign Jews, we are told that the villain, Veitel Itzig, 'used the German language with great facility (*Fertigkeit*), but with an Eastern breath, more larynx than higher grammar':[196] that is, residual Yiddish gives his German a guttural, physical flavour. In Bartsch's *Seine Jüdin* the Christian hero marries a 'Jewess', reassured by her complete assimilation and perfect German; but when their marriage is breaking up, she suddenly refers to Jesus as 'Joisel', thereby revealing not only the hidden language of the Jew but also the shallow, irreligious nature that it expresses.[197] In Bahr's *Die Rotte Korahs*, the trial of the Jewish financier Jason (formerly Jakobson), is interrupted when Jason, in the throes of a fatal seizure, bursts out 'in loathsome jargon'.[198] Here again, the 'true' language of the Jew emerges in a crisis.

The second convention presupposes that, since the Jew's public language is false, Jews only tell the truth among themselves, and we can only hear it by eavesdropping. This assumption underlies Sessa's *Unser Verkehr*, which purports to show us the shameless greed exhibited by Jews in private, and Heine's poem 'Erlauschtes' ('Overheard'), where we eavesdrop on a conversation in a Hamburg street between two Jews about the dowry one paid to marry off his daughter:

[195] Freud, *SE* viii. 81; cf. *Studienausgabe*, ed. Alexander Mitscherlich *et al.*, 10 vols. (Frankfurt, 1970), iv. 78.
[196] Freytag, *Soll und Haben* (Munich, 1978), p. 107. On the question of antisemitism here, see George L. Mosse, 'The Image of the Jew in German Popular Literature: Felix Dahn and Gustav Freytag', in his *Germans and Jews* (New York, 1970), pp. 61–76; Richter, *Sprache*, pp. 187–214.
[197] Bartsch, *Seine Jüdin*, p. 214.   [198] Bahr, *Die Rotte Korahs*, p. 164.

'Jake, you smart fellow, how much did you pay
For that lanky Christian there,
The husband of your eldest girl?
She was getting a bit threadbare.'[199]

Similarly in Fontane's last novel, *Der Stechlin* (1898), the Jewish merchant Baruch Hirschfeld maintains a friendship with the aged Junker Dubslav von Stechlin, but when he is alone with his son Isidor we overhear the two plotting to buy up Dubslav's estate.[200] Other writers imagine Jews dropping into *Jargon* when no Gentiles are present: in Wilhelm von Polenz's *Der Büttnerbauer* (*Farmer Büttner*, 1895), Samuel Harrassowitz, the dealer who drives the upright farmer into bankruptcy and suicide, uses Yiddish expressions in his private conversations with Isidor Schomberger and other Jewish associates;[201] and in Dinter's *Die Sünde wider das Blut* (*The Sin against the Blood*, 1917) the villainous Jewish Kommerzienrat, absurdly, writes letters in *Jargon* to a business colleague with whom he is plotting to Judaize the world. Elsewhere Dinter lets us eavesdrop on two converted noblemen, Baron v. Oppenheimer and Baron v. Werheim: when the latter receives a letter from his fiancée breaking off their engagement, the former relapses into linguistic Jewishness, uttering 'the one significant word: "Nebbich!"'[202]

Along with Freytag, it was Wilhelm Raabe who created the most memorable image of the dangerous Jew. Just as Veitel Itzig in *Soll und Haben* shadows the virtuous German Anton Wohlfart, so in Raabe's *Der Hungerpastor* (*The Hungry Pastor*, 1864) the profound, confused, inarticulate German pastor Hans Unwirrsch is shadowed by the unscrupulous Moses Freudenstein, who reappears as the cosmopolitan and convert Dr Theophil Stein. Yet Raabe, like Freytag, was a staunch liberal; he disclaimed any antisemitic intention, assuring a distressed Jewish admirer that many of his best friends were Jews and that Moses was a renegade: 'Don't I treat the real Judaea in the *Hungry Pastor* with all

[199] *Complete Poems of Heine*, p. 792; H vi. 277.
[200] Fontane, *Romane, Erzählungen, Gedichte*, ed. Walter Keitel, 6 vols. (Munich, 1962), v. 12–13.
[201] Polenz, *Der Büttnerbauer* (Leipzig, n.d.), pp. 48, 225. On 'Isidor' as a supposedly ultra-Jewish name, see Dietz Bering, *Der Name als Stigma: Antisemitismus im deutschen Alltag, 1812–1933* (Stuttgart, 1987).
[202] Dinter, *Die Sünde wider das Blut*, p. 155.

respect? Is it *my* fault if you count the renegade as one of your own?'[203] In the text Moses is clearly dissociated from the Jewish people by the prophecy that he has become too clever and will betray them (R vi. 119).[204] But the novel counteracts this indication by adopting a fairy-tale mode in which good is pitted against evil, tradition against modernity, Christian against Jew; within these terms it is a highly readable and engaging story, but these terms themselves might be rejected as an over-simple, distorted picture of what purports to be contemporary society.[205]

Discomfort with *Der Hungerpastor* may have led Raabe to atone for its anti-Judaism with the subtle story *Frau Salome* (1875).[206] Baroness Salome von Veitor, the widow of a Berlin banker, is described repeatedly as a 'beautiful Jewess' (R xii. 23, 28, 84), and is clearly intelligent, kind, and motherly. In conversations with her friend Justizrat Scholten, a typical Raabe eccentric, Salome talks repeatedly of the difficulty of assimilating to German society: 'We adapt to the moods of what surrounds us, and it is quite a business—an activity, a labour, in which we spin more melancholy than comfort from storm and stillness, rain and blue sky, sun and shadow' (R xii. 26). Rebutting the stereotype of Jews' effortless adaptability, Raabe instead emphasizes their difference. The German landscape evoked in Salome's words is alien to her. The action occurs on the slopes of the Brocken, the mountain central to German myth and literature as the setting for the Walpurgisnacht orgy of German witches which features in Goethe's *Faust*. Scholten suggests that Salome would look better mounted on a dromedary beneath Oriental palm-trees, and calls her a 'beautiful Semitic sorceress' (R xii. 23, 24). She herself speaks of 'my cool Semitic brain' (R xii. 85) and contrasts the Odyssey, which refreshes German hearts, with the peace of the Judaean desert (R xii. 77–8). These and many other allusions in

---

[203] Letter to Philippine Ullmann, 4 Feb. 1903, in *Briefe*, ii (Göttingen, 1975), p. 445.

[204] References in this form are to Raabe, *Sämtliche Werke*, ed. Karl Hoppe *et al.*, 20 vols. (Göttingen, 1960–).

[205] For a judicious account of the issues, see Jeffrey L. Sammons, *Wilhelm Raabe: The Fiction of the Alternative Community* (Princeton, 1987), pp. 73–87.

[206] See Florian Krobb, *Die schöne Jüdin. Jüdische Frauengestalten in der deutsch-sprachigen Erzählliteratur vom 17. Jahrhundert bis zum Ersten Weltkrieg* (Tübingen, 1993), p. 158.

this densely wrought text place Greek and German culture together in opposition to that of the Orient. The references to Salome's otherness, though harmless, seem compulsive. Finding her reading the newspaper, Scholten asks if she has been studying the Oriental question (R xii. 71). He implies, and she agrees, that her 'hook-nosed relatives' are just as bad as the 'would-be Christian-Germanic Aryan-sniffers', the professional antisemites of the day (R xii. 27–8); and the humiliations she has endured from her relatives are suggested by her references to Heine's poem 'Affrontenburg' (R xii. 67). The narrator reminds us that she has 'Oriental eyes' and, when excited, she relapses into the Jewish accent and syntax (R xii. 31, 67).

While Raabe's intentions were undoubtedly good, and his presentation of the friendship between Scholten and Salome is warm and convincing, we recognize here the exceptionalism of Lessing's *Die Juden*, combined with an obsessive insistence on the hallmarks of Jewish difference and their historical and cultural roots. Salome is exceptional both in being a outsider among modern Jews and in retaining the positive qualities of Old Testament Jews. The climax of the story is a disastrous fire during which Salome not only organizes the rescue services but thinks of her ancestors' encounters with Jehovah:

She looked beyond the nearby flames to distant lightning-flashes and cloudbursts; and old verses from her fathers' psalms went through her mind and became audible on her lips. She stood there like the visionary women of her race when, beneath their feet, battles were fought against the heathen.   (R xii. 94)

Reciting a majestic passage from the Psalms (Ps. 18: 7–15), Salome becomes the embodiment of ancient Hebrew religious and poetic spirit, represented both by the Psalmists and by the singer Deborah (Judges 4). But she involuntarily reminds us of the supposed distance between the ancient Hebrews and their degenerate decendants among whom she has the misfortune to be born, and hence of the obstacles to assimilation that were increasingly presumed to reside in the Jews' innate racial or cultural character. Not dissimilar is the view of Julius Langbehn that such noble Jews as the Psalmist, Spinoza, or Rembrandt's subjects differ widely from the modern mass of Jewish plebeians who are renegades from Judaism.[207]

Conceptions of Jewish assimilation in the late nineteenth century are further illuminated by Ferdinand von Saar's story *Seligmann Hirsch* (1888). Saar, a Viennese writer who abandoned a military career for a literary one, is an underrated but very fine author of *Novellen* which combine a simple beauty of style with a pleasantly worldly atmosphere. In this story, three generations of Jews are viewed by a detached but sympathetic Gentile first-person narrator. Seligmann Hirsch is an elderly Jew whom the narrator meets when both are staying in a hotel. In his appearance, some 'Jewish' features (large nose, fingers overladen with rings, sing-song accent) combine with a strongly-marked face and eccentric clothing (a 'fantastical travelling-cap', wide boots) in an ensemble which is exotic rather than than stereotypical: he resembles 'an Armenian or Bulgarian'.[208] A vigorous, noisy person, insensitive to others, he first inflicts himself on the local card-players, and, when driven away for spoiling their game by his irrepressible comments, implores the narrator to play billiards with him. Clearly, however, Hirsch's intrusiveness is a plea for attention, revealing his desperate insecurity and loneliness. He knows that he is still incompletely assimilated and feels estranged from his children, who in turn find him an embarrassment. He shows acuity in comparing himself to Shakespeare's King Lear, though he admits that his daughter is no 'Recha':[209] this mistake for 'Regan' reminds us that his daughter also lacks the filial piety of Lessing's Recha in *Nathan der Weise*. After losing his fortune, Hirsch lived first with his daughter and son-in-law on their Hungarian estate, and was then transferred to his son and daughter-in-law in Vienna; neither arrangement has been success-ful, and finally the son, Bernhard, a highly successful business-man, dumps his father with another family in Venice, where the old man eventually cuts his own throat. The comparison with King Lear (so much apter than the clichéd Shylock would have been) raises Hirsch's story from a Jewish family dispute to a more universal and tragic plane.

---

[207] [Langbehn], *Rembrandt als Erzieher*, p. 242.

[208] Saar, *Seligmann Hirsch*, ed. Detlef Haberland (Tübingen, 1987), p. 13.

[209] Ibid. 24. On the Shakespeare allusion, see Roger Paulin, *The Brief Compass: The Nineteenth-Century German Novelle* (Oxford, 1985), pp. 88–9.

Nevertheless, *Seligmann Hirsch* is very much a Jewish story. It is presented to us by the narrator, who, though irritated by old Hirsch's pushiness, recognizes his warmth and vitality and sympathizes with his loneliness. Instead of being the predictable orthodox Jew, Hirsch, though from Galicia, presents himself as enlightened, with no scruples about eating pork, and tells how his behaviour scandalized his late wife Gittel, a strictly observant Hasid. The process of assimilation has already begun. It has gone much further with his daughter Sarah (her husband Aron calls himself 'Aladar' and evidently lives like a Magyar landowner) and his son Bernhard, a slight, inconspicuous, bespectacled, insincere character who does not want his social position endangered by his embarrassing father. However, in one of Saar's characteristically subtle switches of perspective, Hirsch's end is recounted by another Jewish figure, a man-about-town who, having squandered his inheritance on 'noble passions' and relying on support from relatives, avenges himself by denouncing Jews as bitterly as an antisemite. This unappealing character takes the side of Bernhard Hirsch, who by now has acquired the title of Baron Hirtburg, and ridicules Seligmann's affection for his family. He also informs us about the third generation: Seligmann's grandson looks extremely Jewish, while the granddaughter is developing into an outstanding beauty. Although the narrator refrains from comment, the story hints that assimilation is a bad bargain: to accomplish it, Jews estrange themselves from the warmth, energy, and close family ties of earlier communities, becoming cold-hearted opportunists or, like the man-about-town, obsessed with the Jewishness they despise.

In this richly textured story Saar has interwoven the story of Jewish assimilation with another, Darwinian narrative. By having young Hirsch ennobled, Saar recalls Jewish families who were ennobled like the Wertheimsteins and the Hofmannsthals; but by having old Hirsch come from Galicia, he recalls the numerous Jewish immigrants who came to Vienna from eastern Europe in the liberal era—the Freud family from Galicia, the Kraus family from Moravia—whose children would be the creators of Viennese modernism. But Saar had also read Darwin, who is mentioned in his story. Old Hirsch is a living fossil, unable to adapt to the modern world, as out of place in Venetian exile as 'a rhinoceros in an aquarium'.[210] His adaptable children manipulate, reject, and defeat him. But evolution takes its revenge by giving Bernhard not only a daughter (a 'beautiful Jewess'?) who seems likely to marry into the Gentile aristocracy, but a son whose strongly Jewish appearance suggests—at least to the antisemitic man-about-town—a Darwinian throwback to his grandfather. And this narrative strand increases the story's emotional complexity by arousing, in the detached narrator, compassion for those like Hirsch who are doomed to extinction at the hands of unpleasant survivors. The story hints at the coming *Verjudung* of Europe, but its narrative framework artfully disclaims standard prejudicial reactions by displacing them onto a Jewish antisemite.[211]

Thomas Mann

Thomas Mann's remarks on the Jewish problem, and his fictional portrayal of Jews, reveal a deep ambivalence. In 1907, asked to comment on the 'Jewish question', he proclaims himself a philo-semite, asserts that the 'exodus' desired by the Zionists would impoverish European culture, and looks forward to the 'ennoble-ment' of the Jews that will remove all their repellent mannerisms (M xiii. 459–62).[212] This harks back to the philosemitism of Lessing and Dohm; it invites the Jews into European society on condition that they cease to be Jews. However, Mann also values the Jews' specific contribution to culture. In later public utterances he often quotes Riemer's remark about how well Jews appreciated Goethe, and applies it also to himself. He was supportive towards Jewish writers like Samuel Lublinski (a critic who praised *Buddenbrooks*) and Jakob Wassermann. But they remain a pictur-esque, half-alien element whose function apparently is to serve and enrich German culture. Their love for the spirit ('Liebe zum Geist', M xiii. 475) makes them a necessary ingredient in a

---

[210] Saar, *Seligmann Hirsch*, p. 35; on Saar's Darwinism, see ibid., 201–11.

[211] On Saar's alleged latent antisemitism, contrast Norbert Miller, 'Das Bild des Juden in der österreichischen Erzählliteratur des Fin de siècle', in Herbert A. Strauss and Christhard Hoffmann (eds.), *Juden und Judentum in der Literatur* (Munich, 1985), pp. 172–210 (p. 187), with Haberland in *Seligmann Hirsch*, pp. 142–8; a judicious view in Egon Schwarz, 'Jüdische Gestalten bei Marie von Ebner-Eschenbach und Ferdinand von Saar', *German Quarterly*, 63 (1990), 173–86.

[212] References in this form are to Mann, *Gesammelte Werke*, 13 vols. (Frankfurt, 1974).

Germany too ready to relapse into the provincial crudity represented by antisemites. They form part of 'the Mediterranean,
European, Oriental, the truly human and universalistic element'
(M xiii. 483) that saves German culture from nationalistic
narrowness. Writing for American readers in November 1922,
he cited Mahler's *Lied von der Erde*, based on Chinese poems,
to rebut Spengler's claim that different cultures could not mix:
here the Jewish composer serves to mediate between Germany and
China (M xiii. 267). In exile, he attacked Nazi maltreatment of
Jews, urged Western democracies to allow unrestricted Jewish
immigration, denounced antisemitism, and protested against the
United States' withdrawal of approval for a Jewish state in
Palestine.[213]

At times, though, Mann had reservations. He was understandably alarmed by the Jewish revolutionaries who took part in the
Russian Revolution and, far nearer home, in the Munich Soviet of
1919. In figures like Eugen Leviné, executed by the White troops
who captured Munich that April, Mann sensed an explosive
combination of abstract intellectuality and religious fanaticism.[214] He considered such Jewish men of letters as Alfred
Kerr, Theodor Lessing, and Kurt Tucholsky to be impertinent
and shallow. Both Kerr and Lessing had attacked him scurrilously
in print; Mann briefly contemplated revenge by making Lessing
the model for the contemptible protagonist of *Ein Elender* (*A
Miserable Specimen*), a story eventually ascribed to Aschenbach
in *Death in Venice*.[215] It was with Kerr and Lessing in mind that
he said in 1936 that Jews had always been among his worst
enemies as well as his best friends (M xii. 783). In 1933 he did
not object to their removal from print, nor to the 'de-Judaization
of the law' (*Entjudung der Justiz*).[216] 'The revolt against the
Jewish element would, up to a point, have my sympathy,' he wrote
in his diary on 20 April 1933, 'if the end of a Jewish check on the

[213] For a positive account of Mann's attitude to Jews, see Anthony Heilbut, *Thomas Mann: Eros and Literature* (London, 1996), esp. p. 396.

[214] Mann, *Tagebücher 1918–1921*, ed. Peter de Mendelssohn (Frankfurt, 1979), p. 223.

[215] M viii. 450; see Hans Wysling, '"Ein Elender". Zu einem Novellenplan Thomas Manns', in Paul Scherrer and Hans Wysling, *Quellenkritische Studien zum Werk Thomas Manns* (Berne and Munich, 1967), pp. 106–22.

[216] Mann, *Tagebücher 1933–1934*, ed. Peter de Mendelssohn (Frankfurt, 1977), p. 46.

German spirit were not so worrying for the latter and if the
German national spirit (*das Deutschtum*) were not so stupid as
to put my type in the same boat and send me into exile as well.'[217]
Yet Mann's wife, Katia Pringsheim, was of Jewish descent, though
her family was thoroughly integrated into German society.[218]
Mann's father-in-law, Alfred Pringsheim, was professor of mathematics at Munich University, and an enthusiastic Wagnerian.
After his first encounter with the Pringsheim family, Mann wrote
to his brother Heinrich: 'With these people one never even thinks
about Jewishness.'[219]

A further complication in Mann's portrayal of Jews is most
apparent from his early works. In 1907 Mann gives this description of the typical Jew:

Recognizable everywhere as a stranger, with the pathos of the exception
in his heart, he represents one of the extraordinary modes of existence
that survive within civil life, distinguished from the common norm in a
sublime or sordid sense, despite all humane and democratic levelling-
down.   (M xiii. 459)

This romanticized portrayal of the Jew not only preserves the
sense of Jewish distinctness inscribed in German legislation, but
is also a projection of Mann's conception of the artist; one need
only think of the permanent outsider Tonio Kröger. It suggests
another figure: the homosexual. Mann's homosexuality is amply
clear from his diaries and, when one reads it without prejudice,
from his fiction. The stigma attaching to Mann's artist figures
covertly describes that of the homosexual.[220] Mann's artists are
stigmatized by conventional society as sick and degenerate, if not
criminal; they have to be continual play-actors in order to disguise
their inner nature (and this applies not only to Tonio Kröger and

[217] Mann, pp. 54.
[218] Thomas Mann's most meticulous biographer does not say when the Pringsheims
converted; but Katia's paternal grandfather, who was professor of botany at Jena and
then at Berlin, must have benefited from either his own or his father's conversion. On
the maternal side, Katia Pringsheim's great-grandfather had converted to Protestantism
in 1827 and assumed the name Franz Dohm, no doubt after the philosemite C. W. von
Dohm. See Peter de Mendelssohn, *Der Zauberer: Das Leben des deutschen Schriftstellers Thomas Mann. Erster Teil: 1875–1918* (Frankfurt, 1975), pp. 541–52.
[219] Thomas Mann and Heinrich Mann, *Briefwechsel 1900–1949*, ed. Hans Wysling
(Frankfurt, 1984), p. 50.
[220] See Karl Werner Böhm, *Zwischen Selbstzucht und Verlangen: Thomas Mann
und das Stigma Homosexualität* (Würzburg, 1991).

Gustav von Aschenbach but also to Thomas Buddenbrook, who is unfitted for his bourgeois calling by a dose of decadence). The homosexual needs a mask in order to pass in a homophobic society, just as the Jew must suppress his original traits in order to be accepted in Western society. And for both the homosexual and the Jew, their contribution to society depends on their *not* being fully assimilated. To succeed as they do in the professions open to them, Mann says, the Jews need obstacles to overcome (M xiii. 460); this implies that complete assimilation would deprive the Jews of their distinctive character and turn them into ordinary ungifted people. As for the homosexual: he is distinguished, in Mann's portrayals, by his special capacity for love. Tonio Kröger's love for Hans Hansen, and Aschenbach's love for Tadzio, are intense and pure because the object is unattainable. This love is sublimated into creativity: for Tonio it becomes 'good and fruitful' (M viii. 338); in Tadzio's presence Aschenbach is inspired to write the 'page and a half of choice prose' (viii. 493) which, ironically, will later be much admired by people who would be shocked if they knew what stimulated it. The stigmas attaching to the Jew and the homosexual guarantee their creativity.

There is, however, an important difference between Mann's conceptions of the Jew and of the homosexual, and it can be revealed by examining the scandalous story *Wälsungenblut* (*The Blood of the Volsungs*), which Mann wrote in 1905 but withdrew from publication at the last moment. It is set in a wealthy Jewish household in Berlin, whose name, Aarenhold, recalls an actual clan of Jewish entrepreneurs called Arnhold but has been extended to include 'Aar', the poetic and ultra-Germanic word for 'eagle'. The Jewishness of the Aarenhold family is conveyed by repeated heavy hints, rather than by the 'ironic discretion' Mann claimed.[221] Herr Aarenhold comes from a remote eastern locality, and has made a fortune by dubious but large-scale business deals

---

[221] Thomas Mann and Heinrich Mann, *Briefwechsel*, p. 65. For commentary on the story, see especially Jens Malte Fischer, *Fin de Siècle: Kommentar zu einer Epoche* (Munich, 1978), pp. 233–41; Heide Eilert, *Das Kunstzitat in der erzählenden Dichtung. Studien zur Literatur um 1900* (Stuttgart, 1991), pp. 268–80; Mark M. Anderson, '"Jewish" Mimesis? Imitation and Assimilation in Thomas Mann's "Wälsungenblut" and Ludwig Jacobowski's *Werther, der Jude*', GLL 49 (1996), 193–204.

and by his indomitable determination; Frau Aarenhold embarrasses everyone by her foreign appearance, elaborate hairdo, ostentatious jewellery, and Jewish syntax and vocabulary. The children, who despise their parents and their own Jewish blood, have ultra-Germanic names—Kunz, Märit, Siegmund and Sieglinde—and Jewish physiques: protruding lips, hooked or flat noses, and dark hair and eyes. Their conversation is relentlessly intellectual and sophisticated; Kunz's duelling scar, Märit's militant feminism, and the general taste for combative arguments, convey an aggressiveness which, the narrator reflects, may stem from being habitually on the defensive (M viii. 382). Sieglinde's intended, the non-Jew von Beckerath, whom Siegmund sarcastically speaks of as 'this Germanic type' ('dieses Germanen', M viii. 395), is wholly out of his depth amid the Aarenholds' inimitable cultivation and self-assurance.

Siegmund, the principal focus, is nevertheless troubled by the emptiness of his life. His intellectualism and aesthetic cultivation have, he feels, cut him off from raw experience and creative vitality. He is sharply conscious of his Jewish appearance, 'the badges of his blood' (M viii. 408), which his elegance cannot conceal. He feels imprisoned in witty, logical, superficial intellectuality, incapable of deeper experiences, and hopelessly uncreative. Despite his arrogant veneer, he represents a touching portrayal of an inwardly vulnerable character who, like so many figures in Mann's early works, feels out of touch with robust and passionate life. Although he and his siblings talk the language of Social Darwinism, insisting on struggle and achievement, Siegmund lacks the impetus to be anything more than a dilettante, and his twin sister is resigned to marrying a man she despises. In short, Siegmund is the Jew described by Wagner in 'Judaism in Music'. But the solution to Siegmund's plight comes from Wagner's music-drama. A week before Sieglinde's wedding, she and Siegmund attend a performance of *Die Walküre*. Mann's quietly witty description contrasts Wagner's outcast twins with the tediously respectable Hunding. Back home, Siegmund and Sieglinde re-enact the Wagnerian act of incest. And in the original ending, Siegmund gives the following answer to Sieglinde's question 'What about Beckerath?':

'Nun,' sagte er, und einen Augenblick traten die Merkzeichen seiner Art sehr scharf auf seinem Gesichte hervor, 'was wird mit ihm sein? Beganeft haben wir ihn,—den Goy!'[222]

'Well,' he said, and for a moment the distinguishing marks of his race stood out very sharply on his face, 'what about him? We've jewed him— the goy!'

Thus, after the only intense experience of his life, Siegmund relapses into his mother's Jewish-German, implying that this is the true language of the would-be German Jew. It contrasts with the stilted, artificial language in which the twins normally talk. Siegmund's only escape from his uncreative life is incest, but even that is an imitation of German art.

In the imitation of Wagner, however, Jewishness and German-ness meet. Recounting *Die Walküre*, which ends with Brünnhilde's punishment for saving Sieglinde, the narrator says:

> Yet in the womb of the woman she had found time to rescue it continued to germinate, the hated, impious and divinely chosen race, from which a pair of twins had been brought together by their plight and their suffering in such free ecstasy.   (M viii. 405)

By this deliberately ambiguous reference, Mann unleashes some unexpected meanings.[223] The Volsungs are momentarily equated with the Jews. The Volsungs are Wotan's chosen race, yet he is compelled to harass and punish them, just as Jehovah has subjected the Jews to suffering. Moreover, Siegmund's attraction to his slender, boyish-looking sister has undertones of homosexuality, suggesting that they have the special, outcast existence of the homosexual. Their incest is an act of revenge against the Gentile and heterosexual world in the person of Beckerath, whom Siegmund deprives of Sieglinde's virginity (and perhaps of fatherhood).

The original ending of *Wälsungenblut*, quoted above, alarmed Oscar Bie, the editor of the *Neue Rundschau*, who asked Mann to change it. Mann reluctantly substituted: 'he should be grateful to us. He will lead a less trivial existence from now on' (M viii. 410). However, before the story could be published, its contents became known in Munich, because some faulty proofs were used as

---

[222] Thomas Mann and Heinrich Mann, *Briefwechsel*, p. 355.
[223] See his essay 'Zur jüdischen Frage' (1921), M xiii. 466–75.

packing-paper and sent to a Munich bookshop, where they were
discovered and pieced together by an employee. Rumours circulated that Mann had taken revenge for humiliations supposedly
endured in the household of his wealthy Jewish in-laws. No doubt
these rumours were distorted and exaggerated; but from Mann's
letter of 27 February 1904 to his brother Heinrich it is clear that
the wealthy and cultured Pringsheim household was intimidating
enough to put Mann on his social mettle. He summed them up as
'Tiergarten mit echter Kultur':[224] that is, the kind of wealthy
Jewish family who might live in the Tiergarten district of Berlin
(like the Aarenholds), but who (unlike the Aarenholds) were
genuinely cultured and had no sign of Jewishness. Nevertheless,
the similarities between the fictional Berlin Aarenholds and the
real Munich Pringsheims extend even to details: both have a room
hung with Gobelin tapestries; Katia even had a twin brother. After
withdrawing the story from publication, Mann still had to endure
a scene with his enraged father-in-law who had unwittingly
supplied the expression 'beganeft'. The story circulated surrepti-
tiously; it was privately published in a limited edition in 1921. It
may seem strange that Mann was so insensitive as not to realize
what offence this story might cause. However, he had drawn freely
on his own family's history in *Buddenbrooks*, and would do so
again in *Doktor Faustus*. As for the Jewish stereotypes in *Wälsungenblut*, they were such a standard form of literary expression that
Mann evidently had difficulty in associating them with actual
Jews.

The Jews are represented in *The Magic Mountain* (1924) by
Leo Naphta, a convert and Jesuit, whose lurid background
includes a talmudic education in a Russian shtetl. Naphta's father
was, implausibly, both a ritual slaughterer and also a Hasidic
tsaddik who communed with God and performed miraculous
cures; but he was charged with the ritual murder of Gentile
children and crucified against his own front door.[225] Naphta,
like Raabe's Moses Freudenstein, is a renegade to his people, a
convert and a Jesuit, who claims that revolutionary terror can
restore medieval theocracy; he transmutes his father's ritual

---

[224] Thomas Mann and Heinrich Mann, *Briefwechsel*, p. 49.
[225] On the associations of slaughter, ritual murder, and Naphta's tuberculosis, see
Sander L. Gilman, *Franz Kafka, the Jewish Patient* (London, 1995), pp. 141–3.

violence into aggressively logical argumentation. He typifies the mixture of religious fanaticism and rootless intellectuality that Mann associated especially with Russian Jews like Leviné. He is also a distinct religious type, sharply recalling the travesty of St Paul presented so bitterly by Nietzsche in *The Antichrist*. Nietzsche's Paul is deeply Jewish, the successor to the power-hungry Jewish priesthood: a 'genius of hatred', a cynical manipulator and nihilist, he distorted what was valuable in Jesus' message and reduced it to a demagogic formula.[226]

Ritual slaughter appears elsewhere in the novel. Lost in the snow, Hans Castorp has a twofold hallucination. First he sees young people playing and dancing on a sunlit shore which he intuitively recognizes as Mediterranean. Then he enters a massive, Mycenaean-looking temple that broods over the scene:

The bronze door of the sanctuary stood open, and the poor soul's knees all but gave way beneath him at the sight within. Two grey old women, witchlike, with hanging breasts and dugs of finger-length, were busy there, between flaming braziers, most horribly. They were dismembering a child. In dreadful silence they tore it apart with their bare hands— Hans Castorp saw the bright hair blood-smeared—and cracked the tender bones between their jaws, their dreadful lips dripped blood. An icy coldness held him. He would have covered his eyes and fled, but could not. They at their gory business had already seen him, they shook their reeking fists and uttered curses—soundlessly, most vilely, with the last obscenity, and in the dialect of Hans Castorp's native Hamburg.[227]

This is a strange way to represent the interdependence of life and death. Is it not forced and arbitrary to represent our common fate by a grotesque atrocity? What wider significance does this image have? Castorp attributes his dream to the collective soul of humanity. The graceful 'children of the sun' embody the Apollonian side of Greek life as described by Nietzsche in *The Birth of Tragedy*. No doubt the temple also has a Greek aspect: Mann had read in Erwin Rohde's *Psyche* about female demons that devoured children.[228] But it does not suggest the Dionysiac ecstasy which was the other half of Nietzsche's polarity. And why do the old

[226] Nietzsche, *Werke*, VI iii. 213–15, 245.

[227] Mann, *The Magic Mountain*, tr. H. T. Lowe-Porter (London, 1945), p. 494; M iii. 683.

[228] See Peter Pütz, 'Thomas Mann und Nietzsche', in *Nietzsche und die deutsche Literatur*, ed. Bruno Hillebrand, 2 vols. (Munich, 1978), ii. 121–55 (p. 140).

women speak modern German dialect? In dismembering a child, they are performing a ritual murder such as Jews—including Naphta's father—were charged with, and their use of German reminds us that such charges were still brought in Imperial Germany; the child's 'bright hair' suggests a blonde German victim. The word 'Blutmahl' ('blood-feast', M iii. 684), used in Castorp's reflections, links this murder with such phenomena as the Passover meal and the Christian Eucharist. Such a link was asserted by Nietzsche, who in *The Antichrist* identifies early Christianity with Judaism and mentions among its barbaric features 'the blood-drinking in the Communion'.[229] Its presence here is supported by the fact that Naphta, like his model St Paul, is both Jew and Christian, while his antagonist Settembrini stands for classicism and humanism. Hence, if the 'children of the sun' represent the union of body and spirit envisaged by Settembrini, the atrocity in the temple typifies the sick, destructive core of Naphta's religiosity; and it is contrasted with the ultimately sterile, but far more attractive combination of Dionysian mysteries and Eucharistic unity later associated with Peeperkorn. Evidently the dream was meant to give historical depth to Mann's antithesis of life and death, associating them respectively with the Greek and Judaeo-Christian sources of Western civilization.

Mann returned more seriously to the Old Testament in his *Joseph* tetralogy and in the Novelle *Das Gesetz* (*The Law*, 1944). The former work is too vast to be considered here; but though the humanism which structures the life of Joseph as a divine comedy may seem weak in the age of death camps, it was at least to Mann's credit that he found his exemplars of humanity among the Jewish people.[230] *Das Gesetz* is short, pithy, and disturbing. Here Mann ironically retells the story of Moses up to the promulgation of the Ten Commandments. Moses finds among the Midianites the conception of an invisible God, perceives its implications, and makes it central to his thought and activity. By speaking in the name of the invisible God, who supposedly manifests His power in the eruption of the Sinai volcano, Moses manages to impose his authority and inculcate

---

[229] Nietzsche, *Werke*, VI. iii. 187.

[230] See Ruth Klüger, 'Thomas Manns jüdische Gestalten', in *Katastrophen: Über deutsche Literatur* (Göttingen, 1994), pp. 39–58 (esp. p. 54).

morality among the recalcitrant and sensual people. The narrative illustrates the origins of civilization, with powerful echoes of Nietzsche and Freud.

Mann inherited various conceptions of Moses from German classicism: Herder's wise legislator, Schiller's enlightened charlatan, Goethe's clumsy hot-head. He also read Freud's *Moses*; and he later acknowledged the unconscious influence of Heine's portrayal of Moses (M xi. 154).[231] In Heine he found, first, a clear suggestion that Moses' God was only the projection of Moses himself:

God pardon me the sin, but sometimes I fancy that this Mosaic God is only the reflected radiance of Moses himself, whom he so much resembles, both in wrath and in love—It would be a great sin, it would be anthropomorphism, to assume such an identity between God and his prophet—but the resemblance is striking. (H vi. 480–1)

In Mann's story it is made ironically clear that the hot-tempered Moses conceives his God in his own image, and that the Ten Commandments represent Moses' own attempts at self-control. Though not quite a charlatan, Moses takes advantage of the eruption of Sinai to quell opposition and claim divine sanction, and his acolyte Joshua, who secretly brings Moses food on Sinai in order to make his sojourn there appear miraculous, is shameless in manipulating his image.

Second, Mann found in Heine the image of Moses as sculptor working on the flesh of his people:

[. . .] despite his enmity to art, Moses was himself a great artist and possessed the true artistic spirit. Only in him, as with his Egyptian compatriots, this artistic spirit was focused only on the colossal and imperishable. Unlike the Egyptians, however, he did not shape his artistic works from brick and granite; rather, he built human pyramids, he chiselled human obelisks, he took a poor pastoral tribe and made it into a nation that would likewise bid defiance to the centuries—a great, everlasting, holy nation, a nation of God, that could serve as a model to all other nations, and indeed as a prototype to the whole of mankind: he created Israel! (H vi. 481)

---

[231] See Volkmar Hansen, *Thomas Manns Heine-Rezeption* (Hamburg, 1975), pp. 251–65.

Similarly, Mann's Moses exploits the authority gained by leading the exodus from Egypt in order to begin shaping the 'formless body of his people' (M viii. 846), which is 'mere raw material of flesh and blood' (M viii. 847), to be cleaned, carved, and chipped with a metaphorical chisel. His instruction begins with toilet training and elementary hygiene and works up via the dietary laws to chastity, honesty, and piety. Thus a whole psychosocial process, in which the polymorphous body of the child is trained and disciplined, is condensed into the Israelites' brief sojourn in the oasis of Kadesh. No wonder that while Moses is on Sinai they relapse into worshipping the Golden Calf. Their infantile regression is described farcically as a return to practices of incest, defecation, and eating worms. Cultural taboos are not yet effective in the absence of Moses' personal authority. Their dance recalls the Dionysiac orgy that Aschenbach dreams about in *Death in Venice*, and the erotic gambollings of Heine's poem 'The Golden Calf'.[232] The tables of the Law are needed as a substitute for Moses' presence; and the commandments incised in the stone express metaphorically the harshness with which Moses inscribes his ethical will on the body of his people.

The image of the sculptor has further alarming resonances. It was well established to describe how a dictator reshapes society. In Büchner's disillusioned drama of the French Revolution, *Danton's Death* (1835), the imprisoned Danton remarks: 'These days everything is fashioned out of human flesh. And now my body's to be used as well.'[233] Nietzsche in *The Genealogy of Morals* spoke of the politician as an artist working on human material and shaping it with the hammer-blows of his 'artistic violence'.[234] Mussolini talked of the masses being 'like wax in my hands', and said: 'Lenin is an artist who has worked in men as others have worked in marble and metal.'[235] So Mann's Moses, even if a benevolent dictator, disturbingly resembles the malevolent dictators against whom the book was directed. The Ten Commandments are a 'Diktat', i.e. something dictated by God to Moses and by Moses to his people (M viii. 860, 863, 864, 872). His civilizing efforts

---

[232] *Complete Poems of Heine*, p. 586.
[233] Georg Büchner, *Complete Plays, 'Lenz', and Other Writings*, tr. John Reddick (London, 1993), p. 49.   [234] Nietzsche, *Werke*, VI, ii. 341.
[235] Quoted in J. P. Stern, *Hitler: The Führer and the People* (Glasgow, 1975), p. 45.

are enforced by Joshua's troop of young men, the Angels of Death, who execute the worshippers of the Golden Calf.

Mann's portrayal of the dictator Moses recalls Freud's desire for a dictatorship of reason. Both writers posit a wide gulf separating the rational and moral authority from the irrational, sensual mass on which it is to be imposed. Rather than awakening among the Israelites a latent desire for goodness and purity, Moses inscribes these values brutally on their stubborn flesh. His dictatorship also recalls Nietzsche's account in *The Genealogy of Morals* of how a priestly caste imposes a bad conscience on people previously guided by natural impulses and of the pain required to imprint commandments on the body of recalcitrant humanity. Thus, if Moses represents the spirit ('Geist'), then the spirit appears as a tyranny. Instead of a humanist vision in which carnal desires are purified by the influence of the spirit, we have a harsh vision in which an inhuman technology, in the service ostensibly of God but perhaps only of a strong-willed individual, cuts into the vulnerable living flesh of the desiring body and ruthlessly subjects it to a severe moral order. And here we have two Jewish stereotypes pushed to an extreme. On the one hand, we have the rationality of the Jew, originally propagated by Mendelssohn but reinterpreted by antisemites like Chamberlain as an iron will to calculate and dominate. On the other, this rationality is imposed on the natural Jew, who is an entirely sensual being, as indifferent to civilized taboos as the incestuous pair in *Wälsungenblut*.

Mann's doubts about Jews reappear in *Doktor Faustus* (1947). No sooner has the 'good German' narrator Zeitblom expressed cautious dissent from Hitler's treatment of the Jewish question, than he adds that some specimens of that stock ('Exemplare jenes Geblütes') have aroused confusion and antipathy in him (M vi. 15). This applies chiefly to Dr Chaim Breisacher, a polymath and an intellectual opportunist with a nose for ultra-modern fashion. Even before the First World War he dumbfounds conservatives by an out-and-out primitivism, as in the brilliant comic scene where the hapless General von Riedesel learns from Breisacher that King Solomon was a decadent, the Psalmist an impious Enlightener, and prayer a mere rationalization of magic (M vi. 371–8). After the War Breisacher reappears among the Kridwiss circle, who are Mann's chief examples of intellectuals toying with barbarism. In both respects Breisacher contrasts with the authentic German artist Leverkühn. While Breisacher is a performer and charlatan, Leverkühn is a recluse; while Breisacher seizes on others' ideas, Leverkühn is a true innovator whose artistic achievements cost him his health, his peace of mind, and possibly his soul. And while Breisacher dabbles in politics, Leverkühn is resolutely unpolitical, despite the deeper homology between his uncompromising modernism and the anti-humanism of contemporary German politics. Breisacher is based on the eccentric Bible scholar, Oskar Goldberg, whose notions about archaic Judaism, set down in his *Die Wirklichkeit der Hebräer* (1925), will be glanced at in Chapter 5.[236] A strange diary entry of 15 July 1934 reveals that Mann actually regarded Goldberg as a typical Jewish intellectual, and hence as a typical Jew:

Thought about the absurdity whereby the Jews, who are being deprived of their rights and expelled from Germany, have a major share in the intellectual matters that find (admittedly distorted) expression in the political system and to a large extent must be considered as having prepared the way for the anti-liberal turn.[237]

Goldberg is then cited as an example, along with Karl Wolfskehl and Theodor Lessing. It is extraordinary to generalize about Jews, even about Jewish intellectuals, from so few and such eccentric examples. There may be projection at work: Mann is projecting on to the 'Jews' his own earlier anti-democratic, nationalistic sentiments, and thus, in a remarkable feat of blaming the victims, giving the Jews partial responsibility for Nazism.

The other major Jewish character, Saul Fitelberg, is an impresario from Paris who visits Leverkühn's Bavarian retreat in the vain hope of luring him into the cosmopolitan music industry. Here Mann adopts the Wagnerian topos of the Jew's alienation from language. Originally from Poland, Fitelberg speaks a mixture of German and French which marks him out as a rootless cosmopolitan, in contrast to the quintessentially German Leverkühn. It also shows him to be, as Mann admitted, a literary descendant of Lessing's dishonest Frenchman Riccaut (M xi. 280). Fitelberg is a skilful imitator who has learnt, by adjusting his language, manners, and dress, to move in high society as though born to

[236] On Mann and Goldberg, see Stéphane Mosès, *Spuren der Schrift: von Goethe bis Celan* (Frankfurt, 1987), pp. 111–33.
[237] Mann, *Tagebücher 1933–1934*, p. 473.

it. He himself is uncreative; through the international entertainment business he reduces art to a commodity. Yielding to his blandishments and accompanying him to Paris would mean the loss of Leverkühn's integrity as a German artist. And yet the scene is deeply ambivalent, for Leverkühn's seclusion represents a rejection of European contacts and a retreat into an introverted, unbalanced German identity.[238] The scene is also, as Egon Schwarz says, 'the allegory of the failed German–Jewish experiment'.[239] Fitelberg talks with evident feeling about the affinity between Germans and Jews:

Why should we Jews, who are a priestly people, even when we are minaudering about in Parisian salons, not feel drawn to the Germans? [. . .] The Germans should let the Jew be the médiateur between them and society, be the manager, the impresario. He is altogether the right man for it, one should not turn him out, he is international, and he is pro-German. Mais c'est en vain. Et c'est très dommage![240]

But such an experiment could only fail, for it accepts the stereotypes of the creative, emotional, inarticulate German (going back to Fichte) and of the nimble, cosmopolitan, uncreative Jew whose predestined task is service to German culture. This task is illustrated by a minor character, Kunigunde Rosenstiel, a Jewish businesswoman who supports Leverkühn's musical career. Her portrayal begins with clichés: a 'bony Jewess' with 'woolly hair' and eyes whose 'primeval sadness' betrays the 'daughter of Zion' (M vi. 417); but Mann reverses Wagner's stereotypes by telling us that Kunigunde, like most Jews, is very musical, and that she wins Leverkühn's favour by her command of pure German. Her devotion to Leverkühn, though, represents a Jew's loyalty to the German art which she cannot create.

Should we agree with Egon Schwarz that Mann colluded with antisemitism by presenting unattractive Jewish figures in a novel purporting to account for the German catastrophe? Granted, Breisacher and Fitelberg are great comic characters. But Mann is

---

[238] See Hans Rudolf Vaget, 'Kaisersaschern als geistige Lebensform', in Wolfgang Paulsen (ed.), *Der deutsche Roman und seine historischen und politischen Bedingungen* (Berne and Munich, 1977), pp. 200–35.

[239] Schwarz, 'Die jüdischen Gestalten in Thomas Manns *Doktor Faustus*', *Thomas Mann Jahrbuch*, 2 (1989), 79–101 (p. 93).

[240] Mann, *Doctor Faustus*, tr. Helen Lowe-Porter (London, 1949), pp. 407–8; M vi. 541–2.

playing a double game by exploiting their self-dramatizing charlatanry for novelistic effect while implicitly censuring them for this very quality. Mann pointed out that the novel contains no sympathetic characters except Zeitblom and Frau Schweigestill; otherwise it is a gallery of eccentrics, 'an aquarium of fish in fantastic shapes'.[241] That does not account, however, for the exceptional comic gusto with which Breisacher and Fitelberg are portrayed. They are products of the long-standing view, traced back to Dohm and the beginnings of emancipation, of Jews as essentially different, as set apart by their Jewishness, not as individuals who incidentally happen to be Jews. They are dramatic performers: Breisacher dominates a salon, Fitelberg dumbfounds Zeitblom and Leverkühn with his unstoppable, multilingual monologue. This dramatic presentation suggests that the comic Jew has been transferred from the stage to the novel. On the page, the Jew dramatically enacts the difference which is imposed on him by a well-established mentality and which underlies the portrayal of the Jew in realist fiction from Raabe to Mann. It would be wrong, I believe, to see Mann as tainted by antisemitism. But there is a tension between the novelist's task of entertaining the reader with vivid characters and the other task of leading us through empathy to appreciate the shared humanity of people who are outwardly different.

[241] Letter to Agnes Meyer, 7 Sept. 1948, in *Briefe*, ed. Erika Mann, 3 vols. (Frankfurt, 1962–5), iii. 49.

4

Assimilation

Dual Identity

The establishment of the German Empire in 1871 brought with it the extension of full civil rights to all the Jews in its territory. The Jews of the Habsburg Empire had gained full civil rights through the new liberal constitution four years earlier. At last the Jews' legal rights were commensurate with their economic and social success. As Zygmunt Bauman puts it: 'In Germany and the Austro-Hungarian Empire the emancipation of the Jews was a story of uninterrupted and astounding success by all standards accessible and deemed relevant at the time.'[1] And yet the 1870s were the decade in which the 'Jewish question' became a subject of debate, the word 'antisemitism' was coined and came into wide use, and Treitschke could claim that most Germans considered the Jews a national misfortune. Their very success, as we have seen, made Jews seem to typify the negative aspects of capitalist modernity, and called forth a new antisemitism that protested against supposed Jewish domination.[2] How did German and Austrian Jews respond to this Janus-faced situation?

Many Jews understood their situation as the triumph of liberalism. This meta-narrative underlies the much-read German-Jewish histories by Heinrich Graetz and Ludwig Geiger.[3] In their narratives, pre-emancipation Jewry was sunk in superstition: 'demoralised and despised', dominated by 'childish dotards', afflicted by 'the superstitious errors of the Kabbala' and 'the

---

[1] Bauman, *Modernity and Ambivalence* (Cambridge, 1991), p. 164.
[2] The tensions are well summarized by Reinhard Rürup, 'Emancipation and Crisis: The "Jewish Question" in Germany 1850–1890', *LBY* 20 (1975), 13–25.
[3] See David Sorkin, 'Emancipation and Assimilation: Two Concepts and their Application to German-Jewish History', *LBY* 35 (1990), 17–33 (p. 21).

mud-streams of Sabbatian fanaticism'.[4] Jews were liberated from superstition and gained access to European culture through proponents of the Enlightenment such as Frederick the Great and Moses Mendelssohn, who 'aroused the slumbering genius of the Jewish race' and initiated an 'intellectual and spiritual rebirth'.[5] These historians celebrate the attachment to tradition shown by the development of its scholarly study, and the renewal of tradition typified by Reform Judaism. Above all, they extol Gabriel Riesser for restoring Jewish self-esteem by his proclamation in 1831 that Jews were Germans who subscribed to the 'Mosaic confession'.[6]

Thus this narrative culminated in acceptance as simultaneously Jewish and German. Similarly, liberals like Riesser and Jacoby had sought acceptance as German Jews, though the content of their Jewishness was to be accommodated to the demands of modernity. 'As I am simultaneously a Jew and a German, the Jew in me cannot become free without the German, nor the German without the Jew', wrote Jacoby in a letter of May 1837; 'as I cannot divide myself, no more can I divide the freedom of the one from that of the other within myself.'[7] Riesser's words, 'If anyone disputes my German identity, I consider him a murderer', were often quoted.[8] They wished to be respected as Jews who were imbued with the German spirit. The psychologist Moritz Lazarus argued in response to Treitschke that since *Volk* was an intellectual construct based on language, Jewish descent was no obstacle to Jews' becoming Germans, any more than Kant was disqualified as a German by his Scottish ancestry: 'Our mother tongue and fatherland are German: both are the progenitors of our inner life.'[9] Gustav Landauer said in 1913 that he was neither a German Jew nor a Jewish German, but both equally: 'I am aware of no dependent or adjectival relationship; [. . .] my Germanness and Jewishness do each other no harm and give each other much

---

[4] Graetz, *History of the Jews, from the Earliest Times to the Present Day*, ed. and tr. Bella Löwy, 5 vols. (London, 1891–2), v. 211, 213, 219.

[5] Graetz, *History*, v. 310; Geiger, *Geschichte der Juden in Berlin*, i. 74 (chapter heading).

[6] Graetz, *History*, v. 640–4; Geiger, *Geschichte der Juden in Berlin*, i. 183.

[7] Quoted in Weber, *Jacoby*, p. 38.

[8] e.g. in Blumenfeld, *Erlebte Judenfrage*, p. 45.

[9] Lazarus, 'Was heißt national?' (lecture delivered on 2 Dec. 1879), in *Treu und Frei* (Leipzig, 1887), pp. 53–113 (p. 71).

help.'[10] Moritz Heimann declared in 1917 that he had been a
Zionist even before he heard the term, yet felt no contradiction
between his Jewish sympathies and his German cultural identity:
'There is nothing unnatural in following an orbit with two
centres; some comets do it, and all the planets.'[11] Admitting
that German antisemitism seemed incorrigible, Jakob
Wassermann in 1921 persisted in affirming: 'I am a German,
and I am a Jew, the one as much and as completely as the
other.'[12]

Yet the liberal Jewish self-conception as equally Jewish and
German ran counter to the belief held by non-Jewish liberals
since Kant, Dohm, and Humboldt that Jewish emancipation
meant being absorbed into the cultural melting-pot and losing
their distinctive Jewish identity. Thus the historian Theodor
Mommsen replied to Treitschke's antisemitism by arguing that
just as the separate Germanic tribes had been absorbed into a
single nation, and the seventeenth-century French Huguenot
immigrants had been assimilated, so the Jews would simply
add a flavour to the new national compound; indeed, he resorted
to one of the biological analogies ubiquitous at this period by
calling the Jews a powerful agent of decomposition, dissolving
regional identities into the new homogeneous German nation.[13]
But while Mommsen and other non-Jews understood Jewish
assimilation as absorption into the national whole, liberal Jews
took assimilation to mean their social acceptance with a distinct
cultural identity. They used the word to mean what would now
be called 'acculturation': acceptance of a common culture by a
social group that remains distinct.[14] Accordingly, historians now
see acculturated German Jews as forming a subculture: 'a sub-
group in society, recognizable by its ethnic origin, its economic

[10] Landauer, 'Sind das Ketzergedanken?' [1913], in *Der werdende Mensch*, ed.
Martin Buber (Potsdam, 1921), pp. 120–8 (p. 126).
[11] Heimann, 'Zionismus und Politik' [1917], in *Was ist das: ein Gedanke? Essays*,
ed. Gert Mattenklott (Frankfurt, 1986), pp. 181–91 (p. 183).
[12] Wassermann, *Mein Weg als Deutscher und Jude* [1921], in *Deutscher und
Jude: Reden und Schriften 1904–1933*, ed. Dierk Rodewald (Heidelberg, 1984),
p. 130.
[13] Mommsen, *Auch ein Wort über unser Judenthum* (Berlin, 1880), repr. in
W. Boehlich (ed.), *Der Berliner Antisemitismusstreit* (Frankfurt, 1965), pp. 210–25.
[14] See Sorkin, 'Emancipation and Assimilation', p. 20.

concentration, its comparative social isolation, and by its non-conformist minority religion'.[15]

These features, however, were not all present in equal strength. Social isolation diminished only slowly, while (except among the strictly Orthodox) attachment to religious Judaism, or to any cultural distinctiveness, was in decline. Residual allegiance to Jewish culture was often half-hearted and embarrassed. 'In my boyhood,' recalled Max Mayer, 'a knowledge of Judaism and its teachings, the very consciousness of being Jewish, were to me something supplementary, rather a domestic matter and of little practical significance outside the family circle.'[16] Wassermann, brought up in the ancient Jewish community of Fürth, recalls that after his mother's death, when he was 9, he had to say *kaddish* for her twice a day for a year in the company of a *minyan* of ten elderly men, but that his father gradually abandoned religious practice apart from following the dietary laws and observing festivals: 'In reality we were Jews only in name and through the hostility, alienation or rejection received from our Christian surroundings.'[17] Max Brod recalled how in his childhood in Prague, around 1890, Jewish festivals survived in shadowy, barely understood forms: the Feast of Tabernacles was reduced to a series of hasty visits from an elderly man carrying a palm-branch and a citron (*ethrog*) over which his father would pronounce a blessing; lights were still kindled at Hanukkah, and a feast was held at Passover, though the children were not encouraged to take the prayers seriously.[18]

Traditional Jewish learning was imparted only in the form of Hebrew lessons which seem usually to have been badly taught and to have left little impression but repugnance. Fritz Mauthner says that the religious instruction he received in Prague around 1860 was divided between moral platitudes too simple for a 9-year-old, and Hebrew lessons that would have puzzled a trained Orientalist.[19] Arthur Ruppin, brought up in Prussian Poland, recalled his

[15] Katz, *Out of the Ghetto*, p. 213; see Sorkin, *The Transformation of German Jewry*, and for the application of this model to Vienna, Steven Beller, *Vienna and the Jews 1867–1938: A Cultural History* (Cambridge, 1989).

[16] Mayer, 'A German Jew goes East', *LBY* 3 (1958), 344–57 (p. 344).

[17] Wassermann, *Mein Weg*, p. 41.

[18] Brod, *Streitbares Leben* (Munich, 1960), p. 347.

[19] Mauthner, *Prager Jugendjahre* (Frankfurt, 1969), pp. 112–14.

Hebrew instruction as 'very superficial'; Julius Braunthal remembered his Torah school, which he attended in Vienna around
1900, as a nightmare.[20] Arnold Zweig, a Berliner, recalls 'the
disgracefully dreary lessons which nobody spoke of with respect
and which were imposed on us by the most wooden and
incompetent pedagogues'.[21] Karl Kraus, remembering his
religious instructors in the Franz-Josefs-Gymnasium in Vienna,
called them effective propagandists for conversion: 'How many
may subsequently be grateful to their orthodox tormentors who so
zealously propagated baptism and involuntarily planted the seeds
of a healthier outlook in the boys' brains.'[22] 'Strangely enough,'
writes Wassermann, 'I have seldom heard of a humane or kindly
teacher of Jewish religion; most are cold zealots and half-
ridiculous figures.'[23] No wonder, therefore, that in 1934 Rabbi
Joachim Prinz could lament the extraordinary disappearance of
Jewish learning which had made biblical research the province of
Protestant theologians: 'The "people of the book", as the Jews are
known, has long since forgotten its own books and left them lying
in lumber-rooms.'[24]

Recent studies of Jewish life in Vienna and Prague show that
many Jews continued to live in largely Jewish neighbourhoods. In
1867, 68 per cent of the Berlin Jews lived in Alt-Berlin and the
adjacent districts.[25] In 1900, 55 per cent of all Viennese Jews
lived in three districts of the city: Innenstadt, Leopoldstadt, and
Alsergrund.[26] Upwardly mobile Jews tended to leave traditional
residential areas, only to cluster afresh in wealthier districts. It was
often easy to think of oneself as solely German while one's main
social contacts were largely with other German Jews. Fanny
Lewald was brought up in a fully acculturated family which socialized mainly with other Jews, yet it was only pious relatives and

---

[20] Ruppin, *Briefe, Tagebücher, Erinnerungen*, ed. Schlomo Krolik (Königstein,
1985), p. 44; Braunthal, *In Search of the Millennium* (London, 1945), pp. 24–5.

[21] Zweig, *Caliban*, p. 156.

[22] Kraus, 'Jüdischer Religionsunterricht', *Die Fackel* (Aug. 1899), 27–30 (p. 30).

[23] Wassermann, *Mein Weg*, p. 39.

[24] Prinz, *Wir Juden* (Berlin, 1934), pp. 57–8.

[25] Steven M. Lowenstein, 'Jewish Residential Concentration in Post-Emancipation
Germany', *LBY* 28 (1983), 471–95 (p. 478).

[26] Marsha L. Rozenblit, *The Jews of Vienna, 1867–1914: Assimilation and Identity*
(Albany, NY, 1983), p. 76. For Prague, see Gary B. Cohen, 'Jews in German Society:
Prague, 1860–1914', *Central European History*, 10 (1977), 28–54.

hostile schoolchildren who told her that they were Jews.[27]
Norbert Elias recalled that during his upbringing in Breslau,
his family felt no conflict between their German and their
Jewish identities, thought of themselves as Germans, visited
the synagogue on festival days, but in fact belonged to 'good
Jewish society [which] formed a closely knit kind of bourgeoisie'.[28] Hans Mayer describes how his parents in Cologne 'lived,
without knowing it, at least without wanting to know it, in a
German-Jewish ghetto'.[29] A recurrent scene in German-Jewish
autobiography tells how the child learns of his or her Jewish
identity from Gentiles, because the parents no longer have any
positive conception of Jewishness. Thus Kurt Blumenfeld as a
child was told by a Catholic maidservant that one of the sins
she confessed to her priest was working for Jews, because the
Jews had crucified Christ.[30] Hannah Arendt, brought up, like
Blumenfeld, in Königsberg, did not know that she was Jewish
until she heard antisemitic insults.[31] Ernst Toller, born in the
German-speaking town of Samotschin in Prussian Poland,
records as his earliest memory how another child's nursemaid
said about him: 'Don't stand there, that's a Jew', words whose
meaning he did not understand.[32] Margarete Susman, brought
up in a secure middle-class home in Hamburg in the 1870s,
knew the word 'Jew' only from a children's story featuring a
villainous Jew who robbed a tree of its golden leaves; after her
unconverted family had celebrated Christmas, young Margarete,
charmed by the Christmas tree, exclaimed: 'I don't want to be a
Jew, I want to be a Christian', and was deeply upset to be told
by her nanny that she was ineluctably a Jew and thus akin to
the thief.[33]

Jewish families were not always cold-shouldered by their non-
Jewish neighbours. In Ruppin's home town, Rawitsch in Posen,
Jews in the 1880s co-operated amicably with German Protestants

---

[27] Lewald, *Meine Lebensgeschichte*, p. 43.
[28] Elias, *Reflections on a Life*, tr. Edmund Jephcott (Cambridge, 1994), p. 6.
[29] Mayer, *Ein Deutscher auf Widerruf: Erinnerungen* [1982], 2 vols. (Frankfurt, 1988), i. 61.   [30] Blumenfeld, *Erlebte Judenfrage*, p. 27.
[31] See Richard J. Bernstein, *Hannah Arendt and the Jewish Question* (Cambridge, 1996), p. 14.
[32] Toller, *Eine Jugend in Deutschland* ([1933]; Reinbek, 1963), p. 12.
[33] Susman, *Ich habe viele Leben gelebt: Erinnerungen* (Stuttgart, 1964), p. 17.

and Polish Catholics.[34] Moritz Heimann, brought up in a Prussian village in the 1870s, recalled:

In my childhood, as the only Jewish family in the village and following the strict ritual law, we were completely absorbed into our Christian, German environment, not despite our Jewish difference but *because* of it.[35]

The Socialist politician and theorist of post-Marxian revisionism, Eduard Bernstein, the son of a Jewish engine-driver, was brought up in a district of Berlin with few Jews. His parents were Reform Jews who observed Sunday and did not keep kosher. This, Bernstein thinks, is why they were accepted: 'Separation at meals and the celebration of a different day of rest are often felt by the populace to be a dividing wall that prevents the development and establishment of a true sense of social cohesion.'[36] But he also thinks that his parents attained social acceptance at the cost of reducing their Jewish identity to a set of ethical precepts almost devoid of any religious basis. Despite their acceptance, his Jewishness was brought home to him and his siblings by mockery from other children and by the habit among his parents' non-Jewish friends of threatening their children with the words 'The Jew's coming'. In adult life, he did not wish to deny his Jewishness, but it did not prevent him from becoming a patriotic German liberal and later Socialist with deep worries about the share of Jewish capital in supporting financial speculation and influencing the press. Writing in wartime, with antisemitism increasing, Bernstein understandably plays down its presence in the past; even so, he conveys that Jewish children could not remain unaware of their difference, and that adults had to minimize the difference in their customs in order to find acceptance outside the subculture.

The Jewish subculture was kept in being both by internal solidarity and by more or less subtle mechanisms of exclusion. Particular pessimism about assimilation is expressed in 1911 by Friedrich Blach, who shows his yearning for this ideal by adopting the unusual self-description 'a Jewish German' (instead of the normal 'German Jew'). He says that Jews are typically in one of

[34] Ruppin, *Briefe, Tagebücher, Erinnerungen*, p. 32.
[35] Heimann, *Was ist das: ein Gedanke?*, p. 183.
[36] Bernstein, 'Wie ich als Jude in der Diaspora aufwuchs', *Der Jude*, 2 (1917–18), iii. 186–95 (p. 188).

two situations, both unfavourable for assimilation. If a Jew lives in
a city, he mixes mostly with other Jews and does not learn German
ways. If he lives in a small town, he is dependent on non-Jews, but
is liable to be embittered by repeated rebuffs.

After numerous failures on entering new circles the Jew ends by always
conducting careful tests, and especially by examining every individual
with suspicion. For nothing is so infectious as antisemitism. This
constantly repeated dilemma makes him gradually unsure of himself.
His outward appearance and manner may be impeccable, but inwardly
he is always on the *qui vive*. The consequence is a nervousness that most
readily afflicts those for whom absorption into German identity
(*Deutschtum*) is a truly heartfelt need.[37]

Milder but pervasive social unease is expressed in the diaries kept
in the 1920s by Victor Klemperer, professor of Romance
philology at Dresden. A convert, he rarely reveals his Jewishness.
Getting into conversation with pleasant but right-wing Germans,
he guiltily colludes in their discreet antisemitism: 'a swastika angel
passed through the room'.[38] At a conference, he notes the Jewish
appearance of colleagues: one is clearly a Viennese Jew despite his
duelling scars, another has 'bow legs, Jewish face', another 'looks
like a Talmudist'.[39] He enjoys 'nice Jewish evenings' with his
familiar circle; Gentile friends are felt as 'foreign bodies', and
the rest feel more relaxed after their departure; at one such
evening, Klemperer's Gentile wife (evidently acculturated to her
surroundings) contributes to the 'Jewish tone' by making a cross-
word puzzle composed of Yiddish expressions.[40] Yet Klemperer
dislikes the wrong kind of Jews—showy and ostentatious types.[41]
The subculture was not homogeneous.

Even on the highest social level, complete social acceptance
seemed unattainable. What *arriviste* ever arrived more definitively
than Gerson Bleichröder, who was appointed Bismarck's banker in
1859, was the only Jew present at the Versailles negotiations
following the Franco-Prussian War in 1871, and was raised to
the hereditary nobility in 1872? Admittedly, Bleichröder was

---

[37] [Blach], *Die Juden in Deutschland. Von einem jüdischen Deutschen* (Berlin,
1911), p. 73.
[38] Klemperer, *Leben sammeln, nicht fragen wozu und warum: Tagebücher 1918–
1932*, ed. Walter Nowojski, 2 vols. (Berlin, 1996), i. 621.
[39] Ibid. i. 362–5.   [40] Ibid. i. 661; ii. 61, 17.   [41] Ibid. i. 888–9.

ennobled largely because he had helped to salvage the fortunes of Prussian junkers threatened with ruin by the collapse of the Romanian railway projects organized by the Jewish financier Strousberg. He was one of the two richest men in the Empire, the other being Alfred Krupp; he was a personal friend of Bismarck; he entertained lavishly, and was reputed to invite only Gentiles; remaining a loyal Jew, he donated millions of marks to Jewish and Christian charities. Yet he pleased neither community. His children all converted and married non-Jews, and led at best undistinguished lives (his son Hans was idle in business and was cashiered as an officer). He was not socially accepted, but seen as a parvenu. When he was abused personally by Stöcker in 1880, he sent the Kaiser a petition requesting protection for himself and other Jewish subjects, but it was not till seven months later that he received any reply, and then only six bland lines. 'Genuine acceptance by the highest levels of German society was a mirage that lured Gerson and his children ever deeper into a wilderness of unrealizable ambitions from which there was no return.'[42]

Many Jews sought assimilation through conversion. 'In the early 1880s, there were at least two hundred conversions a year [in Germany]; twenty years later, over five hundred. In relative terms, this means that in the 1800s there was one conversion a year for every 2,200 Jews in Germany; in the early 1900s, one for every 1,100 Jews. More significantly, in Berlin, the center of gravity of German Jewry, the ratios were much higher: about one for every 600 to 650 Jews in the period 1882 to 1908.'[43] These figures do not include those who adopted Catholicism, nor the numerous parents who, without themselves converting, had their children baptized in order to spare them difficulties in later life. Some converts were sincere, like the philosopher Edmund Husserl, who became a Lutheran while a student. But most were motivated by expedience, not devotion. Missionary societies made pitiably few converts, and recognized that most of their applicants sought 'work, shelter,

---

[42] Fritz Stern, *Gold and Iron: Bismarck, Bleichröder, and the Building of the German Empire* (London, 1977), p. 466.

[43] Todd M. Endelman, 'The Social and Political Context of Conversion in Germany and England, 1870–1914', in Endelman (ed.), *Jewish Apostasy in the Modern World* (New York and London, 1987), pp. 83–107 (p. 85).

bread, but not Christian truth'.[44] But conversion did not secure one against racially based antisemitism.

Not only unconverted but also converted Jews were liable to experience rejection in their professional lives. During the nineteenth century, as we saw in Chapter 2, German and Austrian Jews largely entered the middle class. Increasingly they sought not the economic success available to the self-employed, but acceptance within an established profession. The frequent barriers they encountered can be attributed to antisemitism, not necessarily as a full-blown ideology, but as a more subtle mechanism of exclusion encouraged by the 'anti-modern mentality' which identified Jews with an unwanted modernization. It was difficult under the German Empire for Jewish lawyers to be appointed to official positions such as those of notaries, state prosecutors, or judges, though practice varied widely in different states. Before 1918 only one unbaptized Jew became a Cabinet Minister: Moritz Elstätter, Minister of Finance in Baden from 1868 to 1893 and delegate to the Bundesrat (the Upper House of the Imperial Parliament).[45] Despite legal entitlement, unbaptized Jews were from 1885 on excluded (except in Bavaria) from becoming army officers or joining the prestigious reserve officer corps.[46] Austria was more tolerant, admitting Jews both to the officer corps (though not always to the 'best' regiments) and to the reserve, of which in 1897 Jews formed 18 per cent.[47] While many Jews studied medicine, they were less likely to pursue prestigious careers like surgery than to enter clinical practice, and they often adopted relatively unattractive specialisms like dermatology, venereology, and—eventually—psychoanalysis.[48]

Access to the academic profession was also difficult for Jews. The Prussian 'lex Gans', debarring unbaptized Jews from academic posts, was suspended only in 1847, and not until then was an unconverted Jew, the physiologist Robert Remak, appointed (though only as *Privatdozent*) at a Prussian university. The first

[44] Quoted in Clark, *The Politics of Conversion*, p. 249.

[45] Pulzer, *Jews and the German State*, p. 91.

[46] Werner T. Angress, 'Prussia's Army and the Jewish Reserve Officer Controversy before World War I', *LBY* 17 (1972), 19–42.

[47] See István Deák, *Beyond Nationalism: A Social and Political History of the Habsburg Officer Corps, 1848–1918* (New York and Oxford, 1990), p. 175.

[48] See Efron, *Defenders of the Race*, pp. 30–1; Weindling, *Health, Race and German Politics*, p. 34.

Jew to become a full professor in Germany was the mathematician Moritz Abraham Stern at Göttingen in 1859; the first in Berlin was the medical scientist Ludwig Traube in 1872. By the end of the 1870s there were about twenty unbaptized Jewish professors in Germany.[49] Their numbers increased only slowly. Moritz Lazarus, the distinguished founder of *Völkerpsychologie*, made his early career in Switzerland, moved to Berlin out of patriotic enthusiasm when the Empire was founded in 1871, and received many honours, but never an actual professorial appointment (*ordentliche Professur*).[50] Freud recalls in 'An Autobiographical Study' how, on arriving at Vienna University in 1873, 'I found that I was expected to feel myself inferior and an alien because I was a Jew' (*SE* xx. 9). He spent seventeen years as a 'Privatdozent' before being appointed a professor, and owed his appointment only to some determined string-pulling.[51] The distinguished neo-Kantian philosopher Hermann Cohen was appointed to the Chair of Philosophy at Marburg only at the second attempt, thanks to intervention by Prussia's liberal Minister of Education, Adalbert Falk.[52] Another philosopher, Ernst Cassirer, needed the support of Wilhelm Dilthey to become even a *Privatdozent* in 1906, and had to wait till the advent of the Weimar Republic to obtain a Chair in 1919.[53] The sociologist Georg Simmel, though a second-generation convert, had to wait even longer for a Chair: he was in his mid-fifties when appointed professor at Strasbourg in 1913, and his professional isolation resulted from a bias against sociology in general, a distrust of his unorthodox and literary approach to the subject, and an antisemitism which was at times made explicit: his appointment at Heidelberg was prevented, in part, by a letter from a fellow-academic describing him as 'an

[49] Pulzer, *Jews and the German State*, pp. 92–3.

[50] Belke, 'Einleitung', in Lazarus and Steinthal, *Die Begründer*, p. xl.

[51] Gay, *Freud: A Life for our Time*, pp. 136–9. For other examples of professional difficulties experienced by unconverted Jewish academics, see Endelman, 'The Social and Political Context of Conversion', pp. 89–90.

[52] Pulzer, *Jews and the German State*, p. 93.

[53] David R. Lipton, *Ernst Cassirer: The Dilemma of a Liberal Intellectual in Germany, 1914–1933* (Toronto, 1978), pp. 8–9. On academic appointments, particularly Cassirer's, see the revealing correspondence between Husserl and Paul Natorp in Husserl, *Briefwechsel*, ed. Karl Schuhmann, 10 vols. (Dordrecht, 1994), v. 132–62.

Israelite through and through'.[54] Paul Ehrlich, who developed salvarsan as a cure for syphilis, was awarded the Nobel Prize for Medicine in 1908, but could obtain a Chair only at the University of Frankfurt, privately founded in 1914; the highest state post he held was that of director of the Institute for Experimental Therapy at Frankfurt.[55] The unconverted Eduard Berend, later the first scholarly editor of Jean Paul, gave up hope of an academic career in 1920 after three unsuccessful attempts to have his post-doctoral thesis accepted.[56] Max Weber said in 1918 that a commitment to an academic career was a 'mad hazard' for any young scholar, but 'if he is a Jew, of course one says *lasciate ogni speranza*'.[57]

Another source of discontent and disadvantage was the exclusion of Jews from student corporations (*Studentenverbindungen*). These corporations, with their bizarre drinking and duelling rituals, were a major form of student sociability which sheltered their members against the loneliness and insecurity of late adolescence.[58] Although many Jewish students were admitted in the mid-nineteenth century, by the 1890s they were normally excluded; and in 1896 a Viennese student assembly went further by enunciating the 'Waidhofen Principle' which declared Jews to be racially incapable of appreciating the German concept of honour and therefore unfit to duel with an Aryan.[59] Exclusion from these

[54] Quoted in Dirk Käsler, *Die frühe deutsche Soziologie 1909 bis 1934 und ihre Entstehungs-Milieus: Eine wissenschaftssoziologische Untersuchung* (Opladen, 1984), p. 381. On his Strasbourg appointment, see Hans Simmel, 'Auszug aus den Lebenserinnerungen', in Hannes Böhringer and Karlfried Gründer (eds.), *Ästhetik und Soziologie um die Jahrhundertwende: Georg Simmel* (Frankfurt, 1976), pp. 247–68 (pp. 264–6). [55] Pulzer, *Jews and the German State*, pp. 110–11.
[56] Hanne Knickmann, 'Der Jean-Paul-Forscher Eduard Berend (1883–1973). I', *Jahrbuch der Jean-Paul-Gesellschaft* 1994, 7–91. Walter Benjamin's 'Habilitation' thesis, later published as *Der Ursprung des deutschen Trauerspiels*, was rejected by examiners, one of whom judged it partially unintelligible: see Burkhardt Lindner, 'Habilitationsakte Benjamin', *LiLi: Zeitschrift für Literaturwissenschaft und Linguistik*, 53–4 (1984), 147–65.
[57] Weber, 'Science as a Vocation', in *From Max Weber: Essays in Sociology*, tr. H. H. Gerth and C. Wright Mills (London, 1947), pp. 129–56 (p. 134). For further examples, see Notker Hammerstein, *Antisemitismus und deutsche Universitäten 1871–1933* (Hamburg, 1995), p. 73.
[58] See Peter Gay, *The Cultivation of Hatred* (New York, 1993), pp. 9–33; Ute Frevert, *Ehrenmänner: Das Duell in der bürgerlichen Gesellschaft* (Munich, 1991), pp. 132–59.
[59] See R. G. S. Weber, *The German Student Corps in the Third Reich* (London, 1986), pp. 48–53; Frevert, *Ehrenmänner*, pp. 158–9. Schnitzler comments indignantly

corporations, complained Friedrich Blach in 1911, obliged Jewish students either to forgo an important part of student life or to found their own corporations which were a poor imitation of the real thing.[60] Moreover, they were excluded from the old-boy networks of influence that corporations established and sustained. Hermann Cohen, writing in 1916, urged that after Germany's victory in the First World War the exclusion of Jewish students from corporations should cease, as being contrary to the national honour.[61] However, the exclusion of Jewish students no doubt saved them from drunkenness and enabled them to work harder. Franz Held remarks in 1890 that Jewish students are 'almost the only German students who really study'.[62]

Similar rituals existed in professional life. Arthur Ruppin, as a trainee lawyer (*Referendar*), had to participate in *Stammtisch* rituals modelled on those in student corporations; when he announced that he was a Jew, the atmosphere became frosty, and people tried to get him drunk, but he gained respect by holding his drink and by mentioning that he was a good shot with a pistol.[63] Even informal associational life tended increasingly to exclude Jews. 'Many middle-class societies, choirs, gymnastic associations, and cycling clubs, which would never have dreamt of such a thing in the past, now strictly reject Jews', complained 'Benedictus Levita' in 1900.[64] The antisemitic cycling club in Schnitzler's *Der Weg ins Freie* need not be an invention.

A less visible but equally lasting means of discrimination was based on names that were (not always correctly) recognized as characteristically Jewish. From an early stage in the history of emancipation, Jews often discarded conspicuously Jewish names. Thus Lippmann Zunz changed his name to Leopold about 1815, eliciting from his ex-headmaster S. M. Ehrenberg the comment that such changes were futile: 'I cannot stand it when Jews change

on the Waidhofen resolutions in *Jugend in Wien*, pp. 155–6, though at the time his diary mentions them only briefly and parenthetically (*T* 30 Mar. 96).

  [60] [Blach], *Die Juden in Deutschland*, p. 54.
  [61] Cohen, 'Deutschtum und Judentum', in his *Jüdische Schriften*, 3 vols. (Berlin, 1924), ii. 237–301 (p. 279).
  [62] Held, 'Die Mission des Judentums', *Die Gesellschaft*, 6 (Apr. 1890), 555–66 (p. 564).   [63] Ruppin, *Briefe, Tagebücher, Erinnerungen*, pp. 105–7.
  [64] Benedictus Levita, 'Die Erlösung des Judenthums', *Preußische Jahrbücher*, 102 (Oct. 1900), 131–40 (p. 132).

their forenames in order to erase all traces of their origin. The dyed-in-the wool Jew is not helped by his concealment, and for an educated man to deny his origin is disgraceful.'[65] Later in the century we find many Jewish writers changing their names: Max Goldmann became Max Reinhardt; Georg Levin became Herwarth Walden; Alfred Kempner became Alfred Kerr; Egon Friedmann became Egon Friedell; Siegmund Salzmann became Felix Salten; Richard Engländer became Peter Altenberg; and Maximilian Simcha Südfeld ('Southfield') went through 180 degrees to become Max Nordau ('Northmeadow'). These changes were part of an assimilatory project, a 'life-plan'.[66] To discard a recognizably Jewish name was a way of distancing oneself from the Jewish community. Some Jews even adopted the names of Enlightenment luminaries, as did the forebears of Theodor Lessing, of the Hebrew author Schlomoh Schiller, and of Kafka's friend Robert Klopstock.[67]

Dietz Bering has tried to reconstruct the system within which certain first and family names were strongly marked as 'Jewish' and hence, in the eyes of antisemites, as hateful or ridiculous. He draws on the applications for change of name during the periods 1840–67 and 1900–32 which survive in Prussian archives. He also surveys the relevant legislation, whose most important landmark is probably the decree of 12 March 1894, declaring that the desire to escape antisemitic pressure or professional hindrances was insufficient reason for changing one's name: official policy was to keep the Jews, even after conversion, as a distinct and stigmatized group. Bering's researches produce a table listing 'Jewish' names in descending order of opprobrium. Cohn leads the field, followed by Levy (and its variants), Moses, Itzig, Salomon, and Schmul. Some of these are far more prominent than their frequency in the population would suggest, a sign that they were indeed stigmatized. Moreover, the often circumstantial petitions preserved in the archives provide cameos of lives blighted by names: a young man denied employment because his

---

[65] Ehrenberg, letter to I. M. Jost, 31 Aug. 1815, in *Leopold and Adelheid Zunz: An Account in Letters*, p. 2.

[66] Edward Timms, 'Peter Altenberg: Authenticity or Pose?' in G. J. Carr and Eda Sagarra (eds.), *Fin de Siècle Vienna* (Dublin, 1985), pp. 126–42 (p. 131).

[67] Lessing, *Einmal und nie wieder*, p. 34; for Schiller, see Buber, *Briefwechsel*, i. 219. Cf. Brod, *Streitbares Leben*, pp. 167–8.

surname was Itzig; a Jew who could marry a Catholic only if, as her relatives demanded, he gave up the surname Cohn. Both these applications were refused.[68] Bering also draws on contemporary cartoons, satires, and newspaper reports to suggest that a tendency to regard markedly 'Jewish' names as contemptible increasingly permeated everyday life and contributed to the indifference with which the broad German population regarded the persecution of the Jews under Hitler. Since many Jewish writers had changed their names, a standard ploy in antisemitic polemics was to refer to them by their original names (often getting these wrong): thus the *Semi-Kürschner* lists 'Harden, Maximilian, gebor. Isidor Witkowski'; 'Ludwig, Emil, gebor. Kohn', calling the later name a 'Trugname' or 'deceitful name'.[69] At a 1936 conference, Carl Schmitt repeatedly referred to the legal philosopher Hans Kelsen as 'Kelsen-Kohn'.[70] Onomastics were unreliable in practice. There were Gentiles called Kohn and Jews called Hitler.[71] And some Jews, even before the cult of Wagner, adopted emphatically Germanic names like Siegfried: Brecht plays on this practice in his anti-Nazi play *Furcht und Elend des Dritten Reiches* (*Fear and Misery in the Third Reich*, 1938), where a jeweller called Arndt (the name of a nineteenth-century German nationalist) is said to be a Jew—'as his very name shows'.[72]

In the late nineteenth century, these and other veiled restrictions caused some German and Austrian Jews to regard the subculture negatively. Instead of a means of access to German culture, it was seen as a new ghetto with invisible walls. Theodor Herzl's pre-Zionist play *Das neue Ghetto* (*The New Ghetto*), which had its première in 1897, helped to publicize this phrase. The 'new ghetto' is Herzl's term for the condition of emancipation without assimilation. The Jews are legally free, but they have not become integrated into the wider community. Where the fault lies is unclear. In February 1882 he uses the image and explains it: the Jews are a deformed finger on humanity's hand; their growth has been deformed by a ring, symbolizing the Jews' belief in their

[68] Bering, *Der Name als Stigma*, pp. 298, 302–3.
[69] Stauff (ed.), *Semi-Kürschner*, part I, cols. 149 and 285.
[70] Käsler, *Die frühe deutsche Soziologie*, p. 375.
[71] Bering, *Der Name als Stigma*, p. 170; Brigitte Hamann, *Hitlers Wien: Lehrjahre eines Diktators* (Munich and Zurich, 1996), p. 69.
[72] Brecht, *Gesammelte Werke*, 20 vols. (Frankfurt, 1967), iii. 1105.

election as God's chosen people. This is a curious transformation of Lessing's parable in which the desired ring made its possessor beloved in the sight of God and man. In Herzl's version, the Jewish ring does the opposite.

Without the dull pressure and prison of the ghetto, which persisted long after its tangible walls had fallen—like a tight ring that still seems perceptible on one's finger, even some time after it has laboriously been removed or filed off—without the ghetto, which survives incorporeally in the short-sighted opinions held by the populace and by many of the 'educated', without this evil ghetto of modern and previous ages, the ring finger on humanity's hand, known as Judaism, would not have assumed the form, or rather the deformity, that it has done.[73]

In 1882 Herzl still thought that the removal of legal restrictions would eventually admit the Jews to full and real membership of the community. By 1894, however, he had become more pessimistic. He now thought that even if outward pressures such as anti-semitism were removed, the Jewish people were inwardly damaged and would be unable to overcome their psychological deformity. Herzl says that he was inspired to write his play after a conversation in October 1894 with the sculptor Samuel Friedrich Beer, in which both agreed 'that it does not help the Jews if they become artists and free from money. The curse sticks. We never get out of the ghetto' (*BT* ii. 50). And his play depicts a hero trapped in Jewishness by the fateful idealism which distinguishes himself from his cynical Gentile surroundings.

The play opens just after Jakob Samuel, a Jewish lawyer, has married Hermine Hellmann, daughter of a wealthy businessman. Soon afterwards Jakob suffers an emotional blow when his Gentile friend Franz Wurzlechner formally terminates their friendship on the grounds that friendship with Jews will damage his intended political career. Jakob's brother-in-law Rheinberg is involved with an aristocrat, Rittmeister von Schramm, in selling shares in an unprofitable coal-mine. Jakob is sensitive towards Schramm, for years earlier, when Schramm challenged him to a duel over a trifle, Jakob, whose father was gravely ill, apologized instead of fighting, and he has felt ashamed ever since. He agrees to defend the miners in their complaints against dangerous work-

---

[73] Herzl, *Briefe und Tagebücher*, ed. Alex Bein *et al.*, 7 vols. (Berlin, Frankfurt, Vienna, 1983–96), i. 610. Henceforth quoted as *BT*.

ing conditions. In an accident, many miners are killed; Schramm is ruined, and Rheinberg is in danger of ruin. Jakob tells Schramm that he is to blame for maltreating his employees; Schramm angrily replies 'Judenpack!' ('Jewish scum!') and alludes to Jakob's earlier apology, whereupon Jakob strikes him. A duel is inevitable; Schramm wounds Jakob almost fatally. At the end of the play, Jakob is brought in, dying; his last words are: 'Ich will— hinaus! Hinaus—aus—dem—Ghetto!' ('I want to get—out! Out—of—the ghetto!' (ZW v. 124).[74]

The idealist Jakob owes much to the Jewish ethical tradition embodied by his affectionate parents, who have taught him to be upright and honourable, and who are sharply conscious of the difficulties of Jewish life. Herr Samuel knows that the customers in his shop distrust him as a Jew; Frau Samuel warns her worldly daughter-in-law that Jewish men need special emotional support in their conflicts with the Gentile world: 'A Jewish wife must be even more to her husband than a Christian wife. For our men have much to endure when they go outside' (ZW v. 23). The Samuel parents have acculturated themselves with some effort, adopting High German to spare their son embarrassment. He is sufficiently embarrassed, however, by his brother-in-law Rheinberg, a cynical businessman; by Rheinberg's snobbish wife; and by Rheinberg's agent Wasserstein, a comically unacculturated Jew who, while waiting for the guests to return from Jakob's wedding, cannot refrain from pricing the furniture under the suspicious eye of the Gentile maid. Later in the play, however, when the tables have turned and Wasserstein is the wealthy patron of the ruined and obsequious Rheinberg, he has enough self-knowledge to realize that he is respected only for his money and enough decency to admire in Jakob a heroism of which he knows himself to be incapable. The official moral authority, Rabbi Friedheimer, thinks it salutary for Jews to be segregated from the Gentile world by an invisible ghetto, and warns Jakob against leaving it. Yet, on the play's showing, the invisible ghetto nurtures a complacent, cynical materialism, and Jakob's tragedy is that despite his idealistic rebellion against his environment, his loyalty to Jewry dooms him to be identified by the outside world with its persistent faults.

---

[74] References in this form are to Herzl, *Gesammelte zionistische Werke*, 5 vols. (Tel Aviv, 1934–5).

The image of the 'new ghetto' surrounding modern Jews was a common one in Herzl's generation. But while the French Jewish publicist Bernard-Lazare applied the phrase to the hostile external force of antisemitism, German and Austrian Jews applied it to the inner condition of the Jewish subculture.[75] Martin Buber says in 1902 that Jews need to overcome 'their narrow life and their narrow minds, the outer and the inner ghetto'.[76] The Jewish bourgeoisie was said to form a new ghetto, cut off from the wider community by its wealth and by the power of the Jewish-owned press. Thus Karl Kraus warns in *Die Fackel* in 1899: 'The bars of gold and newsprint that still enclose the ghetto must come down. Through dissolution to redemption!'[77] Perhaps the harshest criticism of quasi-assimilated Jews, however, came from Walther Rathenau in his pseudonymous article 'Höre, Israel!' ('Hear, O Israel!', 1897). Judged by Rathenau's ideals of Prussian and military manhood, actual Berlin Jews looked and sounded deplorably unmilitary, ill-at-ease, unmannerly, and over-assertive. Instead of absorbing German standards of behaviour, they remained voluntarily separate: 'Closely knit among themselves, strictly secluded from the outside world: thus they live in a semi-voluntary invisible ghetto, not a living limb of the nation but an alien organism within its body.'[78]

Rathenau typifies a much more radical assimilationism than that of Riesser and Jacoby, Geiger and Graetz, outlined at the beginning of this chapter. He sought complete integration into German culture and society while retaining a merely nominal Jewish identity. An earlier spokesman for radical assimilationism, Conrad Alberti, argued in 1889 that Jews could only be absorbed into Germany if they discarded every vestige of Jewishness without converting. He insists that Judaism as a religion is entirely obsolete. Monotheism has been superseded by modern science; the Old Testament's claims to divine authority have been destroyed by biblical scholarship; and the valuable parts of Jewish ethics have been absorbed into modern civilization. Jewry ('das Judentum') is

---

[75] On Bernard-Lazare's article 'Le nouveau ghetto', published in response to anti-Dreyfusard antisemitism, see Ernst Pawel, *The Labyrinth of Exile: A Life of Theodor Herzl* (London, 1990), pp. 204–5.
[76] Buber, *Die jüdische Bewegung: Gesammelte Aufsätze und Ansprachen*, 2 vols. (Berlin, 1920), i. 91.   [77] *Die Fackel*, 23 (mid-Nov. 1899), p. 7.
[78] 'W. Hartenau', 'Höre, Israel!', *Die Zukunft*, 18 (6 Mar. 1897), 454–62 (p. 454).

no longer a religion, a race, or a nation, but merely a clique held together by economic interest. Although Alberti stresses that Jews are not in general worse than Christians, but tend to have different failings, the shortcomings he ascribes to the older generation of Jews strikingly resemble the charges laid by antisemitism. Jews are responsible for corruption in finance, the press, and the theatre. They are too intellectual to appreciate or produce art. Unlike Gentiles, they cannot admit to ignorance, and are therefore inclined to a superficial affectation of culture ('Bildungsheuchelei'). Their powerful urge for self-preservation renders them incapable of self-sacrificing idealism. The younger generation, according to Alberti, lacks these flaws. Young Jews detest their parents' Jewish character: 'I can boldly affirm that of the young generation of Jews steeped in modern culture there is not one who is not profoundly convinced of the superfluity, harmfulness and rottenness of Jewry.'[79] All that prevents their absorption into German identity ('Deutschtum') is antisemitism, which makes it seem shameful to abandon one's nominal Jewish allegiance. Alberti urges the antisemites to cease their agitation and allow Jews to become Germans without the humiliation of having to convert. In the interests of 'Deutschtum' they should instead promote assimilation, admit Jews to the officer class, and, above all, encourage mixed marriages. Similarly, Jakob Fromer, having argued that Jews throughout history always aroused antisemitism, advised his fellow-Jews:

Submerge yourselves, disappear! Disappear, along with your Oriental physiognomies, your character that is so incongruous with its surroundings, your 'mission', and, above all, with your exclusively ethical outlook. Assume the manners, morals and religion of your host nations, seek to mingle with them, and take care to vanish into them without trace.[80]

While Rathenau, Alberti, and Fromer called for radical assimilation, sociologists maintained that it was already happening. Arthur Ruppin argued in 1904 that as traditional Jews encountered western culture, they increasingly adopted its manners, first

---

[79] Alberti, 'Judentum und Antisemitismus. Eine zeitgenössische Studie', *Die Gesellschaft*, 5 (1889), 1718–33 (p. 1719).

[80] Fromer, *Vom Ghetto zur modernen Kultur: Eine Lebensgeschichte* (Charlottenburg, 1906), p. 234.

to supplement their traditional practices, then to supersede them; finally, several generations on, they broke away from Judaism altogether, adopting Christianity and retaining, at most, a residual Jewish identity. He thought it inevitable that in a few more generations Jews not just in Germany, where the process of assimilation was far advanced, but throughout the world would be absorbed into the surrounding population and lose their distinct identity. As Jews became a middle-class people, their birth rate dropped and intermarriage increased. In 1870 Jews formed 1.25 per cent of the total population of Germany; in 1905, 1 per cent. In North Germany, Vienna, and Budapest, for every ten Jews who married other Jews, from one to three Jews married non-Jews. Children of mixed marriages were seldom brought up as Jews.[81] Only immigration from eastern Europe sustained their numbers. Other demographers concurred. Felix Theilhaber provided statistical evidence that German Jews were threatened with extinction by the low birth rate characteristic of city-dwellers and by absorption into the rest of the population.[82] After surveying the population statistics from western Europe, particularly Germany, Maurice Fishberg concluded: 'The effects of this violent race suicide are evident in the censuses of the Jewish population in those countries. The number of native Jews is decreasing in rapid strides to an extent unknown in the history of any civilized people.'[83]

These sociologists did not foresee how Jewish identity would be reinvented, nor that a racial definition of Jewishness would eventually be forced on Jews who thought themselves fully assimilated. We now need to look in detail at what 'assimilation', in the nineteenth-century sense, or rather acculturation, actually meant in practice, and to examine the tensions to which it gave rise in everyday life: above all, the tension between German *Bildung* and a residual and problematic Jewishness.

---

[81] Ruppin, *The Jews of To-Day*, tr. Margery Bentwich (London, 1913), pp. 83, 170. (Originally published as *Die Juden der Gegenwart* (Berlin, 1904).) Similar statistics in Fishberg, *The Jews*, pp. 196–9; Brunner, *Der Judenhaß und die Juden*, p. 7.

[82] Theilhaber, *Der Untergang der deutschen Juden* (Munich, 1911).

[83] Fishberg, *The Jews*, p. 235. This book was soon translated into German, and can be considered part of the German debate on racial and demographic questions.

Acculturation

Under the 'emancipation contract', it was by absorbing German culture that the Jews could prove their fitness for membership of German society. One's social life was supplied by one's subculture. One acquired the majority culture through one's upbringing and one's education.

The first agency of acculturation was the family. Jews entering the middle class readily adopted the lifestyle of nineteenth-century bourgeois domesticity, in which the wife, instead of taking part in the family business, retreated into the shelter of the home and concentrated on the sufficiently arduous task of running the household and bringing up the children.[84] The classic division of gender roles was formulated in Schiller's much-loved poem 'Das Lied von der Glocke' ('The Song of the Bell'), in which the man ventures out 'into hostile life' where he 'must struggle and strive', while the 'modest housewife' runs the home.[85] Dirt and smells (dreadful reminders of unassimilated Jewish life) were anxiously eliminated. The housewife supervised the furnishing and decoration of the home, and Jewish wives tended to be in the forefront of fashion; around 1900 they often acquired telephones before their Gentile neighbours, who would call to use their telephone and, while doing so, either admire the solid comfort of the Jewish home or (enviously) despise its ostentation.[86] The favourite icons of domesticity were Moritz Oppenheim's hugely popular paintings, *Bilder aus dem alt-jüdischen Familienleben* (*Pictures from Old Jewish Family Life*), which project the domestic idyll back into the idealized past; and favourite reading included the *Gartenlaube* (*The Summer-House*), a mass-circulation liberal weekly which celebrated family values.[87]

---

[84] See Ingeborg Weber-Kellermann, *Die deutsche Familie. Versuch einer Sozial-geschichte* (Frankfurt, 1974), pp. 102–18.

[85] Schiller, *Sämtliche Werke*, i. 432. Schnitzler cynically parodies this ideal in the marital scene in *Reigen*, where the adulterous husband quotes Schiller in order to impress traditional values on his adulterous wife. To make matters yet worse, the wife almost certainly transfers to her husband the syphilis acquired from her lover, who in turn acquired it from his parlour-maid . . . (*E* i. 353).

[86] Marion Kaplan, *The Making of the Jewish Middle Class* (New York and Oxford, 1991), p. 32.

[87] See Ismar Schorsch, 'Art as Social History: Moritz Oppenheim and the German Jewish Vision of Emancipation', in his *From Text to Context: The Turn to History in Modern Judaism* (Hanover, NH, and London, 1994), pp. 93–117; Henry Wassermann, 'Jews and Judaism in the *Gartenlaube*', *LBY* 23 (1978), 47–60.

Jewish wives may have received more respect than their Gentile counterparts: according to Marion Kaplan, the patriarchal tyrant who inspires cringing fear and secret enmity, familiar from such German dramas as Hebbel's *Maria Magdalene*, is rare in German-Jewish memoirs.[88] Instead of the severe discipline that was apparently common in the German Gentile family, these memoirs portray a nurturing and loving environment whose members were tied together not by external discipline but by the internalized bonds of affection.

However, family reminiscences should be read with caution. They may be coloured by nostalgia and piety. Besides, authoritarian fathers certainly feature in some German-Jewish memoirs, notably those of Theodor Lessing, son of a distinguished and autocratic doctor, and Ernst Fischer, whose father was an officer in the Austrian army frustrated by slow promotion.[89] Paul Celan's father, Leo Antschel, was a forbidding figure who habitually punished his son for trivial offences.[90] Paternal tyrants are also prominent in German-Jewish fiction: one thinks of Kafka's *Das Urteil* (*The Judgement*, 1912), of Franz Werfel's *Nicht der Mörder, der Ermordete ist schuldig* (*Not the Murderer but the Victim is to Blame*, 1920), of Walter Hasenclever's play *Der Sohn* (*The Son*, 1914), and of Ludwig Winder's Expressionist novel *Die jüdische Orgel* (*The Jewish Organ*, 1922) with its domestic tyrant Wolf Wolf who simultaneously embodies a repressive Orthodox Judaism. All these works are fantasies of parricide. Confronting his father, Kafka's protagonist finds himself involuntarily thinking: 'what if he fell and smashed himself to pieces!'[91] The journalist Anton Kuh traced such works back to the stifling atmosphere he ascribed to the Jewish home. His authority is his brother-in-law Otto Gross, the radical psychiatrist who, in a *cause célèbre* of 1913, was imprisoned in a mental asylum at the behest of his

---

[88] See Kaplan, *The Making of the Jewish Middle Class*, pp. 54–63. As fictional examples of non-Jewish domestic authoritarianism, Kaplan cites Gabriele Reuter's *Aus guter Familie* (1895) and Heinrich Mann's *Der Untertan* (1918), though the parents in Reuter's novel are not so much authoritarian as over-possessive.

[89] See Lessing, *Einmal und nie wieder*; Fischer, *An Opposing Man*, tr. Peter and Betty Ross (London, 1974).

[90] Israel Chalfen, *Paul Celan: Eine Biographie seiner Jugend* (Frankfurt, 1979), p. 36.

[91] Kafka, *The Transformation and Other Stories*, tr. Malcolm Pasley (London, 1992), p. 46.

notoriously authoritarian father.[92] According to Gross, the root of all evil is sexual violence which has brought about the institution of marriage as the foundation of the authoritarian state, which was projected as an authoritarian God. The Jews first created such a state, and their patriarchal order is embodied in the Jewish family, against which Kuh delivers a furious diatribe:

The father, the primal possessor, brandishes the rod that sustains his family. The mother, crippled by happiness, preserves the children as cripples; the daughters are prepared for burial while still alive, goods displayed for sale like potted plants; and the sons—read what they say in their own writings, in so far as they, squeezed between deed and terror, are committed to the word: how they shake their limbs to get rid of that limiting awareness of humanity's littleness in the parlour, as they shake the fetters of memory with foam-flecked lips and blood-shot eyes, how their boldest voyage round the world was undertaken in sheer defiance, and how, thinking back, they still feel the rising tears.[93]

Kuh goes on to argue that the activism of Jewish Expressionists like Werfel and Hasenclever is really an attempt to overcome their domineering fathers. The attempt often fails, and the insecurity of Jewish intellectuals results from their inability to break away from the patriarchal family: one thus remains adolescent, disguising one's lack of experience by a precocious intellectuality which becomes a substitute for experience.

Moreover, even accepting the emphasis on ties of affection found in family memoirs, one should remember that affection can be a still more effective means of control than external discipline, for internalized emotional ties can engender dependence and guilt. The middle-class housewife invested a large, sometimes excessive quantity of spare emotion in her children. Jewish autobiography and fiction repeatedly emphasize 'that intense intimacy which is characteristic of Jewish families'.[94] Such intimacy, familiar from more recent novels like Philip Roth's *Portnoy's Complaint* and its German counterpart, Rafael Seligmann's *Rubinsteins Versteigerung* (1989), became more intense as the outside world became more hostile. This hothouse atmosphere is described by

[92] See Jennifer E. Michaels, *Anarchy and Eros: Otto Gross' Impact on German Expressionist Writers* (New York, Berne, Frankfurt, 1983).
[93] Kuh, *Juden und Deutsche* (Berlin, 1921), pp. 23–4.
[94] Paul Frölich, *Rosa Luxemburg: Her Life and Work*, tr. Edward Fitzgerald (London, 1940), p. 15.

Arnold Zweig in his 1927 treatise on antisemitism and Jewish life, *Caliban*:

A kind of powerful, over-stimulating intimacy, like an incubator, is beamed incessantly at the children, and the more intensely their parents have to struggle to make a living, the easier it is for them, as a normal emotional attitude, to switch from violent anger with the child to an equally violent demonstration of love. As a result, the child takes for granted the continual alternation of hot and cold that he has experienced with his parents and incorporates it into his life.[95]

Compared to this intense atmosphere, the outside world seems chilly, especially if one meets with hostility as a Jew. Dividing the world into the sheltering home and the hostile exterior, the Jew himself becomes a divided personality. He acquires an inferiority complex vis-à-vis the outside world which makes him try to satisfy its demands but may send him into neurosis or madness: 'This type still believes himself to be physically inferior, and to belong to a morally inferior race, and, what is more, obliged repeatedly to prove that he is not harmful to the community, but a useful citizen who must be tolerated.'[96]

One would expect this emotional intensity to surround not only the father but, still more, the mother, the child's main agent of acculturation.[97] Extraordinary tensions between sons and mothers can be found in the searing poems written about his mother by the lawyer Ludwig Bendix and published by the latter's son; in the life of Kurt Tucholsky, who described his mother as a domestic tyrant of Strindbergian proportions; and in the autobiography of Elias Canetti, whose newly widowed mother (herself an admirer of Strindberg) taught him German (the language she had shared with his father) in four weeks by a process of unremitting terror.[98] The intense atmosphere of conflict and domination within the family is sharply present in the early fiction of Kafka.

[95] Zweig, *Caliban*, p. 190.   [96] Ibid. 187–8.

[97] See Ritchie Robertson, 'Mothers and Lovers in Some Novels by Brod and Kafka', *GLL* 50 (1997), 475–90.

[98] Reinhard Bendix, *Von Berlin nach Berkeley: Deutsch-jüdische Identitäten*, tr. Holger Fliessbach (Frankfurt, 1985), pp. 58–60; Michael Hepp, *Kurt Tucholsky: Biographische Annäherungen* (Reinbek, 1993), pp. 25–35; Canetti, *Die gerettete Zunge: Geschichte einer Jugend* (Munich, 1977), pp. 98–102. On Benjamin's domineering mother, see Momme Brodersen, *Walter Benjamin: A Biography*, tr. Malcolm R. Green and Ingrida Ligers (London, 1996), p. 12.

While Kafka's father is well known as a domestic tyrant, thanks largely to the publication of his son's 'Letter to his Father', less is known about the authority exercised by his mother; yet, as Elizabeth Boa has pointed out, Julie Kafka stole her son's letters in order to find out about his relationship with Felice Bauer and hired a detective to check up on Felice's character, thereby using unscrupulous means to guard domestic proprieties.[99] An alliance between paternal and maternal forms of domination is subtly depicted in *Das Urteil*. Georg Bendemann, who has taken over the family business from his widowed father, is about to marry and make himself independent. His father is old and frail; Georg, with an unctuous and unconvincing display of filial compassion, promises to include him in the new household, and meanwhile puts him to bed like a child; whereupon the story moves from apparent realism into Expressionist distortion as the old man suddenly regains his strength, leaps upright on his bed, and denounces the cowering Georg for selfishly planning to marry. Georg's friend in Russia, who has featured as a mysterious obstacle to his marriage, is now described by the father as 'a son after my own heart': sick, lonely, and a failure, the friend would not have excited the jealous rage that Georg does. In opposing his son, however, the father is acting as intermediary for his dead wife. He keeps a corner of his room as a shrine to her memory. Strangely, he refers to her as 'our mother': she is thus desexualized by being described as the mother not only of her son but also of her husband, while Bendemann senior, calling himself 'I from whom you proceeded', implies that *he* somehow gave birth to his son. Georg's sexuality is attacked when his father alleges that his fiancée allured him by shamelessly lifting her skirts and when he cryptically accuses Georg of 'violating his mother's memory'. Finally his father sentences Georg to death by drowning, and as Georg carries out the sentence his last words express his submission to both his parents: 'Dear parents, I have really always loved you.' Thus the affection so often celebrated in the Jewish family is expressed here only as an admission of defeat in a life-and-death conflict between a son

---

[99] Boa, *Kafka: Gender, Class, and Race in the Letters and Fictions* (Oxford, 1996), pp. 53–5.

and a father, where the latter also represents the doubly un-challengeable authority of the deceased mother.

The family, with its powerful emotional bonds, joined with the wider Jewish public sphere in inculcating secular culture and good manners, a task performed ever since the Enlightenment. Jewish women, denied the religious education reserved for men, compensated by acquiring secular culture which they could transmit to their children. They also drilled their children in manners, often making the family dinner-table a scene of relent-less discipline. 'Through his *pince-nez*', recalls Ernst Fischer, 'my father kept a sharp eye on the way we used our knives, forks and spoons, making sure that we ate our soup without lowering our heads towards our plates, that we wiped our mouths without needlessly soiling the table-napkins, and so forth and so on.'[100] Children were admonished to speak properly and avoid raising their voices, gesticulating, drawing attention to themselves in public—all the solecisms ascribed to Jews by non-Jews and to unassimilated Jews by the more assimilated. Throughout the nineteenth century, the importance of respectable, decent be-haviour was inculcated through journals and sermons.[101] Thus the editors of the periodical *Sulamith*, founded in 1806 to promote the enlightenment and education of the Jews, insisted that Jews should enter German society as Jews, professing the universal humane values that were at the core of Judaism, avoiding both orthodox fanaticism and cynical scepticism. It promoted the 'civil improvement of the Jews' not only by uplift-ing exhortations but by a regular feature entitled 'Gallery of harmful abuses, indecent customs and absurd ceremonies among the Jews' which satirized such things as the behaviour of profes-sional marriage-brokers and the custom of holding wedding processions led by a jester.[102] Yet the civilizing mission repre-sented by *Sulamith* was highly problematic. For if the moral values it preached were universal, then what was specifically Jewish about them? And the example of indecency just cited

---

[100] Fischer, *An Opposing Man*, pp. 31–2. Cf. Kafka's letter to his father in *Nachgelassene Schriften und Fragmente II*, ed. Jost Schillemeit (Frankfurt, 1992), pp. 155–6.   [101] See Sorkin, *The Transformation of German Jewry*, pp. 81–104.
[102] David Fränkel, 'Über die jüdischen Heurathsstiftungen und Hochzeitsfeste', *Sulamith*, 1 (1806), 165–83, 222–45.

suggests that the goal of acculturation was not higher morality but bourgeois respectability.[103]

Acculturation meant, among other things, losing a distinctive 'Jewish' speech and body language, and acquiring a new set of conventional manners. The linguistic situation in the mid-nineteenth century was described by the psychologist Heymann Steinthal, born in Dessau in 1823:

We children were aware of four varieties of German. Our parents spoke authentic Jewish-German with occasional Hebrew words which in living speech were often pronounced differently than in Hebrew prayer. The Christian boys spoke the popular dialect of Central Germany. We Jewish boys did not speak like our fathers and mothers, nor like the Christian children, who of course spoke just like their parents. It was a modified Jewish German (*Judendeutsch*). I must add that many of the older Jews and Jewesses who had some education, including my father, who had even learnt French and wrote a fairly correct German, spoke just like Christians when in contact with them: they spoke dialect with ordinary citizens, and pure or approximately pure German with dignitaries.[104]

Testimonies differ on how common it was for assimilated Jews to acquire a local dialect. Moritz Goldstein recalled that 'a Jew reared in Berlin spoke or could speak the genuine Berlin dialect, a Munich Jew the Munich dialect, a Königsberg Jew the Königsberg dialect, and so on'.[105] However, the Viennese Socialist Julius Braunthal tells us in his memoirs that instead of having a Viennese accent he spoke 'High German' (*Hochdeutsch*); and Jakob Loewenberg, brought up in rural Westphalia, recalls that Jewish families spoke High German among themselves, though they could talk Low German dialect (*Plattdeutsch*) when dealing with outsiders.[106] While showing how adaptable Jews could be, this

---

[103] See George L. Mosse, 'Jewish Emancipation: Between *Bildung* and Respectability', in Reinharz and Schatzberg (eds.), *The Jewish Response to German Culture*, pp. 1–16.

[104] Lazarus and Steinthal, *Die Begründer*, p. 375.

[105] Goldstein, 'German Jewry's Dilemma before 1914: The Story of a Provocative Eessay', *LBY* 2 (1957), 236–54 (p. 240).

[106] Braunthal, *In Search of the Millennium*, p. 41; Loewenberg, *Aus zwei Quellen: Geschichte eines deutschen Juden* ([1914]; Paderborn, 1993), p. 47. That assimilated Jews generally spoke educated *Hochdeutsch* rather than dialect is maintained by Jacob Toury, 'Die Sprache als Problem der jüdischen Einordnung in den deutschen Kulturraum', in Walter Grab (ed.), *Gegenseitige Einflüsse deutscher und jüdischer Kultur von der Epoche der Aufklärung bis zur Weimarer Republik* (Tel Aviv, 1982), pp. 75–95.

situation also discloses scope for embarrassment. The familiar language of the home is distinguished from the 'proper' language of the outside world. Even if one remains bilingual, one will attach different values to the two languages. The outside language is correct and creditable but emotionally unsatisfying; one's feelings remain attached to the disreputable language of the home. Yiddish or Jewish-German soon came to be despised. In the later nineteenth century it is usually referred to as *Jargon* or *Mauscheln*.

There are, however, difficulties in judging acculturation by conformity to a standard language. The notion of a standard language, whether in German or English, is delusive. It purports to be a neutral form of communication, mastery of which admits one to a linguistic community of equals; but in practice a standard language exists primarily as an ideal to which speakers approximate in varying degrees. The real standard language is constantly though unobtrusively changing and thus providing new criteria for excluding those less successful at speaking it.[107] Since those with a sharp ear can always detect linguistic differences, there was ample scope for the widespread notion, investigated in detail by Sander Gilman, that Jews, even when they spoke and wrote impeccable German, were somehow still using a hidden language which marked and polluted their use of the majority language. We have already noted Wagner's claim that the Jew can never speak a language quite like a native. Similarly, Richard Andree maintains that Jews can never quite pass as native speakers of their acquired languages: 'Even the majority of our "educated" Jews have a peculiar lisping or abrupt language, from which the Jew can instantly be recognized, even if you close your eyes and cannot see his physiognomy.'[108]

Jews themselves agreed. The Zionist and Yiddishist Nathan Birnbaum says that Jews' language is always recognizable:

I do not mean 'Mauscheln'—the ugly rudiment of a language that has developed so beautifully in the East—but that peculiar, intellectual emphasis that rests upon the Jew's German, no matter how German his language may be. Anyone who moves among German-speaking Jews and non-Jews must know the difference between the German of

---

[107] See Lynda Mugglestone, *'Talking Proper': The Rise of Accent as Social Symbol* (Oxford, 1995), pp. 55–6.   [108] Andree, *Zur Volkskunde der Juden*, p. 116.

the one group and that of the other, a difference that can scarcely be defined in rules and can be perceived only by one's emotions and one's taste.[109]

On first hearing his voice recorded, Schnitzler was struck by 'the decidedly nasal, Jewish character of my voice' (*T* 19 Mar. 1907). However, while Birnbaum and Schnitzler did not mind speaking like Jews, assimilationists deplored verbal traces of Jewishness. Walther Rathenau lists distinctively Jewish expressions (especially interjections conveying disparagement or scorn) that he finds irritating:

You have certainly enriched the German vocabulary with the interjections 'Kunststück!' 'Kleinigkeit!' 'Zustand!' and many others. Nevertheless, it is irritating when in conversation one is alternately favoured with the address 'Sehr geehrter Herr' (My dear sir) and the question 'Verstehen se [*sic*] mich?' (D'you get me?) It is hard for you to strike a mean between cringing submissiveness and odious arrogance.[110]

The expressions Rathenau dislikes either express emotion or strengthen the link with one's interlocutor, thereby disturbing the cool, restrained demeanour he preferred.

Friedrich Blach also deplored Jewish gesticulation:

Even in the best-educated Jewish circles the most unspeakable *Jargon* expressions can be found. Affirmation is expressed like negation, negation like affirmation. The answer is a new question. As soon as a conversation becomes animated, somebody's hands are always waving about in the air.[111]

Thus, even if one controlled one's speech, one might still have to worry about one's body-language. Non-Jews were sharp-eyed. Fontane gently mocked the extreme demonstrativeness of Jewish families.[112] Cosima Wagner complains of 'the fidgetiness of these people' and of the 'excitable Jewish character' and 'inability to listen in silence' of Jewish acquaintances.[113] Coudenhove-Kalergi

---

[109] Birnbaum, *Die jüdische Moderne: Frühe zionistische Schriften* (Augsburg, 1989), p. 123.   [110] 'W. Hartenau', 'Höre, Israel!', p. 459.

[111] [Blach], *Die Juden in Deutschland*, p. 24. Cf. the detailed description of 'the organic link between paper German and gestural language' in Kafka's letter to Max Brod, June 1921: Max Brod and Franz Kafka, *Eine Freundschaft*, ii: *Briefwechsel*, ed. Malcolm Pasley, (Frankfurt, 1989), p. 359.

[112] Letter of 11 Sept. 1855, quoted and discussed in Paulsen, 'Theodor Fontane', p. 317.

[113] Cosima Wagner, *Diaries*, i. 280 (8 Oct. 1870); i. 531 (31 Aug. 1872); i. 194 (28 Feb. 1870).

remarks that the gestures appropriate to a kaftan-wearer become
ridiculous when the kaftan has been replaced by a frock-coat. He
instances 'the skipping movement of the feet that is so common
among Jews, their way of turning their palms outwards, extending
their fingers, and raising them to shoulder height, and their
frequent stooping posture'.[114] An admirer of Georg Simmel
claims that his Jewish origins were apparent from the lively
gestures that 'seemed to express the action of thinking' when he
delivered lectures.[115] A writer in the Zionist periodical *Ost und
West* maintains that facial expressions are far more reliable signs
of Jewishness than physical features:

Certain inimitable facial expressions are peculiar to the Jew. Think of
the expression that accompanies the untranslatable word 'nebbich', of
the glance of mutual understanding that only Jews exchange when they
have reached a conclusion about a third party; think of their looks
expressing tenderness and sorrow, their look on scenting danger, their
expression when some manoeuvre in a game has succeeded, and so
on.[116]

More recent semioticians have confirmed the existence of distinctively Jewish gestural languages. In the 1930s David Efron
contrasted the sign-languages of Eastern Jewish and southern
Italian immigrants in New York, showing that the Italians' signs
were pictorial, corresponding to the objects talked about, whereas
the Jews' signs were 'logico-topographic'. While the Italian
illustrates by gesture the objects he is talking about, the Jew
uses his arm 'as a pointer, to link one proposition to another, or
to trace the itinerary of a logical journey; or else as a baton, to
beat the tempo of his mental locomotion'.[117] More generally,

---

[114] Coudenhove-Kalergi, *Das Wesen des Antisemitismus*, p. 249.

[115] Elias Hurwicz, 'Georg Simmel als jüdischer Denker', *Neue Jüdische Monats-
hefte*, 3/9–12 (10–25 Feb. and 10–25 Mar. 1919), 196–8 (p. 196). Simmel's gesticu-
lations while lecturing must have been famous, for they are also mentioned by Friedrich
Gundolf in a letter of 1905: Stefan George, Friedrich Gundolf, *Briefwechsel*, ed. Robert
Boehringer and Georg Peter Landmann (Munich and Düsseldorf, 1962), p. 165; and by
Margarete Susman, *Ich habe viele Leben gelebt*, p. 51.

[116] Quoted in Zollschan, *Das Rassenproblem*, p. 44.

[117] Efron, *Gesture, Race and Culture: A Tentative Study of some of the Spatio-
Temporal and 'Linguistic' Aspects of the Gestural Behavior of Eastern Jews and
Southern Italians in New York City, Living under Similar as well as Different Environ-
mental Conditions* (The Hague and Paris, 1972), p. 98. First published as *Gesture and
Environment* (New York, 1941). I owe this reference to Paul Connerton.

Efron noticed unacculturated Jews supporting their arguments with gestures that invaded the opponents' personal space:

In the course of our exploration of the swarming streets of the lower East Side, we soon became accustomed to the idea of seeing a person firmly grasping the coat-lapel of his companion with one hand, while the other was describing all kinds of arabesques in the immediate vicinity of his nose. No less frequent was the spectacle of an individual seizing the wrist of his opponent, or boring with the index-finger through the buttonhole of his coat. Pulling or shaking the body of the conversational adversary are also habitual procedures in the gesture technique of the ghetto Jew.[118]

Outside the family, acculturation was promoted through what remained of religious practice. Reform Judaism aimed at social as well as theological innovation, seeking to bring religious worship closer to the sedate and decent forms of worship associated with German Protestantism, with German sermons, organ music, and sometimes confirmation instead of bar mitzvahs. Not only the Orthodox, but also Jews inclined to Zionism, deplored these adaptations. In thus 'Protestantizing' Judaism, wrote the disillusioned Rabbi Joachim Prinz in 1933, the Reformers took away its colour, destroyed its connections with ancient tradition, and introduced an easy religion requiring no sacrifices.[119] 'Benedictus Levita', who advocated Jewish conversion to an undogmatic but ethically stringent Protestantism, likewise dismissed the ethics of Reform as too easygoing, 'the ideal of a man who wants to cultivate his vineyard in peace, enjoy a sound sleep and a good digestion, but be spared disagreeable pangs of conscience'.[120] After attending a Reform *Einsegnung* (confirmation), Moritz Heimann thought its dreariness was equalled only by the Lutheran baptism, with a clergyman 'in a well-cut frock-coat', described in Thomas Mann's domestic epic *Gesang vom Kindchen*.[121] Joseph Roth describes modern piety sarcastically:

They no longer pray in synagogues and prayer-houses, but in dreary temples, in which the divine service is as mechanical as in any better-class Protestant church. They become temple Jews (*Tempeljuden*), that is, well-bred, smooth-shaven gentlemen in frock-coats and top hats who pack their prayer-books in the editorial of their Jewish family newspaper

[118] Efron, *Gesture, Race and Culture*, p. 89.   [119] Prinz, *Wir Juden*, pp. 65–8.
[120] 'Die Erlösung des Judenthums', p. 136.
[121] Heimann, *Was ist das: ein Gedanke?*, p. 205.

because they think they will be less recognizable from this editorial than from the prayer-book. In the temples you can hear the organ; the cantor and the preacher wear headgear that makes them resemble Christian clergymen. Any Protestant who strays into a Jewish temple must admit that there is no great difference between Jew and Christian and that one should really give up being an antisemite, if only the Jews' business competition were not so dangerous.[122]

In domestic life, Jewish celebrations were often superseded by non-Jewish ones like Christmas, which could be celebrated in a virtually secular manner. As early as 1832, S. M. Ehrenberg complained that most Jews celebrated Christmas and the Christian New Year.[123] Freud's mother celebrated these festivals, ignoring Jewish feasts.[124] Walter Benjamin said that even his grandparents had celebrated Christmas, though as a 'German popular festival' (*Volksfest*) rather than a Christian one.[125] These concessions shocked the Orthodox: in 1895 Rabbi Güdemann of Vienna was displeased to find Herzl preparing a Christmas tree for his children (*BT* ii. 288); and the scholar Eduard Berend recalled how his parents had to hide the Christmas tree when expecting a visit from his Orthodox grandfather.[126]

A major means of acculturation was of course education.[127] Traditionally, literacy was high among both male and female Jews. Even around 1800, when three-quarters of the German population may still have been illiterate, Jewish men learnt at least enough Hebrew to understand prayers, and women learnt to read Yiddish. Reading began early: Lazarus Bendavid tells us that he could read Hebrew at 3 and was taught by his mother to read German when he was 4.[128] The value formerly attached to Jewish learning was transferred to secular culture: Arthur Ruppin read all Goethe's works at the age of 12; the pianist Karl Tausig

[122] Roth, 'Juden auf Wanderschaft', in *Werke*, ed. Klaus Westermann and Fritz Hackert, 6 vols. (Cologne, 1989–91), ii. 838.
[123] *Leopold and Adelheid Zunz: An Account in Letters*, p. 62.
[124] Martin Freud, *Glory Reflected: Sigmund Freud—Man and Father* (London, 1957), p. 11.
[125] Gershom Scholem, *Walter Benjamin: Die Geschichte einer Freundschaft* (Frankfurt, 1975), p. 49.
[126] Knickmann, 'Der Jean-Paul-Forscher Eduard Berend (1883–1973)', p. 44.
[127] See Beller, *Vienna and the Jews*, ch. 7, for an amply-documented survey.
[128] Bendavid, 'Selbstbiographie', pp. 6–7. For other examples, see Gunnar Och, 'Jüdische Leser und jüdisches Lesepublikum im 18. Jahrhundert. Ein Beitrag zur Akkulturationsgeschichte des deutschen Judentums', *Menora*, 2 (1991), 298–336.

'worked through' Schopenhauer at the age of 16.[129] Offspring of the *Bildungsbürgertum* often benefited from well-stocked parental libraries, like that of Karl Popper's father, a Viennese lawyer with a strong interest in history and philosophy.[130] Jewish children received as birthday and bar mitzvah presents not only the German classics and fairy-tales but also, judging from memoirs and surviving personal libraries, much conservative and even anti-semitic German fiction, including especially Freytag's *Soll und Haben* and Raabe's *Hungerpastor*.[131]

The high proportion of Jews in urban grammar-schools (*Gymnasien*) and universities has been amply documented. In Prussia in 1906, Jews provided 6.5 per cent of pupils at *Gymnasien*, but little more than one per cent of the general population.[132] In the late nineteenth century Jews formed some 10 per cent of the population of Vienna, but accounted for 30 per cent of pupils at the city's eleven *Gymnasien*.[133] The figures for Jewish attendance at girls' schools are even more striking: in 1909–10 over 40 per cent of girls at secondary schools in Vienna and Lower Austria were Jewish.[134] This predominance results from the large proportion of Jews within the liberal bourgeoisie, and testifies not only to the parents' social position but to the enlightened outlook which made them value education for both sexes. At universities, Jewish students were four to five times more numerous than the Jewish proportion of the general population would suggest. They were most numerous at the Universities of Berlin (17 per cent in 1886–7) and Vienna (about 25 per cent in 1900).[135] Jewish students were especially drawn to the study of medicine, though when restrictions on legal practice by Jews were withdrawn, medicine was overtaken by law as a 'Jewish' subject. Jewish graduates were likely to be self-employed, Gentile

---

[129] Ruppin, *Briefe, Tagebücher, Erinnerungen*, p. 50; Cosima Wagner, *Diaries*, i. 392. Other examples in Beller, *Vienna and the Jews*, pp. 99–100.

[130] Popper, *Unended Quest: An Intellectual Autobiography* (Glasgow, 1986), p. 11.

[131] See Chaim Schatzker, 'Die Jugendliteratur als Sozialisationsagentur', in Hans Jürgen Schrader, Elliott M. Simon and Charlotte Wardi (eds.), *The Jewish Self-Portrait in European and American Literature* (Tübingen, 1996), pp. 73–81 (p. 74).

[132] Monika Richarz, 'Berufliche und soziale Struktur', in Michael A. Meyer (ed.), *Deutsch-jüdische Geschichte in der Neuzeit*, 4 vols. (Munich, 1996–7), iii. 57.

[133] Rozenblit, *The Jews of Vienna*, pp. 102–5; confirmed by Beller, *Vienna and the Jews*, ch. 4. [134] Hamann, *Hitlers Wien*, p. 529.

[135] Richarz, 'Berufliche und soziale Struktur', p. 58.

graduates to become state officials. The expansion of the press provided employment for many Jewish arts graduates; though perceptions of Jewish press domination may have conflated Jewish-owned press concerns like those of Ullstein and Mosse, where Jewish journalists were not particularly numerous, with the large number of Jewish journalists on liberal or left-wing papers.

German and Austrian Jews participated in the consumption and promotion of culture to an extent that corresponds to their educational ideals and to their large representation within the liberal bourgeoisie.[136] They included eminent patrons like the Wittgensteins in Vienna and the Cassirers in Berlin. The industrialist Karl Wittgenstein (father of the philosopher) hosted performances by musicians from Brahms to Bruno Walter, and hired the modernist architect Josef Hoffmann to build his country house, while his daughter Margarete had her portrait painted by Gustav Klimt.[137] The art dealer Paul Cassirer was the first gallery-owner in Germany to display works by Manet, Monet, and Van Gogh, and he later supported the sculptor Ernst Barlach, though Cassirer's civilized values differed widely from Barlach's professed primitivism: 'He has the "cultured" viewpoint, which I can't share,' wrote Barlach to the right-wing propagandist Moeller van den Bruck, 'for to my feelings there are better things than culture. I can't do without barbarism.'[138] The influence of the wider Jewish public is attested by many contemporaries. Ernst von Wolzogen, no friend to the Jews, conceded in the 1890s: 'It was nearly always the Jews who started, or at least supported, the literary unions, the free theatres, the ethical societies, as well as the periodicals devoted to the spiritual revolution.'[139] Paul Amann maintained in 1919, appealing not to statistics but to personal observation and booksellers' anecdotes, that Jews constituted a significant part of Germany's more selective and cultivated reading public. Jewish readers seldom asked a bookseller to recommend

[136] See Peter Gay, 'Encounter with Modernism: German Jews in Wilhelminian Culture', in his *Freud, Jews and Other Germans* (Oxford and New York, 1978), pp. 93–168.

[137] Brian McGuinness, *Wittgenstein: A Life*, i.: *Young Ludwig (1889–1921)* (London, 1988), pp. 17–20.

[138] Letter of 26 Dec. 1911, in Barlach, *Die Briefe*, ed. Friedrich Dross, 2 vols. (Munich, 1968), i. 390.

[139] Quoted in Ernest K. Bramsted, *Aristocracy and the Middle-Classes in Germany: Social Types in German Literature 1830–1900*, 2nd edn (Chicago, 1964), p. 263.

'something humorous', but were generally open to new literary developments, while the older Germans in particular concentrated on Goethe and such favourites as Raabe, Keller and Storm.[140] Arnold Zweig asserts that the theatregoing public was predominantly Jewish.[141] A notorious poem by Fontane, 'An meinem Fünfundsiebzigsten', tells how he was taken aback to find that the congratulatory messages marking his seventy-fifth birthday came not from the Prussian aristocrats whom he had celebrated in print but from readers whose names revealed their Jewishness.[142] The poem's ending, 'Kommen Sie, Cohn' ('Come along, Cohn') has generally been interpreted as a disappointed and grudging acceptance of Cohn's homage which does not compensate Fontane for his rejection by the aristocracy.[143]

German-Jewish memoirs, letters, and biographies display a love of books which seems admirable, touching, yet sometimes excessive. At the age of 13, following the precedent of Esau and Jacob, Aby Warburg sold his birthright to his younger brother Max in return for the promise that Max would always buy him all the books he wanted.[144] Max agreed, not foreseeing that he had thus committed himself to funding what became an outstanding scholarly library. Walter Benjamin, reporting the birth of his son to his friend Gershom Scholem, deals with this event in a short paragraph, remarks that his feelings have been anticipated in a famous letter by Lessing, and continues: 'I am reading a *heap* of enormously interesting things and there are still more of the same on my desk [. . .]'.[145] Should the world of the mind receive quite such priority? Peter Kien, the professorial protagonist of Canetti's

---

[140] Amann, 'Westjüdische Dynamik', *Der Jude*, 4 (1919–20), iv. 144–51 (p. 150).

[141] Zweig, *Bilanz der deutschen Judenheit: Ein Versuch* ([1934] Leipzig, 1991), p. 205.   [142] Fontane, *Romane, Erzählungen, Gedichte*, vi. 340–1.

[143] Oppeln-Bronikowski calls the ending 'bitter' (*Antisemitismus?*, p. 58); Fritz Kahn calls the poem 'sarcastic' (*Die Juden als Rasse und Kulturvolk*, 3rd edn. (Berlin, 1922), p. 230); Blumenfeld says that he would have refused Fontane's invitation because it implies that Jews do not belong in Germany (*Erlebte Judenfrage*, p. 57); and more recently Wolfgang Paulsen has called the poem an 'outburst of bitter resentment' against the aristocracy with whom Fontane had identified, while its address to Cohn is an 'offensive slap on the shoulder' ('Theodor Fontane', pp. 312–13). On Fontane's rejection by the aristocracy, see Bramsted, *Aristocracy*, pp. 263–8.

[144] Ernst Gombrich, *Aby Warburg: An Intellectual Biography*, 2nd edn. (London, 1986), p. 22.

[145] Benjamin, *Briefe*, ed. Gershom Scholem and Theodor W. Adorno, 2 vols. (Frankfurt, 1966), p. 186 (17 Apr. 1918).

Die Blendung (1935), is explicitly not a Jew; but in describing the arid book-lined paradise from which Kien is expelled by his combination of selfishness and sexuality, Canetti does seem to be satirizing the bookishness which was part both of his own character and of his culture.

Contemporaries noted the conspicuous part played by Jews in the administration of culture: as publishers, theatre directors, critics, editors, and biographers. Some interpreted this as part of their reverent homage to German culture.[146] Thus Kant found Jewish expositors from Maimon and Bendavid down to Hermann Cohen, Georg Simmel, and Ernst Cassirer.[147] Schopenhauer called his Jewish editor Julius Frauenstädt his apostle. Otto Brahm directed innovative plays by Gerhart Hauptmann and wrote an early study of Kleist. Karl Emil Franzos was the first scholarly editor of Büchner. Among publishers, the S. Fischer Verlag supported Thomas Mann and many other major novelists, while Georg Bondi sustained the writings of the Stefan George circle. Distinguished Jewish critics included Samuel Lublinski, Arthur Eloesser, Moritz Heimann, and Alfred Kerr. The list of Jewish performing artists—actors, conductors, and singers—is immense.[148]

Particularly noteworthy is the prominence of Jews among admirers, propagators, commentators, and editors of Goethe.[149] As Wilfried Barner points out, Goethe was never a popular, accessible author, as Schiller was. While Schiller was widely read by self-educating Jews in eastern Europe, and invited a straightforward identification with his values, the study of Goethe was reserved for those who had reached the pinnacle of acculturation. One of Goethe's earliest devotees was Rahel Varnhagen, née Levin. Beginning in the 1790s, when Goethe's reputation had declined

---

[146] See Hermann Goldschmidt-Faber, 'Von Deutschen und Juden. Eine Entgegnung', *Preußische Jahrbücher*, 163 (Jan.–Mar. 1916), 257–80 (esp. p. 267); Zweig, *Bilanz*, pp. 197–8.

[147] See Jürgen Habermas, 'Der deutsche Idealismus der jüdischen Philosophen', in his *Philosophisch-politische Profile* (Frankfurt, 1971), pp. 37–66.

[148] See Siegmund Kaznelson (ed.), *Juden im deutschen Kulturbereich*, 2nd, enlarged edn. (Berlin, 1959), especially Arthur Eloesser, 'Literatur', pp. 1–67.

[149] Wilfried Barner, *Von Rahel Varnhagen bis Friedrich Gundolf: Juden als deutsche Goethe-Verehrer* (Göttingen, 1992), correcting the inadequate account of the Jewish reception of Goethe in Wolfgang Leppmann's *The German Image of Goethe* (Oxford, 1961).

after the early fame brought by *Götz* and *Werther*, she established a cult of Goethe. He represented for her an image of wholeness and harmony that contrasted poignantly with the frustrations of her own life. The *Wilhelm Meister* novels in particular offered an image of self-development and social assimilation, culimating, however, in the concept of *Entsagung* (renunciation) to which Rahel Levin, like Henry James's similarly high-minded Olive Chancellor, was much attached.[150] 'He was forever my one and only, most certain friend; the guarantor that I need not be afraid amid ghosts; my superior Master, my most touching friend', she wrote in 1808.[151] Goethean textual scholarship began with the extremely interesting and readable book by Michael Bernays, the converted son of the Chief Rabbi of Hamburg (and brother of the classical philologist Jacob Bernays; both were uncles of Martha Bernays, who married Sigmund Freud). Bernays's motives for this study are explicitly patriotic. He has dedicated his scholarship to the service of the national poet. Hence Bernays has to demonstrate his fitness for this patriotic task by warning against over-ingenuity: '[The critic] will be strong and abstemious enough to resist the temptations of idle, playful ingenuity; he will give uncompromising priority to the sense of truth that must be dominant in him.'[152] Bernays, that is, feels obliged to distance himself from the stereotype of the hair-splitting Talmud scholar.

The *Goethe-Jahrbuch* was founded on 28 August 1879, Goethe's 130th birthday, by Ludwig Geiger, son of the pioneer of Reform Judaism, Abraham Geiger, and already known as author of a minutely documented history of the Jews in Berlin. The Goethe-Gesellschaft was founded in 1885, with the distinguished conservative judge Eduard Simson (a convert) as its first president. Albert Bielschowsky wrote the immensely popular biography *Goethe: Sein Leben und seine Werke* (*Goethe: His Life and Works*, 1896), which, Barner says, became a favourite book of the German *Bildungsbürgertum* and a frequent

---

[150] Käte Hamburger, afterword in Rahel Varnhagen, *Gesammelte Werke*, ed. Konrad Feilchenfeldt *et al.*, 10 vols. (Munich, 1983), x. 194–5; Henry James, *The Bostonians* (London, 1967), p. 93; Habermas, 'Der deutsche Idealismus', p. 52.

[151] Rahel Varnhagen, *Briefwechsel*, ii. 20.

[152] Bernays, *Über Kritik und Geschichte des Goetheschen Textes* (Berlin, 1866), p. 8.

present for confirmation or bar mitzvah;[153] subsequent popular biographers include Emil Ludwig and Richard Friedenthal.

Not only Goethe scholarship, but more philosophical or intuitive studies, came especially from Jews, above all from Georg Simmel, Friedrich Gundolf, and Walter Benjamin. All these respond to the intuitive biographism pioneered by Wilhelm Dilthey in *Das Erlebnis und die Dichtung* (*Experience and Poetry*, 1905), which sought to understand a poet's works as the products of crucial experiences. All try to correct or improve on Dilthey's approach. Simmel criticizes Dilthey's search for an originating experience as merely a sophisticated version of genetic criticism, and seeks instead to apprehend the 'life-process' ('Lebensprozeß') from which all Goethe's works proceed and which they express.[154] Gundolf's massive book was an attempt at heroic biography which sought to refine on Dilthey's conception of 'Erlebnis' by distinguishing Goethe's profound 'Urerlebnisse' (primal experiences) from his merely external 'Bildungserlebnisse' (cultural experiences).[155] Earlier, Gundolf had himself worried that his Jewish descent might exclude him from deep emotional experiences and deprive him of 'instinct'.[156] In his treatment of Goethe, he was implicitly opposing the antisemitic denial that Jews could appreciate German culture by claiming an intuitive inwardness with Goethe that was itself no mere *Bildungserlebnis* but the final proof of Jewish intimacy with German culture at its greatest. While Benjamin's essay on *Elective Affinities* explicitly attacks Gundolf's heroic biography for exalting the author's life above his works, it also trumps Gundolf by claiming an insight, not into Goethe's character, but into the metaphysical structure of his novel, understood as the interplay of mythic forces.[157]

All this activity on behalf of German writers and composers, however, often seemed to confirm doubts about Jewish creativity. What about the Jewish production of German culture? Peter Gay

[153] Barner, *Von Rahel Varnhagen bis Friedrich Gundolf*, p. 33.
[154] Simmel, *Goethe* (Leipzig, 1913), p. 16.
[155] Gundolf, *Goethe* (Berlin, 1916), p. 27.
[156] See his letter to Wolfskehl, 19 Dec. 1900, in Karl and Hanna Wolfskehl, *Briefwechsel mit Friedrich Gundolf, Castrum Peregrini*, 123–5 (1976), p. 88.
[157] Benjamin, 'Goethes *Wahlverwandtschaften*', in his *Gesammelte Schriften*, ed. Rolf Tiedemann and Hermann Schweppenhauser, 7 vols. (Frankfurt, 1972–89), i. 123–201 (esp. pp. 158–61).

has rightly warned against exaggerating the Jewish share in modernism.[158] Many Jewish writers found a large readership with fiction of high quality and relatively conservative technique, though flexible enough to accommodate, for example, Schnitzler's experiments with stream-of-consciousness narrative or the famous defamiliarizing description of a soldier at the beginning of Arnold Zweig's *Der Streit um den Sergeanten Grischa* (*The Dispute over Sergeant Grischa*, 1927). Their work has been underrated by literary historians concerned with the obviously modern. Jakob Wassermann, Georg Hermann, and later Stefan Zweig, Franz Werfel, and Lion Feuchtwanger also belong in this group. Among self-consciously modern writers, Jews are most prominent in the Expressionist movement: from Jakob van Hoddis (Hans Davidsohn), whose poem 'Weltende' was widely taken as emblematic of the new poetry, via the poets Ernst Blass, Alfred Lichtenstein, Alfred Wolfenstein, and Albert Ehrenstein, the dramatists Walter Hasenclever and Paul Kornfeld, to the post-War activist writers Ludwig Rubiner and Ernst Toller. However, this roll-call includes a great many writers of the second and third rank, alongside towering figures like Kafka, Lasker-Schüler, and Kraus who are not easily identified with any movement. Gay remarks that 'the Jewish poets in the Expressionist avant-garde found that the non-Jewish poets in their camp wrote, on the whole, much better than they did'.[159] If Jews entered the world of culture in disproportionate numbers, then they must have been correspondingly numerous among minor talents and in the supporting roles which require skill and adaptability rather than genius. This situation confirms the intense desire of educated Jews to realize their varied abilities in German culture.

The high visibility of Jews in German literary culture was noted, and its implications explored, by Moritz Goldstein in a controversial article of 1912. Goldstein, an assimilated Berlin Jew, had studied German literature at the University there and been recommended by the distinguished Germanist Erich Schmidt as editor of Bong's Goldene Klassiker-Bibliothek, a much-purchased series of editions of classical German authors. Yet he sympathized with Zionism, though he had no intention of separating himself from German culture. His essay explores the ambiguity of his

---

[158] Gay, *Freud, Jews and Other Germans*, p. 131.   [159] Ibid. 133.

position. He points out that although Jews dominate many aspects of German culture—the press, the theatre (as directors, actors, and audience), and, increasingly, the academic study of German literature—their presence is only superficially accepted and, deep down, resented. Hence the paradox: '*We Jews administer the intellectual property of a nation that denies our right and ability to do so.*'[160] Goldstein also thinks that the antisemitism widespread among the German public causes the achievements of Jews to be belittled and probably prevents gifted Jewish writers from achieving their full potential; to that extent charges of Jewish uncreativity may be justified, for the uneasy situation of German Jews is unfavourable to the emergence of the '*personality of genius*' and the '*productive character*'.[161] The only solution Goldstein sees is for Jewish writers to take up Hebrew and compose modern Hebrew literature; but he realizes that German Jewish writers are so firmly attached to their country that this is utopian: it is undeniable '*that German culture is in no small measure Jewish culture*'.[162]

It may be added that the Jewish culture exemplified by Goldstein was also German culture, in incorporating certain assumptions that belonged firmly to eighteenth- and nineteenth-century Germany. Thus Goldstein evidently thinks that a culture should be homogeneous, sharing Herder's belief in the distinctive integrity of each culture; and that only such a culture can bring forth the exceptional individuals who illustrate genius through their persons as well as their works, a conception of genius which can be traced back to the *Sturm und Drang* drama of the 1770s with its worship of great men. Unlike many present-day critics, and indeed unlike the post-War Thomas Mann, Goldstein does not think that cultural hybridity, with the stimulus of several interacting cultures, might itself be productive. He implicitly shares Treitschke's antipathy to the prospect of 'a German-Jewish hybrid culture (*Mischcultur*)'.[163] He even agrees with antisemites in suggesting that the true language of the Jew is Hebrew. Hence, just as the reactionary Langbehn thought that geniuses like Rembrandt developed from the homogeneous setting of northern

---

[160] Goldstein, 'Deutsch-jüdischer Parnaß', *Der Kunstwart*, 25/ii (Jan.-Mar. 1912), 281–94 (p. 283). Emphasis in original.   [161] Ibid. 288; emphasis in original.

[162] Ibid. 291; emphasis in original.

[163] Treitschke, 'Unsere Aussichten', p. 573.

Germany, so Goldstein wants a new Hebrew culture as the setting in which Jewish writers can realize their potential.

Goldstein's article aroused much indignation from assimilationists. Ernst Lissauer, already well known for his patriotic poems, maintained that German Jews must either become completely German or else emigrate.[164] Jakob Loewenberg, a progressive schoolteacher and poet who was enthusiastic about medieval German history and culture but had also affirmed his Jewishness by publishing a book of poems entitled *Lieder eines Semiten* (*Songs of a Semite*, 1892), replied by declaring his combined loyalty to Germany and Jewry:

Here lie our dead, and here is the home (*Heimat*) of our soul. *We are Germans, and we want to remain Germans.* We love our fatherland with all the strength of our sorely tried hearts, and if Goldstein says this is an unhappy love and unworthy of a man, then we reply with Goethe: 'If I love you, what's that to you?'[165]

Yet Loewenberg's semi-autobiographical novel *Aus zwei Quellen* (*From Two Sources*) culminates in a scene in which the protagonist, told that as a Jew he cannot teach history to Christian schoolchildren, not only refuses to convert but denounces the discrimination continually visited upon German Jews: 'Who can understand what we endure every time we cross the street, enter the inn, or open the newspaper?'[166] Thus Loewenberg involuntarily concedes the truth of Goldstein's analysis. And in retrospect, the Zionist Kurt Blumenfeld felt that the article had uttered what many contemporaries dimly sensed.[167]

The Jewish Family Novel

The tensions of assimilation and acculturation are explored in a number of novels which criticize the Jewish subculture by focusing on the family. The following types—many anticipated in Herzl's

[164] Lissauer, 'Deutschtum und Judentum', *Der Kunstwart*, 25 (Apr.–June 1912), 6–12.

[165] *Der Kunstwart*, 25 (Aug. 1912), 248; emphasis in original. Loewenberg's quotation (see DKA I. ix. 597) itself illustrates his dual allegiance, for Goethe took it from Spinoza: see *Dichtung und Wahrheit*, DKA I. xiv. 681.

[166] Loewenberg, *Aus zwei Quellen*, p. 149.

[167] Blumenfeld, *Erlebte Judenfrage*, p. 58. For other responses, see Goldstein, 'German Jewry's Dilemma before 1914'.

Das neue Ghetto—occur repeatedly. Older Jews, parents or grandparents, remain loyal, if not to orthodox practice, at least to traditional Jewish values, and often embarrass their children by their incomplete linguistic and social acculturation. The next generation shows merely external adherence to Judaism and is materialistic, snobbish, and amoral. Other members of this generation, or those of the next, react against empty materialism and seek to be accepted as Germans, to form friendships with Germans, or to provide a new content for their inescapable Jewish identity. Very often, too, these families have unacculturated relatives who turn up from Poland or Galicia and cause embarrassment by embodying the Gentile image of the hateful Jew from which the assimilationists are desperately trying to distance themselves. These works cluster around the turn of the century. Obvious examples are Ludwig Jacobowski's *Werther, der Jude* (1892); Jakob Wassermann's *Die Juden von Zirndorf* (1897); Georg Hermann's *Jettchen Gebert* (1906); Schnitzler's *Der Weg ins Freie* (1908); Auguste Hauschner's *Die Familie Lowositz* (1908); Adolf Dessauer's *Großstadtjuden* (1910); and Max Brod's *Jüdinnen* (1911). The list could be multiplied, but this sample, representing quasi-assimilated Jewish communities in Berlin (Jacobowski, Hermann), Fürth (Wassermann), Vienna (Schnitzler, Dessauer), and Prague (Hauschner, Brod), covers the spectrum.

Although these are all novels of merit and interest, some of their authors are now little remembered. Ludwig Jacobowski (1868–1900), the son of a rather unsuccessful small businessman from Strelno (Posen), suffered numerous misfortunes: his much-loved mother died when he was 12; a conspicuous squint and an incurable stutter caused constant embarrassment; he himself died of meningitis at the age of 32. He studied at Berlin and Freiburg, moved into Berlin literary life, in 1898 becoming editor of *Die Gesellschaft*, and also worked for the Verein zur Abwehr des Antisemitismus.[168] Auguste Hauschner (1850–1924), born into a German-speaking Prague Jewish family, spent most of her life in Berlin, where she presided over a salon frequented by such literary friends as Gustav Landauer, Maximilian Harden, and Max

---

[168] See Fred B. Stern, *Ludwig Jacobowski: Persönlichkeit und Werk eines Dichters* (Darmstadt, 1966).

Brod.[169] Georg Hermann (the pseudonym of Georg Borchardt) was much better known. In his day Hermann was called the Jewish Fontane.[170] This seems an overestimate of his pleasant but wordy novels. Unlike Fontane, Hermann always retains a stranglehold over his characters: he is sparing with dramatic dialogue, preferring reported speech and chatty authorial comment. But it is hard to remain unaffected by the hideous irony that this spokesman for Jewish assimilation survived to see his hopes confounded by Nazism and met his death in Auschwitz.

A high degree of acculturation is represented by the Gebert family in Hermann's best-selling and still popular *Jettchen Gebert*, which, set in 1839, projects the conflicts of Wilhelmine Germany back into the Biedermeier period to which Hermann was strongly attached. The Geberts are patriotic Germans. Jettchen's uncle Jason was wounded in the War of Independence; her father was killed two years later at Ligny. Yet although they retain very few Jewish customs, a residual loyalty to an indefinable Jewishness makes them forbid Jettchen to marry a non-Jew, and pride in their Jewishness has restrained them from converting: a choice more likely in 1906 than in 1839. Financial prudence and instinctive clannishness further encourage them in opposing Jettchen's desire to marry Fritz Kössling, an impractical man of letters. Jettchen's uncle Jason tells Kössling: 'With *us*, *nobody* breaks loose from the family, not with *us*.'[171] And the family, however restrictive, is indispensable, for the outside world is not friendly: all Jettchen's non-Jewish school friends have lost touch with her.

The Jewishness of the older generation in these works is usually overlaid by materialism. Jettchen's relatives regard her marriage as a commercial transaction and feel justified in pressuring her to marry her unattractive but (supposedly) wealthy cousin Julius Jacoby (Hermann seems to have adapted Thomas Mann's triangle of Toni Buddenbrook, Morten Schwarzkopf, and Bendix Grünlich

---

[169] See Ritchie Robertson, 'National Stereotypes in Prague German Fiction', *Colloquia Germanica*, 22 (1989), 116–36 (on novels by Hauschner, Mauthner, and Brod).

[170] e.g. by Schnitzler: 'Jüdischer Fontane (cum grano)' (*T* 1 Aug. 1921). See Hans Otto Horch, 'Über Georg Hermann. Plädoyer zur Wiederentdeckung eines bedeutenden deutsch-jüdischen Schriftstellers', in Horch (ed.), *Judentum, Antisemitismus und europäische Kultur* (Tübingen, 1988), pp. 233–53.

[171] Hermann, *Jettchen Gebert*, Volksausgabe (Berlin, 1932), p. 123.

to a Jewish milieu).[172] She herself says emphatically that, having been brought up by her aunt and uncle, she must now repay them by marrying the man of their choice: 'I existed for twenty years, so I had to pay the bill.'[173] The family atmosphere is unpleasant, malicious, and philistine. Jason and Jettchen are the only members who read books. Hermann encourages the reader to despise the Geberts' ignorance by larding his text with half-submerged quotations from Goethe, Schiller, and even Klopstock, which he assumes the reader will recognize; eight lines from Eichendorff are used to prop up an idyllic love-scene. Philistinism is similarly attacked by Auguste Hauschner in *Die Familie Lowositz*, a novel that received moderate praise from Kafka.[174] The older members of the Lowositz family regard books, including the works of Goethe and Schiller, simply as commodities to be bestowed as bar mitzvah presents. Hauschner, who shows her protagonists responding to Czech nationalism, contrasts the importance of poets in the consciousness of the Czech national movement. Elsewhere the Jewish loyalty of the older generation displays little content. In Schnitzler's *Der Weg ins Freie* old Ehrenberg, a loyal Jew, is outraged by the extreme acculturation of his foppish son Oskar, whom he sees emerging from a Catholic church. Yet Ehrenberg's ostentatious Jewishness seems to have little point save to annoy and embarrass his family. Dessauer's *Großstadt-juden*, which reads like an unbalanced imitation of *Der Weg ins Freie*, presents Viennese Jewish society as desperate to curry favour with Gentiles. Here the bookseller Josef Kastner has recently changed his name from Kohn to please his snobbish wife and son; the latter, like Oskar Ehrenberg, is a Jewish antisemite who first affects Viennese dialect, then suddenly adopts a pseudo-aristocratic way of speaking. Frau Jordan does her best to cultivate Gentiles, conceals her Jewishness, carefully monitors her own language and gestures, and favours characteristically Christian expressions like 'Es ist ein wahres Kreuz' ('It's a real cross to bear'), while her son prides himself on his self-control and freedom from 'Jewish' excitability.[175]

---

[172] See the study of this novel by Russell A. Berman, *The Rise of the Modern German Novel: Culture and Charisma* (Cambridge, Mass., 1986), ch. 7.

[173] Hermann, *Jettchen Gebert*, p. 403.

[174] See Kafka, *Briefe an Felice und andere Korrespondenz aus der Verlobungszeit*, ed. Erich Heller and Jürgen Born (Frankfurt, 1967), p. 731.

[175] Dessauer, *Großstadtjuden* (Vienna and Leipzig, 1910), pp. 130, 140.

The most sweeping attack on Jewish society is to be found in *Die Juden von Zirndorf,* which Wassermann wrote as a young and impoverished author anxious to make a sensation. In the foreground, Wassermann shows us traditional Jewry, including such unattractive figures as the old usurer Enoch Karkau and the money-grubbing marriage-broker David Krailsheimer; but there are also unattractive assimilated Jews, like the rich, snobbish banker Baron Löwengard and the feeble decadent Edward Nieberding. The degenerate present is condemned by a prophetic standard, invoked in the novel's prelude which deals with the seventeenth-century messianic movement inspired by Sabbatai Zvi. The central character is a modern prophet with the incongruously classical and Jewish name Agathon Geyer (anticipating, and perhaps inspiring, Mann's Tonio Kröger). Agathon detests the Jews of the present day: he is expelled from school for declaring that he is no longer a Jew; and the narrator reports his thoughts as follows:

He felt himself firmly bound to his people, and yet he hated this people,—more now than ever. And he hated all those who had dispensed with the religious garb and drifted like the ruins of a great building, abandoned on the ocean of life, despised or powerful, but always parasites on a foreign host. A foreign people in the midst of German life, full of forced merriment, in an invisible ghetto. The old idea of magnificence has faded and they play the masters while their bodies bear the marks of two thousand years of misery. Jocular or sharp-witted masters, abjectly submissive or full of vile presumption, but always boundless in their ambition.[176]

Agathon represents an extreme and fantastic alternative to the ossified Jewry portrayed in these texts. As a prophetic figure, contrasted with Jews who have abandoned their faith for shallow atheism, he evidently has the task of restoring a truly religious foundation to a Jewish world which is either desiccated or secularized. We last see him surrounded by women, including his mother, sister, and lover, symbolizing his identification with the feminine, imaginative, gentle dimension instead of the authoritarian world of the father. He reappears in the sequel, *Renate Fuchs,* but only as a dying man full of spiritual authority.

An alternative chosen by the younger generation in some of

---

[176] Wassermann, *Die Juden von Zirndorf* [1897] (Munich, 1996), p. 201.

these novels is identification with 'German' values. In Jacobowski's *Werther, der Jude*, the young hero, Leo Wolff, believes himself to be free from 'Jewish' qualities. In contrast to the ambition supposedly characteristic of Jews, he neglects his university studies, considering himself a dreamy, weak-willed, and instinctive person. He belongs to a duelling fraternity and participates enthusiastically in their heavy drinking sessions and ritual language. Like young Rudolf in *Die Familie Lowositz*, who writes dramas of Schillerian idealism, Leo is represented as an idealist who as a boy admired Schiller's Marquis Posa and now imagines the ideal Jew as a combination of Jesus and Spinoza. Quoting from Goethe's 'Das Göttliche', a key text of Enlightenment humanism, he declares his wish to be 'ein Jude, edel, hilfreich und gut' ('a Jew, noble, helpful and good').[177] Like Dohm a century earlier, he preaches the ethical reformation of the Jews. Ironically, the need for reform is demonstrated by his father and his cousin Siegmund, who have invested the savings of various non-Jewish fellow-citizens in a joint-stock company which goes bankrupt, but have rescued their own property. Delighted to have outwitted the despised Gentiles, they cannot understand Leo's objections. The narrator enters the father's consciousness to inform us that Leo's alien standpoint 'reminded him of the stupid honesty of the "Gojim"'.[178]

Yet if Leo's relatives exploit the Gentiles financially, Leo exploits them sexually. As a token of his assimilation, he has a blonde Gentile girlfriend, a shop-assistant called Helene. The fellow-members of his duelling fraternity, who spend their drinking sessions boasting of their sexual prowess, taunt him for not having slept with her. His prolonged campaign to break down her resistance, however, seems also motivated by her casual reference to somebody else as an ugly Jew. His sexual conquest has the character of revenge. His attitude to her is entirely chauvinistic: 'He could not imagine love without the woman's complete submission and subordination.'[179] He also has a neurotic and egoistic desire to torment her. If this is the sadistic aspect of Leo's sexuality, however, there is also a masochistic side, which appears in his

---

[177] Jacobowski, *Werther, der Jude* ([1892]; Berlin, 1898), p. 168. See Anderson, '"Jewish" Mimesis?'   [178] Jacobowski, *Werther, der Jude*, p. 334.
[179] Ibid. 163.

powerful attraction to the young wife of his revered former head-master. In Frau Erna's presence he feels like a schoolboy, confronted with her 'demonic' personality. His desire makes him feel guilty: 'Even a single impure thought attached to her, to the spouse of his revered and exceedingly good-hearted teacher made him blush with shame.'[180] Jacobowski is depicting, as peculiarly Jewish, a tormented and ambivalent sexuality: Leo wants to conquer and punish the Gentile world in the person of Helene, but also to submit helplessly to it in the person of Erna. He gets Helene pregnant and, in his obsession with Erna, so neglects her that in despair she drowns herself. The novel conveys the clear message that Jews, even those with high moral ideals like Leo, are either corrupt or neurotic and can do Gentiles only harm.

In his introduction to the third and subsequent editions, Jacobowski says that his opinion on the Jewish question has not changed since he wrote it, and that he still advocates complete assimilation to 'German spirit and German mores (*Gesittung*)'. Despite this, the novel can easily be read as warning Germans of the fatal consequences of accepting Jews, and hence as an anti-semitic text. Contemporaries, however, did not read it that way. It was well received by reviewers and translated into six languages, including Yiddish. The longest and most thoughtful review, by Karl Busse, interpreted Leo as a tragic figure caught between the generations: able to imagine a regenerated Jewry, but too imbued with the sins of the fathers to realize it himself. At the end of the novel, Leo's Gentile friend Richard Manzow, absent hitherto, turns up just in time for Leo to die in his arms. This, Busse argues, is a glimpse of the future, corresponding to Moses' dying glimpse of the Promised Land: 'The young Jew passes away in the arms of the young Christian, *young Jewry perishes and simultaneously is absorbed within idealized young Christianity—Christianity understood not as an ecclesiastical and religious concept, but as an ethical one*.'[181] As with Herzl's Jakob Samuel, the women in Leo's life are less important than the ultimate love-object, the Gentile man.

[180] Jacobowski, 164.
[181] Busse, 'Ein moderner Roman', *Die Gesellschaft*, 9 (1893), 76–84 (p. 79); emphasis in original.

Leo's friend Richard and his cousin Siegmund embody two antithetical types often found in this body of fiction: the Gentile friend and the Eastern Jewish relative. The former is an ideal, regarded with helpless love; the latter represents the hideous reality from which the hero is trying to escape through acculturation. In *Der Weg ins Freie* the Gentile protagonist, Georg von Wergenthin, gradually comes to understand Jewish life through his uneasy friendship with Heinrich Bermann, and serves as the lens through which the Jewish characters are presented to the reader. In *Großstadtjuden* Dessauer goes further by making his Gentile character, Artur Gschmeidler, pass authoritative judgements on Jewish life. Disgusted at the flight from Jewishness, Gschmeidler and his Jewish fiancée Lotti conclude that the only thoroughgoing antisemites are Jews.

Schnitzler uses the fictional convention of friendship between Gentile and Jew to gain not one but two vantage-points on the Jewish subculture depicted in *Der Weg ins Freie*. As Georg gradually overcomes his initial naïvety about Jews (as when he imagines old Ehrenberg to be pious) and his irritation with their hypersensitivity, his reactions serve to enlighten the reader. He gets to know a whole gallery of characters seeking to escape from Jewishness into Socialism (Therese Golowski, who displays the histrionic quality Schnitzler associated with politicians); into exaggerated acculturation (the dandified Oskar Ehrenberg); into Zionism (Leo Golowski); and into sheer cynicism, as with the novelist Edmund Nürnberger. The major development is the increase in Georg's sympathy for Heinrich Bermann, the Jewish intellectual who delivers sharp criticisms of the Jews. At first Georg is impatient with the insecurity of his Jewish acquaintances, and feels that Heinrich's behaviour confirms the antisemitic remarks that he has heard made about him. Only later, during a conversation about Zionism, does Georg come to see his Jewish acquaintances in a new light: 'For the first time the name "Jew", which he himself had often used so casually, mockingly and contemptuously, began to take on a new and more sombre meaning. He began dimly to understand this people's mysterious fate, which somehow expressed itself in every one sprung from it' (*E* i. 722).

It is common to observe that, despite their friendship, the strands of the novel that centre on Georg and Heinrich respectively

have not been fully interwoven.[182] Georg's rather aimless social
life takes him through a number of social events—informal
gatherings in people's homes, parties, outings—where he meets
numerous Jewish types and arguments occur which expose different aspects of the Jewish problem. However, the relationship
between Georg and his girlfriend Anna Rosner develops apart
from the social gatherings, even though both are present at
several; none of the social occasions is the setting for a crucial
step in their relationship. Georg's private and social lives could
have been more neatly integrated had Schnitzler made his lover a
Jew; but he insisted to Georg Brandes that he always imagined
Anna as a Catholic.[183] At least this enables him to introduce an
antisemite in the person of Anna's brother. And it means that the
structure of the novel conveys an important message: that social
integration, like narrative integration, is incomplete; that the
Gentile upper and middle classes (the Wergenthins and the
Rosners) stand somewhat apart from the Jewish bourgeoisie of
Vienna.[184] As we saw in Chapter 2, the novel leaves both Heinrich
and Georg arguably guilty of wrongdoing towards the women in
their lives. Anna has died bearing her and Georg's child; Heinrich's
girlfriend has committed suicide. But while the fortunate Georg
escapes to a new job in Germany with a relatively untroubled
conscience, Heinrich remains trapped in spirals of futile self-
torment. For him there is no 'road to the open'.

If, in these family novels, the Gentile friend represents an ideal,
the Polish or Galician cousin represents the hated Jewish identity
that characters want to escape from. In *Jettchen Gebert*, the
Geberts evidently do not look Jewish, but Cousin Julius Jacoby,
whom Jettchen is compelled to marry, resembles a Jewish caricature, small and plump with bristly hair and crafty little eyes.
Julius, whose name is really Joel, speaks with a recognizably
Jewish accent; although he claims to come from Posen, he really
comes from a village called Benschen, and Uncle Jason, who is the
moral and intellectual authority-figure in the novel, foretells that
eventually he will claim to be a Berliner born and bred:

---

[182] See Kenneth Segar, 'Aesthetic Coherence in Arthur Schnitzler's Novel *Der Weg
ins Freie*', *MAL* 25 (1992), iii/iv. 95–111.

[183] Schnitzler, *Briefe 1875–1912*, p. 580 (4 July 1908).

[184] See Klüger, *Katastrophen*, pp. 67–9.

And if anyone asks him in five years' time, he'll say that he does come from Posen, but was taken to Berlin when he was a little chap and has only dim memories of his home town. And if anyone asks him in ten years' time, he'll reply by asking if it isn't obvious that he's from Berlin.[185]

Joel is an Eastern Jewish upstart, contrasted with the quasi-aristocratic Western Jews (and thus again a figure more typical of the period when the novel was written than of that in which it is ostensibly set). Even worse is the cousin from Posen, Siegmund Königsberger in *Werther, der Jude*, who speaks with a nasal accent and rejoices in the credulity of Gentiles.

The obstinately unacculturated Jew can also be a positive figure, like Wasserstein in Herzl's *Das neue Ghetto* (and his ancestor Hirsch in Heine's *Die Bäder von Lucca*). Dessauer similarly shows how the Kastner family live in fear of being embarrassed by Uncle Jakob Weintraub, a shameless *Schnorrer* with over-familiar manners. He thrusts himself into a social gathering, seizes by the hand a high-ranking civil servant whom the family wish to impress, and nonchalantly assumes that the Baroness von Hebenstreit is the civil servant's wife. But in his refusal to be impressed by such dignitaries, Uncle Jakob embodies a kind of integrity which the other characters admire despite their horror: 'Leopold saw with shuddering admiration how Aryan descent, high rank and nobility, advantages which separately inspired him with such awe, even when they were combined had no effect on his uncle.'[186]

Max Brod put a new twist on the Jewish family novel by contrasting two Jewish women in *Jüdinnen*. Here the nervous, ill-looking, intelligent, domineering Prague Jewess Irene Popper is contrasted with the healthy, practical, modest country girl Olga Grosslicht. Both are seen from the viewpoint of the schoolboy Hugo Rosenthal. Against her parents, who typify the older generation by talking loudly and simultaneously in ungrammatical German, Irene reacts by adopting an intellectual manner which gains her the reputation of a bluestocking and is easily perverted into petty sadism. She organizes a game which consists in uttering rude remarks about the other participants, who then confess

---

[185] Hermann, *Jettchen Gebert*, p. 160.
[186] Dessauer, *Großstadtjuden*, p. 262.

which accusations they find most hurtful, and reveals her own sexual insecurity by accusing Olga of running after all the men. The novel intimates that Irene has mistaken her own character by aspiring to a kind of intellectuality which is not for women. She marries a doctor with vulgar manners and unmistakable masculinity, and ends up looking healthy and youthful. Her brother Alfred is sick in a different way: a German nationalist, a helpless admirer of all things Aryan, and a self-hating Jew who derives his world-view from Weininger. Irene's counterpart, Olga, is practical, cheerful, reliable. Her modesty makes Hugo think of the biblical daughters of Jerusalem, and she also reminds him of the cedars of Lebanon. Her healthy sexuality is discreetly called 'developed womanhood'.[187] She has on Hugo the redemptive effect that women generally have on men in Brod's novels. Learning that she, like him, has experienced unrequited love, he kneels at her feet and bursts into tears. He then goes to Prague and retakes, with outstanding success, the exam he had previously failed. For Brod, a recent convert to Zionism, Irene represents the sick urban Jew, while Olga is the healthy country Jew who can reconnect the Jewish future with the biblical past.

All these texts date from before the First World War, but Schnitzler returned to the theme of the Jewish family in 1924 in his remarkable story *Fräulein Else*. It is technically audacious in its use of interior monologue which shows us that although Else is on holiday while her parents remain in Vienna, she carries her family pressures wherever she goes. The setting is a hotel in the Austrian Alps where the 19-year-old Else and some relatives are staying. She receives an express letter from her mother in Vienna, informing her that her father, a lawyer, is in danger of being arrested for embezzling money. He has to raise a large sum within a very few days. The only way of raising the money is for Else to appeal to an old friend of her father's, a wealthy art dealer called Herr von Dorsday, who happens to be staying in the same hotel. Thus Else finds herself placed under intolerable pressure by her family. She goes to Dorsday, and he consents to supply the money, under one condition: she must allow him to look at her naked. Unable to cope with this demand, Else goes downstairs into the hotel dining-room with nothing on under her coat, and shows herself to

---

[187] Brod, *Jüdinnen* ([1911] Leipzig, 1915), p. 264.

Dorsday like that, in public. She then collapses, is taken to her room, and when nobody is looking she manages to take an overdose of sleeping-pills and drifts off into death.

This story is disturbing enough, but becomes more so when presented through the consciousness of a young woman. A conventional view might see Else as hysterical, but Schnitzler in fact shows how her breakdown results from a combination of physiological and emotional factors. The physiological factor is that, as the text discreetly indicates, this challenge comes just at the onset of Else's monthly period; discomfort makes her sleep badly and explains why she has sleeping-pills at her bedside. But the crucial factor is her emotional isolation, revealed through her stream of consciousness. She sees through her parents, aware that her father has affairs on the side and that her mother is too stupid to know. At the same time, she loves her parents and cannot bear the thought of her father going to prison. But she also knows that her parents are using her. Schnitzler, however, is more subtle than to make her a sexual pawn. It seems she has never met a man who strongly attracted her; her sexual emotions are undeveloped though constantly present. No other life than leisure followed by marriage has ever been suggested to her. In the meantime, she is, and knows she is, an object of display. She exists so that men may look at her. Hence there is much in her thoughts about clothes and self-presentation, and a fatal absence of self-esteem. And since she is an object to be looked at, Dorsday's demand—that she let him look at her naked—makes brutally apparent the status that she, as a woman with no purpose in life of her own, is allowed in this society.

Else's Jewishness creates an unspoken bond between her and Herr von Dorsday. She knows that he is Jewish, and is conscious that her own Jewishness is not perceptible:

No, Mr Dorsday, I don't believe in your elegance or in your monocle or in your nobility. You could be dealing in old clothes as easily as in old paintings.—But, Else! Else, what are you thinking of? Oh, I can get away with it. Nobody notices it in my case. I'm even blonde, auburn, and Rudi looks just like an aristocrat. Of course, with Mummy you notice right away, at least when she speaks. But not with Daddy. Anyway, I don't care if they notice. I don't make a secret of it, and Rudi certainly doesn't. On the contrary. (*E* ii. 333)

This passage illustrates Schnitzler's claim that one Jew does not respect another. Else despises Herr von Dorsday because with his affected elegance he tries to hide his Jewishness. She herself claims to be a self-respecting Jew, but she has the advantage that if she wishes she can pass as a non-Jew, and is obviously glad of the fact. But she and Dorsday are linked not only by their Jewishness but by their blocked sexuality. Else's society has alienated her sexuality from her, turning it into a kind of vicarious narcissism: she has made herself into an aesthetic object for the benefit of others. Dorsday's sexuality remains voyeuristic. His erotic organ is the eye. He wants to aestheticize Else, so that she is not a body to be enjoyed or a person to be known, but an object to be contemplated.

The blocked, merely visual sexuality exhibited in the story is related to Schnitzler's innovative narrative technique. Having internalized the male gaze, Else is split between her publicly visible self and the private self—sexually immature, but precocious in knowledge of the world—that comments cynically and maliciously on other people's behaviour. This split is replicated on the page by the division between her spoken words (in italics) and her thoughts (in roman type).[188] However, the narratorial stance is not similarly divided. By giving us access to Else's full consciousness, the narrator allows us to apprehend her as a whole, embodied person in a way that she cannot experience herself. Schnitzler's narrative technique, which could have been used in an intrusive, voyeuristic way, in fact restores to Else the humanity which her family environment systematically denies her. The story not only exposes and rebukes the restrictions it ascribes to the Jewish subculture, but moves out from the confines of the Jewish family novel to articulate a more general conflict between personal autonomy and familial and economic pressures.

SELF-HATRED

Acculturation without integration made it often difficult for Jews to avoid feeling uneasy in the company of non-Jews. Sooner or

---

[188] See Elisabeth Bronfen, *Over Her Dead Body: Death, Femininity and the Aesthetic* (Manchester, 1992), pp. 282–3.

later one would be reminded that one was a Jew and that, in many people's eyes, this was incompatible with being a German. And the individual's experiences were overshadowed by the assumptions of the 'emancipation contract', whereby Jews were accepted into German society on condition that they behaved themselves properly—that is, did not behave in an obviously 'Jewish' way. Some conspicuous reactions took two linked forms. One could maintain the assimilationist stance and try to become more German than the Germans; or one could internalize antisemitic hostility, believe oneself incapable of assimilation, and transfer the blame to oneself in the attitude known, controversially, as 'Jewish self-hatred'. The two were linked because extravagant devotion to Germany could conceal deep self-distrust. I shall consider here writers in whom 'self-hatred' seems predominant, and then turn to some who display what I shall call hyperacculturation.

The first problem with 'self-hatred' is to identify it; the second, to explain it. Should any strongly worded criticism of Jews by a Jew be attributed to 'self-hatred' or 'Jewish antisemitism'? Do Jews incur suspicions at the present day if they criticize Israel?[189] Or has the term been as discredited as Philip Roth implies by putting it in the mouth of the humourless sabra who tells the masochistic narrator: 'Mr Portnoy, you are nothing but a self-hating Jew'?[190] While using the term sparingly, I shall assume that some extreme and obsessive diatribes against Jews by Jews do merit this label and require investigation.

Next, are we to attribute 'self-hatred' narrowly to a peculiarly Jewish psychopathology? Are we to explain it, more broadly, from mechanisms of projection and interaction that may occur when any two or more social groups are in tension? Or, even if we accept the latter explanation, are we to look for aspects of the Jews' situation in Germany and Austria that made such tensions particularly painful?

An extra difficulty for English-speakers is that 'self-hatred', a rare expression, is used mostly in the phrase 'Jewish self-hatred' to translate German discussions, and therefore implies a fixed propensity of Jews to self-detestation. The German word *Selbsthaß* has wider connotations. It belongs to the Enlightenment

---

[189] See Broder, *Der ewige Antisemit*, pp. 35–9.
[190] Roth, *Portnoy's Complaint* (London, 1971), p. 300.

discourse on melancholy, depression, and 'hypochondria'. Moritz uses it to denote the extravagant self-contempt of a character in a play.[191] Goethe applies it to Byron, whose work initially repelled him 'through hypochondriac passion and violent self-hatred' (DKA I xvii. 271). Hence the term already had psychopathological connotations when it was adopted and given currency by the brilliant and erratic writer Theodor Lessing in his best-known book, *Der jüdische Selbsthaß* (*Jewish Self-Hatred*, 1930). Although Lessing does say that 'self-hatred' is a phenomenon that any human group can exhibit, this disclaimer can easily be obscured by his vigorous attempt to explain 'self-hatred' from Jewish psychopathology. Humankind has a universal need to impose meaning on history; since history consists largely of suffering, this means finding somebody to blame; and the Jews are 'the only nation to have sought the guilt for world history *in themselves* alone'.[192] This explanation seems to be inspired by recollections of the Old Testament prophets, who ascribed attacks on Israel to the nation's own backslidings, and by the psychology of religion offered by Nietzsche in *The Genealogy of Morals*, in which the sick make a virtue of their sickness. The Jews' tendency to blame themselves for their misfortunes, and the resulting predominance of their ethical and intellectual lives over their aesthetic life, form a sickness which Lessing undertakes to diagnose. As with the ethnopsychology of Lazarus and Steinthal, mentioned in connection with Freud in Chapter 2, Lessing presupposes an unchanging, or very slowly changing, Jewish character independent of environment. And he takes over the image of the sick Jew from the array of antisemitic stereotypes surveyed in Chapter 3. His account is too deeply mired in the conflicts it undertakes to analyse.

A more promising approach to 'Jewish self-hatred' via social psychology was undertaken in a well-known paper of 1941 by Kurt Lewin.[193] Lewin explains 'Jewish self-hatred' as typifying the behaviour of members of underprivileged groups. Some members are always ashamed of their membership, anxious to

[191] Moritz, *Werke*, i. 319; cf. i. 190 ('Selbsthasser').
[192] Lessing, *Der jüdische Selbsthaß* ([1930] Munich, 1984), p. 13.
[193] Lewin, 'Self-Hatred among Jews', in his *Resolving Social Conflicts* (New York, 1948), pp. 186–200. I am also indebted to the unpublished survey by Elisabeth Albanis, 'The Concept of "Jewish Self-Hatred" in Historiography'.

join the larger community outside, but kept back because that
community identifies them with the underprivileged group. The
self-hater therefore finds himself in a constant state of frustration
which predisposes him to aggression. Logically he should turn his
aggression against the outside majority which refuses to accept
him. But that majority is too desirable, and too powerful, to be
attacked. So instead the self-hater turns his aggression against
himself, or rather those aspects of himself which he thinks identify
him with the underprivileged group. Such a person sometimes
performs an 'identification with the aggressor', and then we have
the phenomenon of the Jewish antisemite, well described in the
'classic' work of Jewish self-hatred, Otto Weininger's *Geschlecht
und Charakter* (*Sex and Character*, 1903):

whoever hates the Jewish character hates it first and foremost in himself; if
he persecutes it in others, he is only trying to separate himself from
Jewishness by these means; he strives to separate himself from it by locating
it entirely in another person, and thus enjoying the momentary illusion of
being free from it himself. Hate, like love, is a phenomenon of projection:
man hates only those people who remind him unpleasantly of himself.[194]

Thus 'self-hatred' is best understood as the product not of psychopathology but of social interaction. This approach is summed up
by Sander Gilman in his wide-ranging study of the subject: 'Self-
hatred results from outsiders' acceptance of the mirage of themselves generated by their reference group—that group in society
which they see as defining them—as a reality.'[195] After reading an
attack by Theodor Lessing on psychoanalysis as being Jewish,
Freud described such 'self-hatred' as 'an exquisitely Jewish
phenomenon'.[196] Yet there is nothing particularly Jewish about
this process. James Boswell, who was anxious to be accepted in
eighteenth-century London by minimizing his Scottishness,
records in his journal for 24 March 1775: 'I was disgusted by
Fordyce, who was coarse and noisy: and, as he had the Scotch
accent strong, he shocked me as a kind of representative of myself.
He was to me as the slaves of the Spartans, when shown drunk to
make that vice odious.'[197] Boswell hates in someone else the

---

[194] Weininger, *Geschlecht und Charakter* ([1903] Munich, 1980), p. 407.
[195] Gilman, *Jewish Self-Hatred*, p. 2.   [196] Jones, *Freud*, iii. 170.
[197] Quoted and discussed in Pat Rogers, 'Boswell and the Scotticism', in his *Johnson
and Boswell: The Transit of Caledonia* (Oxford, 1995), pp. 171–91 (p. 182).

qualities that he fears others (his admired reference group) will detect in him. His antipathy to Fordyce is really a hatred of (what he thinks others will recognize as) the Scottish traits in himself.

However, interaction and projection do not provide a complete explanation of 'Jewish self-hatred'. Some factors were present in late nineteenth-century Germany and Austria that could make Jews' situation additionally painful. We have already seen how nominal acceptance was in fact undermined by various mechanisms of exclusion, and also that Jewish identity was for many Jews an identity with minimal content. Yet the outside world would not let the Jew give up this identity. In 1912 Schnitzler wrote some drastic reflections on the importance of 'the so-called Jewish question':

It was not possible, especially not for a Jew in public life, to ignore the fact that he was a Jew; nobody else was doing so, not the Gentiles and even less the Jews. You had the choice of being counted as insensitive, obtrusive and cheeky, or as oversensitive, shy and suffering from feelings of persecution. And even if you managed somehow to conduct yourself so that nothing showed, it was impossible to remain completely untouched; as for instance a person cannot remain unconcerned whose skin has been anaesthetized but who has to watch, with his eyes open, how it is scratched by unclean knives, even cut into until the blood flows.[198]

The last image expresses the powerlessness of the Jews: society is damaging them and they cannot resist. One can either react emotionally or with impotent dignity. While the image may be drawn from Schnitzler's medical experience, it also recalls older fantasies of the blood libel, in which Jews cut up Christian children. Schnitzler has retained the cruelty of the image but reversed its thrust: now it is non-Jews who lacerate Jews with poisoned knives.

The painful situation evoked by Schnitzler was often exacerbated by coinciding with a conflict between generations. In his polemic against the Jewish family, Anton Kuh explicitly uses the term—'self-hatred, described by mockers as "Jewish anti-semitism"'—and says it was characteristic of German Jews before 1914.[199] Kuh's theory of self-hatred as inability to escape from the family has, perhaps unwittingly, been revived in a tamer form

---

[198] Schnitzler, *My Youth in Vienna*, pp. 6–7 (trans. modified).
[199] Kuh, *Juden und Deutsche*, p. 9.

by the historian Hans Dieter Hellige, who seeks to explain 'Jewish self-hatred' as a specific form of projection located in the social situation of young Jewish men who came of age towards the end of the nineteenth century. Their fathers were businessmen (on a large or small scale) who very often wished their sons to take over their businesses or pursue similar careers. This created tensions which were exacerbated by the traditional authority of the father in a Jewish household. However, the economic depression inaugurated by the Stock Market crash of 1873 made a business career seem unattractive; the young men mostly enjoyed a good education which made university study and cultural pursuits seem accessible goals; and they were conscious that their identification as Jews brought stigma without any compensations. For several reasons, therefore, they turned against capitalism and adopted cultural and intellectual pursuits; yet, as we have seen, they could not count on acceptance by the surrounding society.[200] Kafka analysed this situation in a letter to Brod:

Rather than psychoanalysis, I prefer in this case the insight that this father-complex, which gives many people their spiritual sustenance, refers not to the innocent father but to the father's Jewishness. Most of those who began writing in German wanted to get away from Jewishness, mostly with the unclear consent of their fathers (it was this unclarity that was infuriating), they wanted to, but their hind legs were still stuck to the father's Jewishness and with their front legs they could find no new ground. Their despair at this was their inspiration.[201]

Such writers found themselves between two worlds: one which they had painfully rejected, and another to which it was painful and laborious to gain access.

Hence we find numerous remarkable statements in which Jews admit their dislike of other Jews, showing that they have internalized the view of themselves held by the people around them. They doubt their own originality, their own creativity. Schnitzler (of all people) speculated that he, and all Jews, were incapable of

---

[200] See Hellige, 'Generationskonflikt, Selbsthaß und die Entstehung antikapitalistischer Positionen im Judentum', *Geschichte und Gesellschaft*, 5 (1979), 476–518; the substance of this article reappears in 'Rathenau und Harden in der Gesellschaft des Deutschen Kaiserreichs', Hellige's introduction to his edition of Walther Rathenau and Maximilian Harden, *Briefwechsel 1897–1920* (Munich and Heidelberg, 1983), pp. 15–299.   [201] Brod and Kafka, *Eine Freundschaft*, ii. 360.

writing a first-rate play (*T* 7 Apr. 1906). Wittgenstein wrote in 1931: 'Even the greatest of Jewish thinkers is no more than talented. (Myself for instance.)'[202] Other aphorisms by him associate genius with primitive energy and imply that he considered Jews too civilized to be creative: 'Within all great art there is a WILD animal: *tamed*. Not with [Felix] Mendelssohn, for example.'[203] S. M. Melamed, in a book-length study of Jewish psychology, argued that Old Testament Jews' law and religion did not develop from natural conditions, but were imposed by a spiritual ukase, so that even the ancient Jews were estranged from material reality, from nature, and from sexuality; and this abstractness was heightened in the Diaspora, where Jewish identity centred on books—the Torah and the Talmud.[204] The historian Hans-Joachim Schoeps wrote of his fellow-Jews in his memoirs: 'Their weakness, which imperils their very life, is the abstract orientation of their minds and, in the vital sphere, the great uncertainty of their instincts. I did not like most Jews, but I decided early on to put up with them for the sake of Judaism.'[205]

Jewishness could be not only unwelcome, but also a source of embarrassment. Here it is helpful to draw on the ideas of Erving Goffman.[206] Goffman is interested in the self as something produced dramaturgically, something staged in a performance before a perhaps unsympathetic audience which has to be won over. Shame and self-hatred are the result of failure to perform acceptably, and a frequent reason for such failure is the possession of attributes to which the audience attaches a stigma. To the extent that the individual has internalized society's norms, he feels ashamed of his attributes even when not on stage. In his contact with other people he is liable always to be insecure. He may vacillate between concealing his stigmatized attribute and flaunting it with bravado. These two attitudes are represented in Schnitzler's *Der Weg ins Freie* by the elder and the younger Ehrenberg. Salomon

---

[202] Wittgenstein, *Vermischte Bemerkungen/Culture and Value*, tr. Peter Winch (Oxford, 1980), p. 18e.

[203] Ibid. 37e. Cf. Wagner's judgement of Mendelssohn: 'A landscape painter, incapable of depicting a *human being*.'—Cosima Wagner, *Diaries*, i. 170.

[204] Melamed, *Zur Psychologie des jüdischen Geistes* (Berlin, n.d. [1913?]).

[205] Schoeps, *Ja—Nein—und Trotzdem: Erinnerungen—Begegnungen—Erfahrungen* (Mainz, 1974), p. 33.

[206] Goffman, *Stigma: Notes on the Management of Spoiled Identity* (Harmondsworth, 1968); *The Presentation of Self in Everyday Life* (Harmondsworth, 1971).

Ehrenberg embarrasses his family by speaking in a Jewish version of German, while his son Oskar affects the manner of an aristocratic Viennese without complete success: Georg von Wergenthin notes that Oskar is dressed 'with an elegance that had much of the senior clerk in a fashion shop, something of a young singer of comic songs, and also something of a young gentleman of good society' (*E* i. 664).

One effect of Jews' unease is said to be nervousness and awkwardness in self-presentation. As early as 1840 Berthold Auerbach comments on his fictional protagonist:

Ephraim knew only two forms of social behaviour: to be either stiff and reserved, or else extremely familiar. This fault will be found among most people who live in restricted circles, and especially among most Jews when they first enter a wider sphere of life.[207]

Since Jews are supposed to be ill-mannered, pushy, and over-effusive, other Jews have perpetual scope for embarrassment at the 'Jewish' behaviour of their fellow-Jews because they think it will annoy Gentile observers and that the stigma will be transferred to them. In diaries of the period, Jews comment minutely on other Jews' bad manners. Schnitzler complains about having entertained Heinrich Mann and 'his fat, fairly impossible wife, a vulgar Prague Jewess' (*T* 31 May 1914). Kafka gives a detailed description of the behaviour of a provincial Jew who attracts others' attention by muttering to himself in the train, and describes Hasenclever as 'Jewish, noisy'.[208] Karl Oppenheimer, a well-known paediatrician, and his wife Clara write in 1919: 'The non-Jew cannot possibly understand the feelings with which we Jews observe the noisy, tactless behaviour of many of our co-religionists on journeys or in public places. We are well aware that every ostentatious toilette, every word spoken too loudly, adds a poisoned arrow to our enemies' over-full quiver.'[209] Martin Freud recalls his father's anger on seeing an obviously Jewish boy disgrace himself publicly by breaking a glass in a beer-garden.[210] From her upbringing in 1930s Vienna, Ruth Klüger mentions a fear of 'auffallen', of conspicuous behaviour: she was forbidden

---

[207] Auerbach, *Dichter und Kaufmann*, in his *Gesammelte Schriften*, xii. 132.
[208] Kafka, *Tagebücher*, pp. 931, 1023.
[209] Karl and Clara Oppenheimer, 'Der Antisemitismus', *Süddeutsche Monatshefte*, 17 (1919–20), ii. 124–9 (p. 127).   [210] Freud, *Glory Reflected*, pp. 100–1.

for this reason to recite poetry while walking along the street: "'Jewish children who behave badly make *rishes* (antisemitism).' Did that still matter when the entire population was aroused against us?'[211] Such conspicuous behaviour need not, however, be specifically Jewish. It is characteristic of the person who, elevated by recent wealth into another social group, has difficulty in adjusting to the manners of the new group, and reveals himself to the expert eye as a parvenu. The psychoanalyst Hanns Sachs was surely right in arguing that certain traits supposed to be typically Jewish—insecurity, affectation, greed for status and titles—were in fact features of the bourgeoisie.[212]

A 'Jewish' appearance could also be a source of discomfort. Caricaturists not only emphasized the hooked nose, hunched back, and flat feet supposedly characteristic of the Jew, but alerted people to seek subtler distinguishing marks. Hermann Cohen wrote in 1880: 'We all wish we had the complete German, Germanic appearance, of which we now bear only the climatic side-effects.'[213] Wassermann says in his autobiography: 'My facial type did not mark me out as a Jew, nor did my behaviour nor my idiom. I had a straight nose and was quiet and modest.'[214] Hedwig Fischer, his publisher's wife, said that with his dark hair and sparkling eyes he resembled a young Savoyard.[215] Freud's children avoided discrimination because they looked Italian.[216] It was of course possible to alter one's appearance surgically: when the historian Lewis Namier was 14, his parents had his eyelids and nose operated on in Vienna, possibly to make him look less Jewish.[217]

Recognizably 'Jewish' language and gestures also annoyed Jews. Thus Schnitzler writes of two women friends:

I did not like Sophie so much today. Noticed today the future old Jewess, the bad race, and a way of letting her left hand flap as she walks. [. . .] She lost by comparison with Frau Bachrach, who represents the good

---

[211] Klüger, *weiter leben* (Göttingen, 1992), pp. 11–12.

[212] Sachs, 'Der Jude und der Bourgeois', *Der Jude*, 3 (1918–19), i. 15–20.

[213] Cohen, 'Ein Bekenntnis in der Judenfrage', *Jüdische Schriften*, ii. 85.

[214] Wassermann, *Mein Weg*, p. 39.

[215] Peter de Mendelssohn, *S. Fischer und sein Verlag* (Frankfurt, 1970), p. 341.

[216] Freud, *Glory Reflected*, p. 101.

[217] Linda Colley, *Namier* (London, 1989), p. 8. On the history of rhinoplasty, see Gilman, *The Jew's Body*, pp. 184–93.

Jewish race and has something charmingly refined in her posture and conversation. (*T* 9 Mar. 1893)

Two contrasts are drawn: between Sophie's idle chatter and Frau Bachrach's speech; and between Sophie's lack of bodily self-control and Frau Bachrach's dignified bearing. Volubility and lack of bodily control are, for Schnitzler, Jewish in a bad sense. Any trace of Yiddish is also unattractive: in his autobiography he recalls Gisela Freistadt, whose family are on the fringe of the ghetto, as 'ein hübsches Judenmädel' ('a pretty Jewish girl', *J* 178), who eventually repels Schnitzler by 'her boring, banal way of speaking, which was not free of jargon'.[218] When he meets 'Fännchen' (Franziska Reich), the object of his puppy-love, later in life and 'possesses' her, he is 'disagreeably affected by her Jew-talk and chatter (*jüdeln und plappern*)' (*T* 22 May 1899). The need to speak proper German enters even a dream about Goethe: Schnitzler, apologizing for having mistakenly dismissed Goethe, feels a need to speak properly and says 'I beg you not to think the worse of me' ('Bitte mir das zu gute zu halten') (*T* 20 Sept. 1900).

Schnitzler, in his diaries and in *Der Weg ins Freie*, analyses why unpleasant behaviour by Jews should particularly annoy other Jews. In the novel, Heinrich Bermann relates a familiar Jewish anecdote: 'You know the story of the Polish Jew who shares a railway carriage with a stranger and behaves very politely until suddenly some remark made by the other discloses that he is also a Jew. Thereupon the Polish Jew says with relief: "ä soi!" and puts his feet up on the seat opposite' (*E* i. 755).[219] Heinrich draws the conclusion that one Jew never shows respect for another: 'for,' he says, 'all emotional relationships are carried on in an atmosphere of intimacy, so to speak, in which respect cannot help being suffocated' (*E* i. 756). This unwanted intimacy is that of Jews who have nothing in common, except that the Gentile world classifies them together as Jews. The more acculturated Jew is disgusted and ashamed to find himself equated with the kind of Jew who talks *Jargon*. In his travelling companion he recognizes the hateful image which, he fears, the Gentile world has of him.

---

[218] Schnitzler, *My Youth in Vienna*, p. 150.

[219] This anecdote is also told by Freud, *SE* viii. 80–1, by Lessing in *Der jüdische Selbsthaß*, p. 30, and (to illustrate Jews' lack of self-confidence) by Trebitsch, *Geist und Judentum*, p. 103.

Moreover, he feels that to such a Jew the culture of the non-Jewish world, the polite manners which he himself has striven to acquire, is of no intrinsic value, simply part of a tedious act which it is necessary to put on in front of strangers. Heinrich provides a further explanation for the Jews' prickliness, in terms of social psychology:

I certainly shan't deny that I am specially sensitive to the faults of Jews. The reason is probably that I and all of us—all of us Jews, I mean—have been systematically brought up to be so sensitive. From our childhood onwards we are dragooned into feeling that Jewish qualities are particularly ridiculous or repulsive, which is not the case with regard to the equally ridiculous and repulsive qualities of others. I won't make a secret of the fact that when a Jew displays bad manners or makes a fool of himself in my presence, I sometimes feel so embarrassed that I should like to perish, to sink into the earth. (*E* i. 756)

Heinrich's embarrassment with conspicuously 'Jewish' be-haviour, and his disgust at Jews' lack of self-respect, find many parallels in Schnitzler's diaries. Schnitzler complains repeatedly about what he calls 'renegade and treacherous Jews' (*T* 2 Jan. 1910), or, less translatably, 'Esoi- und Abfallsjuden' (*T* 24 Dec. 1909): Jews who disclaim their Jewishness. He records a con-versation with Richard Beer-Hofmann and his wife 'about the revolting cowardice of a certain kind of Jews who keep trying to run away from themselves' (*T* 18 Feb. 1909). The anecdote about the Jew in the railway carriage illustrates how a stigmatized person relates to others who are similarly stigmatized. The stigmatized person who has internalized his society's standard of 'normality' will reject the stigmatized attribute in himself and in other people. He will project his insecurity on to them, just as Lewin describes the self-hater projecting his feelings on to other members of the underprivileged group. Thus Karl Löwith tells us that in exile in Rome he and his like-minded friends avoided contact with 'excessively Jewish Jews, who formed a kind of ghetto among themselves', and particularly with 'a typical Frankfurt Jew [. . .] who aroused antisemitic feelings in me'.[220] Hence Lewin's account of self-hatred meshes with Goffman's account of 'the management of spoiled identity'.

---

[220] Löwith, *Mein Leben in Deutschland vor und nach 1933* (Frankfurt, 1989), p. 90.

Self-Hatred and Masculinity: Rathenau and Weininger

Jewish unease about self-presentation could also mesh with worries about masculinity, especially since it was a nineteenth-century commonplace that 'the Jew' (always imagined as male) was in some way less masculine than the Gentile male. The equation of Jewishness and femininity appears in Nietzsche's work as early as section 9 of *The Birth of Tragedy* (1872), where the active, Aryan, masculine myth of Prometheus and his crime of stealing fire from heaven is contrasted with the passive, Semitic, feminine myth of Eve and the sin of the Fall.[221] In 1869 the distinguished Viennese rabbi Adolf Jellinek published a book, *Der jüdische Stamm* (*The Jewish Tribe*), with a chapter headed 'The Femininity of the Jewish Tribe'.[222] Women and Jews, he says, share a quick and lively intellect, but are unsystematic, incoherent, and digressive, receptive rather than original, and hence good at imitating others. In their emotional lives, women and Jews are centred on the heart, prone to affection, gratitude, family love, enthusiasm, but also anger and resentment. Their imaginative disposition favours colour and splendour. Just as women especially like praise and benefits conferred by men, so Jews are especially grateful for praise and help from non-Jews. Thus the relationship of Jews to non-Jews is made analogous to the passive, submissive relationship of women to men. This is supposed to demonstrate Jews' capacity for assimilation through imitation, but Jellinek's argument undoes itself, for, as women cannot become men, so Jews, by implication, cannot become non-Jews; they can only imitate non-Jews, and their capacity for imitation was already being cited by antisemites such as Wagner to prove that they could never get beyond a mere external imitation of Gentile manners.

A feminized Jewish man features in the play *Karla Bühring* (1895) by 'Laura Marholm' (the pseudonym of Laura Hansson, 1854–1905), where the violinist Karla Bühring is attracted to the Jewish intellectual Dr Siegfried Collander. Collander's Jewishness is underlined by the taunts of an antisemite, Eschenmeyer, a former member of a duelling society at Heidelberg, who refers

---

[221] Nietzsche, *Werke*, III i. 66.
[222] Jellinek, *Der jüdische Stamm: Ethnographische Studien* (Vienna, 1869), pp. 89–97.

to his 'different race' and refuses to duel with him.[223] Accused of sleeping with Eschenmeyer's wife, Collander escapes from the situation dishonourably by naming Karla as his alibi. He describes to Karla his own cerebral sexuality: 'Even as a young man I was cold—it is all mental pleasure, cerebral pleasure—a science of enjoyment';[224] to him she is a natural force to which he passively surrenders, thereby establishing himself as feminine in relation to her. His enemy Eschenmeyer describes him thus: 'With his excitability and routine of stimulation and his perpetual lust he is a kind of half-way house and intermediate formation, to put it in scientific terms, between us and the female, and that is why woman like him as a daily stimulant'.[225] This Darwinian language proposes the feminized Jew as a kind of missing link between the Aryan man and the woman. The standpoint of the antisemitic character is not necessarily that offered to the audience, but it seems clear that Collander appeals to Karla because he is in some positive respects a feminized man and different from the aggressive masculinity she sees in people like Eschenmeyer. Similarly, Anton Kuh argued that Jewish men appealed to women because of the feminine component which rendered them gentle and intuitive:

Feminine in their longing for coupling without violence, feminine also in the intuitive pliability of their instinct, they thus come closer to the ideal of manhood than any of the lute-strumming, garter-wearing Thusnelda-abductors. And as the woman perceives this, the hostile front between Jews and Germans is broken open by erotic choice much more often than the latter would like.[226]

Two often-cited examples of Jewish self-hatred, Walther Rathenau and Otto Weininger, define Jewishness as feminine, but by reference to different models of masculinity. Rathenau's model is military. The son of a leading industrialist, Rathenau reacted against his father's materialism and identified strongly with the Prussian military ethos.[227] He was bitterly disappointed

[223] Marholm, *Karla Bühring: Ein Frauendrama in vier Acten* (Munich, 1895), pp. 75, 99. I owe this reference to Sarah Colvin. [224] Ibid. 94.
[225] Ibid. 107.
[226] Kuh, *Juden und Deutsche*, p. 91. 'Thusnelda' was the wife of the ancient Germanic chieftain and modern nationalist hero Hermann.
[227] See Ernst Schulin, 'Walther Rathenau und sein Integrationsversuch als "Deutscher jüdischen Stammes"', in Walter Grab (ed.), *Jüdische Integration und Identität in Deutschland und Österreich 1848–1918* (Tel Aviv, 1984), pp. 13–38. Cf.

when, having done his military service in an exclusive Berlin Guards regiment, he was refused permission to stay in the regiment as an active officer, and was obliged, despite his antipathy to his father, to enter the latter's company. He assiduously cultivated politicians, but with little success. When war broke out in 1914 he persuaded the government to create a special procurement department in the War Ministry, which he headed for a few months; his organizational skills may have prolonged the war by two years, but his Jewishness, his visionary imagination, and his Socialist-sounding commitment to economic planning, kept him an outsider in the bureaucratic and military leadership; and his tenure of high political office, as Foreign Minister in the Weimar Republic, was cut short by his assassination in 1922.[228] Rathenau's identification with militarist masculinity included a cult of duelling, which he considered the test of civilized and masculine values; when he and his friend Maximilian Harden fell out, Rathenau demanded a duel, which Harden refused.

Rathenau's discomfort with his unwanted Jewish identity found notorious expression in the pseudonymous article 'Höre, Israel!' ('Hear, O Israel!'), published in Harden's weekly *Die Zukunft* (*The Future*) in 1897. Here he castigates imperfectly assimilated German Jews (i.e. those whose Jewish traits are still recognizable). He complains that most German Jews are not assimilated to German culture. In particular, he complains of their unmilitary, feminine appearance:

> You must ensure that, amid a race that is bred to strict military discipline, you do not make yourself a laughing-stock by your slovenly, shambling appearance. Once you have recognized your ill-constructed build, your high shoulders, your clumsy feet, the soft roundness of your forms, as signs of physical decay, you will have to spend a couple of generations working on your external rebirth.[229]

He adds that at present Jews imitate the costumes of 'lean Anglo-Saxons' when on holiday on the beach or in the mountains, but are like dachshunds imitating greyhounds. However, he does not think

the experiences of Paul Wallich, recounted in Werner E. Mosse, 'Problems and Limits of Assimilation: Hermann and Paul Wallich 1833–1938', *LBY* 33 (1988), 43–65 (esp. pp. 53–5).

[228] See Mosse, *The German-Jewish Economic Élite*, p. 278.

[229] 'W. Hartenau', 'Höre, Israel!', p. 458.

that Jews should be excluded from the public service and the army, for a few exceptional individuals (like himself!) are bound to qualify for inclusion.

A later essay, 'Of Weakness, Fear and Purpose' (1904), universalizes the contrast between Germans and Jews as an antithesis between strong, brave people and weak, timid people. The latter are cynical, perverse, uncreative, hedonistic, greedy, shallow, and vain, and they have put their stamp on modern civilization. Translated into racial terms, as Rathenau admits, the brave type is best represented by 'that wondrous and mysterious primeval Northern race whose blonde heads we are so glad to crown with all the splendour of humanity'.[230] The almost masochistic identification with Germany that we find here also animated Rathenau's emotionally intense friendship with the Germanophile Wilhelm Schwaner, described by Peter Loewenberg.[231] Schwaner evidently represented to Rathenau the German identity he could never quite attain.

With Weininger we find a different model—one in which the intellect is gendered as male. The creativity of the male intellect is celebrated, and contrasted with woman's merely physical capacity for childbirth. Perhaps the clearest expression of this model is a poem by Stefan George in *Der Stern des Bundes* (*The Star of the Covenant*, 1914):

> Die weltzeit die wir kennen schuf der geist,
> Der immer mann ist:[232]
>
> Our epoch was created by the Spirit,
> Which is forever Man.

Having defined the Spirit or Intellect as male, the poem goes on to identify matter as female. Childbirth merely produces yet more material, physical beings. Only the intellect is creative, because it alone confers spiritual value on material objects.

Weininger glorified the male intellect in his notorious best-seller *Geschlecht und Charakter*, one of the most influential doctoral theses ever written. It was admired by Strindberg, Karl Kraus,

[230] Rathenau, 'Von Schwachheit, Furcht und Zweck', in *Gesammelte Schriften*, enlarged edn., 5 vols. (Berlin, 1925), iv. 11–33 (p. 26).

[231] Loewenberg, 'Antisemitismus und jüdischer Selbsthaß', *Geschichte und Gesellschaft*, 5 (1979), 455–75.

[232] George, *Werke*, 2 vols. (Düsseldorf and Munich, 1958), i. 387.

Kafka, Trakl, Kokoschka, Broch, Musil, Doderer, Tucholsky, Schoenberg, and Wittgenstein.[233] Some of its notoriety came from the fact that a few months after completing it the 23-year-old Weininger committed a dramatic suicide in the Vienna house where Beethoven had died. His suicide encouraged speculation about the personal motives behind his book, which are still obscure. It seems unlikely, as used to be thought, that Weininger was homosexual.[234] His strident identification with a cerebral, unerotic ideal of masculinity seems rather to confirm the contention of his friend Hermann Swoboda that he rejected the body outright: 'he hated sensuality and therefore woman as the object and stimulus to sensuality, as the embodiment of sin'.[235] The book expresses a fear of femininity, justified with a vast panoply of pseudo-scientific and pseudo-philosophical argument, together with a rejection of Jewishness which might tempt one to read it as a rejection of Weininger's father. Again the truth seems more complicated. Weininger's father Leopold, a jeweller, son of a tradesman in Moravia, was a domineering personality with strongly antisemitic views; he was also a Wagner enthusiast who often attended the Bayreuth Festival. The book is rather a symbolic identification with the author's father, and a rejection, above all, of the mother.

Irrespective of its biographical basis, *Geschlecht und Charakter* is an important symptom of its age. It appealed to its readers as a backlash against the nascent women's movement and by offering a gendered critique of modernity, deeply indebted to H. S. Chamberlain.[236] Weininger's heroes are male artists, philosophers, and religious leaders, who are distinguished by a powerful sense of their own personality. Women, by contrast, lack the Kantian intelligible self and are incapable of moral autonomy or rational argument. They are predominantly sexual beings who correspond to one of two types: the mother, to whom sex is a means of producing children, and the prostitute, to whom sex is an

---

[233] See Jacques Le Rider, *Der Fall Otto Weininger. Wurzeln des Antifeminismus und Antisemitismus*, tr. Dieter Hornig (Vienna, 1985).

[234] David Abrahamsen, *The Mind and Death of a Genius* (New York, 1946), p. 132.

[235] Swoboda, *Otto Weiningers Tod* [1910], 2nd edn. (Vienna and Leipzig, 1923), pp. 45–6.

[236] For Weininger's admiration for Chamberlain, see *Geschlecht und Charakter*, p. 405 (future references in text); Le Rider, *Der Fall Otto Weininger*, p. 201.

end in itself. Men are intermittently sexual, women are continuously so; and while men have distinct erogenous zones, women's sexuality is diffused over their entire bodies. Thus for Weininger masculinity is defined by boundaries, like those surrounding the self-aware personality, whereas femininity means a blurring of boundaries in a single sexualized mass.

Weininger's thirteenth chapter maintains with perverse ingenuity that the Jews as a people are predominantly feminine. The Jew has no self and hence no self-respect: hence there cannot be a Jewish gentleman, just as women are incapable of dignity. Instead, Jews display insecurity and pushiness. Admittedly, they also resemble women in relatively seldom committing crimes. But this merely shows that Jews and women have a deficient moral sense: being amoral, they cannot rise even to immorality. Women's taste for matchmaking ('Kuppelei') corresponds to the Jewish use of the male marriage-broker. The Jew is sexually obsessed, but without true masculinity: 'The Jew is always more lustful and sensual, although less sexually potent than the Aryan man' (p. 417). Jews' alleged intelligence consists really in vigilance and adaptability. Both Jew and woman can be adaptable, because neither has any intrinsic character; but while the woman is passively pliable, the Jew is active, indeed aggressive, in assimilating himself. Both have put their stamp on modern civilization, which is Jewish and feminine. And whichever of Weininger's basic feminine types—the mother or the whore— she embodies, the Jewish woman is the woman par excellence: 'no woman in the world represents the *idea* of woman so completely as the Jewess' (p. 429). Thus the influence of women coincides with that of Jews. Both are working to degrade modern culture, to undermine the achievements of the male, Aryan mind and spirit, and to press the claims of the erotic, female, and Jewish body. 'From whatever angle one views it,' affirms Weininger, 'the spirit of modernity is Jewish' (p. 441). He adds that it is also feminine. Firm, objective institutions, like the state and the law, risk being dissolved by an emotional and reductive subjectivity that shows itself in anarchism, in doctrines of free love, and in the artistic impressionism which seeks to reproduce moods. But while woman at least seeks a stable centre outside herself, in the man, the Jew is so mobile and fluid that his influence tends to dissolve all stable antitheses. Weininger's most devastating account of the Jew's effect on modernity is buried in an endnote:

The Jew lacks firmness, but also gentleness—rather, he is tough and soft; he is neither rough nor delicate, neither coarse nor polite. He is not a king or a leader, but neither is he a liegeman or a vassal. He does not know what it is to be profoundly moved; but he is just as lacking in equanimity. He takes nothing for granted, but he is a stranger to true astonishment. He has nothing of Lohengrin about him, but still less of Telramund (who stands or falls by his honour). [. . .] Because he believes in nothing, he takes refuge in the material; that is the sole source of his greed for money: he seeks here something real and wants 'business' to convince him of true being (*von einem Seienden*)—thus the only value he recognizes as real is 'hard-earned' money. And yet he is not even a genuine businessman: for the 'unsound', 'unreliable' manner of the Jewish trader is only the concrete manifestation of the Jewish character which is devoid of *inner identity*. (pp. 591–2)

In Weininger's version of the anti-modern mentality, the Jew is identified with the abstract power of money which makes all commodities equal, and with the new social mobility characteristic of a society being modernized at a breathtaking pace. These qualities are then psychologized as the inner emptiness ascribed to the Jew. His emptiness alienates him from both poles of all familiar antitheses: he can be neither king nor vassal, man nor woman. He can only be destructive, dissolving firm binary orders into a spongy softness which recalls Chamberlain's swirling racial chaos surrounding islands of Aryan integrity and looks forward to the imagery of steel-hard masculinity versus liquid femininity traced by Klaus Theweleit in right-wing novels of the 1920s.[237]

Where does this analysis leave Weininger himself? His well-known footnote—'The author must here remark that he is himself of Jewish descent' (p. 406)—seems intended to lend his arguments credibility by supplementing scientific objectivity with rigorous self-analysis. However, his analysis could itself be seen as part of the destructive effect of the Jewish spirit, in which case Weininger's suicide was grimly logical.

---

[237] See Klaus Theweleit, *Male Fantasies*, tr. Stephen Conway (Cambridge, 1987–9).

Self-Hatred and Cultural Criticism: Harden and Kraus

Two famous journalists who were fierce critics of Germany and Austria respectively have often been claimed as prominent examples of 'Jewish self-hatred'. They are Maximilian Harden, editor of the Berlin weekly *Die Zukunft* from 1892 to 1922, and Karl Kraus, who edited *Die Fackel* (*The Torch*) in Vienna from 1899 to 1936, and from 1910 was its sole author. Both feature in Lessing's *Der jüdische Selbsthaß*. Lessing classifies Harden as a 'self-hating Jew' because of the radical assimilationist stance adopted in *Die Zukunft*, and describes Kraus as 'the most radiant example of Jewish self-hatred' because of his incessant attacks on a literary and journalistic world to which he himself belongs.[238] Lessing pays little attention to the substance of their polemics. Their critiques of culture and civilization spring from a version of the anti-modern mentality described in Chapter 3. Instead of taking over its antisemitism, however, Harden shows an extravagant devotion to aspects of Germany, while Kraus emphasizes those elements which he regards as Jewish. Their polemics also include gendered elements which recall the interplay of self-hatred and gender anxiety in Rathenau and Weininger; Harden, moreover, was a friend of Rathenau, and Kraus an admirer of Weininger. However, their polemics cannot be reduced to a defence mechanism, but must be taken seriously as expressing complex and carefully articulated social beliefs. And while both are intense, obsessive writers, Kraus is much more subtle and underwent more development. If the charge of 'Jewish self-hatred' does apply to him, then it is only to his pre-War writings.

Harden *and* Die Zukunft

As founder and editor of *Die Zukunft*, Harden was perhaps the best-known and most influential journalist in Germany.[239] Originally Felix Ernst Witkowski, he was the son of a silk merchant in Berlin who did not give the family any specifically

[238] Lessing, *Der jüdische Selbsthaß*, p. 43. For earlier descriptions of Kraus as self-hater, see Berthold Viertel, *Karl Kraus: Ein Charakter und die Zeit* (Dresden, 1921), p. 60; Kuh, *Juden und Deutsche*, p. 39.

[239] On him, see Harry F. Young, *Maximilian Harden, Censor Germaniae* (The Hague, 1959); B. Uwe Weller, *Maximilian Harden und die 'Zukunft'* (Bremen, 1970).

Jewish upbringing. On their father's death the young Witkowskis
converted and changed their surname to Witting, except for Felix,
who called himself Maximilian Harden because it sounded 'hard'
and recalled the reforming Prussian politician Hardenberg.[240] He
founded *Die Zukunft*, just as Kraus later founded *Die Fackel*, in
order to attack the corruption of the press, especially the liberal
Vossische Zeitung (which plays a role in Harden's polemics
equivalent to that of the *Neue Freie Presse* in Kraus's). The first
number contains a programmatic article, 'Vom Bel zu Babel', in
which Harden borrows the apocalyptic language of Daniel and the
Book of Revelations: 'Priests have become journalists, and today
Baal is the name for the press.'[241] Thus Harden agrees with the
familiar polemic against a modernity whose main instrument is
the Judaized press. By representing the press as the Semitic god
Baal, Harden implicitly invokes the rectitude of the Jewish
prophets but also casts himself as the Germanic hero opposing
the manifestations of Semitism.

Harden also aspired to intervene in national and even international politics. He became a friend of Bismarck, and visited him
at least fifteen times between 1892 and his death in 1898. He
hated the Kaiser, whom he considered a mere mountebank. His
sharp criticisms of the Kaiser brought him three prosecutions for
lèse-majesté; after two of these he was found guilty and sentenced
to confinement in a fortress. Through his journal he tried to
influence German foreign policy, opposing the Triple Alliance
with Austria and Italy, and advocating closer relations with Russia
(an anti-liberal standpoint). After 1900 Harden supported
German overseas expansion and demanded an aggressive foreign
policy. Although he considered Socialism an important force, he
made enemies of the Social Democratic leaders, especially Bebel
and Liebknecht, by attacking them as 'red prima donnas', maintaining that the 'star system' had been transferred from the theatre
to left-wing orators.[242] His politics were authoritarian. Besides
Bismarck, he admired Nietzsche and Treitschke. He upheld the
Social Darwinist view of the struggle for existence, expressed
alarm about the future of the white race, and gave much space

---

[240] This is Harden's own explanation: see Hellige, 'Rathenau und Harden', p. 45.
[241] 'Apostata' [= Harden], 'Vom Bel zu Babel', *Die Zukunft*, 1 (1 Oct. 1892),
33–40 (p. 37).
[242] 'Die rothen Primadonnen', *Die Zukunft*, 1 (26 Nov. 1892), 385–91.

to the Social Darwinist Alexander Tille and to Houston Stewart Chamberlain.[243] His attacks on the Jewish press early gained him a reputation as a Jewish antisemite, though when told by Hermann Bahr in 1894 that he had this reputation, Harden replied that he was an enemy, not of the Jews, but of corruption.[244] Harden's identification with an authoritarian, illiberal Germany reached its climax on the outbreak of the First World War, when his leading articles issued the most bloodthirsty and sabre-rattling propaganda. On 29 August 1914, he declared that since their opponents called the Germans barbarians, the Germans would act accordingly and conquer the Entente and their Japanese allies as completely as the Germanic barbarians had overwhelmed ancient Rome. 'Get used quickly', he adjured, 'to the knowledge that German soil is inhabited by barbarians and warriors.'[245]

What lies behind Harden's authoritarianism is revealed by his early essay 'Sem' ('Shem'), which discusses Jewish identity. It begins with a familiar anti-modern polemic against the Jews, whose mercantile spirit, evident since the days of Jacob, has been strengthened by antisemitism and now makes them the controllers of international finance. By rejecting assimilation and remaining within an invisible ghetto, they ensure that antisemitism persists. In modern society, the unproductive middleman ('Zwischenhändler') is all-powerful; Jews have a peculiar aptitude for it because of their adaptive capacity for mimicry.

Harden goes on to draw an analogy between Jews and women. Just as Jews, though nominally in an inferior position, dominate the Gentile world and take revenge for their mistreatment, so women, as Strindberg has shown, can use marriage to dominate men and thus compensate for their nominal subjection. This is made possible by the intrinsic femininity of Jews: 'For Shem, as he

---

[243] Chamberlain's first contribution was 'Die Bayreuther Festspiele', *Die Zukunft* (18 July 1896), 97–107; others included '"Christus ein Germane"', *Die Zukunft* (23 January 1904), 139–46, in which Chamberlain defended the *Grundlagen* against misrepresentations, and 'Arisches Denken', *Die Zukunft* (28 October 1905), 139–45, an extract from his book *Arische Weltanschauung*, putting forward ancient Indian religious thought as a superior alternative to the mechanistic Jewish thought said to underlie Christianity, modern philosophy and science.

[244] Bahr, *Der Antisemitismus: Ein internationales Interview*, ed. Hermann Greive (Königstein, 1979), p. 37.

[245] 'Wir sind Barbaren', *Die Zukunft* (29 Aug. 1914), 269–91 (p. 291).

is now known, really is almost feminine in gender, pliant and always ready for impregnation and more inclined to sparkling extremes than to cold objectivity, always led by ardent love and ardent hatred, and attached to the person more than to the thing.'[246] The relationship between Germans and Jews is like that between man and wife, and since no divorce is possible (nobody dreams of expelling the Jews!) in the long run the female partner (the Jews) must adapt to the Germans: the exclusivity of the commercial subculture will have to yield to assimilation.

In Harden's imagery, then, the German is masculine, the Jew is feminine. In demanding assimilation, Harden also renders it impossible, for the feminized Jew cannot become male, but only submit to the male. Where does this leave Harden himself? To show that he is one of the few Jews who actually can assimilate to German society, he has to dissociate himself from Jewishness and femininity, and associate himself with masculinity and power. Ironically, Harden's association with powerful Germans occurred mostly on paper. The social contacts he cultivated were with the Kaiser's Jewish entourage—prominent Jewish industrialists like Albert Ballin, bankers like Carl Fürstenberg, and politicians like Rathenau. Thus, like Rathenau, he found that his contact with German power was almost always mediated by other Jews.

However, Harden made a notorious attempt to exert power through the journalistic exploitation of sex in the Eulenburg affair.[247] He believed that Prince Philipp Eulenburg, formerly German ambassador to Vienna and subsequently, in retirement, a confidant of the Kaiser, headed a homosexual 'camarilla' which dominated the imperial court. In *Die Zukunft* of 27 April 1907, Harden hinted unmistakably at Eulenburg's homosexuality, thereby involving himself in a libel trial and unleashing an anti-homosexual campaign throughout Germany. Harden tried persistently to 'out' Eulenburg, even hiring a detective whose inquiries unearthed a fisherman and a milkman who claimed to have had homosexual intercourse with Eulenburg some twenty years earlier.

---

[246] Harden, 'Sem', in *Apostata*, Neue Folge (Berlin, 1892), pp. 146–56 (p. 155).

[247] See James D. Steakley, 'Iconography of a Scandal: Political Cartoons and the Eulenburg Affair in Wilhelmine Germany', in Martin Duberman, Martha Vicinus, and George Chauncey, Jr. (eds.), *Hidden from History: Reclaiming the Gay and Lesbian Past* (London, 1991), pp. 233–63; Röhl, 'Philipp Eulenburg, the Kaiser's Best Friend', in *The Kaiser and his Court*, pp. 28–69.

Harden's last lawsuit, however, produced no result, for Eulenburg collapsed in court, and the trial was postponed indefinitely because of his ill health.

In using the methods of modern gutter journalism against Eulenburg, Harden displayed faulty judgement and questionable motives. His biographers point out that Eulenburg's influence on the Kaiser actually tended to restrain the latter's erratic and impulsive behaviour. All Harden achieved (apart from causing distress) was to remove Eulenburg's salutary influence and increase the Kaiser's freedom to engage in international brinkmanship. His intervention seems to have been motivated by two crucial resemblances between himself and Eulenburg. First: in influencing public affairs without any elected position, Eulenburg was doing what Harden was aiming to do by means of *Die Zukunft*. Hence Harden seems to have been envious of a more successful rival— and one who, unlike the son of a Jewish silk merchant, had been born into the governing elite. Putting class envy aside, however, it is not clear that a journalist was better qualified than an ex-ambassador to advise on government policy. Secondly: in exploiting the most vulgar sexual prejudice to discredit Eulenburg, Harden displayed a cynicism which was rightly attacked by Kraus. 'Only a Philistine, or a freebooter in journalistic sensations, could argue that a dislike of normal sexual intercourse demonstrates incapacity for holding public office', commented Kraus, adding that the sex lives of heterosexual diplomats were just as likely to affect their political activity as those of homosexuals, but were less rewarding for venal journalism (F 234/5: 6, 30). In Harden we see one kind of outsider, the Jew, trying to strengthen his own position at the expense of another kind of outsider, the homosexual. And this effort was also motivated by Harden's fear of the association of Jews with femininity. What better way to prove his masculinity than to attack, in the most prurient way, a member of another out-group associated with femininity—and one which could not defend itself because its existence was socially inadmissible?

Harden's attempts to identify with Germany came to a sad end after the War. As an editor he was hostile to the Weimar Republic, advocating instead the authoritarian rule of a cross-party government. The Republic had more effective enemies, however, including the National Socialists, in whose newspaper Alfred Rosenberg denounced Harden as 'one of Germany's greatest scoundrels'.[248] On 3 July 1922 (only nine days after the murder of Rathenau) two thugs hired by a paramilitary organization attacked Harden near his home, striking him repeatedly on the head with an iron bar. Able to call for help, Harden was found and taken to hospital. Though his life was saved, he no longer had the strength to continue editing *Die Zukunft*. One of the attackers, and the agent who had hired them, were put on trial. However, the trial was explicitly political, indeed racial. The two accused were tried by an inexperienced and inept Jewish judge (who perhaps was too afraid of showing bias) before an antisemitic petty-bourgeois jury and represented by baptized Jewish lawyers. The defendants made much of their German patriotism. Kurt Tucholsky, who was present, records that one asserted in his own favour that he had at least never seduced a German girl.[249] They were allowed with impunity to refer to Harden as 'Isidor Witkowski', knowing that 'Isidor' was considered by caricaturists the name most character-istic of unassimilated Polish Jews. The defence tried to malign Harden as a 'political pest' ('ein politischer Schädling') and thus effectively to put him on trial. No attempt was made to unearth the real instigators of the crime. The accused got off lightly with sentences of four years nine months and two years nine months respectively, not for attempted murder but for helping to cause grievous bodily harm.

Harden put his own case in a speech described by Tucholsky as the last voice of a vanished society that still believed in justice and fair play. He denounced the political injustice of which he was the victim. It was, he said, an obvious case of attempted murder; the judge was colluding with the defence to play it down as a mere attempt to give him a warning. Both the crime itself and the subsequent perversion of justice were motivated by antisemitism. The court favoured those whose names signalled their German identity and discriminated against Harden because of his Jewishness:

The core of the whole business is this: if these two were called Blumenstock and Veilchenfeld and if the person attacked had had a

[248] Quoted in Weller, *Harden*, p. 82. I follow his account of the trial, pp. 88–94.
[249] Tucholsky, 'Prozeß Harden', in *Gesammelte Werke*, ed. Mary Gerold-Tucholsky and Fritz J. Raddatz, 3 vols. (Reinbek, 1960), i. 1070–8 (p. 1077).

primeval Germanic name that sounded deeply German—let's say Max Klante—do you think that things would be just the same? I don't. The jury has been exposed to the malicious, stupid insinuation: 'This vulgar Jew, un-German, changed his name late in life, and his real name is Isidor!'[250]

Thus Harden pinpointed one of the strategies by which Jews were always placed in the wrong. They changed their names in order to become Germans; then it was said that they could not be real Germans because they had changed their names. To illustrate the identification of Jews with Germany, Harden—true to his search for masculine models—pointed out how many Jews had actively helped Germany's war effort: Rathenau by supplying raw materials, Ballin by building up Germany's merchant fleet, Fritz Haber by inventing poison gas. Nevertheless, Harden concluded, the Germans evidently wished to reject the Jews:

If you don't want me, because I was born a Jewish boy (*Judenknabe*), then that's fine! I used often to say to Rathenau: 'Why do you always write and say "We Germans"? People refuse to count the Jews as Germans. I love the German, but I shan't force myself upon him.'[251]

This forms a sad and ironic end to Harden's public career. After the utmost efforts to identify himself with Germany—his friendship with Bismarck, his attacks on Jewish finance, his support for militarism—he was obliged to dissociate himself from it. Germany did not want him; its self-appointed representatives tried to murder him; and its legal system would not provide a fair trial.

Karl Kraus, Journalism, and Language

Given the complexity of Kraus's attitudes to Jews, Jewishness, and antisemitism, all I can do here is indicate some ways in which Jewish themes are intertwined in some of his writings with questions of linguistic purity and uncertain masculinity.[252] Kraus's starting-point is radical assimilationism. He calls for the dissolution both of the traditional culture of the eastern European

[250] 'Hauptteil der Rede Maximilian Hardens vor den Geschworenen', in Harden, *Köpfe: Porträts, Briefe und Dokumente*, ed. Hans-Jürgen Fröhlich (Hamburg, 1963), pp. 244–52 (p. 247). [251] Ibid. 252.
[252] For a guide to the complexity of the subject, see John Theobald, *The Paper Ghetto: Karl Kraus and Anti-Semitism* (Frankfurt, 1996).

ghetto, and of the invisible ghetto inhabited by modern Western Jews (e.g. *F* 33: 19; *F* 23: 7). He does not consider antisemitism a serious threat, maintaining that the antisemitic slogans of the Christian Social party are merely a disguise for their political vacuity (*FS* ii. 116).[253] He opposes Zionism as a form of Jewish antisemitism:

Disregarding any possibility of political danger, good taste has still a right to protest when the intellectual wealth from which the drunken grocer in Hernals shouts his 'Out with you, Jews!' meets with simple repetition by Zionists, and when their answer 'Yes, out with us Jews!' offers too little variety save in its more solemn tone. (*FS* ii. 312)

However, Kraus differs from the assimilationists discussed earlier in that he does not consider present-day German and Austrian society a worthy object to which to assimilate. He opposes liberalism as a spent political force. He distrusts parliamentary government for giving power to self-seekers, agitators, and ignoramuses: a frequent early target is the deputy Mittermayer, formerly a waiter, who (according to Kraus) was prosecuted for petty theft and 'condemned to several months' hard parliament' (*FS* ii. 33). He disapproves of trial by jury as a 'liberal delusion' (*F* 378/80: 2) which introduces petty-bourgeois prejudices into the workings of justice (K iv. 268–74).[254]

Kraus finds the degenerate character of modernity typified by the Jewish-dominated press. In the opening number of *Die Fackel* Kraus describes the press as 'venal to the bones that are left over from half-decayed liberalism' (*F* 1: 5). Liberal newspapers had a wide circulation in Vienna; in 1889 the three leading papers were the *Illustriertes Wiener Extrablatt* with a circulation of 42,000, the *Neues Wiener Tagblatt* with 35,000, and the *Neue Freie Presse* with 33,000.[255] The last-named, generally acknowledged to be among the best in Europe, was the most influential. Moriz Benedikt, who became its editor-in-chief in 1881, was for a generation one of the dozen most powerful men in Austria.[256]

[253] References in this form are to Kraus, *Frühe Schriften 1892–1900*, ed. J. J. Braakenburg, 2 vols. (Munich, 1979).
[254] References in this form are to Kraus, *Schriften*, ed. Christian Wagenknecht, 20 vols. (Frankfurt, 1989–94).
[255] Figures from Jens Malte Fischer, *Karl Kraus: Studien zum 'Theater der Dichtung' und Kulturkonservatismus* (Kronberg, 1973), p. 106.
[256] See Fuchs, *Geistige Strömungen in Österreich*, pp. 20–4.

The *Times* correspondent described him as 'a journalist of genius—a tyrannical, vindictive genius, under whom his staff and many of his readers groan'.[257] His liberal policies had a right-wing bias: he approved of the Christian Social leadership of Vienna, despite Lueger's antisemitism, and vigorously supported the First World War, enthusiastically endorsing even the most barbaric actions by Germany. He had close ties with the biggest Jewish banking houses. And the 'Feuilleton' of the *Neue Freie Presse* published the best-known writers of Viennese modernism: Bahr, Schnitzler, Hofmannsthal, and Beer-Hofmann. Kraus therefore perceived liberalism, Jewish finance, and commercialized literature as forming a single complex which he was determined to oppose.

But what was Kraus's counter-ideal? In the 1890s he thought that the 'Jewish question' would be solved by Socialism: 'economic antisemitism will be absorbed by Social Democracy, which makes all things equal, even noses' (*FS* ii. 306). He used *Die Fackel* to campaign against financial corruption and against the sexual hypocrisy expressed in legislation against prostitution and homosexuality. His standpoint became increasingly conservative. He admired the Archduke Franz Ferdinand as a consistent opponent of liberalism. Franz Ferdinand wanted to reorganize the Habsburg Empire as a federal state and to rule autocratically. On his assassination, Kraus praised him, not for supporting reaction, but for opposing progress, that is, the liberal inheritance of the Enlightenment. He quotes an ambivalent obituary and adds: 'This speech comes from a representative of the dark world of the Enlightenment, from whose embrace the dead man thought he could liberate God's world' (K iv. 423).

The high point of Kraus's conservative thinking comes in the years before the First World War. After it he actively supported democracy, waging bold and remarkably successful campaigns against the Viennese police-chief Schober and the fraudulent newspaper-owner Bekessy.[258] He tried to make common cause with the Austrian Social Democrats, but was eventually repelled

---

[257] Henry Wickham Steed, *The Hapsburg Monarchy*, 3rd edn. (London, 1914), p. 187.

[258] See Edward Timms, 'The Kraus–Bekessy Controversy in Interwar Vienna', in Robert S. Wistrich (ed.), *Austrians and Jews in the Twentieth Century* (London, 1992), pp. 184–98.

by their inept politics, which he thought played into the hands of the Nazis, and put his support behind Dollfuss's attempt to establish a corporate state as a bulwark against Nazism. His conservatism was very different from the reactionary idea of a 'conservative revolution' which in the 1920s appealed to Hofmannsthal: he had no interest in glorifying the *Volk*, in charismatic leadership, or in restoring feudalism. He had no belief in a revolution of the Right or the Left. He described himself as a right-wing radical who had not yet caught up with the French Revolution (K iv. 337).

Although Kraus's anti-modern polemics have much in common with the anti-modernism outlined in Chapter 3, he is not easily pigeon-holed. He did his best (in 'Er ist doch ä Jud', 1913) to ward off the imputation of Jewish antisemitism. Since he had, somewhat embarrassingly, been praised by the racist Lanz von Liebenfels, he distanced himself emphatically from the kind of Jews who flattered the prejudices of Christian society. He insisted that his literary judgements had nothing to do with the writers' Jewishness:

I do not know whether it is a Jewish quality to find the Book of Job worth reading, or whether it is antisemitic to throw a book by Schnitzler into the corner of the room. Whether it shows Jewish or German feelings to say that the writings of the Jews Else Lasker-Schüler and Peter Altenberg are closer to God and language than anything produced by German literature in the last fifty years.   (K iv. 331)

By contrast with degenerate modern Jews, Kraus associated himself with the Old Testament prophets:

I think I can say of myself that I go along with the development of Jewry up to the exodus, but no longer take part in the dance round the golden calf, and thenceforth am aware only of sharing the qualities that belong to God's defenders who take revenge on a people that has gone astray.   (K iv. 329)

The corruption that incited Kraus's prophetic fury was, above all, linguistic corruption. In his early anti-Zionist satire he maintained that Jews simply needed to master good German in order to attain assimilation. Having heard a Galician Jew declare: 'Sie *brochen* uns nicht' ('They don't *need* us', where German requires 'brauchen'), he concludes: 'I think the entire Jewish question depends on changing this "o"' (*FS* ii. 310). But when acculturated Jews took up journalism, they seemed to Kraus to introduce the hidden Jewish language that expressed their moral corruption. Hence Kraus sometimes engages in something disturbingly like the antisemitic tactic of exposing the concealed Jew. Felix Salten (originally Siegmund Salzmann, 1869–1947), author both of *Bambi* and of the pornographic novel *Josefine Mutzenbacher*, is a frequent target: in 1901, when Salten associates himself with a supposedly ultra-Viennese theatre, Kraus refers to him as Sziga Salzmann (*F* 86 (Nov. 1901), 16).[259] Claiming to live 'in an age that has been journalized through and through', Kraus cultivates verbal precision with an ardour that recalls Flaubert: 'If it said that I take an hour over three pages and three days over one line, this language-forsaken age would be baffled' (K iv. 107). His positive models are German classicism, the Schlegel–Tieck translation of Shakespeare, the simple prose of the Biedermeier age, and the few modernists, like Altenberg and Lasker-Schüler, who satisfy his fine literary judgement.

Kraus eventually turned against his former mentor Harden, seeing him not as an opponent of corrupt journalism but as one of its worst exponents. The two first met in summer 1897, when Harden delivered a lecture in Vienna, and Kraus often visited Harden in Berlin until 1904.[260] Their relations were soured because Kraus disapproved of Harden's conventional sexual morality and especially of his homophobic campaign against Eulenburg. Harden's prurience provoked Kraus into a virtual feud which ran from 1907 to 1912, with Harden as leading representative of the moral and linguistic corruption of the press. In Kraus's attacks on Harden two motifs of his later literary feuds are prominent: language and sexuality. He pilloried Harden's gratuitous displays of knowledge and especially his affected and periphrastic style, calling it 'Desperanto', and compiling parallel columns in which phrases from Harden were matched with translations into plain German. Taking Shakespeare as his linguistic ideal, Kraus translated Mark Antony's speech from *Julius Caesar*

---

[259] For more such examples, see Rolf Max Kully, 'Namenspiele. Die erotische, die polemische und die poetische Verwendung der Eigennamen in den Werken von Karl Kraus', in Joseph P. Strelka (ed.), *Karl Kraus. Diener der Sprache, Meister des Ethos* (Tübingen, 1990), pp. 139–66. Cf. Kraus, 'Jüdelnde Hasen', *F* 820/6 (Oct. 1929), 45–6.   [260] See Weller, *Harden*, pp. 343–52, for an account of their relations.

into Hardenese.[261] When reproached by Harden with betraying their former friendship, he resorted to sexual language. In 1912 he claimed that in his relationship with Harden he had been, so to speak, the stronger and therefore masculine partner, and, as men do in relations with women, projected his fantasies on to his feminine partner: 'No, I bestowed my content on an alien gesture, as men are wont to do. It took imagination to mistake the character of Germany's worst writer' (K iii. 241). This recalls one of Kraus's most cynical aphorisms on erotic matters: 'A woman can sometimes be a useful surrogate for masturbation, though that does require an excess of imagination' (K viii. 33).

One of Kraus's most substantial and amusing satires on Jewish journalism is 'Harakiri und Feuilleton' (October 1912), a dialogue between two Jewish journalists in a Viennese newspaper office. He prefaces it by explaining that its setting is also 'the most extensive milieu of the modern world' (K iv. 140), that its characters speak in a dialect which is that of their souls, and that even had he introduced characters of a different race, he would have wished to make them speak the same dialect; for it is that of the contemporary world, 'the true Volapük of all who live in this age and want to get on in the world' (ibid.). Thus modernity is typified by the newspaper and by Jewish journalists. The subject of the journalists' conversation is the news that a Japanese general has committed hara-kiri upon the death of the Emperor; they keep confusing this with the information that Mendl Singer, another Jew, has been ennobled. The contrast between two concepts of nobility—the self-sacrificing devotion of a feudal officer and the paper title of a self-advancing Jew—is clear. The journalists' German is close to *Mauscheldeutsch* in its word order, vowel-changes, emphases, and occasional vocabulary ('betamt', 'Tineff', 'nebbich').[262] They keep slipping from this into pompous, empty journalese, in which Goethe can only be called 'der Weimaraner' and Vienna the 'Kaiserstadt', and reports are a mosaic of clichés. They refer uneasily to Kraus, absurdly invoking the Jewish curse of anonymity ('Kraus, nicht genannt soll er wern!', K iv. 150). And Kraus deflects the charge of Jewish antisemitism by putting it

---

[261] Kraus, 'Die Forum-Szene (Eine Harden-Erinnerung)', *März*, 2/ii (1908), 140–3.
[262] See Caroline Kohn, 'Der Wiener jüdische Jargon im Werke von Karl Kraus', *MAL* 8 (1975), i. 240–67.

in the mouths of his enemies ('Der greßte Antisemit!', K iv. 147).
Here Kraus is using the eavesdropping technique which in Chapter
3 we saw employed, a century earlier, by Sessa in *Unser Verkehr*,
purporting to show how Jews really talk when they are among
themselves. Like Sessa, Kraus shows the Jews as speaking either a
corrupt Jewish language or a pretentious imitation of German.

Kraus's critique of corrupt Jewish language also appears,
infused with national and gender stereotypes, in one of his richest
and most disturbing texts, 'Heine und die Folgen' ('Heine and the
Consequences', 1910).[263] Here Kraus traces the modern degeneracy of language back to Heine's poetry and journalism. His
language is ornamental and decorative. It lacks the necessity, the
inevitability, of genuine art. His poetry relies partly on the casual
evocation of moods, partly on journalistic reports: it is 'nothing
but metrical journalism' (K iv. 199). In his polemics against Platen
and Börne, Heine invades his opponents' private and even sexual
lives in a way that anticipates the methods of Harden in the
Eulenburg affair (K iv. 203). Before substantiating his case against
Heine by quoting from the latter's inferior works, Kraus sums it
up: 'Without Heine, no weekend supplement ("Feuilleton"). That
is the French disease which he introduced among us' (K iv. 186).

The 'French disease' is syphilis, which was probably the cause of
Heine's debilitating and terminal illness.[264] Here Kraus begins
mobilizing sexual and nationalist discourses in order to attack
Heine as the sick, Frenchified Jew who has bestowed his corruption on the German-language media. Heine acquired from the
French the knack of agreeable writing, and now this can be copied
by any journalist, especially by Jewish journalists:

Nowadays, of course, any clever-dick ('jeder Itzig Witzig') can outdo him
in the skill of rhyming 'ästhetisch' with 'Teetisch' and turning the can-
died husk of an idea into a cracker by rhyme and rhythm.   (K iv. 194)[265]

To write good German, in Kraus's opinion, is far more difficult. It
requires, not journalistic facility, but masculine virility. Like

---

[263] See Leo A. Lensing, 'Heine's Body, Heine's Corpus: Sexuality and Jewish Identity
in Karl Kraus's Literary Polemics against Heinrich Heine', in Mark H. Gelber (ed.),
The Jewish Reception of Heinrich Heine (Tübingen, 1992), pp. 95–112.

[264] See Arthur Stern, 'Heinrich Heines Krankheit und seine Ärzte', *Heine-Jahrbuch
1964*, 63–79.

[265] Kraus is referring to the famous rhyme in Heine's poem beginning 'Sie saßen und
tranken am Teetisch' (H i. 95; *Complete Poems of Heine*, p. 68).

Harden in 'Sem', he regards German identity as masculine, Jewish identity as feminine. All Heine and his successors can do with the German language (personified as a woman) is finger her breasts ('Heine, der der deutschen Sprache so sehr das Mieder gelockert hat, daß heute alle Kommis an ihren Brüsten fingern können', K iv. 190). By implication, only writers like Kraus can actually impregnate her.[266] Kraus maps Heine's Jewishness on to his French associations: 'Heine was a Moses who struck the rock of the German language with his rod. But speed is not magic, the water did not flow from the rock, but he had concealed it in his other hand, and it was eau de Cologne' (K iv. 209). Thus Heine (in contrast to Kraus with his prophetic mantle) was not even an authentic descendant of Old Testament Jewry, but a fraudulent imitator of Moses. Moreover, Heine's concern for the sales of his books—surely forgivable in one who, unlike Kraus, did not have a private income—is held against him and represented as characteristic of Jewish commercialism. Heine's phrase 'meine zarten Reime | aus Veilchenduft und Mondenschein' is turned into the name of an imaginary Jewish publishing firm (K iv. 200—and anyone called Veilchenduft would probably be a Galician Jew, therefore imagined as a sleazy operator).[267] Heine is played off not only against Goethe but against another authentic German, Detlev von Liliencron, who features especially as a poet of nature (K iv. 197). In the 1890s Kraus had praised Liliencron's 'firm loyalty to the earth of his homeland, his healthy love of his *Vaterland*' (FS i. 60), in contrast to the Viennese aesthete Felix Dörmann with his sickly affectation of decadence (FS i. 90).[268] Heine's failure to write nature poetry is held against him. Nature poetry is of course the touchstone of Germanness; Heine thus proves himself to be an urban, cosmopolitan Jew, estranged from nature and the soil.

This view of Heine appears in Kraus's essays on him before and after 'Heine and the Consequences'. In November 1901 Kraus

---

[266] For a similar depreciation of Heine as unmanly, in contrast to the manly Goethe, see Max Fischer, *Heinrich Heine, der deutsche Jude* (Stuttgart and Berlin, 1916), pp. 32–3.

[267] The quotation is from 'Anno 1839', H iv. 379–80; *Complete Poems of Heine*, pp. 369–70.

[268] See Uta Schaub, 'Liliencron und Heine im Urteil von Karl Kraus', *Heine-Jahrbuch* 1979, 191–201.

complains that the Germans and Austrians who attended the unveiling of a monument to Heine in Montmartre cemetery were all Jews and many of them businessmen (*F* 87: 20–1). In 1906, when it was proposed to erect a monument to him in Germany, Kraus blamed Heine's Jewish admirers for kowtowing to Germans by trying to have him recognized as a German poet (*F* 199: 1–6). This essay already criticizes Heine for not being a poet of nature, unlike Goethe or Liliencron; notes contemptuously that he is admired by liberals; and calls him the ancestor of journalism.

Kraus's animus against Heine becomes obsessive in the long essay of October 1915, 'The enemies Goethe und Heine' (*F* 406/ 12: 52–89), for which Kraus has searched Heine's recently published letters to find discreditable matter. In a 'Feuilleton' review in the *Neue Freie Presse*, Hugo Wittmann had said how remarkable it was that Heine, whose early letters contain grammatical mistakes characteristic of Jewish-German, should have become a master of the language: 'There is not a fold of its cloak that his ear does not reconnoitre.'[269] Kraus commented:

That is no such miracle as Herr Wittmann supposes. The more intelligent members of this tribe and class can learn it in a jiffy. They spread out the cloak of language before the customers, even if they did not previously run a factory-goods business. Master of language? Easiest thing in the world. Nothing to it.   (*F* 406/12: 61)

Wittmann's mixed metaphor—Heine's ear reconnoitres the cloak of the German language—enables Kraus, by punning on 'auskundschaften' (reconnoitre) and 'Kundschaft' (customers), to represent Heine as a Jewish shop-assistant displaying his wares— a 'Kommis', as in 'Heine and the Consequences'—and acquiring the German language as quickly as such a person would acquire ingratiating manners, while his real language retains a repellent streetwise smartness (Kraus's original phrase, 'das geht wie geschmiert', suggests a 'greasy Jew'). This image of rapid, cynical, and superficial acculturation was current among antisemites: we have already encountered a blatant example in Sessa's *Unser Verkehr*. By alluding to how the young Heine was set up by his Uncle Salomon in his own business (which soon failed), Kraus further

---

[269] 'W.', 'Der junge Heine', *Neue Freie Presse* (15 June 1914), 1–4 (p. 3).

represents Heine as transferring Jewish commercialism from trade to writing. The Yiddish word *Rachmones* (pity), occurring in a letter from Heine to James Rothschild, also causes Kraus glee. He returns to it the following year, when attacking Jewish charitable activity as a disguise for usury: employing the word 'Rachmones', he parenthetically advises the reader to seek its meaning in Heine, but in the letters to Rothschild, not in the *Buch der Lieder* (F 437/ 42: 65). That is, Heine's lyrics speak the false language of the Jew, behind which lies the Jew's true language and real activity— extorting money.

In his attacks on Heine, Kraus is, with unwitting irony, repeat-ing the polemical strategy which Heine had deployed against his own Jewish antagonists. For example, as part of his feud with the composer Meyerbeer, Heine greeted the première of Meyerbeer's opera *Le prophète* (1849) with a 'Festgedicht' ('Festal Ode') culminating in the appearance of Meyerbeer's publisher, Brandus, who first speaks in the inflated language of advertising and then in the 'true', commercial language of the Jew:

> Hier auf diesem Erdenglobus
> Gibts kein beßres Wasser-Opus!
> Es ist hochsublim poetisch,
> Urtitanisch majestätisch,
> Groß wie Gott und die Natur—
> *Und ich hab die Partitur!*[270]

> From this planet to Canopus
> There's no better water opus!
> Truly it's sublime-esthetic,
> It's titanic, it's poetic,
> Great as God and Nature—quite!
> *And I own the score outright!*[271]

Even the masculine pose which forms part of Kraus's polemic was anticipated by Heine, who, as we saw in Chapter 2, casts his literary persona as masculine and virile by contrast with the homosexual Platen and the quasi-acculturated Jew Gumpelino.

Paul Peters has forcefully argued that by emphasizing Heine's

---

[270] H vi. 297. The corrupt language of the Jew is also a prominent theme in Kraus's polemics against Franz Werfel: see Edward Timms, 'Poetry, Politics and Personalities: the Kraus–Werfel Controversy', in Joseph P. Strelka and Robert Weigel (eds.), *Unser Fahrplan geht von Stern zu Stern. Zu Franz Werfels Stellung und Werk* (Berne, 1992), pp. 111–38.   [271] *Complete Poems of Heine*, p. 791.

commercial character Kraus is using him as a scapegoat and imputing to him the stereotypical qualities of the detestable Jew in order to make clear how remote he, Kraus, is from that image. Similarly, Rathenau in 'Höre, Israel!' describes the repulsive qualities of semi-assimilated Jews in order to convince the reader that he, by contrast, is a truly assimilated Jew. Peters maintains that the polemic against Heine coincides with the development of Kraus's conservative ideology, and that Kraus's dearest wish was to be received into exclusive aristocratic society, an ideal he approached most closely in his relationship with Sidonie Nádherný.[272] This argument is chronologically dubious: Kraus did not meet Sidonie Nádherný until three years after he published 'Heine and the Consequences'.[273] However, Peters's argument can still be accepted that Kraus's attacks on Heine represent an over-compensation for his own Jewishness.

Moreover, Kraus's attacks repeat motifs from the many attacks on Heine issued by antisemites. That Heine helped to introduce the French feuilleton into German journalism was a common-place.[274] The rabid antisemite Adolf Bartels transfers the blame to Heine: the 'Feuilleton' 'is a typically Jewish form; Heine found innumerable successors among fellow-members of his race [. . .] down to the luminaries of the *Berliner Tageblatt*.'[275] Treitschke condemns his 'journalistic poetry' (*Feuilleton-Poesie*) as shallow compared to the emotional depth of truly German lyric poetry.[276] Like Kraus, Treitschke judges Heine by inappropriate criteria of generic purity and rhetorical consistency. Having no room for irony, this aesthetic has to condemn it as shallow and frequently indecent, while Heine is conceded only an external talent for literary form. But Treitschke does grant Heine sensitivity and mastery in the use of German. Bartels, like Kraus, denies him this. Besides examining Heine's life, again like Kraus, in order to find fault, Bartels regards Heine as a Jewish, not a German poet. Heine always uses German as a foreign language and is at best a

---

[272] Peters, *Heinrich Heine 'Dichterjude': Die Geschichte einer Schmähung* (Meisenheim, 1990), p. 140.

[273] See the sensitive account of this relationship in Timms, *Karl Kraus, Apocalyptic Satirist*, ch. 14.

[274] See the attack on Heine in Treitschke, *Deutsche Geschichte*, iii. 712–14.

[275] Bartels, *Heinrich Heine: Auch ein Denkmal* (Dresden and Leipzig, 1906), pp. 116, 140.   [276] Treitschke, *Deutsche Geschichte*, iii. 714.

virtuoso whose main gift is dexterity; his work is '*misappropriation* of alien property'.[277] Contemporaries saw how much Kraus's attacks on Heine resembled those of antisemites: a reviewer in the Expressionist journal *Die Aktion* called Kraus a 'Bartels II', and accused him of chauvinism, over-seriousness, and deficient self-irony.[278] For Kraus, Heine was the poet of Jewish capitalism, liberalism, and journalism. His essay had a prolonged influence, confirming the distaste which many young Jewish intellectuals already felt for Heine.[279] And Kraus's case against Heine haunts the defence by Adorno, in which Heine is implausibly described as mass-producing lyrics by expressing already commodified experiences in a ready-made language: in other words, the inauthentic language of the Jew.[280]

Kraus was inclined to blame not only journalism but the horrors of the First World War on Judaized modernity. He states this most sharply in his wartime poem 'Gebet an die Sonne von Gibeon' (*F* 423/5: 58–64). This alludes to the occasion (Josh. 10: 12) when, in order to assist Joshua and the Israelites in their battle against their enemies, the sun stood still upon Mount Gibeon. Kraus's poem expresses amazement that the sun still shines upon a planet being devastated by human beings. It implores the sun to turn its rays against humankind, extirpate them, and leave the earth to animals and plants. But his interpretation of 'Israel' suggests that Jewish commerce and journalism have now conquered the entire world. After repeating the biblical phrase about Israel raising a great cry, he continues:

> Völker, die es gehört, wurden hörig dem Volk;
> alle schrieen wie es, alles ward Israel.
> Alle Sprachen durchdrang einzig die Melodie,
> deren Schalmei das Geld anlockt.
>
> Und sein Wechsel verlangt anderen Wechsel auch—
> Schwarz von Tinte der Tag, rot vom Blute die Nacht!

---

[277] Bartels, *Heine*, p. 94; emphasis in original.

[278] Anselm Ruest, 'Um Heine', *Die Aktion* (19 June 1911), cols. 556–60. This is an elaborate allusion: in 1794 the Berlin Enlightener Saul Ascher replied to antisemitic remarks by Fichte with a pamphlet entitled *Eisenmenger der Zweite* after the notorious antisemite Johann Andreas Eisenmenger. See Och, *Imago judaica*, p. 39.

[279] Scholem, *Walter Benjamin*, p. 83. On the reception of Kraus's essay see Peters, *Heine*, pp. 158–71.

[280] T. W. Adorno, 'Die Wunde Heine', in *Noten zur Literatur*, ed. Rolf Tiedemann (Frankfurt, 1974), pp. 95–100 (esp. p. 97).

Aber welche es sei: Fluth, die im Wechsel wuchs:
Israel ging trocken durch. (F 423/5: 62)

Nations that heard it succumbed to the one nation;
all cried out alike, all became Israel.
Every tongue was infused by the single melody
whose piping lures forth money.
And this change required that much else change hands—
The day was black with ink, the night was red with blood!
But come what might, though the flood rose with money-changing,
Israel passed through dry-shod.

The 'black ink' (i.e. printer's ink) again alludes to journalism, but now it is juxtaposed with another fluid—blood—which Jews shed profusely; but not, Kraus implies, their own blood.[281]

By the time Kraus completed his great satirical drama *Die letzten Tage der Menschheit* (*The Last Days of Mankind*), his obsession with a Judaized modernity had largely dissipated. He began the play in the summer of 1915, incorporated some anti-military satire written before the War, wrote the bulk of the text in 1915–17, but revised it extensively before publishing it in *Die Fackel* in 1919, and made further revisions before it appeared as a book in 1922.[282] The 'Nörgler' (Carping Critic), who comes close to being Kraus's spokesman in the drama, says that militarism and the press are united in the service of 'Jewish and capitalist world destruction' (K x. 197). The middle-class liberal establishment is satirized with emphasis on its Jewish component. Favourite Jewish targets, identifiable by their Yiddishisms, include the Patriot (always presented in conversation with the Newspaper Subscriber) and 'old Biach', a passionate devotee of the *Neue Freie Presse*, who dies with an editorial on his lips (K x. 575). Moriz Benedikt appears in the phantasmagoric epilogue as the Lord of the Hyenas and the Antichrist. Before that, Kraus juxtaposes 'the praying Benedikt', Pope Benedict XIV, with 'the dictating Benedikt', as the editor dictates an exceptionally tasteless article about the fish of the Adriatic gorging on drowned Italian sailors (K x. 191). Kraus still enjoys exposing the hidden language of the Jew. Thus he lets us eavesdrop on a Viennese couple, the Schwarz-Gelbers, who never miss the chance to be seen at charitable functions; on

---

[281] For a different (but to me unconvincing) reading, see Timms, *Karl Kraus, Apocalyptic Satirist*, p. 340. [282] Ibid. 371–4.

arriving home, they are no sooner alone than they have a furious quarrel adorned by Yiddishisms like 'Tineff', 'Nebbich', and 'Ponem'.[283] And when the patriotic journalist Hans Müller tries out his (wonderfully parodied) rhetoric on a soldier from Berlin who replies by calling him a 'Jew-boy', Müller's language abruptly changes into *Mauscheldeutsch* ('Worauf herauf!' K x. 187).[284] We also find Jews as aggressive journalists, dealers in patriotic pictures, and war profiteers, especially in the semi-fantastic scene in which a café is filled with speculators bearing not only familiar Jewish animal-names like Wolf, Hirsch, and Löw, but weird ones like Nashorn (rhinoceros), Pavian (baboon), Walross, Tapir, and Mastodon (K x. 605–6).

However, the play makes clear that corruption, whether moral, financial, or linguistic, is not a Jewish speciality. Goethe's poem 'Über allen Gipfeln' is parodied, first by two retired Viennese officials (both Gentiles; K x. 266), and then by philosophy students at Jena, who turn it into a prophecy of submarine warfare ('Unter allen Wassern ist—"U"', K x. 331). As this example suggests, Kraus's bitterest satire is reserved for Germans, especially Prussians. They have lost contact with their own language: 'No nation lives at a greater distance from its language, and hence from the source of its life, than the Germans', says the Carping Critic, implicitly confuting Fichte. 'Any Neapolitan beggar is closer to his language than a German professor to his' (K x. 200). Kraus also presents Prussian society as permeated by brutality: from the Kaiser, who plays crude practical jokes on his obsequious generals, via the bloodthirsty Lutheran clergymen Falke, Rabe, and Geier (Falcon, Raven, Vulture), and the Wahnschaffe family whose children play war-games in military jargon, through any number of brutal soldiers down to the loutish Berlin tourists who disgrace themselves in a mosque. Except for a scene with the Bavarian patriot Ganghofer, the only German

---

[283] According to Harriet Anderson, *Utopian Feminism: Women's Movements in Fin-de-Siècle Vienna* (New Haven and London, 1992), p. 105, Mrs Schwarz-Gelber was based on Eugenie Schwarzwald, whose tireless activity was also satirized by Alfred Polgar: see Ulrich Weinzierl, *Alfred Polgar: Eine Biographie* (Vienna and Munich, 1985), p. 118.

[284] Kafka cites this expression, from Kraus's later play *Literatur oder Man wird doch da sehn*, as *Mauscheldeutsch*: see Brod and Kafka, *Eine Freundschaft*, ii. 359. A remarkable sample of Müller's prose may be found in Thomas Mann, Heinrich Mann, *Briefwechsel*, p. 43.

dialect Kraus reproduces is Berlinese. Austrian writers enjoy caricaturing Prussians: one thinks of Hofmannsthal's essay 'Preuße und Österreicher' ('Prussian and Austrian') and his conceited Neuhoff in the comedy *Der Schwierige* (*The Difficult Man*, 1922). Kraus's vision here may be obsessively monocular; but it is that of an irritated Austrian, not a self-hating Jew.

Not only did Kraus lose his obsession with Jewishness, but in his great anti-Nazi polemic, written in 1933 (and published only in 1952), *Dritte Walpurgisnacht* (*Third Walpurgis Night*), he reversed his stance, forging an alliance between the discourse of German classicism and the previously despised language of the Jew. He attacks both the perversion of language by Nazi propagandists and the horrors perpetrated in their concentration camps. The book is full of quotations from Goethe, especially the 'Klassische Walpurgisnacht' in *Faust II*; Shakespeare is also heavily drawn upon, especially *Macbeth* and *King Lear*.[285] After quoting the bombast of a Nazified journalist, Bernhard Diebold, Kraus comments: 'Schulbeispiel dafür, welches Gesumms so ein deutscher Kopf macht mit Termini à la Willensbildung, Wille zur Einheit, Kulturbildung, Kultureinheit, geistige Formung und was es derlei noch gibt, damit letzten Endes ein Tineff herauskommt' (K xii. 52: 'A model instance of what a fuss such a German mind makes about terms like the formation of the will, the will to unity, the formation of culture, cultural unity, intellectual formation and so forth, ending up with *Tineff* [rubbish]'): here the Yiddish word expresses common sense and honesty by contrast with the bombastic German phrases preceding it. Talking about the misfortune of Prussian officers who find themselves collaborating with Nazi thugs, Kraus adds: 'This is a tragically true version of the Jewish anecdote about the boy who is desperate to become a soldier and is shown by his worried father a passing Prussian general, with the words: 'Just look, that's how you'll end up!' ('Siehst du, das wird dein Soff sein!', K xii. 94). The only Jewish writer acceptable to the Nazis is the obscure Emanuel bin Gorion, because of his *völkisch* Zionism and his opposition to assimilation. Kraus makes a Faustian joke on his name: rescued in

---

[285] See Edward Timms, 'Kraus's Shakespearean Politics', in Kenneth Segar and John Warren (eds.), *Austria in the Thirties: Culture and Politics* (Riverside, Calif., 1991), pp. 345–58.

Noah's Ark (along with the other animals), he looks out and cries, 'Bin gerettet! Bin Gorion!' (K xii. 154). In contrast, Kraus acknowledges that he is one of the 'assimilated Jews' ('Assimilationsjuden') whom bin Gorion has opposed.

Kraus now emphasizes that journalism is not intrinsically Jewish, imputing to the Nazis the delusion that by banning Jews they could get rid of 'Jewish' journalism: 'one may suspect that the evil of journalism has not entirely been removed by the racial elimination of its hereditary representatives' (K xii. 19). The bad writing of Nazi sympathizers like Gottfried Benn is journalistic, filled with 'newspaper metaphors devoid of experience' ('unerlebten Zeitungsmetaphern', K xii. 84), further proof that the spirit of bad journalism resides with the Nazis. Thus the technique of Kraus's satire, the analysis of linguistic corruption as a clue to moral depravation, remains constant, but the corrupters of language are no longer Jewish journalists but Nazi propagandists. Given the diversity of Kraus's work and its capacity for growth and development, the charge of 'Jewish self-hatred' seems to apply only to a small portion of it.

Self-Hating Jews in Fiction: Wassermann, Natonek, Canetti

If Harden and Kraus coped with unease about Jewishness by projecting the qualities they disliked onto the vast screen of modern civilization, the three novels to be considered next reveal another way of coping with stigma, one that Goffman calls 'minstrelization'. Instead of concealing or projecting the stigmatized attributes, one displays them, acting them out in public. The pressure to do so was described by Richard Beer-Hofmann in a letter to Martin Buber:

Whether we like it or not, whatever we Jews do takes place on a stage— our destiny has constructed it. The nature of other nations, good or bad, is taken for granted. But the whole world may lounge on their seats and gape at the Jews. Expression, voice, posture, hair colour, physique— everything must be submitted to hostile judges—and woe betide us if we do not tread the boards like demi-gods.[286]

---

[286] Letter of 3 Apr. 1913, in Alexander Kosenina, 'Richard Beer-Hofmanns Briefwechsel mit Martin Buber (1910–1936)', *MAL* 29 (1996), ii. 45–81 (pp. 54–5).

One fictional character who responds to this self-consciousness by minstrelization is Polledi in Max Brod's novel *Schloß Nornepygge* (1908). Though he comes from a poor ghetto family, Polledi is accepted socially because he can adapt himself to any surroundings and because cultivated society welcomes him as a clown.[287] Another is in Joseph Roth's *Zipper und sein Vater* (1928), where Arnold Zipper copes with his professional and marital failures by working as a clown and thus acting out his own self-contempt. Characters in novels who dramatize their own stigmatized Jewishness tend to dominate the other characters and to occupy almost self-contained sections of the text. Thus Thomas Mann's dramatic Jewish characters, Chaim Breisacher and Saul Fitelberg, each appear in self-contained episodes where they dominate the scene by their monologues. It is as though their unremitting inner anxiety has been diverted outwards as the nervous energy required to dominate a captive audience; as though they compensate for an inner sense of powerlessness by bringing other people under their dramatic spell.

Three novels, written within a few years of one another, contain dominating characters who are studies in Jewish self-hatred. These are Georg Warschauer, alias Gregor Waremme, in Jakob Wassermann's *Der Fall Maurizius* (*The Maurizius Case*, 1928); Jakob Dowidal, alias Arnold Widahl, in Hans Natonek's *Kinder einer Stadt* (*Children of One Town*, 1932); and Fischerle, alias Dr Siegfried Fischer, in Elias Canetti's *Die Blendung* (written in 1930–1, published in 1935, and translated into English as *Auto da Fé*). The Warschauer episodes stand out starkly from the rest of Wassermann's novel. Joseph Roth told Natonek how much the Shakespearean figure of Dowidal dominated *Kinder einer Stadt*.[288] And Canetti's commentators have pointed out that the story of Fischerle's attempt to escape from his identity forms almost a self-contained section of the novel, being by far its longest chapter.[289]

---

[287] Brod, *Schloß Nornepygge* (Berlin, 1908), pp. 139–41. On the Jew as clown, see Magris, *Weit von wo*, pp. 75–84.

[288] Roth, *Briefe*, ed. Hermann Kesten (Cologne, 1970), pp. 236–8.

[289] David Darby, *Structures of Disintegration: Narrative Strategies in Elias Canetti's 'Die Blendung'* (Riverside, Calif., 1992), p. 104.

Wassermann

Wassermann differs from an earlier generation of writers in that, although he tried desperately to be accepted as a German writer, he always had deep doubts about whether such acceptance was possible. His autobiography, *Mein Weg als Deutscher und Jude*, is famous as an expression of disillusionment. But his doubts are evident much earlier.

In an essay of 1904 Wassermann faces the fact that anti-semitism seems ineradicable. He refers to the long history of the persecution of the Jews and its most recent examples such as the Polna ritual murder trial and the Kishinev pogrom. The modern emancipation of the Jews has on the whole been a failure. It has been too rapid: Jews released from the ghetto try to absorb Western culture too quickly and achieve nothing. And it has produced an unpleasant Jewish type which has not shaken off the old spirit of subordination but applies it now to German culture: 'those Jews who on seeing a picture of a "Germanic" type (*eines "Germanen"*) roll their eyes and freeze with adoration'.[290] Unable to enter Western culture, the modern Jew is seeks a refuge against isolation in his family, and an escape from isolation in an empty cosmopolitanism. But this intellectual culture is not really a substitute for belonging to a living tradition. It puts the Jew in danger of adopting merely negative ideals, as happened with Weininger, whose philosophy led to suicide. The only solution Wassermann can suggest is to convert this enforced cosmopolitanism into something positive, and so he ends by recommending the Jew to cultivate a supranational humanism. 'Let him forget that his fatherland does not consider him worthy of all official posts and dignities, and if he cannot become a Russian or a German in the fullest sense, let him become all the more a human being.'[291]

In later essays Wassermann shows less interest in this Enlighten-

---

[290] Wassermann, 'Das Los des Juden' (1904), in *Deutscher und Jude*, p. 24. See Hans Otto Horch, '"Verbrannt wird auf alle Fälle . . ." Juden und Judentum im Werk Jakob Wassermanns', in Günter E. Grimm and Hans-Peter Bayerdörfer (eds.), *Im Zeichen Hiobs: Jüdische Schriftsteller und deutsche Literatur im 20. Jahrhundert* (Königstein, 1985), pp. 124–46; Gabriele Leja, 'Jüdische Gestalten im erzählerischen Werk Jakob Wassermanns', in Rudolf Wolff (ed.), *Jakob Wassermann: Werk und Wirkung* (Bonn, 1987), pp. 66–96.

[291] Wassermann, *Deutscher und Jude*, p. 27.

ment humanism and explores two contrary possibilities for the Jew, which, he says in 1929, correspond to the Jew's unique inner duality ('Gegensätzlichkeit geistiger und seelischer Eigenschaften').[292] One of the Jew's inner extremes may be realized by leading a secure life within a social order which may be ancient and traditional, or new and revolutionary. (Thus for Wassermann Zionists can be authentic Jews.) In the Diaspora, only exceptional characters can regain this sense of living within a social order. The Jew who does this is the 'Oriental', a term Wassermann loves to use, though mainly in a metaphorical sense. In his essay, 'The Jew as Oriental', addressed to Martin Buber and published in a Zionist volume in 1913, Wassermann declares that the Jew can only be creative as an Oriental: 'The Jew that I call the Oriental [. . .] is sure of himself, sure of the world and humanity. He cannot lose himself, since a noble consciousness, consciousness of the blood, links him to the past and an immense responsibility gives him a duty to the future. [. . .] He knows his sources, he dwells with the Mothers, he rests and creates.'[293] The allusion to the Mothers in Goethe's *Faust II* associates the Jews both with the greatest German writer and his image of creativity, and with the ancient Eastern past. Evidently Wassermann was very attached to this notion, for in 1918, according to Schnitzler's diary, Wassermann contrasted Schnitzler and himself as follows: 'He tried to account for my "rationalist" and his "metaphysically attuned" character by saying that I was the "Western European", he the "Oriental" Jew' (*T* 10 Dec. 1918). And in his autobiography Wassermann says that his love of storytelling was an Oriental impulse in his blood which he shared with Sheherezade, the narrator of the *Arabian Nights*.[294]

The Jew who does not attach himself to a social order lives a solitary, anarchic, self-centred, and self-destructive existence. He is too often shallow and uncreative, a mere man of letters: 'We know them, dear friend, we know them and we suffer from them, these thousand so-called modern Jews, who gnaw at all foundations because they themselves lack foundations; who today discard what yesterday they conquered, today defile what yesterday they

---

[292] Wassermann, 'Die psychologische Situation des Judentums' (1929), in *Deutscher und Jude*, p. 145.

[293] Wassermann, 'Der Jude als Orientale' (1913), in *Deutscher und Jude*, p. 31.

[294] Wassermann, *Mein Weg*, in *Deutscher und Jude*, p. 49.

loved [. . .].'[295] By 1929, however, Wassermann imagines this type as an almost tragic figure, exemplified by Ahasuerus, the Wandering Jew: 'He is robbed, so to speak, of the idea of existence, and so everything he effects or achieves must be gained by force, by straining his character and his abilities to the utmost; he forms a wretched spectacle of perpetual restlessness and perpetual greed. He yields himself only where he can lose himself, and admires only where he feels himself rejected. [. . .] The spiritual energy squandered on fruitless resistance impoverishes his heart and forces his mind into fields of sterile speculation. But he suffers too, and his suffering is mortal.'[296]

Wassermann regards himself as an 'Oriental' who has attached himself to a literary tradition, that of the European novel from Cervantes to Dostoevsky. His desire to be a novelist is a desire to escape from the model of the Jewish man of letters represented by Heine. He repeats Kraus's case against Heine as a journalistic talent.[297] He wanted to fill a gap in German literature by writing a social novel like those of Dickens or Balzac. His ambitions were high, his vanity sometimes ludicrous. Schnitzler's diary records how, hearing Tolstoy praised, Wassermann became increasingly restless and finally burst out: 'What about me?' (*T* 5 Mar. 1914). He wanted to write a great novel on a thoroughly German subject. His first such effort, *Caspar Hauser oder die Trägheit des Herzens* (*Caspar Hauser or the Inertia of the Heart*, 1908), dealt with the mysterious young man who appeared in Nuremberg in 1828 and was murdered three years later. But, Wassermann complains, 'the German media would not accept that such a peculiarly German book was written by a Jew'.[298]

Wassermann tried again, yet more ambitiously, with *Das Gänsemännchen* (*The Goose-Man*, 1915). Although he thought himself unappreciated, critics lavishly praised the 'German' quality of this book, comparing it especially with E. T. A. Hoffmann.[299] It

---

[295] Wassermann, 'Der Jude als Orientale' (1913), in *Deutscher und Jude*, p. 31.
[296] Wassermann, 'Die psychologische Situation des Judentums' (1929), in *Deutscher und Jude*, p. 146.   [297] Wassermann, *Mein Weg*, p. 75.
[298] Ibid. 95.
[299] It was praised as 'ein sonderbar deutsches Buch' by 'L. S.' in *Die Rheinlande. Monatschrift für deutsche Kunst und Dichtung*, 25 (1915), 388; commended for vividly portraying the Nuremberg region by Oskar Loerke in *Die neue Rundschau*, 26/ii (1915), 1708–10, and by Lion Feuchtwanger in *Die Schaubühne*, 12 (1916), I, 10–13; compared with Hoffmann by Max Herrmann-Neisse in *Sirius. Monatsschrift*

centres on the quintessentially German figure of the Nuremberg musician Daniel Nothafft, a dreamy, Romantic character, who has an antithesis in the red-haired Galician Jewish impresario Wurzelmann. Wurzelmann envies Daniel's creativity: 'the servile little fellow (*das Knechtlein*) was filled by the admiration which the Jew born in poverty and oppression feels for the genius of the other race'.[300] Rejected by Daniel as 'Judas', Wurzelmann takes revenge by becoming a music critic and attacking his works. Later in his career Daniel meets a red-haired Jewish divorcée, Regina Süssmann, whom he finds over-intellectual and affected, without the 'vegetative character' he prefers in women[301]—and who, realizing that her homage is unwelcome, confines herself to supporting him from a distance, like Leverkühn's Jewish patroness in *Doktor Faustus*. Daniel has another Jewish friend, the melancholy biologist Dr Friedrich Benda, who looks like a Dutchman rather than a Jew, and who is clearly a projection of Wassermann: 'Did he believe in those racial differences? No. He felt at home on the soil that fed him, committed to the suffering and happiness of the people, linked in a heart-to-heart affinity to the best of them, with his mind formed by their language, their ideas and their ideals.'[302] He strikes up a close friendship with Daniel, for both are outcasts, the Jew and the artist, from small-town life which Wassermann depicts as consumed by endless petty spite.

A similar friendship exists between a Jew and a Gentile in *Christian Wahnschaffe* (1919), a vast rambling novel with too many undeveloped characters. The unattractive Johanna Schöntag constantly proclaims her wish to be unhappy, and focuses her masochism on her Jewishness: 'I wear the yellow star in my soul.'[303] She cannot reconcile her overdeveloped self-awareness with the physical desire that makes her surrender to a man she despises. Her emotions are focused on the beautiful non-Jewish dancer Eva Sorel, who represents the reconciliation of mind and

---

für Literatur und Kunst (1915–16), 61–3, and by Franz Herwig in *Hochland*, 13 (1915–16), I, 478–82 (p. 482). Of these critiques, the most detailed and sympathetic is Feuchtwanger's, reprinted in *Ein Buch nur für meine Freunde* (Frankfurt, 1984), pp. 332–6. See Martin Neubauer, *Jakob Wassermann: Ein Schriftsteller im Urteil seiner Zeitgenossen* (Frankfurt, 1994).

[300] Wassermann, *Das Gänsemännchen* (Munich, 1990), p. 96.
[301] Ibid. 410.   [302] Ibid. 71.
[303] Wassermann, *Christian Wahnschaffe* (Munich, 1989), p. 300.

body that Johanna thinks only possible for unproblematic Gentiles.

In retrospect, all these minor Jewish characters look like sketches for Warschauer/Waremme in *Der Fall Maurizius*. The title figure of this highly readable detective story, Leonhart Maurizius, has been in prison for eighteen years for shooting his wife Elli in order to pursue an affair with his sister-in-law Anna Jahn. The 16-year-old Etzel Andergast, son of the prosecutor Wolf von Andergast, seeks to prove Maurizius's innocence by tracking down Gregor Waremme, who claims to have witnessed the shooting, and persuading him to admit his perjury. Etzel thus opposes his father, a domestic tyrant who forbids Etzel to see his divorced mother. While Etzel is questioning Waremme in Berlin, his father re-examines the evidence and concludes that the affair is too complex for any one person to be called guilty. He asks for Maurizius to be pardoned. Etzel breaks with his father and returns to his mother. As in *Die Juden von Zirndorf*, maternal values are set in opposition to the rigid, loveless world of the father which in this novel is represented by Andergast and his formalist pursuit of technical 'justice' in contrast to Etzel's almost messianic search for true justice.

In Berlin, Etzel worms his way into Waremme's confidence and extorts from him an astonishing, psychologically subtle auto-biographical confession of Jewish self-hatred. As Georg Warschauer, he was brought up in the Polish city of Thorn (Torun) by Jewish parents who still believed in emancipation. Warschauer soon learnt, however, that Jews were only grudgingly tolerated. Gifted and ambitious, he found that as a Jew he could never attain a high office or have his achievements fully respected. Instead of rebelling against the Germans, however, he transferred his resentment to his fellow-Jews, whom he thought despicably lacking in self-respect: 'I hated them, every one. I hated their idiom, their wit, their way of thinking, their commercialism, their peculiar melancholy, their presumption, their self-mockery.'[304] His love was directed to the Germans by whom he felt rejected. To make an impression on them, he resorted to the skills of the actor. He converted to Catholicism and changed his name; he took advan-

---

[304] Wassermann, *Der Fall Maurizius* (Munich, 1988), p. 309. Future references in text.

tage of his fair hair and un-Jewish appearance to pretend to be the son of a Gentile officer's daughter and a Silesian nobleman; by hard work he acquired a reputation as a brilliant polymath. He dreamt of playing a leading part in a united Europe under the hegemony of Germany and the Catholic Church. He dominated other people by a mixture of charisma and empathy, being able to penetrate their inner privacy because, having denied his Jewishness, he had no privacy of his own but was wholly an actor:

For me communication (*Mitteilung*) was second nature, my real nature, like the beat of my pulse; wherever I could communicate, I promptly identified with the other, it was the sublimest form of love towards both men and women, a tireless appeal to force the other out of his own privacy, out of all boundaries and reserves, for I myself had none, neither boundaries nor reserves. (p. 325)

In particular, Warschauer used his power over women, and found himself in an emotional rivalry with Maurizius, a nonentity subject to his charisma, and Anna Jahn, his 'German Helen of Troy' (p. 327). Anna, the representative of the desired German world, responded to Warschauer's spell but felt vague revulsion at his Jewishness: 'She sensed the alien blood', Warschauer recalls (p. 326).

Warschauer's charisma recalls that of George du Maurier's Svengali. Both are German-speaking Jews from Poland. Svengali is variously described as a 'German Pole' and 'an Oriental Israelite Hebrew Jew' who speaks 'German-Hebrew-French' in a 'hoarse, rasping, nasal, throaty rook's caw'.[305] Both novels feature an Oedipal triangle in which an older Jew and a younger Gentile are rivals for the love of a Gentile woman. Svengali and the English art student Little Billee are rivals for Trilby O'Ferrall; Svengali gains a pseudo-victory by turning Trilby, through his magnetism, into an internationally famous singer who is really a terrified zombie, but his power is broken when, at her London début, he catches sight of Little Billee. Trilby breaks down, and her career is over; but the narrative makes clear that she is redeemed through her ability to love and to inspire love in others. Svengali, however, is incapable of love and instead controls people by his personal magnetism. Warschauer, another inwardly hollow

---

[305] Du Maurier, *Trilby* (1894), Everyman's Library (London, 1931), pp. 25, 288, 51, 105.

character, similarly uses his magnetism to subjugate people who are themselves disposed to reject him.

After the end of his relationship with Anna, Warschauer went to the United States, vaguely hoping to resume there the career as an admired polymath which had been ended by the scandal of the Maurizius case. He found, however, that European culture counted for nothing in America, and to survive there, as a 'master of mimicry', he had to adapt to a quite different way of life typified by the slogan 'Keep smiling' (pp. 334, 335). He stayed for ten years in Chicago, a place of poverty and brutality, dominated by the stockyards, wholly untouched by culture. Here, not sheltered by the mediation of culture, Warschauer experienced human bestiality at its worst when he saw a black friend of his pursued by a lynch mob; but he also experienced childlike goodness in the Californian Hamilton La Due, a Christ-figure without a gospel, who helped the poor out of overflowing generosity. Through La Due, Warschauer came in contact with Jewish immigrants from Russia and came to appreciate their language and culture. His 'rebirth' as Georg Warschauer was an acceptance of his Jewish identity (p. 347).

However, Warschauer's Jewish identity is a deeply damaged one. Wassermann described him as a modern personification of Ahasuerus, the Wandering Jew, unable to regain true contact with Jewish traditions.[306] The power of his personality is conveyed by images of volcanic energy, natural devastation, and primitive animal violence. He is profoundly disillusioned, believing only in humanity's greed and stupidity. To Etzel's passion for justice he replies by cynically describing history as a parade of power and oppression: what just recompense can there be for atrocities like the genocide of the American Indians, the African slave trade, or the Ukrainian pogroms? Evidently Warschauer's inner violence is being projected outward, initially as charismatic power, now as bitter cynicism.

Warschauer's distance from others is conveyed also by the homosexuality which makes him respond to Etzel's curiosity.[307]

---

[306] Wassermann, 'Die psychologische Situation des Judentums' (1929), in *Deutscher und Jude*, p. 145.

[307] And which has particularly shocked some commentators: 'Wassermann cannot be said to break a lance for Jewry in this portrayal of Waremme who is a most reprehensible, repulsive character, selfish, unscrupulous, loathsome and homosexual' (John C. Blankenagel, *The Writings of Jakob Wassermann* (Boston, 1942), p. 276).

When his desire for Etzel is apparent, he reminds the latter of a golem, the legendary clay figure animated by Rabbi Löw of Prague: he displays the 'strange drowsy lustfulness of the awakening golem' (p. 239). He fondles Etzel, makes explicit advances to him, and is finally induced to confess his perjury by the sight of Etzel's naked body, which seems to cast on Warschauer the same spell that he used to exert on other people. Disarmed, Warschauer admits that a 'passion' for Etzel has stirred his 'withered heart' (p. 495). He retains, however, the ironic, menacing mode of speech that links him with Proust's great homosexual figure, Baron Charlus.

If Warschauer represents the rootless modern Jew as conceived by Wassermann, he has a positive counterpart, the Jew connected with tradition, in Melchior Ghisels, a character based on Wassermann's friend the journalist Moritz Heimann. Ghisels appears only briefly when Etzel, who admires his writings, calls on him in Berlin. He is described as a good-looking, elegant, relaxed, kindly and sensitive man whose house offers refuge for people in all sorts of difficulties who seek him out as though he were a physician. On Etzel he exercises a 'magnetic' attraction which offers a relief after the uncongenial fascination exerted by Warschauer (p. 359). In response to Etzel's questions about justice, Ghisels replies only with a confession of his own weakness, and his demeanour reminds Etzel of Grünewald's altar-piece of the crucified Christ; but this weakness is evidently spiritual strength, much deeper than Warschauer's tormented and self-destructive violence, and it empowers Etzel to pursue his quest for justice. Nevertheless, the humane Ghisels is a shadowy figure compared to the demonic Warschauer.

Natonek

Hans Natonek was born in 1892 in Prague.[308] His grandfather was a Hungarian rabbi, but his father, director of an insurance company, was a freethinker who had severed all ties with Judaism. Natonek himself converted in 1918. During the 1920s Natonek established himself as a successful journalist in Leipzig and Berlin.

---

[308] See Jürgen Serke, *Böhmische Dörfer: Wanderungen durch eine verlassene literarische Landschaft* (Vienna and Hamburg, 1987), pp. 86–129.

After the Nazi seizure of power he was dismissed from his job and lived in exile first in Czechoslovakia, then in France. Thanks to Thomas Mann, he managed to get to the USA in 1941. In 1946 he became an American citizen. From 1944 till his death in 1963 he lived in Tucson, Arizona.

Natonek's understanding of the Jewish character was influenced by Martin Buber, who defined it as essentially divided and with a corresponding urge to unity.[309] In 1918 Natonek published in Martin Buber's journal *Der Jude* a curious analysis of the Jewish character which interprets its duality in a more radical and pessimistic manner. Natonek maintains that while the Aryan may be single-minded, driven by an irresistible spiritual imperative, the Jew's soul is always divided between spirituality and acquisitiveness. Part of him wants to rise towards God, but part clings greedily to the earth and is obsessed with money-grubbing. 'We Jews all come from Moses, who broke the tablets in flaming wrath on seeing Aaron dancing round the golden calf; we all come from Aaron, who danced round the golden calf while Moses communed with God.'[310] But the Jew, unlike the Aryan, at least has a choice between these two possibilities. Hence Jewishness is above all the problem of wrestling with one's split character. And even the Jew who evades this problem has more potential than the single-minded Aryan. Curiously, however, the language in which Natonek describes the Jew's divided soul is full of submerged quotations from a quintessentially German (hence 'Aryan') text—Goethe's *Faust*, and especially the monologue in which Faust talks about his divided soul. Thus Natonek is boldly transferring 'Faustian' qualities to Jews and denying them to Aryans.

Like other contributors to *Der Jude*, Natonek dislikes many modern acculturated Jews, and explains that they repress this inner conflict:

I should like to smash to pieces the intellectual and commercial mechanism that calls itself the modern Jew; this mechanism that is proud of being identical to other mechanisms whirring through the world. At the sight of the modern Jew's unparalleled vital energy, his tenacious urge to

---

[309] Buber, *Vom Geist des Judentums* (Leipzig, 1916), pp. 24–5; reviewed enthusiastically by Natonek in *Der Merker*, 8 (1917), 359–60.

[310] Natonek, 'Vom jüdischen Zwiespalt. Anmerkungen zur Problematik der jüdischen Seele', *Der Jude*, 2 (1917–18), v/vi. 318–21 (p. 318).

succeed, his astounding versatility, one can escape loathing only by reflecting that they have the secret of an inner being; they are better than they seem; they have their private 'reality': in reality their strength is their weakness, which must pull together a vast amount of energy in order to overtake those who are by nature strong, single-minded and unreflective. Devotion to what is alien to one's nature gives rise to greater, more intense achievements than those born from lazy unity. The Jew has an advantage because his nature and position place him at a disadvantage.[311]

This reads like a schematic description of Jakob Dowidal in *Kinder einer Stadt*. The enmity between him and the Gentile Egon von Epp obliges Dowidal to muster preternatural energy.

The homoeroticism that emerges gradually between Warschauer and Etzel is clearly present from the opening of *Kinder einer Stadt*. It begins with a fight between two schoolboys, the tall, good-looking Epp and the small Jew Dowidal, over possession of a marble as prize in a game: the spoilt Epp, using to getting what he wants without effort, wants the marble, but Dowidal insists that it is his by right. Here the Gentile's identification of power with possession is neatly contrasted with the Jew's sense of justice. As they wrestle in sand which is 'warm as a bed', Dowidal feels strength entering him from the other's body: 'As he wearied, strength came to him from the other body, which he was holding in an embrace, which was closer to him than ever before and linked as though inextricably . . .'.[312] Here Natonek has created a rich but disturbing image of the relation between the Jew and the German, implying both that Dowidal needs another person to live, and—in an echo of familiar antisemitic imagery—that his relation to Epp is that of a parasitic plant living off the host to which it clings. Dowidal's homoerotic yearning is stressed along with Epp's physical loathing:

Epp found the other's close pressure loathsome. He lost interest in the fight. It's *inconclusive*, he thought. Jakob felt him losing his grip and wrestled with growing fury and secret pleasure. Epp's soft, silky hair swept deliciously over his face. How handsome Epp was. Jakob's half-experienced heart could make nothing of this ambivalent feeling. With a

---

[311] Natonek, 320.
[312] Natonek, *Kinder einer Stadt* (Vienna and Hamburg, 1987), p. 11. Future page references in text.

low cry in which all his strength was gathered, he threw Epp down and lay on top of him, breast to breast. (pp. 11–12)

Epp, however, wins the fight by cheating: he delivers an unexpected punch, frees himself, and swaggers away. The unrequited love of the Jew for the handsome Gentile here recalls Tonio Kröger's surreptitious love for Hans Hansen, but it has further dimensions. Since Epp's father is a prominent Liberal, while Dowidal's is a struggling journalist who eventually commits suicide, their relationship allegorizes the dependence of Jews on Austrian liberalism. And Dowidal is a self-tormenting character who, a few weeks later, defiantly refuses Epp's invitation to a party and chooses gloomy isolation, scorning the guests as a way of 'transferring his sense of misery to others' (p. 35).

This projection of his 'self-hatred' (p. 75) onto others becomes the leitmotif of Dowidal's life. As a schoolboy, he exploits the precocious erotic awareness which he acquired when wrestling with Epp, combined with his force of personality, to corrupt the awakening sexuality of the other boys: since his love for Epp is rejected, he wants to prevent others from enjoying love. His revenge on Epp is sexual. Beginning his sexual experience early with prostitutes, Epp develops the familiar emotional polarization of impure, available women and pure, unavailable women, and believes that the much-admired Valerie Bögendorf belongs to the latter class. Aware of Epp's attraction, Dowidal manages to persuade their class-mates that he has himself enjoyed Valerie, and Epp, deprived of what might have been a valuable illusion, becomes a cynical womanizer.

Dowidal's attitude to the world is aggressive. He maintains that rootless Jews like himself must 'work our way out of nothing with our fists and our teeth' (p. 75). 'I am nothing,' he reflects, 'I have nothing, I have no home, no paternal or maternal house, I haven't had a childhood, I don't know what youth is. But money is home, paternal house and youth and power and everything' (p. 97). After his father's death, he disposes of his mother by having her certified insane and forcibly confined in an asylum. Through sheer effort of will, he takes his *Abitur* by private study, and learns to fence, box, row, and swim. To escape from himself, he becomes a Catholic. He becomes an antisemitic journalist, first under the name Jaques Dowidal, then as 'Germanicus'; after the War, as an owner and editor of right-wing papers in the Weimar Republic, he calls himself Arnold Widahl. As a press tycoon he embodies the worst fantasies about a Jewish-dominated press, deliberately disseminating saleable rubbish and deceiving his readers about their true interests. By now he has changed his appearance: his hair is dyed blond, his tailor supplies him with well-cut suits, he has mastered the arts of disguise and self-control, and his bearing recalls Mussolini (p. 199). The chinks in Dowidal's armour are his relations with his former schoolfellows Epp and Hans Waisl. The latter is a quiet boy of Jewish descent, brought up a Catholic, whose endurance of misfortune, especially a wholly uncongenial military career forced on him by relatives, makes him a kind of holy fool. Crippled in the War, he is employed by 'Widahl' as a journalist; he threatens to reveal Dowidal's true Jewish identity, but, lacking the determination to make good his threat, he allows himself to be bought off. As for Epp, he remains the real target of Dowidal's polemics against liberalism and cultural Bolshevism. His sexuality makes him vulnerable. A respected politician, he is tried and sentenced to a year's imprisonment for seducing a 15-year-old girl, though in fact she tried (unsuccessfully) to seduce him, and it is possible that Dowidal somehow instigated the attempt. Epp's 16-year-old son is drowned while sailing; the boat appears to have been sabotaged. Epp and his wife commit suicide.

The novel is in part about personal truth. All three main characters obscure it by their obsessions: Epp's with women, Dowidal's with self-advancement, Waisl's with self-deceiving saintliness. Epp attains truth when, on the verge of suicide, he admits that his wife Valerie is the only woman he has loved. Strangely, his death liberates Dowidal. Now that their feud is over, Dowidal is no longer emotionally dependent on Epp:

Epp is dead and I am risen from the dead. I'm cured. The fatal wound, which was sure to kill me, is beginning to heal. I was in a state of living death. Epp, without knowing it, forced me to be Widahl, the executor of vengeance. Now I can breathe again.   (p. 343)

This conclusion contrasts Waisl's ineffectual, self-indulgent sainthood with the greater authenticity Dowidal derives from his single-minded hatred. The reconciliation preached by the pious Waisl is dismissed as unrealistic. The only way for Dowidal to free himself from enmity was a fight to the finish in which Epp was destroyed. His hatred could only be assuaged and removed by final victory. But it is also clear that, as in Natonek's abstract psychology of the Jew, Dowidal needed Epp to elicit his energy. If, as he claims, he can now 'be himself', what is left for him to be?

If taken as an allegory of German–Jewish relations, the conclusion is even more alarming. The Jew's unrequited love for the Gentile who despises him has become an obsessive, irreconcilable hatred. The Jewish–German relationship distorts the Jew in a manner which is fatal for both him and the German. Casual antisemitism must rebound upon the German in the form of the Jew's deadly revenge. The novel could be read as a dire rebuke to antisemites, but also as itself an antisemitic warning against Jewish malice, supported by extravagant stereotypes of Jewish cunning and will-power.

Canetti

Canetti's Jewish character, the dwarf, hunchback, ponce, swindler, and would-be chess champion Fischerle, is hardly a flattering portrait of a Jew. David Roberts captures its ambivalence by describing Fischerle as the most fascinating figure in the novel and as a caricature that would have done credit to the Nazi paper *Der Stürmer*.[313] In the most detailed study so far, Nicola Riedner suggests that Fischerle illustrates the notion of 'transformation' which Canetti later developed in *Masse und Macht* (*Crowds and Power*, 1960). By 'transformation' Canetti means a kind of empathy that enables one to transform oneself imaginatively into another person. Fischerle's version of transformation, according to Riedner, is a mistaken one which consists in introjecting the antisemitic stereotypes current in the world around him. Thus he represents a false assimilation; and he represents a warning to assimilated Jews that they too might become victims of antisemitism.[314] This is a promising approach, though perhaps too didactic to do justice to the extraordinary energy that animates

[313] Roberts, *Kopf und Welt: Elias Canettis Roman 'Die Blendung'* (Munich, 1975), p. 53. Cf. Margit Frank, *Das Bild des Juden in der deutschen Literatur im Wandel der Zeitgeschichte* (Freiburg, 1987), p. 196.

[314] Riedner, *Canettis Fischerle: Eine Figur zwischen Masse, Macht und Blendung* (Würzburg, 1994), pp. 136, 140, 143.

Fischerle. His energy is the focus of a more recent and more persuasive approach to the novel by Harriet Murphy, who rebukes critics (including myself) for trying to subsume Fischerle under a general type, underestimating his individuality, and failing to acknowledge his aggressiveness, his self-awareness, and his exuberant, amoral playfulness.[315] Murphy's approach to the novel warns us against trying to enlist Fischerle for a cause. He is not an example of Jewish villainy; but neither, despite his violent death, is he a pathetic example of Jewish victimhood.

One possible explanation for Fischerle's stereotypical Jewish features would be to ascribe 'Jewish self-hatred' not only to Fischerle but to his creator. Canetti would have performed the common manoeuvre of displacing his unease about his Jewishness on to a character who is as different as possible from him while still being a Jew. When Fischerle first meets Peter Kien, the help-less scholar whose fraudulent companion he becomes, he uses the word 'Jewish' to see what effect it has on Kien, in case Kien should be an antisemite: 'You never can tell. The world is crawling with antisemites. A Jew always has to be on guard against deadly enemies.'[316] The narrator makes it clear that this is unnecessary. But insecurity is part of Fischerle's character. When the boys in the park, who have been watching Fischerle learning English, sing 'Yes' in chorus, he thinks they mean 'Jew'.[317] His hypersensitivity about being a Jew amounts to self-hatred. The narrator tells us: 'He believed in nothing, except that "Jew" was one of the crimes that bring their own punishment.'[318] This confirms that Fischerle's own sense of Jewishness is entirely an introjection of the outside world's contemptuous attitude to him. However, he suffers no antisemitic hostility. People consider him a 'shabby Jew', but the regulars in the low pub 'Zum idealen Himmel' treat him indulgently, except for one waiter who objects to serving a Jew. We see no overt antisemitism. Yet Fischerle has heard stories about Jews being buried by collapsing churches into which they had impiously intruded, and this reminder of superstitious anti-semitism picks up an earlier reference to a medieval wood-cut which depicts some thirty Jews being burned alive and praying

[315] Murphy, *Canetti and Nietzsche: Theories of Humor in 'Die Blendung'* (Albany, NY, 1997), p. 153.
[316] Canetti, *Auto da Fé*, tr. C. V. Wedgwood (London, 1946), p. 180.
[317] Ibid. 357.   [318] Ibid. 244 (trans. modified).

amid the flames. The novel reminds us of the possibility of anti-semitic violence; and it shows ample violence of other kinds.

Fischerle's physical appearance is dominated by the 'Jewish nose' dear to caricaturists. His nose is so curved that its point is on a level with his chin, making it impossible for him to kiss anyone. He is dwarfish, virtually a midget: when he first accosts Kien, his voice seems to come from under the table; and he has an immense hump. 'No forehead, no ears, no neck, no chest—the man consisted of a hump, a majestic nose, and two black, calm, sad eyes.'[319] His melancholy eyes, another supposedly Jewish feature, are a kindly touch qualifying what otherwise seems a merciless travesty.

In his behaviour Fischerle exhibits the shallow, uncreative intel-ligence, the commercialism, and the adaptability which, as we have seen, were standard components of antisemitic polemic. He has great faith in his own intellect. Like Weininger, he denies that women have any intellectual powers. He tells Kien: 'Listen, a woman *always* tells lies, and why does a woman always tell lies? Because she's a liar! Now I ask you: Could you tell a lie? Could I tell a lie? Out of the question! And why? because we've got heads on our shoulders (*weil wir beide eine Intelligenz haben*).'[320] Yet his 'intelligence' is mere abstract intellectualism, manifested in his devotion to chess. He dreams of becoming a grandmaster and putting Capablanca, the world champion in the mid-1920s, to shame. When he replays chess tournaments reported in the papers, however, he always cheats; the people in 'Zum idealen Himmel' are too ignorant to notice, but Fischerle is terrified in case anyone who does understand chess may want to take him on. He hates chess champions because they really do what he only pretends to do. Fischerle likewise cheats in commerce. He swindles Kien by getting his four associates to bring the same parcel of books to the pawnshop and inducing Kien to pay them. He also swindles his associates. And his position as a ponce reflects the leading role ascribed to Jews in organizing prostitution.[321]

In many respects Fischerle belongs in the novel's gallery of

---

[319] Ibid. 175 (trans. modified).
[320] Ibid. 184; cf. *Die Blendung* (Munich, 1963), p. 200.
[321] See e.g. Hitler, *Mein Kampf*, p. 63. On Jews' active and passive involvement in prostitution, see Edward J. Bristow, *Prostitution and Prejudice: The Jewish Fight against White Slavery* (Oxford, 1982).

obsessed characters. *Die Blendung* depicts, with satirical exaggeration, a world in which most characters are locked in their private obsessions, unable to communicate. They come together only in order to exploit one another. Sex appears not as communication but as violence. The principal obsessives are Kien and his housekeeper Therese, who deceives him into an unconsummated marriage. Both are modelled on Weininger's character-types: Kien, with his phenomenal memory, seems to be a parody of Weininger's male genius, while Therese represents Weininger's notion of woman as purely sensual.[322] Their relationship is in turn inspired by a painting by Rembrandt, *The Blinding of Samson*, which Canetti saw in Frankfurt in his late teens, and which gives the novel its title (literally 'The Blinding').[323] Canetti tells us that he was alarmed, tormented, and fascinated by the painting. Samson is being blinded: a red-hot iron is being thrust into his eye, and he is writhing in pain. Delilah, who betrayed Samson by cutting off his hair and depriving him of his strength, is watching with satisfied hatred. In *Die Blendung*, Canetti has turned the Jewish Samson and Delilah into a couple who are overtly Gentiles but display caricaturally Jewish traits: Kien the cerebral intellectualism ascribed to Jews, Therese the amoral sensuality which, according to Weininger, is best represented by the Jewish woman.[324] Thus an anxiety about 'Jewishness' has found disguised expression in Kien and Therese, explicit expression in Fischerle.

Unlike most of Canetti's obsessives, however, Fischerle is adaptable. His character changes even while he is with Kien. His language becomes more like educated German. After he has got hold of Kien's money and abandoned him, Fischerle transforms his own appearance by getting a suit specially made to conceal his hump; he buys an English phrase-book and masters its contents in an afternoon. These are preliminary stages to travelling via Paris to America, where he plans to establish himself as the chess

---

[322] See Simon Tyler, 'Homage or Parody? Elias Canetti and Otto Weininger', *Austrian Studies*, 7 (1996), 134–49.

[323] Canetti, *Die Fackel im Ohr: Lebensgeschichte 1921–1931* (Munich, 1980), pp. 133–5.

[324] See Weininger, *Geschlecht und Charakter*, p. 429; and on Kien's 'Jewish' features, Sigurd Paul Scheichl, 'Is Peter Kien a Jew? A Reading of Elias Canetti's *Auto-da-fé* in its Historical Context', in Schrader, Simon, and Wardi (eds.), *The Jewish Self-Portrait*, pp. 159–70.

champion Dr Siegfried Fischer, humiliate Capablanca, marry a millionairess, build a palace, and distribute largesse to suppliants. And it must be stressed that though his dreams are fantastic, he really does contrive, by bragging and lavish spending, to transform not only his physical appearance but also his social status. His fantasies are not offered merely for our ridicule, but, much more, for our enjoyment and appreciation.

However, Fischerle is one of two characters who suggest possible escapes from obsession. The other is Peter's brother Georg, who has made a successful career in Paris and changed his name to Georges (a parallel to Fischerle). He owes his success to his power of empathizing with his patients. Georges has his limitations, and his empathy stops short of understanding his brother's madness, but he comes closer than any other character to embodying the empathetic 'transformation' that Canetti was to explore in *Crowds and Power*. Fischerle is his parody. While Georges transforms himself inwardly in order to approach his patients, Fischerle's transformation is external only. And thus Canetti underlines the stereotype of the merely imitative Jew.

Any inquiry into Canetti's own identity as a Jew must stress that he evaded familiar categories of 'Western' and 'Eastern' (i.e. Polish or Galician) Jews by being a Sephardic Jew from Rustchuk (Ruse) in Bulgaria. His family spoke Ladino, a version of medieval Spanish, but Canetti regarded it as an 'impoverished idiom for children and the kitchen'.[325] The language of culture was German, and his parents were thoroughly acculturated: the Burgtheater in Vienna represented their ideal, but it was a German rather than Austrian culture, with Schiller and Goethe as its main figures. They looked down on actual German Jews, still more on Yiddish-speaking Jews: 'Other Jews were looked down upon with naive arrogance; a word that was always laden with contempt was "Todesco", meaning a German or Ashkenazic Jew. Fischerle is clearly an Ashkenazic Jew.'[326] Canetti apparently never experienced antisemitism in Bulgaria, but he suffered it while at school in Zürich and Frankfurt. The Swiss teachers, as well as his fellow-pupils, resented Canetti's quickness of mind and complained that he was always raising his hand in class to answer the teacher's

[325] Canetti, *Die Fackel im Ohr*, p. 106.
[326] Canetti, *Die gerettete Zunge*, p. 12.

questions. A fellow-pupil in Frankfurt repeated all the antisemitic charges against Jews in a tone of disinterested inquiry ('Why do the Jews curse all other people? Why are the Jews cowardly?' etc.). By his own account, Canetti seems to have been upset and rendered insecure by his classmates' persecution, though it was a brief episode. There could be no question of Canetti's forgetting his Jewishness. But there is no sign that he wanted to. The aphorisms in *Die Provinz des Menschen* (*The Human Province*) demonstrate his solidarity with his fellow-Jews during the Holocaust. However, he did not feel himself to be entirely, or solely, a German Jew. He wrote during the Second World War: 'The language of my intellect will continue to be German, precisely because I am a Jew';[327] but in 1965 he described himself as 'a Spanish writer in the German language'.[328] Even in the twentieth century many of the Bulgarian Jews still considered themselves Spaniards. A number fought against Franco in the Spanish Civil War, among them Dr Janto Caneti (possibly a relative?), who set up a hospital in Spain for the wounded of the International Brigade.[329]

Canetti's identity as a Sephardic Jew may have given him enough detachment from the Viennese 'Jewish question' to use stereotypes as a means of exploration. For there are three ways in which the antisemitic stereotypes are qualified, and perhaps outweighed, by sympathetic feeling. First, although explicit antisemitism is absent from the novel, many of the characters vent their hatred on cripples. The word 'Krüppel' ('cripple') recurs obsessively. Fischerle thinks of himself as a cripple because of his deformity. 'A cripple isn't human,' he says, 'I can't help it.' Kien, too, is referred to by the porter Benedikt Pfaff as a 'cripple' (p. 308). Just before killing Fischerle, Knopfhans says: 'A cripple and dirt are the same thing' (p. 400). And the mob which tears Fischerle's lover, the Fischerin, to pieces is in search of 'cripples', who are to be identified by their humps. What Canetti has done is

---

[327] Canetti, *Die Provinz des Menschen: Aufzeichnungen 1942–1972* (Munich, 1973), p. 73.
[328] Quoted in Martin Bollacher, 'Vom Gewissen der Worte. Elias Canetti und die Verantwortung des Dichters im Exil', in Grimm and Bayerdörfer (eds.), *Im Zeichen Hiobs*, pp. 326–37 (p. 334).
[329] See Vicki Tamir, *Bulgaria and her Jews: The History of a Dubious Symbiosis* (New York, 1979).

to bring home the reality of antisemitism by a kind of alienation-
effect in which antisemitic mass feeling is displaced on to cripples.
Instead of the Jew, the cripple serves as the archetypal outsider,
hated simply for being different. The novel is thus not an expression but an exposure of antisemitism. Such a conclusion matches
the reaction of one of its first readers, Alban Berg: 'I read *Die
Blendung* with pleasure, not only artistic but also human pleasure,
since between the lines of this epic of hatred—a hatred aimed
both at people and their institutions—I continually perceived the
loving heart of the author.'[330]

Second, Fischerle is shown suffering humiliations as grotesque
as his appearance. He is more a victim than an exploiter. When the
woman he lives with brings home clients, Fischerle had in the past
to hide under the bed. His melancholy is justified: his life is a
hopeless one, until Kien happens along. His fantasies of establishing himself in America prove that he is not purely rational. But the
irrational actions which make him likeable also bring about his
death: when he is paying off his fellow-swindlers, he cannot resist
giving the 'blind beggar', Knopfhans, a button; but this insult,
arising from Fischerle's sense of fun, is later horribly avenged. He
could have got away to Paris, but he returns to his room to unearth
the notebook containing the names and addresses of chess
champions, and while doing so he is found and murdered by
Knopfhans.

But, third, Fischerle is not merely a victim. His death is not a
consequence of his downtrodden existence but of the exuberance
with which he masters his existence. His exuberance finds expression not only in fantasies and conspiracies, but in garrulous
monologues which parallel the creative activity of Canetti himself
and thus support Harriet Murphy's contention that 'Canetti is
collaborating with Fischerle, at a very deep level'.[331] A similar
collaboration   underlies   Wassermann's   presentation   of
Warschauer/Waremme and Natonek's presentation of Dowidal/
Widahl. By presenting a character who so extravagantly fulfils
stereotypical notions of Jewishness, the author distances himself
from such conceptions of Jewishness. At the same time, the author

---

[330] Letter to Canetti, 11 Nov. 1935, quoted in Herbert G. Göpfert (ed.), *Canetti
lesen: Erfahrungen mit seinen Büchern* (Munich, 1975), p. 122.
[331] Murphy, *Canetti and Nietzsche*, p. 206.

enjoys letting the imaginary Jew display his supposed characteristics without let or hindrance. Writing about Warschauer, Dowidal, or Fischerle is a vicarious way of *being* Warschauer, Dowidal, or Fischerle: of accepting the image of oneself projected by one's society, then letting rip and living out that image with all its consequences. And this act of imaginatively letting rip accounts for the enormous exhilaration which these characters convey. Self-doubt, of whatever intensity, becomes a kind of self-acceptance.

HYPERACCULTURATION

Insecurity about one's position as a member of a conspicuous and sometimes stigmatized minority could lead to exaggerated attempts to make oneself part of the majority: to hyperaccultura-tion. Two forms of hyperacculturation deserve attention. One is through nationalism: an exaggerated identification with German political goals and with nationalist conceptions of German identity. The other is through friendship: the development of emotional dependency on a representative of the admired German culture.

Nationalism

Hyperacculturation is the logical consequence of assimilation-ism. For the goal of complete assimilation to German society means ceasing to exist as a Jew. The extreme assimilationist Friedrich Blach accepted this consequence in advocating 'complete absorption into the totality, entire inclusion of the Jewish component in the total organism of the German people'.[332] Blach acknowledged the Zionist charge that assimila-tion meant suicide as a Jew:

The Zionists call assimilation suicide. Very well, so it is—free and joyful suicide. For I no longer want to be the self that I was; I want to belong to the magnificent nation in whose midst I was born. 'Die at the right time: thus teaches Zarathustra.' We have hesitated for far too long.[333]

---

[332] [Blach], *Die Juden in Deutschland*, p. 11.   [333] Ibid. 42.

This was no individual eccentricity. The assimilationist policy of the CV led in the same direction. Although it began with Enlightenment principles whereby national identity was equated with legal citizenship, its pathetic avowals of rootedness in Germany helped it to slide towards the *völkisch* conceptions of the Right. In November 1919, in response to charges of sympathy with Bolshevism, the CV published an open letter declaring that its more than 200,000 members were '*German nationalist in their outlook*' ('*national-deutsch orientiert*'), for Jewish life was intrinsically conservative; it concluded: 'If in the last year a number of Russian and German Jews (*mostly hysterical literary types*) have been prominent in the [Bolshevist] movement, the Jewish community is not responsible, especially as most of the gentlemen in question have *long since left the Jewish community*.'[334]

Many Austrian Jews, dissatisfied with what seemed a backward and stagnant Empire, transferred their enthusiasm to Bismarck's new Germany. Fritz Mauthner so worshipped Bismarck that he added to his autobiography the invocation: 'Sancte Bismarck, magister Germaniae, ora pro nobis.'[335] Trying to defend Heine against antisemitic detractors, Mauthner implausibly praises him as a Bismarckian before Bismarck, finding in the political satire *Deutschland: Ein Wintermärchen* 'the wild desire for unification through blood and iron'.[336] Freud's father, on adopting the Gregorian calendar, also changed his date of birth from 18 December 1815 to 1 April—Bismarck's birthday.[337]

We also find Jewish Nietzscheans who sought to overcome their Jewishness by devotion to Nietzsche and his heroic ideals. Such devotion should have been encouraged by Nietzsche's denunciations of antisemitism and his expressed admiration for some Jewish qualities.[338] Nevertheless, his friend Paul Rée regarded his own Jewish origins as a secret stigma. Rée fainted on hearing a casual reference to Jews from Lou Andreas-Salomé, and made

---

[334] Quoted in Oppeln-Bronikowski, *Antisemitismus?*, pp. 21–2. Emphasis in original.

[335] Mauthner, *Prager Jugendjahre*, p. 349. See Joachim Kühn, *Gescheiterte Sprachkritik: Fritz Mauthners Leben und Werk* (Berlin, 1975), esp. p. 258.

[336] Mauthner, 'Heinrich Heine' (1897) in *Gespräche im Himmel und andere Ketzereien* (Munich and Leipzig, 1914), pp. 59–91 (p. 73).   [337] Jones, *Freud*, i. 2.

[338] See Jacob Golomb (ed.), *Nietzsche and Jewish Culture* (New York and London, 1997).

scenes when he inadvertently met Jews socially.[339] Another devoted Jewish Nietzschean was Siegfried Lipiner, one of the circle of Viennese students around Engelbert Pernerstorfer who were critical of Austrian liberalism.[340] He was introduced by Nietzsche's friend the classical scholar Erwin Rohde, who described him as 'one of the most bandy-legged of all Jews, but with quite a pleasant, sensitive look on his horrid Semitic face'.[341] In 1877 Lipiner sent Nietzsche a copy of his play *Der entfesselte Prometheus* (*Prometheus Unbound*, 1876) with a fan letter. Nietzsche admired the play, whose solitary, amoral hero may have influenced *Zarathustra*.[342] He gave a kind reply, stressing his high expectations of talented Jews, which sent Lipiner into ecstasy at 'the blissful thought that I may no longer be unfamiliar and indifferent to the heart of my Nietzsche'.[343] However, Lipiner went too far, trying to persuade Nietzsche to spend a summer holiday with him in the Salzkammergut, and Nietzsche eventually rebuffed his 'impertinence', whereupon Lipiner transferred his enthusiasm to Wagner.[344]

Among Jewish Wagnerians, service often became subservience. Jews who promoted Wagner's work included the conductor Hermann Levi, the writer Heinrich Porges, and the pianist Karl Tausig; the concert impresario Angelo Neumann and George Davidsohn, editor of the *Berliner Börsencourier*; and the academics Max Koch and Richard Sternfeld. Admittedly, enthusiasm for Wagner was also strong among many Jews who had never met the Master and were far from being German nationalists. It was in honour of Wagner that Gershom Scholem's grandfather changed his name from Scholem Scholem to Siegfried Scholem.[345]

---

[339] Andreas-Salomé, *Lebensrückblick*, ed. Ernst Pfeiffer (Zurich, 1951), p. 301.

[340] See William J. McGrath, *Dionysiac Art and Populist Politics in Austria* (New Haven and London, 1974).

[341] Rohde, letter of 29 June 1877, in Nietzsche, *Briefwechsel*, ed. Giorgio Colli and Mazzino Montinari, 3 divisions (Berlin and New York, 1975–84), II. vi. 595.

[342] Curt Paul Janz, *Friedrich Nietzsche: Biographie*, 3 vols. (Munich, 1978), ii. 229.

[343] Lipiner, letter of 10 Sept. 1877, *Briefwechsel*, II. vi. 693.

[344] Nietzsche, letter to his mother and sister, 13 Aug. 1878, *Briefwechsel*, II. v. 346–7.

[345] Scholem, *Von Berlin nach Jerusalem: Jugenderinnerungen*, tr. Michael Brocke and Andrea Schatz (Frankfurt, 1997), p. 12. This enlarged edition of Scholem's memoirs was first published in Hebrew in 1982. The English version, *From Berlin to Jerusalem*, tr. Harry Zohn (New York, 1980), is based on Scholem's earlier, shorter German text.

Julius Braunthal's father was devoted to Wagner's music while detesting his antisemitism; he would sing long passages from Wagner at home, then break off and exclaim scornfully: 'And such a noise Wagner calls music!'[346] In Vienna, Peter Altenberg included Wagner among his 'poet-gods' ('Dichter-Götter').[347] Such enthusiasm lent itself to literary caricature: we have already seen how Thomas Mann's Aarenhold twins in *Wälsungenblut* not only bear the names but imitate the conduct of Wagner's incestuous couple; and Carl Sternheim introduces into his hilarious comedy *Die Hose* (*The Knickers*, 1911) the feeble and consumptive Jewish Wagnerite Mandelstamm, who is outwitted by the robust and philistine German bourgeois Theobald Maske.

The cult of Wagner, however, was usually linked with German nationalism, as Hermann Bahr testifies: 'Nobody since Schiller had been felt so strongly by young Germans to be the figure symbolizing the German essence, the manifestation of our most hidden will. Bismarck and Wagner were the signs of German power over the world.'[348] The committee of the Wagner-Verein had as its only Jewish member Richard Sternfeld, who considered *Tristan und Isolde* not only a musical but a poetic masterpiece surpassing Goethe's *Faust*, and called the Zionist Kurt Blumenfeld an 'arrogant Jew-boy' for criticizing it.[349] Even more subservient was the young Russian Joseph Rubinstein, who, having read Wagner's statement that Jews could be redeemed only if they perished, wrote to Wagner in February 1872, asking him for help as the only alternative to suicide.[350] Wagner took him up, but after Wagner's death Rubinstein did commit suicide. But the extreme example of devotion to Wagner was surely Hermann Levi, who endured much patronizing treatment and brutal teasing about his Jewishness. Wagner called him 'the Assyrian', claimed to intend to have him baptized, and observed in his presence that

---

[346] Braunthal, *In Search of the Millennium*, p. 22.
[347] Andrew Barker and Leo A. Lensing, *Peter Altenberg: Rezept die Welt zu sehen* (Vienna, 1995), p. 194.   [348] Bahr, *Selbstbildnis* (Berlin, 1923), p. 139.
[349] Blumenfeld, *Erlebte Judenfrage*, p. 36.
[350] The letter is quoted in Hartmut Zelinsky, 'Der Kapellmeister Hermann Levi und seine Stellung zu Richard Wagner und Bayreuth oder der Tod als Gralsgebiet', in Walter Grab (ed.), *Jüdische Integration und Identität in Deutschland und Österreich 1848–1918* (Tel Aviv, 1984), pp. 309–51 (p. 319); cf. Cosima Wagner, *Diaries*, i. 464–5 (7 March 1872).

'Jewishness is a terrible curse'.[351] Levi approved of discrimination against Jews and expressed the hope that in twenty years' time they would be 'extirpated root and branch' from public life, especially from audiences of the *Ring*.[352] He directed the première of *Parsifal* at the insistence of King Ludwig: Wagner was reluctant because he wanted the opera to be conducted by a Christian. Thanks to some strange sado-masochistic mechanism, Wagner's growing obsession with the ruinous machinations of Jewry, and his constant references to this subject (no less compulsive than Scholten's allusions in Raabe's *Frau Salome*), seem only to have heightened the devotion of what he called his 'pet Israelites'.[353]

Tensions between German Jews and non-Jews increased during the First World War. When it broke out, most Jews, including Zionists, joined with the general population in supporting it, often with extravagant enthusiasm. The CV called on all German Jews to dedicate themselves to the fatherland; rabbis, like Catholic and (especially) Protestant clergymen, affirmed that God supported the German cause.[354] No doubt they were sincerely convinced of the justice of the German cause, but the war also gave them a long-awaited opportunity to demonstrate their loyalty, and many were glad that Germany had declared war on the notoriously antisemitic Russia. The Zionist Hugo Bergman, convinced of 'the greatness of the work that is to be accomplished', regarded the war as divine punishment for the Russian pogroms at Kishinev and Gomel.[355] In Austria, Jews identified with the Habsburg monarchy and were the most loyal to the war effort, while the Empire's various nationalities became increasingly mutinous. Maximilian Harden's bloodthirsty editorials have already been quoted, but by 1917 he recognized that trench warfare was futile and courageously urged peace.[356] Chauvinistic

[351] Cosima Wagner, *Diaries*, ii. 656 (13 Apr. 1881), ii. 682 (2 July 1881), ii. 1007 (9 Feb. 1883). See Gay, 'Hermann Levi: A Study in Service and Self-Hatred', in his *Freud, Jews and Other Germans*, pp. 189–230; Zelinsky, 'Der Kapellmeister Hermann Levi'; Rose, *Wagner: Race and Revolution*, pp. 119–24.

[352] Cosima Wagner, *Diaries*, ii. 254 (13 Jan. 1879).

[353] Ibid. (14 Jan. 1879).

[354] See Egmont Zechlin, *Die deutsche Politik und die Juden im ersten Weltkrieg* (Göttingen, 1969), pp. 86–100.

[355] Schmuel Hugo Bergman, *Tagebücher und Briefe*, ed. Miriam Samburski, 2 vols. (Königstein, 1985), i. 59.

[356] See Harden, 'Vor dem vierten Tore', *Die Zukunft*, 30 June 1917.

utterances came not only in 1914 but throughout the war from Alfred Döblin, later a Socialist and later still a Catholic convert: in December 1914, after the German bombardment of Rheims Cathedral, he declared that the English and French had lost any claim to being cultured nations because they had black troops, and in February 1918 he maintained that anyone inclined to make peace deserved to be massacred: 'Famine won't make us slack; the triumphant face of the Italians (*Welschen*), the cheering of the Senegal Negroes who are marshalled against us, and the hoarse cries of the British will keep us alert.'[357]

The best-known Jewish celebrant of 1914 was Ernst Lissauer. Son of a Jewish businessman, he was born and brought up in Berlin entirely in a German manner, but at 15 rejected his parents' suggestion of baptism, because (like Rathenau) he thought that would be opportunistic. Yet he rejected the empty Judaism of his parents' generation. His Germanophile publisher, Eugen Diederichs, thought Lissauer a great poetic discovery. Lissauer's pre-war poetry is intensely nationalistic, celebrating the German patriots of 1813 and the German landscape through which he represents himself as wandering like the Wandervögel. 'Wurzel', 'Acker', 'Wandern' are key words. One of his enthusiastic admirers, the Jewish critic Julius Bab, declared that Lissauer's poems had given Germany 'a new religiosity'.[358] When war broke out he surpassed himself with the immensely popular patriotic poem 'Haßgesang gegen England' ('Hymn of Hate against England'); the Emperor decorated him with the Order of the Red Eagle, second class. When the war went wrong, however, Lissauer's Jewishness received hostile comment, and he was accused of deliberately propagating the poem out of self-interest. He moved to Vienna in 1923, where he died. Stefan Zweig describes the incongruously endearing impression made by Lissauer in the flesh: 'there toddled into my room a round little man, a jolly face above a double double-chin, bubbling over with self-importance and exuberance, stuttering in his haste, and so possessed with poetry that nothing could keep him from citing

---

[357] Döblin, 'Drei Demokratien', *Schriften zur Politik und Gesellschaft* (Olten and Freiburg, 1972), p. 38.
[358] Quoted in Benno Diederich, 'Ernst Lissauer, ein Lyriker unserer Zeit', *Preußische Jahrbücher*, 157 (July-Sept. 1914), 193–224 (p. 194).

and reciting his verses again and again.'[359] The final stanza of the 'Haßgesang' may be offered as a piece of self-projection:

> Nimm du die Völker der Erde in Sold,
> Baue Wälle aus Barren von Gold,
> Bedecke die Meerflut mit Bug bei Bug,
> Du rechnetest klug, doch nicht klug genug.
> Was schiert uns Russe und Franzos'!
> Schuß wider Schuß und Stoß um Stoß.
> Wir kämpfen den Kampf mit Bronze und Stahl,
> Und schließen Frieden irgend einmal,
> Dich werden wir hassen mit langem Haß,
> Wir werden nicht lassen von unserm Haß,
> Haß zu Wasser und Haß zu Land,
> Haß des Hauptes und Haß der Hand,
> Haß der Hämmer und Haß der Kronen,
> Drosselnder Haß von siebzig Millionen,
> Sie lieben vereint, sie hassen vereint,
> Sie haben alle nur einen Feind:
> England.[360]

> Take the nations of the earth in fee,
> Pile up gold bars along the sea,
> Cover the ocean with prow on prow,
> For us your reckoning didn't allow!
> The Russians and French are far too slow,
> Shot against shot and blow for blow.
> We'll fight the good fight with bronze and steel,
> And we'll make peace when that's how we feel.
> We'll hate you with a lasting hate,
> We'll never abandon this our hate,
> Hate on the water and hate on the land,
> Hate of the head and hate of the hand,
> Hate of the crowns, the hammers' hate,
> Seventy millions' strangling hate,
> They hate together, and well they know,
> They all have only a single foe:
> England.

---

[359] Zweig, *The World of Yesterday*, p. 179.
[360] Lissauer, *Der brennende Tag: Ausgewählte Gedichte* (Jena, [1916]), pp. 40–2. For his later reflections, see 'Bemerkungen über mein Leben', *Bulletin des Leo Baeck Instituts*, 5/20 (1962), 286–301.

In accusing England of trying to control the world through money and cunning calculation, Lissauer is repeating a familiar stereotype, classically expressed in Werner Sombart's wartime pamphlet *Händler und Helden* (*Traders and Heroes*), of England as shallow, uncultured, commercial, and empirical.[361] But these of course are also stereotypes applied to Jews by antisemites, and the war therefore supplied Lissauer with an occasion to confirm his own Germanness by displacing antisemitic stereotypes onto the enemy. Döblin does the same in describing 'the Englishman' as 'one who sucks the nations dry, a parasite on alien blood'.[362]

The philosopher Hermann Cohen positively affirms nationalistic conceptions of German identity. Admittedly, he avoids Romantic nationalism by insisting that the abstract concept of the state cannot be grounded on the natural reality of the *Volk*: rather, the state is an overarching ethical entity which transcends particular, local identities and thus avoids the dangers of nationalism and racialism. The abstract idea of the state is mediated through a distinct national culture with its poetry and philosophy. Thus Adalbert von Chamisso, a Frenchman by birth, could become a German scientist and poet. Cohen fails to dissolve the tension between the ethical idea of the state as such and the particular character of a given national culture, which might imply different and discordant ethical values. He sidesteps the problem by identifying German national culture with the cosmopolitan humanism of the Enlightenment.[363] That is: nationalism is bad, but German nationalism is permissible because it is simultaneously internationalism. One implication of this argument is to delegitimate all other forms of national identity. For if German nationalism is cosmopolitan, all other national identities, being different from German, must be particular, parochial, and inferior, and unable to contest German claims to supranational status.

To make such claims for *Deutschtum*, Cohen has to give a highly selective answer to the perennial question 'what is German?' He notes with discomfort the anti-modern ideology of many contemporary Germans, but dismisses it as narrow, shallow, and not truly German.[364] It has been urged in Cohen's defence

361 Sombart, *Händler und Helden* (Munich and Leipzig, 1915).
362 Döblin, *Schriften zur Politik und Gesellschaft*, p. 21.
363 Cohen, *Ethik des reinen Willens*, 3rd edn. (Berlin, 1921), pp. 253–9.
364 Cohen, 'Vorrede zur zweiten Auflage (1907)', in *Ethik des reinen Willens*, p. x.

that his concept of true Germanness was not an empirical reality but a regulative idea in accordance with which reality should be judged and amended.[365] However, an idea termed 'Germanness' must have *some* empirical content. Cohen's attachment to German identity leads him, in fact, into the same difficulty encountered over a century earlier by Moses Mendelssohn in trying to reconcile his attachment to Judaism with his respect for universal values. If Judaism coincided with universalism, then what was still Jewish about it? Similarly, if for Cohen 'Germanness' means enlightened cosmopolitanism, then what is still German about it?

In 1915 Cohen undertook to support German war aims with his essay 'Deutschtum und Judentum'. Central to Cohen's conception of *Deutschtum* is idealist philosophy, whose high point is Kant. Cohen takes one's breath away by the coolness with which he identifies German idealist philosophy with modern science, on the grounds that the use of hypotheses is idealist. The only scientist named (apart from a passing reference to Newton) is the German Kepler. Alongside philosophy stands German religion. Cohen voices the 'cultural Protestantism' which was important to the intellectual underpinning of the German Empire.[366] He sees in Lutheran Protestantism a form of idealism, in which the search for moral certainty complements Kant's search for intellectual certainty. German music is also idealist, not only in its abstractness, but in its sublimity. Idealist morality accounts for the excellence of German lyric poetry, which is free from all sensuality, thanks to the influence of Luther's hymns; German *Gedankenlyrik* (poetry of ideas, best represented by Schiller) is of equal excellence.

All these achievements, according to Cohen, are close to the Jewish spirit: there is an inward affinity between *Deutschtum* and *Judentum*. It is wrong to consider Judaism merely legalistic: in the observance of the Mosaic law, duty should coincide with freedom, as in Kantian ethics. The Psalms were the crucial influence on Luther; and music has always been central to Jewish liturgy. Above all, the Jewish messianic spirit corresponds to the civilizing

---

[365] Steven S. Schwarzschild, '"Germanism and Judaism"—Hermann Cohen's Normative Paradigm of the German–Jewish Symbiosis', in David Bronsen (ed.), *Jews and Germans from 1860 to 1933: The Problematic Symbiosis* (Heidelberg, 1979), pp. 129–72.

[366] See Hammerstein, *Antisemitismus und deutsche Universitäten*, pp. 40–4.

mission to surmise the future of a world-wide mission; that in the German spirit we must recognize the *pedagogical spirit of the nations* (*Erziehungsgeist der Völker*), and, with all due sobriety and historical modesty, recognize our historical vocation as schoolmaster to the world.'[367]

This fantasy is interesting for what it suppresses. Cohen insists that German lyric poetry, inspired by Luther and the Psalms, is 'purified from all the ambiguities of eroticism'.[368] Cohen is suppressing the presence of Heine, the immoral, ironic German Jew, who in his *History of Religion and Philosophy in Germany* had disclosed the political programme underlying idealism, had reclaimed the rights of the senses, and had said that Germany's hidden religion was pantheism.[369] One of Cohen's sharpest critics, Jakob Klatzkin, pointed out that pantheism was far more characteristic of Germany than idealism.[370] Cohen was well aware of Heine. In an early essay on him, published anonymously in 1867, Cohen discusses his pantheism and tries to dilute its sensuality by redefining it as a pantheistic monotheism which is closely indebted to Spinoza.[371] By 1915, however, Heine could not be accommodated in Cohen's one-sided and chauvinistic construction of the German cultural tradition, except as having first formulated the analogy between the Jews and the German people in respect of their religiosity.[372]

Discussing the position of Jews in Germany, Cohen acknowledges in veiled language that their formal equality is accompanied by disfavour and hostility, but consoles himself by asserting that Jews actually have more rights in Germany than elsewhere, because their rights are not merely formal but proceed from their share in German morality.

I therefore venture, contrary to the universal prejudice, to assert that the Jews' rights are more deeply rooted in Germany than anywhere else.

[367] Cohen, 'Deutschtum und Judentum', in *Jüdische Schriften*, ii. 237–301 (p. 263).
[368] Ibid. 247.   [369] Heine, *Selected Prose*, p. 250.
[370] Klatzkin, 'Deutschtum und Judentum. Eine Besprechung', *Der Jude*, 2 (1917–18), iv. 245–52, v/vi. 358–70.
[371] Cohen, 'Heinrich Heine und das Judentum', in *Jüdische Schriften*, ii. 2–44 (p. 23).
[372] Ibid. 296. In another piece of war propaganda Cohen was willing to use 'the German poet Heinrich Heine' as bait to appeal to the Jews of America: '"Du sollst nicht einhergehen als ein Verleumder". Ein Appell an die Juden Amerikas', *Jüdische Schriften*, ii. 230.

Everywhere else in the world the Jews may have a larger share in political rights and administrative offices: we German Jews strive for this participation on the basis of our inwardly assured participation in German morality, German religiosity. Hence our path to liberation may be harder and more uneven, because it is linked with the variations in social feeling; but it is historically and culturally more deeply rooted. Hence the limited rights we enjoy as Jews in Germany are of more value for our religious survival than the seemingly absolute civil equality enjoyed by Jews abroad.[373]

In this uncritical acceptance even of German prejudice, there is a hint of masochism which fits also with Cohen's eager identification with Germany's supposed mission to dominate the world. Whatever the shortcomings of Enlightenment universalism, it was surely far preferable to the chauvinism espoused here by a well-intentioned, high-minded, and fatefully gullible intellectual.

A subtler response came from the Zionist Martin Buber. Believing in a German–Jewish symbiosis, and sharing the mood of pro-War solidarity, he thought this mood could be a model for the Jewish community of the future. In a speech delivered in late 1914 and printed in his editorial to the first issue of *Der Jude* in 1916, Buber said that the War had taught the 'atomized' Western Jews a sense of community: 'In the storm of the events the Jew has learnt with elemental force what community is.'[374] Buber neither criticizes nor affirms the war as such, but treats it as an occasion for the individual to rediscover the greater life of the community. The rootless modern Jew could, in Buber's organic imagery, once again put down roots in the soil of the community. Buber's hyper-acculturation is apparent, not in chauvinism, but in his acceptance of the widespread German understanding of the war as something elemental (rather than, say, political). Similarly, a very different writer, Ernst Jünger, was to celebrate it retrospectively as an 'invasion of the elemental'.[375] Buber and Jünger illustrate the long-standing German tendency to dismiss politics as shallow by comparison with deep, archetypal, elemental forces.

After the War, some German Jews joined paramilitary troops. The CV, defending German Jews against imputations of cowardice, said that many Jews had lost their lives defending

[373] Cohen, 'Deutschtum und Judentum', p. 280.
[374] Buber, *Die jüdische Bewegung*, ii. 9.
[375] Jünger, *Der Arbeiter*, in *Sämtliche Werke* (Stuttgart, 1979–83), II. viii. 52.

Deutschtum in Upper Silesia, instancing Rudolf Haase, who was shot by Polish insurgents at the age of 15, and Herbert Cohn, who was killed at the storming of the Annaberg fortress.[376] Some were reluctant to forfeit the wartime experience of military solidarity. On 15 December 1919 the *B.Z. (Berliner Zeitung) am Mittag* reported the suicide of Maximilian Späth, a Munich Jew, who had volunteered for army service in 1914 and been decorated for courage, he was a member of the student society 'Frohe Garde' which suddenly decided to expel its Jewish members, whereupon Späth promptly shot himself. His testament runs in part:

As a German by birth, outlook, feeling and upbringing, I was pained to the depths of my soul by seeing how ominously the spiritual growth of my fellow-nationals (*das geistige Werden meiner Volksgenossen*) is developing. [. . .] Since at present I have no opportunity to purify my honour, which has been trampled upon and betrayed by all my friends, with sword in hand as befits a cavalier, since military courts of honour no longer exist and academic corporations forbid me as a Jew to defend myself in arms, in short, since I am denied the right of satisfaction, every decent person will find it understandable and will not declare me insane if I take the only path that is open to me. I do not wish to become a criminal or to give way to base vindictiveness. Hence nothing remains for me but to have it recorded by my death that a German of Jewish birth, who believes that throughout his life he has striven only for the high ideals of the best humanity and nationhood, despite his faults and failings, can also be a person of honour and decency.[377]

One of the saddest features of this story is that by constructing a militaristic and nationalistic self-image, Späth was revealing, not what might be considered manly independence, but a childish lack of self-reliance that left him helplessly dependent on the reference group represented by the student society and the army.

A number of German Jews devoted themselves to the political Right, not realizing that they were bound ultimately to be rejected because of their Jewish ancestry. Notorious examples include Otto Lubarsch, a distinguished professor of medicine at Berlin, who was of Jewish descent but helped to found the Pan-German League in 1890 and ended by approving of National Socialism and even of

---

[376] *Anti-Anti: Tatsachen zur Judenfrage*, ed. by the Centralverein deutscher Staatsbürger jüd. Glaubens (Berlin, n.d. [1932]), p. 11b.

[377] Quoted in Oppeln-Bronikowski, *Antisemitismus?*, p. 53.

its antisemitism;[378] and Max Naumann, head of the Verband nationaldeutscher Juden (founded in 1921 with some 3,000 members), who insisted that profoundly German Jews like himself, rooted in the German soil, were not to be classed with assimilators, still less with greasy, money-grubbing 'Ostjuden': 'Can one mention us in the same breath as Eastern Jews who arrived in Germany one day, cut off their side-locks, greased their hair, seized the economic boom and became company directors, art critics or composers of popular songs?'[379] While denouncing Zionism as a racist ideology, Naumann in 1932 personally endorsed Hitler's National Socialist Party as the only political organization that could bring about a 'rebirth of Germandom', and urged liberal Jews to ignore the 'regrettable side-effects' of Nazi antisemitism.[380] In *Dritte Walpurgisnacht*, Karl Kraus chides Naumann and other 'nationaldeutsche Juden' for subservience to the Nazis. The utterances he quotes (e.g. K xii. 100) could be called bootlicking, except that, as Kraus notes, Jews in concentration camps had literally to lick their persecutors' boots (K xii. 74).

A few Jews tried to make common cause with the Nazis. The Young Jewish movement, founded in 1930, appealed to Hitler in 1932 to allow the Jewish 'Volksstand' to be represented in Germany by its own political bodies, schools, and university.[381] Since it had only thirty members, however, the movement may be dismissed as eccentric. It is not so easy to dismiss the theologian and historian Hans-Joachim Schoeps, well known in post-1945 Germany for his studies of Prussian history. He was an authoritarian conservative whose real allegiance was to the Hohenzollerns and who regretted even the incorporation of Prussia into a united Germany.[382] In spring 1933 Schoeps composed a memorandum

---

[378] See Jens Malte Fischer, 'Identifikation mit dem Aggressor? Zur Problematik des jüdischen Selbsthasses um 1900', *Menora*, 3 (1992), 23–48; Pulzer, *Jews and the German State*, p. 238.

[379] Naumann, 'Der Weg zum Deutschtum', *Der Jud ist schuld . . . ?*, pp. 303–8 (p. 307).

[380] Quoted in Carl J. Rheins, 'The Verband nationaldeutscher Juden 1921–1933', *LBY* 25 (1980), 243–68.

[381] Karl Lieblich, *Was geschieht mit den Juden? Öffentliche Frage an Adolf Hitler* (Stuttgart, 1932).

[382] See Schoeps, *Ja—Nein—und Trotzdem. Erinnerungen—Begegnungen— Erfahrungen* (Mainz, 1974), pp. 28–31.

('Denkschrift') urging that once Zionists and 'Ostjuden' had emigrated, the long-established German Jews should be recognized as a corporation and integrated into the new social order. He contributed to an official Nazi publication, assuring the world that the maltreatment of Jews was a lie spread by 'Ostjuden' and Socialists.[383] He unsuccessfully sought an interview with Hitler, counting on his psychological skill to cure the Führer's obsessive antisemitism. However, the Night of the Long Knives showed him what was really wrong with the Nazis—they were vulgar: 'I rejected the Nazis not only because they were antisemites, but still more because they were proletarians run wild; that offended my political instincts.'[384] At the end of February 1933 Schoeps founded the Deutscher Vortrupp (German Vanguard), which had no more than 150 members, mostly university students, with (he records proudly) no intellectuals. Their real adversaries were other Jewish organizations. Schoeps attacked the Jüdischer Kulturbund for asserting a Jewish cultural identity which, in the Vortrupp's view, did not exist, and he denounced even Naumann's Verband nationaldeutscher Juden as a repulsive variant of assimilationism. Schoeps was arrested and interrogated at length by the Gestapo, but managed to escape to Sweden in December 1938. His parents perished in concentration camps. Schoeps's attitude to Germany took power-worship to the point of masochism. His pamphlet of June 1934, 'We German Jews', ends with such masochistic declarations as: 'We German Jews do not want our own happiness, but the happiness of our fatherland is our happiness. We do not seek to be free, but to be bound.'[385]

Schoeps did not suffer for his folly, unlike Paul Nikolaus Cossmann, a Catholic convert and founder editor of the *Süddeutsche Monatshefte*. A strong supporter of German nation-

---

[383] *Die Greuelpropaganda ist eine Lügenpropaganda sagen die deutschen Juden selbst* (Berlin-Charlottenburg, 1933), p. 27.

[384] Schoeps, *'Bereit für Deutschland!' Der Patriotismus deutscher Juden und der Nationalsozialismus. Frühe Schriften 1930 bis 1939* (Berlin, 1970), p. 19. See Carl J. Rheins, 'Deutscher Vortrupp, Gefolgschaft deutscher Juden 1933–1935', *LBY* 26 (1981), 207–29.

[385] Schoeps, *'Bereit für Deutschland!'*, p. 225. See now the account of Schoeps by John Dippel, *Bound upon a Wheel of Fire: Why So Many German Jews Made the Tragic Decision to Remain in Nazi Germany* (New York, 1996); and the review of the German translation of Dippel's book by Schoeps' son, the distinguished historian Julius H. Schoeps, in *Die Zeit* (17 October 1997), p. 37.

alism, in 1914 he turned the *Süddeutsche Monatshefte* into a political journal dedicated to supporting Germany's cause. In a notable editorial, he described the Versailles Treaty as a betrayal of German heroes by profiteers which would lead the Germans into slavery, an attempt to secure Germany's existence at the expense of her honour, and as 'das Geschäft des Judas mit den Juden'.[386] Though he admitted that it was wrong to blame all Germany's misfortunes on the Jews, he nevertheless claimed that the internal enemies of the German idea (the Socialists) had gained leaders among Jewish lawyers, money from Jewish capitalists, and propaganda support from the Jewish press. All these had contributed to the stab in the back that had laid Germany low. Despite his hostility to the Weimar Republic, Cossmann also opposed Hitler, since he did not want a right-wing revolution but a conservative restoration, and feared Hitler's personal lust for power. In 1933 he was arrested and imprisoned for more than a year. From 1935 to 1941 he lived in seclusion in Bavaria, but in 1941 he was compelled to go to the Munich ghetto in Berg am Laim, and in 1942 was transported to Theresienstadt, where he died. As no provision was made for converts, he was buried according to Jewish ritual: surely the final irony.

It is easy to look back sceptically at the hyperacculturation that reaches its extreme in the wilful blindness of Schoeps and Cossmann, and salutary, therefore, to turn to a work of literature which, though no masterpiece, does explore sympathetically the tragic ironies and the undeniable dignity in the situation of the Jew who identified with Germany. Friedrich Wolf's *Professor Mamlock* (1934), first performed in Yiddish in Warsaw, was the most famous of all exile dramas. The characters are mostly wooden, but Wolf keeps them in rapid motion with surprising interventions and dramatic confrontations. The exposition tells us that the surgeon Professor Hans Mamlock served throughout the War and was awarded the Iron Cross for bravery in the battle of the Somme. His colleagues praise his iron sense of duty as 'positively Prussian'.[387] His wife is non-Jewish ('née Gildemeister', a

---

[386] Cossmann, 'Der "Friede"', *Süddeutsche Monatshefte*, 16 (1918–19), x. 245–58 (p. 253). See Wolfram Selig, *Paul Nikolaus Cossmann und die 'Süddeutschen Monatshefte' von 1914–1918* (Osnabrück, 1967).

[387] Wolf, *Professor Mamlock*, in *Gesammelte Werke*, ed. Else Wolf and Walter Pollatschek, 13 vols. (Berlin, 1960), iii. 295–365 (p. 298). Page references in text.

stage-direction informs us, p. 309). He works for the re-election of
Hindenburg as President, but opposes racism and demands that
politics be kept out of his clinic. About politics he is naïve and
gullible, thinking it must be true that the Reichstag was set on fire
by a Communist, because the official account says so. The heroic
Communism of his son Rolf and of the underground activist
Ernst, who maintain that Nazism is a class question, is part of
Wolf's implausible uplifting message: Rolf maintains: 'And even if
we perish by thousands and tens of thousands, new people will
emerge, we are only the beginning' (p. 347). After the boycott of
Jewish shops and offices of 1 April 1933, Mamlock insists on
going to his clinic: 'I'm going on duty', he says ('ich gehe zu
meinem Dienst', p. 324); he is beaten up and has a placard marked
'Jew' put round his neck. The following day he is allowed to
return, because he has served in the front line, but falls out with
his Nazi assistant, receives almost no support from his colleagues,
and commits suicide.

Having broken with Rolf because of the latter's Communism,
Mamlock is denounced by his wife for Jewish intellectualism: 'I
know this cold absoluteness that calls itself consistency, these
lifeless slogans, these icy antitheses, all this heartless fanaticism
of yours [. . .] brain, brain, brain, but that is the inheritance of
your race!' (p. 320). Ironically, this cold fanaticism is in fact
exhibited by the Nazis, and Mamlock's sense of duty is contrasted
with the irresponsibility of his non-Jewish associates who
abandon their duties at the clinic in order to pursue Party activities. The only person who does support him is Dr Inge Ruoff,
initially a fanatical Nazi, apparently humanized by sympathy for
Rolf Mamlock; she finds the behaviour of the Nazi doctor
Hellpach, Mamlock's opponent, contrary to Nazi ideals of
upright, soldierly conduct. (As a woman, she is a parallel figure
to Mamlock the Jew.) The play proclaims the anti-essentialist
message that the Jew Mamlock embodies the German ideals of
courage and service which the Nazis betray, and hence that moral
ideals are not the property of any one race (or sex). Wolf declares a
belief in individualism, especially through Mamlock's speech on
the importance of the individual and his beliefs:

MAMLOCK: There will never be a time when a person ceases to have
   his thoughts, *his* doubts, his own belief. There is no building that

consists of a single stone; there is no state that does not consist of people, heads, hearts! Like the arches and cross-beams that connect a great building, so the ideas of justice, humanity, intellectual freedom and intellectual courage are the scaffolding that connects us! (pp. 354–5)

Wolf's play is undermined, however, by the discrepancy between his Communist ideals and his dramatic techniques. His explicit individualism is in conflict both with his personal commitment to Communism and with the doctrine, espoused in the play by Rolf, that the individual is dispensable. More seriously, Wolf was no Brecht: he did not rethink the representation of character in drama, and therefore his anti-essentialist message is in conflict with his method of characterization, which relies on the very stereotyping that he explicitly opposes. It is surprising that Mamlock so suddenly comes to accept his labelling as a Jew ('we Jews', p. 341): this volte-face illustrates Wolf's carelessness about motivating his characters, as does Inge Ruoff's change of heart. These changes can only seem plausible by recourse to stereotyped assumptions about how Jews and women always behave. Thus the demands of the plot, which help to make this a stageworthy play, contradict the beliefs about personality which Wolf wishes to put forward.

Friendship

While the militarism of German Jews often suggests a streak of masochism, more complex emotional exchanges underlie some real and fictional instances of friendship between Jewish and non-Jewish Germans. Such cases support Isaiah Berlin's observation that 'those who belong to minorities which are to some degree excluded from participation in the central life of their community' are liable to regard the dominant majority with 'over-intense admiration or indeed worship'.[388] A classic literary expression of such an unequal relationship, in which intense admiration is met with good-natured indifference, is Thomas Mann's *Tonio Kröger*, with its leitmotif 'zu sein wie du!' ('If only I could be

---

[388] Berlin, 'Benjamin Disraeli, Karl Marx and the Search for Identity', in his *Against the Current: Essays in the History of Ideas*, ed. Henry Hardy (Oxford, 1981), pp. 252–86.

like you!'); another is the relation between Proust's narrator and aristocrats like the Guermantes and Robert de Saint-Loup. Additional pain, however, comes when a Jew is shown yearning to be like the Gentiles. Theodor Herzl presents a fictional German–Jewish friendship in his play *Das neue Ghetto*. His noble hero Jakob Samuel is fatefully lured from the ghetto not only by the sense of social responsibility which makes him adopt the cause of the miners, but by his friendship with the Gentile Wurzlechner. To have a Gentile friend is a powerful symbol of social acceptance. Hence Jakob's feeling of betrayal after Wurzlechner formally breaks off relations:

He was not only a friend to me, but also the 'Christian fellow-citizen' who was glad to have dealings with me. It was so flattering—after all, we still have a bit of the ghetto in ourselves. Gratitude, when we're treated like other people. I wanted to show him gratitude by modelling myself on him, assuming his habits, as far as I could, speaking his language, thinking his thoughts . . . And he's dropped me, he's simply dropped me. (*ZW* v. 52)

He feels as though rejected by a lover. His attachment to Wurzlechner is far stronger than his merely conventional affection for his wife. Their friendship is, however, restored when Wurzlechner acts as Jakob's second in his fatal duel with Schramm. Thus while one Gentile man appears as Jakob's antagonist, challenging his acculturation, the other appears as his principal love-object and witness to the acculturation which Jakob can only demonstrate by his death.[389]

Biographical documents suggest a whole series of ill-requited attachments between Jews and Germans in real life. An eighteenth-century example is the sad relationship, based on mutual misunderstanding, between the Berlin physician and philosopher Marcus Herz and his mentor Kant. Herz corresponded with Kant throughout the 1770s, looked after Kant's students when they visited Berlin, and mediated between Kant and Mendelssohn. Their relations cooled in the late 1770s; Kant did not read the books Herz sent him, and was slow to answer his pathetic letters. When the *Critiques* appeared, Herz confessed himself unable to understand or assimilate Kant's

---

[389] For an excellent post-War treatment of such a relationship, see Fred Uhlman, *Reunion* (Glasgow, 1971).

philosophy. In his account of their relationship, Martin L. Davies concludes that 'Herz seems never to have been able to emancipate himself from his own perception of himself as Kant's pupil' and sees in his letters to Kant 'a form of existential security that turned out to be largely an act of self-deception'.[390]

Masochism was also displayed in the relationship between Theodor Lessing and Ludwig Klages, which provides the over-arching narrative of the former's autobiography. Lessing's child-hood was rendered miserable by the tyranny of his self-centred father, who would inflict humiliating punishments for trifling offences. A sickly, bookish child, Lessing overcompensated by an intense identification with German nationalism and a close friend-ship with Klages, a fellow-schoolboy who also had literary ambitions. Together they devoured the works of the nationalist writer Wilhelm Jordan, who wrote a modern version of the *Nibe-lungenlied* and urged Germans to model themselves on primitive Germanic heroes. Klages advised Lessing to struggle against his 'inborn racial soul'.[391] Their conversations, as Lessing records them, thematized the supposed differences between Germans and Jews: Klages defined himself as an idealist and 'Blutmensch' (sanguinary type), while Lessing was a materialist and 'Nerven-mensch' (nervous type); Klages would humorously denounce the Bible, Lessing the Edda.[392] Thus their friendship did not erase but emphasized German–Jewish differences. As a medical student, he moved to Munich in 1894 to be nearer to Klages, but he could not share Klages' devotion to Stefan George. Under the influence of Alfred Schuler, however, with whom he formed a literary group called the 'Kosmiker' ('Cosmics'), Klages was becoming increas-ingly antisemitic: they developed a mystical vitalism that was accessible only to non-Jews and that no doubt anticipated the irrationalism later proclaimed in Klages' well-known treatise *Der Geist als Widersacher der Seele* (*The Spirit as Adversary of the Soul*, 1929). The breach between Lessing and Klages was connected with the antipathy between Klages and Lessing's wife Maria. Klages wrote Lessing a formal letter requesting that they

---

[390] Davies, *Identity or History?*, p. 40.
[391] Lessing, *Einmal und nie wieder*, pp. 186–9. See Lawrence Baron, 'Theodor Lessing: Between Jewish Self-Hatred and Zionism', *LBY* 26 (1981), 323–40; Rainer Marwedel, *Theodor Lessing 1872–1933: Eine Biographie* (Darmstadt and Neuwied, 1987). [392] Lessing, *Einmal und nie wieder*, pp. 187, 189.

should part. Lessing called on Klages and told him that a necessary parting did not mean they had to be enemies, whereupon Klages burst out: 'You are a loathsome, pushy Jew'.[393] Writing his autobiography many years later, Lessing seems never to have got over their estrangement: he still identifies Klages with Germany, associating him with the North German landscape and apostrophizing him: 'You with your defiant blonde head! You young birch-tree![394]

Houston Stewart Chamberlain represented a Germanic ideal for notorious self-hating Jews in Vienna: not only Otto Weininger but also the semi-insane Arthur Trebitsch. This relationship was more complicated, for Chamberlain, born in England, was an adoptive German who served to convince Trebitsch that he, though a Jew, could also become a German. Trebitsch considered Chamberlain 'the model of a true intellectual German', and a philosopher who provided 'the transition from Kant to myself'; he reproduced portraits of himself and Chamberlain to show how strikingly they resembled each other (in fact they are not at all similar).[395] It is perhaps not surprising that Trebitsch's megalomania went along with paranoid terror which led to his enforced confinement in a sanatorium, nor that soon afterwards he helped to finance Hitler's newly founded National Socialist Party. Hitler's associate Dietrich Eckart recalled that Trebitsch was constantly saying 'We Aryans'.[396]

A still more complex relationship, involving emotional dependence on a favourite who had to remain obedient, existed between Freud and Jung. For Freud it was important to have his ideas confirmed by a Gentile, and he sought confirmation most ardently from Jung. Jung was his 'son and heir', his 'eldest son' and 'Crown Prince', the Joshua to his Moses.[397] Yet after the final breach, marked by Jung's resignation from the presidency of the International Psychoanalytic Association in 1914, Freud expressed satisfaction at being rid of 'the brutal, sanctimonious Jung', and complained of Jung's 'lies, brutality and anti-Semitic condescen-

---

[393] Lessing, 382–3.   [394] Ibid. 172.

[395] Trebitsch, *Geist und Judentum*, p. 195; *Die Geschichte meines 'Verfolgungswahns'* (Vienna and Leipzig, 1923), p. 152.   [396] Hamann, *Hitlers Wien*, p. 332.

[397] Jones, *Freud*, ii. 37; *The Freud/Jung Letters: The Correspondence between Sigmund Freud and C. G. Jung*, ed. William McGuire, tr. Ralph Manheim and R. F. C. Hull (London, 1974), p. 218 (16 Apr. 1909); ibid. 196–7 (17 Jan. 1909).

sion toward me'.[398] While their friendship lasted, its fragility was revealed by Freud's excessive reactions to what seem minor annoyances. He twice fainted in Jung's presence: first in Bremen in 1909, after Jung had been holding forth about prehistoric cemeteries, and again in Munich in 1912, after reproaching Jung for publishing articles about psychoanalysis without mentioning Freud's name. On both occasions Freud thought Jung's behaviour revealed an unconscious desire for Freud's death.[399] Jung, in a rawly aggressive letter, rebuked Freud for treating his followers like patients and children (a revealing equation), thus producing 'slavish sons or impudent puppies' who had to 'blushingly admit the existence of their faults' but dared not 'pluck the prophet by the beard'.[400] Freud had tactical reasons for offering his succession to a non-Jew so that psychoanalysis should not be 'a Jewish national affair'.[401] But he was controlled by alarmingly powerful emotions. After Jung's defection, Freud portrayed himself as a rationalist Jew opposed to an incorrigibly religious Gentile whose 'religious-ethical "crisis"' revealed his innate 'Aryan religiosity'.[402] He thus conceded that their emotional division ran along the Jewish–Gentile fault-line.

Similarly, one may wonder about the relationship between Walter Benjamin and Bertolt Brecht. Was the fastidious, bookish critic attracted to Brecht, with his hard-boiled manner and proletarian affectations, in part by the desire to be taken seriously by a non-Jew? As early as 1930, Benjamin's friends were worried about what Siegfried Kracauer called his 'slavishly masochistic attitude to Brecht'.[403] In the records of his visits to Brecht in Danish exile between 1934 and 1938, Benjamin is markedly submissive, though he suspects that he somehow brings out Brecht's 'demagogic attitude of thought'.[404] This attitude is apparent when

---

[398] Letter to Abraham, 26 July 1914, in *A Psycho-Analytic Dialogue*, p. 186; letter to J. J. Putnam, 8 July 1915, quoted in Gay, *Freud*, pp. 241–2.

[399] Jones, *Freud*, i. 348, ii. 165–6.

[400] Jung, *The Freud/Jung Letters*, pp. 534–5 (18 Dec. 1912).

[401] Letter to Abraham, 3 May 1908, in *A Psycho-Analytic Dialogue*, p. 34.

[402] Quoted in Gay, *Freud*, 241–2; Jones, *Freud*, ii. 353.

[403] Letter quoted in Scholem, *Walter Benjamin*, p. 205. Kracauer also referred to Brecht as Benjamin's 'God': see Martin Jay, *Permanent Exiles: Essays on the Intellectual Migration from Germany to America* (New York, 1985), p. 296; and cf. Richard Wolin, *Walter Benjamin: An Aesthetic of Redemption* (New York, 1982), pp. 140–1.

[404] Benjamin, *Versuche über Brecht*, ed. Rolf Tiedemann (Frankfurt, 1978), p. 161.

Brecht charges Benjamin with promoting 'Jewish fascism' by his essay on Kafka, or dismisses Dostoevsky, whom Benjamin admired, as rubbish.[405] Benjamin responded by heaping praise even on such an inferior work as Brecht's *Threepenny Novel*. The connoisseur of Kafka and Proust treated Brecht's dullest truisms as dialectical subtleties and rated his novel far above Dostoevsky.[406] And while Benjamin had formerly delighted in a magical conception of language derived from Jewish mysticism, he now praised Brecht's functional, colourless language for being 'purified from all magic'.[407] But no matter how hard Benjamin tried to prove himself a Marxist, his essay 'The Work of Art in the Age of Mechanical Reproduction' irritated Brecht by adapting 'the materialistic conception of history' in a 'pretty horrible' form, and while respecting his 'Theses on the Philosophy of History' Brecht deplored their 'metaphors and Judaisms'.[408]

These examples of the Jew's hopeless, masochistic love for the strong, unattainable Gentile are all from relationships between men. What about heterosexual relationships? Hannah Arendt was briefly the lover of her teacher Martin Heidegger, and, despite his support for Nazism, for many years she remained attached to him, supervising the English translations of his works, though with only occasional responses from him. The 'spell' he cast over her awaits thorough investigation.[409]

More fully documented is the spell cast on Kafka by the Gentile Milena Jesenská, with whom he conducted an intense relationship, largely by correspondence, in 1920. Jesenská, a well-educated and independent-minded young woman, was beginning to forge a career as a journalist and asked Kafka if she could translate some of his works into Czech. Reacting against her antisemitic, conservatively nationalist father, Milena was drawn to outsiders, like her Jewish husband Ernst Polak, the converted Jew Hermann Broch with whom she had a brief affair in 1918, and the aristocratic Communist Franz Xaver Schaffgotsch with

[405] Benjamin, 158, 162.
[406] Benjamin, 'Brechts Dreigroschenroman', ibid. 54–63 (esp. p. 61).
[407] Scholem, *Walter Benjamin*, p. 258.
[408] Brecht, *Arbeitsjournal*, ed. Werner Hecht, 2 vols. (Frankfurt, 1973), i. 16, 294.
[409] See Elzbieta Ettinger, *Hannah Arendt, Martin Heidegger* (New Haven and London, 1995) (not the last word on the subject), and the review by George Steiner, *TLS* (13 Oct. 1995), 3–4.

whom she began a relationship late in 1920. Crossing the Gentile–Jewish divide was not a problem for her, but it was for Kafka, who warns her against Jews like himself early in the correspondence and, more obsessively, after their happy few days together in Vienna (29 June to 4 July 1920) made their relationship look more serious. Kafka professes amazement that a 'pure' girl, whom he compares to the Maid of Orleans, should not be afraid of Jews.[410] 'Pure' suggests the racial purity of a territorial nation: later Kafka contrasts Milena's possession of a home, which she is free to discard, with the homelessness of his Jewish friend Max Brod (p. 164). 'Pure' implies also that the Jew's sexuality is impure, and Kafka develops this later in his morbid association of sex, Jewishness, and filth. Describing his first sexual experience with a shop assistant, Kafka tells how his recurrent (and probably quite harmless) desire for a trivially disgusting experience made him like the Wandering Jew, 'wandering senselessly through a senseless filthy world' (p. 198). Here as Elizabeth Boa points out, 'sexual and racial self-disgust mix'.[411] Kafka's aversion to physical sex makes him compare Milena to a Medusa's head and himself to a naughty child confronting its mother. He represents his relationship to her as one of helpless dependency, like Samson's upon Delilah (p. 253). The self-disgust of the letters is heightened latterly by Kafka's experience of antisemitic riots in Prague.[412] Above all, he stresses his insecurity as a Western Jew. Jews are surrounded by threats, real or imaginary: 'From the most unlikely sides the Jews are threatened by dangers, or let's leave out the dangers and say: "threatened by threats"' (p. 26). He represents this insecurity at its most extreme:

We both know plenty of characteristic examples of Western Jews; I am, so far as I know, the most Western Jewish of them; that means, to put it too strongly, that I am not given a single quiet second, I am not given anything, I have to obtain everything, not only the present and future, but also the past. (p. 294)

By contrast, he describes enthusiastically the party of Eastern

---

[410] Kafka, *Briefe an Milena*, ed. Jürgen Born and Michael Müller (Frankfurt, 1983), p. 25. Future references in text. [411] Boa, *Kafka*, p. 93. [412] See Christoph Stölzl, *Kafkas böses Böhmen: Zur Sozialgeschichte eines Prager Juden* (Munich, 1975), p. 99.

Jewish emigrants he has seen at a railway station: 'if I had been given the choice of being whatever I wanted, I'd have wished to be a little Eastern Jewish boy in a corner of the room, without a care in the world' (p. 258). The wish to be a little boy is as significant as the wish to be an Eastern Jew.

After Milena ended the relationship in January 1921, they exchanged occasional further letters. In 1923 Milena published an article on the difficulty of marriage, entitled 'The Devil at the Hearth', arguing that living together was more difficult than living alone, and that couples should make realistic promises about the supposedly superficial details of everyday life.[413] Kafka interpreted her article as the product of a marriage between a moribund Judaism and an angel that promised to rescue it at the last minute. Rewriting part of the essay as dialogue, Kafka puts the objections to marriage into the mouth of 'Judaism', and attributes the proposals for improving it to the angel; but the devil on the hearth sees to it that the angel cannot rescue 'Judaism':

The angel keeps dragging Judaism aloft to the place where it must put up resistance, and Judaism keeps falling back and the angel must fall back too if he is not to let it sink down completely. And neither of the two can be blamed, both are what they are, one Jewish, the other angelic. (p. 310)

Kafka thus rewrites Milena's article as an allegory of the impossibility of Gentile–Jewish intermarriage. The Jew is assigned to the devil who will always frustrate the efforts of the angel to bear him aloft to realms of Gentile purity. There is a disturbing resemblance to the contemporary novels of Bahr, Bartsch, and even Dinter which likewise warned against marriages between Gentiles and Jews.

A subtle fictional counterpart to these masochistic relationships occurs in Lion Feuchtwanger's panoramic novel *Erfolg* (*Success*, 1930). Feuchtwanger's father, who came (like Wassermann) from the ancient Jewish community at Fürth, was an Orthodox Jew of scholarly inclinations who reluctantly took over the family's soap-boiling and margarine-manufacturing business. Lion Feuchtwanger rejected Jewish ceremonial and

---

[413] A long extract is quoted in Mary Hockaday, *Kafka, Love and Courage: The Life of Milena Jesenská* (London, 1995), pp. 97–9.

moved among Munich's bohemians as a left-leaning but non-revolutionary intellectual.[414] His detachment is expressed in his doctoral dissertation on Heine's historical novel *Der Rabbi von Bacherach*, where his identification with Heine's distanced interest in Jewish history prepared him to write his own historical novel, *Jud Süß* (1925). Having begun with a historical novel, Feuchtwanger, like Tolstoy and Fontane, was able to transfer his panoramic technique to the present. *Erfolg*, supposedly written from a detached standpoint a century into the future, surveys Munich in the years 1921–4, leading up to the failed putsch by Hitler, here portrayed as 'Rupert Kutzner', head of the 'Wahrhaft Deutsche' (True Germans). Feuchtwanger skilfully interweaves public and private destinies, especially with his main Jewish character, the lawyer Dr Siegbert Geyer. Dr Geyer has an illegitimate son by a Christian woman. The son, Erich Bonhaak, despises his father, occasionally accepts money from him or exploits him for political purposes, and is a leading figure among the True Germans. Dr Geyer is helplessly devoted to him and even defends a Nazi in court at Erich's request. Erich meanwhile dislikes the idea that his father is a Jew, though he himself is blonde and blue-eyed, and illogically denies his paternity: 'He was fresh, bold, a delight to the eyes of men and women. He surely belonged to the master race that erected the high civilization of the world. The wriggling, hysterical Geyer could not possibly be his father. He fervently despised the old fellow whom his mother had swindled with good Nordic cunning.'[415] Here Erich ascribes to his mother the cunning usually attributed—for example, at the end of Mann's *Wälsungenblut*—to the Jews. When Erich is killed in the failed Munich putsch of 1924, his father mourns, tears his clothing, and speaks Hebrew prayers. For venturing to appear at Erich's funeral he is assaulted by the True Germans. Thereafter he is a broken man.

Here Feuchtwanger has written a small allegory of the relations between Jews and Germans: Germans derive from Jews (from Judaeo-Christian civilization) but do not want to admit it; Jews apprehend German irrationality and injustice, thanks to logic and reason, but are also emotionally dependent on

---

[414] See Lothar Kahn, *Insight and Action: The Life and Work of Lion Feuchtwanger* (Cranbury, NJ, 1975).   [415] Feuchtwanger, *Erfolg* (Frankfurt, 1975), p. 542.

Germans; in fact, they need Germans to supply their own emotional strength. It is a fictional example of the Jewish need for Gentile approval.

These relationships were significantly unbalanced. In the same period, however, there existed a larger network whose members believed in 'the myth of a German–Jewish elective affinity'[416] the circle surrounding the poet Stefan George.

Stefan George was editor of an exclusive journal of the *fin de siècle*, *Blätter für die Kunst*. It came to be the focus for George's circle of younger men with literary interests and, in some cases, considerable poetic or critical talents.[417] They looked up to George as a divinely inspired prophet and considered themselves his disciples. In keeping with the strongly ritual character of his poetry, George often appeared in a black costume like a priest's, and subjected his followers to a severe initiation ritual in which they had to read poetry aloud to his satisfaction. The circle had many features of the *Männerbund* or male group which, in diverse forms, was widespread in early twentieth-century Germany.[418] George called them a 'new nobility' who were 'reshaped, reborn' under his quasi-paternal rule so that from them he might choose his 'lords of the world'.[419] Despite George's authoritarianism, many testimonies agree that the atmosphere within the circle was often informal and humorous.[420] Any member who became engaged, however, incurred the disapproval of the Master and moved to the margins of the group.

A striking proportion of George's admirers, both among his immediate disciples and in their larger penumbra, were of Jewish descent. The thirty-five German contributors to the *Blätter für die Kunst* (which also printed many translations) included seventeen Jews.[421] Among George's close associates were the Jews Friedrich

---

[416] Thomas Sparr, '"Verkannte Brüder". Jüdische George-Rezeption', in Schrader, Simon, and Wardi (eds.), *The Jewish Self-Portrait*, pp. 45–53 (p. 47).

[417] See the (too harshly critical) analysis by the sociologist Stefan Breuer, *Ästhetischer Fundamentalismus: Stefan George und der deutsche Antimodernismus* (Darmstadt, 1995).

[418] Hansjürgen Linke, *Das Kultische in der Dichtung Stefan Georges und seiner Schule*, 2 vols. (Munich and Düsseldorf, 1960), i. 155. See Bernd Widdig, *Männerbünde und Massen: Zur Krise männlicher Identität in der Literatur der Moderne* (Opladen, 1992).

[419] See the poems 'Dies ist reich des Geistes' and 'Neuer adel den ihr suchet', in George, *Werke*, i. 382–3.   [420] Linke, *Das Kultische*, i. 149.

[421] Sparr, '"Verkannte Brüder"', p. 47.

Gundolf, Karl Wolfskehl, Richard Perls, Ernst Morwitz, Berthold Vallentin, and his publisher Georg Bondi. The wider circle of his admirers included Georg Simmel, Margarete Susman, Edith Landmann, Kurt Singer, Erich von Kahler, Ernst Kantorowicz, Werner Kraft, and Walter Benjamin. Some remarkably impassioned tributes come from his Jewish devotees. Edith Landmann, his Boswell, declared that the sight of George taught her what the divine was.[422] The Plato scholar Kurt Singer expressed his conviction that 'today nobody embodies the divine more purely and creatively than George—no, that is not enough: the knot of the age and of renewal is tied in George.'[423] Karl Wolfskehl described him as founding a new humanity ('ein George-Menschentum').[424]

George was emphatically not an antisemite. When criticized for associating with Jews, he replied: 'With Jews like mine, I could have ten more and it would do me no harm.'[425] Despite the hint of patronage here, the contrast between the George circle and the Wagner circle is immense. George detested the boastful Prussian-centred nationalism of Wilhelmine Germany. Partly as aesthetic opposition to Prussian chauvinism, his poems seek to enrich German literature by celebrating Roman remnants like the Porta Nigra at Trier, exploring Romance cultures (especially in his translations from Baudelaire and Dante), and cultivating liturgical rhythms and visual imagery based in part on the practice of the Catholic Church which George knew from his Rhineland upbringing.[426] A poem from *Der Stern des Bundes* (*The Star of the Covenant*, 1914) associates Germans and Jews as being equally remote from the visual, sensual culture of the Mediterranean:

> Ihr Äusserste von windumsauster klippe
> Und schneeiger brache! Ihr von glühender wüste!
> Stammort des gott-gespenstes .. gleich entfernte
> Von heitrem meer und Binnen wo sich leben
> Zu ende lebt in welt von gott und bild!

---

[422] Landmann, *Gespräche mit Stefan George* (Düsseldorf and Munich, 1962), p. 18.
[423] Letter to Buber, 5 Feb. 1916, in Buber, *Briefwechsel*, i. 417.
[424] Wolfskehl, 'Stefan George und der Mythos' (1928), in *Gesammelte Werke*, ed. Margot Ruben and Claus Victor Bock, 2 vols. (Hamburg, 1960), ii. 252–60 (p. 253).
[425] Landmann, *Gespräche*, p. 146.
[426] See Linke, *Das Kultische*; Wolfgang Braungart, *Ästhetischer Katholizismus: Stefan Georges Rituale der Literatur* (Tübingen, 1997).

Blond oder schwarz demselben schooss entsprungne
Verkannte brüder suchend euch und hassend
Ihr immer schweifend und drum nie erfüllt![427]

Ye utmost dwellers of the wind-blown cliff
And snowy heath! Ye of the burning waste
Where dwells the ghostly god .. alike removed
From sea serene and inward realm where life
Is lived entire in world of god and image!
Some fair, some dark, sprung from the selfsame womb,
Mistaken twins who seek yet hate each other,
Forever straying, nevermore fulfilled!

Both the Germans and the Jews suffer from abstraction. George was impressed by the parallel between the Jewish prohibition on making images of God and Tacitus' report that the ancient Germanic gods had no visible shape.[428] He also thought that both Germans and Jews shared a narcissistic tendency to self-hatred.[429] Both peoples, he thought, needed to have their deficiencies corrected by his cultural programme. This might seem, at last, an example of the longed-for German–Jewish symbiosis. But it was an unequal relationship, for it required the submission of his disciples, whether Jewish or Gentile, to the German culture-hero George.

One of George's closest and most gifted devotees was the eminent critic known as Friedrich Gundolf. Born Friedrich Gundelfinger, he received from George, who liked to rechristen his disciples, the name 'Gundolf', under which he subsequently published. On their first meeting, in April 1899, the 18-year-old Gundolf was almost dumb with awe, but did manage to raise the question whether Alexander or Caesar was the greater man.[430] This indicates Gundolf's obsession with great men, no doubt a compensation for the insecurity that made him so susceptible to George's authority ('I am only really happy when I can revere a hero and leader', he later confessed);[431] it also underlay the genre of heroic biography which he pioneered with his studies of Caesar,

---

[427] George, *Werke*, i. 365.

[428] Ernst Morwitz, *Kommentar zu dem Werk Stefan Georges* (Munich and Düsseldorf, 1960), p. 361; cf. Landmann, *Gespräche*, p. 53.

[429] Landmann, *Gespräche*, p. 106.

[430] Stefan George, Friedrich Gundolf, *Briefwechsel*, ed. Robert Boehringer and Georg Peter Landmann (Munich and Düsseldorf, 1962), p. 27.

[431] Letter to Wolfskehl, 15 Aug. 1914, *Castrum Peregrini*, 126–8 (1977), 104.

Goethe, and of course George. His many submissive and affectionate letters to his 'dearly beloved master' show that George did sustain his confidence and thus help his academic career. The advice in George's letters, though somewhat brusquely delivered, is generally sensible, as when he rebukes Gundolf's extreme Francophobia in 1914, advises him in 1917 not to marry a woman he hardly knows, and comments in 1920 on his career plans.[432] The breach came when George disapproved of Gundolf's wish to marry Elisabeth Salomon; though a deeper-seated reason may have been George's increasing dislike of Gundolf's commitment to academic criticism.[433] After long delays and many ructions, Gundolf finally broke with the Master by marrying in 1926. Gundolf's abject poems requesting forgiveness show how much this severance hurt him, and the emotional strain may have helped to shorten his life, for he died on 12 July 1931 (George's birthday) at the age of 51.

How far, if at all, was Gundolf's subservience due to unease over his Jewish ancestry? It certainly contributed to his insecurity. As we have seen (above, p. 270), he confessed to Wolfskehl his fear that he lacked strong emotions and instincts; Wolfskehl's comforting reply made explicit Gundolf's unexpressed anxiety that Jewishness might enable him only to admire others' productivity, and reassured him that this faculty of admiration was a fine Jewish quality: 'reverence is our heritage from the very beginning, this ability to perceive life is our Jewish beauty; shall we, just because we rightly admire other qualities in others, deprive ourselves of our very own quality for the sake of borrowing from strangers?'[434] 'Germanness' was a major theme in his conversations with George from the outset. At an early meeting, which left Gundolf ecstatic, they admired Jean Paul's 'divine Germanness' ('göttliche Deutschheit').[435] He curried favour with George by attributing Hofmannsthal's 'commercial spirit' to the latter's Jewish ancestry.[436]

[432] George, Gundolf, *Briefwechsel*, pp. 263–4, 304, 340–1.

[433] See Claude David, 'Gundolf und George', *Euphorion*, 75 (1981), 159–77 (p. 175). Cf. the prickly conversation about 'Geist' recorded in December 1915 by Landmann, *Gespräche*, p. 29.

[434] Wolfskehl, letter of 26 Dec. 1900, *Castrum Peregrini*, 123–5 (1976), 90–1.

[435] Gundolf, letter to Wolfskehl, 23 Aug. 1899, *Castrum Peregrini*, 123–5 (1976), 49.

[436] George, Gundolf, *Briefwechsel*, p. 174. Cf. Jens Rieckmann, 'Zwischen Bewußtsein und Verdrängung: Hofmannsthals jüdisches Erbe', *DVjs* 67 (1993), 466–83.

He was aware that Jews encountered professional discrimination; after the War, outright antisemitism prevented his appointment as professor at Berlin.[437] Gundolf himself said he felt akin to the Romantics, with their mixture of lyricism, depression, and intellectuality, and that George was the only modern person free from this inner disintegration ('Zersetzung').[438] His extreme chauvinism in 1914, which made him call the Belgians 'real beasts' and desire the annihilation of France, would seem to represent an over-compensation for Jewishness, like the chauvinism of Harden and Döblin.[439]

Moreover, George's philosemitism was not shared by all his followers. The Jewish–German division formed a fault-line along which enmities could open up. Younger members of the circle, as Edith Landmann records, opposed George's Jewish associates, calling them deficient in 'the estimation of vital values, the natural, popular (*völkisch*), hard and soldierly life'.[440] The academic Gundolf offered an easy target for such antisemitism as we find in Ernst Glöckner's letters to Ernst Bertram, where George's dependence on Jews is deplored and the 'coldly analytic' Gundolf is judged unworthy to write about a German author like Kleist.[441] It would seem that Gundolf, in his attachment to the Master, was trying to escape from the self-doubt which his Jewish ancestry caused him, and that his attempt was only temporarily successful.

Karl Wolfskehl seems much more self-assured in balancing the German and Jewish components of his identity. According to family tradition, Wolfskehl's ancestors had lived in Germany for many centuries.[442] They were descended from the Kalonymos family whom Charlemagne summoned from Lucca to settle in

---

[437] Ibid. 193 (Simmel's rejection at Heidelberg 'quod Hebraeus'); p. 340 ('Pogromradau' among Berlin students).   [438] Landmann, *Gespräche*, pp. 96–7.
[439] George, Gundolf, *Briefwechsel*, pp. 263 ('écrasez la France!'), 265 (Belgians). See also his demand that the German spirit ('der deutsche Geist') should direct the future culture of Europe: 'Tat und Wort im Krieg', originally in the *Frankfurter Zeitung* (11 Oct. 1914), repr. in *Der George-Kreis: Eine Auswahl aus seinen Schriften*, ed. Georg Peter Landmann (Cologne, 1965), pp. 240–3; and his wildly chauvinistic correspondence with Wolfskehl in the autumn of 1914, *Castrum Peregrini*, 126–8 (1977).   [440] Landmann, *Gespräche*, p. 158.
[441] Glöckner, *Begegnung mit Stefan George: Auszüge aus Briefen und Tagebüchern 1913–1934* (Heidelberg, 1972), pp. 162–5.
[442] See Paul Hoffmann, ' "—jüdisch, römisch, deutsch zugleich". Karl Wolfskehl', in Grimm and Bayerdörfer (eds.), *Im Zeichen Hiobs*, pp. 98–123.

Mainz. They prospered: Wolfskehl's father was a Liberal council-
lor in Mainz and wealthy enough to leave his son a substantial
private income. This enabled Karl to live at leisure in Munich,
collecting art and books, until his fortune was dissolved by post-
War inflation, whereupon he set to work as a literary journalist.
Karl Wolfskehl affirmed his Jewish identity and sympathized with
Zionism from its beginnings; he was also entranced by Germanic
mythology, wrote a doctoral thesis on medieval German wooing
legends, explored the work of J. J. Bachofen on primitive matri-
archy, and, strangest of all, was associated not only with Stefan
George but with the Munich 'Kosmiker', Klages and Schuler. We
have already met Klages as the object of Theodor Lessing's
unrequited adoration. From Nietzsche, Bachofen, and more
suspect sources he and Schuler concocted a philosophy which
placed supreme value on Dionysiac states of intoxication in which
the soul could attain unity with the cosmos. The soul's aspirations, however, were threatened by the spirit ('Geist'), which they
saw as narrowly intellectual, rationalist, materialist, technical,
and (of course) Jewish. Wolfskehl seems to have been attracted
by Schuler's personal charisma and the sense he gave of contact
with primitive forces. He doubtless helped Wolfskehl to develop
the mythic understanding of Judaism found in his early drama
Saul (1905), especially in the eerie scene in which Saul invokes the
dead. In the long run, however, Wolfskehl found their obsessive
irrationalism uncongenial.

In his appearance, as in his writings, Wolfskehl embodied a
strange Jewish–German synthesis. Theodor Lessing described
him as 'an Assyrian prince of manly beauty'; Margarete Susman,
as 'outwardly and inwardly like the god Wotan'.[443] While exploring Germanic mythology and cosmic mysticism, Wolfskehl was
also writing the poem-cycle 'An den alten Wassern'. These poems,
originally published in the *Blätter für die Kunst*, evoke the wander-
ings of the Israelites through the wilderness, the Babylonian exile,
and the post-biblical Diaspora. Their lamenting, desolate tone,
their appeals to God, are modified only by the last poem, which,
placed in the mouth of the dying Moses as he views the Promised
Land from Mount Nebo, suggests Wolfskehl's Zionist aspirations.

---

[443] Lessing, *Einmal und nicht wieder*, p. 312; Susman, *Ich habe viele Leben gelebt*,
p. 49.

Decades later, the theme of exile became more urgent and painful in 'Die Stimme spricht', a series of dialogues with God written after the Nazi takeover and published in 1934. The persecution of the Jews in Germany is placed within the history of Jewish suffering. The yellow star, worn by Jews in the Middle Ages (and again, as Wolfskehl could not foresee, in Germany in 1941), is proudly invoked. Despite telling himself not to look back, Wolfskehl cannot resist a loving evocation of Munich. Occasionally he suggests the Zionist hope by speaking of a new daybreak in the East; but he also presents Jewish history as aimless wandering and draws on the Kabbalah to project this destiny into the metaphysical realm as the exile of the Shekhinah.[444] Wolfskehl himself went into exile in 1933 on the day after the burning of the Reichstag. He moved first to Italy and then, in 1938, to the country that seemed furthest from Hitler— New Zealand, where he spent the last ten years of his life in virtual isolation in Auckland, 'upon the globe's last island reef'.[445]

The most remarkable expression of Wolfskehl's German-Jewish identity, however, is the poem entitled '"Das Lebenslied". An die Deutschen' ('"Song of Life". To the Germans'), which he began in March 1934 in Rome; he revised the poem until 1947, the year before his death, when it assumed its final form. Like much of Wolfskehl's poetry, it is filled with Germanic archaisms and pseudo-archaisms. This style derives from George's work; it becomes more marked and more awkward in Wolfskehl's exile poetry, sometimes recalling the pseudo-archaic language of Wagner's music-dramas. It certainly defies exact translation into English. Wolfskehl uses this style in 'To the Germans' to recall how his Jewish ancestors moved to Mainz and served the medieval emperors; to evoke his own studies of medieval German poetry; and to underline his own Germanness, albeit in the past tense:

> Ich war Deutsch und ich war Ich.
> Deutscher Gau hat mich geboren,
> Deutsches Brot speiste mich gar,
> Deutschen Rheines Reben goren
> Mir ins Blut ein Tausendjahr.[446]

---

[444] Wolfskehl, 'Schechina', *Gesammelte Werke*, i. 135–6; see Scholem, *Major Trends*, p. 230.
[445] Wolfskehl, 'An Erdballs letztem Inselriff', *Gesammelte Werke*, i. 225.
[446] Wolfskehl, *Gesammelte Werke*, i. 216–18 (p. 216).

I was German, I was I. A German region bore me, German bread nourished me, the German Rhine's vines fermented in my blood for a thousand years.

As the supreme embodiment of Germany in his own day he celebrates Stefan George (who also provides the poem with three epigraphs):

> Und dein Tag gar ist der meine.
> Auch um meine Stirne wand
> Stefan, Flammenhort vom Rheine,
> Heil der Herzen, Er der Eine,
> Unsres Stromes Silberband,
> Duft des schönen, Schau des neuen
> Lebens schenkend, der Gebühr,
> Weihend mich, den Immertreuen,
> Seiner Sende, seiner Kür [. . .]

And your very day is mine. It was around my brow, too, that Stefan, the Rhine's fiery hoard, the hearts' salvation, He the One, wound our river's silver ribbon, bestowing the fragrance of the fair, the vision of the new life, as was due, consecrating me, the ever-loyal, to his mission, his election . . .

Here Wolfskehl associates the Rhinelander George with the treasure hidden in the Rhine that animates the action both of the *Nibelungenlied* and of Wagner's *Ring*. But his most intriguing use of myth comes halfway through the poem, and it works against the notion of a German–Jewish symbiosis which the poem is trying to establish:

> Eure Mär ist auch der meine.
> Vom helldüstern Bruderpaar,
> Blindem, der den Blanken töte,
> Hoeder-Vult, von Speer und Flöte
> Flüstert' ich euch [. . .]

Your tale is also mine. I whispered to you of the bright and gloomy brothers, the blind one who killed the shining one, Hoeder-Vult, and of the spear and the flute . . .

This Scandinavian myth concerns the radiant god Baldur and his blind and dismal brother Hoeder. Since all living creatures loved Baldur too much to harm him, the malicious Loki took advantage of Hoeder's blindness to make him shoot his brother unwittingly. Wolfskehl superimposes this myth onto another fiction about two dissimilar brothers, Walt and Vult in Jean Paul's novel *Flegeljahre* (1804–5). The humorous novelist Jean Paul was a favourite in the George circle. Walt is a good-natured innocent for whom his long-lost brother, the flautist Vult, feels great affection; but Wolfskehl, in an essay published in 1927, strangely interpreted their relationship as fratricidal, on the grounds that, at the end of the novel, 'when Vult leaves him and takes away his brother's youth in the dying tones of his flute, a murder is committed as with Baldur'.[447] To this strained interpretation Wolfskehl adds an explicitly erotic parallel between Vult's flute and Hoeder's spear. What is going on here? Wolfskehl is exploring intimate, sibling relationships in which one member is innocent, loved, and loving, the other an outsider for whom homoerotic love accompanies a secret enmity. This would seem to be Wolfskehl's unacknowledged figure for the German–Jewish relationship. The naïve, lovable German is intimately akin to the more sombre, reflective Jew, who loves the German but is fatal to him; the German is simple, the Jew is tragically divided. Hoeder's blindness alludes also to Wolfskehl's own near-blindness. If this composite myth does express Wolfskehl's interpretation of German–Jewish relations, an understanding which could only find symbolic expression, it also confirms the strength of his attachment to Germany: even when sent into exile by a tyrannical regime, he could not blame the Germans but had instead to imply that the fault must lie with the Jews.

[447] Wolfskehl, 'Dämon und Philister', *Gesammelte Werke*, ii. 274–80 (p. 276).

5

Dissimilation

The First World War was a turning-point in German–Jewish relations. Before it, German and Austrian Jews of the well-to-do classes could lead remarkably sheltered lives, disturbed only by distant antisemitic mutterings. Many memoirs lament this 'golden age of security', as Stefan Zweig called it in *The World of Yesterday*. Their authors grew up in an atmosphere of protected idealism. 'Trust in humanity', recalled Margarete Susman, 'was, little as I knew it, the protective covering that concealed the too sombre reality. The great idealistic dream, the dream of German idealism, that was spread over my life for so long, no doubt had to be torn apart in the most appalling manner, so that I might recognize real life.'[1] Schnitzler's pre-War diaries never discuss public events, apart from noting antisemitism; he does mention an eruption of Vesuvius, but only because he fears his friend Hofmannsthal may have been among its victims (*T* 15 Apr. 1906). Even during the War, Gershom Scholem and Walter Benjamin sedulously avoided discussing its progress.[2] 'Since the declaration of war,' thinks the anti-hero of Siegfried Kracauer's novel *Ginster* (1928), 'people had gone mad; nobody talked about anything important any more.'[3]

Many German Jews shared the euphoric sense of solidarity that greeted the outbreak of the War. Enthusiasm soon turned sour, however, as old antagonisms reappeared in harsher form. At the front, Jews felt estranged from non-Jewish soldiers. Thus the war diary of Julius Marx (which admittedly reads as though revised in retrospect) records in October 1914 that the initial solidarity is

---

[1] Susman, *Ich habe viele Leben gelebt*, pp. 22–3.
[2] Scholem, *Walter Benjamin*, p. 35.
[3] Kracauer, *Ginster*, in *Schriften*, ed. Karsten Witte, vii (Frankfurt, 1973), p. 16.

already dissipating and Gentiles are looking at him askance; and he represents himself as saying in 1916: 'The average German simply doesn't like Jews. I should like to be nothing but a German soldier—but people make sure that I know better!'[4] Schnitzler's diary conveys the torn feelings that Austrian and German Jews at home felt as the war advanced. On 19 May 1915 his dentist told him that a noblewoman who was also among his patients had exclaimed, while reading a list of those killed in battle, 'Another aristocrat has fallen. Soon only Jews will be left.' Schnitzler adds in disgust: 'What is this country to us?' The following day, however, he records a conversation with Richard Beer-Hofmann about Austria's military humiliation, and adds: 'We [. . .] feel this country's fate as deeply as others, perhaps more deeply. How rooted one is in the country that gave one birth! What do our fellow-citizens, diplomats, monarchs matter to us in the end? The land! Our home!' (*T* 20 May 1915). As the war became bogged down and the living conditions of civilians deteriorated, scapegoats were sought, and who better than the Jews to provide them? In response to widespread rumours that German Jews were shirking front-line service, the German War Ministry announced on 11 October 1916 that it would carry out a census of Jews serving in the army. The results were never published, and it seems that the number of Jews who were serving in the front line was if anything disproportionately high.[5]

Though most German Jews were sheltered from violence, the increasingly vocal antisemitism in the Weimar Republic rendered them uneasy, while the First Austrian Republic suffered from the division between its hypertrophic capital Vienna, with a Socialist administration and a largely Jewish intelligentsia, and its conservative provinces. The leading role of Jews in revolutionary upheavals, particularly in the short-lived Munich Soviet Republic of 1919, caused anger among antisemites and apprehension among the majority of Jews who feared being tarred with the revolutionary brush. The antisemitic terrorism of paramilitary organizations

[4] Marx, *Kriegstagebuch eines Juden* ([1939]; Frankfurt, 1964), pp. 32, 129. For many similar examples, see Eva G. Reichmann, 'Der Bewußtseinswandel der deutschen Juden', in Werner E. Mosse (ed.), *Deutsches Judentum in Krieg und Revolution* (Tübingen, 1971), pp. 511–612.

[5] See Werner T. Angress, 'The German Army's "Judenzählung" of 1916: Genesis—Consequences—Significance', *LBY* 23 (1978), 117–37.

such as the Freikorps, the Deutscher Schutz- und Trutzbund, and the Austrian Heimwehr had no pre-War precedent. The rule of law was normally upheld, but Jewish self-defence organizations increased their membership: in 1924 the CV had 72,400 members, almost double the 1914 figure.[6] Moderate antisemitism was widespread in universities, both among professors and among students like those who shouted down Einstein's lectures in February 1920; the universities officially opposed antisemitism, though only a few professors, like the economist Lujo Brentano and the Romance philologist Karl Vossler, were prepared to take an individual stand against it.[7]

After the War, there were already signs of what has usefully been called 'dissimilation'.[8] A remarkable change of heart was announced in 1919 by Georg Hermann, whom we have met celebrating assimilation in his best-selling novels. He recalled that he had always considered himself a German citizen of Jewish faith, thoroughly assimilated to German culture, with his Jewishness only as 'a dash of salt' adding a distinctive flavouring. 'I thought that I was first and foremost a German, retaining some residual Judaism only from old attachment, from piety so to speak, for after all one doesn't want to part with an heirloom that has held an honoured place in the family for three thousand years and more.'[9] Now, however, the Germans' conduct during and after the War had shown that they could not be trusted as guardians of humane values. Hermann therefore announced his returned to a racial Judaism, detecting in the depths of his soul ('Urgründe meines Wesens') a longing to escape from his rootlessness and find a home.[10] Edmund Husserl, who had supported the War and whose younger son had been killed on the French front in 1916, now heard his life's work, phenomenology, denounced as Jewish and felt he was being denied membership of the German nation. 'From my childhood I have been absorbed with infinite love

[6] See Donald L. Niewyk, *The Jews in Weimar Germany* (Manchester, 1980), pp. 75, 86.

[7] Niewyk, *The Jews in Weimar Germany*, pp. 63–7; Fritz K. Ringer, *The Decline of the German Mandarins: The German Academic Community*, 1890–1933 (Cambridge, Mass., 1969), p. 239.

[8] Shulamit Volkov, 'The Dynamics of Dissimilation: *Ostjuden* and German Jews', in Reinharz and Schatzberg (eds.), *The Jewish Response to German Culture*, pp. 195–211.

[9] Hermann, 'Zur Frage der Westjuden', *Neue Jüdische Monatshefte*, 3 19–20 (10–25 July 1919), 399–405 (p. 400).   [10] Ibid. 401.

in the intellectual life (*Geistigkeit*) of the German nation and its endless magnificent horizons', he wrote in 1921; now he felt deprived of a fatherland and a nation ('vaterlands- und volklos'), unable to help the Germans in their hour of need.[11] In the same year Arnold Schoenberg (a convert since 1898) and his family were asked to leave the Austrian holiday resort of Mattsee on the grounds that it was reserved for Gentiles. The shock, combined with the antisemitic propaganda emanating from Hitler, sent Schönberg into near-paranoia but also started him exploring the religious foundation of Jewish identity, beginning with his drama *The Path of the Bible* (begun around 1923) and culminating in his unfinished opera (largely written in the early 1930s) *Moses and Aaron*.[12] By 1933 Alfred Döblin concluded that the entire attempt at assimilation had been a mistake, and one that had been repeatedly made throughout Jewish history: 'Defenceless and deluded, they reeled towards a heathen idol called Western Progress. As usual, they had learnt nothing from history, from Aaron's golden calf down to Hellenism and medieval Spain.'[13] He denounced the emancipation contract as 'a kind of suicide', for it invited the Jews to discard their Judaism and thereby led them into a trap by refusing to accept them as Germans.[14]

Even highly acculturated Jews were shocked into disillusionment by the Nazis' accession to power. 'I no longer believe in national psychology', wrote Victor Klemperer in his diary on 3 April 1933. 'Everything I thought un-German, brutality, injustice, hypocrisy, mass-suggestion to the point of drunkenness, all that is flourishing here.'[15] A greater shock befell the chemist Fritz Haber, a converted Jew who had been appointed director of the Kaiser Wilhelm Institute for Physical Chemistry in 1911, and was largely

---

[11] Letter of 17 Oct. 1921 to Dietrich Mahnke in Husserl, *Briefwechsel*, v. 432–3.

[12] See Schoenberg's letters to Kandinsky of 19 April and 4 May 1923 in Arnold Schönberg, Wassily Kandinsky, *Briefe, Bilder und Dokumente einer außergewöhnlichen Begegnung*, ed. Jelena Hahl-Koch (Salzburg, 1980); Alexander L. Ringer, *Arnold Schoenberg: The Composer as Jew* (Oxford, 1990).

[13] Döblin, *Jüdische Erneuerung* (1933), in *Schriften zu jüdischen Fragen* (Solothurn and Düsseldorf, 1995), pp. 53–4.

[14] Döblin, *Flucht und Sammlung des Judenvolks* (1935), ibid., 118.

[15] Klemperer, *Ich will Zeugnis ablegen bis zum letzten*, i. 18. On Klemperer's emphatically German identity, see Yvonne Rieker, '"Sich alles assimilieren können und doch seine Eigenart bewahren": Victor Klemperers Identitätskonstruktion und die deutsch-jüdische Geschichte', in Hannes Heer (ed.), *Im Herzen der Finsternis: Victor Klemperer als Chronist der NS-Zeit* (Berlin, 1997), pp. 21–34.

largely responsible for the development of poison gas on the German side in the War. In the late 1920s he had advocated an authoritarian solution to Germany's problems, but when it arrived in the form of Nazism, Haber took early retirement, moved to Cambridge, and in August 1933 wrote to Einstein: 'In my whole life I have never been so Jewish as now.'[16] An even worse experience was that of Husserl. In 1933 Husserl was deprived of his status as emeritus professor: he called this 'the most hurtful experience of my life'.[17] We know that his pupil Heidegger, who joined the Nazi Party on 1 May 1933 and was made Rector of Freiburg University, did nothing to hinder his removal.

With the unfair advantage of hindsight, however, it seems that many German Jews were remarkably slow to recognize the character of the National Socialists. Admittedly, in the last years of the Weimar Republic most Jews were sceptical about its prospects.[18] They shared the widespread view that the liberal era was over. There was no political party with which they could identify: many of them, though conservatively inclined, were deterred by anti-semitism from supporting right-wing parties; most of those who voted for the Socialist Party or the Catholic Centre Party had tactical, not ideological reasons. They anticipated a dictatorship of the Right or, worse still, the Left. They thought that at least the former, while dispensing with democracy, would maintain the rule of law (*Rechtsstaat*). Many expected that Hitler would be no worse than Lueger, or at least than Mussolini.[19] Few contemplated emigrating before 1933; after all, besides the huge practical difficulties, they felt they were Germans, identified with Germany, and belonged to it quite as firmly as the National Socialists (and more than the Austrian Hitler). Even after 1933 there was no massive wave of emigration: 37,000 German Jews left Germany in 1933, but then the annual total sank until 1938, when it rose to

[16] Quoted in Fritz Stern, 'Fritz Haber: The Scientist in Power and in Exile', in his *Dreams and Delusions: The Drama of German History* (London, 1987), pp. 51–76 (p. 74).

[17] Letter of 1 July 1933 to Gustav Albrecht, in Husserl, *Briefwechsel*, ix. 92.

[18] See Moshe Zimmermann, ' "Die aussichtslose Republik" — Zukunftsperspektiven der deutschen Juden vor 1933', *Menora*, 1 (1990), 152–83.

[19] See Ingrid Belke, 'Publizisten warnen vor Hitler. Frühe Analysen des Nationalsozialismus', in Hans Otto Horch and Horst Denkler (eds.), *Conditio Judaica, 3: Judentum, Antisemitismus und deutschsprachige Literatur vom Ersten Weltkrieg bis 1933/ 1938* (Tübingen, 1993), pp. 116–76.

40,000, and 1939, when after Kristallnacht it reached a high point of 78,000.[20]

Hopes faded slowly. In February 1933 Martin Buber still thought that the National Socialists would not gain any further power in what was still a coalition government: 'So long as the present coalition lasts, we need not expect Jew-baiting or anti-Jewish legislation, only administrative oppression: anti-Jewish legislation would only be possible if the National Socialists increased their power, but that is hardly likely.'[21] Even after the Reichstag fire, the suspension of the constitution, and the boycott of Jewish shops on 1 April 1933, some Jews—not only hyperacculturated Jews like Hans-Joachim Schoeps—thought they could accommodate themselves to National Socialism. In 1934 Adorno applied (unsuccessfully) to join the Reichsschrifttumskammer, the official writers' organization set up by Goebbels, and advised Benjamin to do likewise.[22] Rabbi Leo Baeck doubtless thought he was doing his best to protect the Jews by contributing to an official publication denying that Jews had suffered any violence, and by accompanying a protest against the boycott of Jewish shops with an assurance that German Jews yearned to 'take part in the renewal and resurgence of the German people'.[23] Was Baeck so blinded by identification with Germany, like Schoeps, that he really thought the Jews would be given a part in the reconstruction of Germany? Or did he overestimate his and others' ability to handle the Nazis? Peter Pulzer implies the latter by his conclusion that 'the principal reason why German Jews underestimated the significance of Hitler's coming to power' was 'their familiarity with prejudice and discrimination. It was there, they had coped with it before and they could cope with it again.'[24] A more radical version of this argument, put forward during and after the Third Reich, charges German Jews with falling back into a ghetto mentality which sought to reach a compromise with the ruling power, just as

[20] Avraham Barkai, 'Jüdisches Leben unter der Verfolgung', in Meyer (ed.), *Deutsch-jüdische Geschichte*, iv. 227.

[21] Buber, letter to Ernst Simon, 13 Feb. 1933, *Briefwechsel*, ii. 466–7.

[22] Letter of 5 Apr. 1934 in Adorno, Benjamin, *Briefwechsel*, ed. Henri Lonitz (Frankfurt, 1994), p. 53; cf. note, p. 55. Adorno repeated his advice on 21 Apr. (pp. 62–3), adding that Benjamin need not scruple to declare his loyalty to the Hitler regime, which was already close to collapse (p. 64).

[23] Quoted in Barkai, 'Organisation und Zusammenschluß', in Meyer (ed.), *Deutsch-jüdische Geschichte*, iv. 255.   [24] Pulzer, *Jews and the German State*, p. 345.

Jews had negotiated with princes in pre-modern Germany, instead of confronting the new regime by opposition, resistance, or concerted emigration. Shortly before his suicide in 1935, Kurt Tucholsky wrote Arnold Zweig an agonized letter denouncing the majority of German Jews for their servile opportunism which condemned them to a ghetto existence: 'Anyone who accepts the ghetto from the outset as something given, will stay in it for ever.'[25] Later, and controversially, the psychoanalyst Bruno Bettelheim charged those Jews who failed to emigrate in time, or to offer resistance like the uprisings in Warsaw and Treblinka, with the ingrained habit of 'ghetto thinking'.[26] On the other hand, the dogged courage required to maintain Jewish social and cultural life under the Third Reich demands admiration, even though to classify such activities as 'resistance', as is now often done, seems an excessive extension of the term.[27] The debate over the conduct of German Jews will doubtless continue.

Among a minority of German Jews, however, the beginnings of dissimilation can be traced back to the 1890s, when Jewish self-esteem made some people, like Rathenau and Lissauer, unwilling to convert, despite the potential advantages of so doing. They felt that in view of antisemitic pressures they were morally obliged to remain nominal Jews. In 1893, similarly, Theodor Herzl told a Viennese anti-antisemite: 'at the age of discretion one cannot abandon the "faith of one's fathers", even if one no longer has it' (*BT* i. 511–12). In 1906, when Margarete Susman was about to be baptized in order to get married, she suddenly felt that conversion would destroy the foundations of her life, and cancelled the ceremony at a few hours' notice.[28] Conversion was coming to seem not only opportunistic but shallow. Hugo Bergman, when advised by the philosopher Franz Brentano to remove a purely external obstacle to his academic career by converting, replied by deploring such trivialization of religion:

[25] Tucholsky, letter of 15 Dec. 1935, in *Ausgewählte Briefe*, ed. Mary Gerold-Tucholsky and Fritz J. Raddatz (Reinbek, 1962), p. 335. Cf. Tucholsky's prophetic sketch of Berlin Jews adjusting to Nazi dictatorship in 'Herr Wendriner steht unter der Diktatur' (1930), *Gesammelte Werke*, iii. 547–50.

[26] Bettelheim, 'Freedom from Ghetto Thinking', in his *Recollections and Reflections* (London, 1990), pp. 243–71.

[27] On this debate, see Michael A. Marrus, 'Jewish Resistance to the Holocaust', *Journal of Contemporary History*, 30 (1995), 83–110.

[28] Susman, *Ich habe viele Leben gelebt*, p. 71.

I know many baptized Jews, I have some in my own family and in that of my wife, and I always noticed that those who took such a step without a fervent conviction then justified themselves in their own and others' eyes by constructing an attitude of jocular scepticism towards religion, maintaining that neither religion, nor any other, had any value and thus the change of religion meant nothing. The truth, however, is that each religion is a valuable institution, provided it is a matter of inner experience.[29]

Such scrupulous people, however, were too few to halt the trend, foretold by demographers like Theilhaber, for the Jewish community to become diluted by conversion and, still more, by intermarriage. In Weimar Germany, 37 per cent of Jewish marriages were with non-Jews, while in Austria, where intermarriage was forbidden, over 17,000 people attained the same end by leaving the Jewish community and assuming 'konfessionslos' status.[30]

Facing such disintegrative pressures, Jews who valued their Jewish identity had to give it a new content. At the beginning of the century, Martin Buber proclaimed a 'Jewish Renaissance', a positive rediscovery and revaluation of Judaism and Jewish tradition. Buber's work, and that of others, bore fruit, as Michael Brenner has recently shown in ample detail, in the revival of interest in Jewish culture.[31] Various local societies for the study of Jewish history and literature formed a national organization in 1893 and, from 1898 on, issued an important annual publication, the *Jahrbuch für Jüdische Geschichte und Literatur*. The Hamburg rabbi Max Grunwald founded a society for the study of Jewish folklore in 1898. Buber founded a Jewish publishing house, the Jüdischer Verlag, in Berlin in 1902. After the War this revival gathered pace. In 1919 the Akademie für die Wissenschaft des Judentums was founded under the leadership of the historian Eugen Täubler to promote the rigorous study of Jewish history and religion in a secular spirit. The Freies Jüdisches Lehrhaus, set up by the Orthodox rabbi N. A. Nobel and directed by Franz Rosenzweig, opened in Frankfurt in August 1920. It aimed to inculcate Jewish learning, not just as an academic subject, but

---

[29] Bergman, *Tagebücher und Briefe*, i. 43–4.

[30] Avraham Barkai, 'Bevölkerungsrückgang und wirtschaftliche Stagnation', in Meyer (ed.), *Deutsch-jüdische Geschichte*, iv. 39.

[31] Brenner, *The Renaissance of Jewish Culture in Weimar Germany* (New Haven and London, 1996), from which the information that follows is largely taken. See also George L. Mosse, *German Jews Beyond Judaism* (Bloomington and Cincinnati, 1985).

as a way of revitalizing Jewish life. New directions were explored by Buber and Scholem. Buber began presenting Hasidism to Western readers by retelling Hasidic stories, beginning with *Die Geschichten des Rabbi Nachman* (*The Tales of Rabbi Nachman*) in 1906, but gradually presenting the stories in a less flowery, more sober style and supplementing them with treatises. Annoyed by Buber's insufficiently historical treatment of his sources, Gershom Scholem began his studies in Jewish mysticism with a critique of Buber's malign influence.[32] Jewish knowledge was assembled in the *Encyclopaedia Judaica*, edited by Nahum Goldmann and Jakob Klatzkin, of which ten volumes appeared between 1928 and 1934, and in Siegmund Kaznelson's four-volume *Jüdisches Lexikon* (1927–30).

Even if a minority of German Jews was involved, and the majority held to ideals of assimilation, this was a significant change of direction. For, as Brenner makes clear, it meant the reinvention of Judaism not as a religion but as 'a cultural realm'.[33] Here Jews whose Jewish upbringing had been scanty or non-existent took an interest in a Jewish culture which was not part of their direct experience but a subject of historical knowledge. Kafka identified one stage in this change of attitude when he noted the indifference with which his relatives regarded his nephew's circumcision and foresaw that such ceremonies would eventually again become interesting, but as historical phenomena.[34] The task of the Jewish Renaissance was to restore such historical phenomena to a present which was shaped by German culture.

Brenner acknowledges only partially how far the Jewish Renaissance in Germany was itself an expression of intellectual and cultural developments in Germany and hence a product of assimilation. The new generation of German Jews were so intimately involved in German culture that they absorbed its tendencies and applied them to their newly discovered Judaism. This reapplication can be illustrated from conceptions of ethnicity, language, and messianic leadership.

---

[32] See David Biale, *Gershom Scholem: Kabbalah and Counter-History* (Cambridge, Mass., 1979), p. 73.

[33] Brenner, *The Renaissance of Jewish Culture*, p. 2; cf. Niewyk, *The Jews in Weimar Germany*, p. 104; Ismar Schorsch, 'German Jewry: From Confession to Culture', in *From Text to Context*, pp. 360–7.

[34] Kafka, *Tagebücher*, p. 312 (24 Dec. 1911).

As Brenner points out, German-Jewish identity in the Weimar Republic was increasingly based on 'common ethnicity rather than individual faith'.[35] From the perspective of the 1990s, with their positive acceptance of ethnic identity, it is tempting to welcome this development. But if one inquires into the foundations proposed for Jewish ethnicity, one may have doubts. For, as we saw in Chapter 3, Germans agreed in understanding identity as racial, and differed only on whether to interpret it in a strong (biological) or weaker (cultural) sense. The ideological space between 'race' and 'culture' was filled by the concepts of *Volk* and *völkisch*.

The new definition of Jewish ethnicity came above all from Buber. He described the pathology of the Western Jew and urged his hearers to rediscover the essential underlying psychology which marked the Jewish character through the ages. Since its dispersion, he maintains, the Jewish people has been a diseased organism. Confinement in the ghetto has estranged the Jews from nature and stunted their aesthetic sense, while the study of the Torah, 'a misunderstood, convoluted, contorted religious tradition', has made them one-sidedly over-intellectual.[36] Assimilation has forced on them an alien culture which they have not had time to absorb, and made them hopelessly tense and nervous.[37] No other nation is so sick as the Jews, because no other nation lacks its own land.

These charges are the common coin of modern antisemitism. Buber adopts them in order to rebut them: they apply only to the assimilated Jew, and they will vanish once the Jews have their own territory. Now that bloodless Enlightenment humanism has been superseded by national self-affirmation, the Jews can again become rounded people whose abilities develop harmoniously. On their own soil, they will have a homogeneous national community led by a creative elite which forms the ganglia to the body of the *Volk*. The return to Hebrew, their ancient language, will restore 'the creative function of the popular spirit (*des Volksgeistes*)' and allow the inmost form of their existence to be Jewish.[38]

To begin this Jewish renaissance, Buber urged Western Jews to

---

[35] Brenner, *The Renaissance of Jewish Culture*, p. 39.

[36] Buber, 'Renaissance und Bewegung' (1903), in *Die jüdische Bewegung*, i. 94.

[37] The Western Jew's proneness to neurasthenia was a commonplace: see Fishberg, *The Jews*, p. 6; Zollschan, *Das Rassenproblem*, p. 271; Trebitsch, *Geist und Judentum*, pp. 92, 149; Gilman, *Freud, Race and Gender*, pp. 94–6.

[38] Buber, 'Die hebräische Sprache' (1909), *Die jüdische Bewegung*, i. 182.

rediscover the Jewishness within themselves. In lectures given in 1909 and 1910 to the Bar Kochba, the Zionist society in Prague, Buber sketched a psychology of the Jew. He tried to define the intrinsic substance (*Substanz*) transmitted down the generations in the blood, defining 'blood' as 'the root-like, nourishing power in the individual'. Buber puts forward a threefold psychology of the Jew: (1) the Jew shows his urge for unity by perceiving wholes rather than parts, woods rather than trees; (2) the Jew has a motor rather than a sensory disposition ('mehr motorisch als sensorisch veranlagt'), emphasizing movement rather than sense-perception, hence in religion inclined to action rather than contemplation; (3) Jews are conscious of time more than of space, and hence are oriented towards the future. The Jew's urge for unity, however, is only one side of his intrinsically divided character. His primal duality ('Urzweiheit'), revealed in the myth of the Fall and estrangement from God, discloses his deep-seated desire for unity, and Jewish activity is fundamentally an effort to overcome this duality. Ethical universalism, messianism, and its secularized descendant, Socialism, are all versions of the search for unity.[39]

Again, Buber has taken an antisemitic image—that of the Jew as semi-assimilated and hence divided, torn between Jewish and German identities—and reinterpreted and revalued it so that it becomes an intrinsic part of the Jewish character, not something imposed from outside, and also a positive instead of a negative quality. Buber's psychology of the Jew accommodates some familiar features of Judaism, at least those that Buber chooses to emphasize, such as its practical character and its messianic element.

Present-day readers find Buber's early writings surprising, uncomfortable, and disturbingly racist in tone. Despite the insistent image of 'blood', however, Buber's psychology is only remotely connected with the nineteenth-century pseudo-science of race. As we saw in Chapter 3, racial scientists did try to make empirical claims, based on skull measurements and so on. It was only when further empirical research nullified these claims that racialists propounded theses about the 'Jewish spirit' which were immune

---

[39] The *Drei Reden über das Judentum* are available in Buber, *Der Jude und sein Judentum: Gesammelte Aufsätze und Reden* (Cologne, 1963; quotation from pp. 13, 36), and discussed in Hillel J. Kieval, *The Making of Czech Jewry: National Conflict and Jewish Society in Bohemia, 1870–1918* (New York and Oxford, 1988), ch. 5.

from empirical testing. Buber is making a similar move. His psychology of the Jew is based not on empirical research but on intuitive insight. In this respect Buber's racial psychology ran parallel to the development of antisemitism and was a product of his time—of the period in which the links between Germans and Jews were beginning to unravel and both sides were proposing theories of ineluctable difference.

Buber's contemporaries were similarly reluctant to classify the Jews as a distinct race by physical criteria. Aron Sandler argues that even if Jewish racial qualities cannot be scientifically demonstrated, there is a Jewish individuality, based on the inheritance of physical and mental features, which can be apprehended as a whole but not analysed.[40] Fritz Kahn maintains that the Jews are both a race and a nation, but interprets them as primarily a cultural entity: 'The combination of various tribes to form a political and cultural community gave rise about 1000 B.C. to the Jewish nation.'[41] These attempts to have one's cake while eating it share the ambiguity of Buber's essentialism.

The position of assimilated German Jews can be traced also in Walter Benjamin's reflections on language. Brought up in a prosperous, assimilated Berlin family, the young Benjamin was aware of Judaism only as 'vague piety'.[42] He initially looked for inspiration to such prophets as Nietzsche, Strindberg, and Tolstoy.[43] In 1915, however, Benjamin met Gershom Scholem, to whom, as he admitted, he owed what knowledge of Judaism he possessed.[44] Scholem drew his attention to the philosophy of language which formed part of Jewish mysticism and thus helped to inspire the essay 'Über Sprache überhaupt und über die Sprache des Menschen' ('On language as such and on the language of humanity', 1916), where, according to his biographer Bernd Witte, the Jewish foundations of his thought are most apparent.[45] Benjamin distinguishes three ranks or tiers of language: the divine language of revelation, the language of human beings, and the unspoken

---

[40] Sandler, *Anthropologie und Zionismus: Ein populär-wissenschaftlicher Vortrag* (Brünn, 1904), p. 7.   [41] Kahn, *Die Juden als Rasse und Kulturvolk*, p. 162.
[42] Letter to Ludwig Strauss, Oct. 1912, in Benjamin, *Gesammelte Schriften*, ii. 836.
[43] Benjamin, 'Dialog über die Religiosität der Gegenwart' (1912), in *Gesammelte Schriften*, ii. 34.   [44] Benjamin, letter of 25 Apr. 1930, *Briefe*, p. 513.
[45] Witte, '"Die Welt allseitiger und integraler Aktualität": Die Säkularisierung jüdischer Motive in Walter Benjamins Denken', *Der Deutschunterricht*, 37 (1985), 26–37 (p. 28).

language of things. None of these is a means of communication. Divine language is creative; human language mirrors it in its chief function, that of giving names; and the speechless language of things is a revelation of their spiritual essence. In Paradise, man named everything by its true name, so that language, as naming, was inseparable from knowledge. Since the Fall, which Benjamin associates with the catastrophe of Babel, language no longer echoes creation but has declined into a mere vehicle for communication and, at worst, mere empty chatter.

These notions have several sources. They are certainly indebted to the Kabbalists, who agreed, Scholem tells us, 'in regarding language as something more precious than an inadequate instrument for contact between human beings' which 'reflects the fundamental spiritual nature of the world'.[46] Benjamin also knew the linguistic theories of Wilhelm von Humboldt and the Romantics.[47] In the 'unspoken language of things' we recognize the conception of the book of Nature, the world as God's unwritten revelation, which originated in the Christian Middle Ages and passed via Goethe and the Symbolists to the German and Austrian *fin de siècle*.[48] The fictitious author of Hofmannsthal's 'Chandos Letter' longs for an unknown language 'in which the speechless things will speak to me'; an early poem by Rilke, after deploring the relentless clarity of people's talk, declares: 'Die Dinge singen hör ich so gern' ('I so like to hear things singing').[49] And for *fin-de-siècle* writers the wordless language of things was a relief from the clamour of the modern mass media. In the language of journalism, Karl Kraus above all saw a corruption which could only be resisted by the most vigilant linguistic purism. And the corruption was in part that of an assimilated, rootless, and immoral Jewry. Benjamin was introduced to Kraus's work by Scholem, and later,

---

[46] Scholem, *Major Trends*, p. 17.

[47] See Winfried Menninghaus, *Walter Benjamins Theorie der Sprachmagie* (Frankfurt, 1980), pp. 12, 27.

[48] See Ernst Robert Curtius, *European Literature and the Latin Middle Ages*, tr. W. R. Trask (New York, 1953), ch. 16: 'The Book as Symbol'.

[49] Hugo von Hofmannsthal, 'Ein Brief', in *Erzählungen, erfundene Gespräche und Briefe, Reisen*, ed. Bernd Schoeller (Frankfurt, 1979), p. 472; Rainer Maria Rilke, 'Ich fürchte mich so vor der Menschen Wort' (1897), in *Sämtliche Werke*, ed. Ernst Zinn, 6 vols. (Frankfurt, 1955), i. 194–5. On Hofmannsthal's magical conception of language, see Manfred Hoppe, *Literatentum, Magie und Mystik im Frühwerk Hofmannsthals* (Berlin, 1968).

in 1931, published a long essay claiming that Kraus returned language to its traditional Jewish purpose of 'sanctifying the Name'.[50] In hankering after a pure language unsullied by communication, Benjamin is transposing Kraus's linguistic purism, itself a product of assimilation, to the theological plane.

Messianism, finally, was reinterpreted by Gershom Scholem, the historian of Jewish mysticism, who made a particularly sharp turn away from assimilation. But its beginnings, now revealed in his fascinating diaries and letters, are complicated. His early diaries show the young Scholem to be a typical God-seeker of the Expressionist generation, searching for community in the Jewish youth movement and for spirituality in such writers as Kierkegaard, Tolstoy, St Francis of Assisi, Rilke, and Buber. Addressing Jung-Juda on 27 January 1915, Scholem praised Buber because 'in Judaism, previously the classic religion of rationalism and logic-chopping, he discovered the irrational, emotion and yearning, which is the mother of renewal'.[51] Soon, however, and probably influenced by Benjamin, Scholem rejected Buber's notion of emotional experience (*Erlebnis*) and sought religious renewal rather in an intellectual grasp of Law (as later of Kabbalistic theosophy) as a metaphysical system independent of any belief in God.[52]

Scholem's preoccupation with Jewish mysticism and messianism, however, originated from his situation as an assimilated Jew steeped in German culture.[53] He had his attention drawn to the Kabbalah by the work of a Christian writer, the German Romantic Franz Joseph Molitor, who in turn was continuing the tradition of Christian interpretation of the Kabbalah and combining it with Romantic idealist philosophy.[54] Nietzsche's *Zarathustra* was for Scholem 'a sacred book' and 'a revolutionary book'.[55] Its influence, alongside that of Buber and the Old Testament, is evident in Scholem's rhapsodic account of a journey through the Alps that he undertook in August 1914.[56] In this passage, however, Scholem also cites the passage from Gerhart Hauptmann's novel *Der Narr*

[50] Scholem, *Walter Benjamin*, p. 136; Benjamin, *Gesammelte Schriften*, ii. 359.

[51] Scholem, *Tagebücher 1913–1917*, p. 112.

[52] See particularly his letter to Gerda Goldberg, 6 Aug. 1917, in Scholem, *Briefe 1914–1947*, ed. Itta Shedletzky (Munich, 1994), pp. 87–91.

[53] See George Mosse, 'Gershom Scholem as a German Jew', in his *Confronting the Nation: Jewish and Western Nationalism* (Hanover, NH, and London, 1993), pp. 176–92.   [54] Biale, *Scholem*, pp. 31–2.

[55] Scholem, *Tagebücher 1913–1917*, p. 207 (18 Dec. 1915).   [56] Ibid. 29–38.

in Christo Emanuel Quint (Emanuel Quint, the Fool in Christ,
1910) where Hauptmann's lonely sectarian leader falls into ecstasies at the sight of the rising sun.[57] And the surprising importance that this entirely non-Jewish novel had for the young Scholem emerges from another diary entry:

Which of us young Jews, I wonder, has not had the same royal dream and seen himself as Jesus and Messiah of the downtrodden? Whether its shaping was unconsciously influenced by Hauptmann and Wassermann, not to mention Buber, I do not know.[58]

Given Scholem's later dislike and incomprehension of Christianity, it is noteworthy that for him the archetypal Messiah should be Jesus; though historians of religion tell us that the biblical conception of the Messiah as royal liberator from the House of David was replaced, early in the Diaspora, by a humbler conception, influenced by Christianity, which imagined the Messiah as the servant of the poor.[59] Scholem's sources of inspiration were Hauptmann's *Emanuel Quint* and the early novels of Jakob Wassermann. Wassermann's first successful novel, *Die Juden von Zirndorf* (1897), has a long prelude telling how the Jews of seventeenth-century Germany were excited by the messianic pretender Sabbatai Zvi; and, as we have seen, the protagonist in the main part of the novel, Agathon Geyer, denounces assimilated Jewry in prophetic tones, and becomes a lonely wanderer, like Hauptmann's Quint, with messianic accents. Many years later Scholem wrote the standard study of Sabbatai Zvi. Ironically, it seems that his interest in this figure was first aroused by a best-selling novelist of the age of assimilation.[60]

Another kind of messianism was to be found in revolutionary Socialism. From Marx onwards, Jews were prominent in Socialist movements: they included Ferdinand Lassalle, Eduard Bernstein, Paul Singer, Rosa Luxemburg; in the Weimar Republic, Rudolf Hilferding, Georg Gradnauer, and Paul Levi; in Austria, Viktor Adler, his son Friedrich Adler, and the important theorist Otto

---

[57] Ibid. 32. See Hauptmann, *Sämtliche Werke*, ed. Hans-Egon Hass, 11 vols. (Berlin, 1962–74), v. 24–5.   [58] Ibid. 116 (22 May 1915).
[59] See Michael Hilton, *The Christian Effect on Jewish Life* (London, 1994). For Scholem's hostility to Christianity, see especially his letter of Jan. 1955 to the Anglican Beatrice Hirsch-Reich, in *Briefe 1948–1970*, ed. Thomas Sparr (Munich, 1995), pp. 34–5.
[60] See Scholem, *Sabbatai Sevi, the Mystical Messiah* (London, 1973).

Bauer.[61] Socialism had a special appeal for Jewish heirs of the
Enlightenment, for it seemed to promise a humane, cosmopolitan
society in which people would no longer be divided by race,
religion, or class. 'For the Jew,' says Jochanan Bloch, 'the social
revolutionary movement was mainly the attempt at a *revolutionary assimilation*. In this way he hoped to attain real emancipation.'[62] A different note, however, was struck by the extreme
Socialist and anarchist revolutionaries who emerged after the
War. Michael Löwy has argued that there is an elective affinity
between Jewish messianism and modern utopian anarchism. Jewish messianism not only seeks to restore a past ideal state, but
also, in a dialectical relation with this ideal, it seeks to bring about
a radically new future; messianic redemption is envisaged as a
public, historical event, a catastrophic irruption into and transformation of history, creating a wholly new world, overthrowing
all present powers and replacing the restrictions of the Law with a
new, libertarian order. Löwy finds 'a remarkable structural homology, an undeniable spiritual isomorphism, between two cultural
universes, apparently set in completely distinct spheres: namely,
the Jewish messianic tradition and modern revolutionary, especially libertarian, utopias'.[63] He detects messianism especially in
the Independent Socialist Kurt Eisner, the anarchist Gustav
Landauer, and the revolutionary and dramatist Ernst Toller.
Eisner, a Berlin journalist who helped to found the far-left USPD
(Independent Social Democratic Party) in 1917, advocated Socialism with explicitly religious zeal, and was charged during and
after his lifetime with 'emotional Socialism' and political unre-
alism.[64] He was elected prime minister of Bavaria in November
1918 by the newly established workers' councils, but severely
defeated in parliamentary elections in January 1919, and assas-

---

[61] For these and many more examples, see Robert S. Wistrich, *Socialism and the
Jews: The Dilemmas of Assimilation in Germany and Austria-Hungary* (London and
Toronto, 1982).

[62] Bloch, 'Sozialismus und Judentum', *Neue Deutsche Hefte*, 93 (May/June 1963),
86–113 (p. 102).

[63] Löwy, *Redemption and Utopia: Jewish Libertarian Thought in Central Europe*, tr.
Hope Heaney (Stanford, Calif., 1992), p. 21.

[64] See Heinz Sproll, 'Messianisches Denken und pazifistische Utopie im Werk Kurt
Eisners', in Walter Grab (ed.), *Gegenseitige Einflüsse deutscher und jüdischer Kultur
von der Epoche der Aufklärung bis zur Weimarer Republik* (Tel Aviv, 1982), pp. 281–
333; York-Steiner, *Die Kunst als Jude zu leben*, p. 295.

sinated the following month. After conflict between the advocates of parliamentary and of revolutionary democracy, the latter, including the idealists Landauer and Toller and the more
sinister Leviné, seized power and proclaimed a Soviet Republic
in April 1919. When (to the relief of many Munich citizens,
including Thomas Mann) their regime was violently overthrown
by government and Freikorps troops, Leviné was shot, Landauer
beaten to death, and Toller sentenced to five years' solitary
confinement.[65]

All these revolutionaries, however, had passed through assimilation. Lacking close ties to Judaism or thorough knowledge
about Jewish religious tradition, they were enlightened Europeans
who encountered messianic, apocalyptic, and utopian ideas, deriving from many sources, within European and especially within
German culture. Hence there is no need to posit a mysterious
'isomorphism' between messianism and revolution. In 1920s
Germany we see what J. P. Stern has called 'a society longing
for transcendence'.[66] Extremists on both Left and Right sought
charismatic leaders who offered utopian visions of transformed
society.[67] The Jewish Expressionist Albert Ehrenstein declared:
'We await him who will order the world and slay the devil; the
new Christ, the Christian Napoleon, who, if necessary with fire
and sword, with gas and poison, will ride into dehumanized
Europe and give the children who are yet to come equality of
birth, education and inheritance.'[68] Stefan George's poem 'Der
Dichter in Zeiten der Wirren' ('The Poet in Times of Tumult',
1921) fits the times by prophesying the arrival of a charismatic
leader with a small band of followers who will restore order, raise
the people's banner ('das völkische banner'), and establish the
New Empire.[69] Robert Musil reflected in 1937: '*Long before
the dictators* our age produced the intellectual worship of dictators. Look at [Stefan] George. Then Kraus and Freud, Adler and
Jung. Add Klages and Heidegger as well. The common feature is

---

[65] See Richard Dove, *He was a German: A Biography of Ernst Toller* (London,
1990), ch. 5, and for a different perspective, Thomas Mann, *Tagebücher 1918–1921*.
[66] Stern, *Hitler*, p. 92.
[67] See Jost Hermand, *Der alte Traum vom neuen Reich: Völkische Utopien und
Nationalsozialismus* (Frankfurt, 1988).
[68] Ehrenstein, *Briefe an Gott* (Leipzig and Vienna, 1922), p. 93.
[69] George, *Werke*, i. 416–18.

no doubt a need for mastery and leadership, for the character of the Saviour.'[70]

Toller's play *Die Wandlung* (written in 1918, first performed in 1919) follows the development of its hero, Friedrich, from gullible nationalist to messianic leader. His initial situation, as the first scene makes explicit, is that of an assimilated Jew who feels rejected, rootless, and divided. He seeks assimilation first through nationalism, enlisting in a colonial war; even there he is regarded as alien, though he volunteers for a dangerous reconnoitring mission of which he is the only survivor. Back in Germany, he retains his nationalist ideals and tries to embody them in a sculpture called 'Victory of the Fatherland', but is disillusioned by encountering a former fellow-soldier who is now mad and crippled, and smashes the statue. After a spiritual rebirth, intimated only by symbolic scenes, Friedrich learns that assimilation can only be attained by joining humanity at large. He attends a political meeting, warns against violent insurrection, and instead summons the people to meet him at noon in the market-place, where he denounces the frustrations that have hindered their humanity and leads them off to revolution.

In very general terms, Friedrich's revolutionary message recalls prophetic visions of the peaceable kingdom to be inaugurated by the Messiah.[71] However, any attempt to link the play more closely with Jewish messianism is contradicted by Toller's biography, by his intellectual sources, and by the text. Brought up in an assimilated family in Samotschin in Prussian Poland, Toller rejected his family's residual Judaism along with its bourgeois values.[72] His conception of non-violent revolution, aimed not just at redistributing power and property but at transforming humanity, derives from Gustav Landauer.[73] Landauer's ethical and mystical Social-

[70] Musil, *Tagebücher*, ed. Adolf Frisé, 2 vols. (Reinbek, 1976), i. 896. Emphasis in original.

[71] See Michael Ossar, 'Die jüdische messianische Tradition und Ernst Tollers *Wandlung*', in Grimm and Bayerdörfer (eds.), *Im Zeichen Hiobs*, pp. 293–308.

[72] See Alfred Bodenheimer, 'Ernst Toller und sein Judentum', in Itta Shedletzky and Hans Otto Horch (eds.), *Deutsch-jüdische Exil- und Emigrationsliteratur im 20. Jahrhundert* (Tübingen, 1993), pp. 185–93.

[73] See Richard Dove, *Revolutionary Socialism in the Work of Ernst Toller* (New York, Berne, Frankfurt, 1986), pp. 73–9; on the sources of Landauer's thought, Eugene Lunn, *Prophet of Community: The Romantic Socialism of Gustav Landauer* (Berkeley and Los Angeles, 1973).

ism was opposed to mechanistic and materialistic versions of Marxism. He emphasized instead the spiritual capacities in humanity which needed only to be awakened in order to transform society. 'Socialism', wrote Landauer, 'is a cultural movement, a struggle for the nations' beauty, greatness, fullness.'[74] He made heavy use of rhetoric featuring such words as 'Geist', 'Volk', 'Wille', 'Freude' (spirit, people/nation, will, joy). Toller's play conveys Landauer's message through similar rhetoric and especially through insistent Christian imagery of spiritual rebirth. Friedrich's symbolic death is a kind of crucifixion. His fellow-sufferers cry: 'Crucified let us free ourselves, crucified let us redeem ourselves, resurrected to higher freedom.'[75] In his final speech he tells the people: 'You have carved Jesus Christ in wood and nailed Him to a wooden cross, because you yourselves did not want to go the way of the Cross that led Him to redemption' (p. 122). Though often crude, the play is intermittently impressive through its imagery of rebirth and the pathos of Friedrich's final speech with its call for emancipation from fear and want. The problem is that Landauer's utopian Socialism could only be realized by imperfect human beings with mixed motives, and Toller's play, with the involuntary honesty of literature, insists on disclosing the complex motives that underlie and vitiate Friedrich's mission.

In becoming a revolutionary leader, Friedrich is responding not only to humane feelings but to his own situation, clearly described in the first scene, as an imperfectly assimilated Jew. His assumption of leadership is a flight forward: finding that his society does not accept him as an equal, he persuades it to accept him as its leader. His previous spiritual rebirth uneasily combines Christian, Nietzschean, and aesthetic components. As a Jew, he borrows Christian imagery in order to avoid the other symbolic identity available to him, that of 'Ahasver', the Wandering Jew. Thus his *imitatio Christi* is a form of assimilation. So is his Nietzscheanism. The time of his meeting in the market-place

---

[74] Landauer, *Aufruf zum Sozialismus*, ed. Heinz-Joachim Heydorn (Frankfurt and Vienna, 1967) p. 75. Jewish ideas, mediated by Buber, entered Landauer's thought only in the last decade of his life: see Norbert Altenhofer, 'Tradition als Revolution: Gustav Landauers "geworden-werdendes" Judentum', in David Bronsen (ed.), *Jews and Germans from 1860 to 1933: The Problematic Symbiosis* (Heidelberg, 1979), pp. 173–208.

[75] Toller, *Prosa, Briefe, Dramen, Gedichte* (Reinbek, 1979), p. 110. Future references in text.

recalls Zarathustra's 'great noontide'.[76] One of the symbolic scenes represents Friedrich and his friend as two mountaineers ascending a rock-face; Friedrich abandons his friend in order not to compromise his own ideals and his own spiritual development—'Because I won't abandon myself | I'm abandoning you . . . | Good-bye!' (p. 117). Thus the *imitatio Christi*, which should centre on humility and self-sacrifice, is incongruously attached to an ideology of personal authenticity. Friedrich also has an aesthetic mission. In the first scene he considers himself a genius like Strindberg, refuses to learn a profession, and lives on his uncle's pocket-money, which he spends on prostitutes. His career as a sculptor prepares him for the more exciting task of remoulding humanity; we have already seen in Chapter 3 how often the dictator has been imagined as a sculptor working in human flesh. Finally, by agreeing to repeated appeals to become a 'leader' ('Führer', p. 115), Friedrich triumphantly overcomes the social exclusion to which he was subject as a Jew.

Toller's play, like many Expressionist 'dramas of annunciation', evokes a mood of revolutionary intoxication as an end in itself, as an aesthetic sensation.[77] The play shares the tendency of all secularized messianism to slip from the prospect of a new society to the intoxication of the revolutionary moment in which utopian transformation seems possible. Reacting against the messianism of the early 1920s, Karl Mannheim acutely described how the chiliast, sensing the presence of the messianic kingdom, abandons real political transformation for a mystical *experience* of transformation: 'He is not actually concerned with the millenium that is to come; what is important for him is that it happened here and now, and that it arose from mundane existence, as a sudden swing over into another kind of existence.'[78] Instead of transforming the world, the chiliast or messianist transforms only himself.

The renaissance of Jewish culture led by Buber, Rosenzweig, and Scholem was a remarkable achievement. But in neither its

[76] On Toller's Nietzscheanism, see Gerhard P. Knapp, *Die Literatur des deutschen Expressionismus* (Munich, 1979), p. 58.

[77] See Eberhard Lämmert, 'Das expressionistische Verkündigungsdrama', in Hans Steffen (ed.), *Der deutsche Expressionismus: Formen und Gestalten* (Göttingen, 1965), pp. 138–56.

[78] Mannheim, *Ideology and Utopia: An Introduction to the Sociology of Knowledge*, tr. Louis Wirth and Edward Shils (London, 1940), p. 195. See also Kochan, 'The Messiah and the Utopian', in *Jews, Idols and Messiahs*, pp. 192–202.

religious, its cultural, or its political versions was it a rediscovery of a primordial Judaism. The forms of Judaism its proponents revived bore the stamp of the German culture in which they were at home as assimilated and highly educated German Jews.

THE EASTERN JEWS

The Shtetl

Early in the twentieth century, acculturated Jews from Germany and Austria discovered another kind of Jew: the traditional communities inhabiting Poland, Galicia, and western Russia. These communities were virtually annihilated in the Holocaust. So it is understandable that the attempt to learn about their life should now often be impeded by a nostalgic haze. One needs to disregard the paintings of Chagall or the impression created by well-known musicals (based on the far from sentimental tales of Sholem Aleichem). One also has to treat sceptically the much-read book about them by two Columbia University anthropologists, folksily entitled *Life is with People*, and now available in German translation. It has a preface by the notoriously gullible Margaret Mead which makes painfully clear its purpose of satisfying nostalgia for 'the form and the content, the texture and beauty, of the small-town life of Eastern European Jews, as it was lived before World War I, in some places up to World War II, as it still lives in the memories of those who were reared in the shtetl, and in the memories of Jews in other lands [. . .]'.[79] Doubts about the book increase when we learn that Zborowski, born in Ukraine in 1908, was a Stalinist agent provocateur who became the most trusted confidant of Trotsky's son Leon Sedov, passed on the contents of Trotsky's confidential archives to the NKVD, and may have helped to kill Sedov in February 1938. After making an academic career in New York he was exposed as a spy and sentenced to a five-year prison sentence in December 1958.[80]

[79] Mark Zborowski and Elizabeth Herzog, *Life is with People: The Jewish Little-Town of Eastern Europe* (New York, 1952), p. 11. On Mead's gullibility, see Derek Freeman, *Margaret Mead and the Heretic: The Making and Unmaking of an Anthropological Myth* (Ringwood, 1996).

[80] See Isaac Don Levine, *The Mind of an Assassin* (London, 1959); Isaac Deutscher, *The Prophet Outcast: Trotsky 1929–1940* (London, 1963).

While respectable, he had every motive for establishing his career by literary opportunism. The book provides a general, timeless account of shtetl life, ignoring regional differences and heavily emphasizing its religious framework. Though published after the Holocaust, it is, amazingly, written in the anthropological present tense. It offers a powerful instrument of denial. Ruth Gay aptly compares it to Moritz Oppenheim's paintings that idealized Jewish life before emancipation.[81]

An idealized view of Eastern Jewish communities would see them as homogeneous villages or small towns (*shtetlekh*) with a strongly religious atmosphere. In fact, like the Jewish communities of Germany before emancipation, they were stratified and divided. Thus Moshe Rosman's study of Miedzybóž, the town where the Ba⁣ᶜal Shem lived, shows that better-off Jews, such as estate managers and innkeepers, were often ruthless in exploiting tradesmen, who, not trusting the *kahal* (governing body of the Jewish community), might appeal over their heads to the local Polish magnate for protection against such extortion.[82] Nor was the shtetl wholly separate from Gentile influences. It normally had a mixed population of Jews and Gentiles. Many Jews were innkeepers who doubled as landlords' agents: besides distilling and selling liquor and accommodating travellers, they ran village shops, collected the landlord's rents from the peasants, and bought grain on behalf of Jewish merchants in neighbouring cities. As a sideline they cultivated small pieces of land and raised vegetables and dairy products for themselves and their dependants. Many Jews scraped a living as pedlars, hawking goods among hamlets and farmsteads. Jews practised a great variety of crafts, but were especially common as tailors, shoemakers, and bakers. Before the advent of railways they were also employed in transport, as coachmen and porters. Very few were primarily occupied with agriculture, though in the eastern foothills of the Carpathians a quarter of the local Jewish population was engaged in primitive farming.[83] Between 1835 and 1850 the Russian government set up colonies including some 30,000 Jewish farmers in the underpopulated region north of the Black Sea; among them was David Bronshtayn, the father of

---

[81] Ruth Gay, 'Inventing the Shtetl', *American Scholar*, 53 (1984), 329–49 (p. 330); cf. Jonathan Boyarin, *Storm from Paradise: The Politics of Jewish Memory* (Minneapolis, 1992), p. 61.   [82] Rosman, *Founder of Hasidism*, ch. 5.
[83] Arthur Ruppin, *Soziologie der Juden*, 2 vols. (Berlin, 1930–1), i. 407.

Trotsky, who farmed some 650 acres on the Kherson steppe.[84]
Trotsky's memoirs are unusual among Jewish autobiographies in
beginning with a description of life on a farm.

By the late nineteenth century, the shtetl was becoming overcrowded. Its inhabitants were moving to urban slums or emigrating to London, Manchester, New York, or Chicago. According to
the 1880 census, 413,000 of the 686,596 Jews in Galicia (i.e. 60
per cent) were living in towns; the Jews made up 11.52 per cent of
the total population, but 40 per cent of the urban population.[85]
The actor Alexander Granach, born in Galicia in 1890, evokes the
Jewish quarter of Horodenka in his childhood in a way that recalls
Börne's description of the Frankfurt ghetto:

The lower lanes were dirty and stank, and if rain and frost had not washed
away the dirt and purified the air, the people would simply have suffocated. The little wooden shacks formed an unbroken line, for it was
cheaper to build on to your neighbour's wall. The houses squeezed,
pressed, leaned against each other like frail, sickly beings who are weak
and cold and afraid of being alone. In these shacks dwelt poverty: cob-
blers, tailors, carpenters, plumbers, barrel-makers, masons, furriers,
bakers, and all manner of coachmen and porters—all hard-working
people who rushed around all day to earn a piece of bread or five kreuzers,
so that their rooms full of children should get something to eat.[86]

The ghetto, formerly a feature of Western towns, now survived
only in the East, except when recreated by immigrants to the
Leopoldstadt in Vienna or the Scheunenviertel in Berlin.

Despite the lure of secular culture, to some extent the traditional religious universe still survived. The community centred on
the *shul* (synagogue) and on the *beys-medresh* (house of study) in
which pious men would pore over the Torah at all hours of the day.
All except the smallest communities would have more than one
beys-medresh; the township of Zetl described by Rachel Ertel,
with a Jewish population of 3,450, had four, besides two small
shtiblekh (oratories). Close by would be the *mikve* (ritual bath).[87]

---

[84] Leon Trotsky, *My Life: An Attempt at an Autobiography* (Harmondsworth,
1975), pp. 6–7.
[85] Abraham Korkis, 'Die wirtschaftliche Lage der Juden in Galizien. 1. Teil', *Der
Jude*, 2 (1917–18), vii. 464–71 (p. 469).
[86] Granach, *Da geht ein Mensch* (Munich, 1990), pp. 70–1.
[87] Ertel, *Le Shtetl: La Bourgade juive de Pologne de la tradition à la modernité*
(Paris, 1982).

These buildings provided the religious topography of the shtetl, while its religious chronology ensured that each day was punctuated by prayers and ritual ablutions, each week by the Sabbath and its ceremonies, and each year by a succession of festivals.

An understanding of religion was transmitted through the *heder* (primary school). Here, as often in present-day teaching practice, the target language, Hebrew, was also the medium of instruction. There were no Hebrew–Yiddish dictionaries. Pupils were supposed to pick Hebrew up by having the prayers and other texts translated. This method had limited success: most males in Jewish eastern Europe could read a prayer-book and the Torah with Rashi's commentary, but had very limited ability to read an unfamiliar text in Hebrew.[88] Given its unsystematic character, in which difficult texts and topics might be introduced without preparation, this form of education was probably stimulating for the gifted, but unrewarding for the average child, and of limited effectiveness as a means of diffusing literacy or religious knowledge.

In most reports the *heder* sounds an unattractive institution. A visitor from Germany, Bertha Pappenheim, describes with horror the unhygienic conditions in which classes of sixty, eighty, or a hundred children were cooped up, in terror of being beaten with a stick or a *Kantuk* (a whip with leather thongs).[89] A more sympathetic observer, himself brought up in Ukraine, says: 'The schools, which resemble holes rather than human habitations, are more designed to send the feeble creatures to the cemetery than to equip them for life.'[90] Joseph Bloch, a distinguished Viennese rabbi who was born in Dukla in Galicia in 1850, comments in his memoirs on the unhygienic character of the *heder*, which he entered at the age of 3. When he was transferred to a *melamed* (teacher) to study the Talmud, conditions were little better: 'Instruction was dispensed in the teacher's house, in a room that served simultaneously as bedroom, living-room and classroom. In this room,

---

[88] See Shaul Stampfer, 'What did "knowing Hebrew" mean in Eastern Europe?', in Lewis Glinert (ed.), *Hebrew in Ashkenaz: A Language in Exile* (New York and Oxford, 1993), pp. 129–40.

[89] Pappenheim, *Zur Lage der jüdischen Bevölkerung in Galizien* (1904), repr. in *Sisyphus: Gegen den Mädchenhandel*, ed. Helga Heubach (Freiburg, 1992), p. 50. See Amy Colin, 'Metamorphosen einer Frau: Von Anna O. zu Bertha Pappenheim', in Jutta Dick and Barbara Hahn (eds.), *Von einer Welt in die andere: Jüdinnen im 19. und 20. Jahrhundert* (Vienna, 1993), pp. 216–31.

[90] M. J. bin Gorion, *Vom östlichen Judentum* (Berlin and Vienna, 1918), p. 13.

therefore, I spent the whole morning, the whole afternoon and finally the evening until ten o'clock, with an hour's break for each meal.'[91] On the other hand, E. M. Lipschütz, while acknowledging that discipline was severe, describes how the children played games, how their teachers told them stories and taught them to swim (as advocated in the Talmud), celebrated the festivals of Passover with them, and followed the custom of taking them out to the fields to practise archery on the festival of Lag Ba-Omer.[92]

When Westerners first became aware of this world in the eighteenth century, they regarded it with the disapproval which the Enlightenment felt towards superstition and obscurantism. Eastern Jews might be seen in Vienna or encountered by Habsburg administrators. In his description of Vienna, the Enlightener Johann Pezzl includes 'Polish Jews' among the diverse nationalities to be seen in the capital's streets: 'The Polish Jews, all robed in black, present themselves as scarecrows, with contorted faces and matted hair, a living satire on their supposed special election.'[93] An attempt at objectivity is made by the administrator Joseph Rohrer, chief of police in Lemberg (now Lviv), who undertook a multi-volume ethnographic study of the peoples of the Habsburg Empire, including a volume on the Jews. For the most part, it is an unusually cool, descriptive, detailed work, by a professed admirer of Dohm and Mendelssohn. Rohrer corrects the stereotyped notion that Jews are all innkeepers or procurers by noting that many are tailors, moneylenders, or dealers in small goods, while in the Bukovina a number practise agriculture.[94] However, his personal, emotional responses form a strange counterpoint to his cool

---

[91] Joseph S. Bloch, *Erinnerungen aus meinem Leben*, 2 vols. (Vienna and Leipzig, 1922), i. 1. Cf. the hostile description of a *heder* in the East End of London, quoted in David Feldman, *Englishmen and Jews* (New Haven and London, 1994), p. 338.

[92] Lipschütz, 'Das Leben des Kindes im Cheder', *Der Jude*, 4 (1919–20), ix. 413–18.

[93] Pezzl, *Skizze von Wien* (Vienna, 1789), p. 64. The 'matted hair' is a symptom of a disease formerly endemic in eastern Europe, known as *plica polonica*, and associated by observers especially with Jews: see Larry Wolff, *Inventing Eastern Europe: The Map of Civilization on the Mind of the Enlightenment* (Stanford, Calif., 1994), p. 30.

[94] Joseph Rohrer, *Versuch über die jüdischen Bewohner der österreichischen Monarchie* (Vienna, 1804), p. 59. On him, see Ritchie Robertson, 'Joseph Rohrer and the Bureaucratic Enlightenment', *Austrian Studies*, 2 (1991), 22–42. For other writers on Galician Jewry, see Wolfgang Häusler, *Das galizische Judentum in der Habsburgermonarchie im Lichte der zeitgenössischen Publizistik und Reiseliteratur von 1772–1848* (Vienna, 1979).

description. For example, after describing the Jews' costume, he says:

If, in addition to this gloomy and heavy garb, one imagines a distraught face in which fear, envy and malice have etched their signs, then one can form some notion of how the sensitive German must feel during the first years of his residence in a country where such a self-disfiguring people plays the leading role amid smiling green meadows![95]

By presenting himself as a sensitive German, responsive to nature, Rohrer lends specious plausibility to his counter-construction of the Jew as aesthetically unpleasing, alienated from nature, and devoted to those passions—fear, envy, and malice—which contradict man's presumed natural goodness.

As an Enlightener, Rohrer dismisses the Talmud as superstitious nonsense, and as a mercantilist, he complains that the Jews are to a large extent employed unproductively, are too unhealthy to make useful soldiers, and are disqualified by their religion from most civil duties. His solution is a drastic one. Jews prepared to take up productive work should be placed in forced labour institutions modelled on English workhouses or the Philadelphia penitentiary. 'Immoral' Jews should be sent abroad to settlements resembling those at Sydney Cove and Norfolk Island, which Rohrer greatly admires; he proposes that Austria should enter into an agreement with a colonial power like Britain or Holland to establish penal settlements overseas. Alternatively, they should be confined in prisons using the Philadelphia system of solitary confinement; if they have to work with other prisoners, these should be forbidden to speak to them. Such drastic philosemitism expresses, as has recently been said, 'a latently totalitarian Enlightenment' which professes tolerance while aiming to remodel unproductive outsiders—here the Galician Jews—and absorb them into the functional machinery of the mercantilist state.[96]

So long as Jewish life remained cordoned off from Gentile influences, the community was also able to avoid internal dissension arising from intellectual frustration. But by cultivating people's intelligence, it unwittingly ensured that when the Haskala (the Jewish Enlightenment) made secular Western texts available

---

[95] Rohrer, *Versuch*, p. 52.
[96] Chris Thornhill, ' "Grenzfälle": Galician Jews and Austrian Enlightenment', *GLL* 49 (1996), 171–81 (p. 172).

in Hebrew or Yiddish, many *yeshive* graduates would be curious to explore them, especially as traditional Jewish life seemed condemned to increasing poverty and discomfort. And since Jewish culture formed a seamless web, enfolding every aspect of life, it could not be combined with Western culture, but had to be accepted or rejected wholesale. Hermann Cohen, who met many Russian and Polish Jews on a lecture tour in May 1914, reported: 'I often observed an intellectual cleavage splitting the mind of the Eastern Jew: there is no way of mediating between orthodoxy and religious indifferentism.'[97] In Cohen's opinion, the vacuum left by abandoning orthodox Judaism was often filled in Russia by nihilism. Certainly, by 1900 many young Jews in eastern Europe were disposed to reject their religion, often in favour of secular causes like Socialism or Zionism.

Western Jews were aware of Eastern Jews mainly as immigrants to German cities. Eastern Jewish refugees began arriving in Germany after the Russian pogroms of 1881. Between then and 1914, some 2,750,000 Eastern Jews left Europe for Britain, the United States, and other overseas destinations, and a high proportion passed through Germany to embark at Hamburg or Bremen.[98] German Jews reacted to them with ambivalence, working and contributing immense sums both to relieve their sufferings and to prevent their settlement in Germany by facilitating their transit to Britain and America. Those Eastern Jews who did settle in Germany—70,000, according to the 1910 census—were not homogeneous. They formed distinct communities of Russian, Romanian, or Galician Jews. Most of them worked as artisans, pedlars, salesmen, or small businessmen, or catered for the German Jewish community as rabbis, teachers, ritual slaughterers, etc. Nevertheless, they often aroused unease and even hostility among Western Jews. To assimilated Western Jews, the Easterners represented the return of the repressed, a reminder of the ghetto past. Feeling their own position in Germany to be precarious, they transferred their aggression from the sacrosanct Germans to the poor Eastern Jews who represented an image

---

[97] Cohen, 'Der polnische Jude', *Der Jude*, 1 (1916–17), iii. 149–56 (p. 152).
[98] Steven E. Aschheim, *Brothers and Strangers: The East European Jew in German and German Jewish Consciousness, 1800–1923* (Madison, Wis., 1982), p. 37. See also Jack Wertheimer, *Unwelcome Strangers: East European Jews in Imperial Germany* (New York and Oxford, 1987).

of the Jew from which Westerners wished to dissociate themselves. Jakob Wassermann lamented in 1925: 'The War and post-War years have allowed much filth and foulness to drift to the surface', including 'the hordes of half-barbaric Polish and Russian Jews, greedy for life and booty, who were imprisoned for generations in the wilderness of the ghetto by a wholly barbaric autocracy and, because of the War, have unfortunately been let loose on Germany, the land of the centre.'[99] Ruth Klüger recalls how, even in a concentration camp, 'emancipated' Jewish women like her mother still felt distaste for Eastern Jewish women: when the latter arrived, 'we immediately became a two-class society. Our side maintained that the others were dirty, and kept themselves aloof.'[100]

These attitudes can be partially explained by considering the construction of the Eastern Jew or *Ostjude*. The term *Ostjude* dates only from the early twentieth century. It reflects above all the self-understanding of acculturated German Jews. Before the age of emancipation, Jews from eastern Europe were not felt to be alien; when they entered western Europe, local Jews integrated them into their own communities. But as emancipation loosened these communities, such visitors were less welcome and more obviously different. The term *Ostjude* was never neutral: it denoted the Jew who failed to measure up to Western standards of acculturation, and was especially used in phrases like *Ostjudengefahr* ('Eastern Jewish peril').[101] People who used it disclosed not their superiority but their insecurity about their own assimilation. As Joachim Prinz wrote in 1933, the agitation against Eastern Jews ('Ostjudenhetze') conducted by Westerners was 'fear of the mirror, fear of the past'.[102]

The projective function of the Eastern Jew can be illustrated from the dispute between Theodor Lessing and Binjamin Segel. In 1909 Lessing published in the *Allgemeine Zeitung des Judentums* what purported to be an account of his tour among Jewish communities in Galicia, though in fact he only visited Cracow. He gives a very hostile and sensational description of the eastern

---

[99] Wassermann, 'Offener Brief an den Herausgeber einer Monatsschrift für "Kulturelle Erneuerung"' (1925), in *Lebensdienst: Gesammelte Studien, Erfahrungen und Reden aus drei Jahrzehnten* (Leipzig and Zurich, 1928), pp. 155–9 (p. 158).

[100] Klüger, *weiter leben*, p. 149.   [101] Wertheimer, *Unwelcome Strangers*, p. 6.

[102] Prinz, *Wir Juden*, p. 51.

Jews' squalor; their air of perpetual watchfulness, in which everyone seemed to be constantly calculating his own advantage; their 'Jargondeutsch'; their practice of prostitution, which Lessing alleges to be consistent with the low status assigned to women in orthodox Judaism; their addiction to empty talmudic disputation; and the 'fanatical' ecstasy of a Hasidic synagogue service. Unable to endure any more of 'people screaming and talking through their noses', twitching convulsively, weeping, sobbing, and 'gesticulating like maniacs', Lessing presently rushed out into the fresh air and felt relieved at seeing 'the clear blue night sky and the great healthy stars'.[103] Thus he implies a contrast between the unhealthy, enclosed, semi-insane religion of the Jews and the healthy natural world outside, which is a traditional topos in Western accounts of Eastern Jews. He also asserts that the material wretchedness of the Eastern Jews compels them continually to lie and cheat.

Although this account of Galician Jewry must have satisfied the preconceived notions held by the *Allgemeine Zeitung*'s assimilationist and conservative readership, Lessing was also charged with inventing the inaccuracies, inconsistencies, and implausibilities in his account. In his feeble reply, Lessing tried to wrong-foot his critics by charging them with a touchiness that was, he said, part of Jewish pathology.[104] It would have been still more difficult, however, to rebut the book-length attack by Segel, which not only points out Lessing's errors in detail but charges him with absorbing and reproducing antisemitic stereotypes. Even the distinction Lessing draws between Western and Eastern Jews arises, so Segel argues, from the antisemitism that is widespread among assimilated Jews in western Europe. Anxious for acceptance in 'Aryan' society, assimilationists project their own self-contempt onto the unassimilated Jews who are several rungs further down the ladder. The construction of the 'Eastern Jew' provides the insecure Western Jew with people to despise:

The same spirit [*scil. the spirit of Jewish antisemitism*] sustains the now widespread distinction between Eastern and Western Jews (*'Ostjuden'*

[103] Lessing, 'Eindrücke aus Galizien', *Allgemeine Zeitung des Judentums*, 73 (3 Dec. 1909), 587–8; (17 Dec.), 610–11; (24 Dec.), 620–2; (31 Dec.), 634–5. Quotations from p. 611.

[104] See S. Kalischer, 'Glossen zu den "Eindrücken aus Galizien"', *Allgemeine Zeitung des Judentums*, 74 (28 Jan. 1910), 45–6; and Lessing's reply, 'Galizien. Zur Abwehr', *Allgemeine Zeitung des Judentums*, 74 (18 Feb. 1910), 77–8.

und 'Westjuden'). The latter think themselves entitled to look down on the former from the height of their European culture and moneybags, just as the true-blooded Aryan looks down on all Jews. Dr Lessing's noble expectorations are merely the most venomous expression of this outlook.[105]

Segel argues further that the distinction between Eastern and Western Jews is modelled on the earlier, equally invidious distinction between Ashkenazim and Sephardim (German and Spanish Jews), in which the latter were supposed to be culturally and physically superior.

We should therefore treat with caution the familiar distinction between *Westjuden* and *Ostjuden*. It is not a neutral description of anthropological facts. It is rather an instrument of perception by which Jews in western European countries defined themselves by contrast to others. The contrast might, as Segel suggests, serve the self-esteem of the European Jews who coined and propagated it. But it could also work the other way, allowing European Jews to express their sense of inferiority by contrast with the supposedly 'authentic' Jews of the East. Thus Kafka recorded in his diary for March 1915 a meeting with Jews from Galicia who had found refuge in Prague:

Eastern and Western Jews (*Ost- und Westjuden*), an evening. The contempt of the Eastern Jews for the Jews here. This contempt is deserved. The Eastern Jews know the reason for this contempt, the Western Jews do not.[106]

Kafka illustrates a major change of perspective. The traditional attitude to Eastern Jews held by Westerners was ill-informed disapproval. Mired in primitive superstition, Eastern Jews should be compelled, for their own good, to adopt Western manners and become productive citizens. A shift in attitude is marked by Heine, who visited Poland in 1822. 'The external appearance of the Polish Jew is terrible,' he writes about his first sight of a shtetl. Then, however, his revulsion is tempered by pity: 'But compassion soon shouldered out disgust when I took a closer look at the way these people lived; when I saw the pigsty-like hovels which they inhabit and in which they jabber, pray, haggle, and are miserable'

---

[105] Segel, *Die Entdeckungsreise des Herrn Dr. Theodor Lessing zu den Ostjuden* (Lemberg, 1910), p. 49.   [106] Kafka, *Tagebücher*, p. 730.

(H ii. 75–6).[107] Thus Heine maintains a complex view of the Polish Jews. He does not idealize them: while they really do talk an unpleasing language ('mauscheln') and engage in petty trade ('schachern'), they are also wretched and deserve our compassion, not our contempt.

The rehabilitation of the Eastern Jews was pioneered by Nathan Birnbaum and Martin Buber. Birnbaum, who, though born in Vienna, became an enthusiast for Yiddish, organized the conference on Yiddish at Czernowitz in 1908, and maintained that the Yiddish-speaking Jews had a cultural integrity which the Westerners had sacrificed to illusory ideals of assimilation:

The Eastern Jew has the sharply distinctive character which an old cultural identity confers on man, whether he is struggling for new values or living by old ones. Lacking this character, the Western Jew has something dull, colourless, I might almost say boring about him, because he has almost entirely lost contact with the Jewish people (*Volkstum*) and not regained it, and, with a very few exceptions, he has not put down roots in a non-Jewish people.[108]

By using words like *Volkstum* and 'roots', Birnbaum is adopting the language of Herderian nationalism, which requires authentic peoples to be rooted in the soil, only to turn it against its anti-semitic users. Instead of seeking an impossible and destructive assimilation to Germany, the Jews, in Birnbaum's opinion, need to recover an authentic national identity by returning to their own roots. But while Birnbaum did induce some German Jews to regard the Easterners more sympathetically, he had less impact on a wide public than did the young Buber.

Buber's main achievement was to present the West with an acceptable image of Hasidism. As a young man he took part in the Zionist movement and also studied mysticism, writing a doctoral dissertation on Jakob Böhme. The five years he spent studying Hasidism enabled him to combine his interest in mysticism with the construction of a new Jewish identity. It resulted not in

[107] Translation from Prawer, *Heine's Jewish Comedy*, p. 61. See Ritchie Robertson, 'Enlightened and Romantic Views of the Ghetto: David Friedländer vs. Heinrich Heine', in Anne Fuchs and Florian Krobb (eds.), *Ghetto Writing: Traditional and Eastern Jewry in German-Jewish Prose* (Columbia, SC, 1999), pp. 26–42.

[108] Birnbaum, 'Etwas über Ost- und Westjuden' (1904), in *Die jüdische Moderne*, p. 154. See E. S. Goldsmith, *Architects of Yiddishism at the Beginning of the Twentieth Century* (Rutherford, NJ, 1976); Wistrich, *The Jews of Vienna*, pp. 381–420.

academic work but in several books in which Buber retold the
parables and stories attributed to the Baᶜal Shem and other Hasidic masters, beginning with *Die Geschichten des Rabbi Nachman*
(1906) and *Die Legende des Baal Schem* (1908). These tales
inspired in many Western Jews an intense interest in what had
hitherto seemed an obscure and embarrassing corner of the Jewish
past. However, they were not based on any close acquaintance
with contemporary Hasidic communities, but on the study and
adaptation of early material. Finding the tales disappointingly
thin, crude, and clumsy, Buber deliberately rendered them in
poetic prose, convinced that in doing so he was getting closer to
the original than the first hearers of the legends, thanks to his
'innate inward affinity to Hasidic truth'.[109] The historian Isaac
Deutscher, who was brought up in a Hasidic community in Galicia,
has recorded the scorn he and some contemporaries felt for
Buber's idealizations of Hasidism: 'Through all the thick gilt
and varnish of romanticists like Martin Buber, we could see,
and smell, the obscurantism of our archaic religion and a way of
life unchanged since the middle ages.'[110] Buber's presentation and
interpretation of Hasidism were to receive detailed and scholarly
criticism from Gershom Scholem.[111] In fairness, however, it must
be said that Buber later rewrote these tales in a simpler style,
and that in presenting the deeds and sayings of Hasidic saints he
was drawing attention to a spiritual tradition within Judaism
that was foreign to those who associated it only with Talmud
study and synagogue observance. His presentation of Hasidism
formed part of Buber's reinterpretation of Judaism as a religion
of inwardness, paralleling the theological explorations of his
friend Franz Rosenzweig. And, though based on very different
assumptions, Buber's work can be placed alongside Scholem's
lifelong commitment to recovering the lost tradition of Kabbalistic
mysticism.

In the wake of Birnbaum and Buber, many German and Austrian
Jews took an increased interest in their Yiddish-speaking fellow-

---

[109] Buber, 'Mein Weg zum Chassidismus' (1917), in *Werke*, 3 vols. (Munich and
Heidelberg, 1962–4), iii. 969.
[110] Deutscher, *The Non-Jewish Jew and Other Essays*, ed. Tamara Deutscher (London, 1968), p. 47.
[111] Scholem, 'Martin Buber's Interpretation of Hasidism', in *The Messianic Idea in
Judaism and Other Essays on Jewish Spirituality* (New York, 1971), pp. 228–50.

Jews. Some, like Arnold Zweig, encountered them during war service on the eastern Front, others, like Kafka and Brod, met them as refugees; some, like Hugo Bergman and Alfred Döblin, travelled to eastern Europe in order to observe their culture; others, like Joseph Roth, celebrated the immigrants they met in western cities. A very few, like Jiři Langer and Max Mayer, gave up Western ways in order to immerse themselves in the life of Hasidic communities.[112] In fiction and drama, Eastern Jews in a Western setting are sometimes presented as melodramatically sinister, like the terrible Simon Kaftan in Walter Mehring's *Der Kaufmann von Berlin* (1929) or the old-clothes dealer Krakauer, described in a stage direction as a 'mythical ghetto figure', in Carl Zuckmayer's *Der Hauptmann von Köpenick* (1931).[113] Sometimes, however, Eastern Jews are mysterious and oracular, like the Berlin immigrants in Döblin's *Berlin Alexanderplatz* (1929) and Hermann Broch's *Huguenau* (1932). Realist portrayals of Eastern Jewish immigrants are rare: the major examples, H. W. Katz's *Schloßgasse 21* and Martin Beradt's *Beide Seiten einer Straße*, were first published long after the Second World War.[114] However, I want now to examine fiction that undertook to depict the Jewish communities of eastern Europe at various stages in their disintegration.

Ghetto Fiction

The change of attitude towards the Eastern Jews heralded by Birnbaum and Buber is also found in ghetto fiction. This body of fiction has two strands: one which treats Jewish life nostalgically, another which treats it critically. Ghetto fiction dates mainly from the nineteenth century, the period in which the assimilation of the Jews to German and Austrian society did, despite setbacks, seem to be taking place.[115] German-Jewish writers had to assist the process of assimilation by contending against fictional conventions

[112] See Langer, *Nine Gates*, tr. Stephen Jolly (London, 1961); Mayer, 'A German Jew goes East'.
[113] Zuckmayer, *Dramen* (Frankfurt, 1960), p. 380. On Zuckmayer's portrayal of Jews, see John R. P. McKenzie, *Social Comedy in Austria and Germany 1890–1933* (Berne, 1992), pp. 142–4.
[114] Katz, *Schloßgasse 21* (Weinheim, 1994); Beradt, *Beide Seiten einer Straße: Roman aus dem Scheunenviertel* (Berlin, 1993).
[115] See Gabriele von Glasenapp, *Aus der Judengasse: Zur Entstehung und Ausprägung deutschsprachiger Ghettoliteratur im 19. Jahrhundert* (Tübingen, 1996).

which represented the Jews as irredeemably alien or as repulsive, dishonest and calculating, like the most memorable creations of Freytag and Raabe. A frequent response was to portray the Jews as possessing all the middle-class German virtues, especially a warm domestic life. Often, however, these domestic scenes are remote in time or space. They can be set in recollections of family life, or in the historic past. The earliest example may be the Passover feast in Heine's *Der Rabbi von Bacherach*, his unfinished novel begun in the early 1820s. Berthold Auerbach gives a pleasant description of the Sabbath evening early in his historical novel *Spinoza* (1837).[116] Besides giving non-Jewish readers a favourable picture of Jewish family life, such scenes satisfied the sentimental nostalgia of Jewish readers for the supposed solidarity of life before emancipation. Presently these scenes become remote in space rather than in time. They are transposed to the relatively unassimilated communities of eastern Europe. As the integration of Jews into German society proceeded, these stories had to be set ever further away. Thus Leopold Kompert, at mid-century, wrote a successful series of Novellen about the Jews of Bohemia, and his imitator Aron Bernstein set the Novellen *Mendel Gibbor* (1860) and *Vögele der Maggid* (1865) in Prussian Poland. Such fiction tends to be sentimental, nostalgic, and idyllic. It tones down the alien character of Jewish culture by representing it as quaint but intelligible. Jewish terms and customs are presented as curious survivals from the past and reassuringly explained by a German translation in brackets, thus: 'Barmizwe (Einsegnung)' or 'Marschallik (Spaßmacher)'.

Different problems were raised, however, when it came to representing the Jewish communities further east in Galicia. The appearance and manners of the Eastern Jews were often felt to be alien and repellent. The critical and ethnographical approach to the Eastern Jews finds its way into literary accounts of them. The book by Leo Herzberg-Fränkel, *Polnische Juden: Geschichten und Bilder* (1867), was published in a series called 'Ethnographische Studien'; it sets out to depict the peculiar customs of the Polish Jews in fictional form. Herzberg-Fränkel is shamelessly tendentious in singling out for depiction those customs of which he most strongly disapproves, such as Talmud study and early marriage.

---

[116] Auerbach, *Gesammelte Schriften*, x. (ch. 2).

His stories are not of much literary interest; their importance lies in anticipating the work of Karl Emil Franzos, the master of ghetto fiction.

I now turn to two novels about Galician life: Karl Emil Franzos's *Der Pojaz* (1905) and Joseph Roth's *Hiob* (1930). While combining nostalgia and criticism in differing degrees, they also present shtetl life in different literary modes. Franzos is a nineteenth-century realist, Roth a self-conscious modernist. In both texts, the literary mode helps to shape and complicate the message that the author seeks to transmit.

Although Franzos gained international fame for his fictional and journalistic accounts of traditional Jewish life, he did not himself belong to such a community. His family observed none of the ritual laws and never attended synagogue, though they ensured that Franzos learnt Hebrew. His father, a doctor, was posted first to Czortkow (now Chortkov) in what was then the eastern extremity of Galicia, where Franzos was born in 1848, and then in 1859 transferred to Czernowitz (the capital of the Bukovina; now Chernovtsy). In Czortkow the young Franzos had little contact with other Jews apart from his Hebrew teacher; later he occasionally visited the important Hasidic community of Sadagóra, near Czernowitz, but only as a spectator. His family's assimilationist ideals were directed towards Germany; Franzos learnt to consider the Austro-Hungarian Empire a backward, corrupt, and redundant state, and Galicia its most benighted province. After his father's death Franzos studied law in order to support his close relatives, but as he could not practise law without converting, he turned to journalism and acquired fame by describing the Eastern Jewish world of which he so disapproved. His most successful collection of stories, *Die Juden von Barnow* (1877), was translated into twelve languages. He coined the name 'Half-Asia' for the vast area of eastern Europe stretching from Poland across Galicia and Ukraine to the Black Sea. In his fiction, essays, and travel sketches, he campaigned for its inhabitants, especially the Jews, to be freed from religious obscurantism and corrupt bureaucracy by the spread of German culture in the emancipatory spirit of Lessing and Schiller.

These ideals find their richest expression in Franzos's novel *Der Pojaz* (*The Clown*). Although he completed it in 1893, it was published only in 1905, the year after his death, perhaps because the spread of antisemitism and the Zionist response had shaken Franzos's faith in his Enlightenment outlook. The novel pays homage to German classicism in centring on a hero who seeks liberation from confining circumstances through the theatre, as, above all, in Goethe's novel *Wilhelm Meisters Lehrjahre* (1795–6). Franzos substitutes a Jewish hero, Sender Glatteis, a gifted boy brought up by a strong-willed foster-mother, Rosel Kurländer, in the harshly repressive shtetl of Barnow. His talent for mimicry finds no outlet except in practical jokes. On a visit to Czernowitz he sees a performance of *The Merchant of Venice*, which so enraptures him that he seeks out the director, an assimilated Jew named Nadler, who recognizes Sender's talent and promises to take him on in two years, provided he learns German in the meantime. Although the strict Jews of Barnow are forbidden to study German, Sender manages to learn it from a student, Heinrich Wild, who is serving in the army as punishment for taking part in the 1848 uprising; then he gains access to the library of the local monastery by bribing the porter, and is helped to understand Schiller by another dissident, Pater Marian, who has been exiled to Barnow for dabbling in the Higher Criticism. He becomes liable for military service, which is allocated by a lottery in which the unlucky winners become recruits. Summoned to the lottery, Sender realizes from the name on the summons that Rosel is not his real mother; he thus simultaneously betrays his knowledge of German to the rabbi, and these two shocks, affecting a constitution weakened by long study in the ice-cold monastery, bring on a haemorrhage. Sender proves to be consumptive. This exempts him from army service but also threatens his intended career as an actor. He does set off to join Nadler's company in Czernowitz, but is halted by floods, so that his foster-mother manages to catch up with him. Realizing that she has devoted her life to him although he was not her flesh and blood, he agrees to return, and manages to save her from a murderous attack by her vagabond husband, receiving a wound of which he dies.

Sender's goal is not in itself unattainable. He has a real-life prototype in the internationally known Jewish actor Bogumil Dawison (1818–72), who was born in Warsaw, joined the Vienna Burgtheater in 1849, and later toured Europe and America; his best roles included Shylock and Franz Moor, parts which also appeal to Sender, and he actually makes an appearance near the end of the novel. And Sender's failure is at least more honourable than that of Anton Reiser, whose theatrical mania leads him into long marches through central Germany trying to catch up with travelling troupes that always turn out to have moved on or dispersed.

The obstacles that defeat Sender are twofold. One is the sheer rigid oppressiveness of his surroundings, which Franzos depicts in accordance with the critical tradition of ghetto realism. Traditional customs are represented not as quaint but as instruments of repression. Thus he inveighs against the *heder*, because children are taught to dispute about absurd questions (how many rungs had Jacob's ladder?) with the aid of brutal discipline: Sender's first teacher actually breaks the child's arm while punishing him. Franzos recommends that the *heder* should be abolished forcibly, with 'the vitriol of force, which can sometimes be very salutary'.[117] He attacks the practice of early marriage and the machinations of the marriage-broker. He describes in horrified detail the activities of the *Fehlermacher*, whose business it is to save young men from military recruitment by inducing illnesses or injuries. Here is an example of the *Fehlermacher*'s sales pitch, addressed to the mother of a potential recruit:

For thirty Gulden I'll cut one of your lad's tendons, so that he'll limp for the rest of his life, or chop off two of his fingers, if you'd prefer that! But if you're prepared to spend more money, we'll do something really high-class that can be cured again. Whatever the boy is like, send him to me! How about chronic stomach trouble—strongly recommended! Or consumption—even better, it can't be told apart from the real thing! (p. 145)[118]

These soul- and body-destroying practices are underwritten by religion. Franzos depicts Hasidim as gloomy fanatics, ruled by power-hungry obscurantists and venal *tsaddikim*. While the rabbi is normally not a sacred figure but a learned man who settles disputes, the Hasidic 'Wunderrabbi' or *tsaddik* is supposed to

[117] Franzos, *Der Pojaz* (Königstein, 1979), p. 36; future references in text. See Fred Sommer, *'Halb-Asien': German Nationalism and the Eastern European Works of Karl Emil Franzos* (Stuttgart, 1984).

[118] Cf. the description of another 'Fehlermacher', Beer Blitzer, in Franzos, *Moschko von Parma: Geschichte eines jüdischen Soldaten* (Leipzig, 1880), pp. 180–1.

have the power of working miracles by intercession with God, and to transmit this power to his heirs. Sadagóra was the seat of a famous dynasty of *tsaddikim*, represented in Franzos's day by Israel Ruzhin Friedmann, who had moved there after getting embroiled with the Russian police across the nearby frontier; they had charged him with ordering the killing of two Jewish informers, one of whom was drowned and the other put in the boiler of the ritual bath. At Sadagóra he kept his court in a luxurious palace surrounded by a park, at the expense of his devoted followers. Franzos gives a biting description of this character in one of his travel books.[119] He also introduces an anecdote about him into *Der Pojaz*. A young man whose wife has not yet borne him any children visits the *tsaddik* to ask for a blessing; the *tsaddik* demands fifty Gulden, but the petitioner beats him down to thirty by threatening to transfer his custom to the *tsaddik* of Nadworna, who for only twenty Gulden will supply a blessing guaranteed to produce twins.

While Franzos's satire on dynasties of *tsaddikim* has substance, it also represents a variant of the Enlightenment anticlericalism which we have seen Schnitzler and Freud applying to the Catholic Church. Franzos's portrayal of Hasidism in general is extremely one-sided. He never mentions, for example, the Hasidic custom of celebrating festivals by dancing, described as follows by Kafka's friend Jiři Langer, who witnessed it in the great Hasidic community of Belz in Galicia:

A hundred men take hold of each other's hands, or put their arms round each other's necks and form a large circle that rotates with a rocking dance-step, slowly at first and then faster and faster. The dancing begins in the Bes Hamidrash, but after a while the whole crowd spreads out on to the square and dances under the rabbi's window. A dance lasts uninterrupted for an hour, or maybe more, till the dancers are exhausted, intoxicated by the endless repetition of the same, mystically coloured, dance melody.[120]

Instead, Franzos follows Enlightenment observers like Rohrer in representing the Hasidim of Barnow as life-denying and unnatural. Describing how the Jews settle down for the winter as

---

[119] 'Der Ahnherr des Messias', in Franzos, *Vom Don zur Donau: Neue Kulturbilder aus Halb-Asien*, 2 vols. (2nd edn., Stuttgart, 1889), ii. 251–70.
[120] Langer, *Nine Gates*, p. 14.

soon as the Feast of Tabernacles is over (i.e. in early October), Franzos comments: 'they are governed in all things not by nature but by the principles of their faith' (p. 255).

If the keynote of Hasidism, as Franzos portrays it, is submission to clerical tyranny, then its antithesis is the practicality and industry displayed by the Misnagdim (anti-Hasidic Jews) of the neighbouring village of Buczacz. Lacking a superstitious belief in miracles or a taste for abstruse disputations, they consider the Ten Commandments far more important than the Talmud. Implausibly, they maintain an excellent *heder* where the teacher loves his pupils and teaches them for only three or four hours a day. Evidently their religion is supposed to exalt rationality and ethics above ritual observance, and thus qualify them for citizenship of an industrious Protestant state like Prussia. The Jews of Barnow and Buczacz, Franzos tells us, differ as do the Moravian Brethren of Herrnhut from the Protestant inhabitants of an industrial town (p. 41). Behind this antithesis, however, one may suspect another. While the Jews of Buczacz represent idealized Protestants, those of Barnow, sunk in superstition and blindly obeying their miracle-working leaders, correspond to Catholics, as seen by Prussian proponents of the 'Kulturkampf'—Bismarck's campaign in the mid-1870s to destroy the secular influence of the Roman Catholic Church. Franzos is thus projecting onto his Galician Jews a crude antithesis deriving from the Prussia with which he identified. His novel is even more tendentious than he acknowledges (p. 6). It cannot be regarded as a remotely faithful depiction of Galician Jewry.

None the less, *Der Pojaz* is both entertaining and moving, thanks to its portrayal of its hero's doomed struggle for emancipation. If Sender's oppressive environment forms one obstacle, another is the inner nobility which makes him sacrifice his ambitions out of gratitude to his adoptive mother. Here, however, we encounter the problems posed by the novel's literary mode. Franzos's realism may seem rather homespun when compared to that of his contemporaries Storm or Fontane. He has no qualms about intervening in the story to provide ethnographic information or to comment, often indignantly, on the characters' behaviour. Besides instructing his readers, he wants to win their sympathy by telling his story in a largely humorous tone. He certainly has a fund of excellent anecdotes on familiar comic subjects, like the wiles of the marriage-broker whose self-betraying sales-talk was to supply Freud with some of the best jokes in *Jokes and their Relation to the Unconscious* (also published in 1905). We saw above how he used grim humour to expose the *Fehlermacher*. A combination of humour and indignation, however, makes an uneasy background to the story of Sender, which would seem to require a tragic realism like that attained by Storm in *Der Schimmelreiter* (1888) and by Fontane when describing the death of Dubslav von Stechlin in *Der Stechlin* (1898).

The conflict between realism and humour is illustrated by the characters' names. Grotesque, comic, or allegorical names are incompatible with serious realism.[121] Joseph II's emancipatory legislation required the Galician Jews to assume surnames instead of patronymics as a first step towards becoming citizens. While many surnames were derived from places (Wiener, Lemberger, Brody) or occupations (Brenner, Nadler, Singer) or were Germanizations of Hebrew names (like Hirsch for Naphtali), some grotesque names were imposed by government officials on those too poor to pay for more euphonious names. Franzos, who had done documentary research on the compulsory adoption of surnames, knew that not all Eastern Jews had odd names like Ochsenschwanz or Singmirwas.[122] Yet, although Sender gets off lightly with the (not inappropriate) name Glatteis ('thin ice'), and his heroic foster-mother has the entirely uncomic surname Kurländer, most of the other characters, major and minor, have names like Itzig Türkischgelb, Naphtali Ritterstolz, Chaim Fragezeichen, and Chane Gurkensalat (Turkish Yellow, Chivalric Pride, Question-Mark, Gherkin Salad). Sometimes these names serve an obvious satiric purpose in deflating the pretensions of authoritarian figures like Rabbi Manasse Kirschenkuchen (Cherry-Cake) or the teacher Elias Wohlgeruch (Fragrance). But their general effect is to make the Jews of Barnow seem quaint and remote, fit subjects for satire

---

[121] See Alastair Fowler, *Kinds of Literature: An Introduction to the Theory of Genres and Modes* (Oxford, 1982), pp. 82–7.

[122] Franzos, 'Namenstudien', in *Aus der großen Ebene: Neue Kulturbilder aus Halb-Asien*, 2 vols. (Stuttgart, 1888), i. 127–49. There are many implausible anecdotes about how Jews were given odd or unpleasant names: for one involving E. T. A. Hoffmann, see Norman Davies, *Heart of Europe: A Short History of Poland* (Oxford, 1986), pp. 245–6; and for a sceptical examination, Bering, *Der Name als Stigma*, pp. 409–10.

but not for a fully serious, let alone tragic, realism. In another story by Franzos, *Leib Weihnachtskuchen und sein Kind* (1896), the hero's absurd name (Christmas-Cake) prevents the story from achieving anything more than mild pathos. Similar self-imposed limitations can be found in greater novelists. The quaint names Scott gives his lower-class characters weaken the pathos when he attempts a serious scene with them: for instance, the bereavement of the fisher family in *The Antiquary* loses something when one is reminded that their surname is Mucklebackit.

Against this semi-comic background, Sender's persistent struggle for education has something heroic, as has his act of renunciation in yielding to his mother's wishes. Moreover, Sender is predestined to failure, and at the same time dignified, by being consumptive. As Susan Sontag pointed out, consumption or tuberculosis was thought in the nineteenth century to be a relatively painless disease which ennobled and spiritualized the patient. The fictional consumptive was typically a child (Paul Dombey) or female (Milly Theale in *The Wings of the Dove*) or both (Little Eva in *Uncle Tom's Cabin*).[123] Jews were often thought to run a high risk of tuberculosis.[124] Sender has a literary prototype in the consumptive Jew Mordecai in *Daniel Deronda*. The 'pathetic stamp of consumption with its brilliancy of glance' ennobles Mordecai, even as it expresses the frustration of his obscure life, and helps him to figure as the prophet whose message Deronda, the healthy Jew, will put into practice.[125] Similarly, in *Der Pojaz*, Sender's consumption ennobles him as the unwitting prophet of an emancipation which others will realize.

Franzos's focus on the noble and pathetic Sender threatens to undermine his plea for assimilation. The more sharply Sender is contrasted with the Barnow community, the more it appears that Sender is exceptional in being assimilable, and that the rest of Barnow is beyond saving. We recall the exceptionalism of Lessing's *Nathan der Weise*. However, Sender's hard-won and tenuous accession to the world of German culture is only one means of freeing oneself from the restrictions of Barnow. The other struggle for emancipation is a practical one, waged unremittingly by his

[123] See Sontag, *Illness as Metaphor* (London, 1979).
[124] Gilman, *Franz Kafka*, pp. 171–3.
[125] George Eliot, *Daniel Deronda*, ed. Terence Cave (London, 1995), p. 495.

foster-mother. As a girl she insists on marrying the man of her choice, and gets away with this breach of tradition because of her mother's sympathy with her feelings. Franzos seems to be hinting that the women of Barnow are secretly dissatisfied with the heavily patriarchal society they inhabit, and that the real potential for revolt against it is to be found among them. Rosel's husband turns out to be a drunkard, and eventually she again proves her strength of character by ordering him to leave and never return. Thereafter she earns her own living as a toll-keeper, ostracized by the villagers, but saved from emotional aridity by her voluntary task of bringing up Sender. She further demonstrates her humanity and courage by rescuing Sender from the local teacher. Although, ironically, she frustrates Sender's own attempts to emancipate himself, she shows how an ordinary member of the community, without artistic gifts but with courage and warmth, can stand up against its oppression amid everyday life. Many present-day readers may wish that Franzos had placed her nearer the centre of the narrative. The narrative seems split between the weak hero in the foreground and the strong heroine in the background.

Franzos's novels and sketches were widely received as authoritative pictures of Eastern Jewish life. They were acceptable partly because of Franzos's literary skill and engaging narrative persona, but partly also because they combined elements already present in the Western image of the Eastern Jew. The term 'Half-Asia' became widespread. Thus the Zionist Franz Oppenheimer spoke in 1903 of the 'Jews of Half-Asia who are reduced to the lowest imaginable level of human misery'.[126] Even before *Der Pojaz* was published, however, Buber had begun his rehabilitation of Hasidism, inspired not least by his encounter as a boy with the Sadagóra dynasty of *tsaddikim* that Franzos described so scathingly. This is Buber's version:

The *rebbe*'s palace, with its showy splendour, repelled me. The prayer-house of the Hasidim, with its ecstatic occupants, frightened me. But when I saw the *rebbe* striding through the ranks of his followers, I felt: 'Leader', and when I saw the Hasidim dancing with the Torah, I felt: 'Community'.[127]

---

[126] Oppenheimer, 'Alte und neue Makkabäer' (1906), in *Erlebtes, Erstrebtes, Erreichtes: Lebenserinnerungen* (Düsseldorf, 1964), p. 282; cf. pp. 229, 299. See Aschheim, *Brothers and Strangers*, p. 31.

[127] Buber, 'Mein Weg zum Chassidismus', p. 964.

A wonder-working *tsaddik* plays a central role in *Hiob* (*Job*, 1930), the novel which generally recognized as marking a turning-point in Roth's fiction.[128] The emotional Socialism apparent in his brilliant early journalism was giving way to disillusionment with mechanized, homogeneous 'civilization', and the clipped, Hemingwayesque concision of his earlier novels was being replaced by a more lyrical, emotional, plangent style. But it would be wrong to credit Roth with simple nostalgia, whether for the disintegrating culture of the Eastern Jews or the vanished world of the Habsburg Empire. His complex irony conveys that the Imperial dynasty and the Galician shtetl are themselves in terminal decline. The yearning of Roth's characters can never be satisfied by any earthly objects, and the later novels are tentative inquiries into the interplay of justice, love, and grace in humanity's apprehension of God.[129]

In *Hiob*, the very title proclaims a theodicy—an inquiry into God's governance of the universe. As its setting, the world of the Eastern Jews is contrasted with the modernity of New York, to which the main character emigrates. The new Job is a simple, devout Talmud teacher called Mendel Singer, whose misfortunes begin when his youngest son, Menuchim, turns out to be an imbecile. A *tsaddik* prophesies that Menuchim will be cured and become a wise and good man. In the meantime, however, Mendel becomes estranged from his wife; his elder sons fight on opposite sides in the First World War, and one goes missing while the other is killed; Mendel's wife Deborah dies of grief; their daughter Mirjam becomes promiscuous and subsequently insane. Overwhelmed, Mendel blasphemes against God and rejects the facile consolations that his friends offer in conscious imitation of Job's comforters. But the story ends with an apparent miracle: a famous conductor who visits New York turns out to be Menuchim, cured by Russian doctors, so that the *tsaddik*'s prophecy is fulfilled.

Born in Brody, on the easternmost extremity of the Austrian Empire, Roth was brought up in an Eastern Jewish setting: not,

---

[128] A longer version of this argument, with a different conclusion, appeared as 'Roth's *Hiob* and the Traditions of Ghetto Fiction', in Helen Chambers (ed.) *Co-Existent Contradictions: Joseph Roth in Retrospect* (Riverside, Calif., 1991), pp. 185–200.

[129] See Esther Steinmann, *Von der Würde des Unscheinbaren: Sinnerfahrung be; Joseph Roth* (Tübingen, 1984).

however, in a close community, but in a modest, isolated middle-class home, with no thorough knowledge of Jewish tradition. Roth seems to have known little about the Talmud: a casual reference to the *Shulhan Arukh* looks like showing off, and Roth's description of this work as 'the religious bon-ton of Jewish orthodoxy in the Diaspora' is an odd way of referring to the important codification of the Mosaic law by Joseph Karo.[130] *Hiob*'s fictional world is literary in origin.[131] Some of the Yiddish classics were available to Roth in German translation, including the works of Mendele Moykher Sforim, translated by Roth's friend Efraim Frisch, and the Hasidic tales of Perets.[132] At least as important, however, are *Hiob*'s affinities with German-Jewish ghetto fiction, especially with its nostalgic tendency, as opposed to the critical tendency represented by Franzos.

In relating his protagonist to a biblical prototype, in the title and in the development of the narrative, Roth has several precursors. In 'Judith die Zweite', Leopold Kompert tells how a Jewish girl saves two people from execution by French troops by offering her body to the French commandant, while S. H. Mosenthal supplies a variation on an Old Testament story in 'Jephthas Tochter'.[133] Since the Novelle is so concise, an allusive title can economically suggest a wider significance, as in Keller's 'Romeo und Julia auf dem Dorf', or Franzos's 'Der Shylock von Barnow'. The Old Testament allusions also suggest continuity between the Jewish present and the seemingly more heroic Jewish past, while assuring us that the present-day Jews are still capable of heroism. By contrast, Franzos's satirical approach denies his characters any heroic potential.

To convey how Eastern Jews still lived, as Roth put it, 'in the truth and warmth of tradition',[134] a familiar means is the description of the Sabbath, evoking the solidarity and piety of the Jewish

---

[130] Quoted in David Bronsen, *Joseph Roth: Eine Biographie* (Cologne, 1974), p. 65.

[131] See Gershon Shaked, 'Wie jüdisch ist ein jüdisch-deutscher Roman? Über Joseph Roths *Hiob, Roman eines einfachen Mannes*', in Stéphane Mosès and Albrecht Schöne (eds.), *Juden in der deutschen Literatur* (Frankfurt, 1986), pp. 281–92; Hans Otto Horch, 'Zeitroman, Legende, Palimpsest. Zu Joseph Roths *Hiob*-Roman im Kontext deutsch-jüdischer Literaturgeschichte', *Germanisch-Romanische Monatsschrift*, NS 39 (1989), 210–26.

[132] Fritz Hackert, *Kulturpessimismus und Erzählform: Studien zu Joseph Roths Leben und Werk* (Berne, 1967), pp. 54–62.

[133] Kompert, *Gesammelte Schriften*, 8 vols. (Berlin, 1882), i. 1–27; Mosenthal, *Gesammelte Werke*, 6 vols. (Stuttgart and Leipzig, 1878), i. 111–62.

[134] Roth, *Werke*, ii. 831.

community. The prototype is the account of Moses Lump in Heine's *Die Bäder von Lucca*. One particularly formulaic example from ghetto fiction may stand for many: it is from Leo Herzberg-Fränkel's story 'Ein Meschumed' (i.e. an apostate from Judaism):

It is Friday evening. The struggles of everyday life have yielded place to a peaceful and joyous quiet; the sweat, the toil and the cares of a long, apprehensive week are now succeeded by an hour of peace and repose. The hunt is interrupted for twenty-four hours, and the weary hunters regale themselves with the week's scanty booty. How the poor man is regaled by the sight of his nearest and dearest in their best clothes, by the bright room, the gleaming wine, the steaming dishes on the snowy table, after he has spent six days panting, dragging his chain, hunted, harried through life, in careworn struggles for the sake of this one cheerful hour amid his nearest and dearest![135]

Roth too has an obligatory Sabbath scene, near the beginning of *Hiob*, but its idealizing tendency is controlled by the description of the difficulty the Singers have in keeping the candles burning, and by Roth's mention of their 'careworn festiveness' ('bekümmerter Festlichkeit').[136] Thus his Sabbath scene conveys a more complex message than is usual in ghetto fiction.

Mendel Singer is a *melamed*, who teaches children the Torah and the Talmud; but he is very unlike Franzos's savage Elias Wohlgeruch. He has only twelve pupils; their voices form a 'sing-song', and a 'clear chorus' which is compared to the sound of bells.[137] What they learn is described as 'knowledge of the Bible';[138] we hear nothing about the intricacies of the Talmud. The impression is a pleasant one; Mendel's class sounds almost like a Christian Sunday school.

Another recurrent figure in ghetto fiction is the physically strong Jew who wants to be a soldier, like Jonas in *Hiob*. In general, military service was regarded by traditional communities as a great misfortune, not only because the recruits underwent physical hardships and separation from their families, but because they were unable to keep the dietary laws. Hence the need for the *Fehlermacher*, and hence Jonas and Schemarjah try

---

[135] Härzberg-Fränkel [*sic*], *Polnische Juden: Geschichten und Bilder* (Vienna, 1867), p. 75. In later publications the author spelt his name Herzberg-Fränkel. Cf. the Sabbath scenes in Franzos, 'Der Shylock von Barnow', *Die Juden von Barnow* (Stuttgart and Leipzig, 1876), pp. 12–13; Kompert, 'Der Dorfgeher', *Gesammelte Schriften*, ii. 5–6.
[136] Roth, *Werke*, v. 5.　　[137] Ibid. v. 5, 12.　　[138] Ibid. v. 3.

to make themselves ill by eating and sleeping too little and by drinking too much coffee. However, Jonas, on being accepted, is glad to become a soldier. The physically strong Jew serves to counteract the stereotyped view of Jews as puny and fit only for commerce. In the nostalgic tradition, the Jewish strong man demonstrates that Jews can excel in professions not usually associated with them, like soldiering or farming: thus Mendel Gibbor, the eponymous strong man in Bernstein's story, finally becomes a farmer. Franzos, in *Moschko von Parma*, describes a Jew who uses his strength first by being apprenticed to a blacksmith, then by joining the army; much emphasis is laid on the community's consternation at these unfamiliar career choices. Roth's ideological purpose is somewhat different. Rather than demonstrating the Jews' fitness to enter Gentile society, his strong Jew illustrates the attraction exercised by Gentile society, even by what might seem its less attractive aspects, and the way in which its attraction is causing the Jewish community to disintegrate.

Writers about Eastern Jewry differ sharply in their estimation of the Hasidic *tsaddik* or miracle-working rabbi. Enlighteners, from Maimon to Franzos, treat such figures scornfully. Roth's attitude is the opposite. While Franzos's *tsaddik* is a corrupt charlatan, the rabbi of Kluczysk, whom Deborah visits, is the chief spiritual authority of *Hiob*; he correctly prophesies the eventual curing of Menuchim. Roth tells us about the crowd of petitioners outside his door. He does not mention that a *tsaddik* normally employed several doorkeepers to keep the crowd at bay, and that admission to the *tsaddik*'s presence often required bribes to the doorkeepers. Roth's positive presentation of the *tsaddik* is no doubt fully serious, for when his wife Friedl became mentally ill in the late 1920s, Roth fetched a Hasidic *Wunderrabbi* from the Jewish quarter of Berlin, to pray and utter formulae in the hope of driving the madness out of her.[139]

More complex is Roth's portrayal of Mendel's daughter Mirjam. Her sexuality is heavily emphasized. We hear first that sexual teasing is her main source of pleasure; thirty pages later she has become completely promiscuous, and the apparent deterioration in Roth's style expresses the torrent of banal emotion to which she has succumbed:

[139] Bronsen, *Joseph Roth*, p. 341.

She loved all men, storms burst from them, yet their mighty hands gently lit flames in her heart. The men were called Stepan, Ivan and Vsevolod. In America there were a great many more men.[140]

There follows a long description of Mirjam sensuously feeling her own body. Recounting her dealings with Russian soldiers, she claims to have taught these rather innocent young men all manner of sexual lessons. When insane, she talks still more shamelessly. The link between Mirjam's promiscuity and her decline into degenerative psychosis has a real-life prototype in the insanity of Roth's wife Friedl. Her obsession with sex seems also to reflect a feature of Eastern Jewish life noted by Bertha Pappenheim on her visit to Galicia. Pappenheim maintains that a vast amount of surreptitious sexual activity went on, resulting partly from the idleness of Jewish women; it amounted to 'covert prostitution', and contributed to the growth of the white slave trade which it was Pappenheim's aim to investigate and combat.[141] Mirjam embodies the conception of the Eastern Jewish woman as sexually disturbed and prone to nymphomania, found also in Arnold Zweig's character Lina Klopfer, a Polish Jew whose promiscuity leads to insanity and who, when cured, becomes a prostitute.[142] Mirjam and Lina are pathologized versions of a well-known literary stereotype, that of the 'beautiful Jewess'. Here is another example from ghetto fiction, taken from a story by Sacher-Masoch set in Galicia, in which the Gentile narrator observes the wife of a Jewish innkeeper:

She was beautiful, I'll wager, when Ikey married her. Now all her features have a repellent sharpness. Pain, disgrace, kicks, and lashes have gnawed at the countenance of her race until it acquired this burning yet withered expression, melancholy yet mocking, servile yet vengeful. She curved her tall spine, her slender, delicate hands played with the measure of brandy, her eyes fastened themselves upon the stranger. A burning, craving soul arose from those large, dark, lascivious eyes, a vampire arising from the grave of a putrefied human nature, and glued itself to the stranger's handsome countenance.[143]

---

[140] Roth, *Werke*, v. 51.   [141] Pappenheim, *Sisyphus*, p. 85.

[142] Zweig, *Aufzeichnungen über eine Familie Klopfer* (Munich, 1911), pp. 28–30.

[143] Leopold von Sacher-Masoch, *Don Juan von Kolomea: Galizische Geschichten*, ed. Michael Farin (Bonn, 1985), p. 23. This story was first published in 1866. See Krobb, *Die schöne Jüdin*, p. 212.

This passage is a fine example of projection: the narrator disclaims his desire for the innkeeper's wife by crediting her with insidious, destructive sexuality; he depersonalizes her by first referring to her as 'the Jewess' and then by calling her a vampire.

Although his portrayal of Mirjam may be thought sensational, the general tendency of Roth's depiction is to idealize Eastern Jewish life. He may well underplay such perils of Eastern Jewish life as antisemitism.[144] However, it would be wrong to see Roth as a sentimental counterpart to the satirist Franzos. His depiction of the Eastern Jews is modernist. It is made out of literary images. While Franzos professes to be reporting on real life in Barnow, Roth arranges a sequence of images already familiar from literature. Similarly, his landscape descriptions are openly formulaic. Here and elsewhere (especially in *Radetzkymarsch* and *Tarabas*), the eastern European plains and marshes are continually haunted by the chirping of crickets and the croaking of frogs. Roth even turns his own characters into types by reintroducing them in different stories. Kapturak, who smuggles deserters across the Russian border, appears frequently, and the Trotta and Chojnicki families from *Radetzkymarsch* also figure in *Die Kapuzinergruft* (*The Imperial Vault*, 1938). But while in Balzac or Trollope recurring characters may suggest a solidly real world, in Roth their reappearances make his fictional world seem more obviously an artificial construction (especially since he sometimes forgets important details, as when Mendel Singer from *Hiob* reappears in *Das falsche Gewicht* (*The False Weight*, 1937) with a different profession, wife, and family). His traditional Eastern world is clearly a literary construct.

This extreme literariness has sometimes been censured. Thus Claudio Magris maintains that instead of evoking the world of the Eastern Jews in realistic detail, the novel reduces it to a set of symbols whose purely abstract and unreal character preserves them from the pressure of reality.[145] However, this technique expresses Roth's sense of modernity. In his novels of the 1920s he depicted the modern world as one in which old values and ways of life dissolve. In *Hotel Savoy* (1924) Eastern Jewish refugees crowd into a hotel, while *Die Flucht ohne Ende* (*Flight without*

---

[144] See G. P. Butler, 'It's the Bitterness that Counts: Joseph Roth's "most Jewish" Novel Reconsidered', *GLL* 41 (1988), 227–34 (p. 228).

[145] Magris, *Weit von wo*, p. 113.

End, 1927) takes its deracinated hero on a tour of the modern world, from the Soviet Union, where even love is dismissed as incompatible with the brave new technocracy, to Germany, where Jewish ritual objects are used by the assimilated generation only as household ornaments. In *Hiob* this sense of universal dissolution, in which 'all that is solid melts into air' (in Marx's phrase), enters the very texture of the novel.[146] As one might expect, Roth presents New York in this formulaic, impressionistic style, especially as it is seen mainly through the eyes of the bewildered immigrant Mendel Singer. But while the eastern European world nominally figures as the traditional contrast with modernity, it is represented not as a substantial traditional world but through literary images, indicating that the warmth and security of tradition have gone for good. Modernity is omnipresent. Even the old world can only be depicted by the techniques of modernism. The novel evokes nostalgia, but it shows through its mode of representation that nostalgia can never really be satisfied.

However, disillusionment and scepticism are not the novel's final message.[147] Like other modernists, Roth needs something permanent to underlie his cascade of impressions, and as Joyce finds his framework in the Ulysses story, Roth finds it in the story of Job. Mendel Singer shares Job's piety, his misfortunes, and his despair. Like Job, he has three friends who offer unavailing consolation. And, just as Job regains his wealth and even acquires a new family, Mendel has his son restored to him, healed and famous. The atmosphere of the Bible appears in several modes. When Mendel crosses the ocean, we are reminded that God's terrifying plaything Leviathan, described in chapter 41 of the Book of Job, lurks in its depths. And Menuchim first reappears as a guest at Passover, recalling the traditional expectation of a visit from the prophet Elijah.

This ending has divided Roth's admirers. Socially conscious readers deplore it as an unpolitical flight into fairy-tale.[148] Roth's biographer defends it as 'a mystery-play in Eastern European Jewish guise'.[149] But it works, I think, precisely because of the novel's ostentatiously literary, modernist character. For if Roth

[146] See Marshall Berman, *All That Is Solid Melts Into Air* (London, 1982).

[147] As is argued by Bernd Hüppauf, 'Joseph Roth: *Hiob*. Der Mythos des Skeptikers', in Grimm and Bayerdörfer (eds.), *Im Zeichen Hiobs*, pp. 309–25.

[148] Magris, *Weit von wo*, p. 113.   [149] Bronsen, *Joseph Roth*, p. 387.

had attempted a piece of traditional realist fiction, Menuchim's quasi-miraculous return would have seemed merely fanciful by contrast with its apparently solid setting. But the very thinness of Roth's realism leaves space for the mysterious and the miraculous. As with Kafka, modernism, which might seem to be the literary mode appropriate for a disenchanted world, in fact allows the spiritual to re-enter, not as a matter of dogmatic certainty, but as a vivid and tantalizing possibility.[150]

THE JEW AS ORIENTAL

In the dispute over Jewish identity, an important contested term was 'Oriental'. Some antisemites applied it to Jews in order to define them as unassimilably alien; some Jews, frustrated in their desire for assimilation, applied it to themselves or to other Jews in a spirit of self-contempt; and yet other Jews accepted the term but either changed its content or valued positively the implications that antisemites regarded negatively.

The term 'Oriental' serves as a marker of difference rather than as an expression of substantive or factual content.[151] It marks a crude binary division between the dynamic, secular West and the unchanging, devout East, where the East usually means the Muslim world but may extend to Persia and India, even to China and Japan. The vagueness, and therefore the flexibility, of Western images of the East is well described by Joseph Roth when he says of Paul Bernheim in *Rechts und Links* (*Right and Left*, 1929): 'In the manner of Europeans, who assign literary value to geographical concepts, he considered the East mysterious, the West ordinary. And the East began just after Kattowitz [Katowice in Poland] and stretched as far as Rabindranath Tagore.'[152]

---

[150] Another important depiction of Galician Jewry is H. W. Katz's *Die Fischmanns* (Weinheim, 1994), first published in 1938. The author is the subject of a doctoral thesis by Ena Pedersen (Oxford). See also her 'The Image of Pre-World War I Austria from a Galician Jewish Perspective: On Henry William Katz's Novel *Die Fischmanns*', in Donald G. Daviau (ed.), *Austria in Literature* (Riverside, Calif., 1998).

[151] See Said, *Orientalism*; Rana Kabbani, *Europe's Myths of Orient* (London, 1986); and for an important critique of the concept, John M. MacKenzie, *Orientalism: History, Theory and the Arts* (Manchester, 1995).

[152] Roth, *Werke*, iv. 750. For many similar examples, see Wolff, *Inventing Eastern Europe*.

To call the Jews 'Oriental', even though they had been settled in Europe for many centuries, meant initially that they could not be Europeans. Thus Herder in *Adrastea* (1801–4) calls the Jews 'an *Asiatic* people *alien* to our continent', an utterance later seized on by antisemites.[153] Schopenhauer concluded that the Jews should not be given civil rights: 'they are and remain an alien, oriental people, and must therefore count only as resident aliens.'[154] Replacing 'people' (*Volk*) with 'race', the historian Theodor Mommsen asserted that the Jews of the Roman Empire were as alien, and hence unassimilable, as those of nineteenth-century Germany: 'At that period, too, we encounter the Occidentals' peculiar antipathy towards this so profoundly Oriental race and its and its alien opinions and customs.'[155] This prejudice was strengthened by the anachronistic association of the East with pastoral and nomadic cultures. Lacking a homeland, and being often obliged by oppression or expulsion to migrate from one country to another, the Jews were readily seen as nomads. Schiller in 'Die Sendung Moses' implausibly says that they retained their nomadic character throughout the four hundred years during which they lived in Egypt, and for that reason were hated by the Egyptians.[156] 'Asiatism is mainly represented in Europe by the Jews, who as nomads embody a revolutionary principle', declared the antisemite Adolf Wahrmund in 1887.[157] Sombart calls the Jews 'an Oriental folk transplanted into an environment both climatically and ethnically strange, wherein their best powers came to fruition'.[158] Rathenau, as we have seen, perceived Oriental qualities in the Jews of Berlin: using a word that specifically recalled the Mongol invasions of medieval Europe, he called them 'an Asiatic horde on the sands of the Mark'.[159]

Other 'Jewish' qualities were readily defined as Oriental. Irony was supposed to be a Jewish and hence Oriental quality in

---

[153] Herder, *Sämmtliche Werke*, ed. Suphan, xxiv. 63; quoted by Chamberlain, *Die Grundlagen des neunzehnten Jahrhunderts* (Munich, 1899), p. 323.

[154] Arthur Schopenhauer, *Parerga und Paralipomena*, ii, sect. 132, in *Sämtliche Werke*, ed. Julius Frauenstädt and Arthur Hübscher (Wiesbaden, 1947), vi. 281.

[155] Mommsen, *Römische Geschichte*, iii. 550.

[156] Schiller, *Sämtliche Werke*, iv. 784–5.

[157] Quoted in Christoph Cobet, *Der Wortschatz des Antisemitismus in der Bismarckzeit* (Munich, 1973), p. 217.

[158] Sombart, *The Jews and Modern Capitalism*, pp. 324, 328.

[159] 'W. Hartenau', 'Höre, Israel!', p. 454.

contrast with German seriousness: Treitschke complained that Jewish writers like Heine had introduced 'Oriental wise-cracking (*Witzelei*)' into German literature.[160] Jews, and especially Jewish women, were credited with alarming 'Oriental' sensuality. In *Dichter und Kaufmann* (1840) Berthold Auerbach describes as follows the heartless, shallow, and sensual Täubchen Löbell, who adopts the ultra-German name Theodolinde, on her wedding-day: 'The gleam of her dark eyes shone forth from beneath her long dark lashes; her dark complexion, her somewhat hooked nose, her round chin, all combined to reveal in her the image of a perfect Oriental beauty.'[161] In Ferdinand von Saar's *Geschichte eines Wienerkindes* (1891) a dishonest speculator takes as his mistress the widow of a stockbroker, a Jewess with 'noble Oriental features' and profuse dark hair, who is alleged to have a 'cold intellect as sharp as a knife', bizarre inclinations (unspecified), and a colossal capacity for spending money. Her presence (on a single page of the Novelle) expresses her companion's corruption and seals his fate.[162]

More worrying still were the Jews of eastern Europe, the region discovered for literature by Franzos under the name 'Half-Asia'. It had been customary since the 1840s to describe them as 'Asiatics'.[163] Even Freud describes a relative from Bucharest as 'half-Asian'.[164] They seemed dangerously alien and unassimilable, and their immigration into Germany, as we have seen, aroused hostility not only from antisemites but among many German Jews. However, an Oriental character could also be attributed to the Eastern Jews by their well-wishers. In his sympathetic and touching portrait of a community on the eve of dissolution, *Das ostjüdische Antlitz* (*The Face of the Eastern Jew*), Arnold Zweig explains that many strange features of their lives become intelligible if seen as Oriental. Communal prayer, for example, repelled many Western visitors (like Theodor Lessing): 'but anyone who was ever allowed into a mosque in an Islamic country during prayer will recognize the Jew as an Oriental'; while the ecstasy felt by devout Jews in

[160] Treitschke, *Deutsche Geschichte*, iii. 704.

[161] Auerbach, *Gesammelte Schriften*, xii. 52–3.

[162] Saar, *Ginevra und andere Novellen*, ed. Karlheinz Rossbacher (Frankfurt, 1983), p. 269. For other examples of 'Oriental' Jewish women, see Krobb, *Die schöne Jüdin*.

[163] Aschheim, *Brothers and Strangers*, p. 20.

[164] *Letters of Freud to Fliess*, p. 311 (27 Apr. 1898).

prayer, and manifested by their prostration and jerky movements, was that of the Muslim dervish; and the Eastern Jews are Oriental likewise in excluding women from the ceremonial dances and in their mourning practices.[165]

Jewish Primitivism

Redefining Jewish identity meant looking afresh at the image of the Oriental Jew. It meant especially re-imagining the biblical period when all Jews actually lived in the Orient. While antisemitism represented Old Testament Jews as nomads, traders, and swindlers, Zionists stressed that they were warriors and farmers. Franz Oppenheimer in 1906 described them in terms which recalled nationalistic descriptions of the ancient Germans, combined with medieval knighthood: 'Our forebears were a noble nation when they burst forth from the desert to conquer the Promised Land, a knightly nation of warriors (*ein ritterlich Kriegervolk*) used to wielding spear and sword, as their history shows—a noble nation with gentle manners and pious hearts.'[166] Buber, in defining the Jew as essentially Oriental, insisted that the ancient Hebrews of the Old Testament were not a nomadic people, as antisemites claimed, but a society of farmers, firmly rooted in the soil: their religious festivals followed the agricultural cycle, and their religion taught 'rootedness in the soil of the homeland' ('die Einwurzelung im heimatlichen Boden').[167] Thus the true, Oriental Jew had the positive qualities that *völkisch* discourse ascribed to the Germans.

But was it possible for the urbanized, intellectual Jews of modern Europe to come to resemble their Old Testament ancestors? Buber claimed they could. In his early Zionist writings, Buber starts from the assumption that the Jews' character has been distorted in the Diaspora by external oppression and by the dominance of the Law. To recover their energy, their creativity, and their religious feeling, Jews must regain their own territory and return to Asia. 'Here we are a wedge driven by Asia into Europe's

---

[165] Zweig, *Herkunft und Zukunft: Zwei Essays zum Schicksal eines Volkes* (Vienna, 1929), pp. 38, 53–4.

[166] Oppenheimer, *Erlebtes, Erstrebtes, Erreichtes*, p. 298.

[167] Buber, 'Der Geist des Orients und das Judentum', *Vom Geist des Judentums*, pp. 37–8.

framework, a cause of ferment and trouble-making', says Buber in
1910.[168] As so often, Buber's reconstruction of Jewish identity
accepts and reinterprets antisemitic stereotypes: they are indeed
trouble-makers, a yeast or catalysing agent that keeps Europe in
constant flux;[169] but only because they are out of place there,
whereas in Asia they will regain a tranquil piety. In 1896, by
contrast, Theodor Herzl had imagined a Jewish state as a European bulwark against Asiatic barbarism: 'we would provide an
advance guard of civilization against barbarism' (ZW i. 45).
Buber, however, rejected civilization and welcomed barbarism;
but by the former he understood a sickly, secular, over-rational
way of life, while the alternative was for him the restoration of an
ancient closeness to the divine. He developed this idea about 1912
in 'Der Geist des Orients und das Judentum' ('The Spirit of the
Orient and Judaism'), in which he grouped all 'Oriental' cultures,
from Egypt to China, together, and contrasted them with Occi-
dental cultures whose prototype was that of the Greeks. The
Greek, in Buber's scheme, regards himself as separate from the
world; he apprehends it primarily through the eye; he objectifies it
and abstracts from it in order to control it. The Oriental feels
himself to be an intrinsic part of the world and apprehends it with
all his senses as an infinite process of movement, though with an
ultimate static centre which Buber calls the 'maternal womb'.[170]

An even stronger fascination with Jewish primitivism was
shown by Oskar Goldberg (1885–1952). Goldberg originally
studied medicine. In 1913–14 he visited Kashmir, Bhutan, and
Nepal, met practitioners of Yoga, and took a keen interest in the
possibility of altering the functioning of the body by spiritual
concentration. His first book, *Die fünf Bücher Mosis ein Zahlen-
gebäude* (*The Pentateuch a Numerical Construction*, 1908),
claimed to demonstrate mathematically that everything in the
Pentateuch was reducible to the numerical values of the letters
IHWH, signifying the name of God. This strange quasi-scientific

---

[168] Buber, *Die jüdische Bewegung*, i. 191, 194.

[169] See Theodor Mommsen, 'Auch ein Wort über unser Judenthum' (1880), in *Der
Berliner Antisemitismusstreit*, pp. 210–25 (p. 217); *Hitler's Table Talk 1941–44*, tr.
Norman Cameron and R. H. Stevens (London, 1973), p. 314.

[170] Buber, *Vom Geist des Judentums*, p. 15. This image invites a sympathetic
exploration of the gendered dimension of Buber's early thought. Both Benjamin and
Landauer called his thinking 'womanly' ('frauenhaft'): see Scholem, *Walter Benjamin*,
p. 42.

literal-mindedness also dominates his major book, *Die Wirklich-keit der Hebräer* (*The Reality of the Hebrews*, 1925).

In this work Goldberg puts forward, with a severely factual air, a new account of the creation myth as part of 'cosmic politics'.[171] There are many worlds, each with its own biological centre or god ('Elohim'). A god needs a nation ('Volk') in order to manifest himself in physical form: god and nation are united in a circulation of energy. Our world, being vacant, was seen by the gods as suitable for colonization (Goldberg's term). Each tried to create beings as his instrument. IHWH won by creating Adam, while the other gods only managed to create various species of animals. In revenge, the others succeeded in bringing about Adam's fall and making him mortal, contrary to IHWH's intention. Adam's expulsion from paradise was not a punishment but a political move; and in leading the Hebrews to the Promised Land, Moses was helping IHWH to reconquer territory seized by the other Elohim.

Goldberg insists that God must be imagined as having a body, a physical dwelling, and certain specific powers. Thus the Hebrews in the wilderness saw God as a pillar of cloud by day and a pillar of fire by night, and his energy was literally present in the Ark of the Covenant. The more spiritual conception of God as omnipotent and omnipresent, found already in the prophecies and Psalms (and culminating, of course, in Reform Judaism), is degenerate: 'The god of the nation, who is present and effectual, the "national god", representing the metaphysical energies of the people, has been turned into the pallid, abstract, universal "good God" who is "everything" and therefore nothing at all.'[172] A moral conception of God is similarly misguided. Originally, religious ritual was a means of manipulating the divine energy. Sacrifice was a practical measure needed to maintain the Elohim in bodily form, that is, the smoke ascending from the appropriate sacrifice. The laws of ritual purity were means of keeping the hostile Elohim at a distance, just as one diverts an electric current into the earth. Ritual was a technical matter, like a chemical experiment; and a mistake could result in death, as when Uzza accidentally touches the Ark (1 Chr. 13:10). Similarly, Goldberg thought the Kabbalah was

---

[171] Goldberg, *Die Wirklichkeit der Hebräer* (Berlin, 1925), p. 35 and elsewhere.
[172] Ibid. 149.

'Götterzwang', a means of conjuring up a god and compelling him to do one's will.[173]

In putting forward these eccentric notions, reminiscent of Spielberg's *Raiders of the Lost Ark*, Goldberg was clearly making an indirect attack on the Judaism of his day, denouncing its rituals as futile because separated from their original purpose, and its moral content as a feeble compensation for the inability to control the divine energy. Superficially his work might seem to resemble that of Rudolf Otto, who in *Das Heilige* (*The Idea of the Holy*, 1917) undertook to recapture the original sense of the numinous that had been diluted in modern, intellectual conceptions of religion.[174] Goldberg had some resonance among Jewish primitivists: Karl Wolfskehl found the book 'enormously interesting' and 'doubtless correct'.[175] However, Goldberg's notion of primitive religion lacks any real sense of the numinous. His creation myth is a shabby and amoral political tussle among rival gods. His theory of divine energy is unimaginatively materialistic, reducing divinity to an electric current and miracles to chemical reactions. It is not religious but magical. That is, while religious ritual is a setting for the unpredictable interaction between the power of God and the faith of the believer, magical ritual is itself a supposed means of operating on or with divine power, irrespective of the spiritual state of the magician. Magical fantasies are corrupted by their focus on power. 'A sound magician is a mighty god', says Marlowe's Dr Faustus. Gershom Scholem, an acute observer, described Goldberg as being 'filled with dreams of magical power'.[176] He called *Die Wirklichkeit der Hebräer* 'the *classic work of Jewish Satanism*'.[177]

Goldberg wanted to exercise real power. During the First World War he tried unsuccessfully through Buber to persuade the German Foreign Office to let him return to India in order to make contact with Mahatmas whose spiritual powers might enable Germany to win the war.[178] In American exile he continued

---

[173] Goldberg, *Die Wirklichkeit der Hebräer* (Berlin, 1925), p. 145.

[174] Otto, *The Idea of the Holy*, tr. John W. Harvey (London, 1926).

[175] Wolfskehl, letter to Gundolf, 13 May 1929, *Castrum Peregrini*, 126–8 (1977), 181.   [176] Scholem, *Von Berlin*, p. 184.

[177] Scholem, *Briefe 1914–1947*, p. 230; emphasis in original. See his long critique of the book in a letter to Rosa Okun, 23 Aug. 1928 (ibid. 235–9).

[178] Scholem, *Von Berlin*, p. 186; Werner Kraft, *Gespräche mit Martin Buber* (Munich, 1966), p. 33.

his materialist approach to spiritual matters by trying to photo-graph ghosts. He wrote in his article 'Rules for Research in Hauntings': 'Since we live now in a technical culture, we must prove immortality by technical means.'[179] While still in Germany he dominated a circle of young intellectuals by a personal char-isma which Scholem calls 'magnetic' and 'demonic'.[180] Others found Goldberg repulsive: Walter Benjamin could not even shake hands with him because of his 'impure aura'.[181] Thomas Mann portrayed Goldberg as 'Dr Chaim Breisacher' in *Doktor Faustus*. Since Goldberg was in no way involved with Nazism, this was a little unfair (though it must be added that Mann helped the exiled Goldberg by publishing four of his articles in the exile journal *Maß und Wert* and providing him with a letter of recommendation for use in America).[182] However, Mann was doubtless right in identifying Goldberg as a sinister phenom-enon. Even *Die Wirklichkeit der Hebräer* is strangely spine-chilling when its author imagines an amoral pantheon creating different species (human beings, animals, insects) in a competition for power. Goldberg was among the numerous charismatic figures who flourished under the Weimar Republic. His example shows that primitivism, indulged by Buber as a means of restoring religiosity, can license the unscrupulous to cast away civilized constraints and yield to an obsession with power.

Buber's Orientalism was differently and more engagingly devel-oped by Theodor Lessing in his eccentric, scrappy, yet original book *Europa und Asien* (*Europe and Asia*, 1916). It begins with an eloquent account of Europe's global conquests, anticipating more recent animus against Eurocentrism. It contrasts the active, progressive, individualistic European spirit, governed by the will to power, which has conquered the globe and exterminated many of its inhabitants, with the passive, contemplative, collective Asi-atic spirit, in which the individual is important only as a member of the family or the species, and which has a 'will to redemption'

---

[179] Quoted in Manfred Voigts, *Oskar Goldberg, der mythische Experimentalwis-senschaftler: Ein verdrängtes Kapitel jüdischer Geschichte* (Berlin, 1992), p. 294, from the *New York Spiritualist Leader*, 22 Aug. 1943.
[180] Scholem, *Von Berlin*, pp. 182–3.
[181] Ibid. 183. On the connection between Benjamin's conception of the 'aura' and occultism, see Braungart, *Ästhetischer Katholizismus*, pp. 122–7.
[182] See Voigts, *Oskar Goldberg*, p. 245.

('Wille zur Erlösung'). The Jews are the representatives of Asia in Europe. Despite their superficial appearance of rationality and industry, the Jews' essential character is Asiatic and religious. Even the Jewish and Christian injunction to love one's neighbour as oneself is a version of the Hindu principle (familiar to the West via Schopenhauer) of 'tat twam asi' ('that art thou').[183]

As this suggests, Lessing is working with a crude antithesis in which 'Asia' includes Judaism, Hinduism, Buddhism, the cultures of China and Japan, and Islam (though little is said about the last). This antithesis enables him to go well beyond Buber in countering antisemitic stereotypes of the over-civilized Jew by representing the Jews as primitive. Far from being a religion of reason, Judaism actually contains more primitive myth than Christianity, and the mission of the Jews may really have been to preserve some primitive warmth ('Naturwärme') within the coldly logical, arrogant and power-crazed civilization erected by Christianity. Admittedly, the Jews have been tragically estranged from their 'elemental maternal basis' ('elementarem Mutter-grunde').[184] However, their original ties to nature are preserved in their festivals: thus Sukkoth, the Feast of Tabernacles, was originally a kind of Dionysiac festival, corresponding to the Germanic festival of the summer solstice; while Hanukkah, the Feast of Lights, held in the winter, is identified with pagan Yule. European thought is abstract, Jewish thought is sensuous ('sinn-fällig'); and while Christianity believes in personal immortality, Judaism, like other Asiatic religions, stresses the family or larger collective entity. In short, Lessing, with disarming boldness, replaces the stereotype of the rational Jew with that of the over-rational and imperialistic Christian. In this picture, it is the Jews who have retained the primitive and pagan vitality that has vanished from Christian rationalism.

The Oriental essence of the Jew was also asserted by Max Brod when writing about Mahler. Brod accepts Buber's account of creativity as rooted in the *Volk*, and its 'blood-well of vital-ity' ('Blutbrunnen der Vitalität')[185] Although opposed to quasi-biological theories of race, Brod thinks that racial differences suffice to make different nations incapable of mixing, and that

---

[183] Lessing, *Europa und Asien*, 2nd edn. (Hanover, 1923), p. 289.
[184] Ibid. 311.   [185] Brod, *Heine*, p. 307.

one's racial basis must make itself felt in artistic creation, which taps into the irrational. Thus although Mahler had never heard Eastern Jewish folk-songs, his occasional march-rhythms betray an affinity to Hasidic songs, for Mahler could not help composing 'from the same unconscious primal depths (*Urgrund*) of his Jewish soul [. . .] that generated the most beautiful Hasidic songs which he probably did not know'.[186] And by setting Chinese poems to music in the *Lied von der Erde*, Mahler shows that this Jewish soul is Oriental: he was seeking his roots 'in the primal homeland of Asia' ('in der Urheimat Asien').[187]

Such fantasies are double-edged. Clearly the notion of regaining contact with Asia, insistently imagined as maternal, carries a heavy psychological freight; and Brod deepens the fantasy by dimly conjuring a vast Asian heartland stretching from Palestine to China. Besides indulging in such pleasing fantasies, however, Brod, in arguing for Mahler's essential Jewishness, is reversing the stereotype of the unmusical Jew established almost a century earlier by Wagner. We noted in Chapter 3 Wagner's claim that when a Jew tries to compose Western music he is really though involuntarily inspired by synagogue music, and that, in music as in speech and song, the hidden language of the Jew always breaks through the mask of assimilation. The Zionist Brod agrees with the antisemite Wagner: a Jew cannot assimilate; his hidden language, which is his true language, is the hallmark of his Jewish identity. Similarly, the Zionist Arnold Zweig agrees with Hermann Bahr, discussed in Chapter 3 as representing cultural antisemitism, that the Jews belong in Asia. Bahr, among the extraordinary tirades of Jewish antisemitism attributed to his Dr Beer in *Die Rotte Korahs*, includes the claim that Jews are unsuited to European life: 'We cannot do without Asia. We shall never be redeemed until we are back home there.' A Jew assimilated to Europe has betrayed Asia, 'the inner Orient in which he is rooted'.[188] In Zweig's *Aufzeichnungen über eine Familie Klopfer* (1911), the hero, an immigrant in Palestine, describes himself as the last European, while his fellow-immigrants are turning into Asiatics: 'The future belongs to the Asiatics.'[189]

---

[186] Brod, 'Jüdische Volksmelodien', *Der Jude*, 1 (1916–17), 344–5 (p. 344).
[187] Brod, *Heine*, p. 307. [188] Bahr, *Die Rotte Korahs*, pp. 106, 107.
[189] Zweig, *Aufzeichnungen über eine Familie Klopfer*, p. 104.

Feuchtwanger's Jud Süß

The inner Orient of the Jew is explored in Feuchtwanger's historical novel *Jud Süß* (*Jew Süss*, 1925). In adopting a fictional genre
that for some decades past had been largely abandoned to anti-
quarians and nationalists, Feuchtwanger was following the
example of Alfred Döblin, who had revived the historical novel
in *Wallenstein* (1920). He followed Döblin also in his scepticism
about historical meaning and in his attraction to Oriental doctrines of world-renunciation. Feuchtwanger admired the portrayal
of the Taoist philosophy of non-resistance in Döblin's first major
novel, *Die drei Sprünge des Wang-lun* (*The Three Leaps of Wang-
lun*, 1915), and the mystical detachment attained by the Emperor
Ferdinand in *Wallenstein*.[190] This conception of a generalized
'Oriental', passive, mystical, world-renouncing philosophy reflects
the work of Schopenhauer in mediating aspects of Hinduism and
Buddhism to a wide audience, as well as the widespread tendency,
shared by Feuchtwanger, to imagine Asia as a monolithic 'other' to
Europe. The scepticism about history goes back to Nietzsche's
efforts to offer an alternative to historical thinking. Rather than
finding meaning in history, or believing one could penetrate the
past, Feuchtwanger was disposed to use historical material as a
disguise for personal concerns.[191]

The historical material treated in *Jud Süß* certainly suggested,
and not only to Feuchtwanger, analogies to assimilation and dissimilation in Weimar Germany. Joseph Süss Oppenheimer, born in
Heidelberg either in 1692/3 or 1698/9, became court factor to
Prince Karl Alexander in 1732. When Karl Alexander became
Duke of Württemberg in 1733, he placed Süss in charge of financial affairs. Süss helped the Duke in his attempt to introduce
absolute government and a mercantilist economy. Süss established
new sources of state revenue by leasing enterprises and properties
to Christians and Jews, supervising the division of private property in cases of marriage or inheritance, and controlling the
appointment of government officials. As a supporter of the absolutist rule of his Catholic master, he attracted special enmity from
the largely Protestant population. He adopted the luxurious life-

---

[190] See Feuchtwanger's review of *Wang-lun* in *Ein Buch*, pp. 328–31.

[191] Feuchtwanger, 'Vom Sinn und Unsinn des historischen Romans' (1935), *Ein
Buch*, pp. 494–501 (p. 495).

style of a nobleman and even made two unsuccessful applications to the Emperor for noble status. Contemporaries agree that there was nothing Jewish about his accent or his body language. He lived in such magnificence that his biographer Selma Stern compares him to 'the Caliph in an Oriental fairy-tale'.[192] After the Duke's sudden death on 12 March 1737, Süss was promptly charged with embezzling state income and endangering the country's rights. Although the charges were never properly substantiated, and the accusation of sleeping with Christian women was used against him, Süss was condemned to death, hanged on 4 February 1738, and his remains exhibited in an iron cage. While in prison he became a pious Jew: he prayed, requested kosher food, and rejected offers to save his life on condition that he converted. He died reciting the Shema.

A modern counterpart to Süss—another Jew enjoying precarious power over a largely hostile population—seemed to be Walther Rathenau. Feuchtwanger wrote his novel in 1922, the year of Rathenau's assassination, and at one time thought of writing about Rathenau directly.[193] The comparison between Rathenau and the historical Süss also occurred to Karl Wolfskehl, who, reviewing Stern's biography, saw Süss as an Oriental figure, a vizier raised by his special talents to the immediate service of a potentate who tried to rule as absolutely as a sultan. 'He was a Jew, but not as the ghetto [. . .], but a Jew as the Orient, as an outbreak, a nourishing and devouring flame, an accident, a fairy-tale.'[194] More generally, the book's turbulent opening may well invite comparison with the Republic's early years.[195] Feuchtwanger uses a modern cliché pointedly when he says of Süss's unjust judges: 'they knew that the people and its healthy feeling ('das Volk und sein gesundes Empfinden') were on their side'.[196]

Beyond his contemporary relevance, however, Süss was intended as an exemplary figure. Selma Stern represents the historical Süss as a forerunner of Jewish emancipation who has discarded the passivity of the ghetto and created 'a new, richer Jewish human

---

[192] Stern, *Jud Süß*, p. 134.   [193] Feuchtwanger, *Ein Buch*, p. 497.
[194] Wolfskehl, 'Sultan und Wesir im Schwabenland', in *Briefe und Aufsätze* (Hamburg, 1966), pp. 226–30 (p. 226).
[195] See Paul Gerhard Klussmann, 'Lion Feuchtwangers Roman *Jud Süß*. Gedichtete Psychologie und prophetischer Mythos des Juden', *ZfdP* 97 (1978), Sonderheft, 87–107.
[196] Feuchtwanger, *Jud Süß* (Frankfurt, 1976), p. 484.

type full of emotional tension and breadth'.[197] Feuchtwanger, however, uses Süss for the opposite purpose. Evidently touched by the post-War mood of cultural pessimism, Feuchtwanger, by his own account, intended Süss to illustrate how Europeans should abandon their obsession with power and learn from 'Asia's doctrine of non-willing and non-action'.[198] The Jews were specially equipped to learn this lessson by their position between Europe and Asia, between the world of action and 'the world of non-action, of overcoming the will, of absorption in Nirvana'.[199] Süss exemplifies the duality of Europe and Asia, first in his furious struggle for power and pleasure, and finally in his no less whole-hearted submission to God.

In the novel itself the identification of the Jewish character with Oriental passivity seems somewhat strained. The vindictive Süss betrays the Duke's plans to destroy the Württemberg constitution. When the Duke dies of a heart attack, Süss tries to savour his revenge, but finds it unsatisfying, and is suddenly overcome by a loss of will which he finds a relief. Thereupon he allows himself to be arrested. Soon afterwards Feuchtwanger inserts a passage about the character of the Jewish people:

[The Jewish people] transforms into its own, self-created words the clear, resonant doctrine of action, the dull, smouldering doctrine of defiance to immortality, the gentle, murmuring doctrine of the bliss of non-willing and non-action. And the little nation writes the two books that more than any others have changed the face of the world, the great book of action, the Old Testament, and the great book of renunciation, the New. (pp. 432–3)

Unafraid of the oddity of claiming that the Jewish character is more truly expressed in the New Testament than in the Old, Feuchtwanger goes on to maintain that Jews are 'not quite at home in action, their home is on the bridge between action and renunciation' (p. 433), and that basic to the Jews' character is an Oriental passivity, an urge to renounce the world.

These narratorial observations do not explain, however, the nature of the link between activity and passivity. Is Feuchtwanger,

[197] Stern, *Jud Süß*, p. 141.
[198] Feuchtwanger, 'Über *Jud Süß*' (1929), *Ein Buch*, p. 381.
[199] Feuchtwanger, 'Die Verjudung der abendländischen Literatur' (1920) in *Ein Buch*, p. 435; similarly in 'Der historische Prozeß der Juden' (1930), ibid. 460.

like Buber, constructing a psychology of the Jew as divided and dualistic? If not, what feature of the Jew's character, as constructed by Feuchtwanger, enables him to move from the first to the second? One clue may lie in the novel's numerous references to the Kabbalah. John Milfull has argued that these point to a doctrine that one must plunge into the world and its corruption, as Süss does, in order to free oneself from it.[200] Feuchtwanger certainly entertains the notion of transmigration of souls (*gilgul*) from the Lurianic Kabbalah.[201] Are we, however, to go further and discern in the text the heretical notion of redemption through sin?[202] Are we to think that Süss's immersion in the world is a necessary precondition of his redemption? Or are we to see Süss as redeemed through suffering?

While the novel's esoteric subtext doubtless deserves further exploration, I want to suggest that its Oriental discourse provides a link between the activity and passivity in Süss's character. The link lies in Süss's sensuality and its interpretation. Süss's Uncle Gabriel, a Kabbalist who embodies Süss's conscience, discerns that his sensuality has not extinguished his religious urge: 'He was lying on the naked, impudent breasts of Lilith, but he yearned and reached out towards the Upper World' (p. 415). Another Kabbalist, antithetical to the severe Gabriel, is Süss's daughter Naemi. Naemi is not only beautiful and delicate, but learned in the Kabbalah (p. 144). She is also a 'schöne Jüdin'; her sensuality is suggested when she reads the Song of Solomon, and after listening to Rabbi Gabriel's allegorical interpretation she continues to understand it in literal and sensual terms: she is anxious for a lover (p. 109). Like so many literary (and pictorial) *belles juives*, Naemi represents the sensual Oriental woman. Her virtue, however, is confirmed by her death. One of Süss's enemies, out of revenge, leads the Duke to Naemi's secluded house and encourages him to rape her; Naemi avoids this fate by suicide. This episode recalls C. F. Meyer's story *Der Heilige* (*The Saint*, 1879), where the King rapes Thomas Becket's daughter Grace (Gnade) who is

---

[200] Milfull, 'Juden, Christen und andere Menschen. Sabbatianismus, Assimilation und jüdische Identität in Lion Feuchtwangers Roman *Jud Süß*', in Grimm and Bayerdörfer (eds.), *Im Zeichen Hiobs*, pp. 213–22.

[201] Feuchtwanger, *Jud Süß*, pp. 218, 307; cf. Scholem, *Major Trends*, pp. 281–4.

[202] See Scholem, *Major Trends*, pp. 310–20. Unlike the practitioners of this heresy, Süss does not commit sins for their own sake, nor does he apostatize.

likewise kept in seclusion. Since Meyer represents Becket as originally an Arab from Moorish Spain, this literary model confirms the 'Orientalism' of Naemi.[203] However, she is more than a stereotype. Learned, beautiful, and virtuous, she embodies a spiritualized sensuality free from grossness. Her Oriental associations imply that such a sensuality is part of the Oriental nature of the Jew, as is the disposition to renounce the world. Süss's own sensuality is very evident. In indulging it, however, he is not really turning away from the Upper World. In exploring the sensual part of his nature, he is unwittingly approaching the time when his passive, world-renouncing character will be realized. In Süss, Feuchtwanger presents us with a rounded Jewish figure whose sensual appetite paradoxically supports his deep-seated 'Asiatic' urge to renounce the world.

Else Lasker-Schüler: 'Gottosten'[204]

Else Lasker-Schüler (1869–1945), the greatest woman poet of early twentieth-century Germany, looked to an imaginary Orient in order to heal her own sense of split identity. In 1920 she provided Kurt Pinthus, who included her work in his famous anthology of Expressionist poetry, *Menschheitsdämmerung* (*Twilight of Mankind*), with the following autobiographical note:

I was born in Thebes in Egypt, even if I first saw the light of day at Elberfeld in the Rhineland. I went to school till I was 11, became Robinson [Crusoe], lived for five years in the East, and have vegetated ever since.[205]

Her creativity was nourished by emotional damage. Her parents took her away from school when she was 11 because she developed St Vitus's dance or chorea. This may in turn, as Jakob Hessing surmises, have been brought on by antisemitic harassment.[206] If

---

[203] On Meyer's Orientalism, see Robert C. Holub, *Reflections of Realism: Paradox, Norm, and Ideology in Nineteenth-Century German Prose* (Detroit, 1991), ch. 6.

[204] 'God-East': from the poem 'Joseph' (also known as 'Joseph wird verkauft') in Lasker-Schüler, *Gedichte*, ed. Karl Jürgen Skrodzki, 2 vols. (Frankfurt, 1996), i. 211.

[205] *Menschheitsdämmerung: Ein Dokument des Expressionismus*, ed. Kurt Pinthus (Reinbek, 1959), p. 352.

[206] Hessing, *Else Lasker-Schüler: Biographie einer deutsch-jüdischen Dichterin* (Karlsruhe, 1985), pp. 32–42.

so, the difference becomes all the greater between the harsh outside world and the warm and secure family environment which
Lasker-Schüler celebrates throughout her prose and poetry. Like
other figures in this study, however, Lasker-Schüler suffered the
trauma of banishment from this haven. Her dearly loved brother
Paul died in 1882, her mother died in 1890, and her father in
1894. She seems to have felt her mother's loss most deeply: 'When
my mother died, the moon was shattered', she wrote much
later.[207] Neither of her marriages provided a substitute for family
life. Not much is known about her first husband, Berthold Lasker,
a Berlin physician whom she married in 1894; but the intriguing
fact that he taught chess to his younger brother Emanuel, who
later become world grandmaster, invites one to see him as an
extreme rationalist who could hardly be a suitable husband for
someone so imaginative. Presumably because she disliked him, she
maintained that he was not the father of her son Paul; she said the
father was a Greek prince called Alcibiades de Rouan, but it is not
certain that such a person ever existed, for Lasker-Schüler, like
Joseph Roth, was a compulsive myth-maker.[208] After her divorce
from Lasker in 1900, she married in 1903 Georg Levin, a musician who worked devotedly to promote modernism in the arts and
is best known for founding and editing the Expressionist journal
Der Sturm under the pseudonym Herwarth Walden. This name
came from Lasker-Schüler, who gave all her friends sobriquets: she
called Gottfried Benn 'Giselheer', Karl Kraus the 'Dalai Lama'.
She was divorced from Levin/Walden in 1912.

Whatever the reasons for the failure of these marriages, they
signalize Lasker-Schüler's inability to find a secure place either
among the Berlin Jewish bourgeoisie or in its antithesis, the Berlin
Bohemia. Although she always proudly affirmed her Jewishness,
she did not like the available ways of being Jewish. The split in her
Jewish identity is apparent from a furious letter (beginning 'Honoured Lord of Zion' and signed 'Your Prince of Thebes') which she
sent Martin Buber in 1914 after an argument in which Lasker-
Schüler had (wrongly) maintained that Stefan George was a Jew:

---

[207] Lasker-Schüler, *Prosa und Schauspiele*, ed. Friedhelm Kemp (Munich, 1962), p.
758. Henceforth cited as *PS*.

[208] See Sigrid Bauschinger, *Else Lasker-Schüler: Ihr Werk und ihre Zeit* (Heidelberg,
1980), p. 28.

A wolf came to see you—a High Priest with arrowed teeth, a Basileus with a wild heart, a praying fist, a sea without a shore, a bed that drank itself—and—you talked about literature—you read poems and I don't like that. You are ashamed that George is a Jew—and you are the lord of Zion? I *hate* the Jews, since I was David or Joseph—I hate the Jews, because they despise my language, because their ears are closed and they listen for dwarfishness and Yiddish (*Gemauschel*).[209]

This letter not only reveals Lasker-Schüler's dislike, shared by many contemporaries, for incompletely assimilated modern Jews, but also contains several of the motifs from which she constructed a counter-identity. Her Jewishness is focused on the Old Testament: she identifies herself with 'David or Joseph', presents herself as a High Priest, and calls Buber, as a religious writer, 'lord of Zion'. Her ideal is aristocratic: she and Buber are lords, priests, and kings ('Basileus' is the Greek word for 'king') in contrast to the undifferentiated 'dwarfish' mass of modern Jews. Against mere 'literature', she invokes the primitive, aggressive, and elemental energies: the wolf, the fist, the sea; she herself is at once a priest, a king, and a wild animal. Finally, her identification with 'David or Joseph' implies the androgyny which appears both in her books and in her public persona. She was a conspicuous figure, usually dressed in baggy trousers, with a turban and a mass of imitation jewellery. Some people found her embarrassing; Stefan Zweig described her as 'the comedian of her genius'.[210] Her appearance was not exactly 'cross-dressing', as a recent critic maintains;[211] it was rather the creation of a new identity outside gender stereotypes.

Similarly, Lasker-Schüler constructed Jewishness from various components, among which literary Orientalism was prominent. Her family had largely abandoned Jewish tradition. Although her essay 'Der Versöhnungstag' enthusiastically recalls the celebration of Yom Kippur, she confuses the Day of Atonement with Passover and wrongly says that the vacant place left at the *seder* is for the Messiah instead of the Prophet Elijah.[212] She knew the Old

[209] Buber, *Briefwechsel*, i. 353–4; also in *Lieber gestreifter Tiger: Briefe von Else Lasker-Schüler*, ed. Margarete Kupper, vol. i (Munich, 1969), p. 117.

[210] Zweig, *Tagebücher*, p. 304.

[211] Donna K. Heizer, *Jewish-German Identity in the Orientalist Literature of Else Lasker-Schüler, Friedrich Wolf, and Franz Werfel* (Columbia, SC, 1996), p. 40.

[212] PS 750, corrected by Bauschinger, *Lasker-Schüler*, p. 164.

Testament, had some inkling of the Kabbalah, and read Buber's accounts of Hasidism. She also quotes frequently though inaccurately from the New Testament, and describes Jesus as a prophet and even as the Messiah.[213] This eclectic religiosity is combined with Oriental imagery from the *Arabian Nights* and from the German tradition of Oriental poetry outstandingly represented by Goethe's *West-östlicher Divan* (1819).

Lasker-Schüler's Orient is composite. Just as Stefan George invented a composite Romance language (besides another which only he could understand), Lasker-Schüler invented a language called 'Asiatic'. A poem which she published in this language looks vaguely like Arabic; its title, and last word, are 'Elbanaff', and it begins:

> Min salihihi wali kinahu
> Rahi hatiman
> fi is bahi lahu fassun . . .[214]

At other times she claimed to have translated her poems into Syrian and to recite them in Arabic.[215] More likely, however, these are only sound-patterns, like the sound-poems composed by the Dadaists Hugo Ball and Hans Arp.[216] Her private language looks like an attempt to recreate the security of childhood in a private space to which the harsh world can have no access.

As an imaginative means of overcoming racial and gender polarities, the composite Orient features in Lasker-Schüler's early prose works *Die Nächte des Tino von Bagdad* (*The Nights of Tino of Baghdad*, 1907) and *Der Prinz von Theben* (*The Prince of Thebes*, 1914). Its main localities, not clearly distinct, are Egypt, Arabia, and Baghdad. Morocco, Afghanistan, Greece, and an Islamic Constantinople (inhabited by the Grand Mogul of Philippopolis) are not far away. Time is also vague: the atmosphere of the

---

[213] See *PS* 724 (Rev. 3:16, misattributed to Jesus); *PS* 740 ('bread of life', John 6:35); *PS* 750 (Matt. 5:17); *PS* 869 (John 21:15–17). On her eclecticism, see Wolf Kaiser, *Palästina—Erez Israel: Deutschsprachige Reisebeschreibungen jüdischer Autoren von der Jahrhundertwende bis zum Zweiten Weltkrieg* (Hildesheim, 1992), p. 342.

[214] *PS* 520; supposedly a translation of her poem 'Weltflucht'.

[215] See letter of 22 Mar. 1910 to Jethro Bithell, in *Lieber gestreifter Tiger*, pp. 55–6; letter of 8 Apr. 1910 to Max Brod, in *Wo ist unser buntes Theben: Briefe von Else Lasker-Schüler*, ed. Margarete Kupper, vol. ii (Munich, 1969), p. 26.

[216] Bauschinger, *Lasker-Schüler*, p. 105; on George, Ball, and Arp, see Leonard Forster, *The Poet's Tongues: Multilingualism in Literature* (Cambridge, 1970).

Arabian Nights accommodates references to European tourists, gas-lighting, and Imperial Berlin, as well as mosques, dervishes, fakirs, slaves, eunuchs, dromedaries, rich clothes, opium, obeisances, and bloodthirsty executions. The Jews form part of this Orient: we hear of an Indian, Chandragupta, with a Jewish mother, and of the friendship between a narrator's great-grandfather, the Sheik, and the Jewish sultan Mschattre-Zimt, who after death rises from his grave wearing Moses' turban. There is no consistent narrative thread or narrating voice. Both personae, Tino and the Prince, are of ambiguous gender. Tino, though 'the poetess of Arabia' with several husbands and lovers, has a name with a masculine ending. She dislikes wearing a veil and being a woman: 'and she cursed her brown long hair and all that she had inherited from Eve' (*PS* 82). Her lovers include the son of a Jewish general, 'Abdul Antinous', whose second name is that of the boy loved by the Emperor Hadrian (*PS* 72, 76). The Prince of Thebes, Jussuf (a name by which Lasker-Schüler herself liked to be called), is the third of three rulers, each of whom takes the female name Abigail. Abigail I, a poet, stays in his mother's womb for twenty years, unwilling to face life, until he accidentally kills her with a kick and is born as she dies. This story seems to express both the desire for a sheltering maternal environment and some ambivalence towards the mother who provides it. Abigail II, an elderly man, is stabbed by Jussuf, who ascends the throne as Abigail III and leads 25,000 young men in a campaign to make old citizens ('alte Bürger') release their sons from imprisonment (*PS* 123); this Expressionist theme, familiar from Walter Hasenclever's contemporary play *Der Sohn* (*The Son*, 1914), confirms Lasker-Schüler's hostility to her own family background. Of the 'wild Jews' whom he anoints as his chieftains, Jussuf's favourite is Salomein (a combination of Solomon and Salome). However, everyone, including Salomein, is distanced from Jussuf by awe at his bloodless military success: 'Thus Abigail the Loving became a lonely prince and he remembered painfully the nights when he wrapped himself in the skins of sweet bodies' (*PS* 125). This sentence reveals much of the motivation behind Lasker-Schüler's writing. Lovers are imagined as a refuge: one wraps oneself in their bodies in order to recreate the lost security of home. The lonely prince could well be the author of Lasker-Schüler's own love poetry, which, rich and intense as it is, is really about the desire to be in love. It seeks to create a warm, intimate, shared space as a substitute for the lost world of childhood.

In the *Hebräische Balladen* (*Hebrew Ballads*), first published in 1913, Lasker-Schüler manages to combine and universalize her various preoccupations. First, by linking her exotic Orientalism firmly to the Old Testament, she creates a new, primitive kind of Jew, the 'wild Jew' or 'Hebrew'. Once, when annoyed by the banality of her contemporaries, she burst out: 'We must abolish the word Jew. They should become Hebrews!'[217] The travel book she wrote after visiting Palestine in 1934 is accordingly entitled *Das Hebräerland* (*The Land of the Hebrews*), sustaining the fantasies which were disappointed by the real Palestine; sadly, she spent the last six years of her life there as an exile, living in an unheated flat in a Jerusalem which felt to her like a tomb.[218] Secondly, Lasker-Schüler increasingly managed to understand her personal trauma as typifying the universal yearning for a lost paradise, which, after learning something about the Kabbalah, she later identified with the divine radiance of the Shekhinah: 'the primal light (*Urlicht*) the loving face of the origin', as she called it in her essay 'Paradiese' (*PS* 710).[219] In the *Hebrew Ballads* she transmutes her own experience into a grandiose myth of a separation from God and nature which can possibly be restored through love.

There are three editions of *Hebrew Ballads*, each with differing contents.[220] I shall concentrate on the second edition, as its poems are more homogeneous than those in the third, much enlarged edition. The first poem, 'Mein Volk' ('My People'), ostensibly a lament, in fact helps the reader to bridge the gulf from the degenerate present to the world of the Old Testament. The Jewish nation, which provides the poet's inspiration, is crumbling:

---

[217] Quoted in Hans W. Cohn, *Else Lasker-Schüler: The Broken World* (Cambridge, 1974), p. 119.

[218] See Alfred Bodenheimer, *Die auferlegte Heimat: Else Lasker-Schülers Emigration in Palästina* (Tübingen, 1995); on *Das Hebräerland*, Kaiser, *Palästina—Erez Israel*, pp. 339–58.

[219] On Lasker-Schüler and the Kabbalah, see Cohn, *Lasker-Schüler*, pp. 130–7.

[220] See *Gedichte*, ii. 25–6, 32. The first volume is cited henceforth as *G* and page number. For a poem-by-poem commentary in English, see Leon I. Yudkin, *Else Lasker-Schüler: A Study in German Jewish Literature* (Northwood, 1991), pp. 21–41.

Der Fels wird morsch,
Dem ich entspringe
Und meine Gotteslieder singe . . .   (G 157)

The rock begins to crack
From which I spring
And my divine songs sing . . .   (DD 247)[221]

The Jewish people are now 'the crumbling skeleton of stone'; the poet is a trickle of water flowing over 'grieving stone' ('Klagegestein', suggesting 'Klagemauer', the Wailing Wall) towards the sea, but still connected with 'my blood's early fermentation'. The contrasting imagery of stone and liquid expresses a paradox. What might seem the solid, timeless stone is now crumbling and is associated with grief; the continuity of the Jewish people rests with something so fleeting and vulnerable as a trickle of water. But that slender trickle connects the immensity of the sea with the primal energies of the blood. The frail poet has the power to connect ends with origins.

Origins are invoked in the poem 'Im Anfang' ('In the Beginning'), written as far back as 1902 but introduced here to link childhood and God. The poet recalls how, when the world itself was still a child, she was 'God's naughty child', swinging on a swing pushed by her young father God, attended by the sun and moon as grandparents, and playing tricks on God and the Devil which make them laugh heartily. God's familiarity with the Devil conveys playfully a possibility further explored in 'An Gott' ('To God'): that good and evil might not really be separate. 'To God' is addressed to Him from a position of estrangement. The speaker sees that God allows both good and evil to happen: 'Du wehrst den guten und den bösen Sternen nicht' ('You don't hold back the good or the evil stars'), and her reflections on the alarming freedom permitted by God lead to the question: 'God, where are You?' and to a longing for reunion:

Ich möchte nah an deinem Herzen lauschen,
Mit deiner fernsten Nähe mich vertauschen,
Wenn goldverklärt in deinem Reich
Aus tausendseligem Licht
Alle die guten und die bösen Brunnen rauschen.   (G 160)

---

[221] DD refers to *Your Diamond Dreams Cut Open My Arteries: Poems by Else Lasker-Schüler*, tr. Robert P. Newton (Chapel Hill, NC, 1982).

I should like to listen close to your heart, to exchange myself for your
more distant closeness, when in your kingdom, transfigured in gold, from
thousandfold blessed light all the good and evil springs murmur.

The imagery here, as often in Lasker-Schüler, recalls German
Romanticism and particularly Eichendorff's poem 'Sehnsucht'.[222]
But it expresses a mysterious conjecture: whereas in the fallen
world evil apparently operates without God doing anything to
ward it off, in His kingdom evil may coexist harmoniously with
good, as innocently as springs of water.

The fall into separation from God is prefigured in Adam's
uneasy dreams whose groans disturb Eve as she bends over him
('Eva'), and its consequences are seen in 'Abel': 'Aber durch Kains
Leib führen die Gräben der Stadt' (*G* 164)—'But the city ditches
pass through the body of Cain' (*DD* 249). Here, by a bold metaphor, the veins and arteries running through Cain's body are
identified with the 'Gräben der Stadt' which could be the moats
and ditches defending a fortified town from its enemies or the
complicated system of channels and sewers lying underneath a
modern city. While Abel's face is 'a golden garden', as befits a
pastoralist, all of civilization is implicit in Cain's act of murder.

Piety and violence are brought together, not as antitheses but in
a closer, more uneasy relationship, in 'Abraham und Isaak', which
deserves to be quoted in full:

Abraham baute in der Landschaft Eden
Sich eine Stadt aus Erde und aus Blatt
Und übte sich mit Gott zu reden.

Die Engel ruhten gern vor seiner frommen Hütte
Und Abraham erkannte jeden;
Himmlische Zeichen ließen ihre Flügelschritte.

Bis sie dann einmal bang in ihren Träumen
Meckern hörten die gequälten Böcke,
Mit denen Isaak opfern spielte hinter Süßholzbäumen.

---

[222] Available with translation in *The Penguin Book of German Verse*, ed. Leonard
Forster (Harmondsworth, 1959), pp. 318–19. The affinity with Romanticism was
ignored by early commentators who credited Lasker-Schüler with innate Orientalism:
e.g. Meir Wiener, 'Else Lasker-Schüler', in Gustav Krojanker (ed.), *Juden in der
deutschen Literatur: Essays über zeitgenössische Schriftsteller* (Berlin, 1922), pp.
179–92. Contrast Gay, *Freud, Jews and Other Germans*, pp. 143–5; Heinz Politzer,
'The Blue Piano of Else Lasker-Schüler: "a Hebrew poetess in the German tongue"',
Commentary, 9 (Jan.–June 1950), 335–44.

Und Gott ermahnte Abraham:
Er brach vom Kamm des Meeres Muscheln ab und Schwamm
Hoch auf den Blöcken den Altar zu schmücken.

Und trug den einzigen Sohn gebunden auf den Rücken
Zu werden seinem großen Herrn gerecht—
Der aber liebte seinen Knecht.²²³

Abraham built himself on Eden's sod
A city raised of earth and leaf
And practised converse with his God.

The angels pleased to rest before his holy home
And Abraham knew every one;
Their wingèd steps left symbols in the loam.

Until they then once heard in fearful dreams
The bleating of tormented rams
Where Isaac was playing sacrifice behind the liquorice trees.

And God admonished: Abraham!
From the ridge of the sea he broke off sponge and clam
To trim the altar towering up in stone.

And bound on his back he bore his only son
Since that his Lord's command did him compel -
The Lord, however, loved his servant well.

(DD 251)

At the beginning of history, Abraham still communicates with God and receives visits from angels. He founds a city, but unlike those prefigured by Cain, it is built only of earth and leaves (perhaps suggested by the oaks of Mamre in Gen. 18:1) and it is still located in the region of Paradise. The central line of the poem, however, with its emphatic stresses and its framing assonance of 'Meckern' and 'Böcke', introduces evil where, hitherto, one would least have expected it—in the 'verts paradis des amours enfantins' and behind the liquorice trees ('Süßholzbäume') which not only suggest a child's fantasy of sweets growing on trees but include the word 'süß' (sweet) which constantly occurs in Lasker-Schüler's evocations of love. Isaac is a nasty little boy who likes torturing animals under the pretence of playing at sacrifice. Has he seen sacrifices performed? Or does the sacrifice of live beings really spring from a childish sadism which can only too easily be disguised as religious zeal? Is this the *yetser ha-ra*, the evil impulse

²²³ Later editions give line 10 as 'Und Gott ermahnte: Abraham!' and have in line 13 'auf dem Rücken', which is grammatically preferable (G ii. 188).

debated in rabbinic theology, already at work? It seems as if God's command to Abraham to sacrifice his son is not just a trial of his obedience but a punishment for Isaac: having invented sacrifice, he must be its first victim. The penultimate line reads literally: 'to do justice to his great Lord'. Thus Lasker-Schüler introduces an element of justice into a Bible narrative from which it seems perplexingly absent. Fortunately, there is also mercy, and Isaac is let off for Abraham's sake. But what will happen when humanity has moved further away from God and its evil impulses have freer rein?

Lasker-Schüler suggests several answers. On the one hand, she values the primitive, animal side of human nature exemplified by the 'wild Jew Joshua' and by Moses, who dies 'when his tired lion's soul cried out to God' (*DD* 259). Another poem represents Jacob as a powerful buffalo who is humanized when he feels pain from monkey-bites:

> Durch die müden Schmerzen in den Knöcheln
> Sank er vor dem Himmel fiebernd nieder
> Und sein Ochsgesicht erschuf das Lächeln.   (*G* 158)

> Fever forced him to sink down a while,
> Under heaven, to rest his painful bones,
> And his ox-face bore the world's first smile.   (*DD* 255)

It is when pain and the need for rest take him out of the world of primitive energies that Jacob is humanized by becoming aware of heaven ('vor dem Himmel' implying both sky and heaven) and learning to smile. For wildness is dangerous: in 'Jakob und Esau' the two brothers are at first united in love for Rebecca's handmaid, but Esau gives up his birthright for her sake, and the poem ends: 'Um seine Schultern schlägt er wild das Dickicht' ('Bursts shouldering through the thicket and away', *DD* 253).

On the other hand, Lasker-Schüler repeatedly imagines the quiet (rather than passionate) union of two lovers, using pastoral as opposed to animal imagery. Ruth gives Boaz 'golden corn-flowers' to appeal to his heart, which 'surges high in its corn gardens' ('Boas', *G* 165), images suggested by the harvest in Ruth 2. Esther is 'as slender as a palm of the field' (*G* 158). David and his 'playmate' Jonathan are 'like the buds on the love-psalms' (*G* 161, *DD* 261); in another poem about them, David addresses Jonathan as 'blood of the sweet fig' (*G* 205). The most passionate, complex, and inventive of these poems is 'Pharao und Joseph'.

Spoken by Joseph (the figure with whom Lasker-Schüler identified), it describes Pharaoh's head giving off a scent of corn as it
rests on Joseph's shoulder 'in the wheat of our morn', and combines the images of blood and water as does 'Mein Volk': Pharaoh's eyes are like waves of the Nile, his heart 'lies in my blood'
and 'roars on my riverbed' (G 159, DD 257). Violence is suggested by Pharaoh's anger against Joseph's brothers, the 'ten
wolves' who threw him into the pit. The lovers' union has quiet-
ened but not removed Pharaoh's own potential for violence. The
suggestions of blood and anger hint at physical passion, whereas
in 'Sulamith', despite its basis in the Song of Songs, passion is
etherealized: Sulamith feels how 'the night cloud drinks my deep
dream of cedars', and feels herself fading into the evening colours
of the sky over Jerusalem (G 165). The poem 'Versöhnung', finally,
defies expectations, for while the title evokes the Day of Atonement ('Versöhnungstag'), the poem evokes the not quite complete
or secure union of two lovers. The female speaker refers to what
will or should happen:

> Es wird ein großer Stern in meinen Schoß fallen . . .
> Wir wollen wachen die Nacht.   (G 166)
>
> A great star will fall into my womb . . .
> Let us stay awake through the night.

She asks for rest and reconciliation amid a sense of God's tranquil
plenitude ('So much God spills over'); she wonders why her lover is
reluctant to kiss her; and she says, most revealingly:

> Wir wollen uns versöhnen die Nacht,
> Wenn wir uns herzen, sterben wir nicht.
>
> Let us be reconciled tonight,
> If we cuddle each other, we won't die.

Under the guise of a love-poem, this seems really to be a child's
wish for security. The first line just quoted could also mean 'Let us
reconcile the night to ourselves', thus expressing a wish to pro-
pitiate the night, the dark threatening external presence which
could bring loneliness and death. Lasker-Schüler's greatness as a
poet lies partly in her ability to tap into the feelings of a child and
express them in an arrestingly simple form. In the *Hebrew Ballads*
she managed both to use biblical figures as correlatives for her own

emotions, and to draw out implications latent in the biblical myths.

Beer-Hofmann and the Election of Israel

After long neglect, Richard Beer-Hofmann is emerging as one of the most important, accomplished, and influential writers of the Viennese *fin de siècle*.[224] Beer-Hofmann accepted aspects of the 'Oriental' stereotype, notably religiosity and sensuality, and explored them in unprecedented depth. His father, a Viennese lawyer, had abandoned Jewish religious practice and severed all links with the Jewish community. Since Richard's mother died at his birth, he was brought up and later adopted by her sister Berta and her husband Alois Hofmann, whence the double name. None of his family were observant Jews except his paternal grand-mother, Katherina Beer, whom Richard describes reading a prayer-book by candlelight on Friday evenings.[225] In 1895 he met the 16-year-old Paula Lissy, a Gentile shop-assistant; she was the love of his life, and it was evidently their relationship, and the birth of their children, that awakened Beer-Hofmann's sense of Jewish identity. She converted to Judaism, and they were married in a Jewish ceremony, with Schnitzler as one of the wit-nesses, in 1897. After the birth of their first child, Beer-Hofmann wrote a great and haunting poem, 'Schlaflied für Mirjam' ('Lullaby for Miriam'), which deserves partial quotation not only for its merits but because it expresses a sense of Jewishness that resonated with many members of Beer-Hofmann's generation. Early stanzas evoke the isolation of the individual. The last stanza runs:

> Schläfst du, Mirjam?—Mirjam, mein Kind,
> Ufer nur sind wir, und tief in uns rinnt

---

[224] See the important study in Jacques Le Rider, *Modernity and Crises of Identity: Culture and Society in Fin-de-Siècle Vienna*, tr. Rosemary Morris (Cambridge, 1993), ch. 14. The major book by Stefan Scherer, *Richard Beer-Hofmann und die Wiener Moderne* (Tübingen, 1993), has relatively little on Beer-Hofmann's Jewishness, while Ulrike Peters, *Richard Beer-Hofmann. Zum jüdischen Selbstverständnis im Wiener Judentum um die Jahrhundertwende* (Frankfurt, 1993), is a theological rather than a literary study. See also Scherer, 'Richard Beer-Hofmann und das Judentum', in Norbert Otto Eke and Günter Helmes (eds.), *Richard Beer-Hofmann (1866–1945): Studien zu seinem Werk* (Würzburg, 1993), pp. 13–33.

[225] Beer-Hofmann, *Gesammelte Werke* (Frankfurt, 1963), p. 691. Henceforth cited as BH.

Blut von Gewesenen—zu Kommenden rollts,
Blut unsrer Väter, voll Unruh und Stolz.
In uns sind *Alle.* Wer fühlt sich allein?
Du bist ihr Leben—ihr Leben ist dein -
Mirjam, mein Leben, mein Kind—schlaf ein!   (BH 654)

Are you sleeping, Miriam, my child?
We are but banks, and in us there flows
Blood of the past—to the future it goes,
Blood of our fathers, proud, restless and wild.
All are within us. Who feels alone?
You are their life—their life is your own—
Sleep, my Miriam, my life, my own!

Here, at the climax of the poem, Beer-Hofmann finds an escape from isolation in the unity of the race. The familiar nineteenth-century assumption that ancestral residues linger in the recesses of the individual consciousness is here transposed into a biological key by Beer-Hofmann's emphasis on blood, recalling at the same time that Jewish identity is transmitted through biological descent. In this sense, our ancestors can be imagined as still present in our physical being, as in Hofmannsthal's poem 'Terzinen über Vergänglichkeit'. And this continuity, uniting Beer-Hofmann also with his daughter, enables him to lull her to sleep, confident in the future of the race.

Jewish themes increasingly absorbed Beer-Hofmann's subsequent writing. Although his play *Der Graf von Charolais*, premièred in 1904, is adapted from a seventeenth-century English drama by Massinger, *The Fatal Dowry*, Beer-Hofmann rather incongruously introduces into the first act a Jewish creditor, 'der rote Itzig' (Red Ikey), who possesses the corpse of the old Count Charolais as security for a debt. When the young Count appeals to Itzig's humanity, Itzig replies with a Shylock-like tirade in which he recalls how *his* father was burnt by the Inquisition. Still more remarkable is the fact that Itzig's language, a modified form of the *Mauscheldeutsch* conventionally placed in the mouths of unassimilated literary Jews, is given the dignity of blank verse.[226] Beer-Hofmann had more ambitious plans, however: from 1898 on he contemplated a pentalogy of biblical dramas with the title *His-*

---

[226] See Viktor Žmegač, *Der historische und der typologische Jude: Studien zu jüdischen Gestalten in der Literatur der Jahrhundertwende* (Tübingen, 1996), pp. 56–67.

torie von König David. From 1909 to 1915 he worked on the prelude, *Jaákobs Traum* (*Jacob's Dream*), which had its première in the Vienna Burgtheater in 1919. A slow worker, and side-tracked by ill health and literary commissions (such as a stage adaptation of Goethe's *Faust* I and II), Beer-Hofmann completed the next portion, *Der junge David* (*Young David*), only in 1933. While *Jaákobs Traum* is a taut metaphysical drama, *Der junge David*, an immense play in seven long scenes, is disappointing: its dramatic interest is diffused among far too many characters, and the fussy stage directions, which tell us how each person speaks, seem intended to compensate for the deficient expressive power of their language. Both plays, though, are expressions of Beer-Hof-mann's sense of being simultaneously a Jew and an Austrian. 'In substance I very much a Jew,' he once said, 'and functionally very much an Austrian.'[227] Especially in *Jaákobs Traum*, the severity of the Old Testament narrative is in productive tension with the elaborate theatrical devices borrowed from the Counter-Reformation traditions of Austrian drama—for example, the successive arrivals of the archangels that are carefully described in the stage directions.

First, though, we need to consider the affirmation of Jewishness articulated in another of Beer-Hofmann's masterpieces, his Impressionist novel *Der Tod Georgs* (*The Death of George*, 1900). The novel is virtually without action. We are admitted to the consciousness of the hero, Paul, at four moments of an emotional crisis: a summer evening when his friend Georg is staying with him; an elaborate dream that night in which Paul intuits Georg's death; a few days later, when Paul is travelling by train to Vienna to bring back Georg's coffin; and several months later, an autumn day on which Paul, walking in a park, at last overcomes his sense of bereavement. Paul's inner life is explored through memories and sense-impressions, and the latter especially are conveyed in rich, sensuous, and melodious language, so that they serve as metaphors for emotional states and nuances.

Some of Paul's experience is conveyed by the topoi of 1890s aestheticism. His emotional recovery is presented as a return from death to life; he feels that events take place on a stage, and that life

[227] Quoted in Harry Zohn, '*ich bin ein Sohn der deutschen Sprache nur . . .*': *Jüdisches Erbe in der österreichischen Literatur* (Vienna, 1986), p. 35.

is commanding him to join in the action. Hence he is recognizable as a *fin-de-siècle* aesthete, seeking to escape from aestheticism, like Claudio in Hofmannsthal's *Der Tor und der Tod* (*The Fool and Death*, 1893).[228] But there is also a more oblique narrative in which Paul rediscovers his Jewish identity. This is first indicated in the complicated dream which forms section 2 of the story. Having that evening looked longingly at a passing girl, he dreams that he has been married to her for seven years and is now waiting for her to die. (Since the dying girl represents the dying Georg, this suggests the homoerotic element in Paul's relationship with Georg.) During their marriage Paul, by his scepticism, has deprived the girl of her (apparently Christian) religious faith: 'He took away her belief in a kindly God who guided her fate, and left her only a consuming yearning for faith' (BH 535). This identifies Paul as a sceptical Western Jew who puts all faith in doubt by examining it coldly. That he lives under the shadow of Christian society is suggested by the repeated image of the 'Fensterkreuz', the crossbars separating the window-panes, that casts a shadow into his bedroom.[229]

Paul's dream also contains a long and intense description of the temple of Hierapolis in Syria.[230] The goddess Astarte recalls figures beloved of the *fin de siècle* like Gustave Moreau's Salome or Walter Pater's evocation of the Mona Lisa:

Surrounded by golden statues of the gods, the great goddess sat on a chariot drawn by lions; she was hung with precious stones and wore a crown shaped like a fortress on her head. By night, when the flashing of her water-blue and fire-coloured gems was dimmed in slumber, an unknown jewel in her crown lit up the temple. The goddess's open eyes gazed into the eyes of whoever was permitted to approach and followed him steadily through the room, wherever he might turn.   (BH 542)

Insistently associated with the hardness of stone and an ineluctable gaze, the goddess is no doubt a mother-figure such as Johann

---

[228] See Walter H. Sokel, 'Narzißmus und Judentum. Zu Richard Beer-Hofmanns *Der Tod Georgs*', *Literatur und Kritik*, 221/222 (Feb./Mar. 1988), 8–20.

[229] BH 529, 567, 569. The 'Fensterkreuz' often serves an allegorical purpose in German fiction: see Friedrich Spielhagen, *Sturmflut*, 3 vols. (Leipzig, 1877), i. 114–15; Jakob Wassermann, *Joseph Kerkhovens dritte Existenz* ([1934]; Munich, 1989), p. 55.

[230] On this passage and its *fin-de-siècle* affinities, see especially Le Rider, *Modernity and Crises of Identity*, pp. 141–3; for an interpretation of the novel's affirmation of Jewishness, ibid. 275–84.

Jakob Bachofen, the Swiss lawyer and mythographer who deeply influenced modern conceptions of the feminine, supposed to have been worshipped by the matriarchal cultures that had given way to the civilizing influence of patriarchy. But she is a terrifying, phallic mother, who both licenses and suppresses sexuality. She suppresses it among her eunuch priests, who torture and mortify their bodies, and licenses it among the crowd of worshippers who, on the meadow before her temple, engage in a sexual orgy that erases individuality. Imagining himself as a participant, Paul does not realize that the woman he is making love to is dying in his embraces: as in the earlier part of the dream, she recalls the dying Georg, but also reminds us of the sadism which expresses Paul's desire to free himself from women and perhaps indeed from all personal attachments.

The luxurious evocation of the temple, recalling the exoticism and sadism of Flaubert's Carthaginian novel *Salammbô* (1862), is a fascinating exercise in Orientalism. It implies that, despite the scepticism of his conscious mind, in the depths of his soul Paul is attracted to a sophisticated and sensual Oriental type of religiosity. His Oriental affinities confirm his profoundly Jewish character. Beer-Hofmann is thus contradicting the image of the rational Jew so laboriously propagated in the Enlightenment by Mendelssohn and his followers. Instead, he is suggesting, the Jew is in contact with primordial, Dionysiac forces. It is not reason and morality, but rather the body and the senses, that make the Jew who he is.

These themes, lightly touched on in the dream, are developed more clearly in the final section. Paul not only feels (like many heroes in the literature of the turn of the century) part of all-encompassing life; more particularly, he feels connected by his blood to his ancestors; and these ancestors are clearly identified as Jews, believing in justice and thus following a more austere faith than Christians, whom Beer-Hofmann dismisses as believing in a comfortable God of mercy:

Forebears who wandered and roved, the dust of all highways in their hair and beards, in rags and tatters, spat upon, disdained; everyone against them, despised even by the lowest—but never despising themselves; never so beggarly as to honour their God according to His gifts; calling in their suffering not to a merciful God, but to God the just. (BH 621)

Evidently Beer-Hofmann's image of the Jew as Oriental in the novel is ambivalent. On the one hand, Paul is linked by his blood, by his racial instinct, to the orgiastic practices of the ancient Near East; on the other, he inherits the Jewish desire for purity, to escape from such practices into the worship of an invisible and single God of uncompromising justice. A similar ambivalence can be found in Freud: we saw in Chapter 2 how he associated Judaism with ethical monotheism, but when investigating hysteria he thought his patients' sexual reminiscences were 'like a remnant of a primeval sexual cult, which once was—perhaps still is—a religion in the Semitic East (Moloch, Astarte)'.[231]

While walking in the park, Paul also reflects on names: 'A hero's deeds were concealed in a name—given to a child, it was at once a promise and a burden' (BH 617). Applied to Paul, this reminds us that he bears the name of a convert from Judaism. His very name shows that he inhabits an alien society. Georg, who never appears in his own right, and whose only function in the book is to die, is evidently a Gentile: his rapid medical career, with a professorship only four years after graduating, indicates as much. Paul's love for Georg is the hopeless and envious love of the quasi-assimilated Jew for the completely secure Christian, like that of Jacobowski's Leo Wolff for his friend Richard Manzow. But whereas Leo's death signalizes the failure of assimilation, in Beer-Hofmann's novel it is the Jew who survives and the Gentile who dies. Georg's death is sacrificial: he has to die so that Paul can be liberated from his assimilationism and gain self-respect as a Jew. The novel ends with Paul entering a new life by going through the park gate into the open ('ins Freie'), an image anticipating Schnitzler's novel *Der Weg ins Freie* published eight years later. The last paragraph repeats the image of blood, familiar from 'Schlaflied für Mirjam', as the connection with the Jewish race and the guarantee of security.

Theology is taken very seriously by Beer-Hofmann in *Jaákobs Traum*, a gripping spiritual drama which focuses on Jacob, grandson of Abraham and father of the founders of Israel's twelve tribes, in order to inquire into the election of the Jewish people. Jacob's brother Esau (here called Edom, cf. Gen. 25:30) is often taken to typify the Gentiles (as in Heine's early poem 'An Edom').

---

[231] *Letters of Freud to Fliess*, p. 227 (24 Jan. 1897).

Hence the play also deals with the contrast between the Jews and their neighbours, in keeping with the Lord's prophecy to Rebekah in Gen. 25:23: 'Two nations are in thy womb, and two peoples shall be separated even from thy bowels: and the one people shall be stronger than the other people; and the elder shall serve the younger.' The crucial problem is that Jacob obtained his father's blessing deceitfully by disguising himself as his elder brother and thus misappropriating the latter's birthright. Thus the dominion of Israel over Edom rests on wrongdoing which nevertheless has divine approval.

The play falls into two parts. In the first and shorter, Jaákob has already received his father's blessing and set out for Haran (Beer-Hofmann has telescoped the more leisurely action of Gen. 25–8); the slaves discuss the incident before the return of Edom, who remonstrates with Rebekah and resolves to pursue Jaákob with hounds that are to tear him to pieces. The imagery represents the blessing almost as an organic process: whatever Isaac's intentions, the blessing is valid, just as a union based on mistaken identity still produces a living child; it can no more be undone than a stream can reverse its course; its seed is now growing in Jaákob. But while God's purposes are said to be unfathomable, the transference of the blessing to Jaákob is clearly linked with his moral superiority. Edom is a brutal, violent, sensual man, who invokes pagan goddesses as he sets out to hunt down his brother; Jaákob is described, by his and Edom's mother, as a man of active piety and universal compassion:

> *He* does not banish God to distant heavens,
> But wrestles with Him daily, heart to heart!
> *You* merely hunt, make sacrifices, *murder*!
> *He* blenches at the suffering of all beings,
> He speaks to all, and all things speak to him . . .
> Hence *he* bears both the blessing and its burden!   (BH 29)

The meaning of 'its burden' is explained in the second part, set on the night when Jaákob, on his way to Haran, sleeps on the hill later called Beth-El. Beer-Hofmann endows Jaákob with compassion. In contrast to the pitiless Edom, who first appears with a slaughtered gazelle, Jaákob saves and feeds a young lamb; he also sets free his slave Idnibaál. Edom arrives and repeatedly challenges Jaákob to fight, but Jaákob, by standing unmoved and unafraid, eventually obliges Edom to kneel before him and plead for reconciliation. Jaákob offers him the ceremony of blood-brotherhood and declares that he does not consider himself superior to his brother: the two are simply different, but no more superior or inferior than two plants. This reassurance is undermined, however, by the elaboration of Jaákob's religious mission and its location in a scheme of religious development. Idnibaál tells Jaákob how the gods who sprang from the primal chaos imprisoned their monstrous progenitor under the mountain at 'Uru-Schalim' (Jerusalem), where it continued to demand blood-sacrifices. Recognizing this mountain as Mount Moriah, Jaákob recalls how, on that very spot, Abraham's sacrifice of Isaac was prevented by the substitution of a ram. This supersession of human sacrifice by symbolic offerings is associated with the lamb saved by Jaákob. When Edom aims an arrow at Jaákob, it hits the lamb instead: Jaákob interprets the lamb's death as re-enacting that of the ram and as showing that he, Jaákob, is not to expiate his deceit by being sacrificed: 'The Lord won't *take* me as an offering!' (BH 54).

Here Beer-Hofmann seems to be showing us a fork in the path of humankind's religious development. One response to the primitive violence embodied in Edom was to sublimate violence by expiatory sacrifice, as in the story of Isaac. The death of the lamb points forward to a further stage of development, the self-sacrifice of God in the person of Christ, the Lamb of God (Rev. 5:6), prefigured by the Suffering Servant 'like a lamb that is led to the slaughter' (Isa. 53:7). It might be maintained, however, that humankind's innate violence is in no way diminished by the substitution of a surrogate victim: instead, the institution of sacrifice, even in its Christian form, merely admits that the cycle of murderer and victim is unending, like the cycle of legal violence which Walter Benjamin in 'Zur Kritik der Gewalt' ('Critique of Violence', 1921) contrasts with divine violence.

In rejecting sacrifice, Jaákob is starting on another historical track, that of complete non-violence. While Christians symbolically re-enact Christ's self-sacrifice in the Eucharist, Judaism was obliged to abandon sacrifices when the Temple was destroyed in AD 70, and to substitute prayer, fasting, and the keeping of the Torah.[232] This development of Judaism into a non-sacrificial

---

[232] See E. O. James, *Sacrifice and Sacrament* (London, 1962).

religion is projected by Beer-Hofmann back to the story of Jaákob. Instead of expiating his deceit by dying at Edom's hands, he has to go on living, to grow in moral authority, and to accept his guilt. His election separates him from the cycle of violence and sacrifice. It also accompanies his acute awareness of the suffering that pervades the world.

> Am I elected so that every being
> That suffers may send me its supplication?
> Even the dying gaze of helpless beasts
> Silently asks me '*Why?!*'   (BH 58)

Accordingly, the dream that forms the core of the play, based on Jacob's dream of angels ascending and descending the heavenly ladder in Genesis 28:12, centres on the question of God's responsibility for suffering. As he dozes, Jaákob hears the lyrical voices of the stone beneath his head and the nearby spring, reminding him that even the inanimate creation suffers. In his dream he is visited by the four archangels, Gabríel, Raphaél, Uríel, and Micháel, and the fallen angel Samáel. The four archangels assert that all things and all events are unwittingly part of a divine plan. They preach submission to the divine will and rebuke Jaákob for his reluctance to accept his election as progenitor of Israel. Jaákob, however, feels a strange affinity with Samáel, who expresses his horror at the amount of suffering involved in the world God has created and defiantly asserts that God has made the world badly. Jaákob repeats his concern with suffering. He does not envy the worldly power of kings or the spiritual happiness of the archangels: '*Could* I be happy in a world of pain?' (BH 75). As he understands it, his mission is to share and alleviate the suffering from which God has retreated into heaven. While Micháel proclaims the positive aspect of Israel's election as 'a light to the nations' (cf. Isa. 49:6), Samáel grimly foretells that the fate of the chosen people will be exile, contempt, and massacre. Accepting the ambivalence of his calling, Jaákob is prepared neither to occupy a humble place in the heavenly hierarchy, as the archangels expect, nor to follow Samáel's warning to reject his mission. Instead, he asserts a peculiar relationship to God, one of questioning and combative loyalty. And if, as Samáel claims, God is guilty, Jaákob will embrace God's guilt:

> And, *if* You're bowed by guilt, I'll help to bear it:
> Upon my shoulders place Your guilty load!　　(BH 80)

Although the outraged archangels condemn Samáel's prophecy as a lie, the Lord's voice from heaven confirms its truth. He accepts Jaákob's offer:

> When others kneel to me and beg for grace,
> I spare them, as a lord his slave; but *you*
> Shall stand before your Father face to face
> And get no mercy! Ask me for your *due*!
> In my name you shall suffer woes beyond all count,
> But, even in torment, you shall know that you're my own!
> My debt of guilt to you, my son, must always mount,
> Till high above all others I raise you—to atone!　　(BH 81)

By confronting God, Jaákob exemplifies the calling of the Jews and earns the right to call himself, as he does in the play's closing line, Israel ('Jísro-El').

In this strange and magnificent attempt at a theodicy, Beer-Hofmann challenges the notion that the sufferings of the Jewish people cast doubt on God's goodness. He implicitly opposes the view, common among assimilators, that Jewishness is deplorable, shameful, or otherwise undesirable—'the thousand-year-old family affliction', as Heine called it.[233] He also opposes the long-standing Christian view of the Jews as accursed for rejecting Christ. Instead, Beer-Hofmann represents the Jews' suffering as the very sign of their election. If God has mercy on other people, that shows that He regards them as mere bondsmen, too weak to endure the suffering imposed on the Jews. The image of the lamb shot by Edom might be taken to imply that Christianity is a religion for weak people who escape from suffering through substitutive sacrifice, whereas the Jews are paid the supreme compliment of being denied any such easy option. On the contrary, as an early admirer pointed out, the Jewish people are dignified by being shown to have chosen suffering:

The central significance of this night on Beth El is the horrifying and magnificent idea that this man and this nation were free to choose the unbearable grandeur of their unique fate.[234]

---

[233] 'The New Israelite Hospital in Hamburg', *Complete Poems of Heine*, p. 398; H iv. 420.

[234] Oskar Baum, 'Richard Beer-Hofmann', in Gustav Krojanker (ed.), *Juden in der deutschen Literatur* (Berlin, 1922), pp. 198–206 (p. 205).

By accepting suffering, moreover, the Jews confirm their special relationship to God. Only the accuser Samáel actually states that God is at fault for creating a world of suffering: Jaákob's formulation is hypothetical, '*if* You're bowed by guilt'; but God's voice acknowledges that He is guilty in making the Jews suffer and that His elevation of them is a form of atonement. Nor does He reject Jaákob's offer to assume the guilt that God has incurred. Beer-Hofmann, unavoidably no doubt, obscures the origins of evil, and leaves evil, suffering, and atonement joined in an inextricable nexus. His contrast between Christianity and Judaism resembles Freud's argument in *Moses and Monotheism* that Judaism is the more challenging religion because it denies man the easy absolution made possible by the Christian doctrine of redemption.

Although the events are taken from Genesis, Beer-Hofmann's theodicy is based on the Book of Job. Just as Job, deprived of his children, his servants, and his property, and smitten with an agonizing disease, refuses to accept that he must somehow have sinned and insists on challenging God's injustice, so Jaákob also disputes with God. And just as Job's wranglings are more acceptable in God's sight than the pious platitudes offered by his neighbours and would-be comforters, so God rebukes the orthodox archangels, explains His purposes to Jaákob, and confers on His impious antagonist a special status. The fallen angel Samáel recalls the Satan who in the Book of Job enters heaven among the sons of God and undertakes to provoke Job into cursing God. And of course for Beer-Hofmann, a Jew steeped in German culture, the Book of Job is refracted through a later text modelled on it, Goethe's *Faust* and particularly the 'Prologue in Heaven'. It was a strange and bold undertaking to put forward an interpretation of Judaism based on the Book of Job, which is so alien to the general tenor of the Bible that it might seem, as Heine said, to have been inserted as a homoeopathic cure for man's inclination to question God's goodness (H v. 190–1). And yet Beer-Hofmann's uncompromising emphasis on Jewish suffering anticipates the problems faced by post-Holocaust theology, in which some Jewish thinkers have even seen the exceptional sufferings of the Jewish people as renewed confirmation of its election.[235]

---

[235] See Oliver Leaman, *Evil and Suffering in Jewish Philosophy* (Cambridge, 1995).

As if rewriting the Book of Job were not bold enough, however, Beer-Hofmann undertakes a further task. Besides inquiring into the meaning of unjust suffering among humankind, he also asks about the suffering that pervades nature. In the play, even the stone on which Jaákob lays his head laments its fate as a meteor cast down to earth. The problem of why animals suffer (let alone plants and stones) has had a far smaller place in the great Western religions than in those of the East. Deutero-Isaiah prophesies a time when the lion, instead of being carnivorous, 'shall eat straw like the ox' (65:25). Hosea reports a divine covenant with the beasts, birds, and insects (2:18). Occasionally in Judaism, and frequently in Christianity, nature is thought to have become 'red in tooth and claw' as a side-effect of Adam's fall.[236] The *locus classicus* is Rom. 8:22: 'For we know that the whole creation groaneth and travaileth together in pain until now.'[237] In the nineteenth century, greater compassion towards the natural world emerged from within Judaeo-Christian traditions; Schopenhauer transmitted to German readers Indian doctrines of universal pity; and some Darwinists reinterpreted biblical history and Christian ethics in order to give love a central place within a universe of which humankind now formed an inseparable part.[238]

Hence the Judaism that Beer-Hofmann presents in *Jaákobs Traum* is both ancient and modern. He goes back to a vividly imagined ancient Orient as the setting for his Job-like theodicy; but he also presents Judaism as an ultra-modern religion, whose concern for the suffering of all creation makes it suitable for the age of Schopenhauer and Darwin.

---

[236] See N. P. Williams, *The Ideas of the Fall and of Original Sin* (London, 1927), p. 77; Milton, *Paradise Lost*, ix. 782–4, x. 710–12 ('Beast now with beast gan war').

[237] See Wilhelm Kühlmann, 'Das Ende der "Verklärung". Bibel-Topik und prädarwinistische Naturreflexion in der Literatur des 19. Jahrhunderts', *Jahrbuch der Deutschen Schiller-Gesellschaft*, 30 (1986), 417–52. It has been argued (by Sol Liptzin, 'Richard Beer-Hofmann and Joseph Viktor Widmann', *MAL* 8 (1975), iii/iv. 74–80) that Beer-Hofmann took this theme of the suffering of creation from the drama by J. V. Widmann, *Der Heilige und die Tiere* (Frauenfeld, 1908). The resemblance, however, is not close.

[238] See Keith Thomas, *Man and the Natural World* (London, 1983), pp. 180–1; Alfred Kelly, *The Descent of Darwin: The Popularization of Darwinism in Germany 1860–1914* (Chapel Hill, NC, 1981), pp. 82–8 (on Wilhelm Bölsche).

ZIONISM

Herzl as Visionary

Theodor Herzl, the creator of Zionism as a mass movement, was an imaginative genius whose energies produced political visions that eventually became reality. After early but ephemeral success as a dramatist, he devoted his literary talents to exploring and proclaiming his political message. He analysed the shortcomings of Jewish emancipation in the play *Das neue Ghetto* (discussed in Chapter 4) and described the Jewish state of the future in the utopian novel *Altneuland* (1902). But though he reportedly thought himself an unrecognized literary genius, it is in *Der Judenstaat* and, still more, in the unrestrained visions of his diaries that his imagination really flourishes.[239]

The prophet of the Jewish state, who was born in Budapest and spent most of his adult life in Vienna, had a deep imaginative commitment to Germany. As a young man he was a German nationalist.[240] His Jewish upbringing was residual. Although he attended a Jewish school in childhood, he knew virtually no Hebrew and little about Jewish ritual, law, or history. At the synagogue in Basle, he was called on to pronounce the 'B'roche', and had it whispered to him by an acquaintance (*BT* ii. 545). Herzl's family were among the few Hungarian Jews who resisted Magyarization and remained loyal to German language and culture. Herzl himself was among the many liberals in the Habsburg Empire who wished to assert their German identity and establish German hegemony over the other nations within the Empire.

As a student of law in Vienna Herzl joined the Akademische Lesehalle, which by the late 1870s was dominated by German nationalism. In 1881 the Lesehalle was dissolved after an inflammatory speech by the Pan-German politician Georg von Schönerer. Meanwhile, in autumn 1880, Herzl had joined the duelling fraternity 'Albia'. This small society, with only about fifteen active members, was held together by ritualized drinking and duelling,

---

[239] On Herzl's literary vanity, see Schnitzler's diary, 7 Aug. 1904; Max Jungmann, *Erinnerungen eines Zionisten* (Jerusalem, 1959), pp. 44–5. On Herzl's fantasies, see Peter Loewenberg, 'Theodor Herzl', in *Decoding the Past: The Psychohistorical Approach* (Berkeley, 1984), pp. 101–35.

[240] See Jacques Kornberg, *Theodor Herzl: From Assimilation to Zionism* (Bloomington and Indianapolis, 1993).

uniforms and secret signs, and ideological conformity. Jews were acceptable only on condition of being good Germans: Herzl had the double task of overcoming his Jewish identity and his Hungarian background, and the resulting inner conflict led to an explosion. On 5 March 1883 the Verein deutscher Studenten in Wien, an umbrella organization to which 'Albia' belonged, held a *Kommers* (drinking session) in memory of the recently dead Wagner. Among the speakers was a representative of Albia, Hermann Bahr, who undertook to honour Wagner by a public profession of antisemitism. On hearing about this, Herzl sent Albia a letter of protest, requesting to be released from membership. The Albia committee at first wanted to expel Herzl dishonourably, but finally informed him simply that his name had been removed from the list of members; they refused to record that he had resigned voluntarily.[241]

Herzl's hyperacculturation and his idealization of the military ethos of honour and manliness invite comparison with Walther Rathenau. Just as Rathenau was bitterly disappointed by his exclusion from an elite Guards regiment, so Herzl was embittered by antisemitism in 'Albia'. Herzl, as we shall see, criticized the assimilated Jews of his day as mercilessly as Rathenau had done in 'Höre, Israel!' Yet stubborn pride made both reject the obvious option of conversion. And both revelled in grandiose imperial schemes, appropriate to the age of Rhodes, Kipling, and Buchan.[242] Rathenau, already an industrial magnate, was keenly interested in the German colonial empire and made two trips to its southern African outposts. However we may deplore the unscrupulous European conquest of the earth, we cannot understand Herzl unless we feel the imaginative power of schemes like the great canals and railway projects intended to unify the tropical empires. At the age of 10, Herzl was inspired by the fame of Ferdinand de Lesseps, the engineer of the Suez Canal, to imagine himself building a canal through the Panama isthmus and thus becoming the de Lesseps of the New World.[243] His imagination was caught by technology. The sight of the Suez Canal impressed him far more than the Acropolis, partly because of the powerful

[241] See Alex Bein, *Theodor Herzl: Biographie* (Vienna, 1934), pp. 66–7.
[242] See Geoffrey Wheatcroft, *The Controversy of Zion* (London, 1996), pp. 73, 84–5.
[243] 'Selbstbiographie' (1898), in ZW i. 11–16 (p. 11).

will he sensed behind it: 'Of course human lives and money were stolen and squandered in building the Suez Canal, and yet one must admire the colossal will that realized the simple idea of digging it out of the sand', he wrote (*BT* ii. 674). He felt an affinity with another strong-willed visionary, Cecil Rhodes, and drafted a letter to him, requesting help, in which he said: 'You, Mr Rhodes, are either a politician full of fantasy or a practical fantasist' (*BT* iii. 327); but Rhodes died before the two could enter into contact. Herzl's Jewish state was modelled on Rhodesia, in so far as Rhodes's Chartered Company suggested the settlement by formal charter, guaranteeing the settlers' rights, that Herzl proposed to the Sultan of Turkey in 1899. Herzl also compares his project to Stanley's quest for Livingstone and to the exploitation of goldmines on the South African Rand (*BT* ii. 43–4, 79).

Throughout his life Herzl was fascinated by Prussianism. He confided to his diary: 'If I could be whatever I liked, I should be a Prussian nobleman of ancient lineage' (*BT* ii. 210). His early plays contain idealized aristocratic figures.[244] In *Altneuland* the Jewish hero forms a close friendship with a Prussian aristocrat, originally called Königshoff, who has made a fortune in America and changed his name to Kingscourt. In his negotiations with European potentates over the Jewish state, Herzl assumed that it would be predominantly German, and therefore pointed out to the Grand Duke of Baden 'that the Jews would bring an element of *German* culture into the Orient' (*BT* ii. 606). During the period when he was negotiating with German politicians, he would have liked the Jewish state to be a German protectorate, an idea which found favour with the Kaiser, or so Eulenburg, the German ambassador in Vienna, told him.[245] Under the spell of Eulenburg's Prussian decisiveness and frankness, Herzl wrote: 'To be under the protectorate of this great, strong, moral Germany, with its practical administration and strict organization, can have only the most salutary effect on the character of the Jewish people' (*BT* ii. 635). He reflected: 'Zionism will enable the Jews once more to love Germany, to which our hearts belong despite everything' (*BT* ii. 636). How far was his Zionism at bottom a defiant response to finding his love unrequited?

---

[244] See Kornberg, *Herzl*, pp. 64–5.
[245] See John C. G. Röhl, 'Herzl and Kaiser Wilhelm II: A German Protectorate in Palestine?', *Austrian Studies*, 8 (1997), 27–38.

Unable to become a Prussian aristocrat, Herzl compensated by elaborating stories about his descent from noble and dignified Sephardic Jews of Spain. In fact his family, as far as it can be traced, is firmly rooted in Bohemia and Moravia; but to acknowledge this would have brought Herzl too close to the Eastern Jews for whom he felt conventional dislike. In contrast to Ashkenazic (German and Polish) Jews, who were thought to be small, stout, and red-haired, Sephardic Jews were believed to be physically as well as culturally superior: 'Their special features are long black hair and beard, large almond-shaped eyes, a melancholy cast of countenance, with an oval face and a prominent nose,—in short, the type of Jews represented in the paintings of Rembrandt.'[246] Herzl's propensity for personal myth-making gives him an affinity with Heine, who similarly fantasized about his Spanish descent, and with the romancing of Joseph Roth, who sometimes exaggerated the poverty of his Galician upbringing and sometimes denied it by claiming to be of mixed Russian and Austrian descent and to have spent the First World War as a Habsburg officer.[247] A touch of self-contempt, a wish to transcend one's mundane Jewish origins, led all three to construct Freudian family romances. This may seem a strange foible, but it testifies to the imagination which was indispensable for Herzl's visionary plans.

Entranced by his role as leader, Herzl compares himself, repeatedly, to Moses, and he was pleased to learn from a friend about Sabbatai Zvi, the pseudo-messiah who came forward as a leader of the Jewish people in the seventeenth century (*BT* ii. 139). At the age of 12 he had a dream about the Messiah, who introduced him to Moses and foretold that he would accomplish great deeds.[248] At a working-men's club in the East End of London Herzl was compared to Moses and Columbus (*BT* ii. 403). Contemporary analogies, like that with a famous Irish nationalist, also occurred to him: 'I shall be the Jews' Parnell' (*BT* ii. 256). He realized that he was already becoming a legend: 'A faint mist is beginning to surge around me; it may become the cloud in which I walk' (*BT* ii. 405). He liked imagining himself as a leader. He has often wept

---

[246] Fishberg, *The Jews*, p. 106. Cf. Schorsch, 'The Myth of Sephardic Supremacy', in *From Text to Context*, pp. 71–92.

[247] See Philipp F. Veit, 'Heine: The Marrano Pose', *Monatshefte*, 66 (1974), 145–56; Bronsen, *Joseph Roth*, pp. 34–6, 174–8.

[248] See Joseph Nedava, 'Herzl and Messianism', *Herzl Year Book*, 7 (1971), 9–26.

over Jewish suffering, he recalls; 'But when I lead my people, I must not show a tear. The leader must have a hard gaze (*einen harten Blick*)' (*BT* ii. 131). The ideal leader for him was Kaiser Wilhelm II. When they met, Herzl felt sympathy for him, noticing his embarrassment at having a withered arm, and tried not to look at this deformity: 'I therefore looked steadily into his beautiful, free, charming and yet bold eyes, which held me positively spellbound' (*BT* ii. 664). He dwells on the swift glance ('Blick') with which the Kaiser indicated approval. Herzl's remarkable empathy implies self-projection. The Kaiser, as ideal leader, also embodied Herzl's personal ideal: he was Prussian, had a hard and commanding look, and had overcome a defect; Herzl's attention to the Kaiser's withered arm perhaps conveys a lingering unease about his own Jewishness which had previously brought him into conflict with German nationalism.

Very important in Herzl's plans was the mass journey to the new land. He conceived of this exodus in operatic terms: 'Compared to this, the exodus of Moses was like a Shrovetide play compared to a Wagnerian opera' (*BT* ii. 74). He realized the importance of ceremonial music, and resolved to ensure that festivals were accompanied by solemn marches. Knowing that modern mass politics demand emotional manipulation by symbolism and spectacle, he carefully stage-managed the First Zionist Congress, choosing an appropriate hall, praising his associate David Wolffsohn for modelling the new Zionist banner on the traditional prayer-shawl, and insisting on evening dress for the opening ceremony. No detail was too small: when he met Wilhelm II in Constantinople, his preparation for the interview included choosing gloves of the right shade of grey.

While writing *Der Judenstaat*, Herzl drew strength from Wagner: 'my only recreation in the evenings consisted in listening to Wagner, especially to *Tannhäuser*, of which I never missed a performance. Only on the evenings when there was no opera did I feel any doubt about the correctness of my ideas' (*ZW* i. 14). Herzl's enthusiasm for Wagner, and for *Tannhäuser* in particular, has aroused surprise and controversy. Did Tannhäuser's return to the grotto symbolize the acceptance of Jewish identity which Herzl was undertaking in planning a Jewish state? Or did Herzl equate Tannhäuser's thraldom in Venus's grotto with the servitude of European Jews, seeing the escape not in Tannhäuser's failed revolt but in the moral idealism represented by Elisabeth's redemptive suicide?[249]

Herzl's fascination with *Tannhäuser* does give us access to some deep layers of his imagination; but I think the clue lies in an episode that does not occur in the opera, Tannhäuser's interview with the Pope. Tannhäuser was told that he could no more be saved from damnation than the Pope's staff could burst into leaf. When he is about to return defiantly to Venus's grotto, he is saved by Elisabeth's death and intercession, and as Tannhäuser himself dies, a group of pilgrims fresh from Rome announce that the Pope's staff has indeed produced leaves, attesting to Tannhäuser's redemption. Thus Tannhäuser gains a moral victory over his antagonist the Pope.

Herzl's imagination linked him with Tannhäuser through his Prussophilia. Even in his teens he identified with another antagonist of the Pope—Bismarck. During the *Kulturkampf* of the 1870s, in which he sought to break the authority of the Catholic Church over education and church administration in Germany, Bismarck's most famous utterance was: 'We shall not go to Canossa!' It was at Canossa that the German Emperor Heinrich IV did penance before Pope Gregory VII in the winter of 1077. The young Herzl responded to Bismarck with a poem called 'Nach Canossa gehn wir nicht!' ('We shall not go to Canossa!') which recalls the Emperor's humiliation by the 'dark and treacherous hand of Rome', and praises Luther's reassertion of the German spirit.[250] In a letter of 24 August 1880 'Canossa' appears as a half-joking code-word for humiliation when Herzl, requesting his friend Heinrich Kana to criticize his style, invites him to be 'my own little Canossa' (*BT* i. 96). In later life he regarded Bismarck as a model, once writing to him for advice, and comparing his own plans with the unification of Germany. If in his imagination Herzl is Bismarck challenging the Pope, the Pope easily stands in for Herzl's father. As Peter Loewenberg points out, Herzl idealized his parents, always referring to them in saccharine terms as 'my good parents', 'my good father'; in his diary he decides that his father

---

[249] See Schorske, *Fin-de-Siècle Vienna*, p. 163; Steven Beller, 'Herzl's *Tannhäuser*: The Redemption of the Artist as Politician', in Robert S. Wistrich (ed.), *Austrians and Jews in the Twentieth Century* (London, 1992), pp. 38–57.

[250] Quoted in Amos Elon, *Herzl* (London, 1975), p. 25.

shall be the first senator of the Jewish state.[251] Herzl's unacknowledged ambivalence towards his father is projected onto the Pope.
Tannhäuser both craves the Pope's approval, defies him, and gains
a moral victory over him.

One side of Herzl's ambivalence towards the father-Pope finds
expression in his love of religious ceremonial. His Jewish state,
incongruously, was to include bishops: Güdemann, the Chief
Rabbi of Vienna, was to be made 'first bishop of the capital'
(*BT* ii. 73); the *tsaddik* of Sadagóra was to be made 'a kind of
bishop of a province' (*BT* ii. 70); and the new state was to contain
'a finer Sadagóra' which should be a centre of pilgrimages like
Lourdes (*BT* ii. 176). The Pope features most dramatically in
Herzl's scheme of arranging for the bulk of the Austrian Jews to
convert to Catholicism in a public ceremony in St Stephen's
Cathedral, while Herzl and their other leaders should demonstrate
their own integrity by remaining Jews. He vividly imagined himself in conversation with the Pope and other Church dignitaries,
who would express their deep regret that Herzl himself insisted on
remaining a Jew (*BT* ii. 47). Thus Herzl would enlist the Pope for
his own purposes while denying the Pope a personal triumph over
him.

This ambivalence reappears in Herzl's favourite fantasy of negotiating with potentates. Here he is both rising to their level and
imposing his will on them. 'I shall mix with the masters of the world
as one of themselves', he announces (*BT* ii. 78). He imagines himself
negotiating first with the Tsar, then with the German Emperor, then
with Austria and France, for the release of their Jewish populations,
and he reflects on how to enhance his own dignity: 'To be respected
at courts, I must receive the highest decorations. English ones to
begin with' (*BT* ii. 87). Normally one would think such self-
glorifying visions hardly more sensible than the fantasies of
Schiller's Spiegelberg. Yet Herzl's position as a leading journalist
on one of Europe's major newspapers made politicians willing to
receive him.[252] And his plan for a Jewish state, which seemed no
less wild than these fantasies, did become reality. Any study of him
must acknowledge that his extravagant imagination, his propensity

---

[251] Loewenberg, *Decoding the Past*, p. 108; *BT* ii. 77.
[252] See Edward Timms, 'Ambassador Herzl and the Blueprint for a Modern State',
Austrian Studies, 8 (1997), 12–26.

for myth-making, and his frank egoism, were combined with a realism that changed them from weaknesses into strengths. Without them he could not have succeeded in his mission.

Herzl's later diaries centre on a series of negotiations leading up to audiences and interviews with political leaders. In these negotiations Herzl single-handedly represented the Jews, a role which satisfied both his political imagination and his theatricality. He had repeated contacts with Eulenburg, the German ambassador in Vienna; he met the German Chancellor Hohenlohe, and eventually the Kaiser himself. On 19 May 1901, in Turkey, he actually had an audience with Sultan Abdul Hamid, whom he considered the hapless tool of an unscrupulous camarilla, but who made him a Commander of the Mejidiye order (less of an honour than it seems, since decorations had become so common at the Ottoman court as to be valueless).[253] He had meetings with Joseph Chamberlain, the British Colonial Secretary, in London, with Lord Cromer, the British Consul-General, in Cairo, and with the Russian ministers Plehve and Witte in St Petersburg. His diplomatic adventures culminated in a visit to Rome where he had an audience first with King Victor Emmanuel III and later, on 25 January 1904, with Pope Pius X. Herzl did not kiss the Pope's hand, and thought afterwards that this had ruined the interview, for the Pope refused to support Jewish immigration to Palestine. However, Herzl made a better impression than he realized: a few weeks later his associate York-Steiner had an interview with the secretary of state, Cardinal Merry del Val, who had also met Herzl, and who told him that the Vatican now had no objection to Jewish settlement in Palestine.[254] These meetings were Herzl's own trips to Canossa, where, unlike Heinrich IV, he avoided humiliation—he was prepared even to imperil his mission by refusing to pay homage to the Pope—but, like Bismarck, treated potentates as equals and retained his self-respect.

The Regeneration of the Jews

Herzl believed that centuries of confinement in ghettos had endowed the Jews with serious shortcomings which would grad-

---

[253] David Vital, *The Origins of Zionism* (Oxford, 1975), p. 296.
[254] York-Steiner, *Die Kunst als Jude zu leben*, pp. 306–8.

ually disappear once Jews were admitted to a full range of activities; the 'Jewish question' would be solved by intermarriage and assimilation, described in naïvely Darwinian terms: 'Crossing the western races with the so-called Oriental ones on the basis of a shared state religion—that is the great, desirable solution!' (*BT* i. 610). His experience of antisemitism in the early 1880s, and especially the shock of rejection by the group whose acceptance he so much wanted, seem to have initiated the preoccupation with the 'Jewish problem' that became explicit a decade later. His concern about antisemitism was strengthened, but not caused, by the Dreyfus affair.[255] He thought antisemitism had its good side, since it might 'break the insolence of the purse-proud and the ruthlessness and cynicism of Jewish financiers' (*BT* i. 507). To combat the antisemitic movement, however, another movement would be necessary, and for a while Herzl thought the answer lay in Socialism. He also contemplated public duels with noted antisemites: 'Half a dozen duels would raise the social position of the Jews considerably' (*BT* i. 516). In his diaries he records a fantasy of fighting a duel with Schönerer or Lueger; in case he were killed he would leave behind a letter which would shock humanity into rejecting antisemitism; if he killed his opponent and were put on trial, he would deliver an impassioned speech to the jury and be acquitted, whereupon he would be offered a Parliamentary seat by grateful Jews but nobly refuse it on the grounds that he could not enter Parliament over someone's dead body (*BT* ii. 113).

Herzl's critique of quasi-assimilated Jewry in his play *Das neue Ghetto*, discussed earlier, closely resembles the critiques which have incurred the charge of Jewish self-hatred. The same charge has been levelled at sweeping criticisms of the Jewish bourgeoisie made by Herzl and other Zionists. Herzl's diaries contain personal confessions which often take one aback. They include the statement: 'I am the man who makes aniline out of rubbish' (*BT* ii. 72). Aniline is a colourless oily liquid, present in coal tar, which was used as the basis of early synthetic dyes. The implication is clear and shocking: Herzl is extracting something valuable from human rubbish. Similarly disparaging is another diary entry, made just before the First Zionist Congress:

---

[255] See Kornberg, *Herzl*, ch. 8: 'The Dreyfus Legend'.

The truth is, though I don't tell anyone, that I have only an army of scroungers (*Schnorrer*). I am only at the head of boys, beggars and hacks. Many of them are just using me. Others are already envious or disloyal. The third category will abandon me as soon as they find a little career. Only a few are unselfish enthusiasts. And yet this army would be perfectly adequate, if only I had some success to show. Then they would soon become a regular disciplined army. (*BT* ii. 535)

Just after the Congress Herzl published the essay 'Mauschel' (1897), which, to one biographer, 'reads like a piece of anti-Semitic horror propaganda'.[256] 'Mauschel' typifies the Jew without self-respect or honour, with no cultural or spiritual ideals beyond material profit; like Rheinberg in *Das neue Ghetto*, he is servile in poverty, arrogant in prosperity: 'When poor, Mauschel is a pitiful beggar; when rich, he is an even more pitiful show-off (*Protz*)' (*ZW* i. 210). Such people reject Zionism, thereby proving that they are not true Jews and depriving the Zionists of any reason to maintain a solidarity with them. While Herzl's over-statement may be attributed partly to the strain of the Congress, the essay also represents the counterpart in his work to Rathenau's 'Höre, Israel!' In it, Herzl severs himself violently from the image of the assimilated Jew held by antisemites.

These remarks are drastic reformulations of the conviction, already illustrated, that centuries of European oppression have subjected the Jews' character to deformities which it will take a long time, or drastic action, to amend. Among these deformities we have seen that Herzl included lack of public spirit, cowardice, materialism, snobbery, and deficient self-respect. Another trait he complains of is 'Jewish' irony: 'This Jewish mockery (*Judenspott*) really represents the powerless attempt by captives to look as though they were free' (*BT* ii. 133). One may think this an inadvertently defensive comment on Herzl's own lack of humour; but visionaries cannot afford to laugh at themselves, and it is true that the self-irony Herzl rejects, that of the Jewish *schlemiel* from Sholem Aleichem's Menachem Mendel down to Woody Allen, is always a means of coping with failure.[257]

Such rejections of the stereotypical assimilated Jew were common among the new Zionist generation. By contrast, the Berlin

[256] Elon, *Herzl*, p. 251.
[257] See Ruth R. Wisse, *The Schlemiel as Modern Hero* (Chicago, 1971).

Jewish intellectuals who formed a Zionist group before Herzl were assimilationists who felt no contradiction between German and Jewish identity. Thus the liberal socialist Franz Oppenheimer felt his Jewish 'Stammesbewußtsein' (tribal consciousness) to be compatible with his German 'Volksbewußtsein' (folk consciousness), and regarded a Palestinian homeland as necessary not for German Jews but for the oppressed Jews of eastern Europe.[258] 'You must realize', he explained in 1909 to the younger Zionist Kurt Blumenfeld, 'that Zionism is a project managed by ourselves, with the Eastern Jews merely as the actors.'[259] Max Nordau similarly thought that German Jews would guide and instruct the confused Eastern masses: 'They press forward in a disorderly, disoriented fashion. We show them the path they must follow.'[260]

The new generation, however, put forward what Kurt Blumenfeld called a 'post-assimilatory Zionism' and a merciless critique of assimilated Western Jews.[261] They argued that the Jews were a distinct nation from the Germans, and that all Jews ought to move to Palestine and rediscover their true Jewish identity. Nordau, in keeping with his wholesale critique of modern civilization, denounced Jewish emancipation as a delusion inherited from 'Mendelssohnian soft-soap and enlightenment (*der Mendelssohnschen Schönrednerei und Aufklärung*)'.[262] He told the First Zionist Congress in 1897 that the rise of antisemitism had revealed to the Jew his true situation, suspended between two communities:

He has discarded his specific Jewish identity; the nations tell him that he has not acquired their identity. He flees his fellow-Jews because antisemitism has made them loathsome in his sight; his fellow-countrymen reject him when he seeks to join them. He has lost his home in the ghetto; the land of his birth refuses to be his home.[263]

As a substitute for communal life, the Diaspora had promoted a one-sided intellectuality, both by confining the Jews to commerce and by admitting them only to the narrow rationality of the

---

[258] Oppenheimer, *Erlebtes, Erstrebtes, Erreichtes*, pp. 211–12.
[259] Blumenfeld, *Erlebte Judenfrage*, p. 52. See Aschheim, *Brothers and Strangers*, pp. 93–9.
[260] Nordau, *Zionistische Schriften* (Cologne and Leipzig, 1909), p. 304.
[261] Blumenfeld, *Erlebte Judenfrage*, p. 12.
[262] Nordau, *Zionistische Schriften*, p. 21.   [263] Ibid. 50–1.

Enlightenment, of which modern liberalism was a continua-
tion.[264] Buber declared that Jews were deformed by the constraints he labelled 'Ghetto' and 'Golus' (exile): 'Ghetto, the
unfree intellectuality and the compulsion exerted by a meaningless
tradition, and Golus, the slavery of an unproductive money economy and the hollow-eyed homelessness that corrodes all single-
minded determination (*allen einheitlichen Willen*).'[265] Writing in
Buber's periodical *Der Jude*, Herman Glenn complained of 'the
behaviour of the many upstarts and "civilized" people who
thought they could only seal their allegiance to European culture
by discarding their Jewishness'.[266] Daniel Pasmanik, in a book
inspired by Nietzschean vitalism, agreed that the emancipation
initiated by Mendelssohn had had a 'nationally corrosive effect'
and brought about 'a dismal self-division within the Jewish
people's organism' in which the Jews' self-distrust made them
incapable of creativity. Hence the antisemitic image of the
uncreative Jew was accurate—but only for the Diaspora Jew:
restored to Palestine, Jews would regain their powers.[267] Hugo
Bergman, later Professor of Philosophy at the Hebrew University
of Jerusalem, asserted in a letter to the Berlin psychologist Carl
Stumpf that the Jews have not become organically integrated
into European culture; they have merely appropriated its achievements and, having lost their own spiritual balance, now exercise
a pernicious effect on their surroundings: 'These gifted Jews are
the advance guard of atheism and materialism, revolutionaries
and demagogues, they are found wherever it matters to be ultra-
modern, i.e. to destroy century-old values. Jews—even women—
are marching at the head of the agitation against marriage and
the family, and share, both as leaders and followers, in all the
perversities of present-day urban society.'[268] If these criticisms
recall the extreme denunciations issued by 'self-hating Jews',
then Bergman confirms the resemblance by saying in his diary
that Weininger's critique of the Jews applies accurately to the
emancipated, and every Jew should read him thrice daily in

---

[264] See e.g. Moses Calvary, 'Das neue Judentum und die schöpferische Phantasie', in
Vom Judentum: Ein Sammelbuch (Leipzig, 1913), pp. 103–16 (p. 107).
[265] Buber, *Die jüdische Bewegung*, i. 12.
[266] Glenn, 'Westöstliches Sein', *Der Jude*, 1 (1916–17), xi. 724–7 (p. 727).
[267] Pasmanik, *Die Seele Israels*, pp. 59, 69.
[268] Bergman, *Tagebücher und Briefe*, i. 51.

order to acquire enough self-loathing to undertake the task of self-renewal.[269]

To many early Zionists, then, the Western Jew was either a materialistic, snobbish philistine or a rootless hyper-intellectual without a home in Western society. Zionism offered a return to the soil, to manual labour, and to a sense of community. It was not just a practical move but offered a rebirth, a renaissance of the Jewish people. Herzl thinks that the failings and vices produced by exile can be amended, above all, by setting Jews to physical labour. Access to financial operations will be strictly controlled; those who have hitherto worshipped the Golden Calf, as Herzl puts it, will not be admitted to the stock exchange in the new state. Herzl imagines himself saying in Parliament: 'That was all very well for captivity. Now we have the responsibilities of freedom. We must be a people of inventors, warriors, artists, honest businessmen, rising workers, etc.' (*BT* ii. 88). Herzl imagines the gradual settlement of the Jewish state being planned by a Society of Jews and carried out by a Jewish Company. First (he says airily) the poorest Jews will go as labourers to render the land cultivable, build roads, and regulate rivers; this will create the basis for commerce and markets, which will in turn attract middle-class Jews. Herzl attaches great importance to the principle of the seven-hour working day. Labourers will work in two shifts of three and a half hours each, separated by an equal period, so that the total working day will be fourteen hours but each individual will have plenty of time to relax. They will not be labour slaves ('Arbeitssklaven') and no non-Jewish labourers will be employed (*ZW* i. 67). His notes go into more detail. Unskilled labourers will form a 'labour army' which will be as military as possible, led by a 'labour marshal' (*BT* ii. 96); labour battalions will march off to work with a fanfare of trumpets. The labour army will consist largely of Russian Jews (*BT* ii. 99, 115). The centrality of work will be symbolized on the flag, which will have seven golden stars on a white background, representing the seven-hour working day. Herzl seems to have had such a flag made and carried it around to show to potential sympathizers. He thinks physical labour will create a new race of Jews: 'I believe that a race of wonderful Jews will grow from the earth. The Maccabees will come back to life' (*ZW* i. 104); 'Thus

---

[269] Ibid. i. 80.

our people will regain its efficiency (*Tüchtigkeit*) in the land of the seven-hour working day' (ZW i. 76). The word *Tüchtigkeit* has connotations of racial hygiene: it appears in the title of the recently published book by Alfred Ploetz which proposed selective breeding as the means of restoring humanity from the degeneration produced by capitalistic individualism.[270]

Herzl's concern with work was widely shared. Supporters of practical Zionism, who favoured small-scale colonization projects, pointed out, as Franz Oppenheimer did in 1903, that many Diaspora Jews were engaged in trade or other unproductive jobs and if transported to semi-desert Palestine would simply starve. Therefore, Oppenheimer insisted, it had to be an agricultural colony which would attach colonists firmly to the soil, not a settlement for unproductive traders and sweated labourers: otherwise, 'we should bring all the horrors of the East End of London with its sweatshops, and all the dirty hardship of Galician shtetls and huge Russian villages full of dirt and brutality, wrongly known as cities, into the land of the Lord'.[271] Here practicality is mixed with prejudice, as it is in the sceptical view of Zionism expressed by the Viennese businessman and politician Sigmund Mayer: 'The Jewish state will always lack two things: useful land and useful Jews!'[272]

The Zionist concern with labour was more than practical. Labour was to change the character of the Jews by restoring them to a natural way of life. Aharon David Gordon, a former estate manager who emigrated from Russia to Palestine in 1904 and worked as an agricultural labourer, preached that only manual labour could transform the 'damaged, divided, unnatural' Diaspora Jew into a free Jew who was 'natural, healthy, true to himself'. The mere physical presence of Jews in Palestine was insufficient to bring about the 'redemption of the land'.[273] He opposed the frequent practice of buying estates from Arab landowners and having them worked by cheap Arab labour. Unless

---

[270] See Weindling, *Health, Race and German Politics*, pp. 123–5.

[271] 'Der Aufbau einer jüdischen Genossenschaftssiedlung in Palästina', in Oppenheimer, *Erlebtes, Erstrebtes, Erreichtes*, pp. 281–96 (p. 286).

[272] Mayer, *Die Wiener Juden: Kommerz, Kultur, Politik 1700–1900*, 2nd edn. (Vienna and Berlin, 1918), p. 481 n.

[273] A. D. Gordon, *Erlösung durch Arbeit: Ausgewählte Aufsätze*, tr. Viktor Kellner (Berlin, 1929), pp. 58, 62. On Gordon, see Shlomo Avineri, *The Making of Modern Zionism: The Intellectual Origins of the Jewish State* (London, 1981), pp. 151–8.

Jews themselves did manual labour, he warned, they would lead the same parasitic existence, centred on commerce, as in the Diaspora. Only labour could restore the Jews to health and nature: 'Only by elevating labour in itself into an ideal, or rather, by developing the ideal of labour, can we recover from our sickness and close the gap that separates us from nature.'[274]

The salvation of the Jews was thought to lie in returning to the soil of Palestine. Just as Langbehn found German virtue in the soil of Schleswig-Holstein, so Buber thought the creativity of the Jewish people came from the soil of Palestine and could be renewed only on its home ground.[275] The early Zionist Nathan Birnbaum maintained in his pamphlet *Die nationale Wiedergeburt des jüdischen Volkes* (*The National Rebirth of the Jewish People*, 1893) that emigrants to Palestine would become attached to the soil by farming: 'Through agriculture he will gain that love for the soil which preserves a land for its people, and will find that physical and moral health which must be the true goal of all Jewish endeavours.'[276] Visiting Jewish settlements in 1924, Felix Salten noted the feverish urge of over-intellectual Jews to 'return to the simplicity of the soil'.[277] Eugen Hoeflich likewise uses the language of agrarian romanticism to urge 'absorption into the land, growing into oneness with the soil' and declares that: 'the concept of homeland (*Heimat*) includes an emotion directed to eternity and an outlook that is stronger than the present-day outlook placing "I" above "We"';[278] but he does so in order to make a very serious point: unless Jews do the actual physical labour on the soil, they will simply be colonists, not essentially different from Dutch colonists in Sumatra or British administrators in the Sudan.

In order to complete the regeneration of the Jews, Herzl envisages not only that there will be a professional army, but that all able-bodied men will receive military training and patriotic education. Young men will play cricket, girls will play tennis; gambling will be forbidden, because it diverts intellectual powers and adventurous spirit from more important tasks (*BT* ii. 100–1). On his

---

[274] Gordon, *Erlösung*, pp. 70–1.   [275] Buber, *Die jüdische Bewegung*, i. 191.
[276] Birnbaum, *Die jüdische Moderne*, p. 25.
[277] Salten, *Neue Menschen auf alter Erde: Eine Palästinafahrt* ([1925]; Königstein, 1986), p. 59.
[278] Hoeflich, 'Jüdische Bauern', *Der Jude*, 4 (1919–20), i/ii. 92–3 (p. 92).

visit to Palestine in 1898, Herzl and his companions met at Rehovoth some twenty young Jewish men on horseback singing Hebrew songs; they reminded Herzl of the American cowboys whom he had seen in Paris. 'Wolffsohn, Schnirer, Bodenheimer and I had tears in our eyes as we saw these brave, agile horsemen, into which the trouser-selling youths can transform themselves', he recalls, quoting Treitschke's famous polemic against Jewish immigrants from Poland (*BT* ii. 677).[279]

In his address to the Second Zionist Congress, Max Nordau coined the term 'Muskeljudentum' ('muscular Jewry').[280] In response, young Zionists founded the gymnastic association 'Bar Kochba', named after the second-century resistance leader, and following the example of the German gymnastic associations founded after the War of Liberation. Its gymnastic evenings began with songs from a special song-book of 'Turnlieder'. It presented its first public display of Jewish gymnastics in March 1900. In May the first issue of its magazine, the *Jüdische Turnzeitung*, appeared, setting out its programme to improve the Jews' physique, enhance their sense of national identity, and combat antisemitism. '*We are combating the one-sided development of the mind* which has produced our nervousness and intellectual lethargy!' it proclaimed.[281] In the second issue, Nordau described (almost as graphically as Rathenau in 'Höre, Israel!') how confinement in ghettos had weakened the Jews' physique, and urged them to return to pre-exilic traditions: 'Let us resume contact with our most ancient traditions; let us again become deep-chested, firm-limbed, boldly gazing men!' His model was the second-century anti-Roman rebel Bar Kochba, praised as 'the last embodiment in world history of war-hardened, weapon-loving Jewry'.[282]

Another German model which young Jews followed was the *Wandervogelbewegung*, the group of hiking associations in which mainly middle-class teenagers sought communion with nature and

---

[279] Cf. Treitschke, 'Unsere Aussichten', p. 572.

[280] Nordau, *Zionistische Schriften*, p. 72.

[281] 'Programm des Turnvereins "Bar Kochba"', in Jehuda Reinharz (ed.), *Dokumente zur Geschichte des deutschen Zionismus 1882–1933* (Tübingen, 1981), p. 55. Emphasis in original.

[282] 'Muskeljudentum', originally published in the *Jüdische Turnzeitung*, June 1900; in Nordau, *Zionistische Schriften*, pp. 379–81 (quotations from p. 380).

a sense of community.[283] A wide range of Jewish youth movements developed. In the 1920s they included about one-third of young German Jews.[284] Gershom Scholem, an active member of the 'Jung-Juda' group, reflected in his diary on the paradox of transforming an intensely German movement for Jewish purposes: 'Hebrew songs are sung in German forests, and on the hill where yesterday the solstice fires of the Germanic tribes burned, there flicker today the Hanukkah fires of the Jews.'[285] In 1912 young Zionists founded their own hiking association, the Wanderbund 'Blau-Weiss', in order to regenerate young Jews who had been brought up with deficient physical training, estranged from nature, and taught meekly to ignore antisemitic insults. It aimed to revolutionize the emotional lives of Jews by restoring contact with nature and inculcating the virtues of discipline, honesty, reliability, comradeship, and modesty (all, by implication, lacking in assimilated Jewish society); it had no militaristic or doctrinaire aims, but it wanted to inculcate 'a natural Jewish self-confidence'. Its founding document described the physical and moral condition of the younger generation with the familiar Zionist critique of assimilated Jewry:

Our young people are in general physically less efficient (*untüchtiger*) and more nervous than others; a relatively much greater part suffers under the harmful influences of urban life. Having grown up surrounded by adults who think and act materialistically, by sceptical, ironic, joyless people alienated from nature, in the atmosphere of Jewish wit and Jewish self-mockery, our boys and girls are *a generation whose general human outlook on life has already been corrupted in the parental home.*[286]

Many Jewish youth movements were intended as preparation for life in Eretz Israel, and produced pioneers (*chalutzim*) who emigrated and founded kibbutzim; this applied especially to the Galician-based movement Ha-Shomer Ha-Tzair, whose members

[283] See Walter Laqueur, *Young Germany: A History of the German Youth Movement* (London, 1962); Chanoch Rinott, 'Major Trends in Jewish Youth Movements in Germany', *LBY* 19 (1974), 77–95; Arnold Paucker, 'Zum Selbstverständnis jüdischer Jugend in der Weimarer Republik und unter der nationalsozialistischer Diktatur', in Hans Otto Horch and Charlotte Wardi (eds.), *Jüdische Selbstwahrnehmung* (Tübingen, 1997), pp. 111–28, a personal account with extensive references.

[284] Brenner, *The Renaissance of Jewish Culture*, p. 47.

[285] Entry of 12 Dec. 1915 in Scholem, *Tagebücher 1913–1917*, pp. 197–8.

[286] 'Leitfaden für die Gründung eines Jüdischen Wanderbundes "Blau-Weiß"', in *Dokumente zur Geschichte des deutschen Zionismus*, p. 115. Emphasis in original.

sought to be 'young Hebrews' on biblical models.[287] But some shared authoritarian tendencies with their German prototypes: in 1922 Scholem again attacked the Blau-Weiss after its leader Walter Moses, who later ran a cigarette factory in Palestine, had restructured it along military lines and demanded soldierly faith in 'the victory of power'.[288]

Another aspect of the physical renewal of Jewish life was the reform of sexuality. What Buber called 'the fundamental ailment of the modern Jew, the excessive development of the nerves', could not but affect sexual life.[289] This became a prominent theme after the First World War. Arnold Zweig's essay *Das ostjüdische Antlitz* praised traditional Jewry for sublimating the senses but deplored its accompanying failure to cultivate erotic life, so that marriages were often sexually lukewarm, men were clumsy, women frigid, and the aesthetic value of the body was unappreciated.[290] Zweig's solution was to restore the Mediterranean character of the Jews, encouraging a frank and happy sensuality as well as the talent for rhetoric and eloquence, the expressive body-language, and the clear, rational thought, that the Jews shared with the French, the Italians, and the Greeks; and this could best be done by transporting them to the eastern coast of the Mediterranean.[291] More conservatively, the Orthodox Jew Hans Goslar polemicized against the sexual degeneracy of assimilated Jewry. Having adopted the standards of middle-class Europeans, German Jews now marry late and have small families, so that their birth-rate is decreasing; instead of being valued as wives and mothers, women are degraded into prostitutes or effete, incompetent 'ladies'; and the physical quality of children is in decline. Goslar advocates a return to the traditional Jewish practice of early marriage (at 18 for men, earlier for women), and recommends that sexual indulgence should be moderate; he attacks Freud for claiming that sexual abstinence creates neurosis, and attributes it rather to the

---

[287] See Hermann Meier-Cronemeyer, 'Deutschlands jüdische Jugendbewegung. Versuch eines Fazits', *Emuna*, 8 (1973), 358–70; Chaim Schatzker, 'Martin Buber's Influence on the Jewish Youth Movement in Germany', *LBY* 23 (1978), 151–71; Elkana Margalit, 'Social and Intellectual Origins of the Hashomer Hatzair Youth Movement, 1913–1920', in Jehuda Reinharz and Anita Shapira (eds.), *Essential Papers on Zionism* (London, 1996), pp. 454–72.

[288] Quoted in Biale, *Scholem*, p. 68.   [289] Buber, *Die jüdische Bewegung*, i. 36.

[290] Zweig, *Herkunft und Zukunft*, pp. 90–2, 132–3.

[291] See Zweig, *Das neue Kanaan* (1925) in *Herkunft und Zukunft*, pp. 177–83.

abstraction and over-intellectuality promoted by life in the Diaspora. The solution is Zionism, which 'seeks to transform the type of pure intellectual, a bundle of nerves worn out by abstract theorizing, back into a blood-filled man close to pure nature'.[292] He also opposes mixed marriages, on the grounds that their motive is the increased erotic attraction felt by members of different races, which is no foundation for a lifelong partnership. Goslar's prescriptions are addressed only to male readers, and might offer little to women who do not wish to begin motherhood in their teens. Later Zionists, however, were hardly more successful in reconciling the power of erotic desire with the restrictions of communal life and the equality of men and women. Some offered Lawrentian celebrations of virility, others practised an uncomfortable asceticism in which exposure to naked bodies was expected to remove their erotic appeal.[293] Arthur Koestler's account of his disillusioning stay on a commune in 1926 mentions how sexual appetite was blunted by fatigue and over-familiarity, so that men and women on the same commune were separated by 'a kind of incest-barrier'.[294]

Alongside practical and physical changes, Herzl also planned to restore the Jews' self-respect. He intended that, in the Jewish state, duelling would be allowed in order to improve the quality of officers and the refinement of society, and in *Der Judenstaat* he spends a page and a half, obviously with great enjoyment, working out the rules (*ZW* i. 65–6). Evidently compensating for his own exclusion, he assumes that students will belong to a duelling society ('Couleur', *BT* ii. 150). This ideal was shared by the members of Kadimah, the first Jewish national student society in western Europe, founded in 1882: in response to aggressiveness from German nationalists, they resolved to disprove the imputation of cowardice by transforming themselves into a duelling society and demanding satisfaction for insults.[295] Herzl considered the duel essential to produce a well-bred officer class: 'I need the duel in order to have decent officers and to refine the tone of

[292] Goslar, *Die Sexualethik der jüdischen Wiedergeburt: Ein Wort an unsere Jugend* (Berlin, 1919), p. 41.
[293] See David Biale, *Eros and the Jews: From Biblical Israel to Contemporary America* (New York, 1992), ch. 8: 'Zionism as an Erotic Revolution'.
[294] Koestler, *Arrow in the Blue: An Autobiography* (London, 1952), p. 128.
[295] See Wistrich, *The Jews of Vienna*, pp. 347–80 (esp. p. 366).

good society in the French manner' (*BT* ii. 92). Commercial honour entered into his plans as well, for he intended Jews to demonstrate their honour by paying expropriated Palestinians the full value of their estates: 'We shall teach the world something that was thought impossible for two thousand years: Jewish honour' (*BT* ii. 130).

Self-respect was also to be restored through national cere-monies. For the installation of the leader Herzl imagined a parti-cularly fine and moving ceremony, modelled on the coronation of the Doge of Venice: 'For the popular understanding, such ideas must be represented in the simple and moving form of symbols. And so when we go in procession to the Temple to crown the prince, we shall all wear magnificent ceremonial garb, except that in our midst a man will walk in the wretched and shameful costume of a medieval Jew, with the pointed hat and yellow star. And that man will be our prince. Only when we reach the Temple shall we place a princely robe round his shoulders and a crown on his head' (*ZW* ii. 189). Another scene Herzl loved to imagine was the 'Landnahme', the solemn taking possession of the new land, at which all those taking part would wear the yellow star (*BT* ii. 120). The highest decoration in the Jewish state should be a yellow ribbon, thus converting a badge of shame into a mark of honour (*BT* ii. 187). Similarly, when he founded the Zionist newspaper *Die Welt* in 1897, Herzl decided that it should have a yellow cover, in order to recall the yellow star and turn it into a badge of dignity.[296]

Language also needed regeneration. Herzl never thought that the language of the new state would be Hebrew. 'Who among us knows enough Hebrew to ask for a railway ticket in that lan-guage?' he asks in *Der Judenstaat* (*ZW* i. 94; cf. *BT* ii. 190). A state whose language was Hebrew might confine itself in a linguis-tic ghetto, like modern Greece. And if Hebrew was impracticable, Yiddish was despicable: it was a deformed language which Jews confined in the Diaspora had stolen from their captors (*BT* ii. 75). Nordau agreed, saying of the Eastern Jews: 'They stammer their laments in a gibberish that is unintelligible to cultivated people. We lend them civilized languages.'[297] Herzl imagined the state as

---

[296] York-Steiner, *Die Kunst als Jude zu leben*, p. 460.
[297] Nordau, *Zionistische Schriften*, p. 304.

a multilingual federation like Switzerland, where eventually the most useful language would become dominant: English and French were acceptable, but the official language was most likely to be German (*BT* ii. 90–1). This contempt for Yiddish was deeply rooted among Zionists: in 1927 there was what Scholem called 'chauvinistic' opposition to the founding of a chair of Yiddish philology at the Hebrew University.[298]

The regeneration of the Jews began with Herzl himself. He was conscious that his strikingly 'Jewish' appearance exposed him to antisemitic insults (*BT* ii. 45). Increasingly, he made a virtue of necessity by cultivating 'Jewish' looks which were as different as possible from German-Jewish stereotypes. Contemporaries were vastly impressed by his appearance, which reminded some of the ancient Jewish kings or of the prophets, and struck others as 'Chaldean'.[299] Max Brod described him as 'a king with a flowing Assyrian beard, a demi-god, but in modern dress'.[300] By his appearance Herzl exploited the idea that the Jews, as a 'Semitic' people, were akin to the highly cultured and conquering peoples of the ancient Middle East. His looks were fully used in the iconography of the Zionist movement, notably in the deservedly famous photograph by E. M. Lilien that shows Herzl leaning over the Rhine bridge at Basle and meditating on past and future. His appearance assisted his charisma. Hearing him address a crowded meeting in Berlin, Elias Auerbach perceived a 'mystical radiance' and explains: 'Herzl was the best-looking man I ever met in my life. The surviving photographs of Herzl do not give an adequate impression.'[301] Even knowing Herzl's appearance only from photographs, the normally sober Arnold Zweig, who was particularly impressed by the beard, thought it the first face of a leader ('Führerantlitz') that the Jewish world had produced since Sabbatai Zvi.[302]

In keeping with his self-image, Herzl imagined the Jewish state as led by a new Jewish aristocracy. For its political organization,

[298] Biale, *Scholem*, p. 179.

[299] See David Vital, *Zionism: The Formative Years* (Oxford, 1982), pp. 81, 114; Michael Berkowitz, *Zionist Culture and West European Jewry before the First World War* (Cambridge, 1993), pp. 136–7; Zangwill quoted in David J. Goldberg, *To the Promised Land: A History of Zionist Thought* (London, 1996), p. 43.

[300] Brod, *Streitbares Leben*, p. 69.

[301] Auerbach, *Pionier der Verwirklichung* (Stuttgart, 1969), p. 91.

[302] Zweig, *Caliban*, p. 301.

he favoured an aristocratic republic which would resemble Venice but avoid its faults (*ZW* i. 94; *BT* ii. 189). However, aristocracy will not be hereditary. Yet when he visited the English Zionist Colonel Goldsmid in Cardiff, he imagined Goldsmid's daughters Rahel and Carmel as future aristocrats: 'I was already looking at aristocratic Jewish women of the future. Delicate beings, with an Oriental touch, gentle and dreamy' (*BT* ii. 286).

The regeneration of the Jews is fully imagined in Herzl's utopian novel *Altneuland*. At the beginning, the hero, Friedrich Löwenberg, feels out of place among young under-employed Jewish graduates who will degrade the professions they enter by introducing a spirit of commercial competition into law or journalism. There follows an unflattering portrayal of a social evening in Jewish high society, with ostentatiously bejewelled women, men who talk about their business connections, and the rival wits Grün and Blau, who illustrate the self-defeating 'Jewish' irony that Herzl disliked. The girl Friedrich loves is married off to a business associate of her father's, and Friedrich reflects: 'In this circle, where people appreciated only pleasure and self-interest, money was everything' (*ZW* v. 144). This harsh and clichéd critique, like that in 'Mauschel', could hardly be surpassed by an antisemite. Firmly alienated from the Jewish bourgeoisie, Friedrich discovers an unexpected solidarity with a poor family from Galicia; he gives them his remaining money before leaving Europe in the company of Kingscourt, a millionaire who has wearied of civilization and wants a companion with whom to spend the rest of his life on a remote Pacific island.

On the way to the Pacific they visit the Palestine of 1902, which proves desolate and miserable. The port of Jaffa is described in Oriental clichés of dirt, squalor, idleness, and passivity. After twenty years without even seeing a newspaper, they return through the Red Sea and find, in place of the former decay, a magnificent port with an international population, though the predominant impression is European. Most of the novel henceforth consists of tourism interspersed with lectures. It appears that the Jews were driven from Europe, not by violence, but by antisemitic propaganda, commercial boycotts, and professional ostracism. The territory of the state appears to stretch northwards to Damascus and eastwards to the Euphrates. There is a wonderful description of the railway network, connected to Europe by a railway bridge

across the Bosporus and stretching down through Africa, which
has Jerusalem as its nodal point and has almost emptied the Suez
Canal of East-bound transport (*ZW* v. 205). The new state is not
a backward-looking agrarian utopia but ultra-modern in its
imaginative use of technology.[303]

The New Society, as it is called, has brought about the regeneration of the Jews by giving the Jewish intellectual proletariat an
outlet for their talents and a new-found pride in being Jewish. Its
blessings are typified by David Littwak, the Galician boy whose
family Friedrich helped in Vienna. David is now a grown man, a
well-to-do shipowner and politician, who speaks perfect German.
Friedrich reflects: 'What had the beggarly Jew-boy grown into! A
healthy, educated man with a free and serious look, who seemed
to stand firmly on his own two feet' (*ZW* v. 194). Jewish
assimilation, a failure in Europe, has succeeded in Asia. Apart
from some orthodox farmers who still speak *Mauscheldeutsch*,
most of the population have been transformed by democratic
politics (Herzl's dreams of a new aristocracy are absent from
this text), co-operative associations, sexual equality, and public
service. There is no army, but plenty of competitive sport on the
English model, such as cricket, football, and rowing, which,
combined with a healthy environment, has transformed the
Jews' physique. Even Jewish women, pilloried early in the novel
for their showiness, no longer dress ostentatiously: David's modest, simply dressed sister Mirjam is a fantasy compensation, as
Peter Loewenberg points out, for Herzl's pleasure-loving wife
Julie who was the original of Hermine in *Das neue Ghetto*.[304]

The new state is not nationalistic but cosmopolitan. There is a
Jewish Academy, modelled on the Académie Française, which
rewards contributions to the welfare of humanity. The decorations
it confers are modelled on the Légion d'Honneur and consist of a
yellow ribbon, to remind Jews of their ancestors' yellow star. The
newcomers' tour culminates in a visit to the rebuilt Temple in
Jerusalem, whose Old Town is entirely given over to providing for
pilgrims of various faiths. Arabs are welcome as citizens, typified
by Reschid Bey, a Muslim who has studied in Berlin. David tells
Kingscourt: 'my comrades and I make no distinctions among

---

[303] See Timms, 'Ambassador Herzl', pp. 22–5.
[304] Loewenberg, *Decoding the Past*, p. 124.

people. We do not ask what faith or what race anyone belongs to. He must be a human being (*ein Mensch*), that is sufficient for us' (*ZW* v. 190–1). The universal humanism of the Enlightenment, driven from Europe by increasing xenophobia, has found a refuge here. Although the party led by Dr Geyer, formerly an anti-Zionist rabbi, still wants to exclude non-Jews, at the end of the book it is decisively defeated and David Littwak is elected President of the new state.

The New Society represents the solution of the 'Jewish problem' by providing the Jews with a 'normal' modern state. But in what sense is it a 'Jewish' state? Jewish tradition has only a marginal place within it, on a par with any other religion. There is considerable justice in the famous criticisms made by the Russian Zionist Ahad Ha'am in a controversial review. He complained that the New Society had nothing Jewish about it: its denizens did not even speak Hebrew; the Temple was merely a Reform synagogue on Viennese lines; the only recognizably Jewish character was the hateful Orthodox rabbi; the other characters seemed anxious to conceal their Jewishness and to practise a vacuous tolerance.[305] The liberal universalism, which Herzl thought among the Jews' greatest achievements, seemed to Ahad Ha'am a way of selling out the Jews by erasing their character.

Jews and Arabs

In *Altneuland* Herzl wanted to combine the cosmopolitanism of the Enlightenment with the secular nationalism inspired by Herder and the Counter-Enlightenment. Zionism, as Hugh Trevor-Roper has argued, was a secular nationalist movement like those of 'non-historic peoples' like the Czechs and the Southern Slavs.[306] The proto-Zionism of Moses Hess was explicitly modelled on the Italian Risorgimento and the Polish and Hungarian liberation movements.[307] Herzl's letter to Lord Rothschild of 22 August 1902 shows that he thought of Zionism as another modern nationalist movement: 'In our own time Greeks, Rumanians, Serbs, Bulgarians have established themselves—so why shouldn't

---

[305] Summarized in Steven Beller, *Herzl* (London, 1991), pp. 108–10.
[306] H. R. Trevor-Roper, 'Jewish and other Nationalisms', *Commentary*, 35 (Jan.–June 1963), 15–21.   [307] See Hess, *The Revival of Israel*, pp. 35–7.

we be able to?' (*BT* iii. 455). Recent studies of nationalism stress its imposition of cultural homogeneity in the service of political and economic integration.[308] Herzl thought that the hegemony of western European, especially German, Jews would gradually spread their culture through the Jewish masses who would come largely from Galicia and Russia. He foresaw neither the mass immigration of North African and Middle Eastern Jews, nor the discontent that would be felt by Arabs at the presence, and later the rule, of Jewish settlers.

Immigrants from Europe had difficulty in establishing a relationship with the Jews already living in the East. Some Zionists rejected them, like Israel Auerbach, who complains that the Asian Jew 'is the pure Oriental. Contented, because lacking in aspirations; peaceful, because indolent; uncomplaining, because submissive; dying with reverence before money, splendour, dignity, titles, because of centuries of despotism; cautious, indeed mistrustful and devious, because used to being surrounded by spies; mainly poor and uneducated, because lacking social organization; unpolitical, unenterprising, unfree, because politics, courage and freedom were forbidden by the lords of the Orient.'[309] Such indictments recall the negative description of European Jews as 'Oriental' by antisemites like Treitschke and Jewish critics like Rathenau. On the other hands, efforts were made to identify the Asian Jews with the Oriental basis of the Jewish people, especially by Eugen Hoeflich. Hoeflich was born in 1891 to an assimilated Jewish family in Vienna, served as an Austrian liaison officer with Turkish troops in Jerusalem in 1917 and emigrated to Palestine in 1927, where, as Moshe Ben-gavriêl, he became a popular writer. He describes two weddings he attended in Jerusalem, the first among Yemenite Jews, the second among Hasidim from Poland, and describes how the latter once more became so 'primitively joyful, child-like and natural, and gave themselves up to enjoyment that no stranger would have recognized the timid, excluded Polish Jew in these dancing and singing

---

[308] See Benedict Anderson, *Imagined Communities: Reflections on the Origin and Spread of Nationalism* (London, 1983); Ernest Gellner, *Nations and Nationalism* (Oxford, 1983).

[309] Israel Auerbach, 'Vom orientalischen Judentum', *Der Jude*, 4 (1919–20), x. 433–46 (p. 434).

semi-Orientals'.[310] The Jews, according to Hoeflich, are basically
an Oriental people, with the desert in their blood. The Jew is at
heart a Bedouin. He therefore proposed a 'Panasianist' ideology
which imagined a union of Jews and Arabs. Auerbach and
Hoeflich exhibit the the two sides of the primitivism that we
have earlier seen being applied to the Jews of eastern Europe.
On the one hand, the Asian Jews are seen as backward and
shiftless; on the other, as natural and vital.

Coexistence with Arabs formed a yet more intractable problem
for both sides. The immigration of Jews to Palestine began after
the Russian pogroms with the First Aliya of 1882, when some
thirty thousand settlers, inspired by the Russian movement Hibbat
Zion (Love of Zion), arrived in Palestine. They founded over
twenty agricultural colonies, often buying land from absentee
landowners whose Arab tenants naturally resented being dispossessed and turned into labourers. The Second Aliya (1904–14),
of about the same size, differed in being led by young people
with revolutionary ideas (including David Ben-Gurion and A. D.
Gordon) who wanted to build a Jewish society. Believing in the
regenerative effects of manual labour, they were reluctant to
employ Arab workers. While Herzl had assumed that the development of Palestine would benefit all the inhabitants and thus
reconcile the Arabs to the Jews' presence, as it does Reschid Bey in
Altneuland, the settlers tried increasingly to construct a closed
economy and society. They also wanted to remain culturally distinct from the Arab majority, and since Hebrew was inculcated
through education, there was no integration between Jews and
Arabs in schools. Nor was there political integration. Though
socialist in various degrees, the political parties founded by the
Second Aliya settlers, Poalei Zion and the more moderate workers'
party Ha-Poel Ha-Tzair, were also Zionist and closed to Arabs.
Similarly, and despite counter-proposals by Ben-Gurion, Arabs
were excluded from the Histadrut, the Jewish trade union movement formed in 1920 at the time of the Third Aliya; though it is
admittedly hard to imagine that Arabs would have wanted to join

---

[310] Hoeflich, 'Hochzeiten in Jerusalem', *Der Jude*, 3 (1918–19), iii. 127–30 (p.
129). On Hoeflich, see Kaiser, *Palästina—Erez Israel*, pp. 243–66; Armin A. Wallas,
'Der Pförtner des Ostens. Eugen Hoeflich—Panasiat und Expressionist', in Mark H.
Gelber, Hans Otto Horch, and Sigurd Paul Scheichl (eds.), *Von Franzos zu Canetti:
Jüdische Autoren aus Österreich* (Tübingen, 1996), pp. 305–44.

these organizations even if they could. In keeping with this exclusivism, many Zionist photographs of Palestine leave the Arabs out or treat their culture, represented by mosques, merely as picturesque parts of the landscape.[311] Yet even by 1914 the Yishuv (the Jewish community in Palestine) numbered only some 90,000, amid an Arab population of 590,000.

Early theoreticians of Zionism often sketched grandiose colonial plans which treated the Arabs with remarkable and fateful insouciance. When preparing for his audience with the Kaiser during the latter's journey to the Near East in 1898, Herzl resolved to ask for territory 'from the Brook of Egypt to the Euphrates' (*BT* ii. 650). Oscar Straus, the American ambassador in Constantinople, suggested that the Jewish state should be located in Mesopotamia, 'Israel's ancient home', where the Christian Churches would have no reason to interfere; nothing was said about the Muslim inhabitants (*BT* iii. 79). Such large territories would be required especially to accommodate the millions of oppressed Jews from Russia. Even in 1919 Hans Goslar thought Palestine could accommodate 'a Jewish farming population of several million', and that as the population grew it could expand into Turkish territory.[312] (He ignored both the fate of the Turkish Armenians and the militant nationalism of Mustafa Kemal.) Max Brod thought Palestine alone could accommodate a population of six million.[313] Still more extravagantly, the German Zionist Joseph Bloch imagined the Jewish state eventually becoming part of a socialist 'Pan-Semitic Empire' encompassing North Africa and the Middle East.[314]

The realities of settling in a small territory with an Arab majority created divisions among Zionists. Birnbaum proposed a national centre which would not absorb the entire Jewish population but provide a sense of national identity for them all.[315] The Russian Zionist Ahad Ha'am warned in 1894 that Palestine was too small to accommodate all Jews and could only be a spiritual centre, which would counteract the Jews' fatal talent for imitation and the consequent danger of complete assimilation by setting a

---

[311] Berkowitz, *Zionist Culture*, p. 150.   [312] Goslar, *Sexualethik*, p. 47.
[313] Brod, 'Die jüdische Kolonisation in Palästina', *Die neue Rundschau*, 28 ii (1917), 1267–76 (p. 1272).   [314] See Wistrich, *Socialism and the Jews*, p. 169.
[315] Birnbaum, *Die jüdische Moderne*, p. 24.

standard of Jewish life.[316] 'Practical Zionists', heeding his message, advocated small-scale immigration, while 'political Zionists' wanted to colonize an extensive territory on both banks of the Jordan. After the Arab riots of May 1921 in Jaffa, the Revisionist movement led by Vladimir Jabotinsky, a spell-binding figure comparable to Herzl, demanded the protection of Palestine by an 'iron wall' manned by a Jewish Legion.[317] Another possibility, advocated by Ben-Gurion and Mapai (the Labour Party), was the reconciliation of Jews and Arabs within a territorial federation. The Arabs, however, insisted on their exclusive right to inhabit Palestine, demanded an end to Jewish immigration, and complained of being impoverished by Jewish economic competition. Their fears were intensified by the sharp increase in Jewish immigration from the increasingly tyrannical Europe of the 1930s: the Yishuv grew from 175,000 in 1931 to almost 400,000 in 1936. With the Arab uprising of 1936–9 it became apparent that in reaction to the organization of the Yishuv the Palestinian Arabs had formed their own nationalist movement under the charismatic leadership of the Grand Mufti of Jerusalem, Haj Amin al-Hussaini, who headed the Supreme Muslim Council from 1922 until his dismissal by the British authorities for helping to foment the Arab insurrection.[318]

Integration between Jews and Arabs found few proponents. As early as 1907, the Russian-born educator Yitzhak Epstein, who had come to Palestine with the First Aliya, argued that the Zionist project could only be realized with the consent of the Arabs, and proposed that all the institutions introduced by settlers, from schools to cheap restaurants, should be equally open to the Arab population.[319] In the same year, at the Eighth Zionist Congress, Moses Gaster, the chief Sephardic rabbi of London, hoped that the

---

[316] Ahad Ha'am, 'Imitation and Assimilation' (1894), in his *Selected Essays*, tr. Leon Simon (Philadelphia, 1962), pp. 107–24.

[317] On Jabotinsky, a figure influenced by Nietzschean vitalism and the milder forms of European fascism, see Avineri, *The Making of Modern Zionism*, pp. 159–86, and the sympathetic personal account in Koestler, *Arrow in the Blue*, pp. 106–10.

[318] On him and his career, including his attempts at collaboration with the Axis powers and his acceptance of crude antisemitism, see Zvi Elpeleg, *The Grand Mufti: Haj Amin al-Hussaini, Founder of the Palestinian National Movement*, tr. David Harvey (London, 1993).

[319] See Yosef Gorny, *Zionism and the Arabs, 1882–1948: A Study of Ideology* (Oxford, 1987), pp. 42–4.

Jewish settlers would draw on the achievements of Islamic civilization.[320] However, many early settlers lived in constant fear of
Arab attacks. In self-defence, the Second Aliya established the
underground military organization Ha-Shomer ('The Watchman')
which would ultimately form the nucleus of the Israeli army. Even
some liberal settlers saw the Arabs as 'a semi-savage people'
combining primitive truculence with modern corruption and
wallowing in 'lying, cheating, suspiciousness, and slander'.[321]

The main spokesmen for integration were a group of Central
European Zionists, mostly intellectuals and academics, who from
1925 to 1933 formed the discussion forum Brit Shalom ('Covenant of Peace').[322] Its first president was Arthur Ruppin and its
core members included Hans Kohn, Hugo Bergman, and Robert
Weltsch, all of whom had belonged to the Prague Bar Kochba
society, along with Judah Magnes, the first president of the
Hebrew University. Later they were joined by Gershom Scholem
and Ernst Simon. Their European mouthpiece was the *Jüdische
Rundschau* edited by Robert Weltsch. They were influenced by the
moderate socialism of Ha-Poel Ha-Tzair, by the ideals of personal
regeneration represented by Buber and Gordon, and by their European experience of nationalist conflict, especially in pre-War
Prague, where Jews had been trapped between increasingly chauvinistic Czechs and Germans. True to the enlightened liberalism of
Central European Jewry, they wanted to base their Jewish identity
on culture rather than politics.[323] After the Arab–Jewish clashes of
1929, Hugo Bergman deplored the tendency of many Zionists to
repeat the mistakes of European nationalism: 'When they speak of
Palestine, of our country, they mean "our country", that is to say
"not *their* country". This viewpoint is borrowed from Europe at
the time of its decline.'[324] Alluding to Jabotinsky's Revisionism,
Gershom Scholem declared in the same year: 'The Zionist ideal is
one thing and the messianic ideal another, and the two do not
meet except in the pompous phraseology of mass rallies.'[325] Brit

---

[320] Berkowitz, *Zionist Culture*, p. 114.
[321] Moshe Smilansky in 1914, quoted in Gorny, *Zionism and the Arabs*, pp. 63–4.
[322] See Hagit Lavsky, 'German Zionists and the Emergence of Brit Shalom', in
Reinharz and Shapiro (eds.), *Essential Papers on Zionism*, pp. 648–70.
[323] See Mosse, *Confronting the Nation*, p. 187.
[324] Quoted in Gorny, *Zionism and the Arabs*, p. 123.
[325] Biale, *Scholem*, p. 177.

Shalom proposed a bi-national state in which Jews and Arabs should enjoy equal rights irrespective of numbers; as many Jews should be admitted as possible, but they need not constitute a majority. However, if a bi-national state were set up while Arabs formed the majority, they would, as Ruppin admitted in a letter to Kohn, do their best to hinder the Jews' economic development, and might well be dominated by demagogues.[326] Like Herzl in *Altneuland*, Brit Shalom wanted to transport the liberalism which had failed in Europe to a new home in Palestine. Not surprisingly, it found little support. The ideals descended from the Enlightenment could not easily be transplanted to such a different setting. A civilized cultural nationalism, marked by a reverence for *Bildung* and an aversion to politics, might be admirable in itself, but it was hardly suitable for a beleaguered community whose very existence depended, for better or worse, on sustaining nationalist fervour.

Arnold Zweig: The Return to History

The greatest German novelist to adopt Zionism was Arnold Zweig. A Socialist and, thanks to his service on the Western Front in the First World War, a pacifist, he thought Zionism the only way in which Jews could combine Socialism with the retention of a Jewish identity. This is the conclusion of *Das ostjüdische Antlitz*, the occasionally romanticizing but usually perceptive analysis of Eastern Jewish life founded on Zweig's experience later in the War, when, along with some other artists and intellectuals, he was employed in the press division of the Supreme Commander of the 'Ober-Ost' division in Kovno (Kaunas).[327] Long before actually visiting Palestine, Zweig developed this argument in *Das neue Kanaan (The New Canaan*, 1925), where, as we have seen, he

---

[326] Letter of 30 May 1928 in Ruppin, *Briefe, Tagebücher, Erinnerungen*, p. 400–4; discussed in Gorny, *Zionism and the Arabs*, pp. 125–6.

[327] For Zweig's biography, see Manuel Wiznitzer, *Arnold Zweig: Das Leben eines deutsch-jüdischen Schriftstellers* (Königstein, 1983); also id., 'Er war ein Wanderer zwischen zwei Welten. Arnold Zweig und das Judentum', in Wilhelm von Sternburg (ed.), *Arnold Zweig: Materialien zu Leben und Werk* (Frankfurt, 1987), pp. 308–30. His views on Socialism and Zionism are conveniently summarized in Klara P. Carmely, *Das Identitätsproblem jüdischer Autoren im deutschen Sprachraum: Von der Jahrhundertwende bis zu Hitler* (Königstein, 1981), pp. 75–80, 114–31. On his fiction, see David R. Midgley, *Arnold Zweig: Eine Einführung in Leben und Werk*, 2nd edn. (Frankfurt, 1987).

foretold that the return to Palestine would restore the Mediterranean character—eloquent, expressive, sensual, and rational—that the Jews shared with the Greeks and the Latin peoples. For him, the Jew is by nature an 'Aufklärer', that is, a proponent of the southern European Enlightenment celebrated by Heinrich Mann and gently caricatured by Thomas Mann in the person of Settembrini in *Der Zauberberg*. Hence the Jew feels out of place amid the turbid spirituality of the Germans. Zweig's essay ends in a marvellous evocation of Palestine as prefiguring a new society where humanity will be at ease with itself and at home in the cosmos: it recalls both the utopian vision that opens Heine's *Deutschland: Ein Wintermärchen* and also the tradition of 'Südweh', longing for the sensuous atmosphere of the Mediterranean, that runs through German literature from Goethe's *Römische Elegien* to Nietzsche, Stefan George, and Gottfried Benn.

Experience was not to confirm this prophecy. A visit to Palestine in the spring of 1932 left Zweig with mixed feelings. After Hitler's assumption of power he was among the few German writers who emigrated to Palestine, but he soon regretted his move, finding himself cut off from German culture, unable to learn Hebrew, and denied the recognition he undoubtedly deserved.[328] In 1948, on the day the State of Israel was proclaimed, Zweig—now, it must be remembered, an elderly man with failing health—left the country and went via Prague to East Germany, where he was celebrated as the grand old man of German letters. Here, apart from occasional and obligatory eulogies of Stalin, he behaved with dignity; but some self-abasement is visible in the letter to Feuchtwanger where he says that he is now revelling in Marx and has discarded 'Zionist rubbish' ('Zionistenkram').[329]

Zweig's engagement with Zionism finds oblique and complex expression in two of his great novels, *Der Streit um den Sergeanten Grischa* (*The Dispute over Sergeant Grischa*, 1927) and *De*

---

[328] On the discomfort often felt by German émigrés in Palestine, see Eva Beling, *Die gesellschaftliche Eingliederung der deutschen Einwanderer in Israel: Eine soziologische Untersuchung der Einwanderung aus Deutschland zwischen 1933 und 1945* (Frankfurt, 1967).
[329] Letter of 25 Aug. 1951 in Feuchtwanger and Zweig, *Briefe 1933–1958*, 2 vols. (Berlin, 1984), ii. 143. See Karl Kröhnke, 'Arnold Zweigs teurer Traum. Politische Überlegungen zu seinem Leben und zu seinem Werk', in Sternburg (ed.), *Arnold Zweig*, pp. 255–81.

Vriendt kehrt heim (*De Vriendt goes home*, 1932). *Grischa* draws on Zweig's experience on the Eastern Front. It is based on the actual case of the Russian sergeant Grisha Paprotkin, who in 1917 escaped from a German prisoner-of-war camp in the German-occupied part of western Russia, was captured and unjustly condemned to death as a spy, and was finally executed after prolonged attempts to obtain his release. In Zweig's novel, Grischa's helpers include both Western and Eastern Jews, and a synthesis is implied between their values. The injustice done to Grischa symbolizes the corruption of the German Empire and lets Zweig predict its supersession by a new political order in which the Jews will come into their own.

For much of the text, interest is displaced from Grischa onto the conflict between the liberal and humane members of the occupying forces who try to obtain his release and the authority of the Commander of the German forces in the 'Ober-Ost' division, Erich von Ludendorff, called in the novel Albert von Schieffenzahn. Grischa's would-be helpers include the Jewish writer and soldier Werner Bertin (Zweig's own surrogate, who appears in several other novels) and, most importantly, the army lawyer Posnanski, an Orthodox Jew from Berlin, who is steeped in the German classics and, like Zweig himself, admires Freud. Posnanski displays a passion for justice, based on the Torah, which extorts perplexed admiration from his commanding officer, the decent, Fontanesque General von Lychow. 'These Jewish lawyers', meditates Lychow. 'I could swear that some love justice (*das Recht*) for its own sake, as we love our estates and fields.'[330]

In case we are tempted, however, to see Posnanski, Bertin, and Lychow as embodying a successful German–Jewish symbiosis, we need to remember, not only that they fail to prevent Grischa's execution, but that they are contrasted with the traditional Jews of the region, above all with the carpenter Täwje Frum who helps Grischa confront his death.[331] Täwje admonishes Grischa: 'Anyone who spills man's blood will have his own blood spilt by men'

---

[330] Zweig, *Der Streit um den Sergeanten Grischa* (Potsdam, 1927), p. 130. Future page references in text.

[331] See Jörg Schönert, '". . . mehr als die Juden weiß von Gott und der Welt doch niemand." Zu Arnold Zweigs Roman *Der Streit um den Sergeanten Grischa*', in Grimm and Bayerdörfer (eds.), *Im Zeichen Hiobs*, pp. 223–42 (p. 229), disputing an argument put forward by Marcel Reich-Ranicki.

(p. 321). Grischa comes to accept this pacifism and to see his own death as a punishment for his misdeeds as a soldier—not a particularly bad or inhuman soldier, but one who necessarily was involved in bloodshed. He believes, not in God, but in resurrection, as a natural process represented by the growth of plants in the spring; and this process is symbolized by the birth of Grischa's daughter within a few minutes of his death. One of Zweig's finest pieces of writing is the minute description of Grischa's death, an attempt to render the consciousness of a dying person, which forcefully reminds us of the enormity of cancelling out a human life. Strangely, however, Zweig ascribes the serenity of Grischa's final moments to his unconscious awareness of the basic continuity embodied in the germ-plasm. The germ-plasm was postulated by the biologist August Weismann in the 1870s as the part of a germ-cell which transmits hereditary factors while itself remaining immortal and immutable. Zweig was evidently attracted by the notion that the germ-plasm, as the fundamental constituent of life, might be the object of religious devotion. In his treatise *Caliban* he asserts: 'God is the reflection of living plasm in human levels of consciousness.'[332] This effort to translate religion into the terms of scientific naturalism sits uneasily with the devoutness of Täwje Frum; but Zweig's honest confrontation with Grischa's death firmly relativizes the liberal optimism of Posnanski and Bertin, who feel unable to attend his execution. Unable to confront the existential fact of death, these characters are perhaps *too* civilized.

While the life of the individual Grischa is portrayed against the First World War, that in turn is placed in a wider historical context. German military conquests in the Baltic region recall the early medieval schemes of Henry the Lion; Schieffenzahn hopes to press through Russia to India and succeed where Alexander and Napoleon failed; the ruins of Brest-Litovsk recall (to the Dutch Red Cross official van Rijlte, a civilized collector of Hebrew manuscripts) the rise and fall of Corinth and Jerusalem, Alexandria and Rome. Within this historical context, the public meaning of Grischa's execution is enunciated, first of all, by Posnanski. Grischa's death is an indictment of Germany. It illustrates the shortcomings of a Germany whose material power has increased as its moral standing has declined. All powerful states

---

[332] Zweig, *Caliban*, p. 231; cf. *Grischa*, p. 533.

become similarly demoralized, Posnanski says, and the Jews' task is 'to lead the nations to feel justice hanging in the stars above them' (pp. 484–5). Posnanski is speaking as a Jew who identifies Judaism with morality and justice; in the novel he represents a moral authority which transcends politics and is universal. By this universal standard Germany is judged and condemned. A minor character, Sergeant Laurenz Pont, who is briefly presented as an embodiment of the Germans' history as soldiers from the Roman legions to the present, reflects on the greater maturity of the non-militaristic Jews: 'They've long since grown out of playing at soldiers, he thinks' (p. 515). Germany, like all other states, must go through a process of decline and be replaced by another, in which the higher values anticipated by the Jews can finally be realized.

This historical process is interpreted with particular authority by the Kabbalist Täwje Frum. Täwje has a detached view of Germany, for in his long historical and biblical perspective Xerxes is present along with Napoleon, and he sees that Germany, a young nation, has not yet learnt the futility of conquest. He thinks Germany will be destroyed as Sodom and Gomorrah were. Zweig is at pains to remind us of the antiquity of the Jews, adopting the familiar topos that modern Jews resemble those depicted on reliefs in Hittite temples (p. 89). But he also evokes the Jews' future by having Grischa executed on 2 November 1917, the day of the Balfour Declaration, which ran in part:

His Majesty's Government views with favour the establishment in Palestine of a national home for the Jewish people, and will use its best endeavours to facilitate the achievement of this object, it being clearly understood that nothing shall be done which may prejudice the civil and religious rights of existing non-Jewish communities in Palestine, or the rights and political status enjoyed by Jews in any other country.[333]

On the same day, a group of pious orthodox Jews in the novel, who have finished studying the entire Talmud, discuss the death of Grischa and the significance of the Declaration. Täwje, accepting the Kabbalistic doctrine of reincarnation, thinks that Grischa's soul must have done evil in previous lives. The others ask about the meaning of this crime in this particular historical crisis, for an

---

[333] Quoted from David Vital, *Zionism: The Crucial Phase* (Oxford, 1987), p. 293.

English General is about to ride into Jerusalem and fulfil the prophecies of Daniel by restoring it to the Jews. They interpret history as the rise and fall of a series of empires, beginning with Egypt of the Pharaohs, then Assyria, Babylon, the empire of Alexander the Great, then the Roman Empire; each empire falls because its people ignore the law; the present age is dominated by the German and Russian Emperors, but the beginning of the seventh empire is heralded by the Balfour Declaration with its promise that the Jews will return to Jerusalem: 'The seventh Empire will begin, perhaps, when a Jew again reigns in Jerusalem (*Jeruschalajim*)' (p. 489).

Thus the novel, like many others of the 1920s, focuses on a case of politically motivated injustice. But, ambitiously, it uses this case for a critique of German power. It introduces Jewish values as an absolute standard by which to judge Germany's abuse of power. And it implies that this abuse of power is connected with Germany's defeat in the war, placing these events in the context of world history, the rise and fall of empires.

While in Palestine in 1932 Zweig began writing *De Vriendt kehrt heim*, in which his future disillusionment with Zionism is already foreshadowed.[334] The first few pages allude to the Balfour Declaration and the conflict between Zionists and Arab nationalists. The main centre of consciousness is neither an Arab nor a Jew but a British secret policeman, an attractive though somewhat idealized figure with the unlikely name of Lolard B. Irmin. And the action turns on conflict among Jews, for the title figure, an ultra-orthodox Dutch Jew, poet, and militant anti-Zionist, is murdered by a fanatical young Zionist who has just arrived from Poland. Jizchak Josef de Vriendt's real-life prototype, Jacob Israel de Haan, was murdered in 1924; since he was known to have homosexual relations with young Arabs, he was thought to have been killed by an Arab, but, as Zweig learnt on his visit, the murderer was a Jew whose identity was an open secret. Zweig transfers the murder to 1929 so as to associate it with the violence between Arabs and Jews which broke out that August because of disputes over access to the Wailing Wall and Arab rumours that the Jews were planning to take over the Dome of the Rock.

---

[334] See Wilhelm von Sternburg, '*De Vriendt kehrt heim* oder Arnold Zweigs langer Abschied vom Zionismus', in id. (ed.), *Arnold Zweig*, pp. 181–93.

Zweig's novel is carefully structured. The murder of de Vriendt occurs exactly halfway through, in the central chapter of the central section. Until then, the community of settlers in Palestine is not presented directly. Instead we have a series of conspiratorial conversations among small groups: Irmin and his police assistants; Irmin and other administrators at their club; de Vriendt and his ultra-orthodox associates; the young Zionist immigrants; and the Arab leaders who are plotting the disturbances. The latter are presented in a particularly bad light, as landowners who pay no taxes, exploit their labourers, fear that the higher wages earned by Jews will cause discontent among their own workers, and wish to foment unrest which they can then blame on the Zionists. To portray the Arabs, Zweig employs the literary technique which in Chapter 3 I called eavesdropping: he admits us to the private deliberations of people who, it is assumed, lie to the outside world but tell the truth to each other. In nineteenth-century realism, the eavesdropping technique, applied to Jews, expressed the assumption that they were liars who only told the truth to each other. Here Zweig, a Jewish novelist, applies it to Arabs. To be fair, however, the difference between Zweig's Arabs and his other characters is only one of degree, for in the first half of the novel all the groups described are busy with plotting and counter-plotting.

De Vriendt himself cannot tell the whole truth to anyone, for he is a deeply divided character. He can neither resist nor accept his homosexuality, nor can he understand why God should have given him such an affliction. His extreme piety masks an inner scepticism which finds expression only in his secret poems. Each facet of de Vriendt uses a different language. With his ultra-orthodox associates he converses in Yiddish and prays in liturgical Hebrew. His poems are written in Dutch, his mother's language and that of his most intimate feelings. He talks with his lover Saûd in Arabic, a foreign language which reveals his estrangement from his own sensuality, and with Irmin in English, the language of administration. The language he will not use is modern Hebrew, for he regards it as profane, just as he considers Zionism an impious attempt to anticipate the coming of the Messiah.

The linguistic divisions within de Vriendt correspond to the divisions within the Zionist community which become apparent in the second half of the novel. The settlers are diverse in origins and outlook; only the use of Hebrew, the language de Vriendt rejects, will weld the next generation into a single nation:

The difference between German, Austrian, Russian, British Jews could be felt even in Jerusalem and lasted till the grave; and what alien character might be expected to separate the Nordic from the Oriental Jews? Had it not been for the children, the future would have looked worrying. They, however, were growing together in the streets to form a Hebrew-speaking horde, irrespective of ranks, classes, origins, and occupations; they were weaving a net of similar outlooks, similar ideals, similar defiance and similar talent throughout the country and ensuring the nation's survival for ages to come.[335]

These reflections are ascribed to Dr Heinrich Klopfer, a German Jew who teaches philosophy at the Hebrew University and whose phlegmatic, thoughtful nature is contrasted with the fiery temperament of his friend the engineer Eli Saamen, a Russian Jew who has been inured to violence ever since, in his teens, he killed a pogromist who had just murdered his father.[336] When the riots break out, Klopfer, Saamen, and the rest of the Zionist community are united in self-defence. Zweig tells us that while 130 Jews are killed, mostly defenceless old people, at least 116 Arabs are killed, almost all fighting—that is, the Jews are braver and more honourable fighters (p. 233). Their antagonists expected the Jews to offer no resistance, but Jews have changed: 'They stand up very straight, they hit back, and their blows leave a mark' (p. 240).[337]

The friendship between Klopfer and Saamen is evidently meant to foreshadow the future of the Jewish people. The bookish, reflective German Jew combines with the practical, insouciant Russian Jew to form a new type. Instead of the timid, passive Jew of the Diaspora ghetto, we have now the active, combative Jew

---

[335] Zweig, *De Vriendt kehrt heim* (Berlin, 1932), p. 203. Future references in text.

[336] Heinrich Klopfer appeared already as an immigrant to Palestine, descended from a line of Polish-German Jews, in *Aufzeichnungen über eine Familie Klopfer*; but there he was a decadent figure, resolved not to perpetuate his family because he loved only his sister and because he knew he had only five years to live before succumbing to dementia.

[337] By implication, Zweig enormously exaggerates the effectiveness of Jewish self-defence. The 116 Arabs were killed by the British troops and police without whom the Jews would have been virtually helpless. See Roger Friedland and Richard D. Hecht, 'Divisions at the Center: The Organization of Political Violence at Jerusalem's Temple Mount/*al-haram al sharif*—1929 and 1990', in Paul R. Brass (ed.), *Riots and Pogroms* (London, 1996), pp. 114–53.

who stands up to his enemies. Here, no doubt, Zweig has identified a real historical change, and one that had to happen if the
Jewish community in Palestine, later Israel, was to survive in
hostile surroundings. But Zweig is too good a novelist to write
propaganda, even if he wants to. His forecast is disturbing as well
as triumphant. The link between Klopfer and Saamen typifies the
male bonding which in the Germany of the 1920s was widely seen
as a social cement equally important to, and sometimes more
valuable than, that of the family. An elite of closely linked men
was thought uniquely qualified to lead a mass movement.[338]
Despite Zweig's commitment to democracy, there are hints in
De Vriendt kehrt heim of this male social model, especially
when Irmin adopts the role of an older male educator towards
young men: he breaks the news of de Vriendt's death to the boy
Saûd, whose courageous response shows 'that he had in him the
stuff of which real men were made', and since the young murderer,
Mendel Glass, cannot be brought to justice for lack of evidence,
Irmin inflicts a private punishment by making him jump out of a
boat on the Dead Sea and swim to the shore (pp. 185, 332).
Moreover, the novel contains only one female character, Judith
Kawa, who is having an affair with Saamen while her husband is
in London. However attractive she may be, she comes across as a
frivolous person without commitments of her own (and no
family), who lives only for the convenience of men. Rather than
German ideals of *Bildung*, Zweig transfers German ideals of
military masculinity to Palestine and presents them as the safeguard of the nation's future (failing to foresee the role of women in
the Israeli army).

In presenting us with a new kind of Jew, the ultra-masculine
fighting Jew, Zweig discloses explicit misgivings. Saamen is quite
confident: discussing with Klopfer how the Jews are to become
one people, he opines that political violence, however undesirable,
is needed to found the nation. But while Saamen recalls how
Moses killed the Egyptian (Exod. 2:12), Klopfer thinks with
alarm of the fratricidal pairs Cain and Abel and Romulus and
Remus. 'Whenever a state is founded, it begins with fratricide', he
reflects (p. 206). The reference to fratricide indirectly recalls de
Vriendt's murder by another Jew, and the mention of Romulus, the

---

[338] See Widdig, *Männerbünde und Massen*.

founder of Rome, hints that the future Jewish polity may develop into yet another world empire resting on naked power, a suspicion strengthened by Saamen's advocacy of power without scruples as the only basis for the Jews' future in Palestine. Instead of the ethical, supra-historical perspective of Posnanski in *Grischa*, the Jews in *De Vriendt* are plunging back into history and preparing to commit the mistakes of previous states.

While the Zionists' self-defence is presented in the perspective of the future as a crucial episode in the forging of a people, the Arabs' riots are described not as an episode in Palestinian nationalism but as a familiar expression of antisemitism, a Russian-style pogrom: 'Instead of a national uprising, an attack on the possessing classes by the dispossessed, a rebellion against the mandatory power, it is a simple pogrom, familiar from Jewish history; but this time it takes a different course from before: the victims, these Jews, have changed completely' (p. 240). One could object that pogroms tend to be sudden outbursts of violence, whereas Zweig himself represents the riots as carefully planned (much more so than would seem to have been the case in reality).[339] But hindsight permits a more serious objection: Zweig's novel places the 1929 disturbances in the context of a Jewish history with a long past and an ambivalent future; but by explaining the Arabs' actions as just another pogrom, it takes them out of history and makes them into a mechanical expression of timeless antisemitism. By attributing the riots to a mere conspiracy by landowners, it rejects Arab nationalism as a meaningful context in which to explain them. It denies the Arabs any history of their own. Even later, in an essay written after Zweig's move to Palestine and during the much more serious Arab uprising of 1936–9, Zweig compared the Arabs to people living in a dilapidated house who might understandably resent uninvited strangers moving in, even if the strangers tidied up the house and improved the sanitation.[340] He still did not treat the Arabs' hostility as the expression of a political force.

Zweig's outlook was shared by many people in the Zionist labour movement, notably its 'spiritual leader' Berl Katznelson,

[339] See Bernard Wasserstein, 'Patterns of Communal Conflict in Palestine', in ed. Reinharz and Shapira, *Essential Papers on Zionism*, pp. 671–88.

[340] Zweig, 'Das Skelett der Palästina-Situation' (1938), in his *Jüdischer Ausdruckswille* (Berlin, 1991), pp. 143–58 (p. 157).

who refused to recognize Arab resistance as a national move-ment.[341] David Ben-Gurion, on the other hand, recognized the political and national character of Arab resistance and argued that the Jews could only counter it by forming a clear majority in Palestine. In a wider perspective, the disagreement between Katznelson and Ben-Gurion might be seen as typifying the conflict between two understandings of 'the Jewish return into history': the prophetic and the pragmatic. The Jews might be seen as having a special mission to re-establish themselves in their ancestral homeland, just as previous generations had credited them with a special relationship to God, or, in the diluted version widespread among German Jews in the age of emancipation, with a special ethical mission. Alternatively, their return into history might be seen as making them one nation among many, obliged to hold their own by the same methods of diplomacy, compromise, and occasional violence as their neighbours. Just as Zweig's earlier novel, *Grischa*, set the Jews' restoration to Palestine within a history of rising and declining empires, so his *De Vriendt kehrt heim* adumbrates the political and moral dilemmas that would arise from the Jews' homecoming.

[341] Gorny, *Zionism and the Arabs*, pp. 218–20; Boas Evron, *Jewish State or Israeli Nation?* (Bloomington and Indianapolis, 1995), pp. 146–7.

Select Bibliography

PRIMARY

ALSBERG, MORITZ, *Rassenmischung im Judenthum* (Hamburg, 1891).

ANDREE, RICHARD, *Zur Volkskunde der Juden* (Bielefeld and Leipzig, 1881).

Antisemiten-Spiegel: Die Antisemiten im Lichte des Christenthums, des Rechtes und der Wissenschaft, 2nd edn. (Danzig, 1900).

AUERBACH, BERTHOLD, *Gesammelte Schriften*, 20 vols. (Stuttgart and Augsburg, 1858).

BAHR, HERMANN, *Die Rotte Korahs* (Berlin, 1919).

BARTELS, ADOLF, *Heinrich Heine: Auch ein Denkmal* (Dresden and Leipzig, 1906).

BARTSCH, RUDOLF HANS, *Seine Jüdin* (Leipzig, 1921).

BEER-HOFMANN, RICHARD, *Gesammelte Werke* (Frankfurt, 1963).

BENDAVID, LAZARUS, *Etwas zur Charackteristick der Juden* (Leipzig, 1793).

—— 'Selbstbiographie', *Bildnisse jetzt lebender Berliner Gelehrten mit ihren Selbstbiographien* (Berlin, 1806).

BENJAMIN, WALTER, *Briefe*, ed. Gershom Scholem and Theodor W. Adorno, 2 vols. (Frankfurt, 1966).

—— *Gesammelte Schriften*, ed. Rolf Tiedemann and Hermann Schweppenhauser, 7 vols. (Frankfurt, 1972–89).

BERGMAN, SCHMUEL HUGO, *Tagebücher und Briefe*, ed. Miriam Sambursky, 2 vols. (Königstein, 1985).

BIRNBAUM, NATHAN, *Die jüdische Moderne: Frühe zionistische Schriften* (Augsburg, 1989).

[BLACH, FRIEDRICH], *Die Juden in Deutschland. Von einem jüdischen Deutschen* (Berlin, 1911).

BLÜHER, HANS, *Secessio Judaica. Philosophische Grundlegung der historischen Situation des Judentums und der antisemitischen Bewegung* (Berlin, 1922).

—— *Die Rolle der Erotik in der männlichen Gesellschaft. Eine Theorie der menschlichen Staatsbildung nach Wesen und Wert*, ed. Hans Joachim Schoeps (Stuttgart, 1962).

BLUMENFELD, KURT, *Erlebte Judenfrage: Ein Vierteljahrhundert deutscher Zionismus* (Stuttgart, 1962).

BOEHLICH, WALTER (ed.), *Der Berliner Antisemitismusstreit* (Frankfurt, 1965).

Börne, Ludwig, *Sämtliche Schriften*, ed. Peter and Inge Rippmann, 5 vols. (Dreieich, 1977).

Braunthal, Julius, *In Search of the Millennium* (London, 1945).

Brod, Max, *Heinrich Heine* (Amsterdam, 1935).

—— *Streitbares Leben: Autobiographie* (Munich, 1960).

—— and Kafka, Franz, *Eine Freundschaft*, ii: *Briefwechsel*, ed. Malcolm Pasley (Frankfurt, 1989).

Brunner, Constantin, *Der Judenhaß und die Juden* (Berlin, 1918).

Buber, Martin, *Vom Geist des Judentums: Reden und Geleitworte* (Leipzig, 1916).

—— 'Mein Weg zum Chassidismus' (1917), in *Werke*, 3 vols. (Munich and Heidelberg, 1962–4), vol. iii.

—— *Die jüdische Bewegung: Gesammelte Aufsätze und Ansprachen*, 2 vols. (Berlin, 1920).

—— *Briefwechsel aus sieben Jahrzehnten*, ed. Grete Schaeder, 3 vols. (Heidelberg, 1972–5).

Canetti, Elias, *Die Blendung* ([1935] Munich, 1963).

—— *Auto da Fé*, tr. C. V. Wedgwood (London, 1946).

—— *Die gerettete Zunge: Geschichte einer Jugend* (Munich, 1977).

Chamberlain, Houston Stewart, *Die Grundlagen des neunzehnten Jahrhunderts* (Munich, 1899).

—— *The Foundations of the Nineteenth Century*, tr. John Lees, 2 vols. (London, 1911).

Cohen, Hermann, *Jüdische Schriften*, 3 vols. (Berlin, 1924).

Coudenhove-Kalergi, Heinrich Graf, *Das Wesen des Antisemitismus*, reissued with preface by R. N. Coudenhove-Kalergi (Leipzig and Vienna, 1932).

Darwin, Charles, *The Descent of Man, and Selection in Relation to Sex*, 2 vols. (London, 1871; repr. Princeton, 1981).

Deniker, J., *The Races of Man: An Outline of Anthropology and Ethnography* (London, 1900).

Der Jud ist schuld . . . ? Diskussionsbuch über die Judenfrage (Basle, 1932).

Dessauer, Adolf, *Großstadtjuden* (Vienna and Leipzig, 1910).

Dinter, Artur, *Die Sünde wider das Blut. Ein Zeitroman* (Leipzig, 1921).

Döblin, Alfred, *Schriften zur Politik und Gesellschaft* (Olten and Freiburg, 1972).

Dohm, Christian Wilhelm von, *Über die bürgerliche Verbesserung der Juden* (Berlin and Stettin, 1781).

Dühring, E., *Die Judenfrage als Racen-, Sitten- und Culturfrage. Mit einer weltgeschichtlichen Antwort*, 2nd edn. (Karlsruhe and Leipzig, 1881).

FEUCHTWANGER, LION, *Jud Süß* ([1925] Frankfurt, 1976).

—— *Erfolg* ([1930] Frankfurt, 1975).

—— *Ein Buch nur für meine Freunde* ([1956] Frankfurt, 1984).

FISCHER, ERNST, *An Opposing Man*, tr. Peter and Betty Ross (London, 1974).

FISHBERG, MAURICE, *The Jews: A Study of Race and Environment* (London, 1911).

FONTANE, THEODOR, *Briefe an Georg Friedländer*, ed. Kurt Schreinert (Heidelberg, 1954).

—— *Romane, Erzählungen, Gedichte*, ed. Walter Keitel, 6 vols. (Munich, 1962).

FRANZOS, KARL EMIL, *Der Pojaz* (Königstein, 1979).

FREUD, MARTIN, *Glory Reflected: Sigmund Freud—Man and Father* (London, 1957).

FREUD, SIGMUND, *The Standard Edition of the Complete Psychological Works of Sigmund Freud*, ed. James Strachey, 24 vols. (London, 1953–74).

—— *Letters 1873–1939*, ed. Ernst L. Freud (London, 1961).

—— *A Psycho-Analytic Dialogue: The Letters of Sigmund Freud and Karl Abraham, 1907–1926*, ed. Hilda C. Abraham and Ernst L. Freud, tr. Bernard Marsh and Hilda C. Abraham (London, 1965).

—— *The Letters of Sigmund Freud and Arnold Zweig*, ed. Ernst L. Freud, tr. W. and E. Robson-Scott (London, 1970).

—— *The Freud/Jung Letters: The Correspondence between Sigmund Freud and C. G. Jung*, ed. William McGuire, tr. Ralph Manheim and R. F. C. Hull (London, 1974).

—— *The Complete Letters of Sigmund Freud to Wilhelm Fliess, 1887–1904*, tr. and ed. J. M. Masson (Cambridge, Mass., and London, 1985).

—— *Jugendbriefe an Eduard Silberstein 1871–1881*, ed. Walter Boehlich (Frankfurt, 1989).

[FRIEDLÄNDER, DAVID], *Sendschreiben an Seine Hochwürden, Herrn Oberconsistorialrath und Probst Teller zu Berlin, von einigen Hausvätern jüdischer Religion* (Berlin, 1799).

GEIGER, LUDWIG, *Geschichte der Juden in Berlin*, 2 vols. (Berlin, 1871).

GEORGE, STEFAN, *Werke*, 2 vols. (Düsseldorf and Munich, 1958).

—— and GUNDOLF, FRIEDRICH, *Briefwechsel*, ed. Robert Boehringer and Georg Peter Landmann (Munich and Düsseldorf, 1962).

The Life of Glückel of Hameln, written by herself, tr. and ed. Beth-Zion Abrahams (London, 1962).

GOEBBELS, JOSEPH, *Michael: Ein deutsches Schicksal in Tagebuchblättern* ([1929] Munich, n.d.).

GOETHE, JOHANN WOLFGANG, *Werke*, Hamburger Ausgabe, ed. Erich Trunz, 14 vols. (Hamburg, 1949–60).

—— *Sämtliche Werke: Briefe, Tagebücher und Gespräche*, Deutsche Klassiker-Ausgabe, 40 vols. (Frankfurt, 1986–).

GOLDBERG, OSKAR, *Die Wirklichkeit der Hebräer* (Berlin, 1925).

GOLDSTEIN, MORITZ, 'Deutsch-jüdischer Parnaß', *Der Kunstwart*, 25/ii (Jan.-Mar. 1912), 281–94.

—— 'German Jewry's Dilemma before 1914: The Story of a Provocative Essay', *LBY* 2 (1957), 236–54.

GORDON, A. D., *Erlösung durch Arbeit: Ausgewählte Aufsätze*, tr. Viktor Kellner (Berlin, 1929).

GOSLAR, HANS, *Die Sexualethik der jüdischen Wiedergeburt: Ein Wort an unsere Jugend* (Berlin, 1919).

GRAETZ, H., *History of the Jews, from the Earliest Times to the Present Day*, ed. and tr. Bella Löwy, 5 vols. (London, 1891–2).

GRÉGOIRE, *Essai sur la régénération physique, morale et politique des juifs* (Metz, 1789; facsimile reprint, Paris, 1968).

'HARTENAU, W.' (WALTER RATHENAU), 'Höre, Israel!', *Die Zukunft*, 18 (6 Mar. 1897), 454–62.

HEIMANN, MORITZ, *Was ist das: ein Gedanke? Essays*, ed. Gert Mattenklott (Frankfurt, 1986).

HEINE, HEINRICH, *Sämtliche Schriften*, ed. Klaus Briegleb, 6 vols. (Munich, 1968–76).

—— *The Complete Poems of Heinrich Heine*, tr. Hal Draper (Oxford, 1982).

—— *Selected Prose*, tr. Ritchie Robertson (London, 1993).

HENSEL, SEBASTIAN, *Die Familie Mendelssohn 1729–1847*, ed. Konrad Feilchenfeldt (Frankfurt, 1995).

HERDER, JOHANN GOTTFRIED, *Sämmtliche Werke*, ed. Bernhard Suphan, 33 vols. (Berlin, 1877–1913).

—— *Werke*, ed. Günter Arnold et al., 10 vols. (Frankfurt, 1985–).

HERMANN, GEORG, *Jettchen Gebert*, Volksausgabe (Berlin, 1932).

HERZL, THEODOR, *Gesammelte zionistische Werke*, 5 vols. (Tel Aviv, 1934–5).

—— *Briefe und Tagebücher*, ed. Alex Bein et al., 7 vols. (Berlin, Frankfurt, Vienna, 1983–96).

HESS, MOSES, *The Revival of Israel: Rome and Jerusalem, the Last Nationalist Question*, tr. Meyer Waxman (Lincoln, NB, and London, 1995).

HITLER, ADOLF, *Mein Kampf* (Munich, 1943).

HUMBOLDT, WILHELM VON, 'Über den Entwurf zu einer neuen Konstitution für die Juden', in his *Werke*, ed. Andreas Flitner and Klaus Giel, 5 vols. (Darmstadt, 1964), iv. 95–112.

HUSSERL, EDMUND, *Briefwechsel*, ed. Karl Schuhmann, 10 vols. (Dordrecht, 1994).

JACOBOWSKI, LUDWIG, *Werther, der Jude* ([1892] Berlin, 1898).

JUDT, J. M., *Die Juden als Rasse: Eine Analyse aus dem Gebiete der Anthropologie* (Berlin, n.d. [1903?]).

'JUNIUS', *Das Judenthum und die Tagespresse: Ein Mahnwort in ernster Stunde* (Leipzig, 1879).

KAFKA, FRANZ, *Briefe an Milena*, ed. Jürgen Born and Michael Müller (Frankfurt, 1983).

—— *Tagebücher*, ed. Hans-Gerd Koch, Michael Müller, and Malcolm Pasley (Frankfurt, 1990).

KAHN, FRITZ, *Die Juden als Rasse und Kulturvolk*, 3rd edn. (Berlin, 1922).

KANT, IMMANUEL, *Werke*, ed. Wilhelm Weischedel, 6 vols. (Frankfurt, 1964).

—— 'An Answer to the Question: What is Enlightenment?', in *Political Writings*, ed. Hans Reiss, tr. H. B. Nisbet, 2nd edn. (Cambridge, 1991), pp. 54–60.

KATZ, H. W., *Die Fischmanns* ([1938] Weinheim, 1994).

KAYSERLING, M., *Moses Mendelssohn: Sein Leben und seine Werke* (Leipzig, 1862).

KITTEL, GERHARD, *Die Judenfrage* (Stuttgart, 1933).

KLEMPERER, VICTOR, *Ich will Zeugnis ablegen bis zum letzten. Tagebücher 1933–1941, 1942–1945*, ed. Walter Nowojski, 2 vols. (Berlin, 1995).

—— *Leben sammeln, nicht fragen wozu und warum. Tagebücher 1918–1932*, ed. Walter Nowojski, 2 vols. (Berlin, 1996).

KLÜGER, RUTH, *weiter leben: Eine Jugend* (Göttingen, 1992).

KOESTLER, ARTHUR, *Arrow in the Blue: An Autobiography* (London, 1952).

KOMPERT, LEOPOLD, *Gesammelte Schriften*, 8 vols. (Berlin, 1882).

KRAUS, KARL, *Frühe Schriften 1892–1900*, ed. J. J. Braakenburg, 2 vols. (Munich, 1979).

—— *Schriften*, ed. Christian Wagenknecht, 20 vols. (Frankfurt, 1989–94).

KUH, ANTON, *Juden und Deutsche* (Berlin, 1921).

LANDMANN, EDITH, *Gespräche mit Stefan George* (Düsseldorf and Munich, 1962).

[LANGBEHN, JULIUS], *Rembrandt als Erzieher. Von einem Deutschen*, Illustrierte Volksausgabe (Weimar, 1922).

LANGER, JIŘÍ, *Nine Gates*, tr. Stephen Jolly (London, 1961).

LASKER-SCHÜLER, ELSE, *Prosa und Schauspiele*, ed. Friedhelm Kemp (Munich, 1962).

—— *Lieber gestreifter Tiger: Briefe von Else Lasker-Schüler*, ed. Margarete Kupper, vol. i (Munich, 1969).

LASKER-SCHÜLER, *Your Diamond Dreams Cut Open My Arteries: Poems by Else Lasker-Schüler*, tr. Robert P. Newton (Chapel Hill, NC, 1982).
—— *Gedichte*, ed. Karl Jürgen Skrodzki, 2 vols. (Frankfurt, 1996).
LAZARUS, MORITZ, AND STEINTHAL, HEYMANN: *Die Begründer der Völkerpsychologie in ihren Briefen*, ed. Ingrid Belke (Tübingen, 1971).
LESSING, GOTTHOLD EPHRAIM, *Lessing's Theological Writings*, ed. Henry Chadwick (London, 1956).
—— *Werke*, ed. Herbert G. Göpfert *et al.*, 8 vols. (Munich, 1970–9).
Lessing-Mendelssohn-Gedenkbuch. Zur hundertfünfzigjährigen Geburtsfeier von Gotthold Ephraim Lessing und Moses Mendelssohn, sowie zur Säcularfeier von Lessing's 'Nathan', herausgegeben vom Deutsch-Israelitischen Gemeindebunde (Leipzig, 1879).
LESSING, THEODOR, *Europa und Asien oder Der Mensch und das Wandellose*, 2nd edn. (Hanover, 1923).
—— *Der jüdische Selbsthaß* ([1930] Munich, 1984).
—— *Einmal und nie wieder* ([1935] Gütersloh, 1969).
LEVITA, BENEDICTUS [pseudonym for Adolf Weissler], 'Die Erlösung des Judenthums', *Preußische Jahrbücher*, 102 (Oct. 1900), 131–40.
LEWALD, FANNY, *Meine Lebensgeschichte*, ed. Gisela Brinker-Gabler (Frankfurt, 1980).
—— *Jenny*, ed. Ulrike Helmer (Frankfurt, 1988).
LOEWENBERG, JAKOB, *Aus zwei Quellen: Geschichte eines deutschen Juden* ([1914] Paderborn, 1993).
MAIMON, SALOMON, *Lebensgeschichte*, ed. Jakob Fromer (Munich, 1911).
MAIMONIDES, MOSES, *The Guide for the Perplexed*, tr. M. Friedländer (New York, 1956).
MANN, THOMAS, *Gesammelte Werke*, 13 vols. (Frankfurt, 1974).
—— *Tagebücher 1933–1934*, ed. Peter de Mendelssohn (Frankfurt, 1977).
—— *Tagebücher 1918–1921*, ed. Peter de Mendelssohn (Frankfurt, 1979).
—— and MANN, HEINRICH, *Briefwechsel 1900–1949*, ed. Hans Wysling (Frankfurt, 1984).
MARHOLM, LAURA, *Karla Bühring: Ein Frauendrama in vier Acten* (Munich, 1895).
MARR, W., *Der Sieg des Judenthums über das Germanenthum. Vom nicht confessionellen Standpunkt aus betrachtet* (Berne, 1879).
MAUTHNER, FRITZ, *Prager Jugendjahre* ([1918] Frankfurt, 1969).
MAYER, MAX, 'A German Jew goes East', *LBY* 3 (1958), 344–57.
MENDELSSOHN, MOSES, *Gesammelte Schriften*, vii: *Schriften zum Judentum I*, ed. Simon Rawidowicz (Berlin, 1930).
—— *Jerusalem, or On Religious Power and Judaism*, tr. Allan Arkush (Hanover, NH, and London, 1983).

MOMMSEN, THEODOR, *Römische Geschichte*, iii. *Von Sullas Tode bis zur Schlacht von Thapsus*, 10th edn. (Berlin, 1909).

MORITZ, KARL PHILIPP, *Werke*, ed. Horst Günther, 3 vols. (Frankfurt, 1981).

NATONEK, HANS, *Kinder einer Stadt* ([1932] Vienna and Hamburg, 1987).

NIETZSCHE, FRIEDRICH, *Werke*, ed. Giorgio Colli and Mazzino Montinari, (Berlin and New York, 1972–).

—— *Briefwechsel*, ed. Giorgio Colli and Mazzino Montinari, 3 divisions (Berlin and New York, 1975–84).

NORDAU, MAX, *Zionistische Schriften* (Cologne and Leipzig, 1909).

OPPELN-BRONIKOWSKI, FRIEDRICH VON, *Antisemitismus? Eine unparteiische Prüfung des Problems* (Charlottenburg, 1920).

—— *Gerechtigkeit! Zur Lösung der Judenfrage* (Berlin-Wilmersdorf, 1932).

OPPENHEIMER, FRANZ, *Erlebtes, Erstrebtes, Erreichtes: Lebenserinnerungen* (Düsseldorf, 1964).

PAPPENHEIM, BERTHA, *Sisyphus: Gegen den Mädchenhandel*, ed. Helga Heubach (Freiburg, 1992).

PASMANIK, DANIEL, *Die Seele Israels: Zur Psychologie des Diaspora-judentums* (Cologne and Leipzig, 1911).

PRINZ, JOACHIM, *Wir Juden* (Berlin, 1934).

RAABE, WILHELM, *Sämtliche Werke*, ed. Karl Hoppe *et al.*, 20 vols. (Göttingen, 1960–).

REINHARZ, JEHUDA (ed.), *Dokumente zur Geschichte des deutschen Zionismus 1882–1933* (Tübingen, 1981).

RIESSER, GABRIEL, *Gesammelte Schriften*, ed. M. Isler, 4 vols. (Frankfurt and Leipzig, 1867–8).

ROTH, JOSEPH, *Briefe*, ed. Hermann Kesten (Cologne, 1970).

—— *Werke*, ed. Klaus Westermann and Fritz Hackert, 6 vols. (Cologne, 1989–91).

RUPPIN, ARTHUR, *Briefe, Tagebücher, Erinnerungen*, ed. Schlomo Krolik (Königstein, 1985).

SAAR, FERDINAND VON, *Seligmann Hirsch*, ed. Detlef Haberland (Tübingen, 1987).

SCHILLER, FRIEDRICH, *Sämtliche Werke*, ed. Gerhard Fricke and Herbert G. Göpfert, 5 vols. (Munich, 1958).

SCHNITZLER, ARTHUR, *Die Erzählenden Schriften*, 2 vols. (Frankfurt, 1961).

—— *Die Dramatischen Werke*, 2 vols. (Frankfurt, 1962).

—— *Aphorismen und Betrachtungen*, ed. Robert O. Weiss (Frankfurt, 1967).

—— *Jugend in Wien*, ed. Therese Nickl and Heinrich Schnitzler (Vienna, 1968).

SCHNITZLER, ARTHUR, *My Youth in Vienna*, tr. Catherine Hutter (London, 1971).

—— *Briefe 1875–1912*, ed. Therese Nickl and Heinrich Schnitzler (Frankfurt, 1981).

—— *Briefe 1913–1931*, ed. Peter Michael Braunwarth *et al.* (Frankfurt, 1984).

—— *Tagebuch* (Vienna, 1981–).

SCHOLEM, GERSHOM, *Walter Benjamin: Die Geschichte einer Freundschaft* (Frankfurt, 1975).

—— *Briefe 1914–1947*, ed. Itta Shedletzky (Munich, 1994).

—— *Tagebücher 1913–1917*, ed. Karlfried Gründer and Friedrich Niewöhner (Frankfurt, 1995).

—— *Von Berlin nach Jerusalem: Jugenderinnerungen*, enlarged edn., tr. Michael Brocke and Andrea Schatz (Frankfurt, 1997).

[SESSA, KARL BORROMÄUS ALEXANDER], *Unser Verkehr: Eine Posse in einem Akt*, in *Deutsche Schaubühne; oder dramatische Bibliothek der neuesten Lust- Schau- Sing- und Trauerspiele*, vol. xxx (Augsburg and Leipzig, n.d. [1815?]).

SOMBART, WERNER, *The Jews and Modern Capitalism*, tr. M. Epstein (London, 1913).

SPINOZA, BENEDICT DE, *A Theologico-Political Treatise; A Political Treatise*, tr. R. H. M. Elwes (New York, 1951).

STAPEL, WILHELM, *Antisemitismus und Antigermanismus: Über das seelische Problem der Symbiose des deutschen und des jüdischen Volkes* (Hamburg, 1928).

STAUFF, PHILIPP (ed.), *Semi-Kürschner oder Literarisches Lexikon der Schriftsteller, Dichter, Bankiers, Geldleute, Ärzte, Schauspieler, Künstler, Musiker, Offiziere, Rechtsanwälte, Revolutionäre, Frauenrechtlerinnen, Sozialdemokraten usw., jüdischer Rasse und Versippung, die von 1813–1913 in Deutschland tätig oder bekannt waren* (Berlin, 1913).

STRATZ, C. H., *Was sind Juden? Eine ethnographisch-anthropologische Studie* (Vienna and Leipzig, 1903).

SUSMAN, MARGARETE, *Ich habe viele Leben gelebt: Erinnerungen* (Stuttgart, 1964).

TINDAL, MATTHEW, *Christianity as Old as the Creation* (London, 1730; repr. New York and London, 1978).

TOLLER, ERNST, *Prosa, Briefe, Dramen, Gedichte* (Reinbek, 1979).

TREBITSCH, ARTHUR, *Geist und Judentum: Eine grundlegende Untersuchung* (Vienna and Leipzig, 1919).

TREITSCHKE, HEINRICH VON, *Deutsche Geschichte im neunzehnten Jahrhundert*, 5 vols. (Leipzig, 1879–94).

—— 'Unsere Aussichten', *Preußische Jahrbücher*, 44 (Nov. 1879), 559–76.

TUCHOLSKY, KURT, *Gesammelte Werke*, ed. Mary Gerold-Tucholsky and Fritz J. Raddatz, 3 vols. (Reinbek, 1960).

VARNHAGEN, RAHEL, *Briefwechsel*, ed. Friedhelm Kemp, 4 vols. (Munich, 1966–7).

WAGNER, COSIMA, *Diaries*, ed. Martin Gregor-Dellin and Dietrich Mack, tr. Geoffrey Skelton, 2 vols. (London, 1978–80).

WAGNER, RICHARD, 'Das Judenthum in der Musik', in *Gesammelte Schriften und Dichtungen* (Leipzig, 1887; repr. Hildesheim, 1976), v. 66–85.

—— *Judaism in Music and Other Essays*, tr. W. A. Ellis (Lincoln, Nebr., and London, 1995).

WASSERMANN, JAKOB, *Der Fall Maurizius* ([1928] Munich, 1988).

—— *Deutscher und Jude: Reden und Schriften 1904–1933*, ed. Dierk Rodewald (Heidelberg, 1984).

WEININGER, OTTO, *Geschlecht und Charakter* ([1903] Munich, 1980).

WOLF, FRIEDRICH, *Professor Mamlock* (1934), in *Gesammelte Werke*, ed. Else Wolf and Walter Pollatschek, 13 vols. (Berlin, 1960), iii. 295–365.

WOLFSKEHL, KARL, *Gesammelte Werke*, ed. Margot Ruben and Claus Victor Bock, 2 vols. (Hamburg, 1960).

—— and WOLFSKEHL, HANNA, *Briefwechsel mit Friedrich Gundolf, 1899–1931*, ed. Karlhans Kluncker, *Castrum Peregrini*, 123–5 (1976), 126–8 (1977).

YORK-STEINER, HEINRICH, *Die Kunst als Jude zu leben* (Leipzig, 1928).

ZAPP, ARTHUR, *Das neue Ghetto: Ein Roman aus der Zeit* (Berlin-Nowawes, n.d. [1922?]).

ZOLLSCHAN, IGNAZ, *Das Rassenproblem unter besonderer Berücksichtigung der theoretischen Grundlagen der jüdischen Rassenfrage* (Vienna and Leipzig, 1910).

Leopold and Adelheid Zunz: An Account in Letters 1815–1885, ed. Nahum N. Glatzer (London, 1958).

ZWEIG, ARNOLD, *Aufzeichnungen über eine Familie Klopfer* (Munich, 1911).

—— *Caliban oder Politik und Leidenschaft* (Potsdam, 1927).

—— *Der Streit um den Sergeanten Grischa* (Potsdam, 1927).

—— *Herkunft und Zukunft: Zwei Essays zum Schicksal eines Volkes* (Vienna, 1929).

—— *De Vriendt kehrt heim* (Berlin, 1932).

—— *Bilanz der deutschen Judenheit: Ein Versuch* ([1934] Leipzig, 1991).

ZWEIG, STEFAN, *The World of Yesterday* (London, 1943).

—— *Die Dramen*, ed. Richard Friedenthal (Frankfurt, 1964).

—— *Novellen*, 2 vols. (Berlin and Weimar, 1980).

—— *Tagebücher*, ed. Knut Beck (Frankfurt, 1984).

Secondary

ALBRIGHT, WILLIAM FOXWELL, *History, Archaeology and Christian Humanism* (London, 1965).

ALTMANN, ALEXANDER, *Moses Mendelssohn: A Biographical Study* (London, 1973).

ANDERSON, MARK M., '"Jewish" Mimesis? Imitation and Assimilation in Thomas Mann's "Wälsungenblut" and Ludwig Jacobowski's *Werther, der Jude'*, GLL 49 (1996), 193–204.

ASCHHEIM, STEVEN E., *Brothers and Strangers: The East European Jew in German and German Jewish Consciousness, 1800–1923* (Madison, 1982).

AVINERI, SHLOMO, *The Making of Modern Zionism: The Intellectual Origins of the Jewish State* (London, 1981).

BARNER, WILFRIED, *Von Rahel Varnhagen bis Friedrich Gundolf: Juden als deutsche Goethe-Verehrer* (Göttingen, 1992).

BAUMAN, ZYGMUNT, *Modernity and the Holocaust* (Cambridge, 1989).

BAUSCHINGER, SIGRID, *Else Lasker-Schüler: Ihr Werk und ihre Zeit* (Heidelberg, 1980).

BELLER, STEVEN, *Vienna and the Jews, 1867–1938: A Cultural History* (Cambridge, 1989).

BERING, DIETZ, *Der Name als Stigma: Antisemitismus im deutschen Alltag, 1812–1933* (Stuttgart, 1987).

BERKOWITZ, MICHAEL, *Zionist Culture and West European Jewry before the First World War* (Cambridge, 1993).

BIALE, DAVID, *Gershom Scholem: Kabbalah and Counter-History* (Cambridge, Mass., 1979).

BOA, ELIZABETH, *Kafka: Gender, Class, and Race in the Letters and Fictions* (Oxford, 1996).

BOTSTEIN, LEON, 'Stefan Zweig and the Illusion of the Jewish European', in Marion Sonnenfeld (ed.), *Stefan Zweig: The World of Yesterday's Humanist Today* (Albany, NY, 1983), pp. 82–110.

BRAMSTED, ERNEST K., *Aristocracy and the Middle-Classes in Germany: Social Types in German Literature 1830–1900*, 2nd edn. (Chicago, 1964).

BRAUNGART, WOLFGANG, *Ästhetischer Katholizismus: Stefan Georges Rituale der Literatur* (Tübingen, 1997).

BRENNER, MICHAEL, *The Renaissance of Jewish Culture in Weimar Germany* (New Haven and London, 1996).

BREUER, MORDECHAI, *Jüdische Orthodoxie im Deutschen Reich 1871–1918: Sozialgeschichte einer religiösen Minderheit* (Frankfurt, 1986).

BRODER, HENRYK M., *Der ewige Antisemit: Über Sinn und Funktion eines beständigen Gefühls* (Frankfurt, 1986).

BRONSEN, DAVID, *Joseph Roth: Eine Biographie* (Cologne, 1974).

CARMELY, KLARA, 'Wie "aufgeklärt" waren die Aufklärer in Bezug auf die Juden?', in Ehrhard Bahr, Edward P. Harris, and Laurence G. Lyon (eds.), *Humanität und Dialog: Lessing und Mendelssohn in neuer Sicht* (Detroit and Munich, 1982), pp. 177–88.

CLARK, CHRISTOPHER M., *The Politics of Conversion: Missionary Protestantism and the Jews in Prussia 1728–1941* (Oxford, 1995).

COHN, HANS W., *Else Lasker-Schüler: The Broken World* (Cambridge, 1974).

DAVIES, MARTIN L., *Identity or History? Marcus Herz and the End of the Enlightenment* (Detroit, 1995).

EFRON, JOHN M., *Defenders of the Race: Jewish Doctors and Race Science in Fin-de-Siècle Europe* (New Haven and London, 1994).

ELON, AMOS, *Herzl* (London, 1975).

ENDELMAN, TODD M., 'The Social and Political Context of Conversion in Germany and England, 1870–1914', in id. (ed.), *Jewish Apostasy in the Modern World* (New York and London, 1987), pp. 83–107.

FIELD, GEOFFREY G., *Evangelist of Race: The Germanic Vision of Houston Stewart Chamberlain* (New York, 1981).

FUCHS, ALBERT, *Geistige Strömungen in Österreich 1867–1918* ([1948] Vienna, 1984).

GAY, PETER, *Freud, Jews and Other Germans* (Oxford and New York, 1978).

—— *Freud: A Life for our Time* (London, 1988).

GILMAN, SANDER L., *Jewish Self-Hatred: Anti-Semitism and the Hidden Language of the Jews* (Baltimore and London, 1986).

—— *The Jew's Body* (London, New York, 1991).

—— *Freud, Race, and Gender* (Princeton, 1993).

—— *Franz Kafka, the Jewish Patient* (London and New York, 1995).

GOLDHAGEN, DANIEL JONAH, *Hitler's Willing Executioners: Ordinary Germans and the Holocaust* (London, 1996).

GORNY, YOSEF, *Zionism and the Arabs, 1882–1948: A Study of Ideology* (Oxford, 1987).

GRESSER, MOSHE, *Dual Allegiance: Freud as a Modern Jew* (Albany, NY, 1994).

GRIMM, GÜNTER E., and BAYERDÖRFER, HANS-PETER (eds.), *Im Zeichen Hiobs: Jüdische Schriftsteller und deutsche Literatur im 20. Jahrhundert* (Königstein, 1985).

HABERMAS, JÜRGEN, 'Der deutsche Idealismus der jüdischen Philosophen', in id. *Philosophisch-politische Profile* (Frankfurt, 1971), pp. 37–66.

HAMANN, BRIGITTE, *Hitlers Wien: Lehrjahre eines Diktators* (Munich and Zurich, 1996).

HAMMERSTEIN, NOTKER, *Antisemitismus und deutsche Universitäten 1871–1933* (Hamburg, 1995).

HELLIGE, HANS DIETER, 'Rathenau und Harden in der Gesellschaft des Deutschen Kaiserreichs', in Rathenau/Harden, *Briefwechsel 1897–1920*, ed. Hellige (Munich and Heidelberg, 1983), pp. 15–299.

HONIGMANN, PETER, 'Über den Unterschied zwischen Alexander und Wilhelm von Humboldt in ihrem Verhältnis zum Judentum', in Renate Heuer and Ralph-Rainer Wuthenow (eds.), *Konfrontation und Koexistenz: Zur Geschichte des deutsche Judentums* (Frankfurt and New York, 1996), pp. 46–81.

JONES, ERNEST, *Sigmund Freud: Life and Work*, 3 vols. (London, 1953–7).

KAISER, WOLF, *Palästina—Erez Israel: Deutschsprachige Reisebeschreibungen jüdischer Autoren von der Jahrhundertwende bis zum Zweiten Weltkrieg* (Hildesheim, 1992).

KAMPMANN, WANDA, *Deutsche und Juden: Die Geschichte der Juden in Deutschland vom Mittelalter bis zum Beginn des Ersten Weltkrieges* ([1963] Frankfurt, 1979).

KAPLAN, MARION A., *The Making of the Jewish Middle Class* (New York and Oxford, 1991).

KÄSLER, DIRK, *Die frühe deutsche Soziologie 1909 bis 1934 und ihre Entstehungs-Milieus: Eine wissenschaftssoziologische Untersuchung* (Opladen, 1984).

KATZ, JACOB, *Out of the Ghetto: The Social Background of Jewish Emancipation, 1770–1870* ([1973] New York, 1978).

KATZ, STEVEN T., *The Holocaust in Historical Context*, i: *The Holocaust and Mass Death before the Modern Age* (New York and Oxford, 1994).

KLÜGER, RUTH, *Katastrophen: Über deutsche Literatur* (Göttingen, 1994).

KNICKMANN, HANNE, 'Der Jean-Paul-Forscher Eduard Berend (1883–1973). I', *Jahrbuch der Jean-Paul-Gesellschaft 1994*, 7–91.

KOCHAN, LIONEL, *Jews, Idols and Messiahs: The Challenge from History* (Oxford, 1990).

—— *The Jewish Renaissance and Some of its Discontents* (Manchester, 1992).

KORNBERG, JACQUES, *Theodor Herzl: From Assimilation to Zionism* (Bloomington and Indianapolis, 1993).

KROBB, FLORIAN, *Die schöne Jüdin: Jüdische Frauengestalten in der deutschsprachigen Erzählliteratur vom 17. Jahrhundert bis zum Ersten Weltkrieg* (Tübingen, 1993).

LE RIDER, JACQUES, *Der Fall Otto Weininger. Wurzeln des Antifeminismus und Antisemitismus*, tr. Dieter Hornig (Vienna, 1985).

—— *Modernity and Crises of Identity: Culture and Society in Fin-de-Siècle Vienna*, tr. Rosemary Morris (Cambridge, 1993).

LEVY, RICHARD S., *The Downfall of the Anti-Semitic Political Parties in Imperial Germany* (New Haven and London, 1975).

LINKE, HANSJÜRGEN, *Das Kultische in der Dichtung Stefan Georges und seiner Schule*, 2 vols. (Munich and Düsseldorf, 1960).

LOEWENBERG, PETER, *Decoding the Past: The Psychohistorical Approach* (Berkeley, 1984).

LOWENSTEIN, STEVEN M., *The Berlin Jewish Community: Enlightenment, Family, and Crisis, 1770–1830* (New York and Oxford, 1994).

MAGRIS, CLAUDIO, *Weit von wo: Verlorene Welt des Ostjudentums*, tr. Jutta Prasse (Vienna, 1974).

MEYER, MICHAEL A., *The Origins of the Modern Jew: Jewish Identity and European Culture in Germany, 1749–1824* (Detroit, 1967).

—— *Response to Modernity: A History of the Reform Movement in Judaism* (New York and Oxford, 1988).

—— (ed.), *Deutsch-jüdische Geschichte in der Neuzeit*, 4 vols. (Munich, 1996–7).

MOSSE, GEORGE L., *Confronting the Nation: Jewish and Western Nationalism* (Hanover, NH, and London, 1993).

MOSSE, WERNER E., *The German-Jewish Economic Élite 1820–1935* (Oxford, 1989).

MURPHY, HARRIET, *Canetti and Nietzsche: Theories of Humor in 'Die Blendung'* (Albany, NY, 1997).

NEUBAUER, HANS-JOACHIM, *Judenfiguren: Drama und Theater im frühen 19. Jahrhundert* (Frankfurt and New York, 1994).

NIEWYK, DONALD L., *The Jews in Weimar Germany* (Manchester, 1980).

OCH, GUNNAR, *Imago judaica: Juden und Judentum im Spiegel der deutschen Literatur 1750–1812* (Würzburg, 1995).

PAULSEN, WOLFGANG, 'Theodor Fontane—the Philosemitic Antisemite', *LBY* 26 (1981), 303–22.

PETERS, PAUL, *Heinrich Heine 'Dichterjude': Die Geschichte einer Schmähung* (Meisenheim, 1990).

POLLACK, HERMAN, *Jewish Folkways in Germanic Lands (1648–1806): Studies in Aspects of Daily Life* (Cambridge, Mass., 1971).

PRATER, D. A., *European of Yesterday: A Biography of Stefan Zweig* (Oxford, 1972).

PRAWER, S. S., *Heine's Jewish Comedy: A Study of his Portraits of Jews and Judaism* (Oxford, 1983).

PULZER, PETER, *The Rise of Political Anti-Semitism in Germany and Austria*, 2nd edn. (London, 1988).

—— *Jews and the German State: The Political History of a Minority, 1848–1933* (Oxford, 1992).

REINHARZ, JEHUDA, and SCHATZBERG, WALTER (eds.), *The Jewish Response to German Culture from the Enlightenment to the Second World War* (Hanover, NH, and London, 1985).

—— and SHAPIRA, ANITA (eds.), *Essential Papers on Zionism* (London, 1996).

RICE, EMANUEL, *Freud and Moses* (Albany, NY, 1990).

RICHTER, MATTHIAS, *Die Sprache jüdischer Figuren in der deutschen Literatur (1750–1933): Studien zu Form und Funktion* (Göttingen, 1995).

RIEFF, PHILIP, *Freud: The Mind of the Moralist*, 3rd edn. (Chicago, 1979).

ROAZEN, PAUL, *Freud and his Followers* (Harmondsworth, 1979).

RÖHL, JOHN C. G., *The Kaiser and his Court: Wilhelm II and the Government of Germany*, tr. Terence F. Cole (Cambridge, 1994).

ROHRBACHER, STEFAN, and SCHMIDT, MICHAEL, *Judenbilder: Kulturgeschichte antijüdischer Mythen und antisemitischer Vorurteile* (Reinbek, 1991).

ROSE, PAUL LAWRENCE, *Wagner: Race and Revolution* (London, 1992).

ROSMAN, MOSHE, *Founder of Hasidism: A Quest for the Historical Ba'al Shem Tov* (Berkeley and Los Angeles, 1996).

ROZENBLIT, MARSHA L., *The Jews of Vienna, 1867–1914: Assimilation and Identity* (Albany, NY, 1983).

RÜRUP, REINHARD, 'The Tortuous and Thorny Path to Legal Equality: "Jew Laws" and Emancipatory Legislation in Germany from the Late Eighteenth Century', *LBY* 31 (1986), 3–33.

SAID, EDWARD, *Orientalism* (London, 1978).

SCHEIBLE, HARTMUT, *Arthur Schnitzler und die Aufklärung* (Munich, 1977).

SCHOLEM, GERSHOM, *Major Trends in Jewish Mysticism* (New York, 1946).

SCHORSCH, ISMAR, *From Text to Context: The Turn to History in Modern Judaism* (Hanover, NH, and London, 1994).

SCHORSKE, CARL E., *Fin de Siècle Vienna: Politics and Culture* (Cambridge, 1981).

SCHRADER, HANS JÜRGEN, SIMON, ELLIOTT M., and WARDI, CHARLOTTE (eds.), *The Jewish Self-Portrait in European and American Literature* (Tübingen, 1996).

SEVENSTER, J. N., *The Roots of Pagan Anti-Semitism in the Ancient World* (Leiden, 1975).

SORKIN, DAVID, *The Transformation of German Jewry, 1780–1840* (New York and Oxford, 1987).

—— 'Emancipation and Assimilation: Two Concepts and their Application to German-Jewish History', *LBY* 35 (1990), 17–33.

—— *Moses Mendelssohn* (London, 1996).

SPARR, THOMAS, '"Verkannte Brüder". Jüdische George-Rezeption', in Hans Jürgen Schrader, Elliott M. Simon, and Charlotte Wardi (eds.), *The Jewish Self-Portrait in European and American Literature* (Tübingen, 1996), pp. 45–53.

STENZEL, JÜRGEN, 'Idealisierung und Vorurteil. Zur Figur des "edlen

Juden" in der deutschen Literatur des 18. Jahrhunderts', in Stéphane Mosès and Albrecht Schöne (eds.), *Juden in der deutschen Literatur* (Frankfurt, 1986), pp. 114–26.

STERN, J. P., *Hitler: The Führer and the People* (Glasgow, 1975).

STERN, SELMA, *The Court Jew* (Philadelphia, 1950).

STERNBURG, WILHELM VON (ed.), *Arnold Zweig: Materialien zu Leben und Werk* (Frankfurt, 1987).

SULLOWAY, FRANK J., *Freud, Biologist of the Mind: Beyond the Psychoanalytic Legend*, 2nd edn. (Cambridge, Mass., and London, 1992).

TIMMS, EDWARD, *Karl Kraus, Apocalyptic Satirist* (New Haven and London, 1986).

——— 'Ambassador Herzl and the Blueprint for a Modern State', *Austrian Studies*, 8 (1997), 12–26.

TURNER, DAVID, *Moral Values and the Human Zoo: The 'Novellen' of Stefan Zweig* (Hull, 1988).

VOIGTS, MANFRED, *Oskar Goldberg, der mythische Experimentalwissenschaftler: Ein verdrängtes Kapitel jüdischer Geschichte* (Berlin, 1992).

VOLKOV, SHULAMIT, 'Antisemitism as a Cultural Code: Reflections on the History and Historiography of Antisemitism in Imperial Germany', *LBY* 23 (1978), 25–46.

WEBER, ROLF, *Johann Jacoby: Eine Biographie* (Cologne, 1988).

WEINBERG, WERNER, 'Language Questions relating to Moses Mendelssohn's Pentateuch Translation', *Hebrew Union College Annual*, 55 (1984), 197–242.

WEINDLING, PAUL, *Health, Race and German Politics between National Unification and Nazism, 1870–1945* (Cambridge, 1989).

WELLER, B. UWE, *Maximilian Harden und die 'Zukunft'* (Bremen, 1970).

WERTHEIMER, JACK, *Unwelcome Strangers: East European Jews in Imperial Germany* (New York and Oxford, 1987).

WIDDIG, BERND, *Männerbünde und Massen: Zur Krise männlicher Identität in der Literatur der Moderne* (Opladen, 1992).

WISTRICH, ROBERT S., *Socialism and the Jews: The Dilemmas of Assimilation in Germany and Austria-Hungary* (London and Toronto, 1982).

——— *The Jews of Vienna in the Age of Franz Joseph* (Oxford, 1989).

WOLFF, LARRY, *Inventing Eastern Europe: The Map of Civilization on the Mind of the Enlightenment* (Stanford, Calif., 1994).

WORBS, MICHAEL, *Nervenkunst: Literatur und Psychoanalyse im Wien der Jahrhundertwende* (Frankfurt, 1983).

YATES, W. E., *Schnitzler, Hofmannsthal, and the Austrian Theatre* (New Haven and London, 1992).

YERUSHALMI, YOSEF HAYIM, *Freud's Moses: Judaism Terminable and Interminable* (New Haven and London, 1991).

ZIMMERMANN, MOSHE, *Wilhelm Marr: The Patriarch of Anti-Semitism* (New York, 1986).

Index